D0904587

FUTURE
English for Results

2

TEACHER'S EDITION
AND LESSON PLANNER

Julie C. Rouse

Series Consultants

Beatriz B. Díaz

Ronna Magy

Federico Salas-Isnardi

PEARSON
Longman

Future 2
English for Results
Teacher's Edition and Lesson Planner

Copyright © 2010 by Pearson Education, Inc.
All rights reserved.
No part of this publication may be reproduced, stored in a retrieval system, or transmitted in any form or by any means, electronic, mechanical, photocopying, recording, or otherwise, without the prior permission of the publisher.

Pearson Education, 10 Bank Street, White Plains, NY 10606

Staff credits: The people who made up the **Future 2** team, representing editorial, production, design, and manufacturing, are Rhea Banker, Peter Benson, Nancy Blodgett, Maretta Callahan, Elizabeth Carlson, Aerin Csigay, Mindy DePalma, Dave Dickey, Nancy Flaggman, Irene Frankel, Mike Kemper, Katie Keyes, Linda Moser, Liza Pleva, and Sherry Preiss.

Cover design: Rhea Banker
Cover photo: Kathy Lamm/Getty Images
Text design: Lisa Delgado
Text composition: ElectraGraphics, Inc.
Text font: Minion Pro

ISBN-13: 978-0-13199149-1
ISBN-10: 0-13-199149-3

1 2 3 4 5 6 7 8 9 10—CJK—14 13 12 11 10 09

Contents

The instructional design of *Future* has been carefully crafted and draws on tried-and-true methods. In *Future*, current research findings are put into practice. Each of the skill sections reflects sound pedagogy and offers a logical progression from unit to unit within a level as well as from one level to the next throughout the series. The instructional design is tailored to meet the interests and needs of students at their language level and, at the same time to fulfill curriculum mandates.

Future has been designed to help students persist in their English studies. The program motivates students to keep coming to class through its situational contexts that reflect students' real lives, its touches of humor, and its community-building group work and team projects. If outside factors cause students to miss classes, the strategies and study skills presented in the Student Book, along with the Practice Plus CD-ROM, help students continue their studies until they are able to return to class.

Future also helps students make a successful transition into academic programs. The levels of *Future* progressively introduce academic skills so that students feel empowered to continue their education. By continuing on into academic programs, students improve their chances of entering the job market with all the skills and tools they need to be successful.

Future is truly an integrated-skills course: listening, speaking, reading, and writing are woven together throughout the lessons, just as they are naturally woven together outside the classroom. For example, students practice their listening skills not just on the Listening page but also in the Life Skills lesson and in other lessons throughout the unit.

Following are some of the key pedagogical features of the skill sections of *Future 2*.

Vocabulary

- **Picture-dictionary layout.** Presenting vocabulary through clear, colorful photos and illustrations helps students quickly understand new words and phrases.
- **Elicitation before presentation.** New words are set to the side of the pictures. Teachers elicit what their students know by using the pictures first, and then focusing on text. This helps teachers to engage their students, and it empowers students by letting them say what they already know.
- **Recycling of new words.** After new vocabulary is introduced, it is used again and again throughout the course, giving students the maximum exposure to the new words in a variety of situations. Current research shows that the more encounters learners have with a target word, the more likely they are to retain that word.[1]
- **Strategies for learning outside the classroom.** Learning Strategies in the Vocabulary lessons support persistence by giving students ideas for continued learning outside the classroom. These strategies can be used with any new words students encounter.

Listening

- **Multiple genres.** Throughout *Future*, students are exposed to a variety of listening types such as conversations, interviews, and radio talk shows.
- **Natural language.** Natural discourse is presented so that students hear authentic models. The listening selections model high-frequency words and expressions from the Longman Corpus of Spoken English database.
- **Pre-listening activities.** Before students listen to each selection, they complete pre-listening activities, which pre-teach new vocabulary and help activate students' background knowledge. Students are also asked to make predictions about what they will hear. This helps develop students' critical thinking skills[2] and is an important strategy for successful listening in a second language.[3]
- **True listening practice.** Students listen to the audio without seeing the audio script on the page. This serves two purposes: 1) It ensures that the listening exercise is truly checking students' listening skills, rather than their reading skills; and 2) It helps students prepare for standardized tests in which they are asked to listen to audio selections and answer questions without seeing the script. Students who need extra support can read the audio script printed in the back of the Student Book.
- **Multiple exposures to the same listening selection.** Students listen to selections multiple times. This helps them develop their listening skills and allows them to be successful with the listening task.
- **A variety of listening tasks.** A wide variety of comprehension exercises check students' understanding of both the meaning and the details of the listening selection.

Speaking

- **Careful scaffolding to promote success.** The Listening lesson that precedes the Speaking lesson exposes students to the language they will use in conversation. Students then practice the model conversation through activities that progress from controlled to more open. Speaking lessons culminate in guided role plays, which allow students to have fun expressing themselves in the new language using vocabulary and structures they are familiar with.
- **Negotiation of meaning.** Many of the exercises in each unit require students to work together to negotiate meaning. Giving students the opportunity to interact and negotiate meaning supports development of their language skills.[4]
- **Problem-solving tasks.** In each unit, students have the opportunity to discuss solutions to a particular problem related to the unit theme. These tasks engage students' critical thinking skills and allow them to focus on fluency.

[2] Bloom, B.S. (1956). *Taxonomy of Educational Objectives, Handbook I: The Cognitive Domain,* New York: David McKay Co Inc.

[3] Rost, M. (2002). *Teaching and Researching Listening.* Harlow, England: Pearson Education.

[4] Mackey, A. (1999). Input, interaction, and second language development: An empirical study of question formation in ESL. *Studies in Second Language Acquisition, 21,* 557–587.

[1] Folse, K. (2006). The Effect of Type of Written Exercise on L2 Vocabulary Retention. *TESOL Quarterly,* Vol. 40, No. 2, 273–93.

Pronunciation

- **Systematic pronunciation syllabus.** Pronunciation presentations and practice exercises precede many of the speaking lessons. Students practice isolated sentences from the model conversation that follows.
- **Focus on stress and intonation.** While some pronunciation lessons highlight specific sounds like *th*, students focus on the natural stress, intonation, and rhythm of the language.
- **Emphasis on receptive skills.** *Future* encourages students to notice the natural patterns of English to aid their comprehension as well as their production.

Grammar

- **Grammar naturally embedded in the spoken language.** Grammar in *Future* is first presented receptively through the conversation in the Speaking lesson. Then grammar charts at the beginning of the grammar lesson explicitly show the target structures.
- **Minimal metalanguage.** The charts use little metalanguage in order to ensure that the forms and the meaning of the target structure are clear and comprehensible.
- **Practice with both meaning and form.** Presentations focus on meaning as well as form, a practice that can help learners incorporate more new structures into their language use.[5]
- **Progression from controlled to open practice.** Practice activities progress from very controlled to open, providing ample written and spoken practice in the target structure.
- **Contextualized activities.** Exercises are contextualized, recycling themes and vocabulary from the unit, so that grammar practice is authentic and meaningful.
- **Numerous pair and group activities.** Pair and small group work allows students to work with new language structures in a safe, motivating environment, as well as offering further opportunities for them to negotiate meaning.
- **Opportunities for students to show what they know.** *Show What You Know* activities at the end of every grammar lesson allow students to put together the vocabulary, structures, and competencies they have learned.

Reading

- **High-interest, useful articles.** The reading articles in *Future* present interesting, useful information related to the unit theme. The structures and vocabulary in the texts are controlled so students can be successful readers.
- **Pre-reading activities.** As in the Listening lessons, the Reading lessons have pre-reading activities to help build students' cultural schema, an important factor in successfully completing a reading task.[6] New vocabulary is also pre-taught so that students can focus on improving their reading fluency and skills.

- **Recorded reading selections.** The readings in *Future* are recorded so that students can listen as they read along. Research has shown that listening while reading can have a positive effect on reading fluency.[7]
- **Opportunity to apply the information.** A *Show What You Know* activity at the end of the reading lesson allows students to synthesize and apply the information they have just learned through a writing task.
- **Building of reading skills.** Skills such as finding the main idea, identifying the topic, and scanning for information are explicitly presented and then practiced through pre-reading or comprehension tasks.
- **Inclusion of document and environmental literacy.** In addition to high-interest articles, *Future* gives students practice reading and completing forms and other documents that they are likely to encounter in their everyday lives.

Writing

- **Personal writing.** Students learn to write short paragraphs using material they are familiar and comfortable with. This material is connected thematically to the reading lesson. Personal writing is also integrated throughout the lessons of *Future*.
- **Step-by-step writing syllabus.** Offered in a natural progression, writing tips introduce students to the mechanics of writing.
- **Modeling of writing tasks.** Models for all writing activities in *Future* allow students to complete each task successfully.
- **Authenticity of purpose.** In addition to the personal writing, students complete several authentic genres such as forms, lists, notes, and journals.

Review and Assessment

- **Checkpoints to track progress.** Every unit begins with a list of competencies to be covered. As students complete each lesson, they check off the goal they have completed. At the end of the unit, students are directed to review the goals list to see their progress. Keeping track of goals completed motivates students and reinforces their sense of success and accomplishment.
- **End-of-unit review.** Every unit in *Future* ends with a review of the language and skills presented in that unit. By re-visiting the vocabulary, structures, and competencies they have learned, students can retain the information more easily and assimilate it into their pre-existing knowledge.
- **Opportunities for ongoing assessment.** The *Show What You Know* activities at the end of most lessons and at the end of every unit can be used by teachers to assess their students' progress in particular language skills and competencies. For teachers who want to do a more formal assessment of what their students have learned, the *Tests and Test Prep Book* provides unit tests as well as a midterm and a final test.

[5] Ellis, R., Basturkmen, H., & Loewen, S. (2001). Learner uptake in communicative ESL lessons. *Language Learning, 51,* 281–318.

[6] Burt, M., Peyton, J. K., & Adams, R. (2003). *Reading and adult English language learners: A review of the research.* Washington, D.C.: Center for Applied Linguistics.

[7] Kruidenier, J. (2002). *Research-based principles for adult basic education reading instruction.* Washington, D.C.: National Institute for Literacy, Partnership for Reading.

Each unit begins with a **list of course components** that can be used in class or assigned for homework.

7

Health Watch

Classroom Materials/Extra Practice

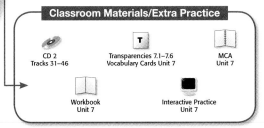

CD 2
Tracks 31–46

Transparencies 7.1–7.6
Vocabulary Cards Unit 7

MCA
Unit 7

Workbook
Unit 7

Interactive Practice
Unit 7

Unit Overview

Goals
- See the list of goals on the facing page.

Grammar
- Prepositions of time: *at / by / in / on / from . . . to*
- Simple past: Irregular verbs
- Ways to express reasons (*because* + a subject and a verb; *for* + a noun)

Pronunciation
- Linking a consonant to a vowel sound
- Pronunciation of *t* between two vowel sounds
- Pauses to organize sentences into thought groups

Reading
- Read an article about ways to manage stress
- *Reading Skill:* Using formatting clues

Writing
- Write about the stress in your life
- Write about an injury

Life Skills Writing
- Complete a medical history form

Preview
- Set the context of the unit by asking questions about health (for example, *How do you feel today? What do you do when you're sick? Do you go to the doctor?*).
- Hold up page 125 or show Transparency 7.1. Read the unit title and ask the class to repeat.
- Explain: Health Watch *means paying attention to your physical condition and to medical information.*
- Say: *Look at the picture.* Ask the Preview questions: *Where is the person?* (She's at home. / She's on the sofa.) *What is she doing?* (She's eating soup / drinking orange juice / reading / watching TV.) *How does she feel?* (bad / sick)
- Write the word *health* on the board and check that students understand (for example, T [pointing to the picture]: *Is she in good health?* Ss: *No, she's sick.* T: *What do people do when they have health problems?* Ss: *Go to the doctor. / Take medicine. / Rest. / Miss work.*).

Goals
- Point to the Unit Goals. Explain that this list shows what the class will be studying in this unit.
- Tell students to read the goals silently.
- Say each goal and ask the class to repeat. As needed, explain: *An injury:* what happens when you get hurt; for example, you can have an injury to your arm or leg
- Tell students to circle one goal that is very important to them. Call on several students to say the goal they circled.

A comprehensive **list of competencies and skills** provides an overview of the unit.

Teaching ideas for the unit opener picture help teachers establish the context of the unit and get students ready for the unit theme.

Teaching notes are organized in a **lesson plan**: Getting Started, Presentation, Controlled Practice, Communicative Practice. **Suggested times** for each part of the lesson plan are based on a 60-minute class. This time may vary depending on class size.

Teaching Tips give helpful teaching techniques and strategies.

Lesson 2 Make a doctor's appointment

Getting Started   10 minutes

1 BEFORE YOU LISTEN

CLASS. Look at the pictures and read the...

- Read the directions.
- Read each sentence and ask the class to repeat.
- Explain any unfamiliar vocabulary through modeling, if possible. For example, to demonstrate *dizzy*, spin around a couple of times, act unsteady, and say: *I'm dizzy.*
- Write the symptoms on the board. Ask: *When do people have these symptoms?* Tell students to review the vocabulary on page 127 for ideas. List students' responses under each symptom (for example, for *dizzy: when they have a headache, when they have an earache*).

Language Note

Point out that the symptoms in Exercise 1 are adjectives, while the health problems on page 127 are nouns.

Presentation   10 minutes

2 LISTEN

A CLASS. Look at the pictures. Guess: Where...

- Read the directions. Ask: *Where is the woman? Where is the man?*
- Call on students to answer. Write guesses on the board (for example, *The woman in an office / in a doctor's office. The man is at home / in bed.*).

B Listen to the conversation. Was...

- Read the directions.
- Play CD 2, Track 33. Students listen.
- Ask: *Where is the woman?* Read the guesses on the board. Elicit and circle the best answer. Repeat with *Where is the man?*

Controlled Practice   10 minutes

Teaching Tip

Optional: Remember that if students need additional support, tell them to read the Audio Script on page 129 as they listen to the conversations.

C Listen again. What is the matter...

- Tell students to look at the pictures again and point to Mr. Cruz. Ask: *What do you think is the matter with him?* (He has a fever.)
- Read the directions and symptoms. Act out each symptom (for example, by placing your palm on your forehead for *He has a fever.*) or call on students to act them out.
- Play Track 33 again.
- To review, ask: *What is the matter with Roberto Cruz?*

D Listen again. Complete the...

- Read the directions.
- Tell students to look at the appointment card and find the checkboxes for the days of the week and the space for the time. Tell students to circle A.M. or P.M. when they write the time.
- Play Track 33 again. Students listen and complete the appointment card.
- To review, ask: *When is Mr. Cruz's appointment?*

Culture Connection

- Tell students to look at the appointment card. Read the notice at the bottom of the card (*If you are unable . . .*). Ask: *If Mr. Cruz can't come to his appointment, when does he need to call?* (before Monday, October 13, at 9:00 A.M.)
- Say: *In the United States, some doctor's offices charge you for missed appointments. To avoid charges, call at least 24 hours ahead of time to cancel an appointment you can't keep.*
- Ask: *In your country, do doctor's offices charge for missed appointments?*

UNIT 7   **T-128**

Language Notes offer insightful and helpful information about English. The notes also offer ideas for **Community Building** in the classroom and **Networking** activities to help students get to know their classmates.

Culture Connections provide the teacher with information about cross-cultural issues, as well as activities that stimulate classroom discussions about culture.

Ideas for multilevel instruction help teachers meet the needs of all learners in a classroom.

Teaching notes for the Life Skills Writing section on page T-xii help teachers work with students on understanding and completing real-life writing tasks.

Lesson 4 Read medicine labels

Presentation   20 minutes

2 READ PRESCRIPTION MEDICINE LABELS

Ⓐ CLASS. Look at the prescription...

- Read the directions. Say: *Point to the prescription. Point to the medicine label.* Ask: *Who gives you a prescription?* (a doctor) *Can you buy this medicine at any drugstore?* (No.)
- Tell students to read the questions silently and look for answers on the prescription and label.
- Read the questions and elicit answers from the class.
- Tell students to cover the medicine label. Say the specific pieces of information from the label in random order. Point to the board and tell students to call out the type of information (for example, T: *Do not take with aspirin.* Class: *Warning*).
- *Optional:* Pair students and tell them to take turns asking and answering the questions.

Ⓑ Read the medicine label in Exercise A again...

- Read the directions. Tell students to look at the example. Read the question and elicit the answer from the class.
- Students compare answers with a partner.
- Write *dosage* on the board. Read item 2 and elicit the answer. Ask the class what *dosage* means and write a definition (for example, *how much medicine you take*). Repeat with *refills.* Read item 5 and elicit a definition (for example, *times that you can get more medicine with the same prescription*).

Ⓒ Listen and check your answers...

- Play CD 2, Track 36. Students listen and check their answers.
- Say: *Now listen and repeat. Practice the questions because you're going to ask them in Exercise 3.* Resume playing Track 36.

Communicative Practice   15 minutes

3 PRACTICE

PAIRS. Take turns being the customer and the...

- Read the directions. Tell students to look at Exercise 2B. Point to the questions and ask: *Who asks the questions?* (the customer) *Who answers the questions?* (the pharmacist)
- Tell students to look at the medicine labels. On the board, write: *an eyedropper, a tube of ointment.* Ask: *What's the picture next to the first label?* (an eyedropper) Ask: *What's the picture next to the second label?* (a tube of ointment)
- Pair students. Say: *Talk to your partner. Decide who's going to be the pharmacist for the eyedrops and who's going to be the pharmacist for the ointment.*
- Tell students to look at the questions in Exercise 2B and find answers to the questions on their label.
- Say: *Take turns being the customer and the pharmacist. The customer asks the questions in Exercise 2B. The pharmacist answers the questions using the underlined information on his or her label.*
- Call on pairs to perform for the class.

MULTILEVEL INSTRUCTION for 3
Cross-ability Tell the higher-level students to play the pharmacist first.

4 LIFE SKILLS WRITING

Turn to page 262 and ask students to complete the medical history form. See pages Txi–Txii for general notes about Life Skills Writing activities.

Progress Check

Can you . . . read medicine labels?
Say: *We have practiced reading medicine labels. Now, look at the question at the bottom of the page. Can you read medicine labels?* Tell students to write a checkmark in the box.

Extra Practice

Interactive Practice   pages 78–79

T-133   UNIT 7

Cross-references to relevant pages in course components at the end of each lesson allow the teacher to plan additional in-class or at-home activities.

Progress checks allow students to reflect on their ability to use the competencies presented in the lesson.

Step-by-step teaching notes help teachers give **clear grammar presentations**. Corresponding **transparencies with discovery exercises** can be found in the *Transparency and Reproducible Vocabulary Cards* component.

Expansions provide more practice with specific skills.

Lesson 6 Talk about an injury

Getting Started — 5 minutes

- Say: *We're going to study the simple past tense of irregular verbs. You heard this grammar in Exercise 3C on page 135.*
- Play CD 2, Track 41. Students listen. Write on the board: *I had an accident, I broke my arm, I hurt my ankle.* Underline *had, broke,* and *hurt.*

Presentation — 15 minutes

Simple past: Irregular verbs

- Write *burn* and *sprain* on the board. Ask: *How do we usually form the past tense?* Elicit the answer and add *-ed* to the words on the board. Say *burned* and *sprained* and ask the class to repeat.
- Say: *Some verbs do not have -ed forms. They have irregular past-tense forms.* Tell students to look at the sentences on the board. Ask: *What is the past-tense form of* have? (*had*) Repeat with *break* and *hurt.* Say: Have, break, *and* hurt *have irregular past-tense forms.*
- Copy the grammar charts onto the board or show Transparency 7.4 and cover the exercise. Point to the right chart and ask: *What other verbs have irregular past-tense forms?* (*cut, fall, get*) Say the irregular past-tense forms and ask the class to repeat.
- Tell students to look at the left chart. Point to the picture of Manolo and Ellie on page 134. Ask: *What happened to Ellie? What happened to Manolo?* Elicit the sentences in the chart. Then read the sentences and ask the class to repeat.
- If you are using the transparency, do the exercise with the class.

EXPANSION: Grammar practice

- Tell students to look at the Grammar Reference on page 286. Say the past-tense forms and ask the class to repeat.
- Give students time to study the irregular past-tense forms on page 136 and in the Grammar Reference on page 286.

- Tell students to close their books. Say base forms in random order and ask the class to call out the past-tense forms.
- Pair students and tell them to quiz each other. Tell students to mark the verbs their partner doesn't know.
- Provide students with index cards or tell them to cut up notebook paper. Tell them to make flashcards for the verbs they need to practice more.

Controlled Practice — 20 minutes

 PRACTICE

A Complete the sentences. Underline the...

- Read the directions. Write the example on the board and point to the answer. Ask: *Is the verb present or past tense?* (present tense) *Why?* (You use *sometimes* with the present tense)
- Say: *Read the sentences carefully before you answer. Decide whether each sentence is present or past tense. Look for clues like* sometimes, today, *and* yesterday.
- Students compare answers with a partner.
- Call on students to read the completed sentences.

B Write sentences about the past. Use a verb...

- Read the directions. Write item 1 on the board and point to the answer. Ask: *Which verb from the box is used?* (*break*) *What is the past-tense form of* break? (*broke*) Read the sentence.
- Say each verb in the box and ask the class to call out the past-tense form.
- Say: *First, choose the correct verb. Then write a past-tense sentence.*
- Students compare answers with a partner. Walk around and spot-check students' spelling of the past-tense forms.
- Call on students to read the completed sentences.

UNIT 7   **T-136**

Persistence Activities give teachers more ideas for community-building, as well as focusing on goal setting and study skills. **Team Projects** help teachers focus on community building and recycling content in every unit.

EXPAND Show what you know!

 ACT IT OUT

STEP 1. CLASS. Review the Lesson 2 conversation...

- Tell students to review the conversation in Exercise 3B on page 129.
- Tell them to read the conversation silently and then practice it with a partner.
- Play CD 2, Track 33. Students listen.
- As needed, play Track 33 again to aid comprehension.

STEP 2. ROLE PLAY. PAIRS. Student A, you are the...

- Read the directions and the guidelines for A and B.
- Pair students. Tell A to make up a medical problem but use real information about his or her schedule. Tell B to think of a name for the doctor's office. Remind pairs to pretend they are talking on the phone.
- Walk around and observe partners interacting. Check pairs' use of prepositions of time when they talk about the appointment time.
- Call on pairs to perform for the class.
- While pairs are performing, use the scoring rubric on page T-xiii to evaluate each student's vocabulary, grammar, fluency, and how well he or she completes the task.
- *Optional:* After each pair finishes, discuss the strengths and weakness of each performance either in front of the class or privately.

3 READ AND REACT

STEP 1. Read about Ramona's problem.

- Say: *We are going to read about a student's problem, and then we need to think about a solution.*
- Read the directions.
- Read the story while students follow along silently. Pause after each sentence to allow time for students to comprehend. Periodically stop and ask simple *Wh-* questions to check comprehension (for example, *Who is Mike? What does Mike often do? Where is Mike going tonight? Who has to cover Mike's hours?*).

STEP 2. PAIRS. What is Ramona's problem?...

- Ask: *What is Ramona's problem?* (Ramona's boss asked her to cover her co-worker Mike's hours. Ramona doesn't want to work late tonight.)
- Pair students. Read the ideas in the list. Give pairs a couple of minutes to discuss possible solutions for Ramona.
- Ask: *Which ideas are good?* Call on students to say their opinion about the ideas in the list (for example, S: *I think she can say, "I'm sorry I can't work late tonight." This is a good idea.*).
- Now tell pairs to think of one new idea not in the list (for example, *She can talk to Mike. She can say, "When you call in sick, I have to work late."*) and to write it in the blank. Encourage students to think of more than one idea and to write them in their notebooks.
- Call on pairs to say their additional solutions. Write any particularly good ones on the board and ask students if they think it is a good idea too (*Do you think this is a good idea? Why or why not?*).

 MULTILEVEL INSTRUCTION for STEP 2
Cross-ability If possible, pair students with the same first language. The higher-level partner helps the lower-level student say his or her idea in English.

4 CONNECT

Turn to page 252 for the Goal-setting Activity and page 280 for the Team Project. See page T-xi for general notes about teaching these activities.

Progress Check

Which goals can you check off? Go back to page 125.
Ask students to turn to page 125 and check off any remaining goals they have reached. Call on students to say which goals they will practice outside of class.

UNIT 7 **T-144**

Students check their progress at the end of each unit by reviewing the vocabulary, grammar, and competencies and then checking off the unit goals.

A **Persistence Activity** and a **Team Project** for each unit of *Future 2* are in the back of the book. Cross-references within the unit indicate at what point each activity should be completed. Following are some general notes that apply to all of the activities within each section.

Persistence Activities: Community Building, Goal Setting, and Study Skills

The Persistence Activities are classroom-tested activities that support students in continuing their studies. Recent research has shown us that students are more likely to persist when they feel they are part of a learning community and when they are able to set educational goals they believe they can achieve. Programs can also support student persistence by showing students how to study efficiently and how to monitor their learning. Each Persistence activity in *Future* fits one of these categories: community building, setting goals, or developing study skills.

Step 1: Introduce the activity
- Say the name of the activity. Then explain the objective of the activity. For example, for Unit 1, say: *We're going to learn each other's names* or, if students have already been introduced to each other, say: *We're going to practice remembering each other's names.*
- Put students in groups, if necessary, for the activity.

Step 2: Get ready
- Read the directions for the first part of the activity and make sure students understand what they need to do.
- Review any language students need for the activity. If necessary, have students take a few minutes to review the unit vocabulary lesson. If students will need to write sentences, write an example sentence on the board.
- Model the activity. If the activity has students working in groups of three, call two on- or above-level students to the front of the room. Model the activity with them, taking one part yourself. If the activity requires students to work independently, write the exercise on the board and call on a few students to give sample responses. Write their responses on the board.

Step 3: Start the activity
- Have students start working in groups or independently, as necessary for the activity. Walk around the room while students are working, checking to make sure they are on task and providing help as needed.
- If the activity has a second part, check to make sure all students have had sufficient time to complete the first part before moving on. When students are ready, repeat Steps 2 and 3 for the second part of the activity.

Step 4: Wrap up
- After students have completed all parts of the activity, call on a few students to share their work with the class.

Team Projects

The Team Projects give students an opportunity to use the language they have learned throughout the unit to produce a product such as a booklet, poster, or chart. Students work in teams. Each team member is assigned a specific role: Captain, Co-captain, Assistant, or Spokesperson. The teacher can assign roles that match each student's strength. For example, since the tasks performed by the Co-captain are not language-intensive, the teacher may want to assign this role to a pre-level student.

Step 1: Introduce the objective
- Explain the objective of the activity. For example, for Unit 1, say: *We're learning about our classmates.*

Step 2: Form teams
- Form groups of 4 students. Assign students the roles of Captain, Co-captain, Assistant, or Spokesperson.
- If necessary, students can share one role. For example, a pre-level student and an above-level student can perform the role of the Assistant together. Also, one student can have two roles if necessary.

Step 3: Get ready
- Gather the materials in the note and have them ready.
- Read the directions for all team members. Go over any examples provided.
- Tell the co-captain to watch the clock to track the time and to tell the team when they have one minute left.
- Have students complete the task. Walk around and help as needed.

Step 4: Create
- Have Co-captains retrieve needed materials.
- Read the directions for the Co-captains and team. Each team can decide who will do what to create the poster, chart, or booklet.
- Have the Co-captain watch the clock and tell the team when they have one minute left.
- Walk around and check that all students have a role. If it seems that a student is not involved, ask the team, *What is _____ doing?*

Step 5: Report
- Call on each Spokesperson to tell the class about the group's project. The goal of the presentation is to make sure the audience (the other students) understands all the information presented.
- Have the other students in the class write down a question for the team that is presenting. Call on students to ask questions that the spokesperson can answer. For example, for Unit 1, a student may ask, *Where does Angela work?*

Speaking and Writing Activities

Future **provides students with multiple opportunities to build their speaking and writing skills.** Speaking tasks are integrated throughout the course, and each unit culminates with a role play and a problem-solving activity. A Writing activity and a Life Skills Writing activity for each unit are in the back of the book. Cross-references within the unit indicate at what point each activity should be completed. If you wish to formally assess students' speaking or writing, you may use the rubrics provided on pages T-xiii–T-xiv.

Life Skills Writing

The Life Skills Writing activities consist of completing forms and other documents. Students first look at a model or work with new vocabulary terms from the document; they then complete the writing task using their own personal information. These activities often appear at the end of the Life Skills Lesson but may appear at different points in a given unit.

Step 1: Introduce the activity
- Say the name of the activity. Then explain the objective of the activity. For example, for Unit 1, say: *You are going to complete an application for a driver's license.*
- Ask students why they might need this kind of form or other document.

Step 2: Complete the pre-writing tasks
- Read the directions for Exercise A in Before You Write. Answer the questions with the class. If there is a model, hold up the page or use the transparency for that page. Have students complete the activity as a class.
- If Before You Read has a second exercise, read the directions for that exercise. Hold up the page as necessary and complete the activity with the class.

Step 3: Complete the writing task
- Read the directions and make sure students understand the task.
- Depending on the level of your class, you may wish to use the transparency to have students complete the task together before having them work independently.
- As students work, walk around the classroom and check for accuracy. Give students help as needed.

Step 4: Check progress
- Say: *Look at the question at the bottom of the page. Can you _____?* For example, for Unit 1, say: *Can you complete a driver's license application?*
- Tell students to write a checkmark in the box.

Speaking Activities

The final page of every unit of *Future* contains an Act It Out activity and a problem-solving activity. These activities offer students an opportunity to practice their spoken fluency and to demonstrate their understanding of the vocabulary, grammar, and competencies from the unit and the course.

After students have practiced the activity in pairs or small groups, allow some students to perform the activity in front of the whole class. If you wish to use this activity for evaluation purposes, use the Speaking Rubric on page T-xiii to make notes about each student's performance. An example of this rubric is shown below. For each category listed in the rubric (Vocabulary, Grammar, Fluency, and Task Completion), include comments about both *strong points* and *weak points*. You can then use those comments to give each student a rating of 1, 2, or 3 for each category.

The purpose of this kind of evaluation is to give fair and clear feedback to students and to give them specific points to work on so they can improve their fluency. It is important to use language that a student can understand and to give examples of what the student did or didn't say when possible. For example, you might say, *You used a lot of vocabulary from the unit* or *You need to work on forms of be. Review the grammar charts in the unit.* Feedback should be given to students in a timely manner in order to be most effective and helpful.

Writing Activities

Each unit of *Future* includes a Writing lesson, which can be found in the back of the book and is thematically related to the article in the Reading lesson. The writing task gives students an opportunity to apply their knowledge of the grammar and vocabulary they have learned in the unit and throughout the course while also allowing them to build their writing skills and develop their writing fluency.

If you wish to give students a formal evaluation of their writing, use the Writing Rubric on page T-xiv to make notes. For each category listed in the rubric (Vocabulary, Grammar, Mechanics and Format, and Task Completion), include comments about both *strong points* and *weak points*. You can then use those comments to give each student a rating of 1, 2, or 3 for each category.

The purpose of this kind of evaluation is to give fair and clear feedback to students and to give them specific points to work on so they can improve their writing skills. It is important to use language that a student can understand and to give examples of what the student did or did not do when possible. For example, you might say: *You used the simple present correctly* or *You need to work on punctuation. Remember to capitalize names.* Feedback should be given to students in a timely manner in order to be most effective and helpful.

Speaking Rubric

Name: _____

Class: _____ Date: _____

Activity: _____ Unit: _____ Page: _____

Vocabulary	Score	Comments
Uses a variety of vocabulary words and expressions from the unit	3	
Uses some vocabulary words and expressions from the unit	2	
Uses few vocabulary words or expressions from the unit	1	
Grammar	**Score**	**Comments**
Uses a variety of grammar points from the unit; uses grammar with control and accuracy	3	
Uses some grammar points from the unit; uses grammar with less control and accuracy	2	
Does not use grammar points from the unit; uses grammar with little control or accuracy	1	
Fluency	**Score**	**Comments**
Speech is authentic and fluent; there is authentic communication with partner	3	
Speech is overly rehearsed at points; not true communication	2	
Speech is not authentic; is not really listening to and communicating with partner	1	
Task completion	**Score**	**Comments**
Student completed the task successfully	3	
Student mostly completed the task; student went off topic at various points	2	
Student was not able to successfully complete the task: see comments	1	

Writing Rubric

Name: _____

Class: _____ Date: _____

Activity: _____ Unit: _____ Page: _____

Vocabulary	Score	Comments
Uses a variety of vocabulary words and expressions from the unit	3	
Uses some vocabulary words and expressions from the unit	2	
Uses few vocabulary words or expressions from the unit	1	
Grammar	**Score**	**Comments**
Uses a variety of grammar points from the unit; uses grammar with control and accuracy	3	
Uses some grammar points from the unit; uses grammar with less control and accuracy	2	
Does not use grammar points from the unit; uses grammar with little control or accuracy	1	
Mechanics (Spelling, Punctuation, Capitalization) and Format	**Score**	**Comments**
Very few or no mechanical errors; follows format of model	3	
Some mechanical errors that do not affect comprehensibility; follows format of model with some errors	2	
Many mechanical errors reduce comprehensibility; does not follow format of model	1	
Task completion	**Score**	**Comments**
Student completed the task successfully	3	
Student mostly completed the task; student went off topic at various points	2	
Student was not able to successfully complete the task: see comments	1	

FUTURE
English for Results

2

Acknowledgments

The authors and publisher would like to extend special thanks to our Series Consultants whose insights, experience, and expertise shaped the course and guided us throughout its development.

Beatriz B. Díaz Miami-Dade County Public Schools, Miami, FL
Ronna Magy Los Angeles Unified School District, Los Angles, CA
Federico Salas-Isnardi Texas LEARNS, Houston, TX

We would also like to express our gratitude to the following individuals. Their kind assistance was indispensable to the creation of this program.

Consultants

Wendy J. Allison Seminole Community College, Sanford, FL
Claudia Carco Westchester Community College, Valhalla, NY
Maria J. Cesnik Ysleta Community Learning Center, El Paso, TX
Edwidge Crevecoeur-Bryant University of Florida, Gainesville, FL
Ann Marie Holzknecht Damrau San Diego Community College, San Diego, CA
Peggy Datz Berkeley Adult School, Berkeley, CA
MaryAnn Florez D.C. Learns, Washington, D.C.
Portia LaFerla Torrance Adult School, Torrance, CA
Eileen McKee Westchester Community College, Valhalla, NY
Julie Meuret Downey Adult School, Downey, CA
Sue Pace Santa Ana College School of Continuing Education, Santa Ana, CA
Howard Pomann Union County College, Elizabeth, NY
Mary Ray Fairfax County Public Schools, Falls Church, VA
Gema Santos Miami-Dade County Public Schools, Miami, FL
Edith Uber Santa Clara Adult Education, Santa Clara, CA
Theresa Warren East Side Adult Education, San Jose, CA

Piloters

MariCarmen Acosta American High School, Adult ESOL, Hialeah, FL
Resurrección Ángeles Metropolitan Skills Center, Los Angeles, CA
Linda Bolognesi Fairfax County Public Schools, Adult and Community Education, Falls Church, VA
Patricia Boquiren Metropolitan Skills Center, Los Angeles, CA
Paul Buczko Pacoima Skills Center, Pacoima, CA
Matthew Horowitz Metropolitan Skills Center, Los Angeles, CA
Gabriel de la Hoz The English Center, Miami, FL
Cam-Tu Huynh Los Angeles Unified School District, Los Angeles, CA
Jorge Islas Whitewater Unified School District, Adult Education, Whitewater, WI
Lisa Johnson City College of San Francisco, San Francisco, CA
Loreto Kaplan Collier County Public Schools Adult ESOL Program, Naples, FL
Teressa Kitchen Collier County Public Schools Adult ESOL Program, Naples, FL
Anjie Martin Whitewater Unified School District, Adult Education, Whitewater, WI
Elida Matthews College of the Mainland, Texas City, TX
Penny Negron College of the Mainland, Texas City, TX
Manuel Pando Coral Park High School, Miami, FL
Susan Ritter Evans Community Adult School, Los Angeles, CA
Susan Ross Torrance Adult School, Torrance, CA
Beatrice Shields Fairfax County Public Schools, Adult and Community Education, Falls Church, VA
Oscar Solís Coral Park High School, Miami, FL
Wanda W. Weaver Literacy Council of Prince George's County, Hyattsville, MD

Reviewers

Lisa Agao Fresno Adult School, Fresno, CA
Carol Antuñano The English Center, Miami, FL
Euphronia Awakuni Evans Community Adult School, Los Angeles, CA
Jack Bailey Santa Barbara Adult Education, Santa Barbara, CA
Robert Breitbard District School Board of Collier County, Naples, FL
Diane Burke Evans Community Adult School, Los Angeles, CA
José A. Carmona Embry-Riddle Aeronautical University, Daytona Beach, FL
Veronique Colas Los Angeles Technology Center, Los Angles, CA
Carolyn Corrie Metropolitan Skills Center, Los Angeles, CA
Marti Estrin Santa Rosa Junior College, Sebastopol, CA
Sheila Friedman Metropolitan Skills Center, Los Angeles, CA
José Gonzalez Spanish Education Development Center, Washington, D.C.
Allene G. Grognet Vice President (Emeritus), Center for Applied Linguistics
J. Quinn Harmon-Kelley Venice Community Adult School, Los Angeles, CA
Edwina Hoffman Miami-Dade County Public Schools, Coral Gables, FL
Eduardo Honold Far West Project GREAT, El Paso, TX
Leigh Jacoby Los Angeles Community Adult School, Los Angeles, CA
Fayne Johnson Broward County Public Schools, Ft. Lauderdale, FL
Loreto Kaplan Collier County Public Schools Adult ESOL Program, Naples, FL
Synthia LaFontaine Collier County Public Schools, Naples, FL
Gretchen Lammers-Ghereben Martinez Adult Education, Martinez, CA
Susan Lanzano Editorial Consultant, Briarcliff Manor, NY
Karen Mauer ESL Express, Euless, TX
Rita McSorley North East Independent School District, San Antonio, TX
Alice-Ann Menjivar Carlos Rosario International Public Charter School, Washington, D.C.
Sue Pace Santa Ana College School of Continuing Education, Santa Ana, CA
Isabel Perez American High School, Hialeah, FL
Howard Pomann Union County College, Elizabeth, NJ
Lesly Prudent Miami-Dade County Public Schools, Miami, FL
Valentina Purtell North Orange County Community College District, Anaheim, CA
Mary Ray Fairfax County Adult ESOL, Falls Church, VA
Laurie Shapero Miami-Dade Community College, Miami, FL
Felissa Taylor Nause Austin, TX
Meintje Westerbeek Baltimore City Community College, Baltimore, MD

Thanks also to the following teachers, who contributed their ideas for the Persistence Activities:

Dave Coleman Los Angeles Unified School District, Los Angeles, CA
Renee Collins Elk Grove Adult and Community Education, Elk Grove, CA
Elaine Klapman Venice Community Adult School, Venice, CA (retired)
Yvonne Wong Nishio Evans Community Adult School, Los Angeles, CA (retired)
Daniel S. Pittaway North Orange County Community College District, Anaheim, CA
Laurel Pollard Educational Consultant, Tucson, AZ
Eden Quimzon Santiago Canyon College, Division of Continuing Education, Orange, CA

About the Series Consultants and Authors

SERIES CONSULTANTS

Dr. Beatriz B. Díaz has taught ESL for more than three decades in Miami. She has a master's degree in TESOL and a doctorate in education from Nova Southeastern University. She has given trainings and numerous presentations at international, national, state, and local conferences throughout the United States, the Caribbean, and South America. Dr. Díaz is the district supervisor for the Miami-Dade County Public Schools Adult ESOL Program, one of the largest in the United States.

Ronna Magy has worked as an ESL classroom teacher and teacher-trainer for nearly three decades. Most recently, she has worked as the ESL Teacher Adviser in charge of site-based professional development for the Division of Adult and Career Education of the Los Angeles Unified School District. She has trained teachers of adult English language learners in many areas, including lesson planning, learner persistence and goal setting, and cooperative learning. A frequent presenter at local, state and national, and international conferences, Ms. Magy is the author of adult ESL publications on life skills and test preparation, U.S. citizenship, reading and writing, and workplace English. She holds a master's degree in social welfare from the University of California at Berkeley.

Federico Salas-Isnardi has worked for 20 years in the field of adult education as an ESL and GED instructor, professional development specialist, curriculum writer, and program administrator. He has trained teachers of adult English language learners for over 15 years on topics ranging from language acquisition and communicative competence to classroom management and individualized professional development planning. Mr. Salas-Isnardi has been a contributing writer or consultant for a number of ESL publications, and he has co-authored curriculum for site-based workforce ESL and Spanish classes. He holds a master's degree in applied linguistics from the University of Houston and has completed a number of certificates in educational leadership.

AUTHORS

Wendy Pratt Long has previously worked as an EFL teacher and administrator. She has taught English to children, adolescents, and adults at all language levels in Mexico and Canada. She earned a master's degree in applied linguistics from the Universidad de las Americas, in Puebla, Mexico. Now working in the field of educational publishing, she has authored and co-authored ancillary materials including *Center Stage 2 Teacher's Edition*, *Summit 2 Workbook*, *Top Notch 2 Workbook*, *Top Notch Copy & Go* (Fundamentals and Level 3), and *Top Notch Assessment Packages* (Fundamentals and Levels 2 and 3). She has collaborated with Pearson Longman on numerous other projects, including the assessment programs for *Center Stage 2* and *Summit 2* and CD-ROMs for multiple levels of the *WorldView* and *Trends* series.

Sarah Lynn has taught ESL and EFL for 20 years in the United States and abroad, and she currently teaches ESL at the Harvard Bridge to Learning and Literacy Program in Cambridge, Massachusetts. Ms. Lynn holds a master's degree in TESOL from Columbia University. She has trained volunteers and given workshops on the teaching of reading, kinesthetic techniques in the classroom, and cross-cultural communication. She has developed curricula for adult education programs in the areas of reading, life skills, and civics, and she is the co-author of *Business Across Cultures*. She has also contributed to numerous teacher resource materials, including those for *Side by Side*, *Foundations*, and *Word by Word*.

Scope and Sequence

UNIT	VOCABULARY	LISTENING	SPEAKING AND PRONUNCIATION	GRAMMAR
Pre-Unit **Getting Started** *page 2*	• Reasons for studying English • Ways to ask for help	• Listen to an introduction • Listen to ways of asking for help	• Introduce yourself • Greet people and ask where they are from • Talk about your goals for learning English • Ask for help	• Simple present of *be*
1 **Making Connections** *page 5*	• Physical descriptions • Personalities	Listen to conversations about: • the way people look • personalities • getting to know someone	• Describe the way people look • Describe people by their personality • Make an introduction • Get to know someone you just met • Recognize appropriate topics for conversation • Word stress • Vowel sounds in unstressed syllables • Sentence stress	• Simple present: *be* + adjective • Simple present: *have* + object • *Be*: Compound sentences with *and/but* • *Be*: Additions with *and...*, *too/and..., not, either* • Simple present tense of *be*: *Yes/No* and information questions
2 **All in the Family** *page 25*	• Family members • Ways to keep in touch with family	Listen to conversations about: • family members • things people have in common • keeping in touch with family Listen to a game show quiz about family members	• Talk about your life and family • Compare families in the U.S. and your country • Talk about what people have in common • Ask about keeping in touch with family members • Word stress • Strong and weak pronunciations of *do*	• Simple present affirmative and negative: *have/live/work* • Simple present: Additions with *and..., too/and... not, either* • Simple present: *Yes/No* and information questions
3 **Lots To Do** *page 45*	• Clothes and materials • Daily errands • Problems with purchases	Listen to conversations about: • clothing someone needs or wants • errands and shopping plans • problems with purchases Listen to a radio interview with shoppers	• Talk about the types of store sales • Describe clothing you need or want • Talk about errands and shopping plans • Describe problems with purchases • Pronunciation of *need to* and *want to* • Pronunciation of *going to*	• Simple present: *want/need* + infinitive • *Be going to* + verb • Adverbs of degree: *very/too*
4 **Small Talk** *page 65*	• Free-time activities • Types of classes • Chores • Reasons to decline an invitation	Listen to conversations about: • weekend activities • likes and dislikes • accepting or declining an invitation Listen to a radio talk show offering tips for doing chores	• Talk about your weekend activities • Communicate your likes and dislikes • Invite someone to do something • Accept or decline an invitation politely • Words with one unpronounced syllable • Pronunciation of *have to* and *has to*	• Adverbs of frequency • Questions with *How often/* frequency time expressions • Simple present: *like/love/hate* + infinitive • Modal: *have to*

LIFE SKILLS	READING	WRITING	NUMERACY	PERSISTENCE
• Ask for help when you don't understand	• Locate the U.S. map and world map in your book	• Write questions to complete a conversation	• Unit and page numbers	• Learn about your book • Meet your classmates • Identify your goals for studying English
• Understand abbreviations on an ID card • Complete an application for an ID card • Complete a driver's license application	• Read an article about ways people learn • Take a quiz about learning styles • Reading Skill: Find the main idea • Problem-solving: Read about responding to impolite questions	• Describe the way people look • Write about your personality • Write learning tips to match your learning style	• Heights and weights • Telephone numbers • Street addresses • Dates • Social Security and ID numbers	• Find classmates with the same learning style and give tips for learning English • Play a game to remember your classmates' names • Make a booklet about the members of your class
• Ask about sending mail • Identify types of mail • Understand post office mailing services • Complete a post office customs form	• Read about a family • Read an advice column about managing responsibilities • Reading Skill: Retell information in your own words • Problem-solving: Read about a conflict with a family member	• Write about your life and family • Write a list of your responsibilities • Describe how people are similar	• Weights of letters and packages • Shipping times for post office mailing services	• Find things you and your classmates have in common • Make a poster about class members' personalities
• Count your change • Read a store ad • Understand types of sales, sale prices, and discounts • Read a sales receipt • Ask about a mistake on a sales receipt • Write a personal check	• Read an article about ways to pay for purchases • Reading Skill: Identify the writer's purpose • Problem-solving: Read about a problem with a purchase	• Write about clothes you need or want • Write about some people's errands • Write about how you will pay for your next big purchase • Write reasons that people are returning clothes	• Count change • Prices in a product ad • Percentages of sale discounts • Amounts of discounts, tax, and total on a sales receipt • Calculations of the cost of different payment methods	• Visualize your goals for learning English • Make a neighborhood shopping guide
• Read a community calendar • Talk about the schedule of an event • Complete a library card application	• Read a bar graph about free-time activities in the U.S. • Read advice about rude and polite behavior on an online message board • Reading Skill: Identify the topic • Problem-solving: Read about declining an invitation politely	• List your weekend plans • Write about your likes and dislikes • Write about what is rude or polite in your country	• Dates on a calendar • Starting and ending times for scheduled events • Amounts and percentages in a bar graph	• Make plans to practice English outside of class • Make a neighborhood activity guide

Text in red = Civics and American culture

UNIT	VOCABULARY	LISTENING	SPEAKING AND PRONUNCIATION	GRAMMAR
5 **At Home** *page 85*	• Home repair problems • Types of repair people • Driving directions	Listen to conversations about: • home repairs • renting an apartment • getting directions Listen to directions on a recorded telephone message	• Describe home repair problems • Ask for information about an apartment • Ask for and give directions to community locations • Stress in two-word nouns • Voiced and voiceless *th* sounds	• Present continuous: Affirmative and negative statements • *There is/There are*: Affirmative and negative statements, questions, and short answers
6 **In the Past** *page 105*	• Events with family and friends • Family activities • Milestones in a person's life • Commuting problems	Listen to conversations about: • events with family and friends • life milestones • a bad day Listen to a radio interview with a famous person	• Talk about past activities • Talk about personal milestones • Talk about a bad day • Extra syllable for *–ed* endings • Intonation of statements repeated as questions	• Simple past: Regular verbs • Simple past: Irregular verbs • Simple past: *Yes/No* questions and short answers • Simple past: Information questions
7 **Health Watch** *page 125*	• Health problems • Symptoms • Common injuries	Listen to conversations about: • making a doctor's appointment • an injury • calling in sick to work	• Describe a symptom • Make a doctor's appointment • Talk about an injury • Report an absence to a work supervisor • Linking a consonant to a vowel sound • Pronunciation of *t* between two vowel sounds • Using pauses to organize sentences into thought groups	• Prepositions of time: *at/by/in/on/ from… to* • Simple past: Irregular verbs • Ways to express reasons: *because* + a subject and a verb; *for* + a noun
8 **Job Hunting** *page 145*	• Job duties • Job skills • Fields of employment	Listen to a job interview about: • job duties and skills • work history • availability	• Talk about your skills at a job interview • Talk about things you can and can't do • Talk about your work experience • Explain your reason for changing jobs • Answer questions about your availability • Pronunciation of *can* and *can't* • Intonation of questions with *or*	• Can to express ability: Affirmative and negative statements, *Yes/No* questions and short answers • Time expressions with *ago, last, in,* and *later* • Ways to express alternatives: *or, and*

LIFE SKILLS	READING	WRITING	NUMERACY	PERSISTENCE
• Read apartment ads • Understand abbreviations in rental ads • Know where to find apartment ads • Complete an application for an apartment • Interpret a map	• Read a U.S. map • Read an article about a U.S. city • **Reading Skill: Skim to get the main idea** • Problem-solving: Read about a problem getting repairs in a rental apartment	• Write about your community • Write driving directions • Write a housing classified ad	• Costs of rent, utilities, fees, and security deposit • Number of rooms in an apartment	• Find a classmate who lives in your area. Discuss what you like and dislike about your community. • Write a daily planner for studying English
• Recognize U.S. holidays • Make a holiday calendar	• Read a biography of Oprah Winfrey • Read a time line of a person's life • **Reading Skill: Scan for information** • Problem-solving: Read about a mistake at work	• Write about your past activities • Write about milestones in your life • Make a time line of your life • Write a short autobiography • Write an absence note to a teacher	• Dates on a calendar • Lengths of time • Times of day	• Set goals to use vocabulary strategies
• Read a medical appointment card • Read OTC medical labels • Read a prescription • Read prescription medicine labels and instructions • Ask questions about taking medicine	• Read an article about ways to manage stress • Take a stress quiz • **Reading Skill: Use formatting clues to find main points** • Problem-solving: Read about a problem with a coworker	• Complete a medical history form • Write about an injury • Write about stress in your life	• Dates and times of appointments • Medicine dosages • Expiration dates • Score a quiz and interpret the results	• Find classmates who share the same sources of stress. Talk about ways to manage stress. • Identify obstacles to class attendance and make plans to overcome them • Make a booklet of home remedies
• Read help-wanted ads • Understand abbreviations in help-wanted ads • Complete a job application	• Read a time line • Read an article about jobs in the U.S. • Read information about job interviews • **Reading Skill: Predict the topic** • Problem-solving: Read about what to say in a job interview when you've been fired	• Write about your dream job • Write about your job skills and work history • Write a time line • Write about a job you want in five years • Write about a person's availability	• Hourly wages • Telephone numbers • Periods of time • Percentages of workers in fields of employment • Starting and ending time of a work shift	• Find classmates who want the same job in five years. Talk about what you need to do to get the job. • Assign jobs to students to assist the teacher in class • Make a job skills booklet

Text in red = Civics and American culture

UNIT	VOCABULARY	LISTENING	SPEAKING AND PRONUNCIATION	GRAMMAR
9 **Parents and Children** *page 165*	• Types of schools • School subjects • Ways children misbehave in school	Listen to conversations about: • a parent-teacher conference and school events • a child's progress in school • a child's behavior in school	• Make plans for school events • Communicate with your child's teacher • Discuss your child's progress in school • Discuss your child's behavior in school • Pronunciation of *will* • The *'s* or *s'* possessive ending	• Future with *will* • Adverbs of manner • Object pronouns • Possessive nouns
10 **Let's Eat!** *page 185*	• Food containers and quantities • Types of food stores • Food on a restaurant menu	Listen to conversations about: • quantities of food • reasons for buying specific brands of food • ordering food at a restaurant Listen to a food commercial	• Talk about the food you need to buy • Compare different brands of food products • Order food at a restaurant • Weak pronunciation of *to, the, a,* and *of*	• Count nouns/Non-count nouns • *How much/How many* • Comparative adjectives with *than* • Quantifiers with plural and non-count nouns
11 **Call 911!** *page 205*	• Medical emergencies • Dangerous situations • Traffic violations	Listen to conversations about: • a medical emergency call to 911 • an emergency situation • a traffic stop Listen to a police officer talk about what to do if you are pulled over for a traffic violation	• Call 911 to report a medical emergency • Describe an emergency situation • Respond to a police officer's instructions during a traffic stop • Stressed syllables • The sound /h/ at the beginning of words	• Present continuous: Statements and questions • *There was/There were* • Compound imperatives
12 **The World of Work** *page 225*	• Job responsibilities • Reasons people change their work schedules	Listen to conversations about: • policies at work • covering a work shift • changing your work schedule Listen to a talk about company policies at a new employee orientation	• Ask questions about company policies • Ask a co-worker to cover your shift • Give reasons for missing work • Request a schedule change • Rising intonation in *Yes/No* questions • Falling intonation in statements and information questions	• Expressions of necessity: *must/have to* • Expressions of prohibition: *must not/can't* • Information questions with *Who* • Information questions with *What/ Which/When/Where* • *Can/Could* to ask permission

Text in red = Civics and American culture

LIFE SKILLS	READING	WRITING	NUMERACY	PERSISTENCE
• Leave and take a telephone message • Complete a telephone message form • Complete a school enrollment form	• Read about parent-teacher conferences and PTOs • Read about ways students can get help with schoolwork • Read an article about the cost of going to college • Interpret a bar graph • Reading Skill: Use information in charts and tables • Read a school newsletter • Problem-solving: Read about a problem with a child's behavior in school	• Write about the progress of students you know • Write about your educational goals	• Dates and times of school events • Telephone numbers • Percentages of students going to college • Costs of tuition and college expenses	• Create a portfolio of your English work • Make a poster about ways to improve your English skills
• Understand the importance of a healthy diet • Read ingredient and nutrition labels • Read food ads • Compare the healthfulness of two food products • Read and order food from a menu	• Read an article about the nutrients in food • Read an article about the effects of caffeine • Reading Skill: Get meaning from context • Problem-solving: Read about a parent's problem providing healthy meals for her family	• Write a food shopping list • Complete a healthy eating log • Compare food in a supermarket ad • Write a radio commercial for a food product • Keep a caffeine journal	• Quantities of food • Amounts on food labels • Prices of food products	• Plan a class picnic • Get to know a classmate over tea and cookies • Make a food shopping guide
• Call 911 to report a medical emergency • Identify fire hazards in the home • Understand fire safety devices and procedures • Create a fire escape plan • Identify ways to avoid accidents at home • Respond to a police officer's instructions • Complete an employee accident report	• Read about 911 calls • Read fire safety tips • Read about a woman's actions during a fire • Read an article about common causes of home injuries • Reading Skill: Identify supporting details • Problem-solving: Read about reporting an accident at work	• Write about what people are doing • Describe emergency situations • Write about the safety of your home	• Street addresses • Numbers of home injuries per year • Percentages of common household injuries	• Identify ways to improve your study skills and habits • Make a fire escape plan poster for your school
• Read a pay stub • Understand payroll deductions and overtime hours • Understand the Social Security program • Complete a vacation request form	• Read an employee manual • Read about overtime hours • Read about a problem at work • Read a FAQ about the Social Security program • Reading Skill: Think about what you know • Problem-solving: Read about a worker's problem with a schedule	• Write about your responsibilities • Write about your life after you retire	• Dates • Amounts of money on a pay stub • Calculations of earnings and deductions on a pay stub • Times on a schedule	• Form into one of three groups: employees, students, and parents. Discuss your responsibilities. • Review the unit goals you have achieved • Make an employee manual

Text in red = Civics and American culture

Correlations

UNIT	CASAS Reading Basic Skill Content Standards	CASAS Listening Basic Skill Content Standards
1	**U1:** 1.1, 1.2, 1.3, 1.4, 2.2, 3.1, 3.2, 3.8; **L1:** 3.12, 6.1; **L2:** 2.5, 2.8, 3.10; **L3:** 2.5, 6.1; **L4:** 2.7, 4.1, 4.6; **L5:** 2.11, 2.12; **L6:** 3.10, 3.14; **L7:** 3.3, 3.6, 7.1; **L8:** 3.12, 6.1; **L9:** 4.1; **SWYK Expand:** 3.3, 3.6	**U1:** 1.4; **L1:** 1.1, 2.3; **L2:** 3.3, 3.4; **L3:** 3.2, 3.3, 3.4; **L4:** 3.4, 3.5; **L5:** 4.2, 4.3, 4.4; **L6:** 3.2; **L7:** 3.4; **L8:** 2.1, 3.3, 3.4; **L9:** 3.1; **SWYK Expand:** 2.1, 3.1, 3.2
2	**U2:** 1.1, 1.2, 1.3, 1.4, 2.2, 3.1, 3.2, 3.8; **L1:** 2.5, 2.9, 3.12; **L2:** 3.12 ; **L3:** 3.12, 4.9; **L4:** 7.1, 7.2, 7.6; **L5:** 3.12; **L6:** 3.12; **L7:** 4.8. 4.10; **L8:** 3.12; **SWYK Review:** 3.11, 4.8; **SWYK Expand:** 3.10, 7.1, 7.8	**U2:** 1.4; **L1:** 1.1, 1.3; **L2:** 1.3, 2.1, 3.1, 3.3; **L3:** 1.3, 2.1, 3.1; **L4:** 1.3, 2.1, 3.1, 3.4; **L5:** 1.3, 2.1, 3.1; **L6:** 3.3; **L7:** 3.3, 3.5; **L8:** 3.3; **L9:** 3.3, 3.4, 3.5; **SWYK Review:** 3.4; **SWYK Expand:** 3.3, 3.4, 3.5
3	**U3:** 1.1, 1.2, 1.3, 1.4, 2.2, 3.1, 3.2, 3.8; **L1:** 3.12; **L2:** 3.12, 4.8; **L3:** 3.12; **L4:** 4.1, 4.4, 4.6, 4.10, 6.2, 7.13; **L5:** 3.14; **L6:** 2.5; **L7:** 4.9, 7.1, 7.2, 7.3, 7.11; **L8:** 2.8, 3.12; **SWYK Review:** 2.11; **SWYK Expand:** 7.1, 7.8	**U3:** 1.4; **L2:** 1.5, 3.3, 3.4; **L3:** 1.5; **L4:** 2.1, 3.3, 3.4, 3.5; **L5:** 1.5, 3.7, 4.1; **L6:** 1.5, 3.4; **L7:** 3.4; **L8:** 3.4, 4.11; **SWYK Expand:** 3.4
4	**U4:** 1.1, 1.2, 1.3, 1.4, 2.2, 3.1, 3.2, 3.8; **L1:** 3.12, 6.1; **L2:** 3.12, 6.1; **L3:** 4.6, 4.8, 4.9; **L4:** 4.6, 6.2; **L5:** 3.12, 6.1, 7.4; **L6:** 4.9, 7.8; **L7:** 3.11, 7.2; **L8:** 3.12; **L9:** 2.8; **SWYK Expand:** 7.8	**U4:** 1.4; **L1:** 1.1; **L2:** 1.3, 3.4; **L3:** 3.5; **L4:** 3.4, 5.1, 6.2; **L5:** 3.4, 6.1; **L6:** 3.4; **L7:** 3.3; **L8:** 1.5, 3.3, 3.4; **L9:** 3.2; **SWYK Review:** 1.5; **SWYK Expand:** 3.1, 3.2, 3.3, 3.4
5	**U5:** 1.1, 1.2, 1.3, 1.4, 2.2, 3.1, 3.2, 3.8; **L1:** 3.12, 6.1; **L2:** 3.12, 6.1; **L3:** 2.8, 3.12; **L4:** 2.3, 2.7, 2.12, 4.6; **L5:** 2.8, **L6:** 2.3, 4.6; **L7:** 4.9, 6.2; **L8:** 4.9; **SWYK Review:** 2.3, 4.9; **SWYK Expand:** 3.12, 7.1	**U5:** 1.4; **L1:** 1.1; **L2:** 5.1, 7.7; **L3:** 4.4; **L4:** 3.4; **L5:** 5.1; **L6:** 1.3, 3.4; **L7:** 3.4; **L8:** 2.6; **SWYK Review:** 2.6; **SWYK Expand:** 4.8, 5.1
6	**U6:** 1.1, 1.2, 1.3, 1.4, 2.2, 3.1, 3.2, 3.8; **L1:** 3.12, 6.1; **L2:** 3.12, 6.1; **L3:** 3.3; **L4:** 3.16, 4.3, 4.6; **L5:** 2.8; **L6:** 2.8; **L7:** 3.10, 7.2, 7.4; **L8:** 3.12, 6.1; **L9:** 3.11; **SWYK Review:** 3.11; **SWYK Expand:** 7.4	**U6:** 1.1, 1.4, 3.4; **L1:** 1.3, 3.4, 3.9; **L2:** 1.3, 3.4, 3.9; **L3:** 1.3, 3.2; **L4:** 5.1; **L5:** 3.6, 4.10, 5.1; **L6:** 3.9; **L7:** 3.4; **L8:** 3.4, 3.8; **L9:** 3.4, 3.8; **SWYK Review:** 3.4, 3.8; **SWYK Expand:** 3.3, 3.4, 3.5
7	**U7:** 1.1, 1.2, 1.3, 1.4, 2.2, 3.1, 3.2, 3.8; **L1:** 3.12, 6.1; **L2:** 3.12, 4.6, 6.1; **L3:** 3.10, 4.6; **L4:** 3.11, 4.6, 7.13; **L5:** 3.11, 3.12, 6.1; **L6:** 3.11, 6.1; **L7:** 4.6, 4.9, 4.10, 6.2, 6.6; **L8:** 3.11; **L9:** 3.9; **SWYK Review:** 3.9; **SWYK Expand:** 3.10, 7.1, 7,8	**U7:** 1.4; **L1:** 1.1; **L2:** 3.4, 4.11; **L3:** 3.4; **L4:** 3.4; 3.5; **L5:** 1.5, 2.1, 4.11; **L6:** 1.3, 3.3; **L7:** 5.1; **L8:** 1.5, 2.1, 5.1; **SWYK Expand:** 3.3, 3.4
8	**U8:** 1.1, 1.2, 1.3, 1.4, 2.2, 3.1, 3.2, 3.8; **L1:** 2.9, 2.11, 3.11, 3.12, 6.1; **L2:** 3.12, 6.1; **L3:** 3.11, 3.12, 6.1; **L4:** 2.6, 2.7, 3.11, 4.6; **L5:** 7.4; **L6:** 7.4; **L7:** 6.1, 7.2; **L8:** 3.11; **L9:** 3.11, 4.6; **SWYK Review:** 3.11, 7.4; **SWYK Expand:** 3.11, 7.8	**U8:** 1.4; **L1:** 3.4, **L2:** 1.5, 4.10; **L3:** 1.5, 3.2, **L4:** 3.4, 4.10; **L5:** 4.10, 5.2, 6.1; **L6:** 3.4; **L7:** 3.4, 4.10; **L8:** 3.3, 3.4, 3.6, 4.7; **SWYK Expand:** 3.3, 3.4, 3.5
9	**U9:** 1.1, 1.2, 1.3, 1.4, 2.2, 3.1, 3.2, 3.8; **L1:** 2.3, 3.12, 6.1; **L2:** 2.6, 4.2, 4.3; **L3:** 3.3, 4.9; **L4:** 4.2, 4.3, 4.6; **L5:** 2.8, 2.9, 6.1; **L6:** 2.8, 2.9, 3.10; **L7:** 4.8, 4.9, 7.1, 7.8; **L8:** 2.8, 3.11; **L9:** 2.8, 3.10; **SWYK Review:** 2.8, 3.10, 4.6 **SWYK Expand:** 4.2, 4.3, 4.8, 7.8	**U9:** 1.4; **L1:** 4.10; **L2:** 4.3, 4.4; **L3:** 3.4; **L4:** 2.5, 3.1, 4.6, 4.10, 6.1; **L5:** 3.1, 4.6, 4.10, 6.1; **L6:** 1.3; **L7:** 4.3, 4.4; **L8:** 3.4; 4.3, 4.4; **SWYK Expand:** 3.4
10	**U10:** 1.1, 1.2, 1.3, 1.4, 2.2, 3.1, 3.2, 3.8; **L1:** 2.3, 3.12, 6.1; **L2:** 3.12, 6.1; **L3:** 2.8; **L4:** 2.7, 4.1, 6.2, 6.6; **L5:** 3.3; **L6:** 2.9, 4.10; **L7:** 3.13, 6.6; **L8:** 2.3; **L9:** 2.8; **SWYK Review:** 2.8; **SWYK Expand:** 2.6, 4.1, 6.6, 7.3	**U10:** 1.4; **L1:** 1.1; **L2:** 4.10; **L3:** 3.4; **L5:** 1.3, 3.3, 4.10; **L7:** 3.4; 4.10; **L8:** 2.1
11	**U11:** 1.1, 1.2, 1.3, 1.4, 2.2, 3.1, 3.2, 3.8; **L1:** 3.12, 6.1; **L2:** 3.12, 6.1; **L3:** 2.5; **L4:** 3.12, 4.9, 6.1, 6.6, 7.8; **L5:** 3.11, 3.12, 4.10, 6.1; **L6:** 2.8, 3.12, 6.1; **L7:** 3.12, 6.1, 7.3; **L8:** 3.11, 3.12, 6.1; **L9:** 3.3; **SWYK Review:** 3.3; **SWYK Expand:** 3.11, 7.8	**U11:** 1.4; **L1:** 1.1; **L2:** 3.4, 5.1, 6.4; **L3:** 3.4; **L4:** 4.10; **L5:** 1.3, 4.4, 4.10, 6.2; **L6:** 3.3, 3.4, 4.4, 4.10; **L7:** 3.3, 3.4 **L8:** 3.3, 4.10; **SWYK Expand:** 4.10, 6.4
12	**U12:** 1.1, 1.2, 1.3, 1.4, 2.2, 3.1, 3.2, 3.8; **L1:** 2.12, 3.12, 6.1; **L2:** 2.12; **L3:** 2.12, 3.11; **L4:** 3.11, 4.1, 4.4, 4.7; **L5:** 7.8; **L6:** 4.8; **L7:** 6.2, 6.5, 6.6; **L8:** 3.11, 4.6; **L9:** 3.3; **SWYK Review:** 3.3; **SWYK Expand:** 7.9	**U12:** 1.4; **L1:** 4.10; **L2:** 3.6, 4.11, 5.4; **L3:** 3.3; **L4:** 3.4; **L5:** 5.2, 6.2; **L6:** 3.4; **L7:** 3.4, 5.1; **L8:** 6.3, 7.1; **L9:** 6.4; **SWYK Expand:** 4.10, 6.4

CASAS Competencies	LAUSD ESL Beginning High Competencies	Florida Adult ESOL Course Standards
U1: 0.1.2, 0.1.4, 0.1.5, 0.1.7, 0.2.1, 0.2.4; **L1:** 7.4.1; **L4:** 0.2.2, 4.1.1; **L6:** 0.2.3; **L7:** 0.2.3, 7.4.1, 7.4.9; **SWYK Review:** 0.1.6; **SWYK Expand:** 4.4.1, 7.1.1, 7.1.2, 7.3.1, 7.3.2, 7.3.3, 7.3.4	3; 4; 5; 6; 7a; 63	3.01.01, 3.01.02, 3.01.03, 3.06.04
U2: 0.1.2, 0.1.4, 0.1.5, 0.1.7, 0.2.1, 0.2.4; **L1:** 6.6.5, 7.4.1; **L4:** 0.2.3, 7.1.1, 7.2.1, 7.5.5; **L5:** 7.5.5; **L6:** 0.2.3; **L7:** 2.4.2, 2.4.3, 2.4.4, 2.4.5; **SWYK Review:** 7.2.3; **SWYK Expand:** 7.1.1, 7.1.2, 7.1.4, 7.3.1, 7.3.2, 7.3.3, 7.4.8, 7.5.3, 7.3.4	4; 5; 7a; 24a	3.01.02, 3.01.03, 3.02.01, 3.02.07
U3: 0.1.2, 0.1.4, 0.1.5, 0.1.7, 0.2.1, 0.2.4; **L1:** 1.2.9, 7.4.3; **L2:** 1.2.9, 1.3.1; **L3:** 1.2.9, 1.31, 1.3.3, 1.6.4, 1.6.5; **L4:** 1.1.6, 1.2.1, 1.2.2, 1.2.4, 1.2.9, 1.3.3, 1.6.3, 1.6.4, 1.8.1; **L5:** 0.2.3, 1.2.6, 1.2.7; **L6:** 1.2.6, 1.2.7; **L7:** 1.3.1, 1.5.2, 1.8.1, 1.8.6; **L8:** 0.1.8, 1.3.3; **L9:** 1.3.3; **SWYK Review:** 1.3.3, 7.1.1; **SWYK Expand:** 1.2.6, 1.2.9, 1.3.3, 7.1.1, 7.1.2, 7.3.1, 7.3.2, 7.3.3, 7.3.4	3; 5; 7a; 7b; 8a; 24a; 27; 32; 33; 62a	3.01.03, 3.02.05, 3.04.01, 3.04.02, 3.04.06, 3.04.08,
U4: 0.1.2, 0.1.4, 0.1.5, 0.1.7, 0.2.1, 0.2.4; **L1:** 0.2.3, 2.6.1, 6.6.5, 7.4.3; **L2:** 2.6.1, 2.6.3, 2.8.2; **L3:** 0.2.3, 2.3.2, 2.6.1, 2.8.2; **L4:** 0.2.2, 2.3.2, 2.6.1, 2.5.6, 2.6.3; **L6:** 0.2.3, 2.6.1, 6.7.3; **L7:** 0.2.3, 7.7.1, 7.7.3, 7.7.4; **SWYK Review:** 2.6.1, 2.6.3, 7.1.1; **SWYK Expand:** 2.6.1, 2.6.3, 7.1.1, 7.1.2, 7.3.1, 7.3.2, 7.3.3, 7.3.4, 7.5.5	5; 7; 7a; 9a; 9b; 9c; 21; 22; 62a	3.01.02, 3.01.03, 3.02.02
U5: 0.1.2, 0.1.4, 0.1.5, 0.1.7, 0.2.1, 0.2.4; **L1:** 1.4.1, 1.4.7, 7.4.1; **L2:** 1.4.1, 1.4.7; **L3:** 1.4.1, 1.4.7; **L4:** 1.4.1, 1.4.2; **L5:** 1.4.1, 1.4.2; **L6:** 1.4.1, 2.2.1; **L7:** 1.4.2, 2.2.1; **L8:** 1.2.7, 2.2.1; **SWYK Review:** 2.2.1; **SWYK Expand:** 1.4.2, 1.4.5, 1.4.7, 5.31, 5.32, 7.3.1, 7.1.1, 7.1.2, 7.1.4, 7.3.2, 7.3.3, 7.3.4	17; 17a; 23a; 23b; 37; 38a; 38b; 38c; 38d; 39; 62b	3.01.03, 3.03.01, 3.04.04, 3.04.05, 3.04.06, 3.06.03
U6: 0.1.2, 0.1.4, 0.1.5, 0.1.7, 0.2.1, 0.2.4; **L1:** 7.1.4, 7.4.1; **L3:** 0.2.3, 7.4.3; **L4:** 2.3.2, 2.7.1; **L7:** 0.2.3, 6.7.1; **SWYK Review:** 0.1.6, 0.1.8; **SWYK Expand:** 0.1.6, 0.1.8, 2.7.1, 4.3.4, 4.4.1, 4.5.1, 4.6.4, 7.1.1, 7.1.2, 7.1.3, 7.3.1, 7.3.2, 7.3.3, 7.3.4, 7.4.1, 7.4.3	4; 5; 7; 7a; 11e; 16b; 25	3.01.02, 3.01.03, 3.02.03, 3.03.09, 3.03.11
U7: 0.1.2, 0.1.4, 0.1.5, 0.1.7, 0.2.1, 0.2.4; **L1:** 3.6.3, 7.4.1; **L2:** 3.1.2, 3.6.3; **L3:** 0.1.6, 3.1.2; **L4:** 0.1.8, 3.2.1, 3.3.1, 3.3.2, 3.3.4; **L5:** 0.1.8, 3.6.2, 3.6.3; **L6:** 0.2.3, 3.6.23, 3.6.3; **L7:** 0.2.3, 3.5.8, 3.5.9, 6.6.5, 7.5.4; **L8:** 0.1.8, 2.1.7, 3.5.4, 4.4.1; **L9:** 0.2.3, 1.2.7, 3.5.4, 3.6.3; **SWYK Review:** 0.1.6, 0.1.8, 3.1.2, 3.1.3, 3.6.3, 3.6.4; **SWYK Expand:** 3.1.2, 3.1.3, 3.3.1, 3.6.3, 3.6.4; 7.1.1, 7.1.2, 7.3.1, 7.3.2, 7.3.3, 7.3.4	10b; 17a; 17b; 42; 43; 44; 46; 47; 55a; 62	3.01.01, 3.01.06, 3.03.10, 3.03.11, 3.04.01, 3.05.01, 3.05.02, 3.05.03
U8: 0.1.2, 0.1.4, 0.1.5, 0.1.7, 0.2.1, 0.2.4; **L1:** 4.1.8, 7.1.1; **L2:** 0.1.6, 4.1.5, 4.1.8; **L3:** 0.1.6, 4.1.5, 4.1.8; **L4:** 4.1.2, 4.1.3, 4.1.6, 4.1.8, 4.2.5; **L5:** 4.1.2, 4.1.6, 4.1.8; **L6:** 4.1.6, 4.1.8, 6.7.3; **L7:** 0.2.3, 4.1.6, 4.1.8; **L8:** 4.1.6, 4.1.8; **L9:** 0.2.3; **SWYK Review:** 0.1.6, 4.1.5, 4.1.6, 4.1.7, 4.1.8; **SWYK Expand:** 0.1.6, 4.1.5, 4.1.6, 4.1.7, 4.1.8; 7.1.1, 7.1.2, 7.3.1, 7.3.2, 7.3.3, 7.3.4	7a; 51; 52a; 52b; 54a; 54b; 54c; 55b; 59a	3.03.01, 3.03.02, 3.03.03, 3.03.10, 3.03.11, 3.03.15
U9: 0.1.2, 0.1.4, 0.1.5, 0.1.7, 0.2.1, 0.2.4; **L1:** 2.8.1, 2.8.3, 7.4.1; **L2:** 0.1.6, 2.8.6; **L3:** 2.8.9, 7.7.4; **L4:** 2.1.7, 2.8.5; **L5:** 0.1.6, 0.1.8, 2.8.7, 7.5.1; **L6:** 0.1.6, 0.1.8, 7.5.1; **L7:** 0.2.3, 2.8.1, 6.6.5, 6.7.2, 7.1.1; **L8:** 0.1.6, 0.1.8, 2.8.6, 2.8.8; **L9:** 2.8.7; **SWYK Review:** 2.5.8, 2.8.3, 2.8.6, 2.8.8, 2.8.9, 5.6.5; **SWYK Expand:** 2.5.8, 2.8.3, 2.8.6, 2.8.8, 2.8.9, 5.6.5; 7.1.1, 7.1.2, 7.1.3, 7.1.4, 7.3.1, 7.3.2, 7.3.3, 7.3.4	13; 14; 17a; 17b; 21; 25	3.01.02, 3.01.04, 3.01.07, 3.02.09
U10: 0.1.2, 0.1.4, 0.1.5, 0.1.7, 0.2.1, 0.2.4; **L1:** 1.1.7, 1.2.8, 7.4.1; **L2:** 0.1.6 1.1.7, 1.2.8; **L3:** 0.2.3, 1.1.7, 1.2.8; **L4:** 1.2.8, 1.6.1, 3.5.1, 3.5.2, 3.5.9; **L5:** 0.1.6, 1.2.1, 1.2.2, 1.2.8, 3.5.2; **L6:** 1.2.1, 1.2.8, 3.5.2; **L7:** 0.2.3, 1.2.1, 1.2.2, 1.2.8, 3.5.2; **L8:** 0.1.6, 1.2.8, 2.6.4; **SWYK Review:** 1.1.4, 1.1.7, 1.2.2, 1.2.8; **SWYK Expand:** 0.1.6, 1.1.4, 1.1.7, 1.2.1, 1.2.2, 1.2.6, 1.2.8, 7.1.1, 7.1.2, 7.3.1, 7.3.2, 7.3.3, 7.3.4	32; 34; 35; 36	3.04.01, 3.04.02, 3.05.05, 3.05.06
U11: 0.1.2, 0.1.4, 0.1.5, 0.1.7, 0.2.1, 0.2.4; **L1:** 0.1.6, 0.1.8, 2.1.2, 2.5.1, 3.6.2, 3.6.4, 7.4.1; **L2:** 0.1.6, 0.1.8, 2.1.2, 2.2.1, 2.5.1, 3.6.2, 3.6.4; **L3:** 0.1.6, 0.1.8, .02.3, 2.1.2, 3.6.2, 3.6.4; **L4:** 1.4.8, 2.5.1, 3.4.2; **L5:** 0.1.8, 1.4.8, 7.3.1; **L6:** 1.4.8, 1.9.7; **L7:** 0.2.3, 1.4.8, 3.4.2; **L8:** 1.9.1, 1.9.7; **L9:** 1.9.1, 1.9.7; **SWYK Review:** 2.1.2, 2.5.1, 4.3.4; **SWYK Expand:** 2.1.2, 2.5.1, 3.4.8, 4.3.4, 4.4.1, 7.1.1, 7.1.2, 7.3.1, 7.3.2, 7.3.3, 7.3.4, 7.4.1	7a; 20; 23b; 42; 45b; 48; 49; 57	3.02.01, 3.03.08, 3.05.01, 3.05.02, 3.06.02, 3.06.04, 3.06.05, 3.07.03
U12: 0.1.2, 0.1.4, 0.1.5, 0.1.7, 0.2.1, 0.2.4; **L1:** 4.1.7, 4.1.8, 4.3.3, 4.4.1, 7.4.1; **L2:** 0.1.6, 4.1.7, 4.1.8, 4.4.1; **L3:** 4.1.7, 4.1.8, 4.4.1; **L4:** 1.1.6, 4.1.6, 4.2.1, 4.2.5, 4.4.3, 6.0.2, 6.6.5; **L5:** 1.1.6, 4.1.6, 4.4.1, 4.8.3; **L6:** 4.1.6, 4.4.3; **L7:** 0.2.3, 4.2.5, 5.5.9; **L8:** 4.1.6, 4.1.8, 4.25, 4.4.1, 4.4.2, 4.6.2; **SWYK Review:** 0.1.6, 4.2.4, 4.2.5, 4.3.2, 4.4.1, 4.4.2, 4.4.3, 4.4.4, 4.5.1, 4.6.1, 4.6.3; **SWYK Expand:** 0.1.6, 4.2.4, 4.2.5, 4.3.2, 4.4.1, 4.4.2, 4.4.3, 4.4.4, 4.5.1, 4.6.1, 4.6.3, 4.2.4, 7.1.1, 7.1.2, 7.1.4, 7.3.1, 7.3.2, 7.3.3, 7.3.4	7a; 8a; 8b; 11d; 11e; 46; 55; 55b; 55c	3.01.03, 3.02.01, 3.03.01, 3.03.02, 3.03.06, 3.03.07, 3.03.09, 3.03.10, 3.03.11

All units of *Future* meet most of the **EFF Content Standards**. For details, as well as for correlations to other state standards, go to www.pearsonlongman.com/future.

To the Teacher

Welcome to *Future*
English for Results

Future is a six-level, four-skills course for adults and young adults correlated to state and national standards. It incorporates research-based teaching strategies, corpus-informed language, and the best of modern technology.

KEY FEATURES

Future provides everything your students need in one integrated program.

In developing the course, we listened to what teachers asked for and we responded, providing six levels, more meaningful content, a thorough treatment of grammar, explicit skills development, abundant practice, multiple options for state-of-the-art assessment, and innovative components.

Future serves students' real-life needs.

We began constructing the instructional syllabus for *Future* by identifying what is most critical to students' success in their personal and family lives, in the workplace, as members of a community, and in their academic pursuits. *Future* provides outstanding coverage of life skills competencies, basing language teaching on actual situations that students are likely to encounter and equipping them with the skills they need to achieve their goals. The grammar and other language elements taught in each lesson grow out of these situations and are thus practiced in realistic contexts, enabling students to use language meaningfully, from the beginning.

Future grows with your students.

Future takes students from absolute beginner level through low-advanced proficiency in English, addressing students' abilities and learning priorities at each level. As the levels progress, the curricular content and unit structure change accordingly, with the upper levels incorporating more academic skills, more advanced content standards, and more content-rich texts.

Level	Description	CASAS Scale Scores
Intro	True Beginning	Below 180
1	Low Beginning	181–190
2	High Beginning	191–200
3	Low Intermediate	201–210
4	High Intermediate	211–220
5	Low Advanced	221–235

Future is fun!

Humor is built into each unit of *Future*. Many of the conversations, and especially the listenings, are designed to have an amusing twist at the end, giving students an extra reason to listen—something to anticipate with pleasure and to then take great satisfaction in once it is understood. In addition, many activities have students interacting in pairs and groups. Not only does this make classroom time more enjoyable, it also creates an atmosphere conducive to learning in which learners are relaxed, highly motivated, and at their most receptive.

Future puts the best of 21st-century technology in the hands of students and teachers.

In addition to its expertly developed print materials and audio components, *Future* goes a step further.

- Every **Student Book comes with a Practice Plus CD-ROM** for use at home, in the lab, or wherever students have access to a computer. The Practice Plus CD-ROM can be used both by students who wish to extend their practice beyond the classroom and by those who need to "make up" what they missed in class. The CD-ROM also includes the entire class audio program as MP3 files so students can get extra listening practice at their convenience.
- The **Workbook with Audio CD** gives students access to more listening practice than ever before possible.
- The **Tests and Test Prep** book comes with the *Future Exam*View® *Assessment Suite*, enabling teachers to print ready-made tests, customize these tests, or create their own tests for life skills, grammar, vocabulary, listening, and reading for students at three levels—on-level, pre-level, or above-level.
- The **Teacher Training DVD** provides demo lessons of real teachers using *Future* with their classes. Teachers can select from the menu and watch a specific type of lesson, such as a grammar presentation, or a specific type of activity, such as an information gap, at their own convenience.
- The **Companion Website** provides a variety of teaching support, including a pdf of the Teacher's Edition and Lesson Planner notes for each unit in the Student Book.

Future provides all the assessment tools you need.

- The **Placement Test** evaluates students' proficiency in all skill areas, allowing teachers and program administrators to easily assign students to the right classes.
- The **Tests and Test Prep** book for each level provides:
  - **Printed unit tests** with accompanying audio CD. These unit tests use standardized testing formats, giving students practice "bubbling-in" responses as required

for CASAS and other standardized tests. In addition, reproducible test prep worksheets and practice tests provide invaluable help to students unfamiliar with such test formats.

  o The *Future* **Exam***View*® *Assessment Suite* is a powerful program that allows teachers to create their own unique tests or to print or customize already prepared tests at three levels; pre-level, on-level, and above-level.

- **Performance-based assessment:** Lessons in the Student Book end with a "practical assessment" activity such as Role Play, Make it Personal, or Show What You Know. Each unit culminates with both a role-play activity and a problem-solving activity, which require students to demonstrate their oral competence in a holistic way. The **Teacher's Edition and Lesson Planner** provides speaking rubrics to make it easy for teachers to evaluate students' oral proficiency.

- **Self-assessment:** For optimal learning to take place, students need to be involved in setting goals and in monitoring their own progress. *Future* has addressed this in numerous ways. In the Student Book, checkboxes at the end of lessons invite students to evaluate their mastery of the material. End-of-unit reviews allow students to see their progress in grammar and writing. And after completing each unit, students go back to the goals for the unit and reflect on their achievement. In addition, the CD-ROM provides students with continuous feedback (and opportunities for self-correction) as they work through each lesson, and the Workbook contains the answer keys, so that students can check their own work outside of class.

Future addresses multilevel classes and diverse learning styles.

Using research-based teaching strategies, *Future* provides teachers with creative solutions for all stages of lesson planning and implementation, allowing them to meet the needs of all their students.

- The **Multilevel Communicative Activities Book** provides an array of reproducible activities and games that engage students through different modalities. Teachers' notes provide multilevel options for pre-level and above-level students, as well as extension activities for additional speaking and writing practice.

- The **Teacher's Edition and Lesson Planner** offers pre-level and above-level variations for every lesson plan as well as numerous optional and extension activities designed to reach students at all levels.

- The **Transparencies and Reproducible Vocabulary Cards** include picture and word cards that will help kinesthetic and visual learners acquire and learn new vocabulary. Teachers' notes include ideas for multilevel classes.

- The **Practice Plus CD-ROM** included with the Student Book is an extraordinary tool for individualizing instruction. It allows students to direct their own learning, working on precisely what they need and practicing what they choose to work on as many times as they like. In addition, the CD-ROM provides all the audio files for the book, enabling students to listen as they wish to any of the material that accompanies the text.

- The **Workbook with Audio CD**, similarly, allows students to devote their time to the lessons and specific skill areas that they need to work on most. In addition, students can replay the audio portions they want to listen to as many times as necessary, choosing to focus on the connections between the written and spoken word, listening for grammar pronunciation, and/or listening for general comprehension.

- The **Tests and Test Prep** book, as noted on page xiv, includes the *Future* **Exam***View*® *Assessment Suite*, which allows teachers to print out prepared tests at three levels (pre-level, on-level, and above-level) and to customize existing tests or create their own tests using the databank.

Future's persistence curriculum motivates students to continue their education.

Recent research about persistence has given us insights into how to keep students coming to class and how to keep them learning when they can't attend. Recognizing that there are many forces operating in students' lives—family, jobs, childcare, health—that may make it difficult for them to come to class, programs need to help students:

- Identify their educational goals
- Believe that they can successfully achieve them
- Develop a commitment to their own education
- Identify forces that can interfere with school attendance
- Develop strategies that will help them try to stay in school in spite of obstacles
- Find ways to continue learning even during "stopping out" periods

Future addresses all of these areas with its persistence curriculum. Activities found throughout the book and specific persistence activities in the back of the book help students build community, set goals, develop better study skills, and feel a sense of achievement. In addition, the Practice Plus CD-ROM is unique in its ability to ensure that even those students unable to attend class are able to make up what they missed and thus persist in their studies.

Future **supports busy teachers by providing all the materials teachers need, plus the teacher support.**

The **Student Book, Workbook with Audio CD, Multilevel Communicative Activities Book**, and **Transparencies and Reproducible Vocabulary Cards** were designed to provide teachers with everything they need in the way of ready-to-use classroom materials so they can concentrate on responding to their students' needs. The **Future Teacher Training DVD** gives teachers tips and models for conducting various activity types in their classroom.

Future **provides ample practice, with flexible options to best fit the needs of each class.**

The Student Book provides 60–100 hours of instruction. It can be supplemented in class by using:
- Teacher's Edition and Lesson Planner expansion ideas
- Transparencies and Reproducible Vocabulary Cards
- Workbook exercises
- Multilevel Communicative Activities
- Tests
- CD-ROM activities
- Activities on the Companion Website (longmanusa.com/Future)

TEACHING MULTILEVEL CLASSES

Teaching tips for pair and group work

Using pair and group work in an ESL classroom has many proven benefits. It creates an atmosphere of liveliness, builds community, and allows students to practice speaking in a low-risk environment. Many of the activities in *Future* are pair and small-group activities. Here are some tips for managing these activities:
- Limit small groups to three or four students per group (unless an activity specifically calls for larger groups). This maximizes student participation.
- Change partners for different activities. This gives students a chance to work with many others in the class and keeps them from feeling "stuck."
- If possible, give students a place to put their coats when they enter the classroom. This allows them to move around freely without worrying about returning to their own seats.

- Move around the classroom as students are working to make sure they are on task and to monitor their work.
- As you walk around, try to remain unobtrusive, so students continue to participate actively, without feeling they are being evaluated.
- Keep track of language points students are having difficulty with. After the activity, teach a mini-lesson to the entire class addressing those issues. This helps students who are having trouble without singling them out.

Pairs and groups in the multilevel classroom

Adult education ESL classrooms are by nature multilevel. This is true even if students have been given a placement test. Many factors—including a student's age, educational background, and literacy level—contribute to his or her ability level. Also, the same student may be at level in one skill, but pre-level or above-level in another.

When grouping students for a task, keep the following points in mind:
- *Like-ability* groups (in which students have the same ability level) help ensure that all students participate equally, without one student dominating the activity.
- *Cross-ability* groups (in which students have different ability levels) are beneficial to pre-level students who need the support of their at- or above-level classmates. The higher-level students benefit from "teaching" their lower-level classmates.

For example, when students are practicing a straightforward conversation substitution exercise, like-ability pairings are helpful. The activity can be tailored to different ability levels, and both students can participate equally. When students are completing the more complex task of creating their own conversations, cross-ability pairings are helpful. The higher-level student can support and give ideas to the lower-level student.

The *Future* Teacher's Edition and Lesson Planner, the Teacher's Notes in the Multilevel Communicative Activities Book, and the Teacher's Notes in the Transparencies and Reproducible Vocabulary Cards all provide specific suggestions for when to put students in like-ability versus cross-ability groups, and how to tailor activities to different ability levels.

Unit Tour

Unit Opener

Each unit starts with a full-page photo that introduces the theme and vocabulary of the unit.

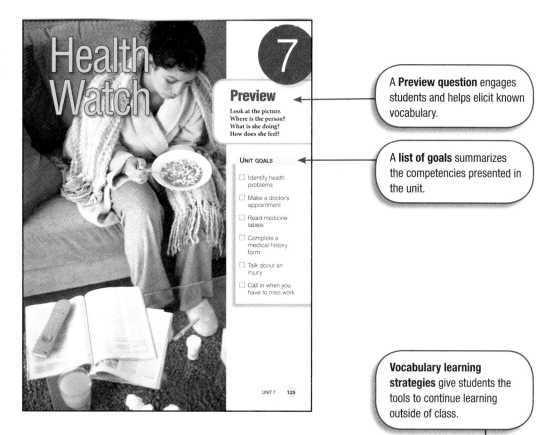

A **Preview question** engages students and helps elicit known vocabulary.

A **list of goals** summarizes the competencies presented in the unit.

Vocabulary learning strategies give students the tools to continue learning outside of class.

Vocabulary

Theme-setting vocabulary is presented in picture dictionary format.

Oral and written activities provide abundant vocabulary practice.

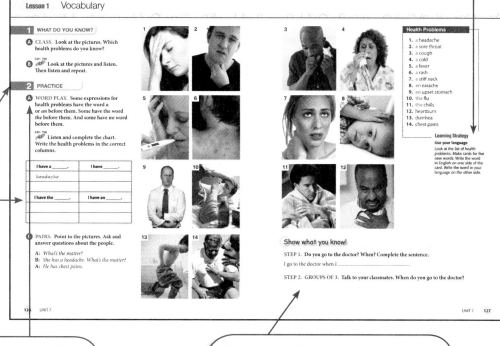

In **Word Play activities**, students use **graphic organizers** to categorize words, helping them to understand and remember new vocabulary.

Show what you know activities allow students to use the new words in conversation and provide an assessment opportunity for the teacher.

Listening and Speaking

Three listening lessons present the core competencies and language of the unit.

Before You Listen activities introduce new language and cultural concepts.

Prediction questions focus attention on the context-setting photo and encourage critical thinking.

The **Pronunciation Watch** and exercises focus on the sound patterns, stress, and intonation of English.

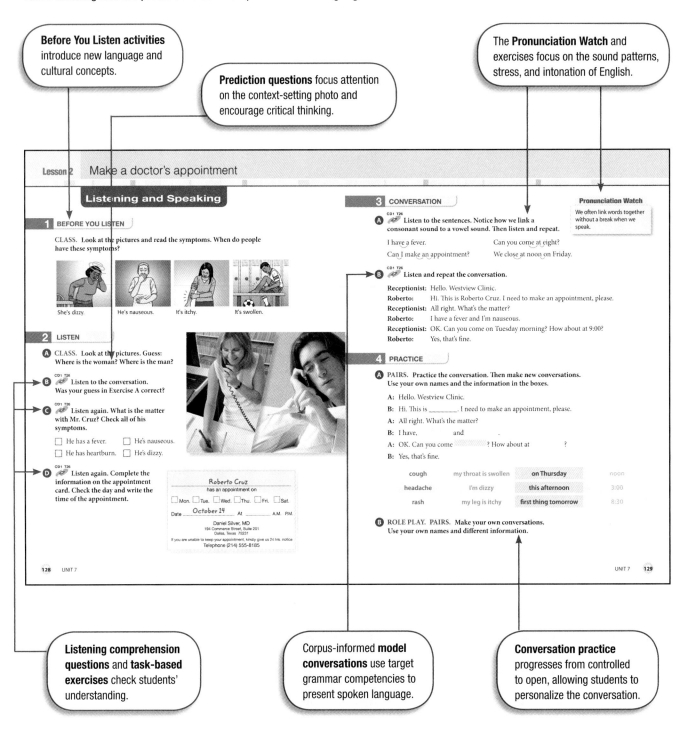

Lesson 2 | Make a doctor's appointment

Listening and Speaking

1 BEFORE YOU LISTEN

CLASS. Look at the pictures and read the symptoms. When do people have these symptoms?

She's dizzy. He's nauseous. It's itchy. It's swollen.

2 LISTEN

A CLASS. Look at the pictures. Guess: Where is the woman? Where is the man?

B CD1 T26 Listen to the conversation. Was your guess in Exercise A correct?

C CD1 T26 Listen again. What is the matter with Mr. Cruz? Check all of his symptoms.

☐ He has a fever. ☐ He's nauseous.
☐ He has heartburn. ☐ He's dizzy.

D CD1 T26 Listen again. Complete the information on the appointment card. Check the day and write the time of the appointment.

Roberto Cruz
has an appointment on
☐ Mon. ☐ Tue. ☐ Wed. ☐ Thu. ☐ Fri. ☐ Sat.
Date _October 14_ At _____ A.M. P.M.
Daniel Silver, MD
194 Commerce Street, Suite 201
Dallas, Texas 75231
If you are unable to keep your appointment, kindly give us 24 hrs. notice
Telephone (214) 555-8185

128 UNIT 7

3 CONVERSATION

A CD1 T26 Listen to the sentences. Notice how we link a consonant sound to a vowel sound. Then listen and repeat.

I have a fever. Can you come at eight?
Can I make an appointment? We close at noon on Friday.

B CD1 T26 Listen and repeat the conversation.

Receptionist: Hello. Westview Clinic.
Roberto: Hi. This is Roberto Cruz. I need to make an appointment, please.
Receptionist: All right. What's the matter?
Roberto: I have a fever and I'm nauseous.
Receptionist: OK. Can you come on Tuesday morning? How about at 9:00?
Roberto: Yes, that's fine.

Pronunciation Watch
We often link words together without a break when we speak.

4 PRACTICE

A PAIRS. Practice the conversation. Then make new conversations. Use your own names and the information in the boxes.

A: Hello. Westview Clinic.
B: Hi. This is _____. I need to make an appointment, please.
A: All right. What's the matter?
B: I have, and .
A: OK. Can you come ? How about at ?
B: Yes, that's fine.

cough	my throat is swollen	on Thursday	noon
headache	I'm dizzy	this afternoon	3:00
rash	my leg is itchy	first thing tomorrow	8:30

B ROLE PLAY. PAIRS. Make your own conversations. Use your own names and different information.

UNIT 7 129

Listening comprehension questions and **task-based exercises** check students' understanding.

Corpus-informed **model conversations** use target grammar competencies to present spoken language.

Conversation practice progresses from controlled to open, allowing students to personalize the conversation.

Grammar

Each unit presents three grammar points in a logical,
systematic grammar syllabus.

Grammar charts present the target grammar point with minimal metalanguage.

Grammar Watch notes call attention to specific aspects of the grammar point.

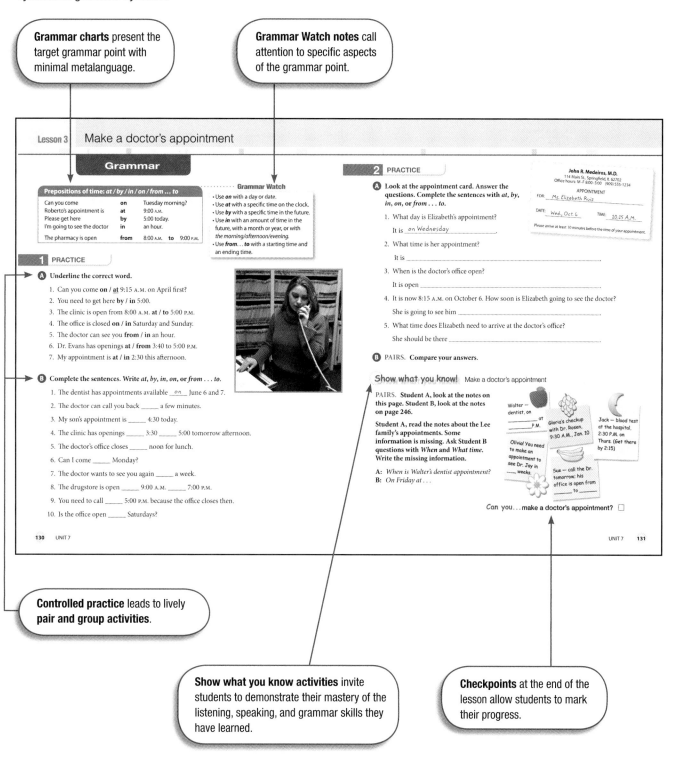

Lesson 3 | Make a doctor's appointment

Grammar

Prepositions of time: *at / by / in / on / from ... to*

Can you come	**on**	Tuesday morning?
Roberto's appointment is	**at**	9:00 A.M.
Please get here	**by**	5:00 today.
I'm going to see the doctor	**in**	an hour.
The pharmacy is open	**from**	8:00 A.M. **to** 9:00 P.M.

Grammar Watch

- Use **on** with a day or date.
- Use **at** with a specific time on the clock.
- Use **by** with a specific time in the future.
- Use **in** with an amount of time in the future, with a month or year, or with *the morning/afternoon/evening.*
- Use *from ... to* with a starting time and an ending time.

1 PRACTICE

A Underline the correct word.

1. Can you come **on** / **at** 9:15 A.M. on April first?
2. You need to get here **by** / **in** 5:00.
3. The clinic is open from 8:00 A.M. **at** / **to** 5:00 P.M.
4. The office is closed **on** / **in** Saturday and Sunday.
5. The doctor can see you **from** / **in** an hour.
6. Dr. Evans has openings **at** / **from** 3:40 to 5:00 P.M.
7. My appointment is **at** / **in** 2:30 this afternoon.

B Complete the sentences. Write *at, by, in, on,* or *from ... to.*

1. The dentist has appointments available __on__ June 6 and 7.
2. The doctor can call you back _____ a few minutes.
3. My son's appointment is _____ 4:30 today.
4. The clinic has openings _____ 3:30 _____ 5:00 tomorrow afternoon.
5. The doctor's office closes _____ noon for lunch.
6. Can I come _____ Monday?
7. The doctor wants to see you again _____ a week.
8. The drugstore is open _____ 9:00 A.M. _____ 7:00 P.M.
9. You need to call _____ 5:00 P.M. because the office closes then.
10. Is the office open _____ Saturdays?

2 PRACTICE

A Look at the appointment card. Answer the questions. Complete the sentences with *at, by, in, on,* or *from ... to.*

1. What day is Elizabeth's appointment?
   It is __on Wednesday__.
2. What time is her appointment?
   It is _____
3. When is the doctor's office open?
   It is open _____
4. It is now 8:15 A.M. on October 6. How soon is Elizabeth going to see the doctor?
   She is going to see him _____
5. What time does Elizabeth need to arrive at the doctor's office?
   She should be there _____

John R. Medeiros, M.D.
114 Main St., Springfield, IL 62702
Office hours: M–F 8:00–5:00 (909) 555-1234

APPOINTMENT
FOR: _Ms. Elizabeth Ruiz_
DATE: _Wed., Oct. 6_   TIME: _10:15 A.M._
Please arrive at least 10 minutes before the time of your appointment.

B PAIRS. Compare your answers.

Show what you know! Make a doctor's appointment

PAIRS. Student A, look at the notes on this page. Student B, look at the notes on page 246.

Student A, read the notes about the Lee family's appointments. Some information is missing. Ask Student B questions with *When* and *What time.* Write the missing information.

A: *When is Walter's dentist appointment?*
B: *On Friday at . . .*

Walter — dentist, on _____ at _____ P.M.

Gloria's checkup with Dr. Rosen, 9:30 A.M., Jan. 10

Olivia! You need to make an appointment to see Dr. Jay in _____ weeks.

Jack — blood test at the hospital, 2:30 P.M. on Thurs. (Get there by 2:15)

Sue — call the Dr. tomorrow; his office is open from _____ to _____

Can you . . . make a doctor's appointment? ☐

130   UNIT 7

UNIT 7   131

Controlled practice leads to lively **pair and group activities**.

Show what you know activities invite students to demonstrate their mastery of the listening, speaking, and grammar skills they have learned.

Checkpoints at the end of the lesson allow students to mark their progress.

Life Skills

The Life Skills lesson in each unit focuses on functional language, practical skills and authentic printed materials such as schedules, labels, and receipts.

> **Functional language** related to the Life Skills topics is modeled and practiced.

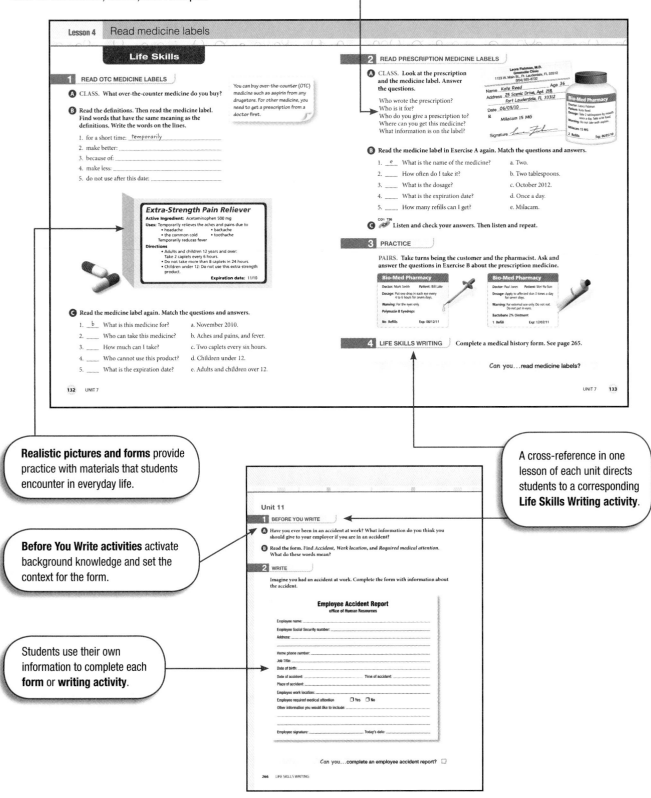

> **Realistic pictures and forms** provide practice with materials that students encounter in everyday life.

> **Before You Write activities** activate background knowledge and set the context for the form.

> Students use their own information to complete each **form** or **writing activity**.

> A cross-reference in one lesson of each unit directs students to a corresponding **Life Skills Writing activity**.

Reading

High-interest articles introduce students to cultural concepts and useful, topical information. Students read to learn while learning to read in English.

Pre-reading questions accompanied by pictures pre-teach vocabulary and activate students' background knowledge.

Essential **reading skills** such as finding the main idea, scanning for information, and getting meaning from context are introduced and practiced.

Comprehension questions check understanding of the article and build reading skills.

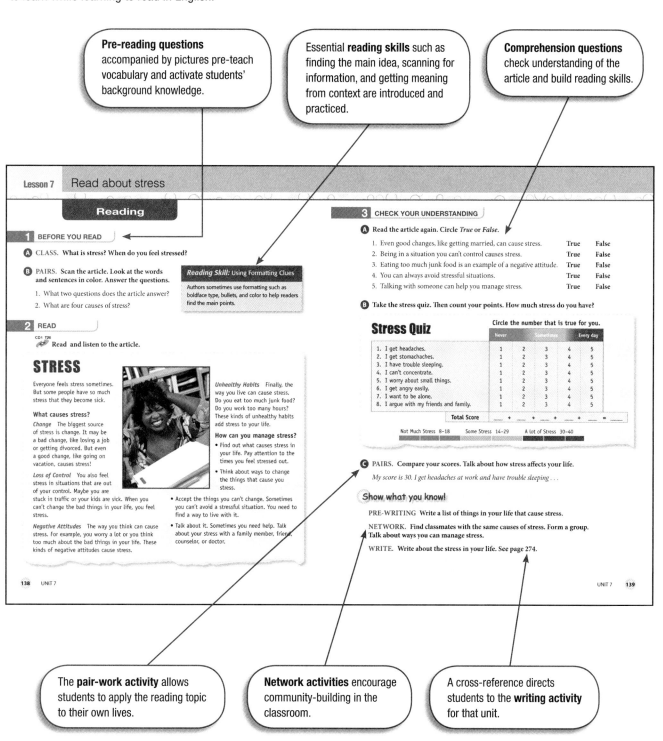

Lesson 7   Read about stress

Reading

1 BEFORE YOU READ

Ⓐ CLASS. What is stress? When do you feel stressed?

Ⓑ PAIRS. Scan the article. Look at the words and sentences in color. Answer the questions.

1. What two questions does the article answer?
2. What are four causes of stress?

Reading Skill: Using Formatting Clues

Authors sometimes use formatting such as boldface type, bullets, and color to help readers find the main points.

2 READ

CD1 T26
Read and listen to the article.

STRESS

Everyone feels stress sometimes. But some people have so much stress that they become sick.

What causes stress?

Change The biggest source of stress is change. It may be a bad change, like losing a job or getting divorced. But even a good change, like going on vacation, causes stress!

Loss of Control You also feel stress in situations that are out of your control. Maybe you are stuck in traffic or your kids are sick. When you can't change the bad things in your life, you feel stress.

Negative Attitudes The way you think can cause stress. For example, you worry a lot or you think too much about the bad things in your life. These kinds of negative attitudes cause stress.

Unhealthy Habits Finally, the way you live can cause stress. Do you eat too much junk food? Do you work too many hours? These kinds of unhealthy habits add stress to your life.

How can you manage stress?

• Find out what causes stress in your life. Pay attention to the times you feel stressed out.

• Think about ways to change the things that cause you stress.

• Accept the things you can't change. Sometimes you can't avoid a stressful situation. You need to find a way to live with it.

• Talk about it. Sometimes you need help. Talk about your stress with a family member, friend, counselor, or doctor.

138   UNIT 7

3 CHECK YOUR UNDERSTANDING

Ⓐ Read the article again. Circle *True* or *False*.

1. Even good changes, like getting married, can cause stress.	True	False
2. Being in a situation you can't control causes stress.	True	False
3. Eating too much junk food is an example of a negative attitude.	True	False
4. You can always avoid stressful situations.	True	False
5. Talking with someone can help you manage stress.	True	False

Ⓑ Take the stress quiz. Then count your points. How much stress do you have?

Stress Quiz

Circle the number that is true for you.

	Never		Sometimes		Every day
1. I get headaches.	1	2	3	4	5
2. I get stomachaches.	1	2	3	4	5
3. I have trouble sleeping.	1	2	3	4	5
4. I can't concentrate.	1	2	3	4	5
5. I worry about small things.	1	2	3	4	5
6. I get angry easily.	1	2	3	4	5
7. I want to be alone.	1	2	3	4	5
8. I argue with my friends and family.	1	2	3	4	5

Total Score _____ + _____ + _____ + _____ = _____

Not Much Stress 8–18   Some Stress 14–29   A lot of Stress 30–40

Ⓒ PAIRS. Compare your scores. Talk about how stress affects your life.

My score is 30. I get headaches at work and have trouble sleeping . . .

Show what you know!

PRE-WRITING Write a list of things in your life that cause stress.

NETWORK. Find classmates with the same causes of stress. Form a group. Talk about ways you can manage stress.

WRITE. Write about the stress in your life. See page 274.

UNIT 7   139

The **pair-work activity** allows students to apply the reading topic to their own lives.

Network activities encourage community-building in the classroom.

A cross-reference directs students to the **writing activity** for that unit.

Review

The Review page synthesizes the unit grammar through contextualized cloze or sentence writing activities.

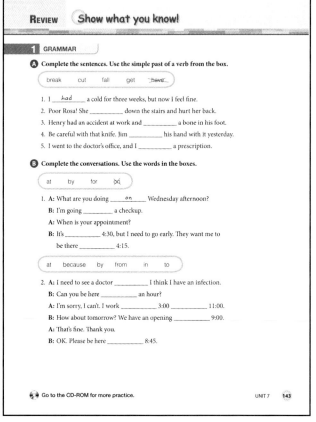

Expand

The final page of the unit allows students to review and expand on the language, themes, and competencies they have worked with throughout the unit.

Lively **role-play activities** motivate students, allowing them to feel successful. Teachers can use these activities to assess students' mastery of the material.

Cross-references direct students to the **Persistence Activity** and **Team Project** for that unit.

Checkpoints allow students to see the unit goals they have accomplished.

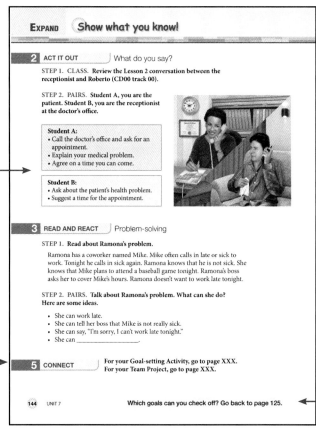

Persistence Activities

Persistence activities build community in the classroom, help students set personal and language goals, and encourage students to develop good study skills and habits.

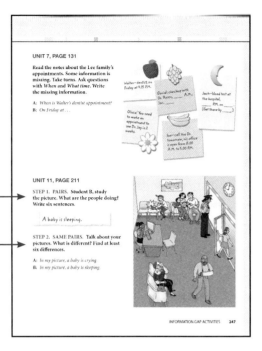

Controlled activities provide scaffolding for the **real-life application activities** that follow.

Writing

After students have their Pre-Writing discussion in the Reading lesson, they are asked to write about the same subject. Topics are interesting and relevant to their lives.

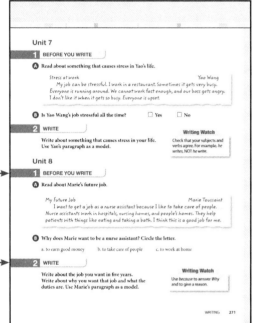

Before You Write activities present a model of the writing activity with comprehension questions to check students' understanding.

Students complete the **writing task** in a few sentences or a short paragraph.

Team Projects

Each unit includes a collaborative project that integrates all of the unit themes, language, and competencies in a community-building activity.

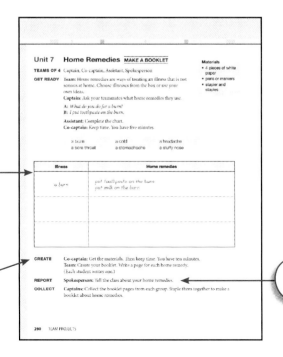

A **graphic organizer** helps students collect the information they need for the task.

Students work in teams to create a **poster, chart, or booklet** that relates to the unit theme.

Teams give **oral presentations** to share their project with the class.

Pre-Unit

Getting Started

Welcome to Class

1 LEARN ABOUT YOUR BOOK

A CLASS. Turn to page iii. Answer the questions.

1. What information is on this page? the contents of the book
2. How many units are in this book? 12
3. Which unit is about food? Unit 10
4. Which two units are about work? Unit 8 and Unit 12

B CLASS. Sometimes you will need to go to the back of the book to do activities. Look at the chart. Find the pages in the book and complete the chart.

Page	Activity
248	Persistence Activities
260	Life Skills Writing
272	Writing
278	Team Projects

C PAIRS. There is additional information for you in the back of the book. Find each section. Write the page number.

Grammar Reference __286__   Map of the U.S. and Canada __311__

Audio Script __297__   Map of the World __312–313__

Word List __291__   Index __308__

Getting Started

Welcome to Class

 LEARN ABOUT YOUR BOOK

Getting Started   10 minutes

> **Community Building**
>
> From the first class, encourage a supportive, friendly classroom by modeling supportive, friendly behavior yourself. Get to know your students' names and things about them. Make sure they know your name and things about you.

- Set the mood for the class. Say: *We're going to meet each other. I'm going to write my name on the board.* On the board, write your name as you want the students to call you.
- Say: *Hello. My name is _____. Nice to meet you, class.*
- Now have students come to the board and write their names. Have them introduce themselves to the class.
- Help each student as needed to say hello and his or her name. When a student says his or her name, encourage the class to say: *Hello _____. Nice to meet you.* You may want to write this on the board for students to read as they say it.

> **Teaching Tip**
>
> If you have more than 15 students in class, break the introductory activity into more than one class meeting. Keep track of which students participated, and call on others to continue at the next meeting. An ideal number of names on the board is between 8 and 15.

- Say: *Now let's learn something about our book.*

Presentation   5 minutes

Ⓐ **CLASS. Turn to page iii...**

- Hold the book up. Say the title. Students repeat.
- Have students turn to page iii.

- Read the questions aloud.
- Write the first question on the board. Read the question aloud. Have students call out what information they see on the page. As they call things out, write the words on the board and point to what they are saying so all students can see.
- Repeat for questions 2, 3, and 4.

> **Culture Connection**
>
> Students come from a variety of educational backgrounds. They may be uncomfortable working together and afraid to take risks. Conduct your classroom so that everyone feels safe to make mistakes. Lead students gently into working in pairs and in groups. As the weeks go on, they will become more and more comfortable with this.

Controlled Practice   10 minutes

Ⓑ **CLASS. Sometimes you will need...**

- Hold up your book. Pointing at the chart, say: *Look at page 248. Do you see the Persistence Activities?*
- Tell students to look at the other pages in the chart and to write the activity they see.
- As you walk around and help, you will begin to see which students may be pre-level, which may be at-level, and which may be above-level.
- Call on volunteers to say what is on each page. Write it on the board.

Ⓒ **PAIRS. There is additional information...**

- Holding up the book, leaf through the back pages. Read the directions out loud.
- Do item 1 together. Read the title. Have students repeat. Tell students to look through the pages and raise their hands when they find it. This is another quick way to begin to identify pre- and above-level students.
- Form pairs. Have students complete the task.
- Call on volunteers to give their answers.

Presentation   5 minutes

- Walk around the class. Stop in front of a student. Say: *Hi. My name is _____.* Hold your hand out to shake hands.
- If the student says hello and says his or her name, continue the conversation. Say: *Nice to meet you.* If the student doesn't say anything, ask: *What's your name?* When he or she answers, say: *Nice to meet you.*
- Talk to five or six more students in this way.

Controlled Practice   10 minutes

Ⓐ Read and listen...

- Read the directions aloud to the class. Point out that the icon means they will listen to a CD.
- Play CD 1 Track 2 twice. Mime shaking hands when the women say *Nice to meet you.*
- Play Track 2 again. This time pause the CD, read the sentence aloud, and have students repeat.

Communicative Practice   15 minutes

Ⓑ PAIRS. Practice the conversation...

- Ask for a volunteer. Holding your book up and encouraging the class to follow in the book, model the conversation. Be sure to shake hands with your volunteer.
- Form pairs. Have them practice the conversation.
- Walk around and help as needed.

  Expansion: Speaking practice for 2A
- Have pairs walk around together and introduce themselves to other pairs.

Community Building

Before leaving class on the first day, ask volunteers to say the name of a classmate they met. This way the students begin to learn each other's names from the beginning.

- Ask the class if anyone knows what *goals* are. Accept any answers you get, and then write on the board: *goals = I want to do this.*
- Ask: *Why do you want to learn English? What is your goal?*
- If some students answer appropriately, write their answers on the board. If no one answers, say: For example, *do you want to learn English to get a good job? Or, to communicate with the doctor?*
- State the objective: *We're going to think and talk about why we want to learn English.*

Ⓐ Why are you studying...

- Read the directions aloud. Draw two square boxes on the board. Say: *Read. If your answer is yes, check the box.* Make a check mark in one box on the board.
- Explain that students will work on their own and check the information about themselves.
- Walk around and help as needed. You can begin to model the language that is coming up by looking at their information. Say, for example: *Oh, you're studying English because you want a better job?*

Ⓑ NETWORK. GROUPS OF 3. Talk about...

- Write the targeted language on the board. Write: *I am studying English because I want to _____.* Say a few examples, pointing out how you are filling in the blank with a goal.
- Form groups of 3. Put students sitting near each other together.
- Walk around and help as needed.
- To review, ask questions about each item, asking for a show of hands. For example: *Who is studying English to get a better job?* You can ask volunteers to read the goal they wrote in the last item.

Teaching Tip

End every class by thanking students for coming and participating. Leave a few minutes at the end of every class to review with the class what you learned. For this class, review students' names and some of their goals.

2 MEET YOUR CLASSMATES

CD1 T2

A  **Read and listen to the conversation.**

Ayida: Hi. My name is Ayida .

Carmen: Hello, Ayida . I'm Carmen .

Ayida: Nice to meet you, Carmen .

Carmen: Nice to meet you, too.

Ayida: Where are you from?

Carmen: Peru . How about you?

Ayida: I'm from Haiti .

B PAIRS. Practice the conversation. Use your own names and information.

3 TALK ABOUT YOUR GOALS

A Why are you studying English? Check the boxes.

☐ to get a job or a better job

☐ to get United States citizenship

☐ to continue my education

☐ to help my children with schoolwork

☐ to get into a career program

☐ other goal: _____

B NETWORK. GROUPS OF 3. Talk about your goals. Do you have any of the same goals?

4 ASK FOR HELP

A Complete the conversations. Use questions from the box.

> ~~Can you speak more slowly?~~
> How do you pronounce this?
> What does this word mean?
>
> Can you repeat that?
> How do you spell that?
> What's this called in English?

1.

Where are you from?

I'm sorry. Can you speak more slowly?

Oh, sorry. Where are you from?

I'm from Korea.

2.

What's this called in English?

It's a pencil sharpener.

Thank you.

3.

Excuse me. How do you pronounce this?

New Student Registration

Registration.

Registration?

Yes. That's right.

4.

Can you help me?

Sure.

What does this word mean?

Occupation? It means a job or career.

5.

Please turn to page 45.

I'm sorry. Can you repeat that?

Sure. Please turn to page 45.

6.

My name is Chiao.

Chiao? How do you spell that?

C-H-I-A-O.

Thanks.

CD1 T3

B 🎧 Listen and check your answers.

C ROLE PLAY. PAIRS. Choose one conversation from Exercise A. Make your own conversation. Use different information.

Presentation   5 minutes

4 **ASK FOR HELP**

- Say: *Sometimes we don't understand something. Then we need to ask questions.*
- State the objective: *We are going to learn some questions to ask when we don't understand something.*

Controlled Practice   15 minutes

Teaching Tip

Ask students to use a pencil to write their answers. This allows them to erase an incorrect answer and clearly mark the correct answer.

Ⓐ Complete the conversations...

- Tell students that in every cartoon box, there is a communication problem. Tell them they will choose a question from the box to ask.
- Read the directions and the questions.
- Hold your book up. Point to the speakers as you read the conversation.
- Check comprehension: *What did the first student ask?* (where the other student was from) *What was the problem?* (the other student didn't understand the question) *What question did he ask when he didn't understand?* (Can you speak more slowly?)
- Do the second cartoon together. Read aloud, mime the actions, and write the answer on the board. Then call on a volunteer to read the conversation with you. Remind students to cross off the phrase they used.

Ⓑ 💿 Listen and check...

- Play CD 1 Track 3. Have students just listen first.
- Play Track 3 again. Have students check and correct their answers.
- To confirm, play Track 3 one more time.

▰▰ Expansion: Reading practice for 4B

- Form pairs. Have students read each cartoon box, alternating the role they read.

Communicative Practice   10 minutes

Teaching Tip

Introduce the activity of role play. Explain to students what it is. Tell them that there are many role plays in the book and that starting with Unit 1, you'll evaluate them when they do them. Tell them it is a great way to practice the language they learned. Explain to them that they will see themselves improve as they do more and more of them.

Ⓒ ROLE PLAY. PAIRS. Choose one conversation...

- Call on a volunteer to model one of the conversations in 4A with you. Write it on the board. Show students how to change the information. Then model the new conversation for the class.
- Walk around and help as needed.
- Call on pairs to role play their conversation for the class.

▰▰ MULTILEVEL INSTRUCTION for 4C

Pre-level You may now have an idea which students need more support, guidance, and practice. Pair these students and have them change the information in cartoon 2 or 5.

Above-level You may now have an idea which students learn quickly, participate willingly, and need to be challenged. Pair these students and have them change as many conversations as they can in the allotted time.

Teaching Tip

End every unit by reviewing what students did and learned. Tell them briefly the theme of the next unit and some of the things they will learn.

Making Connections

Classroom Materials/Extra Practice

CD 1
Tracks 4–20

T
Transparencies 1.1–1.6
Vocabulary Cards Unit 1

MCA
Unit 1

Workbook
Unit 1

Interactive Practice
Unit 1

Unit Overview

Goals
- See the list of goals on the facing page.

Grammar
- Simple present: *be* + adjective, *have* + object; contractions
- *Be*: Compound sentences with *and / but*
- *Be*: Additions with *and . . . , too / and . . . not, either*
- Simple present tense of *be*: *Yes / No* and information questions

Pronunciation
- Word stress
- Vowel sounds in unstressed syllables
- Sentence stress

Reading
- Read an article about ways people learn
- *Reading Skill:* Finding the main idea

Writing
- Describe the way people look
- Write about your personality
- Write a list of learning tips for your learning style

Life Skills Writing
- Complete a driver's license application

Preview
- Set the context of the unit by asking questions about people (for example, *Who do you know in the U.S.? Do you spend your free time with family, friends, or co-workers?*).
- Hold up page 5 or show Transparency 1.1. Read the unit title and ask the class to repeat.
- As needed, explain: Making connections *means* getting to know people.
- Say: *Look at the picture.* Ask the Preview questions: *Where are the people?* (at a backyard party), *What are they doing?* (smiling, shaking hands, greeting each other).

Goals
- Point to the Unit Goals. Explain that this list shows what the class will be studying in this unit.
- Tell students to read the goals silently.
- Say each goal and ask students to repeat. Explain unfamiliar vocabulary as needed:

    An application: a form that you complete to get something such as a driver's license or a job

    Personality: how a person acts, feels, and thinks (Give examples: *friendly, optimistic.*)
- Tell students to circle one goal that is very important to them. Call on several students to say the goal they circled.
- Write a checkmark (✓) on the board. Say: *We will come back to this page again. You will write a checkmark next to the goals you learned in this unit.*

Making Connections

1

Preview

Look at the picture.
Where are the people?
What are they doing?

UNIT GOALS

☐ Describe the way people look

☐ Complete an application

☐ Describe personalities

☐ Get to know someone

1 WHAT DO YOU KNOW?

A CLASS. Look at the pictures. What are some words that describe the people?

Bruno: short, thin

B ^{CD1 T4} Look at the pictures and listen. Listen again and repeat.

2 PRACTICE

A Choose one person in the pictures. Write a list of words to describe that person.
Answers will vary but could include:
Maxim: tall, heavy, blond hair

B PAIRS. Student A, read your list to your partner. Student B, listen and identify the person in the picture.

A: *Short. Curly hair. Slim.*
B: *Bruno?*
A: *Yes.*

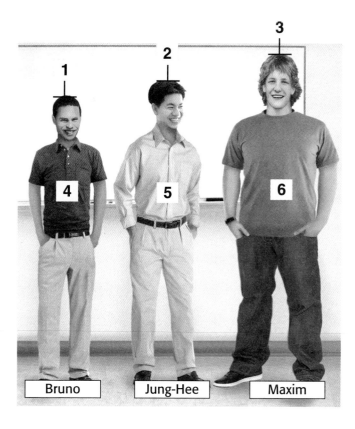

1 2 3
4 5 6
Bruno Jung-Hee Maxim

C WORD PLAY. Look at the underlined words. Which word describes hair length? Which word describes hair type? Which word describes hair color?

He has <u>short</u>, <u>curly</u> <u>brown</u> hair.
     1   2   3

1 = hair length
2 = hair type
3 = hair color

D Write four other phrases to describe hair. Add commas. Answers will vary but could include:

	1	2	3	
She has	shoulder-length,	straight	black	hair.
	long,	wavy	red	
	short,	curly	blond	
	short,	straight	brown	

Lesson 1 Vocabulary

Getting Started   5 minutes

1 WHAT DO YOU KNOW?

A CLASS. Look at the pictures. What are some...

- Show Transparency 1.2 or hold up the book. Tell students to cover the list of words on page 7.
- Point to picture 1 and ask: *What are some words that describe Bruno?* Say: *Look at the pictures. What are some words that describe the other people?*
- Students call out answers. Help students pronounce physical descriptions if they have difficulty.
- If students call out an incorrect description, change the student's answer into a question for the class (for example, *Kwami has a mustache?*). If nobody can identify the correct description, tell students they will now listen to a CD and practice descriptions.

Presentation   10 minutes

B 📀 Look at the pictures and listen....

- Read the directions. Play CD 1, Track 4. Pause after number 16 (*a goatee*).
- To check comprehension, say each physical description in random order and ask students to point to the appropriate picture.
- Resume playing Track 4. Students listen and repeat.
- *Optional:* Say each description and use a gesture or action to indicate its meaning. For example, adjust the height of your hand to show *short, average height,* and *tall.* Ask students to repeat. Use the same gestures or actions in random order and tell students to call out the description.

Controlled Practice   20 minutes

2 PRACTICE

A Choose one person in the pictures. Write a list...

- Read the directions. Tell students to point to Bruno.
- Ask: *What words describe Bruno?* As students call out answers, list them on the board (for example, *short, thin* (or *slim*), *short hair, curly hair, brown hair*).

- Tell students to write their lists. Walk around and check that they are using the vocabulary from the lesson. If students are making spelling mistakes, tell them to check the vocabulary list on page 7.

B PAIRS. Student A, read your list to your partner....

- Read the directions. Read the example with an above-level student. Play Student A and model using rising intonation to guess the person.
- Pair students and tell them to take turns playing A and B.

Language Note

Explain: *You can change a statement into a question by making your voice go up at the end.* On the board, write: *Bruno.* and *Bruno?* Say *Bruno* as a statement and as a question. Ask the class to repeat. Call on several pairs to read the example and practice rising intonation when B guesses *Bruno?*

C WORD PLAY. Look at the underlined words....

- Read the directions and example. Ask: *Which word describes hair length?* (*short*) On the board, write: *1. hair length.* Continue with hair type and hair color.
- Point to 3. Ask: *What words describe hair color?* Make a list on the board. Make sure students know *blond.*
- Tell students to look at the example again. Ask: *Where is the comma?* (after *short / hair length*)

D Write four other phrases to describe hair. Add...

- Read the directions. On the board, write: *She has.* Elicit a hair length, type, and color from the class. Complete the sentence without commas.
- Ask: *Where do I put the comma?* Add the comma to the sentence on the board.
- Walk around and check students' word order and use of commas.

▬▬ EXPANSION: Listening and speaking practice for 2D

- Ask an above-level student to read one sentence out loud. On the board, draw a simple picture of the hair the student describes.
- Pair students and tell them to take turns reading their sentences and listening to and drawing their partner's sentences.

Learning Strategy: Personalize

- Read the directions.
- Model the activity. Say: *I'm thinking of my (wife / brother / friend).* If possible, show a photo. List four vocabulary words to describe that person on the board.
- Walk around as students write their words. If misspellings occur, tell students to check the list on the board or on page 7. Call on a few students to read their descriptions out loud.
- Say: *You can remember new vocabulary when you write descriptions that are important to you.* Tell students they can use this strategy to remember other new vocabulary.

EXPANSION: Vocabulary practice

- Tell students to bring in a picture of a person from a magazine, or provide magazines for students to cut pictures out of. Tell them that they will make a web diagram with their picture.
- Model the activity. Paste a photo of a person from a magazine on a sheet of paper, and draw lines radiating from the photo. Say: *Look at the vocabulary list. Which words describe this person?* Write the physical descriptions you elicit on your web diagram.
- Tell students to paste or tape their photo on a sheet of paper and write at least four physical descriptions on their web diagram.

Communicative Practice   20 minutes

Show what you know!

STEP 1. Look at the list of physical descriptions....

- Say: *Look at the vocabulary list. Which words describe you?*
- Tell students to underline all the vocabulary words that describe them.
- On the board, list the vocabulary words that describe you. Include your hair color.
- Ask: *Which words describe my hair?* Underline them. Then ask the class to put them in the correct order.

- Write this phrase on the board: *long wavy blond hair.* Ask: *Where do I put the comma?* (after *long*)
- Say: *Write the words that describe you on a piece of paper. Be sure to write words describing your hair.* Walk around and collect the papers.

STEP 2. CLASS. Take a piece of paper from the box....

- Read the directions and model the activity. Take a piece of paper, read the description, and try to identify the student (for example, *Ana?*).
- Pass the box to the student you correctly identify. Tell the student to take a piece of paper and read the description. Ask: *Who is it?* The student passes the box to the classmate he or she correctly identifies. Continue until all students have had a turn.
- When a student incorrectly identifies a classmate, point out something about the classmate that doesn't match the description (for example, *David has curly hair, not straight hair.*).

EXPANSION: Vocabulary and writing practice for Step 2

- Tell students to write five sentences describing classmates' hair. Model the activity by eliciting one sentence from the class and writing it on the board. Choose one student to describe and ask: *Do I write He or She?*
- Remind students to start sentences with a capital letter, end with a period, and use a comma.

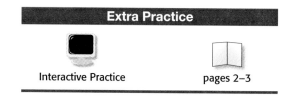

Extra Practice	
Interactive Practice	pages 2–3

Felix   Basia   Ana   Mai

Kwami   Yusef   David

Physical Descriptions

Height
1. short
2. average height
3. tall

Weight
4. thin/slim
5. average weight
6. heavy

Hair Type
7. bald
8. curly
9. wavy
10. straight

Hair Length
11. short
12. shoulder-length
13. long

Facial Hair
14. a beard
15. a mustache
16. a goatee

Learning Strategy

Personalize

Think of someone you know well. Look at the list of physical descriptions. Write four words to describe that person.

Show what you know!

STEP 1. Look at the list of physical descriptions. Which words describe you? Write the words on a piece of paper. Put your paper in a box.

STEP 2. CLASS. Take a piece of paper from the box. Read the description to the class. Who is it?

Listening and Speaking

1 BEFORE YOU LISTEN

PAIRS. Read the words in the box. Then complete the chart.

attractive   beautiful   good-looking   handsome   ~~pretty~~

Words for women only	Words for men only	Words for women and men
pretty beautiful	handsome	attractive good-looking

Some words describe only women. Some words describe only men. Some words describe both women and men.

2 LISTEN

CD1 T5

A Look at the picture. Listen to the conversation between two friends, Tania and Eva. What does Tania want to know more about?

  a. a party   (b.) Eva's friend   c. a teacher

CD1 T5

B Listen again. Answer the questions.

1. Where is Tania going tonight?
  a. to her class   b. to her job   (c.) to a party

2. What does Tania say about Eva's friend?
  a. "He's attractive."   b. "He's good-looking."   (c.) "He's handsome."

3. What does Eva's friend look like?
  a.   (b.)   c.

CD1 T6

C Listen to the whole conversation. Complete the sentence.

Victor is Eva's _____.
  a. friend   b. boyfriend   (c.) brother

Getting Started

1 BEFORE YOU LISTEN

PAIRS. Read the words in the box. Then complete...

- Tell students to look at the words in the box. Pronounce the words and ask the class to repeat.
- Say: *Look at the picture. They are both attractive. They are both good-looking.*
- Say: *Point to the woman in the picture. She's pretty.* Pretty *describes only women. What other word describes only women?* (beautiful)
- Explain the difference between *pretty* and *beautiful.* On the board, write: *pretty = attractive, beautiful = very attractive.*
- Say: *Point to the man in the picture. Do we describe him as* pretty? (No, *pretty* describes only women.) *What word describes only men?* (handsome)
- Pair students and tell them to complete the chart.
- To review, draw the chart on the board. Ask: *Which words describe only women? Which word describes only men? Which words describe both women and men?* Complete the chart on the board. Pronounce the words in each column and ask the class to repeat.

EXPANSION: Listening and vocabulary practice for 1

- Tape several magazine photos of attractive women and men (with a variety of features) to the board. Number the photos.
- In random order, describe each person (for example, *He is tall. He is average weight. He has short, wavy black hair.*).
- Students listen and write the number of the photo you're describing.
- Then tell students to write one of the words from the chart (for example, *pretty* or *beautiful*) next to each number.

Presentation

2 LISTEN

A **Look at the picture. Listen to...**

- Ask students to look at the picture. Say: *This is Tania and Eva. They're friends.*
- Read the directions and the answer choices. Ask: *What does Tania want to know more about?*
- Play CD 1, Track 5. Students listen and circle the letter of the correct answer.
- Elicit the correct answer from the class.

B **Listen again. Answer the questions.**

- Tell students to read the questions and answer choices silently.
- Play Track 5 again. Students circle the letter of the correct answer.
- Students compare answers with a partner.
- Call on volunteers to ask and answer the questions.
- Say: *Tania thinks Eva's friend is good-looking. What does Eva's friend look like?* (He has short black hair.)

Teaching Tip

If students need additional support, tell them to read the Audio Script on page 297 as they listen to the conversation.

C **Listen to the whole conversation....**

- Play CD 1, Track 6. Students circle the letter of the correct answer. To check the answer, ask students to raise their hands for a, b, or c.
- Ask: *What is the name of the guy Tania thinks is good-looking?* (Victor) *Is Victor Eva's friend?* (No, he's Eva's brother.)

EXPANSION: Vocabulary and graphic organizer practice for 2C

- On the board, draw a three-column chart like the one at the top of page 8. Label the columns *Tania, Eva,* and *Victor.* Tell students to copy the chart.
- Pair students and tell them to look again at the pictures, questions, and answers in Exercises 2A, 2B, and 2C. Tell pairs to complete the chart with physical descriptions of Tania, Eva, and Victor and with what they know about each person.

Describe the way people look

3 CONVERSATION

A 💿 **Listen to the words. Then listen and...**

- Tell students to close their books. Write the words they will hear on the board. Pronounce each word slowly and ask students to listen for the break(s).
- Pronounce each word again and draw lines between syllables. Explain: *Each part of a word is a syllable.* Ask: *How many syllables does* party *have?*
- Tell students to open their books. Read the Pronunciation Watch note. Pronounce *par-ty*, stressing the first syllable. Say: *In* party, par *is long and strong. It is the stressed syllable.*
- Play CD 1, Track 7. Students listen to the words.
- Resume playing Track 7. Students listen and repeat.

Language Note

To help students hear stress, tell them to tap the table when repeating the stressed syllable.

Controlled Practice   10 minutes

B 💿 **Listen to the words. Mark (•)...**

- Read the directions out loud. Write item 1 on the board. Pronounce *handsome*. Ask: *Which syllable is long and strong?* (the first syllable) Pronounce *handsome* as many times as needed. Mark the stressed syllable *hand-* on the board.
- Play CD 1, Track 8. Students listen and mark the syllables. Play Track 8 again if students have difficulty identifying the stressed syllables.
- Write items 2–4 on the board. Ask volunteers to mark the stressed syllables on the board. As needed, play Track 8 again.

C 💿 **Listen and repeat the conversation.**

- Note: This conversation is the same one students heard in Exercise 2A on page 8.
- Tell students to find and circle the four words from the pronunciation activities that are in the conversation (*party, tonight, inviting,* and *handsome*). Tell them to underline the stressed syllable in each of these words.
- Play CD 1, Track 9. Students listen and repeat.
- Walk around and help with pronunciation as needed. Pay particular attention to students' pronunciation of *party, tonight,* and *inviting.*

Communicative Practice   15 minutes

4 PRACTICE

A PAIRS. **Practice the conversation. Then make...**

- Pair students and tell them to practice the conversation in Exercise 3C.
- Then, in Exercise 4A, tell students to look at the information in the boxes.
- Copy the conversation onto the board with blanks and read it. Fill in the first two blanks with names from the class. When you come to the next blank, ask what color it is. Point to the box that's the same color and fill in the blank with the first item.
- Point out that students may change *he's* and *he* to *she's* and *she* in Student A's last line.
- Ask a pair of on-level students to practice the conversation on the board for the class.
- Erase the words in the blanks and ask two above-level students to make up a new conversation.
- Tell pairs to take turns playing A and B and to use the vocabulary words to fill in the blanks.
- Tell students to stand, mingle, and practice the conversation with several new partners.
- Call on pairs to practice for the class.

▬▬ MULTILEVEL INSTRUCTION for 4A

Pre-level Tell pairs to fill in the blanks in their book and practice from the conversation.
Above-level After practicing each part, pairs practice without looking at the conversation.

B ROLE PLAY. PAIRS. **Make your own...**

- Say: *Think of someone you want to know more about. Write three words to describe that person.*
- Model the activity. Say: *I'm thinking of . . .* On the board, write three words to describe the person. Play A and practice the conversation in Exercise 4A with an above-level student. Complete A's last line with the information you listed on the board.
- Tell students to practice the conversation in Exercise A with a new partner.

Extra Practice

Interactive Practice

3 CONVERSATION

Pronunciation Watch

A syllable is a part of a word. For example, the word *party* has two syllables: par·ty. In words with more than one syllable, one syllable is stressed. The stressed syllable is long and loud.

A CD1 T7 **Listen to the words. Then listen and repeat.**

par·ty   to·night   beau·ti·ful   at·trac·tive

B CD1 T8 **Listen to the words. Mark (•) the stressed syllable.**

1. hand·some   2. in·vit·ing   3. pret·ty   4. in·tro·duce

C CD1 T9 **Listen and repeat the conversation.**

Tania: Hi, Eva.

Eva: Hi, Tania. Are you coming to my party tonight?

Tania: Of course. Are you inviting your friend?

Eva: Which friend?

Tania: You know—he's handsome and he has short, black hair.

4 PRACTICE

A PAIRS. Practice the conversation. Then make new conversations. Use the information in the boxes and your own names.

> thin
> average height
> average weight

A: Hi, _____.

B: Hi, _____. Are you coming to my party tonight?

> wavy
> long
> curly

A: Of course. Are you inviting your friend?

B: Which friend?

A: You know—he's _____ and he has _____, _____ hair.

> red
> brown
> black

B ROLE PLAY. PAIRS. Make your own conversations. Use different words to describe the friend.

Grammar

Simple present: *be + adjective*

Affirmative			Negative			
I	am		I	am		
They	are	tall.	They	are	not	heavy.
He	is		He	is		

Simple present: *have + object*

Affirmative			Negative				
I	have		I	do			
They		black hair.	They		not	have	black hair.
He	has		He	does			

Grammar Watch

Contractions are short forms. Here are some examples:

• he is not = **he's not / he isn't**
• he does not = **he doesn't**

• they are = **they're**
• they are not = **they're not / they aren't**

For more contractions, see page 286.

1 PRACTICE

A Complete the sentences.

My sister and brother ____are____ very good-looking, but they don't look alike.
                       (is / are)

My sister ____has____ brown eyes, but my brother ____has____ blue eyes. My sister
          (is / has)   (has / have)

____has____ long hair. It ____is____ curly. My brother's hair ____is____
(has / is)   (are / is)   (has / is)

short. And it ____isn't____ curly—it's straight. Also, my sister ____is____ tall, and
              (isn't / is)   (is / are)

my brother ____is____ average height. But my sister and brother ____are____ alike
           (have / is)   (is / are)

in one way: They ____are____ both thin.
                 (are / have)

B Complete the sentences. Write the correct forms of *be* or *have*. Use contractions for the negative sentences.

1. Omar ____has____ brown hair.

2. Na-Young (not) ____isn't____ thin.

3. Jeff and Rob ____have____ blond hair.

4. Josh and his brother ____are____ tall.

5. Amy's hair (not) ____isn't____ curly.

6. Marko's eyes ____are____ green.

7. Ivana and Olga ____are____ very attractive.

8. Steve (not) ____doesn't have____ a beard.

Getting Started   5 minutes

- Say: *We're going to study* be *and* have *in descriptions. In the conversation you listened to in Exercise 3C on page 9, Tania used this grammar.*
- Play CD 1, Track 9. Students listen. Write on the board: *He's handsome and he has short, black hair.* Underline *he's handsome* and *he has short black hair.*

Presentation   15 minutes

Simple present: *be* **+ adjective**

- Copy the top grammar chart onto the board or show Transparency 1.3 and cover the exercise. Read the examples. Ask: *What are the adjectives?* Underline *tall* and *heavy.* Say: *Use* be *with adjectives.*
- Tell students to look at the vocabulary on page 7. Ask: *What are the other adjectives that describe height?* (*short, average height*) *What are the other adjectives that describe weight?* (*thin/slim, average weight*) *What's the adjective that describes a person with no hair?* (*bald*) Tell students to draw a line under number 7, *bald,* dividing the vocabulary box in half, and to write *be* + adjective in the top half of the vocabulary box.

Simple present: *have* **+ object**

- Copy the bottom grammar chart onto the board or show Transparency 1.3 and cover the exercise.
- Read the examples. Ask: *What is the object?* Underline *black hair* in both boxes. Say: *Use* have *with objects.*
- As needed, explain that *black* is an adjective but *hair* is a noun/object. On the board, write: *The cat is black.* (be + *adjective*) and *The cat has black fur.* (have + *object*)
- Tell students to look at the vocabulary on page 7. Ask: *What types of hair do people have?* (curly hair, . . .) *What lengths of hair do people have?* (short hair, . . .) *What facial hair do some men have?* (a beard, . . .) Tell students to write have + *object* in the bottom half of the vocabulary box.
- Read the Grammar Watch note. Ask students to come to the board and rewrite the sentences using contractions.
- If you are using the transparency, do the exercise with the class.

Controlled Practice   20 minutes

1 PRACTICE

A Complete the sentences.

- Read the first sentence. Ask: *Why is the answer* are? (*Good-looking* is an adjective, so the verb is *be.*)
- As needed, review: *What's the subject?* (*My sister and brother*) *Which pronoun is* My sister and brother *the same as?* (*they*) *They is* or *They are?* (*are*) Remind students that *it* uses the same form of the verb as *he/she.* On the board, write: *It is, It has.*
- Walk around and help students complete the exercise as needed.
- Students compare answers with a partner.
- Read the paragraph with the correct answers. Students check their answers.

EXPANSION: Speaking practice for 1A

- Ask students to draw a simple picture of the sister and brother described in Exercise A.
- Above-level students can close their books, look at their drawings, and describe the sister and brother to a partner.

EXPANSION: Graphic organizer practice for 1A

- Tell students to complete a chart like the one on page 8 comparing the sister and brother described in Exercise 1A. Students add adjectives that can only be used for men and ones that can only be used for women.

B Complete the sentences. Write the correct forms...

- Write item 1 on the board. Underline *brown hair* and ask: *Is this an adjective or an object?* Write *object.* Read the completed sentence.
- Before they complete the exercise, remind students to look at the words after the blanks and decide if they are an *adjective* or *object.*
- Students compare answers with a partner.
- Call on students to read the completed sentences. For the negative items, write the contractions on the board and tell students to check their spelling.

Communicative Practice   20 minutes

2 PRACTICE

ⓐ PAIRS. Look at the picture. Describe the people...

- Tell students to look at the picture but cover the names. Say: *They are famous people. Do you know who they are?* Elicit the names students know.
- Tell students to look at the names in the book. Ask: *What do these famous people do? Where are they from?* Make statements and ask the class to identify the people (for example, *She's an actress* and elicit *Zhang Ziyi. They're from the U.S.* and elicit *Venus Williams, Jorge Garcia,* and *Cee-Lo Green.*). Use the following information: Yao Ming—basketball player from China, Venus Williams—tennis player from the U.S., Jorge Garcia—comedian and actor from the U.S., Shakira—singer from Colombia, Cee-Lo Green—singer from the U.S., Zhang Ziyi—actress from China.
- Read the directions and the example.
- Elicit words to describe Yao Ming and list them on the board (for example: *tall, black hair*). Point to *tall* and ask whether to use *be* or *have (be)*. Elicit *Yao Ming is tall* or *He's tall* and write it on the board.
- Pair students and tell them to take turns describing each person in the picture.
- Check student's use of *be* and *have*.

▮▮▮ MULTILEVEL INSTRUCTION for 2A
Pre-level Tell students to write two physical characteristics next to the drawing of each person before they do the speaking activity.
Above-level Students write several physical characteristics for each person.

ⓑ WRITE. Write two sentences to describe each...

- On the board, write: *Shakira has <u>long blond</u> hair. Shakira has <u>long blond wavy</u> hair.* Point to the first sentence and ask: *How many adjectives?* Repeat for the second sentence. Write: *2 adjectives = no commas, 3 + adjectives = 1 comma.* Ask the class where to put the commas in the sentences.
- Read the directions. Remind students to start each sentence with a capital letter, end with a period, and use a comma where necessary.
- Check students' verbs and punctuation.

- Pair students and tell them to take turns reading their sentences to each other.
- Ask for volunteers to read their sentences. Tell them to use *He, She* or *This person* instead of the name. Ask the class to identify the people.

▮▮▮ EXPANSION: Speaking practice for 2B
Students bring in magazines and take turns describing the celebrities pictured.

Show what you know!

STEP 1. WRITE. Describe someone in the class....

- Read the directions. Model the activity by asking the class to describe you. Elicit three sentences and write them on the board.
- Tell students to write three sentences about one person in the class, beginning each sentence with *This person is* .... Tell them not to write the name of the person they're describing.

STEP 2. PAIRS. Student A, read your sentences...

- Read the directions. Play B and model the activity with an above-level student. Direct Student A to read you one sentence at a time and wait for you to guess before reading the next sentence.
- Pair students and tell them to practice the conversation.

▮▮▮ MULTILEVEL INSTRUCTION FOR STEP 2
Pre-level Perform the activity with pairs to make sure they understand what to do.
Above-level Pairs practice the conversation again. They describe a different person but don't write sentences first.

Progress Check

Can you ... describe the way people look?
Say: *We have practiced describing the way people look. Now, look at the question at the bottom of the page. Can you describe how people look?* Tell students to write a checkmark in the box.

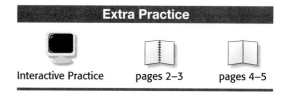

Extra Practice		
Interactive Practice	pages 2–3	pages 4–5

PRACTICE

A PAIRS. Look at the picture. Describe the people. Talk about their height, weight, and hair. There is more than one possible answer.

Shakira has long, wavy, blond hair. She's short and thin.

Yao Ming   Venus Williams   Jorge Garcia   Shakira   Cee-Lo Green   Zhang Ziyi

B WRITE. Write two sentences to describe each person. Use a separate piece of paper.

Show what you know!   Describe the way people look

STEP 1. WRITE. Describe someone in the class. Write three sentences.

| This person is tall and heavy. |

STEP 2. PAIRS. Student A, read your sentences. Student B, guess the person.

A: *This person is tall and heavy.*
B: *Is it Laura?*
A: *No, it isn't. This person has straight, blond hair.*
B: *Is it Sofia?*
A: *Yes!*

Can you...describe the way people look? ☐

Complete an application

Life Skills

1 COMPLETE AN APPLICATION

A **PAIRS.** Read the application for an identification card. Ask and answer the questions.

Name of Applicant			
First	Last	Middle	Suffix (Jr., Sr., III)
Robert	Jones	William	Jr.

Social Security Number (SSN)	Place of Birth	Date of Birth (mm-dd-yyyy)
555-33-4444	Miami, FL	06-07-1975

Sex	Height	Weight	Eye Color	Hair Color
Male ✓ Female ○	5 Feet 9 Inches	190 Pounds	green	blond

Residence Address				
Street	Apt. #	City	State	Zip Code
3602 College Avenue	3A	Clarkston	GA	30021

1. What is Robert's full name?
Robert William Jones, Jr.
2. What is Robert's Social Security number?
555-33-4444
3. When was Robert born?
06-07-1975
4. Where was he born?
Miami, FL

5. How tall is Robert?
5 feet 9 inches
6. How much does he weigh?
190 pounds
7. What color are his eyes?
Green
8. What is Robert's residence address?
3602 College Avenue
Apt. 3A
Clarkston, GA 30021

B Look at Teresa Santos's identification card. Match the abbreviations and the words.

1. __b__ F   a. height
2. __f__ DOB   b. female
3. __e__ BRN   c. black
4. __c__ BLK   d. weight
5. __a__ Ht.   e. brown
6. __d__ Wt.   f. date of birth

Getting Started   10 minutes

Culture Connection

- As needed, familiarize students with the U.S. system of measurement. Tell them to look at the application in Exercise A. Ask: *How tall is Robert Jones?* (5 feet 9 inches) *How much does he weigh?* (190 pounds)
- Write on the board: *5 feet 9 inches = 175 centimeters.*
- Ask: *Who in the class is about 175 centimeters tall?* Ask a student to stand so the class can visualize 5 feet 9 inches.
- Write on the board: *190 pounds = 86 kilograms.* Ask: *Who in the class weighs about 86 kilos?* Ask a student to stand so the class can visualize 190 pounds.
- Ask: *Is Robert Jones short, average height, or tall?* (average height) *Is he thin, average weight, or heavy?* (average weight)

Presentation   15 minutes

1   COMPLETE AN APPLICATION

A PAIRS. **Read the application for an identification...**

- Ask students to look at the application and find *Suffix.* Explain *Jr., Sr.,* and *III*: On the board, write: *Father: Robert William Jones, Son: Robert William Jones.* Say: *The father and son have the same name, so the son is Robert William Jones, Junior.* Add a comma and *Jr.* to the son's name. Say: *If Robert's grandfather also had the same name, Robert would be Robert William Jones the Third.* Cross out *Jr.* and write *III.*
- Tell students to find *Date of Birth* on the application. Write *mm-dd-yyyy* on the board. Label the abbreviations (*mm = month, dd = date, yyyy = year*). Explain that the number of letters equals the number of digits to write (for example, not *9* for September but *09*, not *78* but *1978*). Tell students to write today's date in this format in their notebooks. Ask a volunteer to come to the board and write the date in this format.
- Pair students. Tell them to ask and answer the questions.
- Read each question and call on volunteers to answer. Write the answers on the board and, as needed, point to where the information is found in the application.

Teaching Tip

When new information is presented through an activity, the activity helps students determine the meaning of new words through context. In most cases, students will be able to figure out the answers even though the words are new. However, don't expect students to already know this information. Tell students it's OK if they can't answer all the questions.

Controlled Practice   5 minutes

B **Look at Teresa Santos's identification card. Match...**

- Read the directions. Before students do the matching exercise, tell them to find and circle the abbreviations on the identification card.
- Say: *Point to* F *on the card. What's the word before* F*?* (Sex) *So what do you think* F *means?* (female) *What does* female *mean?* (a girl or a woman)
- Tell students to use the card to figure out the meanings of the abbreviations.
- Students compare answers with a partner.
- To check answers, write the abbreviations on the board. Call on students to say the full words.

Culture Connection

- *Optional:* You may wish to help students convert their height and weight to the U.S. system of measurement and give them the formulas to convert kilos to pounds and centimeters to feet + inches. The examples use the equivalencies from the Getting Started section.

    Weight: Multiply kilograms by 2.2 to convert to pounds.

    Examples: 60 kilograms x 2.2 = 132 pounds

    90 kilograms x 2.2 = 198 pounds

    Height: Multiply centimeters by .3937 to convert to inches. Divide inches by 12 to change to feet; the remainder will be inches.

    Examples: 163 centimeters x .3937 = 64 in.

    64. in./12 = 5 ft. 4 in.

    183 centimeters x .3937 = 72 in.

    72 in./12 = 6 ft.

Communicative Practice   30 minutes

2 PRACTICE

Ⓐ PAIRS. Student A, look at Joseph Smith's...

- As needed, review titles. Ask students to look at Joseph Smith's application and to point to *Title.* On the board, write the headings *Male* and *Female.* Say each title and ask: *Male or female?* Write each title under the appropriate heading. Point to the female titles on the board. Ask: *Which one is for married women?* (*Mrs.*) *For single (not married) women?* (*Miss*) *For either married or single women?* (*Ms.*)

- As needed, review name order on applications. Write your full name on the board. Label the parts *first, middle,* and *last.* Explain: *Your last name is your family name.* Ask students to point to *Name* on the application. Tell students that application forms ask for information in a certain order, so they must read them carefully. Ask them to help you write your name in the order shown on the form.

- Point to the application and ask: *What information is missing?* (title, date of birth, eye and hair color, street address) Write the words on the board. Ask: *What questions can you ask to get this information?* (*What is Joseph's title?*) If necessary, have students review the questions in Exercise 1A on page 12.

- Pair students and assign roles of A and B. Read the first paragraph of the directions. Walk around and check that Student A is looking at the application on page 13 and Student B is looking at the identification card on page 245.

- Say: *Student A, complete the missing information on Joseph Smith's application. Ask questions. Student B, look at Joseph Smith's identification card and answer your partner's questions.*

▮▮▮ MULTILEVEL INSTRUCTION for 2A

Cross-ability The above-level student plays the role of Student A.

Ⓑ SAME PAIRS. Student A. Look at Ana Martinez's...

- Say: *Now, Student B, look at Ana Martinez's identification card on page 245. Ask Student A questions and complete the missing information. Student A, look at Ana Martinez's identification card on page 13 and answer your partner's questions.*

- To check their work, tell Student A to look at Joseph Smith's identification card on page 245 and Student B to look at Ana Martinez's identification card on page 13.

▮▮▮ EXPANSION: Writing practice for 2B

- Tell students to write sentences to describe Ana Martinez or Joseph Smith.

3 LIFE SKILLS WRITING

Turn to page 256 and ask students to complete the driver's license application. See page T-xii for general notes about the Life Skills Writing activities.

Progress Check

Can you . . . complete an application?

Say: *We have practiced completing an application. Now, look at the question at the bottom of the page. Can you complete an application?* Tell students to write a checkmark in the box.

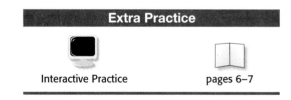

Extra Practice	
Interactive Practice	pages 6–7

A PAIRS. Student A, look at Joseph Smith's application.
Student B, look at Joseph Smith's identification card on page 245.

Student A, ask questions. Complete the missing information
on the application.

Title		Name (Last, First, Middle)		
(Mr.) Ms. Mrs. Miss		Smith	Joseph	Charles

SSN	Sex	Date of Birth (mm–dd–yyyy)
987-65-4321	M ☑ F ☐	02-14-1965

Height	Weight	Eye Color	Hair Color
6 Feet 1 Inches	185 Pounds	Brown	Black

Residence Address

Street	Apt. #	City	State	Zip Code
36 Almond Drive	4E	Chicago	IL	60604

B SAME PAIRS. Student A, look at Ana Martinez's identification card.
Student B, look at Ana Martinez's application on page 245.

Student A, answer Student B's questions.

NEW YORK STATE
IDENTIFICATION CARD
Governor of the State of New York
ID: 123 456 789
Martinez, Ana M
101 Chestnut St.
Yonkers, NY 10701
DOB: 05-07-1987
SEX: F EYES: BRN HAIR: BRN HT: 5-04
ISSUED: 10-20-2006 EXPIRES: 05-07-2011

3 **LIFE SKILLS WRITING**   Complete a driver's license application. See page 256.

Can you...complete an application?   ☐

Describe personalities

Listening and Speaking

1 BEFORE YOU LISTEN

A GROUPS OF 3. **Look at the words to describe people. Read the definitions. Match the words and definitions.**

~~bossy~~   cheerful   laid-back   moody   outgoing   shy   sweet   talkative

1. always tells other people what to do   _bossy_
2. is nervous when speaking to other people   shy
3. likes to talk a lot   talkative
4. changes feelings quickly and often   moody
5. is relaxed and not worried about anything   laid-back
6. is happy and positive   cheerful
7. is kind, gentle, and friendly   sweet
8. enjoys meeting new people   outgoing

CD1 T10

B **Listen and check your answers.**

2 LISTEN

CD1 T11

A **Look at the picture. Listen to more of Tania and Eva's conversation. What are they talking about?**

a. classmates   (b.) Victor   c. friends

CD1 T11

B **Listen again. What is Victor like? Check the words.**

☐ laid-back   ☑ outgoing   ☐ bossy
☑ sweet   ☑ quiet   ☐ moody

CD1 T12

C **Listen to the whole conversation. Read the sentences. Circle *True* or *False*.**

1. Tania is talkative.   (True)   False
2. Tania likes talkative guys.   True   (False)

1   **BEFORE YOU LISTEN**

A   GROUPS OF 3. **Look at the words to describe...**

- Say: *Look at the words to describe people.* Read the words in the box. Tell students to read the definitions silently.
- Tell students to look at the example. Say: *Someone who always tells people what to do is . . . (bossy).*
- Form groups of 3. Together, students match the words and definitions.
- *Optional:* Give students a couple of minutes to study the words and definitions. While students are studying, write the words on the board. Pronounce each word and ask the class to repeat. Tell them to close their books. Read the definitions in random order and ask the class to call out the words.

   EXPANSION: Graphic organizer practice for 1A

- Pair students and tell them to draw a chart like the one on page 8. Tell them to label the columns *Positive, Negative,* and *Positive or negative.* Explain: Positive *means* good *and* negative *means* bad.
- Partners then decide whether each personality trait is positive or negative or could be either. They write each word in the appropriate place on the chart.

Teaching Tip

When words that may be new are presented through a matching activity, teach students the following strategy: Tell students to do the items they're sure of first, cross the words off in the box, and then try to figure out the others.

B   **Listen and check your answers.**

- Play CD 1, Track 10. Students correct their answers.
- Read the answers and ask students to repeat.

2   **LISTEN**

A   **Look at the picture. Listen to more...**

- Point to the photo. Ask: *Who are they?* (Tania and Eva) *What do we know about Eva?* (She has a brother. His name is Victor. She's having a party tonight.) *What do we know about Tania?* (She's going to Eva's party. She says Victor is good-looking.)
- Read the directions and answers. Play CD 1, Track 11. Students circle the letter of the correct answer.
- Ask students to raise their hands if they checked a. Repeat for b and c.
- Ask: *Why are they talking about Victor?* (because Tania is interested in him)

Teaching Tip

Remember that if students need additional support, tell them to read the Audio Script on page 297 as they listen to the conversation.

B   **Listen again. What is Victor like?...**

- Read the directions and the words.
- Play Track 11 again. Student listen and check.
- Check answers by asking a question for each word (for example, *Is Victor laid-back? Is he outgoing?*).

C   **Listen to the whole conversation....**

- Read the directions and items.
- Play CD 1, Track 12. Students listen and circle.
- Read each item and call on students to say answers.
- As a class, change item 2 to make it true. On the board, write: *Tania likes talkative guys.* Cross out *talkative* and add *who* to the end of the sentence. Ask the class to finish the sentence (*. . . listen*).

   EXPANSION: Vocabulary practice for 2C

- Ask students to look at the words in Exercise 1A. Say: *Tania likes guys who listen. Which personality traits do you like?* Students rank the words in order from *1* (best) to *8* (worst).
- Pair students. Partners compare their lists.
- Say each word and tell students to raise their hands if it's their number 1. Tally on the board.

3 CONVERSATION

A 🔘 Listen to the words. Notice...

- On the board, write: *a-bout*. Pronounce *about* and ask: *How many syllables does* about *have?* (two) Pronounce *about* again and ask: *Which syllable is stressed?* Underline *bout*.
- Say: *The vowel sound in a stressed syllable is long and clear.* Mark the stress over the *ou* in *about*. Pronounce *about*, drawing out the *ou* sound.
- Point to *a-bout* on the board. Say: *-bout is the stressed syllable. What is the unstressed syllable?* Circle *a-*.
- Say: *Vowels in unstressed syllables often have a very short, quiet sound.* To demonstrate this sound, say "uh" several times and ask the class to repeat. Then pronounce *about* several times, modeling the "uh" sound of the unstressed syllable.
- Tell students to open their books and read the Pronunciation Watch note silently.
- Read the directions. Point out that the vowel sounds in the unstressed syllables are blue.
- Play CD 1, Track 13. Students listen.
- Resume playing Track 13. Students listen and repeat.

Language Note

Help students articulate sounds they might find difficult to reproduce by having them practice adjusting the position of their tongue. Tell students to place their tongue low, in the middle, and then high in their mouth. Then tell them to place their tongue in the front, center, and back of their mouth. Explain: *To say the "uh" sound, place your tongue in the middle, center of your mouth. Make sure your tongue is relaxed.*

Controlled Practice   20 minutes

B 🔘 Listen and repeat the conversation.

- Note: This conversation is the same one students heard in Exercise 2A on page 14.
- Tell students to read the conversation silently and look for words that they practiced in Exercise 2B (*outgoing, quiet*). Tell them to circle the unstressed vowel in *quiet*.
- Play CD 1, Track 14. Students listen and repeat.

4 PRACTICE

A PAIRS. Practice the conversation. Then make...

- Pair students and tell them to practice the conversation in Exercise 3B.
- Then, in Exercise 4A, tell students to look at the information in the boxes. Say each item and ask the class to repeat.
- Copy the conversation onto the board with blanks and read it. When you come to a blank, fill it in with the first pair of words (*funny* and *tells great jokes*).
- Ask a pair of on-level students to practice the conversation on the board for the class.
- Erase the words in the blanks and ask two above-level students to make up a new conversation.
- Tell pairs to take turns playing A and B and to use the vocabulary lists to fill in the blanks.
- Walk around and check students' pronunciation of the unstressed syllable in *quiet*.
- Tell students to stand, mingle, and practice the conversation with several new partners.
- Call on pairs to practice for the class.

Communicative Practice   10 minutes

B MAKE IT PERSONAL. PAIRS. Talk about...

- Two students read the conversation out loud.
- Play A and practice a conversation with an above-level student (for example, *My husband's name is Robert.*). Prompt the student to ask: *What's he like?*
- Pair students and tell them to take turns playing A and B.
- Tell students to stand, mingle, and practice the conversation with several new partners.

▅▅ MULTILEVEL INSTRUCTION for 4B

Pre-level Before they practice, students list personality traits of a friend or family member.
Above-level Pairs talk about several people.

Extra Practice

Interactive Practice

3 CONVERSATION

CD1 T13

A 🔘 **Listen to the words. Notice the unstressed vowels. Then listen and repeat.**

about   quiet   talkative   beautiful   attractive

CD1 T14

B 🔘 **Listen and repeat the conversation.**

Tania: So tell me more about Victor. What's he like?

Eva: Well, he's outgoing and he has a lot of friends.

Tania: Yeah? What else?

Eva: He's sweet but he's a little quiet.

> **Pronunciation Watch**
>
> The vowel sound in a stressed syllable is long and clear. Vowels in unstressed syllables often have a very short, quiet sound. For example, a·bóut.

4 PRACTICE

A PAIRS. **Practice the conversation. Then make new conversations. Use the information in the boxes.**

A: So tell me more about Victor. What's he like?

B: Well, he's _____ and he _____ .

A: Yeah? What else?

B: He's _____ but he's a little _____ .

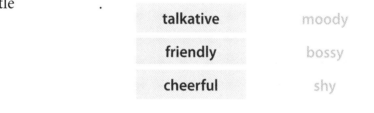

funny	tells great jokes
outgoing	loves adventure
interesting	tells great stories
talkative	moody
friendly	bossy
cheerful	shy

B MAKE IT PERSONAL. PAIRS. **Talk about the personalities of your friends or family members.**

A: *My best friend's name is Marie.*
B: *What's she like?*
A: *She's friendly. She's nice and she isn't bossy.*

Describe personalities

Grammar

Be: Compound sentences with *and* / *but*

He's outgoing	**and**	he has a lot of friends.
He's sweet	**but**	he's a little quiet.

Grammar Watch

- Use *and* to join two sentences with similar ideas.
- Use *but* to join two sentences with opposite ideas.

1 PRACTICE

A Complete the sentences. Write *and* or *but*.

1. He's from Brazil _____but_____ now he lives in the U.S.

2. Sarah is my friend. She's funny _____and_____ she's sweet.

3. My hair is straight _____and_____ it's shoulder length.

4. I'm shy _____but_____ my brother is outgoing.

5. I like long hair _____but_____ my wife's hair is short.

B Write sentences. Use the words in parentheses, the correct form of *be*, and *and* or *but*.

1. (Tina / shy / her sister / talkative) _Tina is shy but her sister is talkative._

2. (Ken / outgoing / he / moody) _Ken is outgoing but he is moody._

3. (The food / delicious / the waiter / friendly) _The food is delicious and the waiter is friendly._

4. (The class / good / the teacher / funny) _The class is good and the teacher is funny._

5. (Emily / cheerful / she / laid-back) _Emily is cheerful and she is laid-back._

C Complete the sentences. Write adjectives to make true sentences. Answers may vary but could include

1. I'm _____shy_____ and I'm _____quiet_____.

2. I'm _____interesting_____ and I'm _____funny_____.

3. I'm _____friendly_____ but I'm _____moody_____.

4. My teacher is _____talkative_____ and he's/she's _____outgoing_____.

D PAIRS. Compare your answers.

Lesson 6 Describe personalities

Getting Started 5 minutes

- Say: *We're going to study* be *in sentences with* and *and* but. *In the conversation you listened to in Exercise 3B on page 15, Eva used this grammar.*
- Play CD 1, Track 14. Students listen. Write on the board: *He's outgoing and he has a lot of friends. He's sweet but he's a little quiet.* Underline *and* and *but.*

Presentation 10 minutes

Be: Compound sentences with *and* / *but*

- Students close their books. Copy the sentences from the grammar chart onto the board, omitting *and* and *but.*
- Read the first statement in the Grammar Watch note. Ask: *Which two sentences have similar ideas?* Write *and* between the first pair of sentences.
- Read the second statement in the Grammar Watch note. Ask: *Which two sentences have opposite ideas?* Write *but* between the second pair of sentences.
- Tell students to open their books and look at the grammar charts or show Transparency 1.4 and cover the exercise. Read each sentence. Tell students that two sentences joined together with *and* or *but* are *compound sentences.*
- On the board, write: *My friend is good-looking and . . . , My friend is good-looking but . . .* Elicit answers.
- If you are using the transparency, do the exercise with the class.

Controlled Practice 15 minutes

1 PRACTICE

A Complete the sentences. Write *and* or *but*.

- Read the directions. Write item 1 on the board. Circle *He's from Brazil* and *now he lives in the U.S.* Ask: *Are these similar ideas or opposite ideas?* (opposite) Write in *but.*
- Walk around and when you spot an incorrect answer, read the two sentences that make up the compound. Ask: *Are these similar ideas or opposite ideas? Should you use* and *or* but?
- Call on students to read the sentences out loud.

B Write sentences. Use the words in parentheses...

- Read the directions. Write item 1 on the board. Underline *Tina / shy.* Ask: *What is the correct form of* be? Write: *Tina is shy.* Underline *her sister / talkative.* Ask: *What is the correct form of* be? Write: *her sister is talkative* a little to the right of *Tina is shy.*
- Read the two sentences. Ask: *Are these similar ideas or opposite ideas? Do I write* and *or* but? Write *but* to complete the compound sentence.
- Walk around and check that students start each sentence with a capital letter and end with a period.
- Call on students to read the answers out loud.

C Complete the sentences. Write adjectives to make...

- Read the directions. Write items 2 and 3 on the board with adjectives that make the sentences true for you.
- Remind students about the list of adjectives in Exercise 1A on page 14.
- *Optional:* Elicit other adjectives to describe people and write them on the board. Explain new words as needed.
- Walk around and prompt students as needed.

D PAIRS. Compare your answers.

- Students compare answers with a partner.
- Call on students to read their answers out loud.

EXPANSION: Listening and speaking practice for 1D

- Play a game. Write item 3 on the board. Say: *You have to listen and remember your classmates' sentences. Then you will complete the sentence yourself.* Procedure:

  - The first student completes the sentence (for example, *I'm nice, but I'm shy*).
  - The second student describes the first student (*[Student 1's name] is nice but she's shy*) and then says his or her own sentence.
  - The third student describes the first student and the second student and then says a new sentence.
  - Continue until a student cannot repeat everyone else's descriptions. That student then starts over.
  - Continue until everyone has had a turn.

Presentation   10 minutes

Be: Additions with *and . . . , too / and . . . not, either*

- On the board, write: *Eva is a student and I'm a student.* Underline *a student* in both parts of the sentence. Say: *The same information is repeated in the second part of the sentence.* Cross out *and I'm a student* and write *and I am, too.*

- Write: *Victor isn't a teacher and I'm not a teacher.* Underline *a teacher* in both parts of the sentence. Say: *The same information is repeated in the second part of the sentence.* Cross out *and I'm not a teacher* and write *and I'm not, either.*

- Circle *and I am, too* and *and I'm not, either.* Explain: *These are called* additions.

- Read the first sentence on the board. Say: *Eva is a student. Is this an affirmative statement or a negative statement?* On the board, write: *affirmative statements—too.*

- Read the second sentence on the board. Say: *Victor isn't a teacher. Is this an affirmative statement or a negative statement?* On the board, write: *negative statements—not, either.*

- Copy the top grammar chart onto the board or show Transparency 1.4 and cover the exercise. Read the examples. Ask: *Do the affirmative additions use contractions?* (No.) *Where is the comma in the affirmative additions?* (before *too*) Say each affirmative addition and ask the class to repeat.

- Repeat for the bottom grammar chart. Ask: *Do the negative additions use contractions?* (Yes.) *Where is the comma in the negative additions?* (before *either*) Say each negative addition and ask the class to repeat.

- Students read the Grammar Watch note silently.

- If you are using the transparency, do the exercise with the class.

Controlled Practice   5 minutes

2 PRACTICE

Complete the sentences. Write the correct forms...

- Read the directions. Write item 1 on the board. Underline *He isn't tall* and ask if it's affirmative or negative. Write the answer without the comma and ask: *Where do I put the comma?* (before *either*)

- Read completed item 1. To check that students understand the meaning of *not either*, ask: *Is he tall?* (No.) *Is his wife tall?* (No.)

- Students compare answers with a partner.

- Call on students to write the answers on the board.

Communicative Practice   15 minutes

Show what you know!

STEP 1. WRITE. Think about your own personality....

- Read the directions. On the board, write: *My personality.* Then write two sentences with *I am* and two sentences with *I'm not.* Use adjectives from page 14. Circle the sentences with *I am* and label them *affirmative.* Circle the sentences with *I'm not* and label them *negative.*

- Tell students to use the adjectives from page 14 or their own adjectives. Check that students write two affirmative sentences and two negative sentences.

STEP 2. GROUPS OF 5. Tell your partners about...

- Read the directions. Tell students to look at your sentences on the board. Ask an above-level student to read his or her sentences out loud. Write the student's name next to any of your sentences that are the same. Repeat with other students.

- Point to the affirmative sentences and names on the board. Make sentences with *too.* Point to the negative sentences on the board. Make sentences with *either.*

- Form groups of 5. Tell students to take turns reading their sentences out loud, listening for sentences that are the same as theirs and writing students' names.

Progress Check

Can you . . . describe personalities?

Say: *We have practiced describing personalities. Now, look at the question at the bottom of the page. Can you describe personalities?* Tell students to write a checkmark in the box.

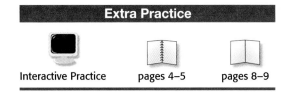

Extra Practice		
Interactive Practice	pages 4–5	pages 8–9

Be: Additions with *and ...*, *too / and ...not, either*

Affirmative statement	Addition		
		I	am, too.
Eva is a student	and	they	are, too.
		he	is, too.

Negative statement	Addition		
		I	'm not, either.
			aren't, either.
Victor isn't a teacher	and	you	're not, either.
		she	isn't, either.
			's not, either.

- Use an addition as a way to avoid repeating the same information in the second part of the sentence.
- Use *too* for affirmative sentences.
- Use *not, either* for negative sentences.
- Use a comma before *too* and *either*.

2 PRACTICE

Complete the sentences. Write the correct forms of *be* and *too* or *either*.

1. He isn't tall and his wife __isn't, either__.

2. Greg is funny and his dad __is, too__.

3. Sun is in my English class and Oscar and Fernando __are, too__.

4. My brothers are not outgoing and I __'m not, either__.

5. My friend is beautiful and her daughter __is, too__.

Show what you know! Describe personalities

STEP 1. WRITE. Think about your own personality. Write four sentences with *be*. Write two affirmative sentences and two negative sentences.

I am outgoing and I am quiet.

STEP 2. GROUPS OF 5. Tell your partners about your personality. Do you have the same personality as other members of your group? Make sentences with *too* or *either*.

Marta is outgoing and I am, too.

Can you...describe personalities? ☐

Reading

1 BEFORE YOU READ

PAIRS. What is your learning style? For example, do you like to study alone or with other people? Do you like to study in a quiet room or in a noisy place?

2 READ

CD1 T15

Listen. Read the article.

What is a Learning Style?

Some people learn best when they study with classmates. Other people like to study alone. Some people learn how to do things by reading books. Other people learn things best by talking to people. There are many ways to learn new information. These ways of learning are called learning styles. Here are some learning styles.

Visual Learners
Visual learners learn best by seeing. They remember new information best when it is in pictures, graphs, and maps. They are also good at spelling and remembering faces.

Auditory Learners
Auditory learners learn best by talking and listening. They remember information best when they hear it. They have a "good ear" for language and remember names easily. They are good at discussions and interviewing. They find it difficult to study in noisy places.

Kinesthetic Learners
Kinesthetic learners learn best by doing things. They like doing projects. They remember new information best if they act it out or role-play. They "speak" with their hands a lot. They find it difficult to sit down and study for long periods.

3 CHECK YOUR UNDERSTANDING

A Read the article again. What is the main idea of the article? How do you know?

a. People learn best by doing things.

b. People learn in different ways.

c. Some people use two learning styles.

Reading Skill: Finding the Main Idea

The main idea is the most important idea in the article. The first paragraph usually tells the main idea.

Getting Started 10 minutes

1 BEFORE YOU READ

PAIRS. What is your learning style? For example...

- Read the directions.
- Say: *Think about who you study with, where you study, when you study, and how you study.*
- On the board, draw a web diagram. Write *study* in the circle. On the lines radiating out from the circle, write: *Who, Where, When,* and *How.* Point to *Who* and ask: *Do you like to study alone or with other people?* Point to *Where* and ask: *Do you like to study in a quiet room or in a noisy place?* Point to *When* and ask: *Do you like to study early in the morning or late at night?* Point to *How* and ask: *Do you like to read, talk about, or write new information?*
- Tell students to copy the diagram and note their study habits.
- To model the activity, tell the class about your study habits: who you study with and where, when, and how you study. Pair students and tell them to talk about their web diagrams.

Presentation 10 minutes

2 READ

 Listen. Read the article.

- Tell students to look at the article. Say: *Look at the photo. What are the people doing?* (studying) *Do they like to study alone or with other people?* (with other people)
- Ask: *What is the title of the article?* (What Is a Learning Style?) Tell students to look at the icons, or small pictures, in the article. Ask: *What are three learning styles?* (visual learners, auditory learners, kinesthetic learners) Say each learning style and ask the class to repeat. Ask: *How do you think visual learners learn?* (by seeing / they look) *How do you think auditory learners learn?* (by listening / they listen) *How do you think kinesthetic learners learn?* (by touching / they touch)

- Play CD 1, Track 15. Students listen and read along silently.
- Tell students to read the article again silently. Tell them to circle how each type of learner remembers new information best.
- Tell students to underline what each type of learner is good at.

EXPANSION: Graphic organizer practice for 2

- On the board, draw a chart with three columns and three rows. Label the columns: *Visual, Auditory, Kinesthetic.* Label the rows: *learn by . . . , remember information best when . . . , good at . . . .*
- Pair students and tell them to complete the chart with the information they underlined in the article.

Controlled Practice 20 minutes

3 CHECK YOUR UNDERSTANDING

Ⓐ Read the article again. What is the main idea...

- Read the Reading Skill note. Tell students to circle the first paragraph of the article. Tell students to read the first paragraph silently and underline the sentence that tells the main idea, or most important idea, of the article.
- Read the first paragraph. Ask: *What sentence did you underline?* Elicit the answer and write it on the board: *There are many ways to learn new information.* Label the sentence: *Main Idea.*
- Read the directions and answer choices.
- To check the answer, ask students to raise their hands for a, b, or c.

B **How do you learn best? Take the quiz.**

- Tell students to read and take the quiz silently. Walk around and help with unfamiliar vocabulary as needed.
- Read the quiz. Say each answer choice and ask students to raise their hands for the answer they chose.
- Tell students to look at item 4 in the quiz. Read the question. Ask: *What does a visual learner do?* (draw a picture) *What does an auditory learner do?* (say the word) *What does a kinesthetic learner do?* (write the word) Elicit answers.
- Say: *Now try the three learning styles.* Write a new word on the board. It should be a difficult word that's easy to draw. Read item 4 again. Say each answer choice and tell students to do what it says with the new word. Ask: *Which way worked best for you? Is it the same as the answer you checked when you took the quiz?*

C **Look at the quiz. How many responses do...**

- Ask: *What do you think your learning style is?* Tell students to read the article again and circle their learning style.
- Read the directions. Students count their responses for each symbol.
- Ask: *What is your learning style? Is it the same as the one you circled in the article? Or is it different?* Ask for a show of hands.
- Read the note. Say: *Raise your hand again if the learning style you circled in the article is different from your quiz result.* Ask: *Do you think you use more than one learning style?*

Communicative Practice   20 minutes

D **PAIRS. Compare your quiz results.**

- Model the activity. Ask an above-level student to ask you the questions from the directions. Talk about the learning style you circled in the article and your learning style according to the quiz. Say whether or not the quiz results surprise you (for example, *I thought I was an auditory learner, but my quiz result is visual learner.*).
- Pair students. Tell them to ask each other the questions in the directions.

Show what you know!

PRE-WRITING. NETWORK. Find classmates...

- Tell students to look back at the article and the quiz. Tell them to note some ways to learn English that are good for their learning style (for example, visual learners can draw pictures to remember information).
- Tell students to stand, mingle, and ask classmates: *What is your learning style?* Tell students to form small groups with classmates who have the same learning style.
- Model the activity. Talk about your learning style and how you learn English best.
- Tell groups to share their notes.

WRITING. Write a list of learning tips for your...

- Ask students to turn to page 268 and write a list of learning tips for their own learning style. See page T-xii for general notes about the Writing activities.

EXPANSION: Vocabulary practice

- Group students with the same learning style. Tell them to identify ways to learn new information that are good for their learning style. Tell them to use these ways to practice the vocabulary on page 7. Suggest that students look at the article and quiz for ideas.
- Visual learners can draw pictures of vocabulary words and make vocabulary cards. Auditory learners can talk about their classmates' physical descriptions and close their eyes and say the words over and over again. Kinesthetic learners can play charades and say the words as they write them over and over again.

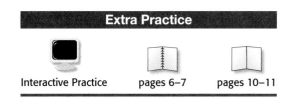

Extra Practice		
Interactive Practice	pages 6–7	pages 10–11

B How do you learn best? Take the quiz.

Learning Styles Quiz

How do you learn new information? What do you do in these situations?

1 You have a new cell phone. You don't know how to use it.

- ☐ I read the instructions in the user's manual.
- ☐ I ask a friend to explain it to me.
- ☐ I play with the phone until I understand how to use it.

2 You're going to a new restaurant in your neighborhood. You don't know exactly where it is.

- ☐ I look at a map.
- ☐ I call the restaurant and ask for directions.
- ☐ I start walking until I find it.

3 You can't remember how to spell a word.

- ☐ I write the word different ways. I choose the way that looks right.
- ☐ I say the word and write the letters as they sound.
- ☐ I use my finger to "write" the word and decide what feels right.

4 You need to memorize a new word.

- ☐ I draw a picture of the work in my notebook.
- ☐ I close my eyes and say the word over and over again.
- ☐ I say the word as I write it over and over again.

C Look at the quiz. How many responses do you have for each symbol? Answers will vary. Write the numbers. The symbol with the most responses is your learning style.

_____ responses = visual learner

_____ responses = auditory learner

_____ responses = kinesthetic learner

Many people use more than one learning style. For example, a person may learn best by talking and doing.

D PAIRS. Compare your quiz results.
What is your learning style? Do the results surprise you?

Show what you know!

PRE-WRITING. NETWORK. Find classmates with the same learning style. Talk about how you learn English best.

WRITING. Write a list of learning tips for your learning style. See page 268.

Get to know someone

Listening and Speaking

1 BEFORE YOU LISTEN

CLASS. Imagine that you are meeting someone for the first time. In this country, which questions are OK to ask? Check the questions.

☑ What do you do?   ☑ Where are you from?

☐ Are you married?   ☐ Where do you live?

☐ How old are you?   ☐ Do you have children?

2 LISTEN

A CLASS. Look at the picture. Who are the people? Where are they?

CD1 T16

B Listen to the conversation. Answer the questions.

1. What's happening?
   a. Victor is asking Tania for a date.
   (b.) Victor and Tania are meeting for the first time.
   c. Tania is saying good-bye.

2. Which questions does Victor ask Tania?
   ☑ Are you a student?   ☑ Where are you from?

   ☐ Is it nice?   ☐ What do you do?

   ☐ Are you from Ecuador?   ☑ What's it like?

CD1 T16

C Listen again. Read the sentences. Circle *True* or *False*.

1. Tania is a student.   (True)   False

2. Eva is a student.   (True)   False

3. Victor is from Ecuador.   True   (False)

CD1 T17

D Listen to the whole conversation. Answer the question.

What is Victor's job? _He is a cook at a restaurant._

Lesson 8   Get to know someone

Getting Started   10 minutes

 BEFORE YOU LISTEN

CLASS. Imagine that you are meeting someone...

- Read the directions. Students read and check the questions silently.
- Read each question. Ask: *Is it OK to ask this here?*
- Introduce yourself to several students. Ask each student one or two of the appropriate questions (for example, *Hi, I'm _____. What's your name? Nice to meet you, _____. Where are you from?*).

Culture Connection

- On the board, write: *How old are you?* Reinforce that in the U.S. it's not polite to ask a person's age.
- Ask: *What other questions are not OK to ask when you are meeting someone for the first time in the U.S.?* (*How much money do you make? How much is your rent? How much did you pay for your car?*) Write the questions on the board under the heading *Not OK*. For emphasis, cross them out.
- Ask: *What questions are not OK to ask in your home country?* Add students' questions to the list on the board.

Presentation   25 minutes

2 **LISTEN**

A **CLASS. Look at the picture. Who are the people?...**

- Ask students to look at the picture. Ask: *Who are the people?* Tell students to label Eva, Victor, and Tania. Write their names on the board. Ask: *Who are Eva and Tania?* (friends) *Who is Victor?* (Eva's brother)
- Ask: *Where are they?* (at Eva's party) *Who's meeting for the first time?* (Victor and Tania)

B **Listen to the conversation. Answer...**

- Read the directions and answer choices.
- Say: *Look at the picture. What do you think is happening? Which questions do you think Victor asks Tania? Now listen and see if you're right.*
- Play CD 1, Track 16. Students mark the answers.

- For item 1, ask students to raise their hands if they circled a. Repeat for b and c.
- For item 2, say: *Victor and Tania are meeting for the first time. What does Victor ask Tania?*

Teaching Tip

Remember that if students need additional support, tell them to read the Audio Script on page 297 as they listen to the conversation.

C **Listen again. Read the sentences....**

- Read the directions and the sentences. Play Track 16 again. Students listen and circle.
- Call on students to read the sentences and say answers.
- On the board, write: *Tania is a student, and Eva _____. Ask the class to complete the sentence. (is, too)*
- Write item 3 on the board. Say: *Rewrite the sentence to make it true.* (*Tania is from Ecuador.*)

D **Listen to the whole conversation....**

- Read the directions and the question. Play CD 1, Track 17. Students listen and write the answer.
- Ask: *Is Victor a student?* (No, he's not.) *What is his job?* (He's a cook.) *Where does he work?* (at a restaurant)

EXPANSION: Speaking practice for 2D

- Pair students and tell them to role-play a conversation between Victor and Tania. The student playing Victor reads the checked questions in Exercise 2B. The student playing Tania answers.

EXPANSION: Speaking practice for 2D

- Ask: *What will happen next with Tania and Victor?* Play Track 17 again. On the board, write:

Victor: No, I'm not. I work at a restaurant. I'm a cook.
Tania:
Victor:
Tania:
Victor:

- Elicit students' ideas to continue the conversation. Write the new lines on the board.
- Ask two above-level students to read the conversation on the board.
- Pair students and tell them to practice the practice the new conversation.

3 CONVERSATION

Ⓐ 💿 **Listen to the sentences. Then listen...**

- Read the directions. On the board, write: *Are you a student, too?* without the stress marks. Read the Pronunciation Watch note. Ask: *What are the important words?* Underline *you, student,* and *too.* Ask: *Which words are not stressed?* (*Are, a*)

- Tell students to close their books. Say: *I'm going to read only the stressed words in the sentence. See if you can still understand the basic meaning.* Say: *you, student, too.*

- Point to the sentence on the board. Pronounce each underlined word and ask: *How many syllables?* Draw a line separating the two syllables in *stu/dent.* Say: *In words with more than one syllable, only one syllable is stressed.* Pronounce *student* and ask: *Which syllable is stressed?* Double underline *stu.*

- Read the sentence on the board. Exaggerate the stress on *you, stu-,* and *too.*

- Tell students to open their books and look at the stressed words in the sentences. Pronounce each stressed word and ask: *How many syllables?* On the board, write: *I work at a restaurant.* Draw lines separating the three syllables in *res/tau/rant.* Pronounce *restaurant* and ask: *Which syllable is stressed?* Double-underline *res.*

- Play CD 1, Track 18. Students listen.
- Resume playing Track 18. Students listen and repeat.

Controlled Practice   15 minutes

Ⓑ 💿 **Listen to the sentences. Mark (•)...**

- Ask students to look at items 1–3. Ask: *What are the important words?*
- Read the directions and play CD 1, Track 19.
- Write items 1–3 on the board. Call on students to mark the stressed words on the board. Correct as needed.

Ⓒ 💿 **Listen and repeat the conversation.**

- Note: This conversation is the same one students heard in Exercise 2D on page 20.
- Say: *Underline the sentences in the conversation that you practiced in Exercises 3A and 3B* (*Nice to meet you. So, are you a student? Where are you from?*). *Now mark the stressed words or syllables.*

- On the board, write: *I want to introduce you to my friend.* Ask: *What are the important words in this sentence?* Underline *want, introduce,* and *friend.* Pronounce each underlined word and ask: *How many syllables?* Draw a line separating the three syllables in *in/tro/duce.* Pronounce *introduce* and ask: *Which syllable is stressed?* Double-underline *tro.* Tell students to underline the first sentence in the conversation and then mark the stress.

- Play CD 1, Track 20. Students listen and repeat.

4 PRACTICE

Ⓐ **GROUPS OF 3. Practice the conversation.**

- Form groups of 3. Tell students to practice the conversation in Exercise 3C, taking turns playing each person.
- Walk around and model the correct sentence stress as needed.

Communicative Practice   10 minutes

Ⓑ **ROLE PLAY. GROUPS OF 3. Student A,...**

- Read the directions. Play A and model the activity with two above-level students. Prompt B to continue the conversation by asking a question from Exercise 1 on page 20. Prompt C to answer and ask another question.
- Form groups of 3. Tell students take turns playing each person. Walk around and help as needed.

▬▬ **MULTILEVEL INSTRUCTION for 4B**

Pre-level Students playing the roles of B and C ask one question each from Exercise 1 on page 20. Before students role-play the conversation, tell them to write answers to each question in Exercise 1 on page 20.

Above-level Students playing the roles of B and C ask several questions and ask partners to elaborate on their answers. They can ask, for example, *What's it like? What's your wife's name? How old are your children?*

Extra Practice
▮
Interactive Practice

3 CONVERSATION

CD1 T18

A 🔘 **Listen to the sentences. Then listen and repeat.**

   ●   ●   ●   ●   ●

Are you a student, too?   No, I'm not.

    ●   ●   ●

I work at a restaurant.   I'm a waiter.

> ### Pronunciation Watch
>
> In English, the important words in a sentence are stressed. They are long and loud. In words with more than one syllable, only one syllable is stressed.

CD1 T19

B 🔘 **Listen to the sentences. Mark (●) the stressed words.**

1. Nice to meet you.   2. Where are you from?   3. How about you?

CD1 T20

C 🔘 **Listen and repeat the conversation.**

Eva: I want to introduce you to my friend. Victor, this is Tania. Tania, this is Victor.

Victor: Nice to meet you.

Tania: Nice to meet you, too.

Victor: So, are you a student?

Tania: Yes, I am. Eva and I are in the same English class.

Victor: Oh, that's nice. Where are you from?

Tania: Ecuador.

Victor: Really? What's it like?

Tania: It's a very beautiful country.

4 PRACTICE

A GROUPS OF 3. **Practice the conversation.**

B ROLE PLAY. GROUPS OF 3. **Student A, introduce Student B to Student C. Continue the conversation.**

   A: *I want to introduce you to my friend. _____, this is _____.*

       _____, this is _____.

   B: *Nice to meet you.*

   C: *Nice to meet you, too.*

   B: *So, _____ . . .*

Get to know someone

Grammar

Simple present tense of *be: Yes / No* and information questions

Yes / No questions with *be*			Short answers						
Are	you	a student?	**Yes,**	I	**am.**	**No,**	I	**am**	**not.**

Information questions with *be*			Short answer
Where	**are**	you from?	Ecuador.

PRACTICE

A Match the questions and answers.

1. __d__ Where is your family from?
2. __a__ Are they students?
3. __f__ What is your country like?
4. __b__ How old is your daughter?
5. __c__ Are you from Russia?
6. __e__ What's your name?

a. Yes, they are.
b. She's four.
c. No, I'm not.
d. Brazil.
e. I'm Jennifer.
f. It's beautiful.

B Read the answers. Write questions about the underlined information.

1. **A:** What is your last name?

   B: My last name is <u>Chow</u>.

2. **A:** What is Pei-Ling's address?

   B: Pei-Ling's address is <u>240 Colson Drive</u>.

3. **A:** Where are they from?

   B: They're from <u>Cuba</u>.

4. **A:** How old is Peter?

   B: Peter is <u>twenty-four years old</u>.

5. **A:** Are his sisters tall?

   B: <u>Yes</u>. His sisters are tall.

6. **A:** Is he outgoing?

   B: <u>No</u>. He's not outgoing. He's really shy!

7. **A:** What is Mike's phone number?

   B: Mike's phone number is <u>555-9874</u>.

8. **A:** Are Ted and Chris students?

   B: <u>Yes</u>. Ted and Chris are students.

C PAIRS. Ask your partner three questions from Exercises A and B.

Lesson 9 Get to know someone

Getting Started   5 minutes

- Say: *We're going to study questions with the verb* be. *In the conversation you listened to in Exercise 3C on page 21, Victor used this grammar.*
- Play CD 1, Track 20. Students listen. Write on the board: *Are you a student? Where are you from?* Underline *are* in each question.

Presentation   10 minutes

Simple present tense of *be*: *Yes / No* and information questions

- Copy the grammar charts onto the board or show Transparency 1.5 and cover the exercise.

Yes/No questions with *be*

- Read the *Yes / No* question and short answers from the top chart. Ask a few students: *Are you a student?* Elicit: *Yes, I am.* Ask a few students: *Are you a cook?* Elicit: *No, I'm not.*
- On the board, write: *Tania is from Ecuador.* With the class, change the statement to a *Yes / No* question. Draw arrows to indicate changing the order of the subject and verb. Write: *Is Tania from Ecuador?* Ask the question and elicit the short answer. Write: *Yes, she is.*

Information questions with *be*

- Read the information question and short answer from the bottom chart. Ask a few students: *Where are you from?* Elicit a short answer.
- On the board, write: *Is Tania from Ecuador?* With the class change the *Yes / No* question to an information question. Cross out *Ecuador* and draw a blank at the beginning of the question. Ask: *What question word do I use?* Write *Where* in the blank and change *Is* to *is*. Read the question and elicit the answer.
- If you are using the transparency, do the exercise with the class.

Controlled Practice   15 minutes

 **PRACTICE**

A Match the questions and answers.

- Read the directions. Tell students to cross out the letter of the answers as they use them.
- Read each question and call on a student to answer.

B Read the answers. Write questions about...

- Tell students they will write information questions for A from B's answers. Help them understand the changes they need to make when they write questions from the answers, as follows:

  -Write item 1 on the board and read B's answer. Point to A's question and ask: *Is this a Yes / No question or an information question?* (information question) Read the answer again. Ask: *What is the question word?* Write *What* on the line. Circle *My last name* and *is* in the answer and draw arrows to indicate students should change the order of the subject and verb.

  -Ask students to look at item 3. Read the answer. Ask: *What's the verb?* On the board, write: *They are from Cuba.* Draw arrows to indicate that students should change the order of the subject and verb.

- Read each question and call on a student to answer.

Communicative Practice   10 minutes

C PAIRS. Ask your partner three questions...

- Pair students and tell them to take turns asking and answering questions from Exercises A and B. Each partner should ask three different questions.

▬▬ MULTILEVEL INSTRUCTION for C
Cross-ability Lower-level students ask questions first. Before switching roles, higher-level students can help lower-level students write answers to three questions.

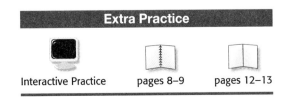

Extra Practice		
Interactive Practice	pages 8–9	pages 12–13

1 GRAMMAR

Ⓐ Complete the conversations. Write the correct...

- Tell students to review the grammar charts on pages 10 (*have* + object) and 22 (*be: Yes / No* and information questions).
- Read the directions.
- Ask students to look at item 1. Ask: *Why is* Are you *the answer? What form of* be *goes with* you? On the board, write: *you are.* Ask: *Is item 1 a question or a statement?* Draw arrows to indicate that students should change the order of *you* and *are.* Write the answer without the capital letter (*are you Anthony Jenkins?*) and ask: *Is this correct?* (No.) Capitalize *are.*
- Walk around and, as needed, ask students what the subject is or whether the item is a question or a statement.
- Call on a pair of above-levels students to read each conversation. Write the answers on the board as the students say them.
- *Optional:* Pair students and ask them to practice the conversations. Call on pairs to perform the completed conversations for the class.

Ⓑ Complete the information. Underline the correct...

- Tell students to look at the photo. Hold up your book, point to the girl on the left, and ask: *What does she look like?* (She has long, straight, brown hair) Point to the girl on the right and repeat. Ask: *Do they look alike?* (Yes.) *Why?* (They're twins.)
- Complete the first sentence with the class. Ask: *Why is* is *the answer?* (We use *be* when we talk about someone's name.)

- Tell students to refer back to the grammar charts on pages 10 (*be* + adjective, *have* + object), 16 (compound sentences with *and / but*), and 17 (*be* + additions) as needed as they do the rest of the exercise.
- Students compare answers with a partner.
- Read the paragraphs with the correct answers and tell students to check their work.

 EXPANSION: Graphic organizer and speaking practice for 1B

- Tell students to use the information from Exercise 1B to complete a chart, like the one on page 8, comparing Ellen and Isabel.
- Pair students. Tell them to close their books, look at their charts, and talk about how Ellen and Isabel are alike and how they're different.

CD-ROM Practice

 Go to the CD-ROM for more practice.

If your students need more practice with the vocabulary, grammar, and competencies in Unit 1, encourage them to review the activities on the CD-ROM. This review can also help students prepare for the final role play on the following Expand page.

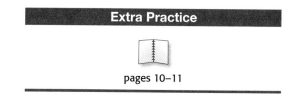

Extra Practice
pages 10–11

1 GRAMMAR

A Complete the conversations. Write the correct forms of the words in parentheses.

1. **A:** Excuse me. ___*Are you*___ Anthony Jenkins?
   (you / be)

   B: No, I __'m not___. Anthony ___is___ the tall guy over there.
   (not / be)   (be)

   He ___has___ short, dark hair.
   (have)

   A: Oh, I see him. Thanks.

2. **A:** You look familiar. ___Are you___ a student at the English Language Center?
   (you / be)

   B: Yes, I ___am___. I __'m_____ in level two.
   (be)   (be)

   A: Me, too. ___Who's___ your teacher?
   (who / be)

   B: Ted Graham. He _'s_____ a really good teacher.
   (be)

B Complete the sentences. Underline the correct words.

My name **has / <u>is</u>** Ellen. **<u>I'm</u> / I have** eighteen years old. This is my sister, Isabel. We're twins. As you can see, we look alike. My hair **<u>is</u> / am** long and brown, **<u>and</u> / but** my sister's hair is, **either / <u>too</u>**. We both **<u>have</u> / are** brown eyes. **<u>I'm</u> / I have** not tall, **but / <u>and</u>** my sister isn't, **too / <u>either</u>**.

We are very similar, **and / <u>but</u>** we're not alike in every way. My sister **<u>is</u> / has** talkative, **<u>but</u> / and** I'm quiet. My sister **has / <u>is</u>** outgoing, **<u>but</u> / and** I'm shy. My sister is always cheerful, **and / <u>but</u>** I am sometimes moody. Oh, and one more difference: I **<u>am</u> / are** sweet, **<u>but</u> / and** my sister **<u>is</u> / are** bossy. Don't tell my sister I wrote that!

2 ACT IT OUT   What do you say?

STEP 1. CLASS. Review the Lesson 8 conversation between Eva, Victor, and Tania (CD 1 track 16).

STEP 2. ROLE PLAY. GROUPS OF 3. Imagine you are at a party.
Student A, introduce Students B and C.
Students B and C, continue the conversation. Make small talk.

3 READ AND REACT   Problem-solving

STEP 1. Read about Victor's problem.

Victor is at work. He meets a new co-worker, Jim, for the first time. First they talk about where they are from. Then Jim asks Victor, "How much money do you make?" Victor doesn't want to answer the question.

STEP 2. PAIRS. What is Victor's problem? What can he do? **Here are some ideas.**

- He can say nothing and then talk about something different.
- He can answer the question and feel bad.
- He can say, "I'd rather not say."
- He can _____.

4 CONNECT

For your Community-building Activity, go to page 248.
For your Team Project, go to page 274.

EXPAND Show what you know!

2 ACT IT OUT

STEP 1. CLASS. Review the Lesson 8 conversation...

- Tell students to review the conversation in Exercise 3C on page 21.
- Tell them to read the conversation silently and then practice it with a partner.
- Play CD 1, Track 16. Students listen.
- As needed, play Track 16 again to aid comprehension.

STEP 2. ROLE PLAY. GROUPS OF 3. Imagine you...

- Read the directions. Model the activity with two above-level students. Introduce the two students to each other. After the students say *Nice to meet you / Nice to meet you, too*, prompt them to make small talk. Remind them that they can ask any of the checked questions from Exercise 1 on page 20.
- Form groups of three and assign roles.
- Walk around and observe students interacting. Check that one student is introducing the other two. Then check that the two who were introduced continue to talk, for example, about what they do and where they are from.
- Tell groups to switch roles so that the student who played A can now play B or C.
- Call on all groups to perform for the class. Each group should perform twice, switching roles as above.
- While groups are performing, use the scoring rubric on page T-xiii to evaluate each student's vocabulary, grammar, fluency, and how well he or she completes the task.
- *Optional:* After each group finishes, discuss the strengths and weakness of each performance either in front of the class or privately.

3 READ AND REACT

STEP 1. Read about Victor's problem.

- Say: *We are going to read about a student's problem, and then we need to think about a solution.*

- Read the story while students follow along silently. Pause after each sentence to allow time for students to comprehend. Periodically stop and ask simple *Wh-* questions to check comprehension (for example, *Where is Victor? Who is Jim? What do Victor and Jim talk about first? What does Jim ask Victor? What is Victor's problem?*).

STEP 2. PAIRS. What is Victor's problem? What...

- Ask: *What is Victor's problem?* (A new co-worker asked him a personal question / a question about money / "How much money do you make?")
- Pair students. Read the list of ideas. Give pairs a couple of minutes to discuss possible solutions for Victor.
- Ask: *Which ideas are good?* Call on students to say their opinion about the ideas (for example, S: *I think he can say, "I'd rather not say" because Jim's question is not polite.*).
- Now tell pairs to think of one new idea not in the box (for example, *He can make a joke and say, "Not enough."*) and to write it in the space. Encourage students to think of more than one idea and to write them in their notebooks.
- Call on pairs to say their additional solutions. Write any particularly good ones on the board and ask students if they think it is a good idea too (*Do you think this is a good idea? Why or why not?*).

▬ MULTILEVEL INSTRUCTION for STEP 2

Cross-ability If possible, pair students with the same first language. The higher-level partner helps the lower-level student to say his/her idea in English.

4 CONNECT

Turn to page 248 for the Community-building Activity and page 274 for the Team Project. See page T-xi for general notes about these activities.

Progress Check

Which goals can you check off? Go back to page 5.

Ask students to turn to page 5 and check off the goals they have reached. Call on students to say which goals they will practice outside of class.

All in the Family

Classroom Materials/Extra Practice

CD 1
Tracks 21–34

Transparencies 2.1–2.6
Vocabulary Cards Unit 2

MCA
Unit 2

Workbook
Unit 2

Interactive Practice
Unit 2

Unit Overview

Goals
- See the list of goals on the facing page.

Grammar
- Simple present affirmative and negative: *have / live / work*
- Simple present: Additions with *and . . . , too / and . . . not, either*
- Simple present: *Yes / No* and information questions

Pronunciation
- Sentence stress
- Strong and weak pronunciations of *do*

Reading
- Read an advice column about managing responsibilities
- *Reading Skill:* Retelling information

Writing
- Write about your life and family
- Describe how people are similar
- Write a list of your responsibilities

Life Skills Writing
- Complete a post office customs form

Preview
- Set the context of the unit by asking questions about family (for example, *Do you have a big family or a small family? Where do your family members live?*).
- Hold up page 25 or show Transparency 2.1. Read the unit title and ask the class to repeat.
- Say: *Look at the picture.* Ask the Preview question: *What do you see?* (a family / a father, mother, son, and daughter)

Unit Goals
- Point to the Unit Goals. Explain that this list shows what the class will be studying in this unit.
- Tell students to read the goals silently.
- Say each goal and ask the class to repeat. Explain unfamiliar vocabulary as needed:

    Customs form: a form that you complete when you send mail to another country
- Tell students to read the goals silently and then to circle one goal that is very important to them. Call on several students to say the goal they circled.
- Write a checkmark (✓) on the board. Say: *We will come back to this page again. You will write a checkmark next to the goals you learned in this unit.*

All in the Family

Preview

Look at the picture.
What do you see?

UNIT GOALS

- [ ] Identify family members
- [ ] Talk about your life and family
- [ ] Talk about what people have in common
- [ ] Ask about sending mail
- [ ] Complete a customs form
- [ ] Ask about family members

1 WHAT DO YOU KNOW?

A CLASS. Look at the pictures of Marta's family. Find Marta in each picture. Guess: Who are the other family members in the pictures? Which family relationships do you know?

I think number 1 is Marta's brother.

CD1 T21

B Look at the pictures and listen. Listen again and repeat.

Manny Tina Manuel Isabel   Marta   Maria Tony Carlos

2 PRACTICE

A PAIRS. Student A, ask a question about Marta's family. Student B, answer.

A: *Who is Marta's mother-in-law?*
B: *Sandra. Who are Marta's grandchildren?*

B PAIRS. Look at the pictures. Student A, say two names and point to the two people in the pictures. Student B, say the relationship.

A: *Ben and Ann.*
B: *Brother and sister.*

Ben   Marta   Tina   Eva   Felix

C WORD PLAY. PAIRS. Look at the list of family members. Which words are for females? Which are for males? Which are for both? Complete the diagram.

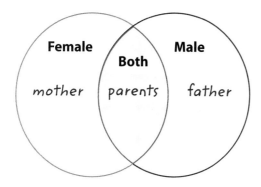

Female **Both** **Male**
mother parents father

Marta   Ben   Sandra   Tom   Ann

Lesson 1 Vocabulary

Getting Started   10 minutes

1 WHAT DO YOU KNOW?

Ⓐ CLASS. Look at the pictures of Marta's family....

- Show Transparency 2.2 or hold up the book. Tell students to cover the list of words on page 27.
- Point to the first picture and ask: *Where is Marta? Who are the other family members in the pictures? Which family relationships do you know?*
- Students call out answers. Help students with pronunciation if needed.
- If students call out an incorrect family member, change the student's answer to a question for the class (for example, *Number 3 is Marta's brother?*). If nobody can identify the correct family relationship, tell students they will now listen to a CD and practice the words for family members.

Presentation   5 minutes

Ⓑ Look at the pictures and listen....

- Read the directions. Play CD 1, Track 21. Pause after number 25 (*grandchildren*).
- Say each family word in random order and ask students to point to the appropriate picture.
- Resume playing Track 21. Students listen and repeat.

> **Language Note**
>
> Write on the board: *Ben is Marta's fiancé. Marta is Ben's fiancée.* Underline *fiancé* and *fiancée*. Ask: *What is the difference in spelling?* (the word for a woman has an extra *e*)

Controlled Practice   20 minutes

2 PRACTICE

Ⓐ PAIRS. Student A, ask a question about...

- Read the directions. Play A and model the example with an above-level student.
- Read each line in the example and ask the class to repeat. Model correct intonation.

- Pair students and tell them to take turns asking and answering questions.

> **Community Building**
>
> Show students how to correct each other's mistakes by modeling the activity again with an above-level student. Ask the student to play A and ask a new question. Play B, as follows:
>
> A: *Who are Marta's grandchildren?*
> B: *Mary and Sue.*
> A: No. [Points to Benny]
> B: *Mary and Benny.*
> A: *Yes. Good!*

Ⓑ PAIRS. Look at the pictures....

- Read the directions.
- Play A and model the example with an above-level student. Point to Ben and Ann in the third picture.
- Pair students and tell them to take turns playing A and B. Tell A to point to two people in the same picture.
- Walk around and check that B is saying what the family members' relationships are to each other, not to Marta.

▬▬ MULTILEVEL INSTRUCTION for 2B

Cross-ability Direct the lower-level student to play A. The higher-level student plays B several times to check that Student A understands the vocabulary before they switch roles.

Ⓒ WORD PLAY. PAIRS. Look at the list of family...

- Copy the diagram and examples onto the board. Say: Mother *is for females.* Father *is for males.* Parent *is for both females and males.*
- Read the directions. Categorize the first five items on the vocabulary list as a class. Say each word and ask: *Is it female, male, or both?* Write each word in the appropriate place on the diagram.
- Pair students. Tell them to draw their own diagrams and write all the vocabulary words in the appropriate place.
- Tell students to switch partners and compare their charts with another classmate.

▬▬ EXPANSION: Vocabulary practice for 2C

- Tell students to look at their diagrams and underline the words that describe them.

Learning Strategy: Personalize

- Teach *brother-in-law*. Point to number 16 in the pictures. Say: *Ann is Ben's brother. She's Marta's sister-in-law. Who is Ben's sister-in-law?* (Tina) *Who is Ben's brother-in-law?* (Manny) Tell students to write *brother-in-law* at the end of the vocabulary list.
- Read the directions and the examples.
- Say: *To remember the words for family members, write the names of your family members and their relationship to you.* Write the names of five people in your own family and their relationship to you.
- Walk around as students work. If misspellings occur, tell students to check the list on page 27.
- Say: *You can remember new vocabulary when you apply it to your own life.* Remind students to use this strategy to remember other new vocabulary.

Communicative Practice   20 minutes

Show what you know!

STEP 1. GROUPS OF 3. Talk about your own...

- Tell students to look at the lists they made in the Learning Strategy activity and to circle the family members who live in this country.
- Model the conversation with two above-level students. Tell one of the students to play A and ask you the question from the example. Point to your list of family members on the board and answer. Say: *Yes, I have . . . .* Then ask the other student the question from the example.
- Form groups of 3 and tell them to take turns asking and answering the questions.

STEP 2. Tell the class about your partners'...

- Read the directions and the example. On the board, write: *Andrea's sister lives here.* Underline the *'s* in *Andrea's* and the *-s* in *lives.* Say the sentence and ask the class to repeat.
- Model the activity with the same two above-level students as in Step 1. Tell the class what you remember about the second student's family. Talk about each family member separately.
- Call on students to tell the class about two members of each partner's families. Listen for the possessive *'s*, the correct possessive pronoun (*his* or *her*), and the simple present verb ending *-s*.

Teaching Tip

Correcting students' grammar indirectly is a good way to model correct usage without making students feel self-conscious about errors or inhibiting them from speaking freely in class. In Step 2 of *"Show what you know!"*, if a student uses the possessive *'s* or the simple present verb ending *-s* incorrectly, rephrase the student's statement as a question, as if asking for clarification. For example, S: *Andrea sister live here.* T: *Andrea's sister lives here?*

▬▬ EXPANSION: Vocabulary practice

- Tell pairs to create a family tree for Marta's family. (Draw your own family tree on the board as an example. Start with your mother and her siblings at the top of the chart.) Tell them to start with Isabel and Maria at the top of the tree and label the tree with Marta's family members' names and each member's relationship to Marta.
- To make the activity more difficult, tell students to label each family member with books closed. Then students open their books to check their answers (including spelling) and fill in missing labels.

▬▬ EXPANSION: Writing practice

- Tell students to write sentences about relationships in Marta's family (two sentences about each picture). First, write two sentences about picture 1 as a class (for example, *Manuel and Isabel are Marta's parents. Carlos is Tony's son.*).

▬▬ MULTILEVEL INSTRUCTION for STEP 2

Pre-level Before they report to the class, students practice talking about their partners' families in groups and write two sentences about each partner under the example.

Above-level Students extend the conversation in Step 1 by asking: *What does your [family member] look like? What is your [family member] like?* In Step 2, students can report this additional information to the class. For example: *Lily's mother lives here. She's short and thin. She has short, straight black hair. She's cheerful and interesting.*

Extra Practice
Interactive Practice   pages 14–15

Tommy   Liz   Marta   Ben

Family Members

1. brother	**14.** mother-in-law
2. sister	**15.** father-in-law
3. father	**16.** sister-in-law
4. mother	**17.** son
5. aunt	**18.** daughter
6. cousin	**19.** children
7. uncle	**20.** parents
8. fiancé	**21.** grandmother
9. fiancée	**22.** grandfather
10. niece	**23.** granddaughter
11. nephew	**24.** grandson
12. wife	**25.** grandchildren
13. husband	

Learning Strategy

Personalize

Look at the list of family members. Think about your family. Write the names of five family members and their relationship to you.

1. Marie: niece
2. Pierre: nephew

Liz   Marta   Ben   Mary   Tommy   Sue   Benny

Show what you know!

STEP 1. GROUPS OF 3. Talk about your own families.

A: *Do you have family in this country?*
B: *Yes, I have a sister and a . . .*

STEP 2. Tell the class about your partners' families.

Andrea's sister lives here. Her brother . . .

Listening and Speaking

1 BEFORE YOU LISTEN

A READ. Look at the picture.
Read about the Garcia family.
Which members of the Garcia
family live together? Who did they
live with in Mexico?

B CLASS. In your country, which
family members usually live together?
Do you think this is the same
for people in the U.S.?

My name is Inez Garcia.
This is a picture of my family.
This is me, my husband,
and my two kids. We live in
an apartment in Los Angeles.
In Mexico, we lived with
my mother and father.

2 LISTEN

A CLASS. Look at the picture of two new
coworkers, Amy and Babacar. What do people
talk about when they are getting to know each
other?

CD1 T22

B Listen to the conversation. Answer
the questions.

1. What size family does Babacar have?
   a. big   (b.)small

2. How many brothers does Babacar have?
   (a.)one   b. two

3. Where do Babacar's sisters live?
   a. Somalia   (b.)Senegal

CD1 T23

C Listen to the whole conversation.
Complete the sentence.

Babacar's brother lives **far from /(with)**Babacar.

Lesson 2 Talk about your life and family

Getting Started
10 minutes

1 BEFORE YOU LISTEN

A READ. Look at the picture. Read about the...

- Tell students to look at the picture. Ask: *What do you see?* (a family/a father, a mother, and two children) *Where is the family?* (in a park)
- Read the paragraph while students read along silently. Then ask students to read it again silently.
- Ask the questions from the directions: *Which members of the Garcia family live together?* (the mother, father, and two children) *Who did they live with in Mexico?* (Mrs. Garcia's mother and father)

B CLASS. In your country, which family members...

- At the top of the board, draw a two-column chart with the headings *In my country* and *In the U.S.*
- Ask: *In your country, which family members usually live together? In the U.S., which family members usually live together?* Write students' answers on the chart.

Culture Connection

- Say: *In the U.S., parents and their children usually live together—like the Garcia family in Los Angeles. In some families in the U.S. and in many other countries, parents, children, grandparents, aunts, uncles, and cousins may live together—like the Garcia family in Mexico.*
- *Optional:* Ask: *Who did you live with in your country? Who do you live with in the U.S.?*

Presentation
25 minutes

2 LISTEN

A CLASS. Look at the picture of two new co-workers...

- Tell students to look at the picture. Ask: *What are they doing?* (eating) *Where do you think they are?* (at work)
- Read the directions. Ask: *Are Babacar and Amy old friends?* (No, they're new co-workers.) *Do they know a lot about each other?* (No.) *What do people talk about when they're getting to know each other?* (work, family, where they're from)

B Listen to the conversation. Answer...

- Read the directions. Read the questions and the answer choices. Play CD 1, Track 22.
- Students compare answers with a partner. Tell them to take turns asking and answering the questions.
- Ask a student to read each question and call on a classmate to answer.
- *Optional:* Ask the class: *How many sisters does Babacar have?* (two) *Where does Babacar's brother live?* (here)

Teaching Tip

Optional: Remember that if students need additional support, tell them to read the Audio Script on page 297 as they listen to the conversations.

C Listen to the whole conversation....

- Read the directions. Play CD 1, Track 23.
- Explain *far from* and *with*. Draw two simple houses with one stick figure each on opposite sides of the board. Label the figures *Babacar's brother* and *Babacar*. Say: *Babacar's brother lives far from Babacar.* Then draw one simple house with two stick figures inside. Label the figures *Babacar's brother* and *Babacar*. Say: *Babacar's brother lives with Babacar.*
- Ask a student to come to the board, read the completed sentence, and point to the corresponding picture.
- *Optional:* Ask the class: *Do Babacar and his brother live in a house or an apartment?* (an apartment) *Where does Babacar's brother work?* (in a hospital)

EXPANSION: Graphic organizer practice for 2C

- As a class, make a web diagram for Babacar. On the board, draw a circle with lines radiating out from it. Write *Babacar* in the middle of the circle.
- Ask: *What do we know about Babacar?* Write information about him at the end of each line (for example, *from Senegal, small family, one brother, two sisters*). Circle *one brother* and *two sisters*.
- Ask: *What do we know about Babacar's brother and sisters?* Draw lines radiating out from these circles and write information about Babacar's siblings at the end of the lines (for example, for *one brother: lives here, works in a hospital, lives with Babacar*).

3 CONVERSATION

A 🔊 **Listen. Then listen again and...**

- Say: *Important words in a sentence are stressed.* On the board, write: *I have a brother and a sister.* Read it and ask: *What are the important words?* Underline *brother* and *sister*.
- Say: *Short "grammar" words—for example* a, the, and *and—are usually short and weak.* Read the sentence again and ask: *What are the weak words?* Circle *a, and,* and *a*.
- Say: *Weak words often have the short, quiet vowel sound "uh."* Pronounce the "uh" sound several times. Read the sentence modeling the "uh" pronunciation of the vowel sounds in the blue "grammar" words.
- Tell students to read the Pronunciation Watch note silently.
- Play CD 1, Track 24. Students listen.
- Resume playing Track 24. Students listen and repeat.

Controlled Practice   10 minutes

B 🔊 **Listen and repeat the conversation.**

- Note: This conversation is the same one students heard in Exercise 2B on page 28.
- Tell students to read the conversation silently. Tell them to look for and circle *a, the,* and *and*.
- Read Babacar's first line and ask students to repeat.
- Play CD 1, Track 25. Students listen and repeat.

4 PRACTICE

A **PAIRS. Practice the conversation.**

- Ask two above-level students to role-play the conversation. Then ask them to switch roles.
- Pair students and tell them to take turns playing A and B.
- Walk around and help with pronunciation as needed.

Communicative Practice   10 minutes

B **MAKE IT PERSONAL. PAIRS. Talk about your...**

- Tell students to look at the picture. Ask: *Is this a big family or a small family?* (a big family) *Do you have a big family or a small family?*
- Read the directions.
- Play B and model the conversation with an above-level student. Use real information to complete B's response.
- Pair students and tell them to take turns playing A and B.

■ MULTILEVEL INSTRUCTION for 4B

Pre-level Before they practice the conversation, tell students to write how they will finish B's response.

Above-level Tell students to also talk about where their family members live.

Teaching Tip

Ask students to bring photographs of their families to class. Bring in your own family photos and use them to model Exercise 4B. Tell partners to show each other their photos as they talk about their families. As pairs practice, walk around and ask questions about the photos (for example, *Who's this? Are they your parents? What's your cousin like? Where does [your partner's] sister live?*). Ask students to keep their family photos in their notebooks for use throughout Unit 2.

■ EXPANSION: Speaking and listening practice for 4B

- Students will use their family photos to play a guessing game.
- Form new pairs. Tell students to lay out their photos.
- Tell A to describe the physical characteristics and personality of a family member. Tell B to point to a photo to guess who it is.
- Students switch roles and repeat.

Extra Practice

Interactive Practice

3 CONVERSATION

CD1 T24

A 🔘 **Listen. Then listen again and repeat the sentences.**

I have a brother and a sister.
We live in the same apartment.
He works in a hospital.

CD1 T25

B 🔘 **Listen and repeat the conversation.**

Amy: Tell me about your family.

Babacar: Well, I don't have a very big family. I have a brother and two sisters.

Amy: Do they live here?

Babacar: My sisters live in Senegal, but my brother lives here.

> **Pronunciation Watch**
>
> Important words in a sentence are stressed. Short "grammar" words—for example, *a*, *the*, and *and*— are usually short and weak.

4 PRACTICE

A **PAIRS.** **Practice the conversation.**

B **MAKE IT PERSONAL. PAIRS. Talk about your own families.**

A: *Tell me about your family.*
B: *I have a very big family. I have …*

Grammar

Simple present affirmative and negative: *have / live / work*

Affirmative			Negative			
I	**have**	two sisters.	I		**have**	a big family.
We	**live**	in New York.	We	**don't**	**live**	in Miami.
They	**work**	in a school.	They		**work**	in an office.
He	**has**	a brother.	He		**have**	a sister.
She	**lives**	in Senegal.	She	**doesn't**	**live**	here.
My brother	**works**	in a hospital.	My sister		**work**	in a hospital.

1 PRACTICE

Grammar Watch

- With *he*, *she*, or *it*, the simple present verb ends in *-s*.

- Use *don't* or *doesn't* to make a sentence negative.

- Use the base form of the verb with *don't* and *doesn't*.

A Complete the sentences. Underline the correct words.

1. My cousin **has** / **have** a wife and two children.

2. They **doesn't** / **don't** have children.

3. Her cousin **work** / **works** in a theater.

4. My mother-in-law **lives** / **live** on South Street.

5. Our grandparents **doesn't** / **don't** live here.

6. We **don't** / **doesn't** work on weekends.

7. Shelly and Kirk **have** / **has** twins.

B Complete the sentences. Write the correct forms of the words in parentheses.

1. Clara (work) _____ works _____ at a beauty salon.

2. His sister-in-law (not have) _____ doesn't have _____ a job.

3. Nina's fiancé (live) _____ lives _____ near the city.

4. Her husband (work) _____ works _____ with her brother.

5. I (not live) _____ don't live _____ with my parents.

6. Our family (live) _____ lives _____ in Colombia.

7. They (not work) _____ don't work _____ in a big office.

8. Emilio (not have) _____ doesn't have _____ any cousins.

Lesson 3 Talk about your life and family

Getting Started 5 minutes

Getting Started   5 minutes

- Say: *We're going to study the simple present of the verbs* have, live, *and* work. *In the conversation on page 29, Babacar used this grammar.*
- Play CD 1, Track 25. Students listen. On the board, write: *I don't have a very big family. I have a brother and two sisters. My sisters live in Senegal. My brother lives here.* Underline *don't have, have, live,* and *lives.*

Presentation   10 minutes

Simple present affirmative and negative: *have / live / work*

- Copy the grammar charts onto the board or show Transparency 2.3 and cover the exercise.
- Read the sentences across both grammar charts, for example, *I have two sisters. I don't have a big family.*
- Ask: *When does the simple present verb end in -s?* On the chart on the board, underline the *-s* in *has, lives,* and *works* and tell students to do the same on the chart in their books. Then read the first item from the Grammar Watch note.
- Ask: *How do you make a simple present sentence negative?* On the chart on the board, underline *don't* and *doesn't* and tell students to do the same on their chart. Then read the second item from the Grammar Watch note.
- On the board, write: *I live in the United States. He lives in Senegal.* Ask the class to make the sentences negative. Elicit *don't* and *doesn't* and then draw a blank after each. Ask: *What verb form do I use with* don't? *What verb form do I use with* doesn't? Fill in the blanks and read the third item from the Grammar Watch note.
- On the board, write: *I, we, they work / don't work* and *he, she, it works / doesn't work.*
- If you are using the transparency, do the exercise with the class.

Controlled Practice   15 minutes

1   PRACTICE

Ⓐ Complete the sentences. Underline...

- Read the directions.
- Write item 1 on the board. Ask: *Why is the answer* has? (because *My cousin* is the same as *he,* and we say *he has*)
- Walk around. If you see an incorrect answer, circle the subject of the sentence and ask the student which pronoun it is the same as.
- Students compare answers with a partner.
- Call on students to read the completed sentences.

Ⓑ Complete the sentences. Write the correct forms...

- Read the directions.
- Write item 1 on the board. Ask: *Why is the answer* works? (because *Clara* is the same as *she,* and we say *she works*)
- Write item 2 on the board. Ask: *Why is the answer* doesn't have? (because *His sister-in-law* is the same as *she,* and we say *she doesn't have*)
- Walk around. If you see an incorrect answer, circle the subject of the sentence and ask the student which pronoun it is the same as.
- Students compare answers with a partner.
- Call on students to read the completed sentences.

▬▬ EXPANSION: Grammar and writing practice for 1B

- Give pairs a magazine photo of an anonymous (not famous) person. Tell pairs to make up information about their person. Tell them to write three affirmative and three negative sentences with *have, live,* and *work.* Write some examples on the board.

Controlled Practice 15 minutes

2 PRACTICE

A Look at the Mendez family tree. Complete...

- Read the directions. Write items 1 and 2 on the board.
- Read item 1. Tell students to point to Alba on the Mendez family tree. Ask: *Does Alba live in Los Angeles?* (No.) Say: *So, the answer is* doesn't live.
- Walk around and check that students are using the family tree to determine whether sentences are affirmative or negative.
- Students compare answers with a partner.
- Call on students to read the completed sentences.
- *Optional:* As a class, change each negative sentence to an accurate affirmative sentence (for example, for item 1, *Alba lives in Chicago.*).

EXPANSION: Vocabulary practice for 2A

- Tell students to choose one member of the Mendez family and to circle the family member on the family tree.
- Then students write the names of all the other family members and their relationship to the person they chose (for example, a student who chose Celia would write *Arturo: grandfather, Sandra: grandmother, Elena: mother,* etc.).

B PAIRS. Make three new sentences about...

- Read the directions and the example.
- Pair students. Walk around and help as needed.
- Tell each student to write a sentence on the board.
- Read each sentence. Ask the class: *Is this correct?* Circle any incorrect sentences and number them. Tell students to rewrite them in their notebooks.
- Elicit the corrections and make them on the board. Reread the corrected sentences.

Communicative Practice 15 minutes

Show what you know!

STEP 1. Complete the sentences about your family....

- Read the directions.

- On the board, complete two sentences with real information about you and one sentence with made-up information. Don't tell the class which sentence is false.
- Walk around and help as needed. Students shouldn't discuss their sentences with each other.

STEP 2. GROUPS OF 3. Play a guessing game...

- Read the directions. Ask two above-level students to read the example out loud.
- Play A and model the conversation by reading your sentences to the class. Prompt the class to play B and guess which of your sentences is false.
- Form groups and tell students to take turns reading their sentences and guessing. Walk around and, as needed, help students guess.

STEP 3. Tell the class about one of your partners.

- Read the directions and the example.
- Tell the class to look at your sentences on the board. Change the false sentence to make it true.
- Tell students to change their false sentence to make it true.
- Point to each sentence on the board and call on an above-level student to say a sentence about you.
- Call on students to tell the class about one of their partners.

MULTILEVEL INSTRUCTION for STEP 3

Pre-level In Step 3, tell students to first write sentences about their partner.

Above-level In Step 3, tell students to also tell the class what's not true about their partner. Tell them to say a fourth sentence with *doesn't* and *have, live in,* or *work in.*

Progress Check

Can you . . . talk about your life and family?

Say: *We have practiced talking about our lives and families. Now, look at the question at the bottom of the page. Can you talk about your life and family?* Tell students to write a check in the box.

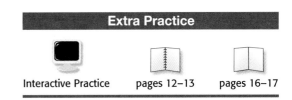

Extra Practice		
Interactive Practice	pages 12–13	pages 16–17

The Mendez Family

A **Look at the Mendez family tree. Complete the sentences. Use the correct forms of the words.**

1. Alba __doesn't live__ in Los Angeles.
   (live)
2. Marcos __lives__ in Lima.
   (live)
3. Elena __has__ a son.
   (have)
4. Marcos __has__ a brother.
   (have)
5. Elena and Pablo __live__ in New York.
   (live)
6. Sandra __has__ three grandchildren.
   (have)
7. Pablo and Marcos __have__ a sister.
   (have)
8. Sandra and Arturo __don't live__ in Dallas.
   (live)

Arturo — Lima, Peru
Sandra — Lima, Peru
Elena — New York
Pablo — New York
Marcos — Lima, Peru
Celia — New York
Alba — Chicago
Sara — Dallas

B **PAIRS. Make three new sentences about the Mendez family.** Answers will vary.

Elena and Pablo have three daughters. They live . . .

Show what you know! Talk about your life and family

STEP 1. Complete the sentences about your family and life. Write two true sentences and one false sentence. Answers will vary.

I have _____ .

I live in _____ .

I work in _____ .

STEP 2. GROUPS OF 3. Play a guessing game. Student A, read your sentences to your group. Students B and C, guess which sentence is false.

A: *I have four sisters. I live in Oak Park. I work in a hotel.*
B: *I think the first sentence is false. I don't think you have four sisters.*

STEP 3. Tell the class about one of your partners.

Manuel has two sisters. He lives in Oak Park. He works in a hotel.

Can you . . . talk about your life and family? ☐

Reading

1   BEFORE YOU READ

PAIRS. Look at the picture. What is the man doing? How does he feel? Do you ever feel like that?

Answers will vary.

2   READ

CD1 T26

Listen. Read the letters in a newspaper advice column.

Dear Kate
Advice for Your Life

Dear Kate,

My husband and I both work. I work days and he works two jobs, days and evenings.

We have three kids (ages 8, 10, and 14). They need a lot of my time. They need me to help them with homework. I take them to school activities and sports events. And then there is all the housework! The cooking, the laundry, the cleaning, the shopping, the bills! I need to do a million things at the same time. Help! I can't do it all!

Tired Tania

Dear Tania,

You're right. You can't do it all. You're trying to do too much.

First, ask yourself, "What is most important?" You can't do everything. Only do the important things.

Second, get help. Ask your children to help with the housework. They can do the dishes, take out the garbage, do the laundry, and do other chores. Ask your husband to help on the weekends.

Third, say no. You already have many responsibilities. When people ask you to do something extra, say, "I'm sorry, but I don't have the time right now."

Finally, take some time for yourself. Make sure you get a little time every day to do something you like. Watch a TV program, take a bath, or read a magazine. Take care of yourself first. Then you will have the energy to take care of others.

Kate

Getting Started
10 minutes

1 BEFORE YOU READ

PAIRS. **Look at the picture. What is the man...**

- Tell the class to look at the picture. Ask: *What is the man doing?* On the board, write: *juggling.* Ask: *How many balls is the man juggling?* (four)

- Ask: *Can you juggle? How many balls can you keep in the air?*

- *Optional:* Bring in several small balls (or use objects in your classroom) and ask a couple of students to demonstrate juggling. Start students off with three balls. Add a ball at a time until students can't keep the balls in the air anymore. Ask: *Is juggling easier or harder with more balls?* (harder)

- Tell the class to look at the picture again. Ask: *What are the words on the balls?* (*work, fun, school, family*) Explain that juggling also means trying to fit two or more jobs or activities into your life.

- Pair students and tell them to look at the man in the picture and to ask and answer the questions next to the picture.

- Ask the class: *How does he feel?* (tired) *Why?* (He has a lot of activities/responsibilities.) Ask: *Do you have a lot activities or responsibilities? Do you ever feel like the man in the picture?* Call on volunteers to answer.

Presentation
20 minutes

2 READ

 Listen. Read the letters in a...

- Tell the class to look at the advice column. Ask: *Who is the woman in the picture?* (Kate) *What does she do?* (She gives advice.) *Who needs advice?* (Tania) *What is Tania's problem?* (She's tired.)

- Play CD 1, Track 26. Students listen. Pause at the end of Tired Tania's letter.

- Tell students to draw a stick figure juggling three balls. Ask: *What three balls is Tania juggling?* Tell students to write Tania's responsibilities in the circles/balls. Review as a class. Check that students write *work, kids/family,* and *housework.*

- Resume playing Track 26. Students read and listen.

- Tell students to draw a fourth ball. Ask: *What other activity does Kate think Tania should try to fit into her life?* Tell students to write the activity in the fourth ball. Review as a class. Check that students write: *time for herself.*

Read about managing responsibilities

Controlled Practice 15 minutes

3 CHECK YOUR UNDERSTANDING

Ⓐ Read Tania's letter to Kate. Then read...

- Tell students to read the first letter again silently.
- Read the directions and have students complete the activity.
- Students compare answers with a partner.
- Ask students to read the sentences and call on classmates to say the answers.
- *Optional:* Tell students to change the false sentences to make them true. Call on students to read the revised sentences. (1. Tania <u>has one job</u>. 2. Tania is <u>not</u> a student. 4. . . . <u>in the evening</u>.).

Ⓑ Read Kate's letter to Tania. Check the...

- Tell students to read the second letter again silently.
- Read the directions and have students complete the activity.
- Students compare answers with a partner.
- Call on students to read the checked items.

Ⓒ PAIRS. Student A, what is Tania's problem?...

- Read the Reading Skill note.
- Read the directions. Pair students and assign roles.
- Say: *Student A, what is Tania's problem? Look at the picture you drew of Tania on page 32. Review Exercise 3A. Read the true sentences about Tania.*
- Say: *Student B, what is Kate's advice? Review Exercise 3B. Read the checked sentences.*
- Pairs cover Exercises 3A and 3B and explain Tania's problem and Kate's advice in their own words.
- Remind students to switch roles and practice both parts.
- Call on a couple of pairs to retell Tania's problem and Kate's advice for the class. For example, Student A: *Tania's husband has two jobs. Tania works. They have three children. The children have a lot of activities, and Tania has a lot of housework. She can't do everything. She needs help!*

  Student B: *Kate's advice is to do the important things, to ask the children to help, to say no, and to take time for herself.*

Ⓓ GROUPS OF 3. Do you agree with Kate's advice...

- Form groups of 3. Ask: *Do you agree with Kate's advice?* Tell groups to discuss each of Kate's four suggestions from Exercise 3B. Tell them to say, *I agree* or *I don't agree* and explain why.
- Model the activity. For example, T: *Kate's advice is to ask for help. I agree. The children are 8, 10, and 14. They can help with the housework. My son is 9, and he takes out the garbage and washes dishes.*
- Ask: *Do you have any other advice for Tania?* Ask one student from each group to write one idea on the board (for example, *limit the children's activities, make a housework chart with each family member's responsibilities, prepare meals for the week on the weekend and freeze them.*).
- Read the ideas on the board. Discuss as a class.

Communicative Practice 15 minutes

Show what you know!

PRE-WRITING. PAIRS. What are your family,...

- Tell students to look at Tania's letter. Ask: *What are her family responsibilities?* On the board, write: *three kids, help them with homework, take them to school activities, take them to sports events.*
- Tell students to draw a stick figure juggling three balls and write *family, school,* and *work* in the balls. Say: *This person is you. What are your family, school, and work responsibilities?* Tell students to draw lines radiating out from the balls and note their responsibilities.
- Pair students. Pairs talk about their diagrams.
- Ask: *Are you juggling too many responsibilities? Are you trying to do too much? Is Kate's advice helpful to you?* Tell pairs to discuss. Tell each partner to note one of Kate's suggestions that they want to try.

WRITE. Write a list of your responsibilities....

Ask students to turn to page 268 and write a list of their responsibilities. See page T-xii for general notes about the Writing activities.

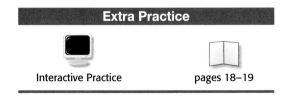

Extra Practice

Interactive Practice   pages 18–19

CHECK YOUR UNDERSTANDING

A Read Tania's letter to Kate. Then read the sentences. Circle *True* or *False*.

1. Tania works two jobs.   True   (False)

2. Tania is a student.   True   (False)

3. Tania has three children.   (True)   False

4. Tania takes care of her kids in the afternoon.   True   (False)

5. Tania takes her children to school activities and sports events.   (True)   False

6. Tania does a lot of housework.   (True)   False

B Read Kate's letter to Tania. Check the advice she gives.

☑ Only do the things that are important.

☑ Ask other people for help.

☐ Go to bed earlier and get more sleep.

☑ Say, "no" when people try to give you more responsibilities.

☐ Make a schedule of your time.

☑ Take a little time each day for yourself.

C PAIRS. Student A, what is Tania's problem? Student B, what is Kate's advice? Explain in your own words.

D GROUPS OF 3. Do you agree with Kate's advice? Do you have any other advice for Tania?

Reading Skill:
Retelling Information

Retell means to say in your own words what you read or hear. The words are different, but the meaning is the same.

Show what you know!

PRE-WRITING. PAIRS. What are your family, school, and work responsibilities? Is Kate's advice helpful to you?

WRITE. Write a list of your responsibilities. See page 268.

Talk about what people have in common

Listening and Speaking

1 BEFORE YOU LISTEN

CLASS. Look at the picture of three brothers. What are some things that family members have in common? Answers will vary.

2 LISTEN

A CLASS. Look at the picture of two neighbors, Ming and Tina. Guess: What are they talking about?

CD1 T27
B Listen to the conversation. Was your guess in Exercise A correct?

CD1 T27
C Listen again. Read the sentences. Circle *True* or *False*.

1. Tina looks like her sister.

   (True)   False

2. Tina has a friend named Lili.

   True   (False)

3. Tina has a lot in common with her sister.

   (True)   False

4. Tina's sister works in a bank.

   (True)   False

5. Tina's sister doesn't have any children.

   True   (False)

CD1 T28
D Listen to the whole conversation. Answer the questions.

1. Does Ming have any sisters?   Yes, she has two sisters.

2. Does Ming have any brothers?   No

Lesson 5 Talk about what people have in common

Getting Started   5 minutes

 1 BEFORE YOU LISTEN

CLASS. Look at the picture of three brothers...

- Tell students to look at the picture. Ask: *What does this family have in common?* As needed, explain: *Some things that people can have in common are interests, physical characteristics, and personalities.*
- Write students' responses on the board. For example, *They look alike. They like soccer.*

Presentation   15 minutes

2 LISTEN

Ⓐ CLASS. Look at the picture of two neighbors...

- Read the directions. Tell students to label *Ming* and *Tina* in their books.
- Ask: *What are they looking at? What do you think they are talking about?* Write students' ideas on the board. Tell students they will listen for the answer in Exercise B.

Ⓑ Listen to the conversation. Was your...

- Read the directions. Play CD 1, Track 27.
- Ask: *Was your guess in Exercise A correct?* Circle the correct answers on the board. (Answers: They are looking at photographs and talking about Tina's family.)
- Ask: *Whose family are they talking about—Tina's or Ming's?* (Tina's family) Play Track 27 again as needed.

> **Teaching Tip**
>
> *Optional:* Remember that if students need additional support, tell them to read the Audio Script on page 297 as they listen to the conversations.

Controlled Practice   10 minutes

Ⓒ Listen again. Read the sentences...

- Read the directions. Tell students to read the items silently.
- Play Track 27 again. Students circle *True* or *False*.
- Students compare answers with a partner.
- Read each sentence and ask the class to call out *True* or *False*.
- *Optional:* As a class, rewrite the false items to make them true (2. Tina has a <u>sister</u> named Lilli. 5. Tina's sister <u>has a new baby</u>.).
- To review, ask: *What do Tina and her sister Lilli have in common?* Elicit and write on the board: *They look alike. They work in a bank. They have new babies.*

Ⓓ Listen to the whole conversation...

- Say: *Now Tina is asking about Ming's family.* Read the directions and the questions.
- Play CD 1, Track 28. Students listen and write the answers.
- Students compare answers with a partner. Walk around and look at students' answers. If you see a lot of incorrect answers, play Track 28 again.
- Read the questions and call on students to answer. Then ask: *How many sisters does Ming have? What do Ming and her sisters have in common?* Elicit and write on the board: *They have two sisters. They don't have any brothers.*
- Ask: *Do you think what Ming says is funny? Why?*

3   CONVERSATION

A Listen. Then listen and repeat...

- Tell students to look at the examples and underline each *do*.
- Say: Do *has two pronunciations—a weak one and a strong one.* Write *do* on the board. Draw two lines branching out from *do* and write *weak* and *strong*.
- Play CD 1, Track 29. Pause after the first pair of sentences. Ask: *Which one has a strong, clear pronunciation of* do? *Which one has a short, weak pronunciation of* do? Write *Yes, I do.* under *strong* in the diagram on the board. Write *Do you have any sisters?* under *weak*. Say the sentences and ask the class to repeat. Say: *"D'ya" have any sisters?*
- Read the first two sentences of the Pronunciation Watch note. Say *"D'ya"* several times and ask the class to repeat.
- Read the last sentence of the Pronunciation Watch note. Say a strong, clear *do* several times and ask the class to repeat.
- Tell students to look at the second pair of sentences. Ask: *Which ones have a strong, clear pronunciation of* do? Write *Actually, we do.* and *She works in a bank, and I do, too.* under *strong* in the diagram on the board.
- Tell students to look at the second pair of sentences again. Ask: *Which one has a short, weak pronunciation of* do? Write *Do you have a lot in common?* under *weak*.
- Resume playing Track 29. Students listen to the second pair of sentences and then listen and repeat all of the sentences.

Controlled Practice   20 minutes

B Listen and repeat the conversation.

- Note: This conversation is the same one students heard in Exercise 2B on page 34.
- Tell students to read the conversation silently and underline each *do*.
- Tell students to circle the word or punctuation that comes after each *do*. Ask: *Which one is weak?* (Do you have a lot in common?) *Which ones are strong?* (Actually, we do. She works in a bank, and I do, too.). Tell students to write *"D'ya"* over *Do you* in the conversation.
- Play CD 1, Track 30. Students listen and repeat.

4   PRACTICE

A PAIRS. Practice the conversation. Then make new...

- Pair students and tell them to practice the conversation in Exercise 3B. Tell them to take turns playing each role.
- Then, in Exercise 4A, ask students to look at the words in the boxes. Say each one and ask the class to repeat.
- Copy the conversation onto the board with blanks. Read through the conversation. When you come to a blank, fill it in with information from the boxes (*niece, niece, restaurant, two kids*).
- Ask two on-level students to practice the conversation in front of the class.
- Tell pairs to take turns playing each role and to use different information from the boxes.
- Tell students to stand, mingle, and practice the conversation with several new partners.
- Walk around and listen to students' pronunciation of *do*. As needed, say the sentences and ask students to repeat.
- Call on pairs to perform for the class.

Communicative Practice   10 minutes

B MAKE IT PERSONAL. PAIRS. Talk about your...

- Pair students and tell them to think of a family member that they have a lot in common with.
- Read the directions. Tell the class about a family member that you have a lot in common with. For example, say: *I have a lot in common with my cousin Kerry. She lives in Philadelphia, and I do, too . . .*

MULTILEVEL INSTRUCTION for 4B

Cross-ability Write on the board: *She / He _____, and I do, too. And we both have _____.* Under the blank in the first sentence, write: *works in . . . / lives in. . . .* Before pairs practice, higher-level students help lower-level students choose a family member and complete the sentences.

Extra Practice

Interactive Practice

3 CONVERSATION

CD1 T29

Ⓐ 💿 **Listen. Then listen and repeat the sentences.**

Do you have any sisters?
Yes, I do.

Do you have a lot in common?
Actually, we do. She works in a bank, and I do, too.

Pronunciation Watch

Do often has a short, weak pronunciation when another word comes after it. *Do you* sounds like "d'ya." *Do* does not not have a weak pronunciation at the end of a sentence or before a comma.

CD1 T30

Ⓑ 💿 **Listen and repeat the conversation.**

Ming: Tina, is this your sister? You two look alike.
Tina: Yeah, that's my sister, Lili.
Ming: Do you have a lot in common?
Tina: Actually, we do. She works in a bank, and I do, too. And we both have new babies.

4 PRACTICE

Ⓐ **PAIRS. Practice the conversation. Then make new conversations. Use the information in the boxes.**

A: Tina, is this your _____? You two look alike.

B: Yeah, that's my _____, Lili.

A: Do you have a lot in common?

B: Actually, we do. She works in a _____, and I do, too. And we both have _____.

niece	restaurant	two kids
aunt	clothing store	a son
cousin	hospital	a boy and a girl

Ⓑ **MAKE IT PERSONAL. PAIRS. Talk about your own family members. Do you have a lot in common?**

I have a lot in common with my sister Anna. She . . .

Talk about what people have in common

Grammar

Simple present: Additions with *and..., too / and...not, either*

Affirmative			Negative		
Lili works in a bank,	**and**	I you we they	Trang doesn't live in Denver,	**and**	I you we they
		do, too.			**don't, either.**
		he she			he she
		does, too.			**doesn't, either.**

1 PRACTICE

A **Complete the sentences. Match the sentence beginnings and endings.**

1. __b__ I speak Farsi, and my husband   a. doesn't, either.

2. __c__ She lives with her parents, and her brothers   b. does, too.

3. __d__ They don't live in an apartment, and we   c. do, too.

4. __a__ Pablo doesn't work in an office, and Ursula   d. don't, either.

> **Grammar Watch**
> - Use *too* for affirmative sentences.
> - Use *not, either* for negative sentences.
> - Use a comma before *too* and *either*.

B **Complete the sentences. Use the words in the box.**

> do, too   does, too   doesn't, either   don't, either

1. Mark has two nephews, and Jason _____ *does, too* _____.

2. They don't work on weekends, and we _____ don't, either _____.

3. My son doesn't live with me, and my daughter _____ doesn't, either _____.

4. My wife works for her father, and my brothers-in-law _____ do, too _____.

5. Todd and Mikah don't have any children, and we _____ don't, either _____.

6. Her sisters-in-law live on Walnut Street, and her father-in-law _____ does, too _____.

7. I don't have any brothers, and Melanie _____ doesn't, either _____.

8. My husband works long hours, and I _____ do, too _____.

9. Marilyn doesn't live in the city, and her sisters _____ don't, either _____.

Getting Started   5 minutes

- Say: We're going to study additions with *and . . . , too* and *and . . . not, either* in the simple present. We use additions to combine two sentences. In the conversation on page 35, Tina used this grammar.
- Play CD 1, Track 30. Students listen. On the board, write: *She works in a bank, and I do, too.* Underline *and I do, too.*

Presentation   10 minutes

Simple present: Additions with *and . . . , too* / *and . . . not, either*

- On the board, write four sentences about the same family member you talked about in Exercise 4B on page 35. Write a pair of affirmative statements and a pair of negative statements with *have, live,* or *work.* The statements should show two things you have in common. For example, *Kerry lives in Philadelphia. I live in Philadelphia. Kerry doesn't have a sister. I don't have a sister.*
- Copy the grammar charts onto the board or show Transparency 2.4. Read some sentences from each chart.
- Point to your examples on the board. Elicit the class's help in combining the pair of affirmative statements. On the board, write: *Kerry lives in Philadelphia and I . . .* Ask the class to complete the sentence. Write *do too.* Then ask where to add commas (before *and* and *too*).
- Point to your examples on the board. Ask for the class's help in combining the pair of negative statements. On the board, write: *Kerry doesn't have a sister and I . . .* Ask the class to complete the sentence. Write *don't either.* Then ask where to add commas (before *and* and *either*).
- Point to the sentence with *too* in the chart. Elicit the class's help in changing the order of the subjects. On the board, write: *I work in a bank and Lili. . . .* Ask the class to complete the sentence. Write *does too.* Then ask where to add commas (before *and* and *too*).
- Point to the sentence with *not, either* in the chart. Elicit the class's help in changing the order of the subjects. On the board, write: *I don't live in Denver, and Trang. . . .* Ask the class to complete the sentence. Write *doesn't either.* Then ask where to add commas (before *and* and *either*).

- Read the Grammar Watch note while students read along silently.
- If you are using the transparency, do the exercise with the class.

Controlled Practice   20 minutes

1 PRACTICE

Ⓐ Complete the sentences. Match the sentence...

- Write item 1 on the board. Underline *speak* and ask: *Affirmative or negative?* Too *or* not, either? Then underline *my husband* and ask: *What pronoun is* my husband *the same as?* (he) *So, do we say* do, too *or* does, too? Read the completed sentence. Explain that Farsi is the language spoken in Iran, Afghanistan, Tajikistan, and Uzbekistan. It is also called Persian.
- Walk around and if students have difficulty, take them through the same steps as above. As needed, pronounce *Pablo* and *Ursula* and ask students to repeat.
- Tell students to compare answers by reading the completed sentences.
- Read each sentence beginning and ask the class to call out the ending.

Ⓑ Complete the sentences. Use the words in the box.

- Write item 1 on the board. Underline *has* and ask: *Affirmative or negative?* Too *or* not, either? Then underline *Jason* and ask: *What pronoun is* Jason *the same as?* (he) *So, do we say* do, too *or* does, too? Read the completed sentence.
- Walk around and if students have difficulty, take them through the same steps as above.
- Students compare answers by reading the completed sentences out loud.
- Read each sentence beginning and ask the class to call out the ending.
- Tell students to check their answers for commas.

Talk about what people have in common

2 PRACTICE

A PAIRS. Look at the Nash family. How are the....

- Read the directions. To explain *similar*, point out two students who have something in common. For example, say: *Ismail has a goatee, and Cesar does, too. They are similar.*
- Tell students to look at the picture. Ask: *What cities do the family members live in?* (Tampa, Vancouver, and Seattle)
- *Optional:* Post a map of the U.S. and Canada and ask students to point out Tampa, Vancouver, and Seattle. Ask: *What state is Tampa in?* (Florida) *What state is Seattle in?* (Washington) *Has anyone been to Tampa, Vancouver, or Seattle? Which city is not in the U.S.?* (Vancouver) *Where is Vancouver?* (in Canada)
- Tell students to point to Douglas and Emily. On the board, write: *Douglas, Emily, gray hair.* Elicit two affirmative sentences from the class and write them on the board: *Douglas has gray hair. Emily has gray hair.* Ask: *Are the sentences affirmative or negative?* (affirmative) *How do we combine them?* Elicit the example in Exercise 2B.
- Repeat with the second example.
- Pair students and tell them to take turns pointing out similarities. Walk around and check that students say both affirmative and negative sentences.

▬▬ MULTILEVEL INSTRUCTION for 2A

Pre-level Direct pairs to first say two names and what's similar (for example, *James and Grace, brown hair*). Then ask them to say a sentence about each person (for example, *James has brown hair. Grace has brown hair.*). Ask: *Are the sentences affirmative or negative?* (affirmative) Tell them to combine the sentences.

Above-level Tell students to use compound subjects (for example, *Brian and Michelle have a daughter, and Brad and Sarah do, too.*).

B WRITE. Write six sentences about the people...

- Read the directions.
- Walk around. As needed, tell students to say the similarity as a pair of statements; then take them through the steps to combine the statements. Check that students use commas correctly.

Communicative Practice   20 minutes

Show what you know!

STEP 1. Complete the questions. Use your own ideas.

- After students complete the questions, write the questions on the board. Call on students to come to the board and fill in the blanks.
- Read each question with the "d'ya" pronunciation of *Do you* and ask the class to repeat.

STEP 2. GROUPS OF 5. Student A, read one...

- Form groups. Each student asks one question from Step 1. All the other students in the group answer. Tell students not to repeat a question that a partner has already asked. Tell students to take notes with their group members' names, questions, and answers and to include their own name and answers.

STEP 3. Tell the class about what the people in...

- Read the directions and the example.
- Tell students to use their notes to write sentences about the people in their group.
- Walk around and check that students are using *too* and *either*. As needed, remind students to use the third-person singular *-s*.
- Tell each student to choose one sentence to tell the class. Say: *Talk to your group. Make sure each person says something different.*
- Call on students to say one sentence each about what two people in their group have in common.

Progress Check

Can you . . . talk about what people have in common?
Say: *We have practiced talking about what people have in common. Look at the question at the bottom of the page. Can you talk about what people have in common?* Tell students to write a checkmark in the box.

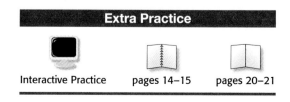

Extra Practice

Interactive Practice   pages 14–15   pages 20–21

A PAIRS. Look at the Nash family. How are the people similar?

Answers will vary.

Tampa ————— Vancouver ——— Seattle ———

B WRITE. Write six sentences about the people. Use *too* and *either*. Use a separate piece of paper. Answers will vary.

> Douglas has gray hair, and Emily does, too.
> Brian doesn't live in Vancouver, and Brad doesn't, either.

Show what you know! Talk about what people have in common

STEP 1. Complete the questions. Use your own ideas.

Do you have any family in _____?

Do you live in _____? Do you work in _____?

STEP 2. GROUPS OF 5. Student A, read one question from Step 1. Other students, answer the question. Give true information.

Tia: *Do you have any family in Chicago?*
Jan: *Yes, my brother lives in Chicago.*

STEP 3. Tell the class about what the people in your group have in common. Use *too* and *either*.

Jan has family in Chicago, and I do, too. In-Ho lives . . .

Can you...talk about what people have in common? ☐

Ask about sending mail

Life Skills

1 ASK ABOUT SENDING MAIL

A PAIRS. Match the pictures with words from the box.

| large envelope |
| letter |
| mailing tube |
| package |
| postcard |

1. *large envelope*
2. mailing tube
3. letter
4. postcard
5. package

B Look at the chart of post office mailing services. Read the sentences. Circle *True* or *False*.

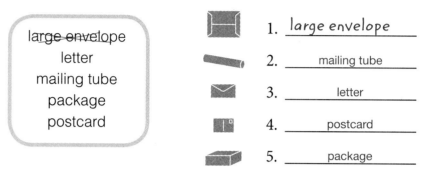

SERVICE	PACKAGE or LETTER	SPEED	SERVICE	PACKAGE or LETTER	SPEED
Express Mail	70 pounds or less	1–2 days	First-Class Mail	13 ounces or less	1–3 days
Priority Mail	70 pounds or less	1–3 days	Parcel Post	70 pounds or less	2–9 days

1. You can send a 30-pound package by Priority Mail. (**True**) False

2. You can send a letter by Express Mail. (**True**) False

3. You can send a 20-pound package by First-Class Mail. True (**False**)

4. You can send a postcard by Parcel Post. True (**False**)

5. It takes three days for an Express Mail package to arrive. True (**False**)

6. It takes two to nine days for a Parcel Post package to arrive. (**True**) False

C PAIRS. Compare your answers.

Ask about sending mail

Getting Started 5 minutes

- Write *mail* on the board. Ask: *Do you write letters to friends and family in your country? Do you send them packages? Where do you go to mail packages?* (to the post office or other parcel service) *What does the clerk do with the package before he or she tells you the cost to mail it?* (weigh it)

Culture Connection

- Help students understand the English system of weight measurement. Tell students to look at the chart of mailing services in Exercise 1B. Ask: *What weights do you see?* Write *13 ounces* and *70 pounds* on the board.
- If possible, bring in an empty cereal box. Point out the weight and say: *This box of cereal is a little more / less than 13 ounces.* Ask: *What else weighs about 13 ounces?* List students' ideas on the board.
- On the board, write: *16 ounces = one pound.* Say: *A student's desk weighs about 35 pounds. A teacher's desk weighs over 140 pounds* (adjust or use different classroom objects as needed). Ask: *What do you think weighs about 70 pounds?* List students' ideas on the board.
- Ask: *In your country, what unit of weight is used for boxes of cereal?* (probably grams) *What unit of weight is used for desks?* (probably kilograms)
- *Optional:* On the board, write: *ounces x 28.35 = grams* and *pounds x .45 = kilograms.* Ask students to convert 13 ounces to grams and 70 pounds to kilograms. Elicit and write on the board: *13 ounces = about 369 grams; 70 pounds = 32 kilograms.* Say: *The weight in kilograms is about half the weight in pounds.*

Presentation 5 minutes

1 ASK ABOUT SENDING MAIL

Ⓐ PAIRS. Match the pictures with words from the box.

- Pair students. Hold up the book and point to the envelope. Ask: *What type of mail is it? Is it a large envelope, a letter, a mailing tube, a package, or a postcard?* Elicit the answer and say: *Match the other numbered pictures with words from the box.*

- Say each item in the box and tell the class to call out the correct number.

Teaching Tip

When new words are presented through an activity, tell students to match the items they know first and cross out the words they use. Direct them to then look for clues to meaning in the words that are left—for example, *tube* in *mailing tube* and *card* in *postcard*—and use the clues to make good guesses.

Controlled Practice 15 minutes

Ⓑ Look at the chart of post office mailing services....

- Say: *Look at the chart of mailing services.* Ask: *How many different ways are there to send a letter or package?* (four)
- Draw a continuum from *slow* to *fast* on the board. Make three marks on the continuum. Point to each mark and ask the class to say the name of the service and the number of days it takes. Label the marks: *Parcel Post: 2–9 days; Priority Mail / First-Class Mail: 1–3 days; Express Mail: 1–2 days.*
- Read the directions and the example. Tell students to point to *Priority Mail* on the chart. Ask: *Can you send a package by Priority Mail?* (Yes.) *What weight package can you send?* (70 pounds or less) *Is 30 pounds less than 70 pounds?* (Yes.)

Ⓒ PAIRS. Compare your answers.

- Form pairs. Say: *Student A, read the true sentences. Student B, read the false sentences.*
- *Optional:* For each false sentence, ask pairs to change the information and say as many different true sentences as they can. Model the activity with item 3. For example, elicit and write on the board: *You can send a 20-pound package by Express Mail. You can send a large envelope by First-Class mail.* Etc.
- Call on students to read the sentences and answers. For each false sentence, elicit a variety of sentences with correct information from the class.

Presentation   20 minutes

Ⓓ PAIRS. Look at the list of extra mailing services....

- Say: *First, you decide how to send your letter or package, for example, by Express Mail or Priority Mail, and you tell the clerk. Then the clerk might ask if you want any extra services. You pay extra for these.*

- Tell students to look at the chart. Ask: *How many different services are there?* (six) Say the name of each service and ask the class to repeat.

- Tell students to read the descriptions of each service silently and to underline the most important words in the descriptions.

- Read the description of Certified Mail and explain *signs for.* Say: *With Certified Mail, the mail carrier won't leave a letter or package unless someone signs their name to show they received it.*

- Read the description of Insurance and explain *lost* and *damaged.* Say: *With Insurance, you get your money back if something bad happens to your package—if it doesn't arrive or it arrives broken.*

- Read the directions. Pair students. Say: *Student A, read what the first customer wants. Student B, say which mailing service is the best for the customer. Switch roles and repeat with the second customer.*

- Call on two pairs to read what each customer wants and suggest a mailing service (for the man: Certificate of Mailing and Delivery Confirmation or Certified Mail; for the woman: Insurance).

▬▬▬ EXPANSION: Graphic organizer practice for 1D

- Draw a chart on the board. The column headings are the first five services; the row headings are *receipt, know when item arrives, know who signs for item,* and *get money back if item is lost/damaged.* Draw lines to separate the five columns and four rows and to create boxes. Pairs read about the extra mailing services again and check boxes to show what each service provides.

- Tell students to think of something they want to mail. Tell them to look at the left side of the chart and note what they want (receipt, when item arrives, etc.). Say: *Student A, tell your partner what type of mail you're sending and what you want. Student B, use your chart to say which mailing service is the best for your partner. Switch roles and repeat.*

Teaching Tip

Enhance the activities on pages 38 and 39 with realia, authentic materials from the real world. Bring in shipping labels for Express Mail, Priority Mail, First-Class Mail, and/or Parcel Post and forms for extra mailing services. In the Expansion activity for Exercise 1D, Student B can suggest a mailing service and hand Student A the correct shipping label and form to fill out.

Controlled Practice   15 minutes

2 PRACTICE

 Listen to a conversation between a...

- Read the directions. Tell students they will listen to the conversation twice. The first time they will just listen; then they will listen and fill in the blanks.

- Play CD 1, Track 31. Students listen.

- Play Track 31 again. Students listen and fill in the blanks. If necessary, pause the CD to allow students more time.

- Now tell students to listen again and check their answers. Tell students to capitalize the names of mailing services. Play Track 31 again.

- Ask one pair to role-play the completed conversation for the class. Correct as needed.

3 LIFE SKILLS WRITING

Turn to page 257 and ask students to complete the post office customs form. See p. T-xii for guidelines.

Progress Check

Can you . . . ask about sending mail?

Say: *We have practiced asking about sending mail. Now, look at the question at the bottom of the page. Can you ask about sending mail?* Tell students to write a check in the box.

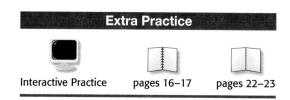

Extra Practice		
Interactive Practice	pages 16–17	pages 22–23

D PAIRS. Look at the list of extra mailing services. Then read what each customer wants. Which mailing service is the best match for each customer?

Extra Mailing Services

Certificate of Mailing
You get a receipt to show you mailed the item on a certain date.

Delivery Confirmation
You can find out when your package is delivered.

Certified Mail
You get a receipt to show you mailed the item. You can find out when the item is delivered and who signs for it.

Insurance
If your package is lost or damaged, you get money back.

Registered Mail
You get a receipt to show you mailed the item. Your item is both certified and insured.

COD (Collect on Delivery)
The person who receives the item pays for the cost of mailing.

I want a receipt to show I mailed this letter today. And I want to know when the letter arrives. I don't need insurance.

Certified Mail

I'm sending a gift to my brother. I want my money back if the package gets lost. I don't need the package certified.

Insurance

2 PRACTICE

CD1 T31

Listen to a conversation between a customer and a post office clerk. Write the missing words.

Customer: Hello. I'd like to mail this ____package____.

Clerk: How do you want to send it?

Customer: How long does ____Parcel Post____ take?

Clerk: Two to nine days.

Customer: OK. I'll send it ____Parcel Post____.

Clerk: Do you want ____Delivery Confirmation____ or insurance?

Customer: Yes. ____Delivery Confirmation____, please.

3 LIFE SKILLS WRITING
Complete a post office customs form. See page 257.

Can you...ask about sending mail? ☐

Ask about family members

Listening and Speaking

1 BEFORE YOU LISTEN

CLASS. Do you watch game shows? Which game shows do you watch?

2 LISTEN

CD1 T32

A 🎧 **Listen to the game show. What is Trevor answering questions about?**

CD1 T32

B 🎧 **Listen again. Match the name and the person's relationship to Trevor.**

1. __d__ Ann   a. brother-in-law
2. __c__ Paul   b. sister-in-law
3. __a__ Alex   c. mother-in-law's brother
4. __b__ Danielle   d. wife

CD1 T32

C 🎧 **Listen again. Answer the questions.**

1. Where do Trevor's wife's grandparents live?
   a. with Trevor   (b.) in San Antonio   c. in a big house

2. How many sisters does Trevor's mother-in-law have?
   (a.) two   b. three   c. five

3. What does Trevor's brother-in-law do?
   a. He's an artist.   b. He's an engineer.   (c.) He's an accountant.

4. When does Danielle work?
   (a.) at night   b. during the day   c. on weekends

Lesson 8 Ask about family members

Getting Started   5 minutes

1   BEFORE YOU LISTEN

CLASS. Do you watch game shows? Which...

- As needed, explain: *A game show is a television program. People play games or answer questions to win money and prizes.*
- Read the directions. Say: *Raise your hand if you watch game shows.* Ask several students: *Which show do you watch?* Write the names on the board.
- Ask: *Do you know these game shows? What do people do? Play games? Answer questions?* Elicit simple descriptions of a few of the shows.

Presentation   15 minutes

2   LISTEN

A 💿 **Listen to the game show. What is...**

- Tell students to look at the picture. Ask: *What's the name of this game show?*
- Write *They're Your Family Now!* on the board. Say: *On this game show, people answer questions. What do you think they answer questions about?* Write students' ideas on the board.
- Tell students to point to the man with the microphone. Say: *He is the host. He asks the questions.* Tell students to point to Trevor. Say: *He is the contestant. He answers the questions.* Write *host* and *contestant* on the board and tell students to label their pictures.
- Play CD 1, Track 32. Students listen.
- Ask: *What do contestants on* They're Your Family Now! *answer questions about?* Read the ideas on the board. Circle any that are correct. As needed, add *their in-laws* or *their wife's or husband's family.*

> **Teaching Tip**
>
> *Optional:* Remember that if students need additional support, tell them to read the Audio Script on page 298 as they listen to the conversations.

Controlled Practice   15 minutes

B 💿 **Listen again. Match the name and the...**

- Read the directions and the names. Tell students to listen for these names.
- Play Track 32 again. Students listen and write the letter of the relationship on the line next to the appropriate name. Play Track 32 as many times as needed.
- Students compare answers with a partner.
- Say each item in the form of a sentence for students to complete. For example, *Ann is Trevor's. . . .* Ask the class to call out the answer.

C 💿 **Listen again. Answer the questions.**

- Read the directions. Tell students to read the questions and answer choices silently.
- Ask: *Where is San Antonio?* (in Texas) If possible, point out the location of San Antonio on a U.S. map.
- Tell students to look at item 3. Say *artist, engineer,* and *accountant* and ask the class to repeat. Say a description of each job and ask the class to call out the job. Say: *designs roads, bridges, machines, etc.* (an engineer); *paints, draws, or sculpts* (an artist); and *keeps records of the money spent or received by a person or company* (an accountant).
- Play Track 32 again. Students listen and circle the correct answers.
- Students compare answers with a partner. Tell them to take turns asking and answering the questions.
- Call on students to ask one question each and then choose a classmate to answer.
- *Optional:* Ask: *Which question did Trevor not answer correctly?* (item 3) *How much money has Trevor won so far?* ($300)

▨ **EXPANSION: Grammar and writing practice for 2C**

- Tell students to write complete sentences to answer the questions in Exercise 2C. For example, *1. Trevor's wife's grandparents live in San Antonio.*
- Tell students to underline the verb in each sentence and check that it's in the correct form.

Lesson 8 Ask about family members

Presentation

5 minutes

3 CONVERSATION

A CLASS. **Look at the pictures. What are some....**

- Read the directions.
- Explain that *keep in touch* means to speak or write to someone when you cannot see them often.
- Say the words in the box and ask the class to repeat.
- Students compare answers with a partner.
- Hold up the book and point to each picture. Ask the class to call out the word.

Controlled Practice

10 minutes

B 🔾 **Listen and repeat the conversation.**

- Tell students to read the conversation silently.
- Ask: *How does Adela keep in touch with her family? How does Emil keep in touch with his family?* Elicit and write on the board *She calls* and *He e-mails.*
- If students don't use the *-s* at the end of the verbs, circle the pronouns, point to the end of the verbs, and ask: *What's missing?*
- Tell students to underline *Do* twice in the conversation. Ask: *What comes after* Do? (*you*) *So, is* do *strong or weak?* (weak) Tell students to write *D'ya* above *Do you* in the conversation.
- Play CD 1, Track 33. Students listen and repeat.

4 PRACTICE

A PAIRS. **Practice the conversation.**

- Pair students and tell them to take turns playing A and B.
- Walk around and check students' pronunciation, especially of "*D'ya*" for *Do you*.

Communicative Practice

10 minutes

B MAKE IT PERSONAL. PAIRS. **Do you keep....**

- Read the directions.
- Say: *Look at the pictures in Exercise 3A. How do you keep in touch with your family? Circle the items.*

- Tell students to look at the conversation in Exercise 3B. Ask: *How often does Adela call?* (once a week) Use a calendar to illustrate the meaning of *once a week* and other phrases students can use to talk about how often, such as *every night, every week, a few times a month, on holidays,* and *a lot.* For example, hold up a calendar, point to and say each day of the week; then say *every day* and write it on the board.
- Tell students to look at the item numbers they circled in Exercise 3A and to draw lines to those pictures. At the end of each line, tell students to write the name and relationship of someone they keep in touch with in that way and to note next to each name how often they communicate with that person.
- Tell students to look at the conversation in Exercise 3B. Tell them to highlight or underline: *Do you keep in touch with your family?, How often?,* and *How about you?*
- Play B and model the conversation with an above-level student. Prompt A to ask you the first two highlighted questions. Respond and then ask *How about you?* and repeat A's two questions (*Do you keep in touch with your family? How often?*).
- Pairs use the highlighted questions in Exercise 3B and their notes from Exercise 3A to practice the conversation. Walk around and help as needed.
- Tell students to stand, mingle, and form new pairs to practice the conversation.

■■■ **MULTILEVEL INSTRUCTION for 4B**

Pre-level Before they practice, students write answers to the questions *Do you keep in touch with your family?* and *How often?*

Above-level Pairs practice the conversation several times. Each time, they talk about different family members and different ways they keep in touch.

Extra Practice

Interactive Practice

3 CONVERSATION

A CLASS. Look at the pictures. What are some ways that people keep in touch with their family and friends? Match the pictures and the words in the box.

| call | e-mail | visit | write |

1. ____call____

2. ____write____

3. ____e-mail____

4. ____visit____

CD1 T33

B Listen and repeat the conversation.

Emil: Do you keep in touch with your family?

Adela: Yeah. I call my parents a lot.

Emil: Really? How often?

Adela: About once a week. How about you? Do you call your family a lot?

Emil: No, not really. I usually just e-mail.

4 PRACTICE

A PAIRS. Practice the conversation.

B MAKE IT PERSONAL. PAIRS. Do you keep in touch with your family? Who do you keep in touch with? How? How often?

I keep in touch with my brother Amir. I usually . . .

Ask about family members

Grammar

Simple present: *Yes / No* questions and answers

Do	you they	**visit** **call**	your family? their parents?
Does	he she	**live** **have**	near you? children?

Yes,	I they	**do.**
	he she	**does.**

No,	I they	**don't.**
	he she	**doesn't.**

Simple present: Information questions and answers

When	**do**	you	**visit**	them?
Where	**does**	he	**live?**	
How	**does**	she	**keep**	in touch?

On holidays
In Vancouver.
By e-mail.

· · · · · · **Grammar Watch**

Other question words
How often do you call?
How many kids do you have?
Which family members live here?

PRACTICE

A Complete the questions. Underline the correct word.
Then match the questions and answers.

1. __c__ **Do** / **Does** you have any sisters?

2. __d__ **Do** / **Does** he visit his family often?

3. __e__ **Do** / **Does** your niece have children?

4. __a__ **Do** / **Does** your parents work?

5. __b__ **Do** / **Does** you and your son live in Dallas, too?

a. Yes, they do.

b. Yes, we do.

c. Yes, I do.

d. No, he doesn't.

e. Yes, she does.

CD1 T34

B Listen and check your answers.

C Complete the questions. Use the correct form of the words in parentheses.

1. What ____do____ your brothers ____do____? (do)

2. How often ____do____ your cousins ____visit____ their parents? (visit)

3. When ____does____ your husband ____go____ to school? (go)

4. How ____do____ you ____keep____ in touch with your family? (keep)

5. Where ____does____ your uncle ____work____? (work)

6. How many kids ____does____ Sharon ____have____? (have)

Getting Started   5 minutes

- Say: *We're going to study* Yes / No *questions and information questions in the simple present. In the conversation on page 41, Emil and Adela used this grammar.*
- Play CD 1, Track 33. Students listen. On the board, write: *Do you call your family a lot?* Underline *do* and *call.*

Presentation   10 minutes

Simple present *Yes / No* and information questions

- Copy the grammar charts onto the board or show Transparency 2.5.
- Read each *Yes / No* question and its corresponding affirmative and negative short answers. For example, *Do you visit your family? Yes, I do. / No, I don't.*
- On the board, write: *Danielle works at night.* Elicit the class's help to change the statement to a *Yes / No* question. Circle *Danielle* and ask: *What pronoun is* Danielle *the same as?* (she) *Do we use* do *or* does? Add *Does* to the beginning of the sentence. Then cross out the *-s* at the end of *works* and add a question mark. Rewrite the question: *Does Danielle work at night?* Read the question and elicit the correct short answer. Write: *Yes, she does.*
- Tell students to cover the information questions on the grammar chart and look only at the answers. Read the information questions in random order. Ask the class to call out the answers. Then tell students to uncover the questions and read the information questions and answers silently.
- Point to the question on the board: *Does Danielle work at night?* Elicit the class's help to change the *Yes / No* question to an information question. Cross out *at night* and draw a blank at the beginning of the question. Ask: *What question word do I use?* Write *When* in the blank and change *Does* to *does.* Read the question and elicit the answer.
- If you are using the transparency, do the exercise with the class.

Controlled Practice   15 minutes

PRACTICE

A Complete the questions. Underline the correct....

- Read the directions.
- Write item 1 on the board. Ask: *Why is the answer Do?* (because the subject is *you*) Circle *you.* Then read the question and elicit the answer.
- Tell students to circle the subject in each question before completing the item.
- *Optional:* Tell them to label the subjects in items 3–5 with the corresponding pronoun.

B Listen and check your answers.

- Read the directions.
- Play CD 1, Track 34. Students listen and make corrections as needed.
- *Optional:* Pair students. Tell partners to take turns asking and answering the questions. Tell them to practice the weak pronunciation of *do* ("D'ya") in the questions and the strong pronunciation of *do* in the short answers.

C Complete the questions. Use the correct form...

- Read the directions.
- Write item 1 on the board. Point to *do* in the first blank and ask: *Why is the answer* do? (because the subject is *your brothers*) Point to *do* in the second blank and *do* in parentheses. Ask: *Does the word in parentheses change?* (No.) Read the question.
- Students compare answers with a partner, taking turns reading the questions.
- Call on students to read the questions.

▬▬▬ **EXPANSION: Writing and grammar practice for C**

- Tell students to write made-up answers to the questions in Exercise C.
- Then tell them to take turns reading the questions and their answers with a partner.

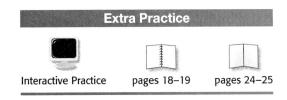

Extra Practice		
Interactive Practice	pages 18–19	pages 24–25

1 GRAMMAR

Ⓐ Complete the questions. Use *do* or *does* and...

- Read the directions. Tell students to refer back to the grammar charts on page 42 (Simple present: *Yes / No* questions and answers).
- Tell students to read the chart in Exercise A silently.
- To check comprehension, ask: *Where does Ji-Na work?* (at a hospital) *How many children does Nu have?* (two) *Where does Rahim live?* (in his own house)
- Read the directions.
- Say the subject in each item and ask the class to call out *do* or *does*. Tell students to check their answers. Tell students to look at the second blank in each item. Ask: *Does the word in parentheses change?* (No.)

Ⓑ PAIRS. Answer the questions in Exercise A. Use...

- Read the directions. Tell students to refer back to the grammar charts on page 30 (Simple present affirmative and negative: *have / live / work*).
- Tell students to look at Exercise A. Read item 1. Tell students to point to Nyoro and Rahim and look at the number of children they have. Repeat the question and elicit the answer: *Yes, they do.*
- Complete item 2 together as a class in the same way. Remind students to add *-s* to the verb or use *has* when they answer information questions about one person.
- Say the names in the chart and ask the class to repeat.
- Pair students and tell them to take turns asking and answering the questions.
- Walk around and check for third-person singular *-s* in answers to information questions. Check for commas in short answers.
- Call on different pairs to ask and answer each question.

Ⓒ Complete the sentences. Use the information in...

- Read the directions. Tell students to refer back to the grammar charts on page 36 (Simple present: Additions with *and . . .* , *too / and . . . not, either*).
- As students complete the task, walk around, and if students have difficulty, take them through steps to arrive at the answer. For example, for item 2, underline *has* and ask: *Is has affirmative or negative? Do we use* too *or* not, either? Then underline *Rahim* and ask: *Do we say* do, too *or* does, too?
- Students compare answers with a partner, taking turns reading the sentences.
- Call on students to read the sentences.

EXPANSION: Graphic organizer, grammar, and speaking practice for 1C

- Tell students to make their own chart like the one at the top of page 43 and to complete it by asking five classmates information questions.
- First, tell students to look at the chart. Ask: *What questions do you need to ask?* Form the questions as a class and write them on the board (*Where do you work? How many children do you have? Where do you live?*).
- Tell students to stand, mingle, ask five classmates the questions, and fill in their charts.
- Extend the activity by having students write *Yes / No* and information questions about their charts. Then tell partners to exchange charts and ask each other their questions.
- Extend the activity further by having students compare classmates by writing sentences with additions.

CD-ROM Practice

 Go to the CD-ROM for more practice.

If your students need more practice with the vocabulary, grammar, and competencies in Unit 2, encourage them to review the activities on the CD-ROM. This review can also help students prepare for the final role play on the following Expand page.

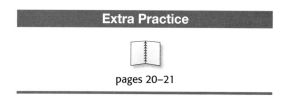

Extra Practice

pages 20–21

1 GRAMMAR

A Complete the questions. Use *do* or *does* and the words in parentheses.

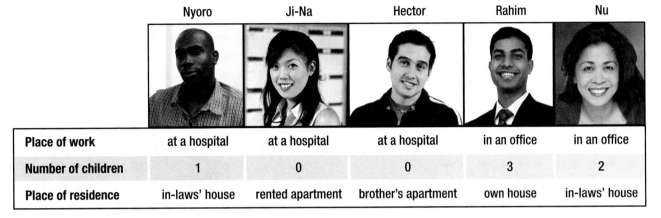

	Nyoro	Ji-Na	Hector	Rahim	Nu
Place of work	at a hospital	at a hospital	at a hospital	in an office	in an office
Number of children	1	0	0	3	2
Place of residence	in-laws' house	rented apartment	brother's apartment	own house	in-laws' house

1. _____Do_____ Nyoro and Rahim _____have_____ children? Yes, they do.
   (have)

2. Where _____does_____ Nyoro _____work_____? He works at a hospital.
   (work)

3. _____Do_____ Nyoro and Nu _____live_____ with their in-laws? Yes, they do.
   (live)

4. _____Does_____ Hector _____have_____ children? No, he doesn't.
   (have)

5. Where _____does_____ Ji-Na _____live_____? She lives in an apartment.
   (live)

6. How many children _____does_____ Rahim _____have_____? He has three children.
   (have)

7. Where _____do_____ Nu and Rahim _____work_____? They work in an office.
   (work)

B PAIRS. Answer the questions in Exercise A. Use the information in the chart.

C Complete the sentences. Use the information in the chart and the words in the box.

> ~~do, too~~   does, too   don't, either   doesn't, either

1. Nyoro works at a hospital, and Ji-Na and Hector _____do, too._____.

2. Nyoro has children, and Rahim _____does, too_____.

3. Ji-Na doesn't work in an office, and Hector _____doesn't, either_____.

4. Nu doesn't live in an apartment, and Nyoro and Rahim _____don't, either_____.

Go to the CD-ROM for more practice.

2 ACT IT OUT   What do you say?

STEP 1. CLASS. Review the conversations in Lessons 2 and 5 (CD 1 tracks 22 and 27).

STEP 2. ROLE PLAY. PAIRS. You are co-workers talking at lunch.

Student A, ask questions about Student B's family or friends.

Student B, answer the questions. Talk about: • where they live and work • what they have in common with each other • who looks alike

3 READ AND REACT   Problem-solving

STEP 1. Read about Jin-Hee's problem.

Jin-Hee is married and has two children. Every weekend Jin-Hee's mother-in-law comes to visit. Her mother-in-law tells Jin-Hee how to cook, how to take care of the children, and how to manage the house. Jin-Hee doesn't like her mother-in-law's advice.

STEP 2. PAIRS. What is Jin-Hee's problem?
What can she do? Here are some ideas.

- She can tell her mother-in-law not to visit anymore.
- She can ask her husband to talk to his mother.
- She can listen to her mother-in-law and then do things her own way.
- She can _____.

4 CONNECT   For your Community-building Activity, go to page 248.
For your Team Project, go to page 275.

EXPAND   Show what you know!

2 ACT IT OUT

STEP 1. CLASS. Review the conversations in Lessons...

- Play CD 1, Tracks 22 and 27. Students listen and read along silently.
- As needed, play the CD again to aid comprehension.

STEP 2. ROLE PLAY. PAIRS. You are co-workers...

- Read the directions and the guidelines for A and B.
- Pair students. Tell A: *Start the conversation by saying* Tell me about your family. *Then ask about where B's family members live and work. Ask whether B and different family members look alike or have a lot in common.*
- Tell B: *Answer with* I have *and the members of your family. Say* lives *and* works *when you talk about one family member. Use* and . . . , too / and . . . not, either *to talk about how family members look alike or what they have in common.*
- Walk around and observe partners interacting. Check that A forms simple present *Yes / No* and information questions correctly. Check that B uses third-person singular *-s* when answering information questions about one person. Check that B uses additions with *and . . . , too / and . . . not, either* correctly.
- Call on pairs to perform for the class.
- While pairs are performing, use the scoring rubric on page T-xiii to evaluate each student's vocabulary, grammar, fluency, and how well he or she completes the task.
- *Optional:* After each pair finishes, discuss the strengths and weakness of each performance either in front of the class or privately.

> **Teaching Tip**
> This is another activity that can be enhanced by the use of students' real family photos.

3 READ AND REACT

STEP 1. Read about Jin-Hee's problem.

- Say: *We are going to read about a student's problem, and then we need to think about a solution.*
- Read the directions.

- Read the story while students follow along silently. Pause after each sentence to allow time for students to comprehend. Periodically stop and ask simple *Wh-* questions to check comprehension (for example, *How often does Jin-Hee's mother-in-law visit? What does Jin-Hee's mother-in-law do? Does Jin-Hee like her mother-in-law's advice?*).

STEP 2. PAIRS. What is Jin-Hee's problem? What....

- Ask: *What is Jin-Hee's problem?* (She doesn't like her mother-in-law's advice.)
- Pair students. Read the ideas in the list. Give pairs a couple of minutes to discuss possible solutions for Jin-Hee.
- Ask: *Which ideas are good?* Call on students to say their opinion about the ideas in the box (for example, S: *I think she can ask her husband to talk to his mother because she will listen to him.*).
- Now tell pairs to think of one new idea not in the box (for example, *She can talk to her mother-in-law.*) and to write it in the blank. Encourage students to think of more than one idea and to write them in their notebooks.
- Call on pairs to say their own solutions. Write them on the board and ask: *Do you think this is a good idea? Why or why not?*

▮▮ MULTILEVEL INSTRUCTION for STEP 2
Pre-level Students work in groups of 4 to come up with an idea.
Above-level Tell pairs to cover the list of ideas and to come up with three of four of their own ideas first. Then they can look at the list in the book to compare.

4 CONNECT

Turn to page 248 for the Community-building Activity and page 275 for the Team Project. See page T-xi for general notes about teaching these activities.

Progress Check

Which goals can you check off? Go back to page 25.
Ask students to turn to page 25 and check off the goals they have reached. Call on students to say which goals they will practice outside of class.

3

Lots to Do

Classroom Materials/Extra Practice

CD 1
Tracks 35–48

T
Transparencies 3.1–3.6
Vocabulary Cards Unit 3

MCA
Unit 3

Workbook
Unit 3

Interactive Practice
Unit 3

Unit Overview

Goals

- See the list of goals on the facing page.

Grammar

- Simple present: *want / need* + infinitive
- *Be going to* + verb
- Adverbs of degree: *very / too*

Pronunciation

- Weak pronunciation of *to*; "wanna" for *want to* in informal conversation
- "Gonna" for *going to* in informal conversation

Reading

- Read an article about ways to pay for things
- *Reading Skill:* Identifying purpose

Writing

- Write about clothes you need or want
- Write about some people's errands
- Write about how you will pay for your next big purchase
- Write reasons that people return clothes

Life Skills Writing

- Write a personal check

Preview

- Set the context of the unit by asking questions about shopping (for example, *Do you like to shop? What do you like to shop for?*).
- Hold up page 45 or show Transparency 3.1. Read the unit title and ask the class to repeat.
- Explain: Lots *has the same meaning as* a lot.
- Say: *Look at the picture.* Ask the Preview questions: *Where are the people?* (in a store) *What are they doing?* (shopping / looking at clothes)

Unit Goals

- Point to the Unit Goals. Explain that this list shows what the class will be studying in this unit.
- Tell students to read the goals silently.
- Say each goal and ask the class to repeat. Explain unfamiliar vocabulary as needed:
    Purchases: things that you buy
- Tell students to circle one goal that is very important to them. Call on several students to say the goal they circled.
- Write a checkmark (✓) on the board. Say: *We will come back to this page again. You will write a checkmark next to the goals you learned in this unit.*

Lots to Do

Preview

Look at the picture.
Where are the people?
What are they doing?

UNIT GOALS

- ☐ Identify clothes and materials

- ☐ Describe your wants and needs

- ☐ Count your change

- ☐ Read a store ad

- ☐ Read a sales receipt

- ☐ Write a personal check

- ☐ Talk about shopping plans

- ☐ Describe problems with purchases

1 WHAT DO YOU KNOW?

A CLASS. **Look at the pictures. Which clothes do you know? Which materials do you know?**

CD1 T35

B  **Look at the pictures and listen. Listen again and repeat.**

2 PRACTICE

A PAIRS. **Talk about the clothes.**

A: *I like this coat.*
B: *It's nice. What's it made of?*
A: *Wool.*
B: *I like these jeans.*

B WORD PLAY. PAIRS. **What clothes are made of these materials? Write the words in the chart.** Answers will vary but could include:

Wool	Leather	Fleece	Cotton
a coat	boots	gloves	a scarf
gloves	a jacket	a sweatshirt	a jacket
a scarf	gloves	a scarf	a sweatshirt

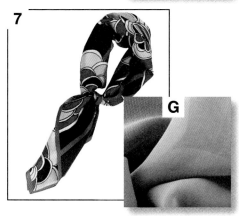

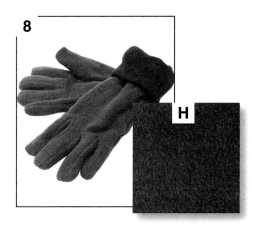

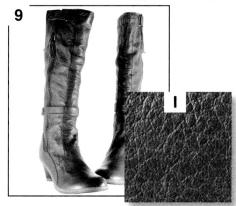

Getting Started 5 minutes

1 WHAT DO YOU KNOW?

A CLASS. **Look at the pictures. Which clothes do you...**

- Show Transparency 3.2 or hold up the book. Tell students to cover the list of words on page 47.
- Say: *Look at the pictures. Which clothes do you know?* Elicit a clothes item (for example, *number 5 is jeans.*).
- Students call out answers. Help students pronounce clothes if they have difficulty.
- Repeat with: *Which materials do you know?*
- If students call out an incorrect clothes item or material, change the student's answer to a question for the class (for example, *Letter C is* leather?). If nobody can identify the correct clothes item or material, tell students they will now listen to a CD and practice the words for clothes and materials.

Presentation 10 minutes

B 🎧 **Look at the pictures and listen....**

- Read the directions. Play CD 1, Track 35. Students look at the pictures and listen. Pause after item 9. (*boots*)
- To check comprehension, say each clothing item in random order and ask students to point to the appropriate picture.
- Resume playing Track 35. Pause after item I. Say each material on the list, tell students to look at the picture, and enlist students' help to find an example of each material in the classroom.
- Say each material in random order and ask students to point to the appropriate picture.
- Resume playing Track 35. Students listen and repeat.

Controlled Practice 20 minutes

2 PRACTICE

A PAIRS. **Talk about the clothes.**

- Read each line in the example and ask the class to repeat. Model correct intonation.

- Play A and model the example with an above-level student. Point to picture 1.
- Continue the conversation. Prompt B to point to a clothes item and say: *I like this . . .* Respond: *It's nice. What's it made of?*
- Write the first two lines of the example on the board. Cross out *coat* and write *jeans*. Ask: *What other changes do I need to make?* Elicit the changes from the class and make them on the board. Then read the new lines: A: *I like these jeans.* B: *They're nice. What are they made of?*
- Tell students to look at vocabulary words 1 to 9. Ask: *What other clothes words are plural?* Write *gloves* and *boots* on the board next to the revised example.
- Pair students and tell them to talk about two pictures each.
- Walk around and check that students make the necessary changes for plural clothes words.

■■■ **MULTILEVEL INSTRUCTION for 2A**

Pre-level Before they practice, students label each picture. Tell them to write *this* or *these* + the clothing item next to each number and the material next to each letter.

Above-level Students can vary the language they use to talk about the clothes. Tell them to point out items they like and don't like. B can respond: *I do, too.* or *I don't, either.*

B WORD PLAY. PAIRS. **What clothes are made of...**

- Read the directions. Write *Wool* and the example on the board. Tell students to look at vocabulary words 1 to 9. Ask: *What other clothes are sometimes made of wool?* Add *a scarf* and *gloves* to the list.
- Explain that *corduroy* and *denim* are made from *cotton*. Pair students and tell them to choose three common clothes items for each material.
- Tell students to switch partners and compare their charts with another classmate.
- To check answers, copy the chart onto the board and complete the chart as a class.

■■■ **EXPANSION: Vocabulary and pronunciation practice for 2B**

- Tell students to look at their clothes. Ask: *What materials are you wearing?* Say the materials in random order. Tell students to stand, point to the item, and repeat if they are wearing the material.

Learning Strategy: Use pictures.

- Read the directions.
- Bring in (or ask students to bring in) clothing catalogs and fashion magazines.
- Distribute the catalogs and magazines. Tell students to cut out five pictures that represent clothes or material from the vocabulary list.
- Provide each student with five index cards or tell students to cut up notebook paper. Tell students to paste the pictures first and then write the words.
- Walk around, and if misspellings occur, tell students to check the list on page 47. Students who finish early can quiz one another with their cards.
- Say: *You can make cards with pictures to remember new words.* Remind students to use this strategy to remember other new vocabulary.

Teaching Tip

If possible, bring in fabric swatches to class. This will help kinesthetic learners to associate the feel of different fabrics with the vocabulary for materials.

Communicative Practice   20 minutes

Show what you know!

STEP 1. Think about your clothes. Make a list...

- Read the directions and the examples.
- Write the first example on the board. Underline *black* and ask: *What comes first?* Under *black*, write: *1. color.* Repeat with *wool* and *coat*. Label them: *2. material, 3. clothes item.*
- If possible, hold up or point to your own clothing item from the vocabulary list. Ask: *What color is it? What material is it? What is it?* Write the words on the board as the class says them. If the item is singular, add *a* or *an.*
- Say: *Now I'm thinking about the clothes in my closet at home.* Write another description on the board. If your first example was singular, make this one plural (for example, *black leather boots*) and vice versa.
- Walk around and check students' word order.
- Encourage students to use clothes and materials from the vocabulary list. Write any other language students use on the board and explain meanings.

STEP 2. PAIRS. Describe your clothes to your...

- Read the directions and ask two above-level students to read the example.
- On the board, write *I have* in front of your own two examples from Step 1. Play A and model the conversation with an above-level student. Read one of your sentences from the board. On the board, write: *I don't* and *Me, too* and prompt B to choose a response. Then ask B to say *I have* and an item from his or her list.
- Pair students and tell them to take turns playing A and B. Say: *Circle any items on your list that your partner also has.*
- Say: *Do you and your partner have any of the same clothes? If not, stand, mingle, and practice the conversation with other partners until you find a classmate who has one of the items on your list.*

STEP 3. Report to the class.

- Read the directions. Ask the student who played Clara in Step 2 to read the example.
- Say: *Look at the circled items on your list.* Call on students to report.

███ **MULTILEVEL INSTRUCTION for STEP 3**

Pre-level In Step 3, direct students to underline *Charles* and *black wool coat* in the example. Tell them to substitute their partner's name and the clothes item they both have.

Above-level In Step 3, ask students to use additions with *and . . . too* to report (for example, *I have a red fleece jacket, and Sung does, too.*).

███ **EXPANSION: Speaking and writing practice for STEP 3**

- Tell students to stand, mingle, and practice the conversation in Step 2 until they find three clothing items they have in common with classmates.
- Then students sit and write three sentences using additions with *and . . . too.*
- Call on students to read their sentences.

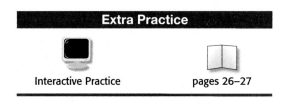

Extra Practice	
Interactive Practice	pages 26–27

2

Things You Wear

1. a coat
2. a jacket
3. a raincoat
4. a windbreaker
5. jeans
6. a sweatshirt
7. a scarf
8. gloves
9. boots

Materials

A. wool
B. corduroy
C. vinyl
D. nylon
E. denim
F. cotton
G. silk
H. fleece
I. leather

Learning Strategy

Use pictures.

Look at the list of clothes and materials. Make cards for five new words. Write the word in English on one side of the card. Paste a picture of the clothes or material to the other side.

4

5

6

Show what you know!

STEP 1. Think about your clothes. Make a list of five items. Include the color and the material.

> a black wool coat
> a blue denim jacket

STEP 2. PAIRS. Describe your clothes to your partner. Do you and your partner have any of the same clothes?

Clara: *I have a black wool coat.*
Charles: *Me, too. I have a . . .*

STEP 3. Report to the class.

Clara: *Charles and I have black wool coats.*

Listening and Speaking

1 BEFORE YOU LISTEN

CLASS. What is a summer clearance sale? What other kinds of sales are there? Do you look for sales when you shop?

2 LISTEN

CD1 T36

A Listen to an interviewer talking to three shoppers at Big Deals clothing store. Match the clothing to the shopper who talks about each item.

1. __a__ Alicia Duran   2. __c__ Gladys Flores   3. __b__ John Nichols

a.    b.    c.

CD1 T36

B Listen again. Look at the chart. Check (✓) the reason each person shops at Big Deals.

	Alicia Duran	Gladys Flores	John Nichols
It's convenient.			✓
They have great prices.	✓		
It's easy to return things.		✓	

Getting Started
5 minutes

1 BEFORE YOU LISTEN

CLASS. What is a summer clearance sale? What...

- Tell students to look at the picture. Ask: *What does the sign say?* Write *SUMMER CLEARANCE SALE* on the board. Point to *SUMMER* and ask: *What clothes do you see?* Write *shorts* under *SUMMER*. Point to *SALE* and ask: *Are prices high or low during a sale?* Write *low prices* under *SALE*.
- Ask: *Are there usually low prices for shorts at the beginning of summer or at the end of summer?* Under *CLEARANCE* write *end of summer*. Say: *Look at the words on the board. What is a summer clearance sale?* (low prices on summer clothes at the end of summer) *Stores have summer clearance sales to make room for fall clothes.*
- Write *clearance sale* on the board. Ask: *What other kinds of sales are there?* Write students' responses on the board. If students have difficulty, provide some examples: *pre-season sale, holiday sale, preferred customer sale, grand-opening sale, going-out-of-business sale.* Explain the meaning of each.
- Ask: *Do you look for sales when you shop?* Ask for a show of hands.

Presentation
10 minutes

2 LISTEN

Ⓐ **Listen to an interviewer talking to...**

- Read the directions.
- Tell students to look at the picture again. Say: *An interviewer is someone who asks people questions.* Point to the interviewer in the picture and ask: *What does she have in her hand?* (a microphone)

- Tell students to look at the exercise. Read the names. Then say each letter and tell the class to call out the clothes.
- Play CD 1, Track 36. Students listen and write the letter of each person's clothes on the appropriate line.
- Students compare answers with a partner.
- To check answers, say: *Alicia Duran wants to buy . . . Gladys Flores needs to return . . . John Nichols needs to buy . . .* Students call out the clothes to complete the sentences.

Controlled Practice
15 minutes

Ⓑ 🔊 **Listen again. Look at the chart. Check...**

- Read the directions.
- To make sure students understand the vocabulary in the chart, ask: *If something is convenient, does it make things easy or difficult for you?* (easy) *When you return something to a store, do you trade it for another item or get your money back?* (get my money back)
- Play Track 36 again. Students complete the chart.
- Students compare answers with a partner.
- To check answers, ask: *Why does Alicia Duran shop at Big Deals?* Repeat with the other two shoppers.

> **Teaching Tip**
>
> If students need additional suport, tell them to read the Audio Script on page 298 as they listen.

▬▬ EXPANSION: Graphic organizer practice for 2B

- Tell students to make their own chart like the one in Exercise 2B. Instead of names of people, tell students to write the names of three stores.
- Students rate each store's convenience, prices, and return policy by checking the boxes.
- On the board, write: *Where do you shop? Why?* Pair students. Tell them to take turns asking one another the questions and to use their charts to answer.

Presentation 10 minutes

3 CONVERSATION

A **Listen. Then listen and repeat.**

- Tell students to look at the examples on the left. Say the verb phrases with a strong pronunciation of *to*.
- Read the first sentence of the Pronunciation Watch note. Tell students to look at the sentences and circle *to*. Ask: *Does another word come after* to? (Yes.) *Does* to *have a strong or a weak pronunciation in the sentences?* (weak)
- Play CD 1, Track 37. Students listen. Pause after *I don't like to shop.*
- Read the second sentence of the Pronunciation Watch note. Resume playing Track 37. Students finish listening and then listen and repeat.

B **Listen and repeat the conversation.**

- Ask students to read the conversation silently. Then tell them to circle *to* in the conversation.
- Ask: *Does another word come after* to? (Yes.) *Does* to *have a strong or a weak pronunciation?* (weak) Say the sentence with a weak pronunciation of *to* and ask the class to repeat.
- Play CD 1, Track 38. Students listen and repeat.

Controlled Practice 10 minutes

4 PRACTICE

A PAIRS. Practice the conversation. Then make new...

- Pair students and tell them to practice the conversation in Exercise 3B. Tell them to take turns playing each role. Walk around and help with pronunciation as needed.
- Then, in Exercise 4A, tell students to look at the information in the boxes. Say each clothing item and ask students to repeat. Ask: *Which one is for hot weather?* (some shorts) *Which one is for cold weather?* (some gloves) *Which one is for cool weather?* (some jeans)
- Read the directions.
- Copy the conversation onto the board with blanks. Read it and fill it in with information from the same row in the boxes (*hot, summer, some shorts*).

- Ask two on-level students to practice the conversation in front of the class.
- Tell pairs to take turns playing each role and to use the words in the boxes to fill in the blanks.
- Walk around and check that students use the weak pronunciation of *to* in *I need to buy some shorts.* As needed, say the sentence and ask students to repeat.
- Tell students to stand, mingle, and practice the conversation with several new partners.

MULTILEVEL INSTRUCTION for 4A

Pre-level Students write the words in the blanks before they practice the conversation. Tell them to use a pencil so they can erase and practice two different conversations.

Above-level After pairs practice the conversation twice, tell them to make a new conversation with *warm*, *spring*, and an appropriate clothes item.

Communicative Practice 20 minutes

B MAKE IT PERSONAL. PAIRS. **Talk about...**

- Write the current season on the board. Ask: *What clothes do you need or want this season?* Tell students to write a short list.
- Ask: *Where do you shop for clothes?* Tell students to write the name of a store. Ask: *Why do you shop there?* Tell students to look at the chart on page 48 and write a reason from the chart or their own reason.
- Read the directions. Ask two students to read the example. Ask the class: *What question can Student A ask next?* (*Where do you shop?*)
- Pair students. Tell them to look at the example and underline the words they need to change to make their own conversation. Ask: *What words did you underline?* (*fall, a new sweater*)
- Walk around and check that A asks all three questions: *What clothes do you need this fall? Where do you shop?* and *Why do you shop there?*

Extra Practice

Interactive Practice

CD1 T37

A Listen. Then listen and repeat.

need to	I need to buy a raincoat.
like to	I don't like to shop.
want to	I want to buy some jeans.

CD1 T38

B Listen and repeat the conversation.

Anwar: Oh, it's so rainy this month!

Maryan: I know! It really feels like spring now. I need to buy a raincoat. Look. Those are nice.

Anwar: Yes, they are. Let's go in and look around.

4 PRACTICE

A PAIRS. Practice the conversation. Then make new conversations. Use the information in the boxes.

A: Oh, it's so _____ this month!

B: I know! It really feels like _____ now.

I need to buy _____ . Look. Those are nice.

A: Yes, they are. Let's go in and look around.

hot	summer	**some shorts**
cold	winter	**some gloves**
cool	fall	**some jeans**

B MAKE IT PERSONAL. PAIRS. Talk about the clothes that you need or want this season. Where do you shop? Why do you shop there?

A: *What clothes do you need this fall?*
B: *I need a new sweater.*

Grammar

Simple present: *want / need* + infinitive

Affirmative			
I They	**want** **need**	**to buy**	a raincoat.
He She	**wants** **needs**	**to exchange**	this hat.

Negative				
I They	**don't**	**want** **need**	**to return**	these boots.
He She	**doesn't**	**want** **need**	**to get**	it now.

1 PRACTICE

A Complete the conversations. Write the correct forms of the verbs in the boxes.

> buy   come   leave   return

> **Grammar Watch**
> - Use *want* and *need* + an infinitive.
> - An infinitive = *to* + the base form of the verb.
> - You can also use *want / need* + a noun.
>   *I want a denim jacket.*
>   *He needs a sweatshirt.*

1. **A:** Denise and I want ___to buy___ a few things at the store later today. Do you want ___to come___ with us?

   B: Sure. I need ___to return___ a blouse that I bought last week.

   A: OK. No problem. What time do you want ___to leave___?

> be   buy   come   go   leave   spend

2. **A:** I want ___to go___ downtown tomorrow morning. Do you want ___to come___ with me?

   B: Well, I need ___to buy___ a birthday present for my mom. But I don't want ___to spend___ a lot of money right now.

   A: Then this is the perfect time to shop—they're having big sales!

   B: Really? That's great!

   A: Yeah. But we need ___to leave___ early. I want ___to be___ home by 12:00.

CD1 T39

B Listen and check your answers.

Getting Started   5 minutes

- Say: *We're going to study* want *and* need *plus an infinitive. In the conversation on page 49, Maryan used this grammar.*
- Play CD 1, Track 38. Students listen. On the board, write: *I need to buy a raincoat.* Underline *need to buy*.

Presentation   10 minutes

Simple present: *want / need* + infinitive

- Point to the following sentence on the board: *I need to buy a raincoat.* Underline *need*. Ask: *What's the infinitive?* Circle *to buy*.
- Read the Grammar Watch note. Say: *You can also say* I need a raincoat.
- Copy the grammar charts onto the board or show Transparency 3.3 and cover the exercise.
- Tell students to look at the grammar charts. Ask: *What are the infinitives?* (*to buy, to exchange, to return, to get*) *Can you think of any other infinitives?* Elicit other infinitives and list them on the board.
- Read the sentences in the chart and ask the class to repeat. Remind students to use *wants* and *needs* with *he, she,* or *it*. Remind students to use the weak pronunciation of *to*.
- If you are using the transparency, do the exercise with the class.

Controlled Practice   20 minutes

1 **PRACTICE**

Ⓐ Complete the conversations....

- Read the directions and the verbs in the boxes. Ask: *What form are the verbs in?* (base form) *How do you make them infinitives?* (add *to*)
- Write A's first line in item 1 on the board and read it. Point to the second blank and ask which verb to use. Write *come* in the blank. Underline *want* and ask: *What do we need to add?* Write *to* before *come*.

■■■ EXPANSION: Grammar and writing practice for 1A

- Tell students to give names to A and B in each conversation in Exercise 1A.
- Then tell them to write a couple of sentences summarizing each conversation. For example, for Conversation 1: *Amy and Denise want to go shopping later, and Beth does, too. She needs to return something.* For Conversation 2: *Alex wants to go downtown tomorrow morning, and Brett does, too. He needs to buy a birthday present for his mom.*

Ⓑ 💿 **Listen and check your answers.**

- Play CD 1, Track 39. Students listen and check their answers.
- Tell students to look at their answers and double check that each one includes *to*.
- *Optional:* Pair students and ask them to practice the conversations. Call on pairs to perform the completed conversations for the class.

2 PRACTICE

Ⓐ Look at the pictures. Write a sentence...

- Read the directions.
- Write item 1 on the board. Tell students to look at the first picture. Ask: *What does Mary need or want to do?* Elicit two possible answers with *go* (*Mary needs to go . . . , Mary wants to go . . .*) and write them on the board.
- Walk around and check that students are using the third-person singular *-s* and *to*.

> **Teaching Tip**
>
> If you notice that students are omitting the third-person singular *-s*, do a mini-review by using examples from the grammar chart on the board.

EXPANSION: Grammar and speaking practice for 2A

- Tell pairs to play the roles of the people in the pictures and say what they need or want to do in the first person (for example, Mary: *I need to go to the shoe store.* Jim: *I want to go to the library.*).

Ⓑ PAIRS. Compare your answers.

- Pair students and tell them to take turns reading the sentences. Remind them that there may be more than one right answer.
- To check answers, call on students to read sentences.

Communicative Practice   20 minutes

Show what you know!

STEP 1. Complete the sentences about your clothing...

- Read the directions.
- Write your own clothes shopping needs and wants on the board as an example.
- Review the difference between *return* and *exchange*.

STEP 2. GROUPS OF 5. Play the Memory Game....

- Read the directions.
- Ask three students seated in a row to role-play the example.
- Ask four above-level students to model the game with you. Read one of your sentences from the board. Prompt the first student to change your sentence to the third person and then read one of his or her own sentences. Continue in this manner with the second and third students. If a student has difficulty, elicit help from the class.
- Form groups. Remind students to say *needs* and *wants* when they talk about each group member.
- If time permits, form new groups and play the game again.

MULTILEVEL INSTRUCTION for STEP 2

Cross-ability Ask one of the above-level students who helped model the game to lead each group. This student should take the last turn and say all group members' clothes shopping needs and wants. You may also want to ask this student to report the group's needs and wants to the class. Pre-level students can take the first turn and read one of their sentences from Step 1.

EXPANSION: Grammar and writing practice for STEP 2

- Ask: *Do you remember your classmates' clothes shopping needs and wants?* Tell students to write as many sentences as they can. As an example, point to one of your own shopping needs or wants. Elicit a sentence and write it on the board.

Progress Check

Can you . . . describe your wants and needs?

Say: *We have practiced describing our wants and needs. Now, look at the question at the bottom of the page. Can you describe your wants and needs?* Tell students to write a checkmark in the box.

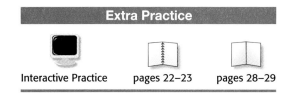

Extra Practice		
Interactive Practice	pages 22–23	pages 28–29

A Look at the pictures. Write a sentence about what each customer wants or needs to do. Use *need* or *want* + an infinitive. There may be more than one right answer.

Answers will vary but could include:

1. Mary __needs to go to the shoe store__.
   (need / want + go)

2. Jim __needs to go to the library__.
   (need / want + go)

3. Larry __wants to buy a coat__.
   (need / want + buy)

4. Ray __needs to get an umbrella__.
   (need / want + get)

5. Hector __wants to return his pants__.
   (need / want + return)

6. Mariko __wants to exchange her shirt__.
   (need / want + exchange)

B PAIRS. Compare your answers.

Show what you know!   Describe your wants and needs

STEP 1. Complete the sentences about your clothing needs or wants. Use *buy*, *get*, *return*, or *exchange*.   Answers will vary.

I need to _____.   I want to _____.

STEP 2. GROUPS OF 5. Play the Memory Game. Talk about shopping for clothes.

Kwon-Su: *I want to buy new gloves.*
Julio: *Kwon-Su wants to buy new gloves. I need to return a wool sweater.*
Silvia: *Kwon-Su wants to buy new gloves. Julio needs to return a wool sweater.*
         I need to get a new umbrella.

Can you…describe your wants and needs?   ☐

Life Skills

1 COUNT YOUR CHANGE

Calculate the change for each purchase. Write the amount on the line.

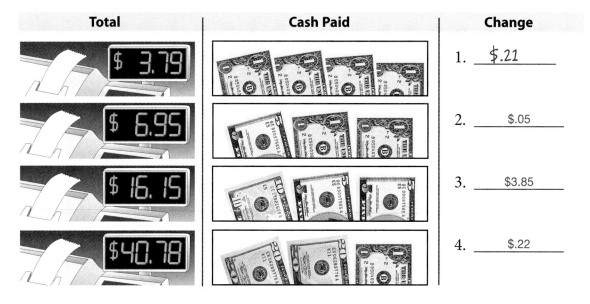

Total	Cash Paid	Change
$ 3.79		1. ___$.21___
$ 6.95		2. ___$.05___
$ 16.15		3. ___$3.85___
$40.78		4. ___$.22___

2 READ A STORE AD

PAIRS. Read the store ad. What's on sale? How much is the discount on each item? swimwear: 30% off   sunglasses: 40% off   flip-flops: 50% off

MAYFIELD Department Store **Summer Sale!**

Wednesday, July 24 – Sunday, July 28

All men's and women's swimwear **30%off**
Regular price: $40
Sale price **$28**

All sunglasses **40%off**
Regular price: $30
Sale price **$18**

All flip-flops **50%off**
Regular price: $5
Sale price **$2.50**

Can you...count your change and read a store ad? ☐

Getting Started — 10 minutes

- Tell students to look at the bills in Exercise 1. Point to each denomination and say: *a twenty-dollar bill, a ten-dollar bill*, etc. Explain that in informal speech, people say: *a twenty, a ten*, etc.
- Ask: *Do you usually pay for things in cash?*

Culture Connection

- *Optional:* Hold up actual U.S. bills. Ask: *Who is pictured on each bill?* List the denominations on the board. Elicit the names students know. Provide the names they don't know: *$1: George Washington* (1st president of the U.S.), *$5: Abraham Lincoln* (16th president), *$10: Alexander Hamilton* (1st secretary of the treasury), *$20: Andrew Jackson* (7th president).
- Ask: *Who's pictured on the money in your country? What are they famous for?*

Presentation — 15 minutes

1 COUNT YOUR CHANGE

Calculate the change for each purchase. Write...

- Tell students to look at the first purchase. Ask: *How much is the purchase?* ($3.79) *How much money did the customer give the cashier?* ($4.00) *How much money does the customer get back?* ($0.21)
- Tell students to look at the first transaction again. Say the amounts in each column and ask the class to repeat. Say: *Three seventy-nine / three dollars and seventy-nine cents, four dollars, twenty-one cents.*
- If students have difficulty, review subtraction or bring in play money and demonstrate how to count back change.

■ EXPANSION: Speaking practice for Exercise 1

- Bring in play money and ask pairs to practice counting back change for each sale. For example,
  A: *Three seventy-nine, please.*
  B: [hands A $4]
  A: *Three eighty* [hands B a penny] *three ninety* [hands B a dime], *four dollars* [hands B another dime].

Controlled Practice — 25 minutes

2 READ A STORE AD

PAIRS. Read the store ad. What's on sale? How...

- Tell students to look at the ad. Ask: *What kind of sale is this?* (a summer sale) *What's the name of the store?* (Mayfield Department Store) *When is the sale?* (Wednesday, July 24–Sunday, July 28)
- Read the directions. Explain that *discount* is the money taken away from the price.
- To model the activity, point to the first item in the ad and ask an above-level student: *What's on sale?* (swimwear) *How much is the discount?* (30%) Write *30%* on the board. Label the % symbol. Say *thirty percent* and ask the class to repeat.
- Tell students to underline the questions *What's on sale?* and *How much is the discount on each item?* in the directions. Pair students and tell them to take turns asking one another the questions about the other two items in the ad.
- *Optional:* Show students how to calculate the discount. On the board, write: *$40 – 30% discount = .* Under that, write: *$40 x .30 = _____.* Ask: *How much is the discount?* Write *$12* on the line. Ask: *What is the sale price?* On the board, write: *$40 – $12 = $28.* Tell pairs to calculate the discount on the other two items (sunglasses, $12; flip-flops, $2.50).

■ EXPANSION for Exercise 2

- Bring in clothing store ads.
- Tell students to circle the clothes they need or want in the ads.
- Hold up your ad. Circle items you want and say: *I need / want to buy . . .*
- Tell students to show their ads to a partner and say: *I need / want to buy . . .*
- Walk around and, when appropriate, ask: *What's it made of?* or *Why do you need / want to buy it?*

Progress Check

Can you . . . count your change and read a store ad?

Say: *We have practiced counting change and reading store ads. Now, look at the question at the bottom of the page. Can you count your change and read a store ad?* Tell students to write a checkmark in the box.

Lesson 4 Pay for things

3 READ A SALES RECEIPT

PAIRS. Read the store sales receipt. Answer...

- Tell students to look at the receipt. Ask: *What is the name of the store?* (Mayfield Department Store)
- Tell students to read the questions and circle the answers on the receipt.
- Point out the difference between *What's the discount?* (30%) and *How much is the discount?* ($9). Explain that *subtotal* is the purchase amount before tax.
- Pair students and tell them to take turns asking and answering the questions.
- Tell students to write the answers next to the questions.
- Ask: *How much is the sales tax?* (6%) *What state is Mayfield Department Store in?* (Florida) *How much is sales tax on clothes in our state?*

4 PRACTICE

A PAIRS. Read the store ad on page 52 again....

- Pair students. Tell them to look at the items and discounts on the receipts and compare them with the discounts in the ad.
- Tell pairs to compare their answers with another pair.

EXPANSION: Vocabulary practice for 4A

- Ask students to bring in receipts—for clothes, if possible.
- Give them a list of things to find: the name of the store, the date of the purchase, the item(s) purchased, the discount(s), the purchase cost before tax, the tax, the cash paid, the change.

Controlled Practice   5 minutes

B Read and listen to the conversation....

- Play CD 1, Track 40. Students read along silently.
- Ask: *Which receipt goes with this conversation?* (Receipt 1) *What's the mistake?* (The ad says all swimwear is 30 percent off. The receipt says 20 percent off.)
- Resume playing Track 40. Students listen and repeat.

Communicative Practice   10 minutes

C PAIRS. Make new conversations. Use the...

- Pair students and tell them to practice the conversation in Exercise 4B and to take turns playing each role.
- Read the directions for Exercise 4C.
- Copy the conversation onto the board. Substitute blanks for the underlined information. Read through the conversation. When you come to a blank, fill it in with information from the receipts (for example, *all flip-flops are $5.00 / $85.00*).
- Ask two on-level students to practice the conversation in front of the class.
- Tell pairs to take turns playing each role and to use information in the incorrect sales receipts.
- Tell students to stand, mingle, and practice the conversation with several new partners.
- Call on pairs to perform for the class.

MULTILEVEL INSTRUCTION for 4C

Pre-level Before they practice, each student chooses a different receipt and fills in A's lines. When it's their turn to play A, students read the lines from their books.

Above-level Pairs practice the conversation again. Tell them to cover the conversation and look only at the receipts.

5 LIFE SKILLS WRITING

Turn to page 258 and ask students to complete the personal check. See page T-xii for guidelines.

Progress Check

Can you . . . read a sales receipt?

Say: *We have practiced reading sales receipts. Now, look at the question at the bottom of the page. Can you read a sales receipt?* Tell students to write a checkmark in the box.

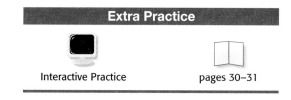

Extra Practice
Interactive Practice   pages 30–31

3 READ A SALES RECEIPT

PAIRS. Read the store sales receipt. Answer the questions.

```
◆ MAYFIELD ◆
DEPARTMENT STORE
      07/28/10

Women's Swimwear
1 swimsuit          $30.00
Discount 30%         -9.00
Subtotal             21.00
FL Sales Tax 6%       1.26
Total                22.26
CASH
                     30.00
Change
                      7.74
```

1. What is the date on the receipt? July 28, 2010

2. What is the discount on the swimsuit? 30%

3. How much does the swimsuit cost before tax? $21.00

4. How much is it after tax? $22.26

5. How much change does the customer get? $7.74

4 PRACTICE

A **PAIRS. Read the store ad on page 52 again. Then check the discounts and prices on the receipts. Circle the three mistakes, according to the information in the ad.**

1.
```
◆ MAYFIELD ◆
DEPARTMENT STORE
     07/25/10

Men's Swimwear
1 swimsuit          $25.00
Discount 20%         -5.00
Subtotal             20.00
FL Sales Tax 6%       1.20
Total               $21.20
CASH                 21.20
Change                0.00
```
ld be 30%

2.
```
◆ MAYFIELD ◆
DEPARTMENT STORE
     07/26/10

Men's Footwear
1 flip-flops        $85.00
Discount 50%        -42.50
Subtotal             42.50
FL Sales Tax 6%       2.55
Total               $45.05
CASH                 50.00
Change                4.95
```
price is $5, and $2.50 on sale

3.
```
◆ MAYFIELD ◆
DEPARTMENT STORE
     07/27/10

Women's Accessories
1 sunglasses        $30.00
Discount 30%         -9.00
Subtotal             21.00
FL Sales Tax 6%       1.26
Total               $22.26
CASH                 23.00
Change                0.74
```
should be 40% off

CD1 T40

B **Read and listen to the conversation. Then listen and repeat.**

A: Excuse me. I think there's a mistake. The ad says all swimwear is 30 percent off.

B: Yes, that's right.

A: But my receipt says 20 percent off.

B: Oh, I'm sorry. I'll take care of that.

C **PAIRS. Make new conversations. Use the information in the incorrect sales receipts in Exercise A.**

5 LIFE SKILLS WRITING

Write a personal check. See page 258.

Can you...read a sales receipt? ☐

Talk about shopping plans

Listening and Speaking

1 BEFORE YOU LISTEN

CLASS. Look at the pictures of someone running errands. Where did the man go? What other errands do people run?

2 LISTEN

CD1 T41

A Listen to the conversation between Debbie and her son Antonio. Complete the sentences.

1. They are talking about plans for _____.
   a. today   (b.) tomorrow

2. _____ is going to relax tomorrow.
   (a.) Antonio   b. Debbie

3. _____ is going to be busy tomorrow.
   a. Antonio   (b.) Debbie

CD1 T41

B Listen again. Number Debbie's activities in the order you hear them.

___3___ go to the supermarket

___1___ go to the ATM

___2___ go to the hardware store

CD1 T42

C Listen to the whole conversation. Complete the sentence.

After the conversation, Antonio _____.
(a.) takes a nap   b. goes to the deli   c. goes to work

Getting Started 5 minutes

1 **BEFORE YOU LISTEN**

CLASS. **Look at the pictures of someone...**

- Say: *Look at the pictures of someone running errands.* On the board, write *run errands* and elicit a definition (for example, *go places and do things you need to do*).
- Say: *Look at the pictures again. Where did the man go to buy meat and cheese?* (the deli) *Where did he go to get money?* (the ATM) *Where did he go to wash clothes?* (the Laundromat) *Where did he go to buy paint and a ladder?* (the hardware store)
- Say the names of the places and ask students to point and repeat.
- Ask: *What other errands do people run?* Write students' ideas on the board (for example, *go to the supermarket, go to the post office, go to the bank*).
- *Optional:* Ask: *What errands do you like to run? What errands do you not like to run?*

Presentation 10 minutes

2 **LISTEN**

A **Listen to the conversation between...**

- Read the directions.
- Say: *Point to Debbie. Point to Antonio.* Ask: *What is their relationship?* (Antonio is Debbie's son. / Debbie is Antonio's mother.)
- Tell students to read the sentences and answer choices silently.
- Play CD 1, Track 41. Students listen and complete the sentences.
- Call on students to read the completed sentences.
- Ask: *Who needs to run a lot of errands tomorrow?* (Debbie)

Teaching Tip

Optional: Remember that if students need additional support, tell them to read the Audio Script on page 299 as they listen to the conversations.

Controlled Practice 10 minutes

B **Listen again. Number Debbie's...**

- Read the directions and the items.
- Play Track 41 again.
- Say: *First, she needs to . . . Then she needs to . . . Then she's going to . . .* and tell the class to call out the errands.
- Ask: *What does Antonio want to do tomorrow?* (nothing, relax)

C **Listen to the whole conversation....**

- Tell students to read the sentence and answer choices silently.
- Play CD 1, Track 42. Students listen and complete the sentences.
- Ask: *Is Antonio going to relax tomorrow?* (No.) *What is he going to do?* (help his mother)
- Read the item and elicit the answer from the class. Ask: *Why?* (He got tired just thinking about tomorrow.) *Do you think Antonio's answer is funny?*

EXPANSION: Listening and writing practice for 2C

- Play Track 42 again.
- Tell students to listen and write a list of errands for Antonio (*1. go to the laundromat, 2. go to the deli, 3. go to the drug store*).
- Students compare lists with a partner.

3 CONVERSATION

A 🔘 Listen. Then listen and repeat.

- Read the Pronunciation Watch note. Tell students to look at the examples and underline *going to*.
- Tell students to look at what comes after *going to*. Ask: *Is there another verb?* Tell students to circle the verbs.
- Check that students circled *relax* and *stop*.
- Tell students to look at the first pair of examples. Ask: *Does* going to *come before another verb?* (Yes.) Say each sentence twice, once with *going to* and once with *"gonna."* Tell students that both are correct.
- Tell students to look at the second pair of examples. Ask: *Does* going to *come before another verb?* (No.) Say the sentence with *going to*. On the board, write and then cross out: *I'm "gonna" the post office.*
- Say *"gonna"* several times and ask the class to repeat. Tell them to use *"gonna"* when they repeat the first pair of examples and *going to* when they repeat the second pair of examples.
- Play CD 1, Track 43. Students listen.
- Resume playing Track 43. Students listen and repeat.

Controlled Practice   20 minutes

B 🔘 Listen and repeat the conversation.

- Note: This conversation is the same one students heard in Exercise 2A on page 54.
- Tell students to read the conversation silently and underline *going to*, and then tell them to look at the words after *going to* and circle any verbs.
- Check that students circled *relax* and *stop*. Ask: *Can these sentences use the pronunciation* "gonna"? (Yes.) Tell students to write *"gonna"* in parentheses above the two sentences.
- Play CD 1, Track 44. Students listen and repeat.

4 PRACTICE

A PAIRS. Practice the conversation. Then make new...

- Pair students and tell them to practice the conversation in Exercise 3B. Tell them to take turns playing each role.

- Then, in Exercise 4A, tell students to look at the information in the boxes. Say each word or expression and ask the class to repeat.
- Read the directions.
- Copy the conversation onto the board and complete it with words from the boxes.
- Play A and practice with a student. Switch roles.
- Tell pairs to take turns playing each role and to use the boxes to fill in the blanks.
- Walk around and listen to students' pronunciation of *"gonna" relax* and *"gonna" stop*. As needed, pronounce the words and ask students to repeat.
- Tell students to stand, mingle, and practice the conversation with several new partners.
- Call on pairs to perform for the class.

Communicative Practice   10 minutes

B MAKE IT PERSONAL. PAIRS. Talk about...

- Tell students to write a list of errands they need to run this week. Write your own list on the board as an example. Remind students that they can use the places in the pictures in Exercise 1 on page 54 and in the boxes in Exercise 4A.
- At the top of your list on the board, write: *I need to go to . . .* Play B and model the conversation with an above-level student. Point to the errands on your list as you answer A's question. Then switch roles and ask the student: *What errands do you need to run?*
- Pair students and tell them to take turns playing A and B.

▬ MULTILEVEL INSTRUCTION for 4B

Cross-ability The above-level student plays B first. After both partners have practiced both roles, the above-level student closes his or her book and the pre-level student asks A's question again.

Extra Practice

Interactive Practice

3 CONVERSATION

A 🔊 **Listen. Then listen and repeat.**

going to   I'm going to relax.
                      I'm going to stop at the bank.

going to   I'm going to the post office.
                      You're going to the store with me.

> **Pronunciation Watch**
>
> In informal conversation, *going to* often has the pronunciation "gonna" when it comes before another verb. It does not have this pronunciation when it is the only verb.

B 🔊 **Listen and repeat the conversation.**

Debbie: So, what are your plans for tomorrow?

Antonio: Nothing. I'm going to relax. Why?

Debbie: Well, I have a lot to do. First, I need to go to the ATM. Then I need to go to the hardware store. Then I'm going to stop at the supermarket.

Antonio: Wow. You're going to be busy.

4 PRACTICE

A **PAIRS. Practice the conversation. Then make new conversations. Use the information in the boxes.**

A: So, what are your plans for tomorrow?

B: Nothing. I'm going to relax. Why?

A: Well, I have a lot to do. First, I need to go to the   .
Then I need to go to the   . Then I'm going
to stop at the   .

B: Wow. You're going to be busy.

library
drugstore
bank

grocery store
deli
post office

bakery
gas station
laundromat

B MAKE IT PERSONAL. PAIRS. **Talk about the errands you need to run this week.**

A: *What errands do you need to run?*
B: *Tomorrow I need to go to my son's school. Then I need to . . .*

Talk about shopping plans

Grammar

Be going to

Affirmative					Negative				
I	**'m**				I	**'m not**			
We				tomorrow.	We	**'re not**			tomorrow.
They	**'re**	**going to**	relax	on Thursday.	They	**aren't**	**going to**	run errands	on Thursday.
				next week.					next week.
He					He	**'s not**			
She	**'s**				She	**isn't**			

1 PRACTICE

A Complete the sentences. Use the correct forms of *be going to*. Use contractions if possible.

Grammar Watch

we are = **we aren't** = **we're not**

he is = **he isn't** = **he's not**

1. She _'s going to_ stop at the post office later.

2. I _'m going to_ cash my check after work.

3. They _'re going to_ return the movies to the video store tomorrow.

4. Dan ___ is going to ___ buy some bread at the bakery tonight.

5. My mom ___ is going to ___ take the car to the car wash this weekend.

6. You _'re going to_ pick up the kids after school tomorrow.

B Complete the sentences. Use the correct forms of *be going to* and the words in parentheses.

1. The clothes are dirty. My brother ___ is going to take ___ them to the laundromat.
   (take)

2. There's a big sale at Griffon's on Saturday. The parking lot ___ is going to be ___ crowded.
   (be)

3. We need to run a lot of errands. We _'re not going to have_ time to relax.
   (not have)

4. Sally ___ is going to work ___ late. She _'s not going to cook_ dinner.
   (work) (not cook)

5. Hector and Maria ___ are going to see ___ a movie tonight. Their kids
   (see)
   ___ are going to stay ___ home with their grandmother.
   (stay)

6. I _'m going to get_ a ride to work tomorrow. I _'m not going to take_ the bus.
   (get) (not take)

Lesson 6 Talk about shopping plans

Getting Started
5 minutes

- Say: *We're going to study* be going to *to talk about the future. In the conversation on page 55, Antonio and Debbie used this grammar.*
- Play CD 1, Track 44. Students listen. On the board, write: *I'm going to stop at the supermarket.* Underline *'m going to.*

Presentation
15 minutes

Be going to

- Copy the grammar charts onto the board or show the charts on Transparency 3.4 and cover the exercise.
- On the board, write: be going to + *base form of a verb*. Say: *Use* be going to *to talk about the future.* Say the future time expressions from the charts (*tomorrow, on Thursday, next week*) and ask the class to repeat.
- Circle *be* in *be going to* on the board. Ask: *What are the forms of* be? Elicit and write *am, is,* and *are.* Say the contractions in the affirmative chart and ask the class to repeat. On the board, write: *You + are = _____* and *It + is = _____.* Elicit and write *You're* and *It's.*
- Read the sentences in the affirmative chart and ask the class to repeat.
- Write *be + not + going to* on the board. Say the contractions in the negative chart and ask the class to repeat.
- Read the Grammar Watch note. On the board, write: *You are not = _____* and *It is not = _____.* Elicit two contractions for each and write them on the board: *You're not / You aren't, It's not / It isn't.* Say: *You can review all of the contractions with* be *on page 286.*
- Read the sentences in the negative chart and ask the class to repeat.
- If you are using the transparency, do the exercise with the class.

Controlled Practice
30 minutes

1 **PRACTICE**

Ⓐ Complete the sentences. Use the correct...

- Read the directions. Tell students to circle *be* in *be going to* in the directions. Say: *Be is the only word you need to change.*
- Write item 1 on the board. Circle *'s* and ask: *Why is this the answer?* (because *is / 's* is the form of *be* that goes with *she*)
- Tell students to use contractions when the subject is a pronoun. Ask: *Which items do not have pronoun subjects?* (items 4 and 5)
- Students compare answers with a partner. Tell them to take turns reading the sentences out loud.

▬▬ **EXPANSION: Grammar practice for 1A**

- Tell students to rewrite the sentences in Exercise 1A in the negative (for example, *She's not going to stop . . .*).
- Then tell students to read their negative sentences to a partner. The partner has to restate the sentence using the other way to construct the contraction with *not* (for example, *She isn't going to stop . . .*).
- Point out that there is only one way to make item 2 negative (*I'm not going to . . .*).

▬▬ **EXPANSION: Writing practice for 1A**

- Pair students and tell them to underline the future time expressions in Exercise 1A.
- Tell them to choose three of the expressions and write their own sentences with *be going to* (for example, *I'm going to make dinner after work.*).
- Students read their sentences to their partner.

Ⓑ Complete the sentences. Use the correct forms of...

- Read the directions.
- Write item 1 on the board. Point to *take* in the answer and in parentheses and ask: *Does the verb after* to *change?* (No.)
- Remind students to use contractions when the subject is a pronoun.
- To check answers, write the numbers from 2 to 6 on the board. Ask students to write only the answers on the board, and ask the class to check them. Make and discuss any necessary corrections.

2 PRACTICE

A PAIRS. Look at the pictures. Talk about what...

- Tell students to look at the pictures. Say each place and ask the class to repeat.
- Read the directions. Pair students and tell them to first brainstorm ideas for each picture (for example, for grocery store: *buy milk, shop for food, pick up something for dinner*).
- Ask an above-level student to read the example. Model continuing the activity by saying another sentence about picture 1 (for example, *He's going to buy stamps.*).
- Form new pairs. Tell partners to take turns saying sentences about each picture and to say as many sentences as they can.
- For each picture, call on a pair to say their sentences.

MULTILEVEL INSTRUCTION for 2A

Pre-level Tell students to look at the example and underline the words they need to change to talk about the other pictures. Check that they underline: *1, man, send a package.* (In picture 3, *is* also changes to *are.*)

Above-level Tell students to say where the person is going (*The woman is going to the ATM.*) and what the person is going to do (*She's going to get cash.*). Tell students to say *going to* in the first sentence and *"gonna"* in the second.

B WRITE. On a separate piece of paper, write a...

- Point to picture 2 in Exercise 2A. Elicit a sentence from the class and write it on the board.
- Walk around and check for the correct form of *be going to* + the base form of a verb.
- Ask students to write any one of their sentences on the board. Read each sentence and ask the class to make any necessary corrections. Then the class guesses the picture by calling out the place.

Communicative Practice   15 minutes

Show what you know!

STEP 1. Think of an errand. Don't tell your classmates....

- Read the directions.
- Brainstorm errands and write them on the board. For ideas, tell students to look at Exercise 2A on page 51, Exercise 1 on page 54, Exercise 4A on page 55, Exercise 1A on page 56, and Exercise 2A on page 57. Begin each errand with the base form of a verb.
- Say the errands on the board and ask the class to repeat.
- Tell students to choose an errand from the board and think about how to act it out.

STEP 2. GROUPS OF 5. Play charades. Student A,...

- Choose an errand from the board to act out (not *stop at the bank*). Act out the errand and then read the example. Play A. Ask an on-level student to play B and an above-level student to play C and make a guess by completing C's line.
- Tell students to highlight or underline *You're going to . . .* in the conversation.
- Form groups of 5. Tell students to take turns acting out an errand. Tell them to use *You're going to . . .* to make guesses and to play three rounds.
- Ask each group to act out an errand for the class to guess.

EXPANSION for STEP 2

- After Step 2, call on students to report what a group member is going to do (for example, *Usman is going to take the car to the car wash.*).

Progress Check

Can you . . . talk about shopping plans?

Say: *We have practiced talking about shopping plans. Now, look at the question at the bottom of the page. Can you talk about shopping plans?* Tell students to write a checkmark in the box.

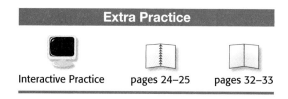

Extra Practice

Interactive Practice   pages 24–25   pages 32–33

A PAIRS. Look at the pictures. Talk about what the people are going to do. There is more than one correct answer.

Answers will vary.

In picture 1, the man is going to send a package.

B WRITE. On a separate piece of paper, write a sentence for each picture in Exercise A.

Show what you know! Talk about shopping plans

STEP 1. Think of an errand. Don't tell your classmates. Think about how you can act it out.

STEP 2. GROUPS OF 5. Play charades. Student A, go first. Act out an errand. Other students, guess the errand.

A: *What am I going to do?*
B: *You're going to stop at the bank.*
A: *No.*
C: *You're going to . . .*

You're going to . . .

Can you...talk about shopping plans? ☐

Reading

1   BEFORE YOU READ

PAIRS. What are the different ways to pay for large purchases, such as a TV or furniture?

2   READ

CD1 T45

Listen. Read the article.

How would you like to pay for that?

Are you thinking of making a big purchase soon, like a big-screen TV or a new computer? What is the best way to pay for it? We interviewed three shoppers who just bought a new $475 Sonpanic TV.

Each shopper paid for the TV in a different way. Read how each shopper paid for the TV. Then compare how much it really cost them. You may be surprised by the differences!

Brian
Advantage

Credit Card

"I paid with my credit card. I like to use my credit card because it gives me time to pay the bill. I can buy something in October, but I don't get the bill until November. <u>I get a month to make my payment</u>. I make sure to pay the total amount on the bill. That way I don't have to pay the credit card company any interest."

Cost of Sonpanic TV	$475.00
5% sales tax	+ $23.75
Total cost of the TV	$498.75

Cindy
Advantage

Credit Card

"I paid with my credit card. I like to pay with credit because I never have enough money to pay for big purchases. The credit card <u>lets me pay just a small amount every month</u>. <u>The problem is that it takes a long time to pay off the whole bill. And I pay a lot of interest to the credit card company.</u>"

Disadvantage

Minimum monthly payment	$10.00
Number of months	× 98
Total cost of the TV	$980.00

Getting Started

1 **BEFORE YOU READ**

PAIRS. What are the different ways to pay...

- Tell the class to look at the picture. Ask: *What is the customer buying?* (a flat-screen TV)
- Pair students and tell them to answer the question in the directions.
- Ask the class: *What are the different ways to pay for large purchases, such as a TV or furniture?* Write students' ideas on the board (for example, *cash, check, credit card, store credit, financing*).
- Explain terms as needed. For example, *financing* means the store or another company such as a bank lends you money and charges you interest.
- Ask: *What are some other large purchases?* Write students' ideas on the board, for example, *appliances (refrigerator, washer and dryer, etc.), a computer, a cell phone.* As needed, point out that *large* refers to the cost, not the size of the product.

Presentation

2 **READ**

 Listen. Read the article.

- Read the title of the article. Ask: *Who says* How would you like to pay for that? (a cashier)
- Play CD 1, Track 45. Students listen and follow along silently.

- Ask: *What did each shopper buy?* (a Sonpanic TV) *How much does a Sonpanic TV cost?* ($475) *How much is the sales tax?* ($23.75) *What's the total cost of a Sonpanic TV?* ($498.75)
- Say: *Point to Brian. How did he pay for the TV?* (credit card) *What does he like about paying with credit?* (It gives him a month to pay the bill.) *Does he pay the whole balance or make the minimum monthly payment?* (He pays the whole balance.) *So, when Brian gets his credit card bill with the TV on it, how much does he pay?* ($498.75)
- Say: *Point to Cindy. How did she pay for the TV?* (credit card) *Why does she like to pay with a credit card?* (She never has enough money for big purchases.) *Does she pay the whole balance or make the minimum monthly payment?* (She makes the minimum monthly payment.) *So, when Cindy gets her credit card bill with the TV on it, how much does she pay?* ($10) *How many payments does she need to make?* (98) *How much does the TV cost her?* ($980.00)
- Say: *Point to Craig. How did he pay for the TV?* (rent-to-own) *Why did he buy his TV at the rent-to-own store?* (because he doesn't have a lot of money and he doesn't have a credit card) *How much does he pay every week?* ($24) *How many payments does he need to make?* (52) *How much does the TV cost him?* ($1,248)
- Ask: *What's the least expensive way to pay for the TV?* (pay the whole balance on your credit card) *What's the most expensive way?* (rent-to-own)

Controlled Practice 20 minutes

3 CHECK YOUR UNDERSTANDING

A Read the article again. What's the purpose of...

- Read the Reading Skill note. Ask: *What are some reasons that authors write articles?* Write students' ideas on the board (for example, *to give information, to express an opinion, to tell a story, to compare and contrast*).
- Ask: *Why did the author write this article?* Students circle the number of the correct answer.
- Read each answer choice. Tell students to raise their hands for the answer they chose.
- Ask: *How do you know? How many different ways to pay does the author write about?* (three) *What do the calculations show?* (the real cost of each way to pay)
- Ask: *What is the real cost of the $498.75 TV when you make the minimum monthly payments on your credit card bill?* ($980) *What is the real cost of the $498.75 TV when you rent-to-own?* ($1,248)

B Underline the advantages and disadvantages of...

- Read the directions. Tell students to look at the chart.
- Ask: *What's good about paying the whole balance on your credit card? What's bad about paying the whole balance on your credit card?* Tell students to write *good* above *Advantages* and *bad* above *Disadvantages.*
- Tell students to read the article again and, if possible, underline the advantages in one color and the disadvantages in another. Students can also underline the words *Advantages* and *Disadvantages* in the chart in their corresponding colors.
- Students compare the advantages and disadvantages they underlined with a partner.
- Say: *Complete the chart. Read the information you underlined in the article. Write notes on the chart.* To model, ask a student to read the advantages he or she underlined for *Credit card (pay the whole amount).* Elicit notes to write in the chart from the class.
- Draw the chart on the board. Call on students to write the advantages and disadvantages. Review as a class.

C PAIRS. Which is the best way to pay for the...

- Tell students to look at the chart and circle the best way to pay for the TV.
- Pair students. Say: *Student A, ask the questions in the directions. Student B, answer with the way to pay that you circled and its advantages.*
- Walk around and help students form sentences from their notes as needed.

Communicative Practice 15 minutes

Show what you know!

PRE-WRITING. PAIRS. **Think about an expensive...**

- Say: *Think about something expensive you want to buy.* Tell students to note the item they want to buy.
- Ask: *How will you pay for it? Will you use one of the ways to pay from the chart? Or will you save up and pay cash? Will you use another way?*
- Pair students. On the board, write: *the purchase you want to make, how you're going to pay for it, and the advantages/disadvantages of your way to pay.*
- Model the activity. Name an expensive purchase you want to make. Talk about the points on the board.
- Tell partners to talk about the points on the board.
- Call on two above-level students to tell the class about the purchase their partners want to make.

■■■ MULTILEVEL INSTRUCTION for PRE-WRITING
Cross-ability The higher-level student asks questions to prompt the lower-level student: *What is the product? How are you going to pay for it? What are the advantages of your way to pay? What are the disadvantages?*

WRITE. **Write about how you are going to pay...**

Ask students to turn to page 269 and complete the activity. See page T-xii for general notes about the Writing activities.

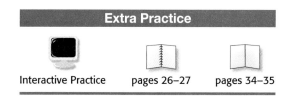

Extra Practice		
Interactive Practice	pages 26–27	pages 34–35

Rent-to-Own

"I bought my TV at the rent-to-own store because I don't have a lot of money right now, and I don't have a credit card. At a rent-to-own store, <u>I can get a new TV and bring it home the same day. If I move, or I don't have enough money, I can return the TV to the store.</u> Every week, I pay $24. <u>At the end of the year, the TV belongs to me.</u>"

Craig

Advantage

Disadvantage

Weekly payment	$24.00
Number of weeks	× 52
Real cost of the TV	$1,248.00

3 CHECK YOUR UNDERSTANDING

Reading Skill:
Identifying Purpose

Authors write articles for different reasons. This is the author's purpose. Knowing the author's purpose helps you understand the main idea.

A Read the article again. What's the purpose of the article? How do you know?

1. To compare the real cost of different ways to pay.
2. To recommend the Sonpanic TV.
3. To tell shoppers to pay for TVs with a credit card.

B Underline the advantages and disadvantages of each way to pay in the article. Then complete the chart. Answers will vary but could include:

Ways to pay	Advantages	Disadvantages
Credit card (pay the whole amount)	• have a month to make payment • don't pay interest	none
Credit card (pay the minimum amount)	• can pay small amount at a time	• takes a long time to pay bill • pay a lot of interest
Rent-to-own	• can bring TV home same day • can return TV	• pay every week • takes a year to own TV

C PAIRS. Which is the best way to pay for the Sonpanic TV? Why?

Show what you know!

PRE-WRITING. PAIRS. Think about an expensive product you want to buy. How are you going to pay for it? Explain your answer.

WRITE. Write about how you are going to pay for your next expensive purchase. See page 269.

Describe problems with purchases

Listening and Speaking

1 BEFORE YOU LISTEN

PAIRS. Look at the pictures. What's the problem with each piece of clothing?
Match the pictures to the reasons for returning clothes.

> There's a hole in it.   It's too tight.   A button is missing.
> They're too loose.   ~~The zipper is broken~~.   A seam is ripped.

1

The zipper is broken.

2

They're too loose.

3

A button is missing.

4

There's a hole in it.

5

A seam is ripped.

6

It's too tight.

2 LISTEN

A   **CLASS.** Look at the picture of two roommates, Shu-Chi and Kelly.
Guess: What are they talking about?

B CD1 T46   Listen to the conversation. Was your guess correct?

C CD1 T46   Listen again. Read the sentences. Circle *True* or *False*.

1. Kelly needs to buy a jacket.   True   (**False**)
2. There is a problem with Kelly's jacket.   (**True**)   False
3. Shu-Chi wants to buy a dress.   True   (**False**)

D CD1 T47   Listen to the whole conversation. Complete the sentence.

Shu-Chi's dress is really a ____shirt____.

Getting Started
10 minutes

1 BEFORE YOU LISTEN

PAIRS. Look at the pictures. What's the problem...

- Tell the class to look at the photos. Elicit the name of each item of clothing (*a jacket, pants, a shirt, a scarf, a sweater, a dress*).
- Read the directions. Ask: *When you return something, where do you take it?* (back to the store where you bought it) *What do you get?* (your money back)
- Read the reasons for returning clothes and ask the class to repeat.
- If necessary, use clothing in the classroom to explain new words such as *hole, loose, tight, zipper, broken, button, missing, seam,* and *ripped.*
- Tell students to look at picture 1. Ask: *What's the problem?* (The zipper is broken.)
- Tell students to match as many pictures and reasons for returning clothes as they can.
- Students compare answers with a partner.
- Ask: *What's the problem with each piece of clothing?* Call on students to say the reason for each picture.
- *Optional:* Elicit other reasons that people return clothes and write them on the board (for example, *It's / They're too big. It's / They're too small. The hem is ripped. There's a spot on it / them.*).

> **Culture Connection**
> - Ask: *Do you sometimes return clothes or other purchases? Do you feel comfortable taking something back to the store where you bought it?*
> - Explain: *In the U.S., it's usually not a problem for customers to return purchases. Most stores have a* return policy, *or rules for returning purchases, posted near the cash registers.*
> - Ask: *What kinds of rules about returns do stores have?* Write *You need to . . .* on the board. Brainstorm and list students' ideas. Then read the sentences out loud (for example, *You need to have a receipt / return items in a certain amount of time / keep tags on the item / keep the item sealed*).
> - Ask: *Is it easy to return purchases in your country? Do stores have similar rules?*

Presentation
15 minutes

2 LISTEN

Ⓐ CLASS. Look at the picture of two roommates....

- Read the directions. Say: *Point to Shu-Chi. Point to Kelly. What is their relationship?* (They're roommates.)
- Read the directions. Ask: *What are they talking about? Guess.* Write students' ideas on the board (for example, *a sale, what Kelly bought, a problem with a jacket*).

Ⓑ 💿 Listen to the conversation. Was your...

- Read the directions. Play CD 1, Track 46.
- Ask: *Was your guess correct?* Circle the correct answer on the board.

> **Teaching Tip**
>
> *Optional:* Remember that if students need additional support, tell them to read the Audio Script on page 299 as they listen to the conversations.

Ⓒ 💿 Listen again. Read the sentences....

- Read the directions. Tell students to read the sentences silently.
- Play Track 46 again. Students listen and circle *True* or *False.* Play the CD as often as necessary to aid students' comprehension.
- To check answers, ask students to read the sentences and call on classmates to say *True* or *False.*
- *Optional:* Tell students to rewrite the false sentences to make them true. (1. Kelly needs to <u>return</u> a jacket 3. Su-Chi wants to <u>return</u> a dress.)
- Ask: *What's the problem with Kelly's jacket?* (The zipper is broken.) As needed, play Track 46 again.

Ⓓ 💿 Listen to the whole conversation....

- Read the directions and the sentence.
- Ask: *What's the problem with Shu-Chi's dress?* (It's too short.) As needed, play Track 46 again.
- Play CD 1, Track 47.
- Call on a student to read the completed sentence.

Describe problems with purchases

Controlled Practice   20 minutes

3 CONVERSATION

Listen and repeat the conversation.

- Note: This conversation is the same one students heard in Exercise 2B on page 60.
- Tell students to read the conversation silently.
- Play CD 1, Track 48. Students listen and repeat.

EXPANSION: Writing practice for 4A

- Before students do Exercise 4A, tell them to close their books. List A's lines and B's lines on the board in random order. Pair students and tell them to write the conversation in order. Tell them that A speaks first.

4 PRACTICE

Ⓐ PAIRS. Practice the conversation. Then make....

- Pair students and tell them to practice the conversation in Exercise 3. Tell them to take turns playing each role.
- Tell students to look at the information in the boxes in Exercise 4A. Say each word or expression and ask the class to repeat.
- Read the directions.
- Copy the conversation onto the board with blanks. Read through the conversation. When you come to a blank, fill it in with a student's name or information from the boxes. As you fill in each blank, say the color of the answer space and point to the same-color word or phrase you choose from the boxes.
- Ask the student whose name you used and another on-level student to read the conversation on the board.
- Tell pairs to take turns playing each role and to use different information from the boxes to fill in the blanks.
- Tell students to stand, mingle, and practice the conversation with several new partners.
- Call on pairs to perform for the class.

Communicative Practice   15 minutes

Ⓑ ROLE PLAY. PAIRS. Make your own....

- On the board, draw a two-column chart with the headings *Singular* and *Plural*. Tell students to look at the reasons in Exercise 1 on page 60. Ask: *Which reasons are only for singular clothing words?* In the left-hand column, write: *There's a hole in it. It's too tight.* Ask: *Which reason is only for plural clothing words?* In the right-hand column, write: *They're too loose.*
- As a class, rewrite the singular sentences to make them plural and vice versa. Write the new sentences across from the original ones on the chart.
- Tell students to look at the conversation in Exercise 4A. Tell them to write *shorts* in B's first blank and *jeans* in A's next blank. Ask: *What other words need to change?* Tell students to circle the words (*this, a, it,* and *It's* in the conversation; *it* in the green box). Elicit the plural equivalents and tell students to write them above the circled words (*these, some / a pair of / them, They're, them*).
- Model the conversation with *shorts* and *jeans* with an above-level student. Make sure the reasons are also plural.
- Pair students and tell them to take turns playing A and B.
- Walk around and check for correct use of singular and plural.
- Call on pairs to role-play for the class. After a pair performs, ask the class: *What does [name] need to return? Why?*

MULTILEVEL INSTRUCTION for 4B

Pre-level Before practicing each part, students write the item of clothing and reason in the conversation. If the clothing word is plural, they also make any necessary changes to other words in the conversation.

Above-level After practicing both parts, each partner thinks of a clothing item and a reason to return it. Then partners close their books and practice the role play again.

Extra Practice

Interactive Practice

CONVERSATION

CD1 T48

Listen and repeat the conversation.

Shu-Chi: Hi Kelly. Where are you going?

Kelly: I'm going to Kohn's. I need to return this jacket.

Shu-Chi: How come?

Kelly: The zipper is broken.

Shu-Chi: That's annoying . . . Um, could you do me a favor?

Kelly: What is it?

Shu-Chi: Could you return a dress for me?

Kelly: Sure. What's wrong with it?

Shu-Chi: It's too short.

4 **PRACTICE**

A PAIRS. **Practice the conversation. Then make new conversations. Use the information in the boxes.**

> **A:** Hi, _____ . Where are you going?
>
> **B:** I'm going to Kohn's. I need to return this _____ .
>
> **A:** How come?
>
> **B:**
>
> **A:** That's annoying . . . Um, could you do me a favor?
>
> **B:** What is it?
>
> **A:** Could you return a _____ for me?
>
> **B:** Sure. What's wrong with it?
>
> **A:** It's too _____ .

blouse
windbreaker
sweater

A button is missing.
A seam is ripped.
There's a hole in it.

sweatshirt
coat
T-shirt

tight
long
big

B ROLE PLAY. PAIRS. **Make your own conversations. Use different items of clothing and reasons. Remember, some clothing words are plural. Make any changes necessary. For example:** *I need to return these pants.*

Grammar

Adverbs of degree: *very* / *too*

| It's | **very** | expensive. (It costs a lot of money.) |
| It's | **too** | expensive. (It's $100, but I only have $90.) |

· · · · · · **Grammar Watch**
- *very* = *a lot*
- *too* = *more than you need or want*

PRACTICE

A Complete the sentences. Underline *very* or *too*.

1. This raincoat doesn't cost a lot. It's **very** / **too** cheap.

2. She wears size 8. That dress is size 6. It's **very** / **too** small for her.

3. The prices at the clearance sale are **very** / **too** good. A lot of people are going to be there.

4. This sweater is **very** / **too** pretty. I want to buy it.

5. I can't wear these shoes. They're **very** / **too** tight.

6. This scarf is **very** / **too** colorful. It looks great with my coat.

B Complete the conversations. Write *very* or *too*.

1. **A:** We can't go to the store now because it's ____too____ late. The store closes in ten minutes.

   B: Well, we can go tomorrow morning. It opens at 8:00.

   A: That's ____too____ early for me. I get up at 9:00 on Saturdays.

2. **A:** The coffee shop on Oak Street is ____very____ good. I get coffee and egg sandwiches for breakfast there sometimes.

   B: I think the service there is ____too____ slow. I'm always late for school when I stop there.

3. **A:** Let me see your new blouse . . . . Oh, it's ____very____ beautiful.

   B: Thanks. But it's ____too____ big. I need to exchange it for a smaller size.

4. **A:** This coat is ____very____ warm. It's perfect for cold winter days.

   B: Are you going to buy it?

   A: No, it's ____too____ expensive. It's $90, and I only have $60.

Getting Started

5 minutes

- Say: *We're going to study* very *and* too. *In the conversation on page 61, Shu-Chi used this grammar.*
- Play CD 1, Track 48. Students listen. On the board, write: *It's too short.* Underline *too*.

Presentation

5 minutes

Adverbs of degree: *very / too*

- Copy the grammar chart onto the board or show Transparency 3.5.
- Circle *expensive* in both examples and write the label *adjective*. Tell the class that *very* and *too* come in front of adjectives.
- Read the Grammar Watch note.
- Read the first sentence in the grammar chart. Say: *But it's possible for me to buy it.* Read the second sentence. Say: *It's impossible for me to buy it.*
- To convey that *too* has negative implications, give several examples: *This skirt is too tight. It doesn't fit. I can't wear it. This food is too hot. I can't eat it.*
- If you are using the transparency, do the exercise with the class.

Controlled Practice

20 minutes

PRACTICE

A **Complete the sentences. Underline *very* or *too*.**

- Read item 1. Ask: *Is it possible to buy the raincoat?* (Yes.) *Is the answer* very *or* too? (*very*)
- Read item 2. Ask: *Is it possible for her to wear the dress?* (No.) *Is the answer* very *or* too? (*too*)

- Students compare answers with a partner. Tell them to take turns reading the sentences.
- To check answers, call on students to read the sentences for the class.

B **Complete the conversations. Write *very* or *too*.**

- Write item 1 on the board and read it. Ask: *Can they go to the store? Is it possible?* (No.) *Is the answer* very *or* too? (*too*)
- Students compare answers with a partner. Tell them to choose roles and read the conversations out loud.
- To check answers, call on pairs to read the conversations for the class.

EXPANSION: Grammar and writing practice for Exercise B

- Brainstorm adjectives and list them on the board.
- Pair students and tell them to choose one adjective and write sentences with *very* and sentences with *too*. For example, for *cold*: *It's <u>very</u> cold today. I'm going to wear my wool coat. / I don't want to go to the beach today. It's <u>too</u> cold.*
- Call on pairs to say their sentences for the class.

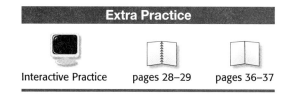

Extra Practice		
Interactive Practice	pages 28–29	pages 36–37

Show what you know!

1 GRAMMAR

Ⓐ Complete the conversation. Use the correct....

- Read the directions. Tell students to refer back to the grammar charts on page 50 (Simple present: *want / need* + infinitive) and page 56 (*Be going to*) as needed.
- On the board, write: want / need + *infinitive*; be going to + *base form of the verb*.
- Tell students to underline the subjects if they have difficulty. Remind them that an *infinitive* is *to* + base form of the verb.
- Students compare answers with a partner. Tell them to read the conversation out loud.
- To check answers, call on a pair to read the conversation for the class. Tell the pair to stop before A's last line. Ask the class: *What's A going to do?* (He's/She's going to run errands.) *What's B going to do?* (He's/She's going to relax at the swimming pool.) Tell A to read the last line and ask: *What's A going to do now?* (He's/She's going to relax at the swimming pool, too.)

Ⓑ WRITE. Look at the picture of customers....

- Read the directions. Tell students to refer back to the reasons for returns in the box on page 60 and the grammar chart on page 62 (Adverbs of degree: *very / too*).
- Tell students to look at what each customer is returning. Tell them to write the clothing word in parentheses next to each item number.
- Remind students to pay attention to whether the clothing word is singular or plural when they write the customer's reason.
- Walk around and check that students wrote singular reasons for items 2, 5, and 6 and plural reasons for items 3 and 4.

Ⓒ PAIRS. Compare your answers.

- Pair students and tell them to take turns pointing to each customer and saying the reason for the return.

▬ Expansion for 4C

- Tell pairs to role-play returning the items. On the board, write:

  Customer:

  Clerk:

  Customer:

- Elicit a model conversation and write it on the board. For example:

  Customer: I want to return this / these _____.

  Clerk: What's wrong with it / them?

  Customer: [Reason]

- Tell students to take turns playing the customer.
- Call on a pair to role-play each return for the class.

CD-ROM Practice

 Go to the CD-ROM for more practice.

If your students need more practice with the vocabulary, grammar, and competencies in Unit 3, encourage them to review the activities on the CD-ROM. This review can also help students prepare for the final role play on the following Expand page.

Extra Practice

pages 30–31

1 GRAMMAR

A Complete the conversation. Use the correct forms of the verbs. Use contractions if possible.

A: I think I _'m going to run_ some errands this afternoon.
(be going to / run)

B: Oh. What do you need to do?

A: First I ___ need to stop ___ at the bank. Then I _'m going to get groceries_.
(need / stop) (be going to / get groceries)

Why? What are your plans for today?

B: Well, I _'m going to relax_ at the swimming pool. I think it's open until 6:00.
(be going to / relax)

A: That sounds great. Can I come with you? Maybe I really ___ don't need to run ___
(not need / run)

any errands today after all!

B WRITE. Look at the picture of customers returning clothes at an exchange counter. Why are the people returning the clothes? Write a reason for each customer.

1. _It's too tight._
2. _The zipper is broken._
3. _The pants are too long._
4. _The shoes are too tight._
5. _The pocket seam is ripped._
6. _The shirt is too big._

C PAIRS. Compare your answers.

Go to the CD-ROM for more practice.

2 ACT IT OUT What do you say?

STEP 1. CLASS. Review the Lesson 2 conversation between Anwar and Maryan (CD 1 track 38).

STEP 2. ROLE PLAY. PAIRS. Talk about the clothes you want and need to buy. Make a list. Look at the pictures or use your own ideas.

3 READ AND REACT Problem-solving

STEP 1. Read about Lan's problem.

Lan's son lives in a city far away. He can't be with her on Mother's Day. He sends Lan flowers. Lan knows that the flowers are expensive. But the flowers are old and not very nice.

STEP 2. PAIRS. What is Lan's problem? What can she do? Here are some ideas.

- She can tell her son about the problem with the flowers.
- She can tell her son, "The flowers are beautiful."
- She can call the flower shop and ask for a refund.
- She can _____.

4 CONNECT

For your Goal-setting Activity, go to page 249.
For your Team Project, go to page 276.

Which goals can you check off? Go back to page 45.

2 ACT IT OUT

STEP 1. CLASS. Review the Lesson 2 conversation...

- Play CD 1, Track 38. Students listen.
- As needed, play Track 38 again to aid comprehension.

STEP 2. ROLE PLAY. PAIRS. Talk about the....

- Read the directions. Ask: *What's the weather like? What season is it? What clothing materials are good for this season?*
- Tell students to look at the pictures and circle the clothes they want or need. Tell them to use the clothes they circled and their own ideas to make a list of *clothes they want* and *clothes they need.* Tell them to add materials before some of the clothes on their lists.
- Pair students. Tell A to talk about the weather. Tell B to respond with clothes he or she needs or wants to buy for this season. Tell A to ask about the color or material of the item B is going to buy.
- Walk around and check that B is using *want / need* + infinitive correctly. Check that A is asking *What color are you going to buy?* or *What material are you going to buy?*
- Call on pairs to perform for the class. While pairs are performing, use the scoring rubric on page T-xiii to evaluate each student's vocabulary, grammar, fluency, and how well he or she completes the task.
- *Optional:* After each pair finishes, discuss the strengths and weakness of each performance either in front of the class or privately.

3 READ AND REACT

STEP 1. Read about Lan's problem.

- Say: *We are going to read about a student's problem, and then we need to think about a solution.*
- Read the directions.
- Read the story while students follow along silently. Pause after each sentence to allow time for students to comprehend. Periodically stop and ask simple *Wh-* questions to check comprehension (for example, *Where does Lan's son live? What does he send her for Mother's Day? What's the problem with the flowers?*).

STEP 2. PAIRS. What is Lan's problem? What....

- Ask: *What is Lan's problem?* (Lan's son sent her a gift of flowers, but there was a problem with the flowers.)
- Pair students. Read the ideas on the list. Give pairs a couple of minutes to discuss possible solutions for Lan.
- Ask: *Which ideas are good?* Call on students to say their opinion about the ideas in the box (for example, S: *I think she can call the flower shop because they made a mistake.*).
- Tell pairs to think of one new idea not in the box (for example, *She can call the flower shop and ask for new flowers.*) and to write it in the blank. Encourage students to think of more than one idea and to write them in their notebooks.
- Call on pairs to say their own solutions. Write them on the board and ask: *Do you think this is a good idea? Why or why not?*

MULTILEVEL INSTRUCTION for STEP 2

Pre-level Ask pairs to agree on one good idea.

Above-level Ask pairs to rank the ideas in the list (including their new idea) on a scale of 1–4 (1 = the best).

4 CONNECT

Turn to page 249 for the Goal-setting Activity and page 276 for the Team Project. See page T-xi for general notes about teaching these activities.

Progress Check

Which goals can you check off? Go back to page 45.

Ask students to turn to page 45 and check off any remaining goals they have reached. Call on students to say which goals they will practice outside of class.

4 Small Talk

Classroom Materials/Extra Practice

CD 1
Tracks 49–65

Transparencies 4.1–4.6
Vocabulary Cards Unit 4

MCA
Unit 4

Workbook
Unit 4

Interactive Practice
Unit 4

Unit Overview

Goals

- See the list of goals on the facing page.

Grammar

- Adverbs of frequency with action verbs and with *be*
- Questions with *How often* / frequency time expressions
- Simple present: *like* / *love* / *hate* + infinitive
- Modal: *have to*

Pronunciation

- Words with one unpronounced syllable
- "Hafta" and "hasta" for *have to* and *has to* in informal conversation

Reading

- Read about rude and polite behavior
- *Reading Skill:* Identifying topics

Writing

- List your weekend plans
- Write about your likes and dislikes
- Write about what is rude or polite in your country

Life Skills Writing

- Complete a library card application

Preview

- Set the context of the unit by asking questions about being social (for example, *Do you like to spend time with friends? What do you talk about? What do you like to do?*).
- Hold up page 65 or show Transparency 4.1. Read the unit title and ask the class to repeat.
- Explain: Small talk *is polite, friendly conversation about unimportant subjects.*
- Say: *Look at the picture.* Ask the Preview questions: *Where are the people?* (at a party, at a friend's house) *What are they doing?* (eating, drinking, talking)
- Ask: *What subjects do people talk about when they make small talk?* (the weather, movies, TV shows, sports, hobbies, weekend plans)

Unit Goals

- Point to the Unit Goals. Explain that this list shows what the class will be studying in this unit.
- Tell students to read the goals silently.
- Say each goal and ask the class to repeat. Explain the following vocabulary as needed:

    When you accept an invitation, you say "Yes."

    When you decline an invitation, you say "No."

- Tell students to circle one goal that is very important to them. Call on several students to say the goal they circled.
- Write a checkmark (✓) on the board. Say: *We will come back to this page again. You will write a checkmark next to the goals you learned in this unit.*

Small Talk

4

Preview

Look at the picture.
Where are the people?
What are they doing?

UNIT GOALS

- ☐ Talk about your weekend activities
- ☐ Plan activities using a calendar
- ☐ Complete a library card application
- ☐ Communicate likes and dislikes
- ☐ Invite someone to do something
- ☐ Accept or decline an invitation

1 WHAT DO YOU KNOW?

A CLASS. Look at the pictures. Which free-time activities do you know?

CD1 T49

B 🔘 Look at the pictures and listen. Listen again and repeat.

2 PRACTICE

A GROUPS OF 5. Play charades. Student A, go first. Act out a free-time activity. Other students, guess the activity.

B WORD PLAY. GROUPS OF 3. Look at the list of free-time activities. Which are outdoor activities? Which are indoor activities? Which can be both? Complete the chart.

Answers will vary but may include:

Indoor | **Outdoor**
Both

go dancing
go out to eat

go swimming
go jogging

go hiking
go fishing

Lesson 1 Vocabulary

Getting Started 10 minutes

1 WHAT DO YOU KNOW?

A CLASS. Look at the pictures. Which free-time activities...

- Show Transparency 4.2 or hold up the book. Tell students to cover the list of words on page 67.
- Read the directions. Elicit a free-time activity (for example, *Number 4 is* go fishing.).
- Students call out answers. Help students pronounce free-time activities if they have difficulty.
- If students call out an incorrect activity, change the students' answer to a question for the class (for example, *Number 2 is* go to the beach?). If nobody can identify the correct activity, tell students they will now listen to a CD and practice the names of the activities.

Presentation 10 minutes

B Look at the pictures and listen....

- Read the directions. Play CD 1, Track 49. Pause after number 12 (go *for a bike ride*).
- To check comprehension, say each free-time activity in random order and ask students to point to the appropriate picture.
- Resume playing Track 49. Students listen and repeat.

> **Teaching Tip**
>
> To make sure students are connecting the new words with their meanings, tell them to point to the pictures as they listen / listen and repeat.

Controlled Practice 15 minutes

2 PRACTICE

A GROUPS OF 5. Play charades. Student A,...

- Read the directions.
- Model the game: Act out a free-time activity (for example, *going jogging*). Ask the class to guess the activity.

- Form groups of 3. Students take turns playing the role of Student A.
- Walk around and check that students who are guessing use question intonation. Model as needed (for example: *Go jogging?*).
- To wrap up, call on a few individual students to act out a free-time activity while the class guesses.

MULTILEVEL INSTRUCTION for 2A
Pre-level Direct students to look at the pictures and the list of activities on page 67 for the first couple rounds of charades. Then tell them to look only at the list of activities and not the pictures when they guess.
Above-level After one round of charades, ask students to close their books when they guess.

B WORD PLAY. GROUPS OF 3. Look at the...

- Read the directions.
- Draw the chart on the board. Point to picture 1 and ask: *What activity is this?* (go hiking) *Is it an indoor activity, an outdoor activity, or can it be both indoor and outdoor?* (outdoor) Write *go hiking* on the right side of the diagram.
- Repeat with pictures 2 and 5 (*go swimming, go dancing*).
- Group students. Tell them to draw their own charts, talk about where people do each activity, and write the activities in the chart.
- To review, assign students numbers from 3 to 12 (skipping 5) and tell them to write the corresponding vocabulary item in the chart on the board.
- Ask the class if the activities are in the correct places in the chart. Point out that there may be different opinions about where to write the activities.

EXPANSION: Vocabulary and speaking practice for 2B

- Extend Exercise 2B. Ask the same groups of 3 to categorize the vocabulary in other ways. For example, ask: *Which activities are good exercise?*
- Give groups a minute to discuss, and then ask another question. Some possible questions: *Which activities are usually free? Which activities are sometimes expensive? Which activities do you like to do alone? Which activities do you like to do with friends or family?*

Communicative Practice   20 minutes

Learning Strategy: Make connections

- Read the directions.
- On the board, rewrite the examples, using the names of places in your community. Tell students to copy these examples into their notebooks. Say: *Thinking about places you know to* go hiking *and to* go swimming *helps you to remember this new vocabulary.*
- Tell students to add five different activities and places to their lists.
- Walk around, and if students misspell activities, tell them to check the list on page 67. Remind students that they can check the spelling of places in the community by asking you or one another: *How do you spell . . . ?*
- Call on students to read their sentences.
- Say: *You can remember new vocabulary when you think about places you know.* Remind students to use this strategy to remember other new vocabulary.

Community Building

- Extend the Learning Strategy activity. Tell students to stand, mingle, and compare the places they wrote.
- Tell them to add the names of other places to their lists. Suggest that students may learn about new places in the community to do the activities they enjoy.

Show what you know!

STEP 1. Look at the list of free-time activities....

- Read the directions.
- Model the step. On the board, write two activities from the list on page 67 that you do in your free time.
- Tell students to write two activities from the list or their own activities.
- Walk around and check spelling of students' own activities. As needed, help students to begin each activity with *go* or the base form of another verb.

STEP 2. GROUPS OF 4. Ask your group members...

- Read the directions. On the board, write *What do you do in your free time?* Say the question and ask the class to repeat.
- Model the step with three above-level students. Point to the question on the board and direct a group member to ask you the question. Answer with *I* + the activities you wrote on the board.
- Ask another group member the question. Write the student's name and activity on the board. Prompt that student to ask the last group member and the last group member to ask the first. Write the two students' names and activities on the board.
- Say: *Make sure each group member takes a turn asking and answering the question.*

STEP 3. Report to the class. What are the three...

- Read the directions.
- Tell students to look at list of people and activities on the board. As a class, decide which three activities are the most popular.
- Write on the board: *The three most popular activities in my group are. . . .* Elicit the complete sentence from the class.
- Ask one member of each group: *What are the three most popular activities in your group?* Students reply using the sentence on the board.

Community Building

- Tell students to stand, mingle, and ask classmates: *What do you do in your free time?*
- Say: *Look at your activities in Step 1. Write down the names of classmates who do the same activities in their free time.*
- *Optional:* Suggest that students make plans to spend free time with classmates who have the same interests.

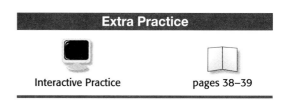

Extra Practice	
Interactive Practice	pages 38–39

3

4

7

8

Free-time Activities

1. go hiking
2. go swimming
3. go shopping
4. go fishing
5. go dancing
6. go jogging
7. go out to eat
8. go to the beach
9. go to the zoo
10. go to the park
11. go for a walk
12. go for a bike ride

Learning Strategy

Make connections

Look at the list of free-time activities. Think about your community. Where can you enjoy these activities? Write five activities and the name of a place where you can do each activity.

> go hiking—Blue Hills State Park
>
> go swimming—Kennedy School Pool

Show what you know!

STEP 1. Look at the list of free-time activities. Write two activities that you do in your free time. Answers will vary.

_____   _____

STEP 2. GROUPS OF 4. Ask your group members, *What do you do in your free time?* Write their names and activities on the lines.

Student 1: _____   _____

Student 2: _____   _____

Student 3: _____   _____

STEP 3. Report to the class. What are the three most popular activities in your group?

Listening and Speaking

1   **BEFORE YOU LISTEN**

A   **CLASS.** Look at the pictures of people taking classes. What other kinds of classes do people take?

B   **CLASS.** What classes do you take?

a guitar class

a computer class

2   **LISTEN**

CD1 T50

A   Look at the picture of Mario and his friend, Bi-Yun. Listen to the conversation. What are they talking about?

  (a.) weekend plans
  b. school
  c. swimming lessons

CD1 T50

B   Listen again. Answer the questions.

1. Who does Bi-Yun usually see on Sunday?

  (a.) her family   b. her friends

2. What does Mario usually do on Saturday mornings?

  a.    (b.)

CD1 T51

C   Listen to the whole conversation. Answer the question.

Which level class do you think Mario is in?

  (a.) beginning   b. intermediate   c. advanced

Talk about your weekend activities

Getting Started   5 minutes

1 BEFORE YOU LISTEN

A CLASS. **Look at the pictures of people...**

- Say: *Sometimes people take classes in their free time. Look at the pictures of people taking classes. What kinds of classes are they?* (a guitar class, a computer class)

- Ask: *What other kinds of classes do people take?* List students' ideas on the board (for example: *an English class, a Spanish class, a photography class, an exercise class, a swimming class*).

B CLASS. **What classes do you take?**

- Tell students to look at the list on the board.
- Ask: *What classes do you take?*
- Students who are not taking a class can talk about a class they would like to take.

EXPANSION: Speaking practice for 1B

- Tell students to choose one class they would like to take in the future. As homework, tell them to research a place in the community that offers the class. Suggest that students ask people, search online, or look in the phone book or newspaper.
- Tell students to contact the place and find out when the class meets, how much it costs, and what students need to bring to class. Tell students to write the information and bring it to class.
- At a later date, follow up by grouping students according to their interests and telling them to share the information they found.

Presentation   25 minutes

2 LISTEN

A **Look at the picture of Mario...**

- Read the directions.
- Say: *Point to Mario. Point to Bi-Yun. What is their relationship?* (friends)

- Play CD 1, Track 50. Students listen and circle the letter of the correct answer.
- Ask: *What are they talking about?* Direct the class to call out the answer.
- Ask the class: *Are they talking about something serious or making small talk?* (small talk)

> **Teaching Tip**
>
> *Optional:* Remember that if students need additional support, tell them to read the Audio Script on page 299 as they listen to the conversations.

B **Listen again. Answer the questions.**

- Read the directions. Tell students to read the questions silently.
- Tell students to look at the answer choices. Ask the class to identify the activities in the photos. (go to the beach, play the guitar / take a guitar class)
- Play Track 50 again. Students circle the letter of the correct answer.
- Students compare answers with a partner. Read the questions and ask the class to call out the answers.

C **Listen to the whole conversation....**

- To make sure students understand the meaning of the answer choices, ask: *Is our English class beginning, intermediate, or advanced?* As a class, discuss and decide whether the class is for students with little or no English, some English, or a lot of English.
- Play CD 1, Track 51. Students listen and circle the letter of the correct answer.
- To review, ask: *Does Mario have little or no guitar experience, some guitar experience, or a lot of guitar experience?* (little or no experience)

EXPANSION: Speaking practice for 2C

- Tell students to think of something they do at a beginning, an intermediate, and an advanced level.
- Group students and tell them to talk about their activities. Model the activity by telling the class about an activity you do at each level (for example: *I play the piano a little. I'm beginning. I take a yoga class. It's intermediate. I'm a great swimmer. I'm advanced.*).

3 CONVERSATION

A 🎧 **Listen. Notice that one syllable...**

- Read the Pronunciation Watch note. Write *family* on the board. Say: *Most people don't say* fa-**mi**-ly *with three syllables. They say* fam-ly *with two syllables.* Cross out the *i* in *family* on the board.

- Play CD 1, Track 52. Tell students to listen and notice that one syllable is not pronounced.

- Write *every* on the board. Say: *Most people don't say* ev-**e**-ry *with three syllables. They say* ev-ry *with two syllables. Cross out the second* e *in* every *on the board.* Repeat with *usually* and *interesting*.

- Resume playing Track 52. Students listen and repeat.

Controlled Practice   15 minutes

B 🎧 **Listen to the words. How many...**

- Tell students to look at the words. Say: *These words have syllables that are not pronounced.*

- Play CD 1, Track 53. Tell students to listen and cross out the vowel that's not pronounced (ev~~e~~ning, fav~~o~~rite, diff~~e~~rent).

- Play Track 53 again. Tell students to listen and write the number of syllables they hear.

- To review, tap on the desk to indicate each syllable as you pronounce *ev-ning, fa-vrite, dif-frent.*

C 🎧 **Listen and repeat the conversation.**

- Note: This conversation is the same one students heard in Exercise 2A on page 68.

- Tell students to read the conversation silently and underline the words *family, usually,* and *every.* Tell students to cross out the vowel that's not pronounced in each word.

- Play CD 1, Track 54. Students listen and repeat.

4 PRACTICE

A **PAIRS. Practice the conversation. Then make...**

- Pair students and tell them to practice the conversation in Exercise 3C.

- Then, in Exercise 4A, tell students to look at the information in the boxes. Say each word or expression and ask the class to repeat.

- Read the directions.

- Copy the conversation onto the board and complete it with words from the boxes.

- Play A and practice with a student. Switch roles.

- Tell pairs to take turns playing each role and to use the boxes to fill in the blanks.

- Tell students to stand, mingle, and practice the conversation with several new partners.

- Call on pairs to perform for the class.

Communicative Practice   15 minutes

B **Think about your plans for this weekend....**

- Read the directions. On the board, list three things you plan to do this weekend.

- Remind students to look at the vocabulary on page 67 for ideas and help with spelling.

- After students list their weekend plans, tell them to note when they are going to do each activity: *Friday, Saturday,* or *Sunday* and *morning, afternoon,* or *evening.*

C **MAKE IT PERSONAL. PAIRS. Talk about...**

- Tell students to look at the activities they listed in Exercise 4B, circle an activity that they usually do on weekends, and write *usually.* Tell them to draw a box around activities they do every weekend and write *every.*

- On the board, write:

  I'm going to _____.

  I usually _____ on _____.

  I _____ every _____.

- Practice the conversation with an above-level student. Tell the student to use Speaker A's first two lines from Exercise 4A. Answer using the fill-in sentences and one of your plans from the board. Point to the information on the board as you say it. Then ask the student *What about you?* and prompt him or her to complete the sentences on the board with one of his or her plans.

- Pair students and tell them to take turns starting the conversation.

Extra Practice

Interactive Practice

3 CONVERSATION

CD1 T52

A Listen. Notice that one syllable is not pronounced. Then listen and repeat the words.

every	usually	interesting
(2 syllables)	(3 syllables)	(3 syllables)

CD1 T53

B Listen to the words. How many syllables do you hear?

1. __2__ evening   2. __2__ favorite   3. __2__ different

CD1 T54

C Listen and repeat the conversation.

Mario: What are you doing this weekend?

Bi-Yun: I'm going to go to the beach with my family.

Mario: Really? Sounds like fun.

Bi-Yun: Yeah. We usually go to the beach on Sunday. What about you?

Mario: Well, I have a guitar class. I have a guitar class every Saturday morning.

Pronunciation Watch

Some words have a syllable that is not pronounced. For example, the word *family* looks like it has three syllables (fam·i·ly) but we pronounce it as two syllables (fam·ily).

---

4 PRACTICE

A PAIRS. Practice the conversation. Then make new conversations. Use the information in the boxes.

A: What are you doing this weekend?

B: I'm going to   with my family.

A: Really? Sounds like fun.

B: Yeah. We usually   on Sunday. What about you?

A: Well, I have a   class. I have a   class every   .

go out to eat
go for a bike ride
go hiking

karate
painting
computer

Friday evening
Saturday afternoon
Sunday morning

B Think about your plans for this weekend. Write three things you plan to do. Answers will vary.

1. _____ 2. _____ 3. _____

C MAKE IT PERSONAL. PAIRS. Talk about your weekend plans with your partner.

Grammar

Adverbs of frequency

	With action verbs					With be			
I We They	**always** **usually** **often**	**go**			I We They	**am** **are**	**always** **usually** **often**		
	sometimes		to the beach.				**sometimes**		at the beach.
He She	**hardly ever** **never**	**goes**			He She	**is**	**hardly ever** **never**		

0%   **100%**

never   hardly ever   sometimes   often   usually   always

Grammar Watch

• Adverbs of frequency go *before* action verbs.

• Adverbs of frequency go *after* forms of *be*.

1 PRACTICE

A Complete the sentences. Underline the correct words.

1. She works on Saturday mornings. She **never** / **often** sleeps late on Saturdays.

2. I can't go to the movies with you Thursday night. I **always** / **hardly ever** take a computer class after work on Thursdays.

3. There are very few good restaurants in my area. I **hardly ever** / **often** go out to eat.

4. Ty is an excellent student. He **always** / **sometimes** does his homework.

5. My friend Tanya is afraid of the water. She **often** / **never** goes swimming.

6. Their son likes video games. He **sometimes** / **never** spends hours on the computer.

B Rewrite the sentences. Use the adverbs in parentheses.

1. (always) The kids are busy. (usually) They get homework help after school.

   The kids are always busy. They usually get homework help after school.

2. (never) Marcus is on time. (sometimes) He gets to class thirty minutes late.

   Marcus is never on time. He sometimes gets to class thirty minutes late.

3. (usually) They go dancing on weekends. (hardly ever) They stay home.

   They usually go dancing on weekends. They hardly ever stay home.

4. (never) They are home on Sundays. (always) They are at their cousin's house.

   They're never home on Sundays. They're always at their cousin's house.

Getting Started   5 minutes

- Say: *We're going to study adverbs of frequency. In the conversation on page 69, Mario and Bi-Yun used this grammar.*
- Play CD 1, Track 54. Students listen.
- On the board, write: *We usually go to the beach on Sundays.* Underline *usually*.

Presentation   10 minutes

Adverbs of frequency

- Copy the *never–always* continuum onto the board or show Transparency 4.3. Pronounce the adverbs of frequency and ask the class to repeat.
- Point to *never* and *always* on the continuum and say: *If you never do something, you don't do it, not at any time. You do it 0% of the time. If you always do something, you do it all the time, or 100% of the time.*
- Pair students. *Say:* Never *is 0% of the time.* Always *is 100% of the time. With your partner, write the percentages for the other adverbs of frequency on the continuum* (hardly ever–20%, sometimes–40%, often–60%, usually–80%).
- Tell students to look at the grammar charts in their books or show Transparency 4.3. Point to the left chart. Ask: *What is the verb?* (go) *Where are the adverbs of frequency?* (before the verb) Read the first point of the Grammar Watch note.
- Point to the right grammar chart. Ask: *What is the verb?* (be) *Where are the adverbs of frequency?* (after be / after the verb) Read the second point in the Grammar Watch note.
- Call on students to read examples from the left chart. Tell them to choose one word from each row (for example, *She always goes to the beach.*).
- Call on students to read examples from the right chart. Tell them to choose one word from each row (for example, *We are hardly ever at the beach.*).
- If you are using the transparency, do the exercise with the class.

▬▬ **EXPANSION: Vocabulary and grammar practice**

- For each adverb on the continuum, tell students to write one activity that they do with that frequency.
- To model the activity, write an activity you never do under *never* on the continuum (for example, *go fishing*). Write an activity you always do under *always* (for example, *eat breakfast*).

Controlled Practice   15 minutes

▮**1** **PRACTICE**

Ⓐ Complete the sentences. Underline the...

- Ask a student to read item 1. Ask: *What does she do on Saturday mornings?* (She works.) *Can she sleep late?* (No.) *So, the answer is . . . ?* (never)
- Tell students to read each item and underline the correct adverb.
- Students compare answers with a partner.
- Call on students to read the completed items.
- Tell students to circle the verb in each sentence. Ask: *Are they action verbs* or be? (action verbs) *Are the frequency adverbs before or after the verbs?* (before)

▬▬ **EXPANSION: Writing and grammar practice for 1A**

- List action verb phrases from Exercise 1A on the board: *sleep late, go to the movies, go out to eat, do homework, go swimming, spend hours*
- Tell students to write sentences about how often they do each activity (for example, *I usually sleep late on weekends.*).
- Tell students to read their sentences to a partner. The partners listen and check that the adverbs of frequency come before the verbs in their partners' sentences.

Ⓑ Rewrite the sentences. Use the adverbs...

- Read item 1. Tell students to circle the verbs (*are, get*).
- Ask: *Is* are *an action verb or a form of the verb* be? (be) *Does* always *go before or after* are? (after) Read the first sentence of the example.
- Ask: *Is* get *an action verb or a form of the verb* be? (action verb) *Does* usually *go before or after* get? (before) Read the second sentence of the example.
- Tell students to circle the verbs in items 2–4 before they rewrite the sentences.
- Walk around and check for correct placement of the adverbs of frequency.
- Students compare answers with a partner.
- Call on students to read their answers.

Presentation · 5 minutes

Questions with *How often* / frequency time expressions

- Copy the grammar charts onto the board or show Transparency 4.3 and cover the exercise.

- Write *exercise* on the board. Say: *Ask me if I exercise.* Elicit and write on the board: *Do you exercise?* Answer: *Yes, I do.*

- Say: *Now you know that I exercise, but you don't know how often I exercise. Do I exercise every day or once a month? To ask about frequency, use* How often. On the board, write *How often* in front of *Do you exercise?* and change *D* to *d*. Answer with a frequency time expression.

- Post a calendar. Use it to point out the meanings of the frequency time expressions in the right chart.

- Point to the question on the board and ask the class: *How often do you exercise?* Tell students to circle one of the time expressions in the right chart or write an answer next to the chart.

- Call on several students and ask: *How often do you exercise?* Then call on different students and ask them to recall their classmates' answers: *How often does [Name] exercise?*

- If you are using the transparency, do the exercise with the class.

Controlled Practice · 10 minutes

2 PRACTICE

PAIRS. Look at Felipe's calendar. Ask and...

- Tell students to look at the calendar but to cover the example. Ask: *How often does Felipe have dinner at his grandma's?* Tell students to circle *have dinner at grandma's* each time it appears on the calendar. Elicit the answer: *Once a week.*

- Pair students and tell them to take turns playing A and B and ask five questions each. Tell them to start each question with *How often does Felipe . . .* and complete it with an activity from the calendar.

- To check answers, call on five students to ask a question. Tell them to call on a classmate to answer. Possible questions and answers: *How often does Felipe play soccer?* (twice a month) *How often does Felipe have a computer class?* (every Monday) *How often does Felipe go jogging with Hong?* (twice a week) *How often does Felipe rent a DVD?* (every Saturday)

Communicative Practice · 15 minutes

Show what you know!

STEP 1. Write three questions with *how often*...

- Read the directions and the example.

- Tell students to begin their questions with *How often do you . . .* and end with an activity. They can use the activities on page 67 or their own ideas.

STEP 2. GROUPS OF 3. Ask your classmates...

- Read the directions. Ask three students to say a question and write each on the board.

- Model surveying the class. Ask a student one of the questions. Write the student's name and answer on the board under the question you asked. Repeat with different students and different questions.

- Tell students to try to ask every classmate a question.

STEP 3. Tell the class about one of your...

- Read the directions.

- Tell students to look at the example. Ask: *What's the verb?* (goes) *What does it end in?* (-s) Tell them to underline the -s. Ask: *What's the frequency time expression?* (once a month) *Where is it?* (at the end of the sentence)

- Point to one name and answer on your chart. Tell the class about this student's activity.

- Tell students to choose one name and answer on their charts. Remind students to use third-person singular -s and to place the frequency time expression at the end of the sentence.

- Call on every student to tell the class about one classmate's activity.

Progress Check

Can you . . . talk about your weekend activities?

Say: *We have practiced talking about weekend activities. Now, look at the question at the bottom of the page. Can you talk about your weekend activities?* Tell students to write a checkmark in the box.

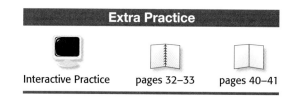

Extra Practice		
Interactive Practice	pages 32–33	pages 40–41

| How often | do | you
they | exercise? |
| | does | he
she | |

Every day.
Every Monday.
Once a week.
Twice a month.

Grammar Watch

once = **one time**

twice = **two times**

2 PRACTICE

PAIRS. Look at Felipe's calendar. Ask and answer five questions with *how often*.

A: *How often does Felipe have dinner at his grandma's?* Answers will vary.
B: *Once a week.*

Felipe's Calendar

Sun.	Mon.	Tues.	Wed.	Thurs.	Fri.	Sat.
1 play soccer	2 have a computer class	3 have dinner at grandma's	4 go jogging with Hong	5	6 go jogging with Hong	7 rent a DVD
8	9 have a computer class	10 go jogging with Hong	11	12 have dinner at grandma's	13 go jogging with Hong	14 rent a DVD
15 play soccer	16 have a computer class	17 go jogging with Hong	18 have dinner at grandma's	19 go jogging with Hong	20	21 rent a DVD
22	23 have a computer class	24	25 go jogging with Hong	26 go jogging with Hong	27 have dinner at grandma's	28 rent a DVD

Show what you know! Talk about your weekend activities

STEP 1. Write three questions with *how often* to ask your classmates about their activities.

How often do you go to the movies?

STEP 2. GROUP OF 3. Ask your classmates your questions from Step 1. Write each person's name and answers on a separate piece of paper.

STEP 3. Tell the class about one of your classmates' activities.

Gigi goes to the movies once a month.

Can you... talk about your weekend activities? ☐

Life Skills

1 PLAN ACTIVITIES

CD1 T55

A ⓐ **Look at the calendar for the Greenville Community Center. Read and listen to how we talk about events. Then listen and repeat.**

- The swim team meets every Saturday from 1:00 to 4:00 P.M.

- The dance class meets on the second Friday of the month at 8:00 P.M.

- The ESL class meets on Mondays and Wednesdays from 7:00 to 9:00 P.M.

East Windsor
Community Center Calendar   **June**

Sunday	Monday	Tuesday	Wednesday	Thursday	Friday	Saturday
	1	2 9:00 – 10:00 A.M. exercise class	3 7:00 – 9:00 P.M. ESL class	4 9:00 – 10:00 A.M. exercise class	5 8:00 P.M. movie club	6 1:00 – 4:00 P.M. swim team
7 8:00 a.m.– 4:00 P.M. hiking club	8 7:00 – 9:00 P.M. ESL class	9 9:00 – 10:00 A.M. exercise class	10 7:00 – 9:00 P.M. ESL class	11 9:00 – 10:00 A.M. exercise class	12 8:00 – 10:00 P.M. dance class	13 1:00 – 4:00 P.M. swim team
14	15 7:00 – 9:00 P.M. ESL class	16 9:00 – 10:00 A.M. exercise class	17 7:00 – 9:00 P.M. ESL class	18 9:00 – 10:00 A.M. exercise class	19 8:00 P.M. movie club	20 1:00 – 4:00 P.M. swim team
21 9:00 A.M.– 12:00 P.M. jogging club	22 7:00 – 9:00 P.M. ESL class	23 9:00 – 10:00 A.M. exercise class	24 7:00 – 9:00 P.M. ESL class	25 9:00 – 10:00 A.M. exercise class	26	27 1:00 – 4:00 P.M. swim team
28	29 7:00 – 9:00 P.M. ESL class	30 9:00 – 10:00 A.M. exercise class				

B **PAIRS. Look at the community calendar again. Circle *True* or *False*. Correct the false information.**

                                       Sunday

1. The hiking club meets on the first ~~Saturday~~ of the month.   **True**   **(False)**
                                 third

2. The jogging club meets on the ~~fourth~~ Sunday of the month.   **True**   **(False)**

3. The dance class meets from 8:00 to 10:00 P.M.   **(True)**   **False**
                             Tuesday   Thursday

4. The exercise class meets every ~~Monday~~ and ~~Wednesday~~.   **True**   **(False)**

5. The movie club meets at 8:00 P.M.   **(True)**   **False**
                         Saturday

6. The swim team meets every ~~Thursday~~.   **True**   **(False)**
                 Mondays   Wednesdays

7. The ESL class meets on ~~Tuesdays~~ and ~~Thursdays~~.   **True**   **(False)**

C **PAIRS. Ask and answer questions about the calendar.**

A: *When does the swim team meet?*
B: *It meets every Saturday from 1:00 to 4:00 P.M. When does the . . . ?*

Presentation 15 minutes

1 PLAN ACTIVITIES

A 💿 **Look at the calendar for the...**

- Tell students to look at the calendar. Tell them to find and circle *swim team* every time it appears on the calendar. Ask: *How many times does the swim team meet in the month?* (four) Repeat with the dance class and the ESL class.
- Read the directions. Play CD 1, Track 55. Students listen and read along silently.
- Resume playing Track 55. Students listen and repeat.
- Tell the class to look at the first sentence. Say: *After every, use singular days of the week—every Saturday, every Tuesday and Thursday.*
- Tell the class to look at the second sentence. Say: *Point to Friday on the calendar. The 5th is the first Friday of the month. What is the date of the second Friday of the month?* (the 12th) On the board, write: *first, second, third, fourth.* Ask a few more questions with ordinal numbers, for example, *What's the date of the third Wednesday of the month?* (the 17th)
- *Optional:* Say the ordinal numbers from 1 to 30 and ask the class to repeat. Then count from 1 to 30 in ordinal numbers as a class.
- Tell the class to look at the last sentence. Say: *Use plural days of the week after* on *when you are talking about an event that happens every week on a certain day—on Mondays and Wednesdays, on Sundays.*
- On the board, write: *at* _____ / *from* _____ *to* _____. Say: *Use at* _____ *with a beginning time. Use from* _____ *to* _____ *with a beginning and end time.*

Community Building

- Tell students to look at the calendar and circle an activity they are interested in.
- Ask: *Are there places that offer activities like these in your community?* Elicit places and costs from the class and write the information on the board.
- Tell students to write the names of any places they are interested in finding out more about. Tell them to ask the classmate who mentioned them how to get a schedule.

Controlled Practice 20 minutes

B **PAIRS. Look at the community calendar...**

- Read item 1. Tell students to point to the first Saturday of the month on the calendar. Ask: *What date are you pointing to?* (June 6th) *Is* Hiking Club *on the calendar for this day?* (No.) Say: *So, the answer is false.*
- Say: *Now we need to correct the false information. Find* Hiking Club *on the calendar. When does it meet?* (on the first Sunday of the month) *Cross out* Saturday *and write* Sunday.
- Pair students. Walk around and remind students to use singular days of the week with *every* and plural days of the week with *on*.
- Ask the class which items are false. Call on students to read the corrected sentences.

C **PAIRS. Ask and answer questions about the...**

- Read the directions.
- Tell students to find *swim team* on the calendar.
- Ask two above-level students to read the example.
- Pair students and tell them to take turns asking and answering questions about the other activities on the calendar. Walk around and check for singular days of the week with *every*, plural days of the week with *on, from . . .* with time frames, and *at* with beginning times.

▬▬ MULTILEVEL INSTRUCTION for 1C

Cross-ability The lower-level student plays Speaker A first. Direct the student to underline *swim team* in the example, substitute different activities on the calendar, and then ask four questions about the calendar. Partners then switch roles. When it's the lower-level student's turn to play Speaker B, he or she will have heard the higher-level student say when most of the activities meet.

▬▬ EXPANSION: Speaking practice for 1C

- Form small groups and tell them to look at the calendar.
- Say: *Which activities are you interested in? Tell your classmates.* On the board, write:

    A: *I'm interested in the [dance class]. How about you?*

    B: *I'm interested in . . .*

- Model the activity with an above-level student. Play A and elicit a response from B.

Lesson 4 Plan activities using a calendar

Controlled Practice   20 minutes

2 PRACTICE

A 🔘 **Listen to the schedule of events....**

- Tell students to listen and write the events on the calendar on all the days each event meets. Tell students to print in small letters, as some days have two events and they will have to add the time later. Suggest that students use pencil so they can correct answers more easily.
- Play CD 1, Track 56. Pause between events to allow students to write the events on multiple days.
- For help with spelling, tell students to check the calendar on page 72. Write *concert* on the board.
- Play Track 56 again. Students listen again and write the times of each event on the calendar.
- As needed, play Track 56 again and allow students to check their own answers before they compare with a partner.

B **PAIRS. Compare your answers.**

- Tell students to look at Exercise 1C on page 72 and to read the example again.
- Pair students and tell them to not to show each other their calendars. Tell them to check their answers by asking and answering questions. Write an example on the board: *A: When does the Lunch Club meet in September? B: It meets on the second Friday of the month at 12:00 P.M.*
- Direct students to circle any answers that are different from their partner's.
- If needed, Play CD 1, Track 56 again. Tell students to listen again and correct their answers.

▮▮ MULTILEVEL INSTRUCTION for 2B

Pre-level Allow students to look at each other's calendars as they compare answers.

Above-level Tell students to add two activities and times to the calendar and not show their calendar to their partner. Partners take turns telling each other what the activities are and when they meet. They write each other's activities on their calendars.

3 LIFE SKILLS WRITING

Turn to page 259 and ask students to complete the library application. See page T-xii for general notes about the Life Skills Writing activities.

Progress Check

Can you . . . plan activities using a calendar?

Say: *We have practiced planning activities using a calendar. Now, look at the question at the bottom of the page. Can you plan activities using a calendar?* Tell students to write a checkmark in the box.

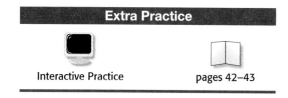

Extra Practice	
Interactive Practice	pages 42–43

CD1 T56

A 💿 Listen to the schedule of events. Write the events on the calendar. Then listen again. Write the times of each event on the calendar.

Greenville September
Community Center Calendar

Sunday	Monday	Tuesday	Wednesday	Thursday	Friday	Saturday
		1	2	3 Dance class 3–4 P.M.	4 Concert Club 7 P.M.	5 Jogging Club 8 A.M.
6	7 ESL class 7–9 P.M. Labor Day	8	9 ESL class 7–9 P.M.	10 Dance class 3–4 P.M.	11 Lunch Club: Hilda's Café 12:00 P.M.	12 Jogging Club 8 A.M. Movie Club 7 P.M.
13	14 ESL class 7–9 P.M.	15	16 ESL class 7–9 P.M.	17 Dance class 3–4 P.M.	18 Concert Club 7 P.M.	19 Jogging Club 8 A.M.
20	21 ESL class 7–9 P.M.	22	23 ESL class 7–9 P.M.	24 Dance class 3–4 P.M.	25	26 Jogging Club 8 A.M. Movie Club 7 P.M.
27	28	29	30			

B PAIRS. Compare your answers.

3 LIFE SKILLS WRITING Complete a library card application. See page 259.

Can you... plan activities using a calendar? ☐

Listening and Speaking

1   BEFORE YOU LISTEN

A   CLASS. Look at the pictures. What are some other activities that people have to do?

B   CLASS. Which activities do you have to do?

cook

vacuum

exercise

iron

2   LISTEN

A   CD1 T57   Listen to an interview on a radio show. What problem do the people discuss?

a. People often don't have a lot of free time.
(b.) People have to do things they don't enjoy.

B   CD1 T57   Read the ideas from the interview. Listen again. Number the ideas in the order you hear them.

a. __3__   After you do something you hate, do something you like.

b. __2__   Put a time limit on the activities you hate to do.

c. __1__   When you need to do something you hate, do something you like at the same time.

C   Read the examples from the interview. Match each example to one of the ideas in Exercise B. Write the letter of the correct idea.

1. __c__   If you hate to wash dishes, then do something you love while you wash the dishes. Wash the dishes and watch TV.

2. __b__   Say it's 1:00 and you need to clean the house. Decide what time you're going to finish cleaning, say, 3:00. When it's 3:00, you stop.

3. __a__   If you hate to do laundry, but you love to read, then say to yourself: "I'm going to do the laundry. Then I'm going to read for half an hour."

Getting Started
5 minutes

 BEFORE YOU LISTEN

Ⓐ CLASS. Look at the pictures. What are...

- Tell students to look at the pictures. Say the activities and ask the class to repeat.
- Ask: *What are some other activities that people have to do?* Elicit answers from the class and write them on the board (for example, *clean the house, wash clothes, do dishes, do homework, work*).

▬▬ **EXPANSION: Writing and Speaking Practice for 1A**

- Form groups of 4. Tell groups to assign one of the pictured activities to each member. Students form a question with *how often* for their activity (for example, *How often do you cook?*).
- Explain that each group member should ask all group members his or her question and note their responses.
- Remind students to answer with adverbs of frequency or frequency time expressions (for example, *I hardly ever cook.* or *I cook twice a month.*).
- Then tell students to write sentences about their group members' activities (for example, *[Name] hardly ever cooks.*). Remind students to use third-person singular *-s*.

Ⓑ CLASS. Which activities do you have to do?

- Ask several students: *Which activities do you have to do? Do you like to do those activities?*

Presentation
10 minutes

2 LISTEN

 Listen to an interview on a radio...

- Read the directions. Ask a student to read the answer choices.
- Play CD 1, Track 57. Students circle the letter of the correct answer.
- To check the answer, ask students to raise their hands if they checked a. Repeat for b.

Ⓑ 💿 **Read the ideas from the interview....**

- Read the directions. Ask three students to read the answer choices.
- Play Track 57 again. Students number the ideas in the order they hear them.
- Call on students to read the items again, this time in the correct order.
- *Optional:* Ask: *Do you think these are good ideas? Why or why not?*

> **Teaching Tip**
>
> If students need additional support, tell them to read the Audio Script on page 300 as they listen.

Controlled Practice
5 minutes

Ⓒ Read the examples from the interview....

- Ask a student to read item 1. Say: *Look at Exercise 2B. Is this the example for idea a, b, or c?* (c) Read idea c and ask: *What is the activity people often hate to do?* (wash dishes) *What is the activity people often love to do?* (watch TV) *According to Dr. Goldberg, when should people do them?* (at the same time)
- Tell students to compare answers with a partner.

▬▬ **EXPANSION: Writing and speaking practice for 2C**

- On a sheet of paper, tell students to write three activities they have to do but don't enjoy and several activities they love to do. Write your own answers on the board.
- Tell students to look at the examples in Exercise 2C and underline the activities.
- Say: *Exchange papers with a partner. Use the language from Exercise 2C and your partner's activities to write advice for your partner. Then read your advice to your partner.*
- To model the activity, read item 1 in Exercise 2C. Substitute two of your own activities on the board for the activities in the sentence.

Communicative Practice   10 minutes

Ⓓ GROUPS OF 3. Look at the picture...

- Read the directions. Ask a student to read the man's problem.
- Form groups of 3. Tell each student to create a solution for the man.
- Ask a student to stand and play the role of the man in the photo. The student says his line and calls on each group to report one solution to the class.

Presentation   5 minutes

3 CONVERSATION

🔘 **Listen and repeat the conversation.**

- Tell students to look at the photo. Ask: *Where are Jane and Karen?* (in a laundromat) *What are they doing?* (talking, doing laundry)
- Tell students to read the conversation silently. On the board, draw a chart:

	Do laundry	*Iron*
Jane hates . . .		
Karen hates . . .		

- Tell students to check the activities each woman hates (Jane: do laundry; Karen: do laundry, iron).
- Play CD 1, Track 58. Students listen and repeat.

Controlled Practice   15 minutes

4 PRACTICE

Ⓐ PAIRS. Practice the conversation. Then...

- Pair students and tell them to practice the conversation in Exercise 3. Tell them to take turns playing each role.
- Then, in Exercise 4A, tell students to look at the information in the boxes. Say each word or phrase and ask the class to repeat.
- Read the directions.

- Tell students to circle one activity in each box that they really don't like to do.
- Copy the conversation onto the board and complete it with words from the boxes.
- Play B and model the conversation with an above-level student. Prompt A to insert the circled activity in the blue box. Ask A if he or she really likes the activity you chose from the green box.
- Tell pairs to take turns playing each role and to use the boxes to fill in the blanks.
- Walk around and remind students to switch roles and practice both parts.
- Tell students to stand, mingle, and practice the conversation with several new partners.
- Call on pairs to perform for the class.

Communicative Practice   15 minutes

Ⓑ MAKE IT PERSONAL. PAIRS. Make your own...

- On the board, brainstorm things people need to do.
- On a sheet of paper, tell students to draw a two-column chart with the headings *Hate* and *Like*. Tell them to choose the activities from the board that they need to do and write them in one of the columns on their chart.
- Pair students and tell them to talk about the activities on their charts. Tell them to use Exercise 3 as a model. Remind students that they can say *Me, too* or *I do, too* to agree with their partner.
- Call on pairs to practice for the class.

▬▬▬ MULTILEVEL INSTRUCTION for 4B

Pre-level Before they practice, tell students to choose an activity from the *Hate* column of their chart. Tell them to write the activity in the conversation in Exercise 4A.

Above-level Tell pairs to continue the conversation by giving each other tips about how to make the things they hate to do more enjoyable.

Extra Practice

Interactive Practice

D GROUPS OF 3. Look at the picture. What is the man's problem? What are some solutions? Use the ideas from the radio show or your own ideas.

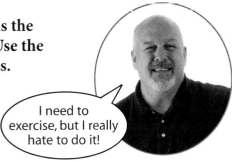

I need to exercise, but I really hate to do it!

3 CONVERSATION

CD1 T58

Listen and repeat the conversation.

Jane: You know, I really hate to do the laundry.

Karen: Me, too. And do you know what else I hate?

Jane: No. What?

Karen: I hate to iron.

Jane: Not me. I actually like it.

Karen: You're kidding.

Jane: No, really. I find it relaxing.

4 PRACTICE

A PAIRS. Practice the conversation. Then make new conversations. Use the information in the boxes.

A: You know, I really hate to   .

B: Me, too. And do you know what else I hate?

A: No. What?

B: I hate to   .

A: Not me. I actually like it.

B: You're kidding.

A: No, really. I find it relaxing.

clean the house
do the dishes
get up early

cook
vacuum
exercise

B MAKE IT PERSONAL. PAIRS. Make your own conversations. Use your own information.

Grammar

Simple present: *like / love / hate* + *infinitive*		
I	like	
You	don't like	**to do the laundry.**
We	love	
They	hate	

	likes	
He	doesn't like	**to iron.**
She	loves	
	hates	

hate = 😫
not like = ☹
like = ☺
love = 😊

1 PRACTICE

A Write sentences. Use the correct form of the verbs *like, love,* or *hate* and an infinitive.

1. My brother / not like / eat vegetables   *My brother doesn't like to eat vegetables.*

2. Mrs. Lynn / love / go to the beach   Mrs. Lynn loves to go to the beach.

3. Her daughters / hate / clean their rooms   Her daughters hate to clean their rooms.

4. Some children / not like / go swimming   Some children do not like to go swimming.

5. Our neighbors / like / have loud parties   Our neighbors like to have loud parties.

6. She / love / go hiking in the mountains   She loves to go hiking in the mountains.

B WRITE. Look at the pictures. Write a sentence for each picture. Use *like, love,* or *hate* and an infinitive. There can be more than one correct answer.

the kids

Niraj   Niraj's Dad

Kyung-Ah

Sally   James

Answers will vary but could include:

1. *The kids love to play soccer.*

2. Kyung-Ah likes to read.

3. Niraj hates to fish with his dad.

4. Sally hates to go to concerts.

C PAIRS. Compare your answers.

Getting Started
5 minutes

- Say: *We're going to study the simple present with* like / love / hate *and the infinitive. In the conversation on page 75, Jane and Karen used this grammar.*
- Play CD 1, Track 58. Students listen. On the board, write: *I really hate to do the laundry.* Underline *hate to do the laundry.*

Presentation
10 minutes

Simple present: *like / love / hate* + infinitive

- Tell students to look at the faces. Say the verbs and ask the class to repeat. Ask: *What are your likes and dislikes?* Tell students to write one activity next to each face.
- Say: *To talk about activities you like and dislike, you use* hate, not like, like, *or* love + *an infinitive.* Ask a student: *What activity do you hate?* Write the student's response on the board (for example, *vacuum*). Ask: *How do you make this an infinitive?* Add *to* to the example on the board.
- Copy the grammar charts onto the board or show Transparency 4.4 and cover the exercise.
- Tell students to look at the left grammar chart. Ask: *How do you feel about doing the laundry?* Tell students to circle the verb that expresses how they feel about doing the laundry.
- Ask a few students: *How do you feel about doing the laundry?* Tell students to use words from the left side of the grammar chart (for example, *I don't like to do the laundry.*).
- Tell students to look at the right grammar chart. Read the sentences and ask the class to repeat.
- Write the names of the students who gave their opinions about laundry on the board. Ask the class to recall their answers. As a class, write a sentence about each person (for example, *[Name] doesn't like to do the laundry.*).
- Tell the class to look at the sentences on the board. Ask: *Do any students have the same opinion about doing the laundry?* As a class, write a new sentence with *they* as the subject (for example, *[Name] and [Name] don't like to do the laundry.*).
- If you are using the transparency, do the exercise with the class.

Controlled Practice
30 minutes

1 PRACTICE

A Write sentences. Use the correct form of the verbs...

- Read the directions. Remind students an *infinitive* is *to* + base form of a verb.
- Tell students to look at item 1. Ask: *What form of* not like *goes with* My brother? (*doesn't like*) *What do you add to* eat *to make it an infinitive?* (*to*) Ask a student to read the example.
- Walk around, and if students have difficulty, repeat the steps from the example.
- Ask students to write the sentences on the board. As a class, correct as needed.

EXPANSION: Grammar and speaking practice for 1A

- Tell students to underline the activities in Exercise 1A.
- Pair students. Say: *Tell your partner whether you like, don't like, love, or hate each activity.*
- Model the activity by telling the class how you feel about the first activity (for example, *I love to eat vegetables.*).

B WRITE. Look at the pictures. Write a sentence...

- Tell the class to look at picture 1. Say: *Point to the face at the top of the page that matches the kids' faces.* Ask a student to read the example. Ask: *Is there another possible answer?* (The kids like to play soccer.)
- Walk around and help as needed. Check for subject-verb agreement and use of *to* before the verb. If you spot an incorrect answer, ask the student to read the answer, identify the error, and correct it.

C PAIRS. Compare your answers.

- Form pairs. Tell students to take turns reading their sentences. Say: *Listen for* to *in your partner's sentences.*
- Say: *If you and your partner have the same sentence, think of a second sentence together. Write the sentence under Exercise 1C.*
- To review, elicit a couple of sentences for each picture.

2 PRACTICE

A READ AND WRITE. Read the information...

- Read the directions.
- Ask: *What is a survey?* Explain that in a survey, you ask a large number of people questions to find out what they think or do.
- Tell students to read the information in the yellow box silently. Ask the class: *What question did the survey ask?* (What's your favorite activity?) *How many people answered the question?* (500)
- Tell students to look at the bar graph to the right of the yellow box. Ask: *What is the title of the bar graph?* (Favorite things to do in the U.S.) Say: *The bar graph shows the results of the survey.* Ask: *What is the most popular thing to do in the U.S.?* (read) *What percentage of people like to read?* (34%) *What is the least popular thing to do?* (use a computer) *What percentage of people like to use a computer?* (7%)
- Tell students to point to the first bar in the bar graph. Ask a student to read the example. Tell students to choose three other activities in the bar graph and write sentences.
- To review, elicit a sentence for each bar on the graph.

B PAIRS. What do people in your country...

- Ask two above-level students to read the question and response.
- Tell students to think about popular activities in their country. Partners then take turns asking and answering the question.
- Ask a few pairs to practice in front of the class.

■ **EXPANSION: Graphic organizer and speaking practice for 2B**

- Ask: *What do you think a bar graph of favorite things to do in your country would look like?* Tell students to list favorite free-time activities in their country, rank them in order, guess a percentage for each activity, and then create a bar graph like the one in Exercise 2A.
- Tell students to explain their bar graph to a partner by pointing to each bar and saying a sentence.

Communicative Practice 15 minutes

Show what you know!

STEP 1. What activities do you like? Love? Hate?...

- Model the activity. Say four sentences about your likes and dislikes. Use *like*, *love*, and *hate*.
- Encourage students to review the free-time activities on page 67.
- Walk around and help as needed. If students ask how to say or spell an activity that's not in the unit, write the activity on the board. Explain the meanings of any activities on the board. Say the activities and ask the class to repeat.

STEP 2. PAIRS. Compare your answers...

- Ask two students to read the example.
- Call on an above-level student to read one sentence from Step 1. Respond truthfully. Say: *Not me* or *Me, too.* Then say one of your sentences from Step 1. To prompt the student to respond to your like or dislike, you can say: *What about you?*
- Call on a few students to report one of their partner's likes or dislikes.

■ **MULTILEVEL INSTRUCTION for STEP 2**

Cross-ability The lower-level student reads each sentence from Step 1, and the higher-level student responds. When partners switch roles, the lower-level student has had appropriate responses modeled.

Progress Check

Can you . . . communicate likes and dislikes?

Say: *We have practiced communicating likes and dislikes. Now, look at the question at the bottom of the page. Can you communicate likes and dislikes?* Tell students to write a checkmark in the box.

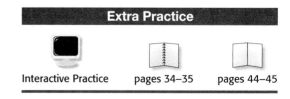

Extra Practice		
Interactive Practice	pages 34–35	pages 44–45

A READ AND WRITE. Read the information. Look at the bar graph.
On a separate piece of paper, write three sentences about the survey.

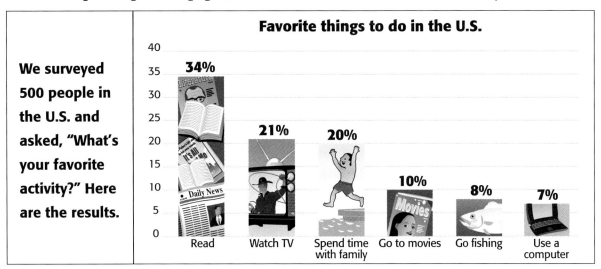

We surveyed 500 people in the U.S. and asked, "What's your favorite activity?" Here are the results.

Favorite things to do in the U.S.

40
35   34%
30
25
20   21%   20%
15
10   10%   8%   7%
5
0
Read   Watch TV   Spend time   Go to movies   Go fishing   Use a
                   with family   computer

Thirty-four percent of the people like to read.

B PAIRS. What do people in your country like to do in their free time?

In my country, a lot of people like to go out to eat.

Show what you know! Communicate likes and dislikes

STEP 1. What activities do you like? Love? Hate? Write four sentences.

1. _____

2. _____

3. _____

4. _____

STEP 2. PAIRS. Compare your answers. Talk about your likes and dislikes.

A: *I love to go fishing.*
B: *Not me. I love to read.*
A: *Well, I like to read, too.*

Can you...communicate likes and dislikes? ☐

Read about rude and polite behavior

Reading

1 BEFORE YOU READ

PAIRS. Look at the picture of people at a movie theater. How is the young man being rude? Do you think this behavior is rude in all countries?

2 READ

CD1 T59

 Listen. Read the online message board posts.

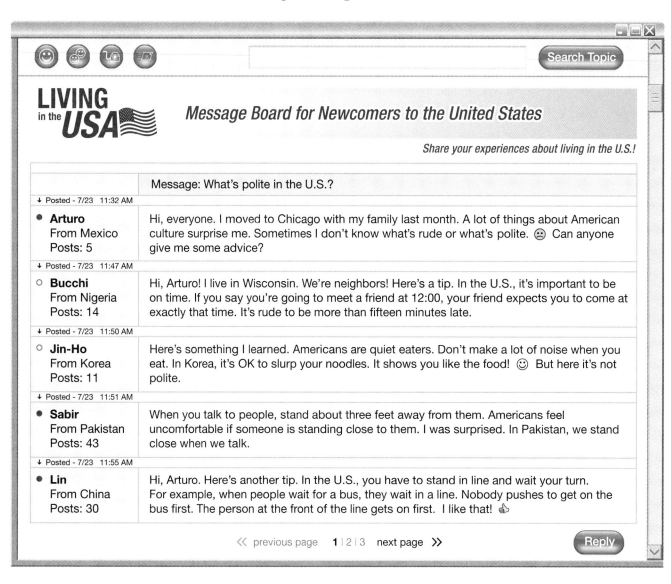

LIVING in the USA 🏴

Message Board for Newcomers to the United States

Share your experiences about living in the U.S.!

	Message: What's polite in the U.S.?
↓ Posted - 7/23 11:32 AM	
● **Arturo** From Mexico Posts: 5	Hi, everyone. I moved to Chicago with my family last month. A lot of things about American culture surprise me. Sometimes I don't know what's rude or what's polite. ☹ Can anyone give me some advice?
↓ Posted - 7/23 11:47 AM	
○ **Bucchi** From Nigeria Posts: 14	Hi, Arturo! I live in Wisconsin. We're neighbors! Here's a tip. In the U.S., it's important to be on time. If you say you're going to meet a friend at 12:00, your friend expects you to come at exactly that time. It's rude to be more than fifteen minutes late.
↓ Posted - 7/23 11:50 AM	
○ **Jin-Ho** From Korea Posts: 11	Here's something I learned. Americans are quiet eaters. Don't make a lot of noise when you eat. In Korea, it's OK to slurp your noodles. It shows you like the food! ☺ But here it's not polite.
↓ Posted - 7/23 11:51 AM	
● **Sabir** From Pakistan Posts: 43	When you talk to people, stand about three feet away from them. Americans feel uncomfortable if someone is standing close to them. I was surprised. In Pakistan, we stand close when we talk.
↓ Posted - 7/23 11:55 AM	
● **Lin** From China Posts: 30	Hi, Arturo. Here's another tip. In the U.S., you have to stand in line and wait your turn. For example, when people wait for a bus, they wait in a line. Nobody pushes to get on the bus first. The person at the front of the line gets on first. I like that! 👍

《 previous page   **1** | 2 | 3   next page 》   **Reply**

Getting Started   5 minutes

1 BEFORE YOU READ

PAIRS. Look at the picture of people...

- Write a definition for *polite* on the board: *acting or speaking in a way that is correct for the social situation you are in, and showing that you are careful to consider other people's needs and feelings.*
- Read the definition. Tell students to look at the picture. Ask: *Is the young man being polite?* (No.) Say: *He's not being polite. He's being rude.*
- Draw a two-column chart with the headings *Polite* and *Rude* on the board. Describe polite and rude actions in the classroom and ask students where to place them on the chart (for example, *coming to class late, raising your hand to speak, talking when someone else is talking*). Brainstorm other actions to add to the chart.
- Tell the class to look at the picture. Ask: *Where is the man?* (in a movie theater) *What is he doing?* As students identify his actions, write them on the board: *putting his feet up on the seat in front of him, eating popcorn, drinking soda, talking on his cell phone.*
- Point to the actions on the board. Ask: *Which of these things is rude / not polite in a movie theater?* Elicit and circle: *putting his feet up on the seat in front of him, talking on his cell phone.* Label these actions *rude.*
- Read each circled action and ask: *Do you think this behavior is rude in all countries?* Ask students to raise their hands for *yes* or *no.* Ask any students who raise their hands for *no* where the behavior is not rude.
- Ask: *What other things are rude to do in a movie theater?* (talking during the movie, coming in late, bringing small children to adult movies)

Presentation   15 minutes

2 READ

 Listen. Read the online message...

- Tell the class to look at the message board. Ask: *Where do you find message boards?* (the Internet)
- Ask: *What is a message board?* Explain that a message board is a website where people from all over the world can post messages that other people can read and reply to.
- Ask: *Do you ever read message boards? Do you ever post messages?* Ask for a show of hands.
- Tell the class to look at the message board. Read the title. Ask: *Who is the message board for?* (newcomers to the United States) *What is the message board about?* (experiences about living in the U.S.)
- Tell the class to look at the message board. Ask: *How many people posted messages?* (five) *Where are the people from?* (Mexico, Nigeria, Korea, Pakistan, China) *Who started this discussion?* (Arturo)
- Tell students to find and circle the three signs or symbols on the message board. Say: *These are called* emoticons. *They are used to show emotions or opinions in e-mail and on the Internet.* Hold up the book, point to each emoticon, and ask the class what they think it means. (unhappy / don't like, happy / funny, agreement)
- Play CD 1, Track 59. Students listen and read along silently. Tell students to circle any unfamiliar vocabulary. Explain / demonstrate new vocabulary as needed, for example, ask a student to act out *slurp your noodles.*

EXPANSION: Graphic organizer practice for 2

- Tell students to read the second, third, fourth, and fifth posts again.
- Draw a two-column chart with the headings *Polite* and *Rude* on the board.
- Tell pairs to copy the chart and write a polite and rude behavior from each post. For example, for the second post, *Polite: be on time / Rude: be more than 15 minutes late.*

Controlled Practice   20 minutes

3 CHECK YOUR UNDERSTANDING

Ⓐ Read the message board posts again. What...

- Read the Reading Skill note and the directions.
- Tell students to read the message board posts again silently. Say: *All of the messages talk about the same topic. What is the topic? Think about it as you read.*
- Tell students to read the answer choices silently and circle the letter of the correct answer.
- Ask a student to read answer choices a, b, and c out loud. Tell students to raise their hand for the answer they chose.

Ⓑ What is the main idea of the message board posts?

- Read the directions.
- Remind the class: *The main idea is the most important idea in the article.*
- Tell students to read the answer choices silently and circle the letter of the main idea.
- Ask a student to read answer choices a, b, and c out loud. Tell students to raise their hand for the answer they chose.

Ⓒ Complete the advice that Arturo received.

- Read the directions.
- *Optional:* Tell students to use the chart they created in the Expansion activity for Exercise 2 on page 78 to complete the sentences.
- To check answers, call on students to read the sentences.

EXPANSION: Grammar practice for 3C

- Say: *Read each tip in Exercise 3C. Then write a sentence about your own behavior. Use adverbs of frequency.* To model the activity, read item 1 and write a sentence about your own behavior (for example, *I'm hardly ever more than 15 minutes late for an appointment with friends.*).
- Remind students that adverbs of frequency go before action verbs and after *be.*
- Pair students and tell them to take turns reading their sentences.

Communicative Practice   20 minutes

Ⓓ PAIRS. Imagine you are writing a post...

- As a class, brainstorm and write on the board other actions that are rude in the U.S. (for example, *littering, staring at people, talking loudly on a cell phone, spitting, smoking in someone's home*).
- Read the directions. On the board, write: *Don't . . .* and *When you . . . , you have to . . .*
- Choose one action from the board and create a post as a class.
- Pair students. Tell them to choose a different action and plan a post. Walk around and help as needed.
- Call on pairs to tell the class their advice.

Show what you know!

PRE-WRITING. PAIRS. Look at the advice in...

- Tell students to read the advice in Exercise 3C again. Ask: *Is this advice correct for your country?* Tell students to write *yes* or *no* next to each item.
- Read item 1. Ask an above-level student: *Is this advice correct for your country?* If the student answers no, ask: *What do people do in your country?*
- On the board, write: *Is this advice correct for your country?* and *What do people do in your country?* If possible, pair students from different countries. Tell A to read each sentence and ask the first question. Tell A to ask the second question when B answers no.
- Ask a few students: *What did you learn about your partner's country?*

WRITE. Write about what is rude or polite....

Ask students to turn to page 269 and complete the activity. See page T-xii for general notes about the Writing activities.

EXPANSION: Writing practice

- Group students from the same country. Tell them to compile their posts and create a message board about living in their country. Post the message boards in the classroom for students to read.

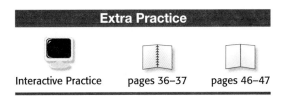

Extra Practice

Interactive Practice   pages 36–37   pages 46–47

CHECK YOUR UNDERSTANDING

A Read the message board posts again. What is the topic of the posts?

a. advice about eating quietly
b. rude and polite behavior in the U.S.
c. surprising things about U.S. culture

Reading Skill:
Identifying Topics

The topic of an article is the subject the author is writing about. Identifying the topic of an article will prepare you to understand it.

B What is the main idea of the message board posts?

a. Americans are quiet eaters.
b. Rude and polite behavior is not the same in all countries.
c. Life in the U.S. is difficult.

C Complete the advice that Arturo received.

1. Don't be more than _____fifteen_____ minutes late for an appointment with friends.

2. Don't make a lot of _____noise_____ when you eat.

3. When you talk to people, stand about _____three_____ feet away from them.

4. When you are at a bus stop or in a store, you have to _____wait_____ your turn.

D PAIRS. Imagine you are writing a post on the message board. What advice will you give Arturo about living in the U.S.?

Show what you know!

PRE-WRITING. PAIRS. Look at the advice in Exercise C. Is this advice correct for your country?

WRITE. Write about what is rude or polite in your country. See page 269.

Listening and Speaking

1 BEFORE YOU LISTEN

Ⓐ CLASS. Look at the pictures. What are some other reasons that people say no to invitations?

I don't feel well.

I'm too busy.

7:30 Meet Tony downtown

I have other plans.

Ⓑ PAIRS. In the U.S., it is polite to give a reason when you decline an invitation. How about in your country?

2 LISTEN

Ⓐ CLASS. Look at the picture of Gloria and Yi-Wen. Where are they?

CD1 T60
Ⓑ Listen to the conversation. What does Gloria ask?

a. "Do you want to get some lunch?"
b. "Do you have time to help me?"

CD1 T60
Ⓒ Listen again. Complete the sentences.

1. **Gloria / Yi-Wen** is very busy.

2. Yi-Wen **can / can't** go with Gloria.

CD1 T61
Ⓓ Listen to the whole conversation. Answer the questions.

1. Who called Yi-Wen?
   a. her husband   b. her friend   c. her co-worker

2. What is Yi-Wen going to do?
   a. finish her work   b. go to lunch with Gloria   c. go to lunch with Bob

Accept or decline an invitation

Getting Started 5 minutes

1 BEFORE YOU LISTEN

A CLASS. Look at the pictures. What are some...

- Say: *Look at some reasons that people say no to invitations.* Say each reason and ask the class to repeat.
- Ask: *What other reasons can you think of?* Elicit students' ideas and write them on the board (for example, *I'm too tired. I don't have any money. I don't like . . .*). Say each reason on the board and ask the class to repeat.

EXPANSION: Vocabulary and graphic organizer practice for 1A

- Form small groups. Assign each group one of the reasons to decline invitations. Tell groups to brainstorm related reasons and write them on small slips of paper (for example, for *I don't feel well: I have a headache. I have a cold. My stomach hurts.*).
- On the board, draw three web diagrams. Write one reason in each circle. Collect the slips of paper and put them in a box or bag. Ask students to draw a slip of paper, read the reason, and write it on the correct web diagram.

B PAIRS. In the U.S., it is polite to give a reason...

- Read the directions. Tell students to underline the word *decline*. Ask: *If you decline an invitation, do you say yes or no to the invitation?* (No.) Write *accept* on the board and say: *When you say yes to an invitation, you accept the invitation.*
- If possible, pair students from different countries.
- On the board, write: *In your country, do you need to give a reason when you decline an invitation?* Tell partners to talk about what is polite in their countries.

Presentation 25 minutes

2 LISTEN

A CLASS. Look at the picture of Gloria...

- Read the directions. Tell students to point to Gloria and Yi-Wen in the picture.
- Elicit an answer to the question (at work).

B Listen to the conversation. What...

- Tell students to look closely at the picture. Ask: *What time is it?* (12:05) *What is Gloria carrying?* (a raincoat / a coat / a jacket) *What does she have over her shoulder?* (her purse)
- Read the directions and the answer choices. Tell students to guess what Gloria asks.
- Play CD 1, Track 60. Students circle the letter of the correct answer.
- Elicit the correct answer from the class. Ask: *Was your guess correct?*

Teaching Tip

Optional: Remember that if students need additional support, tell them to read the Audio Script on page 300 as they listen to the conversations.

C Listen again. Complete the sentences.

- Tell students to look at the picture again. Ask: *What's on Yi-Wen's desk?* (a lot of papers, a phone) *How does Yi-Wen look?* (busy, stressed)
- Play Track 60 again. Students underline the correct words.
- To check answers, call on students to read the sentences.
- Ask: *What does Yi-Wen have to do?* (finish some work)

D Listen to the whole conversation....

- Tell students to read the questions and answer choices silently.
- Play CD 1, Track 61. Students circle the letter of the answers.
- Ask students to read the questions and call on classmates to answer. If an incorrect answer is given, play Track 61 again.

3 CONVERSATION

A Listen. Notice the pronunciation...

- Write *have to* and *has to* on the board. Read the Pronunciation Watch note. Say: *We write* have to *and* has to, *but when people talk they usually say* "hafta" *and* "hasta."
- Tell students to underline *have to* and *has to* in the examples. Play CD 1, Track 62.
- Resume playing Track 62. Students listen and repeat.

Language Note

Read the Pronunciation Watch note again and ask the class: *Why is this?* Tell them to refer back to the Pronunciation Watch note on page 49. Explain that *"wanna," "hafta,"* and *"hasta"* are called *reductions*. Ask: *What other reduction have we practiced?* (*"gonna"*) Pronounce all four reductions and ask the class to repeat.

Controlled Practice   20 minutes

B Listen. Circle the words you hear.

- On the board, write: *a. I have a class tonight. b. I have to go.* (b) Underline *have to* in b and ask: *Is this pronounced* "hafta" *or* "hasta"? (*"hafta"*) Write *"hafta"* in parentheses above *have to*. Read both sentences. Reduce *have to* to *"hafta"* in b. Ask the class to repeat. Remind students that we do not write *"hafta"* or *"hasta."* We only say them in conversation.
- Read the directions. Play CD 1, Track 63. Students listen and circle the words they hear.
- To check answers, play Track 63 again and pause after each item. Elicit the answers from the class.

C Listen and repeat the conversation.

- Note: This conversation is the same one students heard in Exercise 2B on page 80.
- Tell students to read the conversation silently and underline *want to* and *have to*.
- Tell students to write *"wanna"* in parentheses above *want to* in Gloria's first line and *"hafta"* in parentheses above *have to* in Yi-Wen's first line. Say the lines and ask the class to repeat.
- Play CD 1, Track 64. Students listen and repeat.

4 PRACTICE

A PAIRS. Practice the conversation. Then make...

- Pair students and tell them to practice the conversation in Exercise 3C. Tell them to take turns playing each role.
- Then, in Exercise 4A, tell students to look at the information in the boxes. Review the meaning of *deli, errands,* and *make calls.* Say each activity and ask the class to repeat.
- Copy the conversation onto the board and complete it with words from the boxes.
- Play Speaker A and practice with a student. Switch roles.
- Tell pairs to take turns playing each role and to use the boxes to fill in the blanks.
- Walk around. As needed, model correct pronunciation of *"wanna"* and *"hafta"* and ask students to repeat.
- Tell students to stand, mingle, and practice the conversation with several new partners.
- Call on pairs to perform for the class.

Communicative Practice   10 minutes

B ROLE PLAY. PAIRS. Make your own...

- Read the directions. Write the words *accept* and *decline* on the board. Ask: *What does* accept *mean?* (say yes) *What does* decline *mean?* (say no)
- Ask: *How do you accept an invitation?* Point to the yellow note. Say the phrases and ask the class to repeat. Write them on the board under *Accept.*
- Ask: *How do you decline an invitation?* Elicit and write under *Decline:*

    Sorry, I can't. I have to . . .
    I really can't.
    Thanks, but I don't think so. Not today.

- Model the role play: Invite a couple of above-level students to do something. Prompt them to accept or decline using the language on the board.
- Pair students. If time permits, ask students to stand, mingle, and role play with several partners.

Extra Practice

Interactive Practice

3 CONVERSATION

Pronunciation Watch

Pronunciation Watch

In conversation, *have to* usually sounds like "hafta" and *has to* sounds like "hasta."

CD1 T62

A Listen. Notice the pronunciation of *have to* and *has to*. Then listen and repeat.

have to   I have to finish some work.
has to   She has to make some calls.

CD1 T63

B Listen. Circle the words you hear.

1. a. have to   2. (a.) have to   3. (a.) has to   4. a. has to
   (b.) have a   b. have a   b. has a   (b.) has a

CD1 T64

C Listen and repeat the conversation.

Gloria: Do you want to get some lunch?
Yi-Wen: Sorry, I can't. I have to finish some work.
Gloria: Oh. Are you sure?
Yi-Wen: Yes, I'm sorry. I really can't.
Gloria: Well, how about a little later?
Yi-Wen: Thanks, but I don't think so. Not today.

4 PRACTICE

A PAIRS. Practice the conversation. Then make new conversations. Use the information in the boxes.

A: Do you want to   ?

B: Sorry, I can't. I have to   .

A: Oh. Are you sure?

B: Yes, I'm sorry. I really can't.

A: Well, how about a little later?

B: Thanks, but I don't think so. Not today.

walk over to the deli
take a walk
get some coffee

go to a meeting
run some errands
make some calls

B ROLE PLAY. PAIRS. Make your own conversations. Student A, invite your partner to do something. Student B, accept or decline the invitation.

To accept an invitation, you can say:
• Sure. I'd love to.
• That sounds like fun.
• Sounds great.

Grammar

Modal: *have to*

Affirmative				Negative			
I You We They	**have to**	**finish**	some work.	I You We They	**don't have to**	**stay**	at work late.
He She	**has to**	**work**	a lot.	He She	**doesn't have to**	**work**	on weekends.

PRACTICE

> drive   get up   ~~go~~   study   take   visit

Ⓐ Complete the sentences. Use the infinitive forms of the verbs in the box.

1. We don't have _____*to go*_____ to the grocery store. We have a lot of food.

2. He has _____to study_____ tonight. There's a big test tomorrow.

3. Kara doesn't have _____to drive_____ to work. She takes the bus every day.

4. Their flight leaves at 6:00 in the morning. They have _____to get up_____ early.

5. Claude has _____to take_____ his daughter to the doctor. She's sick.

6. I have _____to visit_____ my mother. She's in the hospital.

Ⓑ Complete the sentences. Use the correct forms of *have to* and the words in parentheses.

1. I'm coming home on time tonight. I _*don't have to work late*_ .

                                                (not work late)

2. Alice _____has to stay_____ home with her son. He's sick.

                 (stay)

3. I can watch your kids on Saturday night. You _____don't have to get_____ a babysitter.

                                                       (not get)

4. Monica _____doesn't have to work_____ this weekend. She can go to the zoo with us.

                   (not work)

5. Babu _____has to take_____ the bus to work. He doesn't have a car.

                 (take)

6. The movie theatre is always crowded. We _____have to buy_____ tickets early.

                                          (buy)

Ⓒ PAIRS. Compare your answers.

Getting Started   5 minutes

- Say: *We're going to study* have to. *In the conversation on page 81, Yi-Wen used this grammar.*
- Play CD 1, Track 64. Students listen. On the board, write: *I have to finish some work.* Underline *have to finish*.

Presentation   10 minutes

Modal: *have to*

- Copy the grammar charts onto the board or show the charts on Transparency 4.5 and cover the exercise.
- On the board, write: *I need to finish some work.* Read the sentence. Then cross out *need to* and write *have to*. Say: Have to *and* need to *have similar meanings.*
- Rewrite the sentence: *I have to finish some work.* Read the sentence. Then cross out *I* and write *Yi-Wen*. Ask: *What else do I have to change?* Cross out *have* and write *has*. Rewrite and read the sentence: *Yi-Wen has to finish some work.*
- Call on students to read examples from the grammar charts. Tell them to choose words from each column. For example: *They don't have to work on weekends.* Ask students to say their sentences again with the "hafta" or "hasta" pronunciation of *have to* or *has to*.
- If you are using the transparency, do the exercise with the class.

Controlled Practice   20 minutes

 **PRACTICE**

A Complete the sentences. Use the infinitive forms...

- Read the directions.
- Ask: *You used infinitives in Lesson 6 with* like *and* hate. *What's an infinitive?* (*to* + base form of a verb). Say each verb in the box and ask the class to call out the infinitive (for example, *to drive*).

- Ask a student to read the example. Walk around and check for *to*.
- Call on students to read the completed sentences. Encourage them to use the "hafta" or "hasta" pronunciation of *have to* or *has to*.

B Complete the sentences. Use the correct forms...

- Write item 1 on the board. Ask: *Is it affirmative or negative?* (negative) *What's the subject?* (*I*) Tell students to point to *I* on the right chart. Ask: *What's the correct form of* have to? (*don't have to*)
- Complete item 1 on the board. Call on a student to read the example.
- Walk around and if students have difficulty, take them through the same steps used with the example.
- Tell students to look at their answers and check that each one includes *to*.

C PAIRS. **Compare your answers.**

- Pair students and tell them to take turns reading the sentences. Tell them to practice the "hafta" and "hasta" pronunciation of *have to* and *has to*.
- To check answers, call on a student to read item 2. Tell that student to call on another classmate to read item 3. Continue in the same way with the remaining items.

▇▇▇ **EXPANSION: Grammar and speaking practice for C**

- Tell students to write a to-do list. Write your own to-do list on the board as a model (for example, *go to the laundromat, clean the house, exercise, call my grandmother*).
- Pair students. Say: *Tell your partner about your to-do list. Use* have to. *For example, you can say:* I have to go to the laundromat. I have to clean the house . . .
- Tell students to exchange lists with their partner. Then form new pairs. Say: *Tell your new partner about your first partner's to-do list. Use* has to. Borrow a student's list and model the activity.

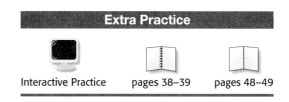

Extra Practice		
Interactive Practice	pages 38–39	pages 48–49

1 GRAMMAR

Ⓐ Complete the conversation. Underline the...

- Tell students to review the grammar charts on pages 70 (Adverbs of frequency), 76 (Simple present: *like / love / hate* + infinitive) and 82 (Modal: *have to*).
- On the board, write:

I	like	
	don't like	
	love	_____ cook dinner.
	hate	
	have	

- Ask students what word goes in the blank. Write *to* in the blank. Ask a few students to say a true sentence using the words on the board.

Ⓑ Listen and check your answers.

- Play CD 1, Track 65. Students listen and check their answers.
- Tell students to read the conversation again silently. Ask: *What does A invite David to do?* (come to his house to watch the game) *Does David accept or decline?* (decline) *What reason does he give?* (He has to go the supermarket because his sister is coming over for dinner.)
- *Optional:* Tell students to practice the completed conversations with a partner.

Ⓒ Rewrite the statements. Use the adverbs in...

- Tell students to review the grammar chart on page 70 (Adverbs of frequency).
- On the board, write item 1 and *My sister is at the mall on weekends.* (*always*) Underline the verb in each sentence. Ask a student to read the Grammar Watch note on page 70. As a class, decide where to place *sometimes* and *always* in the sentences. Read the sentences with adverbs: *I sometimes go to the mall on weekends. My sister is always at the mall on weekends.*
- Tell students to underline the verb in each sentence (*go*, *is*).
- To check answers, ask students who finish early to write a sentence on the board. Read each sentence. As a class, correct as needed.

CD-ROM Practice

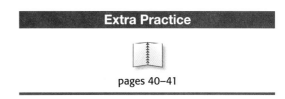 Go to the CD-ROM for more practice.

If your students need more practice with the vocabulary, grammar, and competencies in Unit 4, encourage them to review the activities on the CD-ROM. This review can also help students prepare for the final role play on the following Expand page.

Extra Practice
pages 40–41

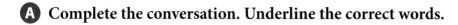

1 GRAMMAR

A Complete the conversation. Underline the correct words.

A: Hi, David. Do you want to come over to watch the game?

B: Sorry, I can't. I **have / <u>have to</u>** go to the supermarket.

A: The supermarket is open late. You can **<u>always</u> / never** go later.

B: Actually, I can't. My sister is coming over tonight and I **have / <u>have to</u>** get food for dinner.

A: OK. Too bad.

B: What about next Saturday? You know I love **watch / <u>to watch</u>** the games on your new TV.

A: Great. Make sure you **don't have / <u>don't have to</u>** run any errands next Saturday!

CD1 T65

B 🔘 Listen and check your answers.

C Rewrite the statements. Use the adverbs in parentheses.

1. I go to the mall on weekends.

   (sometimes) *I sometimes go to the mall on weekends.*

2. Dave works on Tuesday and Thursday mornings.

   (usually) Dave usually works on Tuesday and Thursday mornings.

3. Ted is absent from English class.

   (always) Ted is always absent from English class.

4. My brother cooks breakfast on Sundays.

   (often) My brother often cooks breakfast on Sundays.

5. Ralph eats meat or fish.

   (never) Ralph never eats meat or fish.

6. We are at home during the week.

   (hardly ever) We are hardly ever at home during the week.

 Go to the CD-ROM for more practice.

2 ACT IT OUT   What do you say?

STEP 1. CLASS. Review the Lesson 5 conversation between Jane and Karen (CD 1 Track 58).

STEP 2. PAIRS. Talk about the errands and chores you need to do every week. Talk about which things you like and dislike. Find something you both like to do.

3 READ AND REACT   Problem-solving

STEP 1. Read about Max's problem.

Max has a friend at work named Fran. Fran invites him to go dancing tomorrow night. Max doesn't have any plans tomorrow night but he doesn't want to go dancing.

STEP 2. PAIRS. What is Max's problem? What can he do? Here are some ideas.

- He can say, "Thanks, but I don't want to go dancing."
- He can say, "Thanks, but I have plans tomorrow night."
- He can say yes to the invitation but then not go.
- He can _____.

4 CONNECT   For your Study Skills Activity, go to page 250.
For your Team Project, go to page 277.

2 ACT IT OUT

STEP 1. CLASS. Review the Lesson 5 conversation...

- Play CD 1, Track 58. Students listen.
- As needed, play Track 58 again to aid comprehension.

STEP 2. PAIRS. Talk about the errands and chores...

- Read the directions.
- To prepare for the activity, tell students to write a list of errands and chores they need to do every week. Tell them to draw a face next to each one that shows how they feel about it.
- Pair students. Say: *Talk about your errands and chores.* Use *need to* and *have to. Talk about which things you like and dislike.* Use *hate, not like, like,* and *love and an infinitive.* Use *Me, too.* and *Not me. to agree or disagree with your partner.*
- Walk around and observe partners interacting. Check students' use of *to.*
- Call on pairs to perform for the class. While pairs are performing, use the scoring rubric on page T-xiii to evaluate each student's vocabulary, grammar, fluency, and how well he or she completes the task.
- After each pair performs, ask the class: *What do they both like to do?*
- *Optional:* After each pair finishes, discuss the strengths and weakness of each performance either in front of the class or privately.

3 READ AND REACT

STEP 1. Read about Max's problem.

- Say: *We are going to read about a student's problem, and then we need to think about a solution.*
- Read the directions.
- Read the story while students follow along silently. Pause after each sentence to allow time for students to comprehend. Periodically stop and ask simple *Wh-* questions to check comprehension (for example, *Who is Fran? What does Fran invite Max to do? Does Max want to accept or decline the invitation? Does he have a reason?*).

STEP 2. PAIRS. What is Max's problem? What...

- Read the directions and the question.
- Ask: *What is Max's problem?* (He doesn't want to accept his friend's invitation.)
- Pair students. Read the list of ideas. Give pairs a couple of minutes to discuss possible solutions for Max.
- Ask: *Which ideas are good?* Call on students to say their opinion about the ideas in the box (for example, S: *I think he can say, "Thanks, but I have plans tomorrow night." This is a good idea.*).
- Tell pairs to think of one new idea not in the box (for example, *He can say, "I don't like to dance," and suggest a different activity.*) and to write it in the blank. Encourage students to think of more than one idea and to write them in their notebooks.
- Call on pairs to say their own solutions. Write them on the board and ask: *Do you think this is a good idea? Why or why not?*

▬▬ MULTILEVEL INSTRUCTION for STEP 2

Pre-level Ask: *Which ideas are polite? Which ideas are rude?* Tell students to draw a two-column chart with the headings *Polite* and *Rude.* Tell them to write the ideas from the book and the board in the chart.

Above-level Ask: *Do you think Max doesn't want to go out with Fran or doesn't want to go dancing?* Tell students to write a line for Max to say for each situation.

4 CONNECT

Turn to page 250 for the Study Skills Activity and page 277 for the Team Project. See page T-xi for general notes about teaching these activities.

Progress Check

Which goals can you check off? Go back to page 65.

Ask students to turn to page 65 and check off any remaining goals they have reached. Call on students to say which goals they will practice outside of class.

5 At Home

Classroom Materials/Extra Practice

CD 2
Tracks 2–14

T
Transparencies 5.1–5.5
Vocabulary Cards Unit 5

MCA
Unit 5

Workbook
Unit 5

Interactive Practice
Unit 5

Unit Overview

Goals
- See the list of goals on the facing page.

Grammar
- Present continuous: Affirmative and negative statements
- *There is / There are:* Affirmative and negative statements, questions, and short answers

Pronunciation
- Stress in compound nouns
- Voiced and voiceless *th* sounds

Reading
- Read an article about a U.S. city
- *Reading Skill:* Skimming

Writing
- Write about your community
- Write driving directions
- Write a housing classified ad

Life Skills Writing
- Complete an application for an apartment

Preview
- Set the context of the unit by asking questions about the home (for example, *Where do you live? Do you live in a house or an apartment? Who fixes problems in your home?*).
- Hold up page 85 or show Transparency 5.1. Read the unit title and ask the class to repeat.
- Say: *Look at the picture.* Ask the Preview questions: *What do you see?* (a woman under a sink) *What is the problem?* Elicit or tell the class: *The sink is clogged.* Ask: *What happens when the sink is clogged?* (The water doesn't go down.)

Unit Goals
- Point to the Unit Goals. Explain that this list shows what the class will be studying in this unit.
- Tell students to read the goals silently.
- Say each goal and ask students to repeat. Explain unfamiliar vocabulary as needed:

    Application: a form you complete when you want an apartment, a job, etc . . .

    Directions: instructions about how to get from one place to another

- Tell students to circle one goal that is very important to them. Call on several students to say the goal they circled.
- Write a checkmark (✓) on the board. Say: *We will come back to this page again. You will write a checkmark next to the goals you learned in this unit.*

At Home

5

Preview

Look at the picture.
What do you see?
What is the problem?

UNIT GOALS

- ☐ Describe problems in your home
- ☐ Read apartment ads
- ☐ Complete an application for an apartment
- ☐ Ask about an apartment
- ☐ Get directions

Lesson 1   Vocabulary

1 WHAT DO YOU KNOW?

A CLASS. Look at the pictures. Which household problems do you know?

CD2 T2

B Look at the pictures and listen. Listen again and repeat.

2 PRACTICE

A PAIRS. Student A, point to a picture. Ask, "What's the problem?" Student B, identify the problem.

A: *(points to a picture) What's the problem?*
B: *The ceiling is leaking.*
A: *Right!*

B WORD PLAY. PAIRS. Complete the chart. Use the words in the box. Words can be written more than once.

> ceiling   door   faucet   lock   sink
> toilet   washing machine   window

Answers will vary but could include:

Things that leak	Things that get stuck	Things that get clogged
faucet	window	sink
toilet	lock	washing machine
ceiling	door	toilet

86   UNIT 5

Lesson 1 Vocabulary

Getting Started   5 minutes

1 WHAT DO YOU KNOW?

A CLASS. Look at the pictures. Which household...

- Show Transparency 5.2 or hold up the book. Tell students to cover the list of words on page 87.
- Read the directions. Elicit a household problem (for example, *In number 6, the mailbox is broken.*).
- Students call out answers. Help students pronounce household problems if they have difficulty.
- If students call out an incorrect household problem, change the student's answer to a question for the class (for example, *In number 2, the sink is clogged?*). If nobody can identify the correct household problem, tell students they will now listen to a CD and practice the household problems vocabulary.

Presentation   10 minutes

B Look at the pictures and listen....

- Read the directions. Play CD 2, Track 2. Pause after number 12 (*There's no hot water.*).
- To check comprehension, say each household problem in random order and ask students to point to the appropriate picture.
- Resume playing Track 2. Students listen and repeat.

Controlled Practice   20 minutes

2 PRACTICE

A PAIRS. Student A, point to a picture. Ask, "What's...

- Read each line in the example and ask the class to repeat. Model correct intonation.
- Play Speaker A and model the example with an above-level student. Point to picture 1.

- Continue the conversation. Prompt B to point to a picture and say: *What's the problem?*
- Pair students and tell them to talk about at least three pictures each.
- Walk around and help with pronunciation of the household problems as needed.

MULTILEVEL INSTRUCTION for 2A
Pre-level Allow pairs to refer to the list of words at the bottom of page 87 as needed.
Above-level Tell pairs to cover the list of words on page 87 when they practice.

B WORD PLAY. PAIRS. Complete the chart. Use...

- Pair students. Read the directions.
- Say: *Look at the pictures. Point to a ceiling. Point to a toilet.* Continue in the same way with the other words in the box.
- Tell students to switch partners and compare their chart with another classmate.
- To check answers, copy the chart onto the board. Ask three students to write the words in the chart. Elicit a fourth word for *Things that leak*.
- Point to each word on the chart, say a sentence, and ask the class to repeat, for example: *The faucet is leaking. The door is stuck. The toilet is clogged.*

EXPANSION: Vocabulary practice for 2B
- Tell students to look at the list of household problems on page 87 and the chart in Exercise 2B. Ask: *Which household problems do you have?* Tell students to write a checkmark next to any problems in their home.
- Pair students. Say: *Tell your partner what problems you have.*

Communicative Practice   20 minutes

Learning Strategy: Make labels

- Read the directions. Tell students to look at the vocabulary list and underline the words that name things in their home. Tell them to look at the words that come after *The*.
- Say each noun from items 1–10 and ask the class to call out *a* or *an* and the thing. For example, you say *ceiling* and the class calls out *a ceiling*.
- Tell students to make five cards for things in their house.
- Walk around as students work. If misspellings occur, tell them to check the vocabulary list on page 87.
- Say: *Put your cards on things in your home. Practice saying the words.* Remind students to use this strategy to remember other new vocabulary.

Show what you know!

STEP 1. Look at the list of household problems. Circle...

- Read the directions.
- Ask: *Which household problem do you <u>really</u> not want to have?* Tell students to circle this problem.
- On the board, write the household problem that you think is the worst (for example, *11. There's no heat.*).

STEP 2. GROUPS OF 3. What is the worst household...

- First, group students who chose the same problem. Tell them to brainstorm reasons their problem is bad. Tell them to write the reasons on a sheet of paper and to circle the reason they like the best.
- Form new groups of 3 students who chose different problems and tell them to ask each other: *Which is the worst household problem?*
- With a student, model the activity, for example:

  S: *What is the worst household problem?*

  T: *I think number 11 is the worst problem because I hate to be cold.*

- To wrap up, say each problem from the list and ask students to raise their hands for the problem they chose. Call on a student whose hand is raised to give a reason.

EXPANSION: Vocabulary and listening practice for STEP 2

- Collect one list of reasons from each group. Put the lists in random order and number each sheet. Tell students to number a sheet of paper according to the number of lists you have.
- Say: *I'm going to read the reasons that a group thought a problem was the worst. Guess the problem I'm reading about and write your guess next to the number on your paper. Number 1 . . .*
- Read the reasons again and elicit the answers from the class. Ask if anyone guessed all the problems correctly.

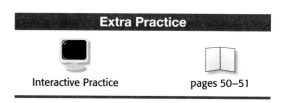

Extra Practice

Interactive Practice   pages 50–51

2

3

5

6

8

9

Household Problems

1. The ceiling is leaking.
2. The faucet is leaking.
3. The toilet is clogged.
4. The sink is clogged.
5. The lock is broken.
6. The mailbox is broken.
7. The window is stuck.
8. The door is stuck.
9. The washing machine isn't working.
10. The stove isn't working.
11. There's no heat.
12. There's no hot water.

Learning Strategy

Make labels

Look at the list of household problems. Think of the things in your home. Make cards for five things. Write the word on a card. Put the cards on the things in your home.

a faucet

Show what you know!

STEP 1. Look at the list of household problems. Circle the problem you think is the worst.

STEP 2. GROUPS OF 3. What is the worst household problem? Explain your answer.

I think number 5 is the worst problem because . . .

Listening and Speaking

1   BEFORE YOU LISTEN

CLASS. Look at the pictures. When there is a problem in your home, who fixes it?

an electrician

a plumber

a locksmith

a building manager

2   LISTEN

A   **CLASS.** Look at the picture of Harry fixing the radiator in his apartment. Guess: Who is he talking to?

a. a plumber
b. the building manager
(c.) his friend

CD2 T3

B   Listen to the conversation. Was your guess in Exercise A correct?

CD2 T3

C   Listen again. What does Joe say?

(a.) Call the building manager.
b. Buy a new radiator.
c. Fix the radiator.

CD2 T4

D   Listen to the whole conversation. Why can't Harry follow Joe's advice?

Harry just became the building manager.

Lesson 2 Describe problems in your home

Getting Started   5 minutes

1 BEFORE YOU LISTEN

CLASS. Look at the pictures. When there is a...

- Tell the class to look at the second picture. Ask: *What's the problem?* (The sink is clogged / leaking.) Tell the class to look at the third picture. Ask: *What's the problem?* (The lock is broken.)
- Tell the class to look at the first picture. Ask: *What isn't working?* (the electricity) Tell the class to look at the fourth picture. Ask: *What isn't working?* (the light)
- Ask: *When there is a problem in your home, who fixes it?* Say each type of repairperson and ask the class to repeat. Explain that if you own your own home, you call an electrician, a plumber, or a locksmith to fix problems. If you rent an apartment, you call the building manager to fix problems.
- As a follow-up, ask: *When the toilet is clogged, who fixes it?* (a plumber) *If the ceiling in your rental apartment is leaking, who fixes it?* (a building manager) *If a light isn't working in a house you own, who fixes it?* (an electrician)

Presentation   10 minutes

2 LISTEN

Ⓐ CLASS. Look at the picture of Harry fixing...

- Read the directions. Tell students to look at the picture and to point to Harry, the radiator, and the phone.
- Ask: *What is Harry doing?* (fixing the radiator, talking on the phone) *If the radiator is broken, what problem does Harry have?* (There's no heat.) *Do you have a radiator in your home?* Ask for a show of hands.
- Ask: *Does Harry live in a house or an apartment?* (an apartment)

- Tell students to read the question and answer choices. Students circle the letter of the answer they think is correct.
- Ask students to raise their hands for the answer they chose. For each answer choice, ask a couple of students who raised their hands to explain their answer.

Ⓑ Listen to the conversation. Was...

- Read the directions. Play CD 2, Track 3.
- Ask: *Is Harry talking to a plumber?* (No, he isn't.) *Is he talking to the building manager?* (No, he isn't.) *Is he talking to his friend?* (Yes, he is.) *What's his friend's name?* (Joe)
- Ask: *Was your guess correct?*

> **Teaching Tip**
>
> *Optional:* If students need additional support, tell them to read the Audio Script on page 300 as they listen to the conversations.

Controlled Practice   10 minutes

Ⓒ Listen again. What does Joe say?

- Read the directions. Ask: *What does Joe think Harry should do about the broken radiator?*
- Play Track 3 again.
- Elicit the correct answer from the class. Ask: *Do you think Joe's advice is good? Why?* (Yes, because Harry rents an apartment.)

Ⓓ Listen to the whole conversation....

- Read the directions. Play CD 3, Track 4. Students write the answer on the lines provided.
- Students compare answers with a partner.
- Ask: *Why can't Harry call the building manager?* Elicit the answer and write it on the board.

Lesson 2 Describe problems in your home

Presentation   5 minutes

 3 CONVERSATION

 Listen and repeat the conversation.

- Note: This conversation is the same one students heard in Exercise 2B on page 88.
- Play CD 2, Track 5. Students listen and repeat.

Controlled Practice   10 minutes

4 PRACTICE

A PAIRS. Practice the conversation. Then make new...

- Pair students and tell them to practice the conversation in Exercise 3. Tell them to take turns playing each role.
- Then, in Exercise 4A, ask students to look at the information in the boxes. Say each word or expression and ask the class to repeat. Then say: *My lock is broken. Who should I call?* (a locksmith) *My bathroom light isn't working. Who should I call?* (an electrician) *My faucet is leaking? Who should I call?* (a plumber)
- Read the directions.
- Copy the conversation onto the board and complete it with words from the boxes.
- Play Speaker B and model a new conversation with an above-level student. Tell the student to look at the blue box and circle one household problem. Use the student's and your name when you complete Speaker B's first line.
- Tell pairs to take turns playing each role and to use the boxes to fill in the blanks.
- Walk around and as needed, remind students to switch roles and practice both parts. Tell them to use a different household problem each time they practice.
- Tell students to stand, mingle, and practice the conversation with several new partners.
- Call on pairs to perform for the class.

Communicative Practice   20 minutes

B ROLE PLAY. PAIRS. Make your own conversations...

- Tell the class that they're going to practice the conversation in Exercise 4A again but with different household problems.
- Tell students to write the following in their notebooks:
  1. a different household problem (not one from the blue box in Exercise 4A)
  2. who they should call to fix this problem
- Pair students. Tell Student B to use the household problem he or she wrote down. Tell Student A to respond with who to call to fix the problem. Say: *If you don't know the name for the correct type of repairperson, you can say* the building manager.
- To wrap up, on the board write some of the errors you heard during the role plays. Ask students to correct the mistakes. Go over the corrections by saying the words or sentences correctly and asking the class to repeat.

MULTILEVEL INSTRUCTION for 4B

Pre-level Student A can show Student B the name for the correct type of repairperson to call.

Above-level Tell Student A not to show Student B the name for the correct type of repairperson to call.

EXPANSION: Vocabulary and graphic organizer practice for 4B

- On the board, draw a web diagram and write *plumber* in the circle. Draw four lines radiating out from the circle.
- Ask students to look at the vocabulary on page 87. Tell them to copy the diagram and write on it the four problems that you should call a plumber to fix (vocabulary items 2, 3, 4, and 12).
- Pairs students and tell them to use the language from the Venn diagram to practice a new conversation like the one in Exercise 4A.

Extra Practice

Interactive Practice

3 CONVERSATION

CD2 T5

Listen and repeat the conversation.

Harry: Hello?

Joe: Hi, Harry. It's Joe.

Harry: Oh, hi, Joe. Can I call you back?

Joe: Sure. No problem.

Harry: Thanks. My radiator is broken and I'm trying to fix it.

Joe: You should call the building manager.

4 PRACTICE

A **PAIRS. Practice the conversation. Then make new conversations. Use your own names and the information in the boxes.**

A: Hello?

B: Hi, ＿＿＿＿＿＿. It's ＿＿＿＿＿＿.

A: Oh, hi, ＿＿＿＿＿＿. Can I call you back?

B: Sure. No problem.

A: Thanks. ＿＿＿＿＿＿ and I'm trying to fix it.

B: You should call ＿＿＿＿＿＿.

My lock is broken	a locksmith
My bathroom light isn't working	an electrician
My faucet is leaking	a plumber

B **ROLE PLAY. PAIRS. Make your own conversations. Use your own names and different information.**

Describe problems in your home

Grammar

Present continuous

Affirmative			
I	**am**		
We	**are**	**fixing**	the radiator now.
He	**is**		

Negative			
I	**am**		
We	**are**	**not calling**	the building manager.
He	**is**		

Grammar Watch

Use the present continuous for events taking place at the present time.

1 PRACTICE

A Complete the sentences. Use the present continuous and the verbs in parentheses.

1. The building manager (help) _____*is helping*_____ the tenant.

2. Thanks for fixing the oven. I (use) _____am using_____ it now.

3. The dishwasher (make) _____is making_____ a loud noise. Can you look at it?

4. That lock is broken. I (try) _____am trying_____ to fix it.

5. That washing machine (not work) _____is not working_____. It's out of order.

6. We (not wait for) _____are not waiting for_____ the building manager to fix the broken light.

   My husband (fix) _____is fixing_____ it right now.

B Read the sentences. Correct the mistake in each sentence.

1. The sink is ~~leak~~ ^leaking, and it's making a big mess.

2. ~~We're~~ We're are looking for a good plumber.

3. ~~I not~~ I'm not calling the building manager.

4. The stove in my apartment ~~not~~ isn't working.

5. The building ~~manager are~~ managers are or manager is fixing the problem.

6. They're not ~~use~~ using the broken sink.

Lesson 3   Describe problems in your home

Getting Started   5 minutes

- Say: *We're going to study the present continuous. In the conversation on page 89, Harry used this grammar.*
- Play CD 2, Track 5. Students listen. On the board, write: *I'm trying to fix it.* Underline *'m trying.*

Presentation   10 minutes

Present continuous

- Copy the grammar charts onto the board or show Transparency 5.3 and cover the exercise.
- Point to the picture of Harry on page 88. Ask: *What is Harry doing?* On the board, write: *Harry _____ fix _____ the radiator.*
- Tell students to look at the left grammar chart. Ask: *What form of* be *goes with Harry?* Write *is* in the first blank in the sentence on the board. Ask: *What do I add to* fix *to form the present continuous?* Write *ing* in the second blank. Read the completed sentence: *Harry is fixing the radiator.*
- Change the subject of the sentence on the board by adding *and I* after *Harry.* Ask: *What else needs to change?* Elicit the answer. Erase *is* and write *are.*
- Point to the picture of Harry on page 88 again. On the board, write: *Harry is calling the building manager.* Ask: *Is this sentence true or false?* (false) *How can I change it to make it true?* Tell students to look at the right grammar chart. Add *not* between *is* and *calling.* Read the new sentence: *Harry is not calling the building manager.* Underline *is not.* Ask: *What's the short form for* is not? Elicit *isn't* and write it above *is not.*
- Read the Grammar Watch note. Say: *Look around the classroom. What's taking place at the present time?* Elicit a few affirmative and negative sentences and write them on the board. Elicit the contractions for the negative sentences (for example, *Ahmed is listening. Amaya and Yoko aren't talking.*).
- If you are using the transparency, do the exercise with the class.

Controlled Practice   20 minutes

1 PRACTICE

A Complete the sentences. Use the present...

- Write item 1 on the board. Ask: *What's the subject?* (the building manager) *What's the correct form of* be? (is)
- Point to the verb *help.* Ask: *How do we form the present continuous?* (is helping)
- Write item 2 on the board. Point to the verb *use.* Ask: *What letter does* use *end in?* (-e) Say: *When a verb ends in* -e, *take off the* -e *before you add* -ing. Cross out the *-e* in *use* and add *-ing.* Then write *using.*
- Walk around and check for the correct form of be and the verb + *-ing.*
- Students compare answers with a partner.
- To check answers, call on students to read the sentences out loud. Elicit contractions as appropriate. Ask the student who reads item 3 how to spell *making.* Write it on the board.

B Read the sentences. Correct the mistake in each...

- Say: *These sentences are in the present continuous. What do you need to form the present continuous?* Elicit and write on the board:

    the correct form of be

    a verb + -ing.

- Read the directions.
- Write item 1 on the board. Ask: *Is the mistake in the form of* be *or in the verb* + -ing? (the verb + -ing)
- Tell students to read each sentence and check for the two things on the board.
- Walk around and, if students have difficulty, tell them to underline the form of *be* and ask: *Is it correct?* Then tell them to underline the verb + *-ing* and ask: *Is it correct?*
- Students compare answers with a partner.
- To check answers, ask students to write the corrected sentences on the board. Ask: *Which items had a mistake in the form of* be? (2, 3, 4, and 5) *Which items had a mistake in the verb* + -ing? (1 and 6)

2 PRACTICE

Complete the e-mail. Use the present continuous and...

- Write the sentence for item 1 on the board. Read the sentence out loud. Ask: *What's the subject?* (Everyone) *What's the form of* be? (*is*) Point out that even though *everyone* refers to many people, it's singular. Underline *one* in *everyone* and say: *The word* one *in* everyone *can help you to remember that it's singular.*

- Ask: *What's the verb in the example?* (*is working*) Say: *Point to the verb* work *in the box. What was added in the example?* (*is* and *-ing*)

- Read the first part of the e-mail. Stop after the sentence that contains item 2. Tell students to look at item 2. Ask: *What's the subject?* (The bathroom sink) *What's the correct form of* be? (*is*) *Which verb in the box goes with* The bathroom sink *and* water all over the floor? (*leak*) *What do you need to add to* leak? (*-ing*)

- Walk around and, if students have difficulty with the correct form of *be*, tell them to underline the subjects.

- Students compare answers with a partner.

- Number from 2 to 7 on the board. Ask students to write answers on the board. If there are any incorrect answers, review the item with the class.

- Tell students to read the e-mail silently. Ask: *What are the problems with the house?* (The bathroom sink is leaking. The kitchen light isn't working. The lock on the front door is broken.)

Communicative Practice   20 minutes

Show what you know!

STEP 1. PAIRS. Student A, look at the picture on...

- Pair students and assign roles of Speaker A and Speaker B. Read the directions. Walk around and check that Student A is looking at the picture on page 91 and Student B is looking at the picture on page 246.

- Remind students: *Don't show your picture to your partner.*

STEP 2. SAME PAIRS. Talk about the pictures...

- Read the directions. Ask a pair to read the example out loud.

- Draw a two-column chart on the board. Label the columns *A* and *B*. In the left column write: *A man is fixing a sink.* In the right column write: *A man is cooking in a kitchen.* Tell students to copy the chart into their notebooks.

- Tell partners to take turns describing their pictures by talking about what a person is doing or a problem. Tell students to write at least four differences in their charts.

- Walk around and check that students are using the present continuous correctly.

- To check answers, call on pairs to say differences. For example,

  A: *In my picture, the stove isn't working.*

  B: *In my picture, the freezer isn't working.*

  A: *In my picture, the ceiling is leaking.*

  B: *In my picture, the window is stuck.*

  A: *In my picture, a woman is calling the building manager.*

  B: *In my picture, an electrician is fixing the electricity.*

Write the differences in the chart on the board.

▄▄▄ MULTILEVEL INSTRUCTION for Step 2

Cross-ability Partners don't look at each other's pictures but can work together to complete the chart. To wrap up, ask a higher-level student to describe Student A's picture for the class. Ask another higher-level student to describe Student B's picture for the class. Tell the class to look at both pictures and point to the activities and problems as they are described.

Progress Check

Can you . . . describe problems in your home?

Say: *We have practiced describing problems in our homes. Now, look at the question at the bottom of the page. Can you describe problems in your home?* Tell students to write a checkmark in the box.

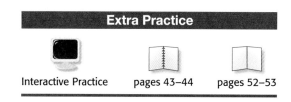

Extra Practice		
Interactive Practice	pages 43–44	pages 52–53

Complete the e-mail. Use the present continuous and the words in the box.

| leak | buy | ~~work~~ | not work | fix | paint | wait |

Hi Linda,

How are you? It's pretty busy around here. Everyone in the family ___is working___ on our
1.
house today. The house is old and there are a lot of problems. The bathroom sink

___'s leaking___ and there is water all over the floor. The light in the kitchen ___isn't working___.
2.   3.
The lock on the front door is broken. Right now my uncle Charlie ___'s fixing___ the sink.
4.
The kids ___are painting___ the living room walls. We ___'re waiting___ for Tom to
5.   6.
get back from the hardware store. He ___'s buying___ a new lock for the front door. There is
7.
so much work to do—I have to go! Talk to you soon!

Elaine

Show what you know! Describe problems in your home

**STEP 1. PAIRS. Student A,
look at the picture on this page.
Student B, look at the picture
on page 246. Don't show your
picture to your partner.**

**STEP 2. SAME PAIRS. Talk
about the pictures. What are the
people doing? What problems
do you see? What are the
differences in your pictures?**

A: *In my picture, a man is fixing
a sink in a kitchen.*
B: *In my picture, a man is
cooking . . .*

Can you . . . describe problems in your home? ☐

Life Skills

1 READ APARTMENT ADS

A Look at the ad for a rental apartment. Read the sentences. Circle *True* or *False*.

Furnished 2-bedroom, 1-bathroom apartment on the third floor of an elevator building. Large living room. Sunny eat-in kitchen with separate dining room. Washer/dryer in basement. Convenient location. Near shopping and public transportation. No pets allowed.

Rent: $1,200/month
Security Deposit: One month's rent
Contact: Joshua 510-555-5432

Fee: One month's rent
Utilities Included: heat, hot water, air-conditioning, and electricity

1. The apartment has two bathrooms.   True   (False)

2. The building has an elevator.   (True)   False

3. The apartment is close to stores and transportation.   (True)   False

4. The rent includes electricity.   (True)   False

5. It's OK to have a pet.   True   (False)

6. The security deposit for this apartment is $1,200.   (True)   False

B PAIRS. Check your answers.

C Look at the abbreviations below. Then look at the ad in Exercise A.
Circle the words for each abbreviation. Then write the words on the lines.

1. A/C _air-conditioning_
2. apt. _apartment_
3. BA _bathroom_
4. BR _bedroom_
5. bsmt. _basement_
6. DR _dining room_

7. EIK _eat-in kitchen_
8. fl. _floor_
9. furn. _furnished_
10. ht. _heat_
11. hw. _hot water_
12. LR _living room_

13. mo. _month_
14. nr. _near_
15. sec. dep. _security deposit_
16. trans. _transportation_
17. util. incl. _utilities included_
18. W/D _washer / dryer_

CD2 T6

D Listen and check your answers. Then listen and repeat.

Getting Started   10 minutes

- Tell the class to look at the ad. Ask: *What is the ad for?* (an apartment) Explain:

  Security deposit: The money that you give to the landlord before you rent an apartment. The landlord returns the money to you when you move out if you have not damaged the apartment. (The *landlord* owns the apartment.)

  Fee: The money that you pay to the agent who shows you the apartment if you decide to rent it. (An *agent* helps people find apartments to rent or houses to buy.)

- Tell the class to look at the ad. Ask: *How much is the rent?* ($1,200 a month) *How much is the security deposit?* (one month's rent = $1,200) *How much is the fee?* (one month's rent = $1,200) *How much does it cost to move into this apartment?* ($3,600)

> **Culture Connection**
>
> - Ask: *To rent an apartment in your country, do you have to pay a fee? Do you have to pay a security deposit?* Discuss as a class.

Presentation   15 minutes

1 READ APARTMENT ADS

Ⓐ Look at the ad for a rental apartment. Read...

- Read the first sentence. Tell students to find and underline the number of bathrooms in the ad. Ask: *What did you underline?* (1 bathroom) *Is the sentence true or false?* (false)
- Tell students to read the sentences, underline information in the ad, and then circle *True* or *False*.

Ⓑ PAIRS. Check your answers.

- Pair students. Say: *Student A, read the sentences. Student B, say the answers. Switch roles after item 3. If you have different answers, look at the information you underlined in the ad.*

- Ask: *Which sentences are false?* (1, 5) Tell pairs to use the information they underlined in the ad and rewrite the false sentences to make them true.
- Call on two students to write the new sentences on the board (1. The apartment has one bathroom. 5. It's not OK to have a pet. / No pets allowed.).

Ⓒ Look at the abbreviations below. Then look at...

- Ask: *Why do classified ads use a lot of abbreviations?* (because people pay for them per line, so longer ads are more expensive)
- Tell students to look at the list. Say: *These are the short forms of words that are often in apartment ads. Look at item 1. Circle* air-conditioning *in the ad.* Ask: *Why is* A/C *the abbreviation for* air-conditioning? (because *air* starts with a and *conditioning* starts with c)
- Read the directions.

Ⓓ 💿 Listen and check your answers. Then...

- Play CD 2, Track 6. Students listen, check their answers, and circle any incorrect answers.

▬▬ EXPANSION: Writing practice for 1D

- Tell students to rewrite the ad for a rental apartment. Tell them to replace the circled words with abbreviations and to pay attention to capitalization and use of periods in the abbreviations. Tell students they shouldn't use articles (*a, an, the*).
- The rewritten ad should look like this:

  Furn. 2 BR, 1 BA apt. on third fl. of elevator building. Large LR. Sunny EIK with separate DR. Washer/dryer in bsmt. Convenient location. Nr shopping and public trans. No pets allowed.
  Rent: *$1,200/mo.*   **Fee:** *One mo.'s rent*
  Sec. Dep.: *One mo.'s rent*
  Util. incl.: *ht., hw, A/C, and electricity included*
  Contact: *Joshua 510-555-5432*

Controlled Practice   25 minutes

2 PRACTICE

A Look at the newspaper apartment ads. Read...

- Say: *Look at the newspaper apartment ads. There is one new abbreviation. Circle it.* Elicit *Pkg.* (in ad b) and write it on the board.
- Point to *Pkg.* and elicit ideas about the word it stands for. Write *parking* next to the abbreviation.
- Call on students to read the answers for one of the three apartments.

EXPANSION: Vocabulary and speaking practice for 2A

- Pair students. Say: *Choose one apartment ad and read it to your partner. Say the full words, not the abbreviations. Choose different ads. Check that your partner substitutes the correct words for the abbreviations.*
- To model the activity, read the first sentence of the first ad: *South End. Large two-bedroom, living room, eat-in kitchen, two bathrooms.*

B GROUPS OF 3. Read about the two families...

- Read the directions. Tell students to read silently about the two families.
- Form groups of 3 and tell them to take out two sheets of paper. Hold up a sheet of paper, turn it horizontally, and point to the left side. Tell groups to list each family's needs on the left side of one sheet and to use abbreviations. To model the activity, elicit one of the Marshalls' needs and write it on the board (for example, *2+ BR*).
- Elicit and write on the board each family's needs. (The Marshalls: *2+ BR; in South End/nr. trans. Rent: $1,250/mo. or less. Sec. dep.: $3,000 or less.* The Wilsons: *2 BR. Pets OK/allowed. Rent: $1,000/mo. or less. Util. incl.*)
- Create charts from the lists of the families' needs on the board. To the right, add columns for: *Apartment a*, *Apartment b*, and *Apartment c*. Tell groups to do the same.
- Tell groups to read each apartment ad and check the things it has that the family needs. To model the activity, ask: *Does Apartment a have two or more bedrooms?* (Yes.) *Is it in the South End?* (Yes.) Put checkmarks in the first two rows under *Apartment a* on the Marshalls' chart.

- Tell groups to complete their charts for both families. Tell them to discuss which apartment is best for each family (The Marshalls: a. The Wilsons: b.).
- As a class, discuss the best match for each family. Ask students to explain their choices.

EXPANSION: Writing practice for 2B

- Tell students to write an ad for their home. Post the ads on the board and number them.
- Say: *Imagine you need to find a new place to live. What are your needs?* Tell students to list their needs and create a chart like the one they completed in Exercise 2B (with their needs as row headings and apartment numbers from the board as column headings).
- Tell students to go apartment / house hunting. Tell them to read the ads on the board and make checkmarks on their chart.
- Form small groups. Say: *Tell your group which home is best for you. Explain why.*

Communicative Practice   10 minutes

C GROUPS OF 3. Look at the list of ways to find...

- Read the directions.
- Form groups of 3. Students discuss the best way to find an apartment.
- Walk around and make sure students explain their answers.

3 LIFE SKILLS WRITING

Turn to page 260 and ask students to complete the application for an apartment. See p. T-xii for general notes about the Life Skills Writing activities.

Progress Check

Can you . . . read apartment ads?

Say: *We have practiced reading apartment ads. Now, look at the question at the bottom of the page. Can you read apartment ads?* Tell students to write a checkmark in the box.

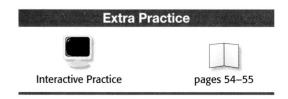

Extra Practice

Interactive Practice   pages 54–55

A Look at the newspaper apartment ads. Read the sentences.
Write the correct letter of the apartment ad next to each sentence.

a.

South End. Large 2 BR, LR, EIK, 2 BA. W/D. Ht. + hw. not incl. Pets allowed. No fee. $1,200/mo. 1 mo. sec. dep. Available immediately. Call Rick 207-555-1212.

b.

Downtown. Sunny furn. 1 BR apt. A/C. Pkg. garage. Nr. trans. Pets OK. $950/mo. Util. incl. No fee. City Properties 207-555-8765.

c.

North Square. Nice 2 BR, LR, DR. No pets. $1,200/mo. Ht. hw. incl. Nr. schools. Fee + 2 mo. sec. dep. Maven Realty 207-555-9989.

1. __b__ It has one bedroom.

2. __b__ It has air-conditioning.

3. __a__ It has a washer and dryer.

4. __c__ No pets are allowed.

5. __a__ It has an eat-in kitchen.

6. __a__ It has two bathrooms.

7. __b__ It is close to transportation.

8. __a__ Utilities are not included in the rent.

9. __b__ It is furnished.

10. __c__ There is a fee.

B GROUPS OF 3. Read about the two families. Which apartment in
Exercise A is best for each family? Explain your answer. Answers will vary but could include:

■ The Marshalls

The Marshalls are a family of four (a mother and three children). Mrs. Marshall works in the South End. She can spend $1,250 a month on rent and utilities. She can pay $3,000 for a security deposit. She doesn't have a car. (c)

The rent is within their budget and it is close to the schools.

■ The Wilsons

The Wilsons are a family of three (a mother, a father, and a six-month-old baby). The parents both work downtown. They have a dog. They have a car. They can spend up to $1,000 a month on rent and utilities. (B)

Dogs are allowed and the rent is in their budget.

C GROUPS OF 3. Look at the list of ways to find an apartment.
Which do you think is the best way? Explain your answer. Answers will vary.

☐ reading newspaper ads
☐ reading Internet postings
☐ going to a real estate agent
☐ talking with friends and neighbors

☐ looking for rental signs in the neighborhood
☐ bulletin boards in supermarkets
☐ other: _____

3 LIFE SKILLS WRITING   Complete an application for an apartment. See page 260.

Can you...read apartment ads? ☐

Ask about an apartment

Listening and Speaking

1 BEFORE YOU LISTEN

CLASS. **Imagine you are calling about an apartment for rent. Read the questions. What other questions can you ask?**

> How much is the rent?
> Is a security deposit required?
> Are utilities included?
> How many bedrooms are there?
> Is it furnished?
> Is there a laundry room in the building?
> Are pets allowed?

2 LISTEN

CD2 T7

A 🔘 **Look at the picture of Paula calling a landlady. Listen to the conversation. Why is Paula calling?**

a. She wants information about an apartment.
b. She has a question about her rent.
c. She has a problem with her apartment.

CD2 T7

B 🔘 **Listen again. Read the sentences. Circle *True* or *False*.**

1. There are two bedrooms.
   True   False

2. There's a large living room.
   True   False

3. There's a laundry room in the building.
   True   **False**

4. There's a park around the corner.
   True   False

CD2 T8

C 🔘 **Listen to the whole conversation. Why isn't Paula interested in the apartment anymore?**

a. She needs three bedrooms.   b. She wants to live near a park.   **c. It is too expensive.**

Lesson 5 Ask about an apartment

Getting Started 5 minutes

1 BEFORE YOU LISTEN

CLASS. Imagine you are calling about an apartment...

- Read the directions. Call on students to read the questions.
- Tell students to look at the ads on pages 92 and 93 for ideas for other questions and write them on the board. (Some other possible questions: *Is there a fee? How many bathrooms are there? Is it near public transportation?*)

Presentation 10 minutes

2 LISTEN

Ⓐ 💿 Look at the picture of Paula...

- Tell students to look at the picture. Say: *Paula is calling a landlady. Point to Paula. Point to the landlady. What is a* landlady? (A woman who owns an apartment or house and rents it to another person.)
- Read the directions and the answer choices. Ask: *Why do you think Paula is calling? Circle the letter of the answer that you think is correct.*
- Tell students to listen to the CD and find out if they are right. Play CD 2, Track 7.
- Elicit the correct answer. Ask: *Who do you call if you have a problem with your apartment?* (the building manager)

Teaching Tip

Optional: If students need additional support, tell them to read the Audio Script on page 301 as they listen to the conversations.

Controlled Practice 10 minutes

Ⓑ 💿 Listen again. Read the sentences...

- Play Track 7 again. Students read the sentences silently and circle *True* or *False*.
- Ask students to read the sentences and call on classmates to answer *True* or *False*. Ask a student to correct the false sentence (There's *no* laundry room . . .).
- Ask: *What is the apartment near?* (a laundromat and a park)

Ⓒ 💿 Listen to the whole conversation....

- Read the question and the answer choices.
- Play CD 2, Track 8. Students listen and circle the letter of the correct answer.
- Ask: *According to the ad, how much is the rent?* On the board, write: *$200/mo.* Ask: *Is the ad correct?* (No.) *How much is the rent really?* On the board, write: *$2,000/mo.* Ask: *What happened? What was the mistake?* (A zero was dropped from the price. / The rent is $2,000, but the ad says it is only $200.)
- Elicit the correct answer.

████ EXPANSION: Speaking practice for 2C

- Pair students and tell them to take turns asking and answering the questions from Exercise 1 about one of the ads on pages 92 and 93.

Lesson 5 Ask about an apartment

Presentation   10 minutes

3 CONVERSATION

A **Listen. Then listen and repeat.**

- Read the Pronunciation Watch note.
- Tell students to look at the nouns in Exercise 3A. Say: *Nouns can be two words, like* bus stop *and* laundry room, *or one word, like* dishwasher. Ask: *Which is stressed,* bus *or* stop? (*bus*) laundry *or* room? (*laundry*) dish *or* washer? (*dish*)
- Play CD 2, Track 9. Tell students to listen for the stress on the first word.
- Resume playing Track 9. Students listen and repeat.

B **Listen and repeat the conversation.**

- Note: This conversation is the same one students heard in Exercise 2A on page 94.
- Tell students to read the conversation silently and to circle the nouns *bedrooms, living room,* and *laundry room.*
- Tell students to underline the stressed word. Check that students underlined *bed, living,* and *laundry.*
- Play CD 2, Track 10. Students listen and repeat the conversation.

Controlled Practice   10 minutes

4 PRACTICE

A **PAIRS. Practice the conversation. Then make...**

- Pair students and tell them to practice the conversation in Exercise 3B. Tell them to take turns playing each role.
- Walk around and check students' pronunciation of *bedrooms, living room,* and *laundry room.* Model the stress as needed.
- Then, in Exercise 4A, ask students to look at the information in the boxes. Ask: *Are there any compound nouns? Circle them and underline the first word in each.* Check that students circled and underlined as follows: <u>bath</u>room, <u>dish</u>washer, <u>parking</u> lot, <u>living</u> room, <u>bus</u> stop, <u>shopping</u> center,

<u>supermarket.</u> Pronounce each compound noun (with the stress on the first word) and ask the class to repeat.
- Read the directions.
- Copy the conversation onto the board and complete it with words from the boxes.
- Ask two above-level students to model a new conversation. Say: *Student A, you're the landlord. What does your apartment have? Choose one thing from the blue box and one from the red box. Student B, you're calling about the apartment. What do you hope the apartment has? Choose one thing from the green box and one thing from the yellow box.*
- Tell pairs to take turns playing each role and to use the boxes to fill in the blanks.
- Walk around and check that students are properly substituting information into the conversation. Model stress in compound nouns as needed.
- Tell students to stand, mingle, and practice the conversation with several new partners.
- Call on pairs to perform for the class.

Communicative Practice   10 minutes

B **ROLE PLAY. PAIRS. Make your own...**

- Pair students and tell them to take turns playing Speakers A and B.
- Say: *Student A, imagine you are going to rent your house or apartment to someone. Write the number of bedrooms and two other nice things it has. Student B, you want to rent a house or apartment. What do you want the house or apartment to have? What do you want to have nearby? Write two things to ask about.*
- Tell pairs to use their own information in the conversation in Exercise 3B and to make changes as needed. Tell Student A to answer Student B's questions truthfully, either *yes* or *no.* Ask an above-level pair to model the role play. Help them use their own information.
- Walk around and help as needed.

Extra Practice

Interactive Practice

T-95   UNIT 5

3 CONVERSATION

Sometimes we put two words together to make a noun. The first word is usually stressed.

CD2 T9

A Listen. Then listen and repeat.

• bus stop • laundry room • dishwasher • living room

CD2 T10

B Listen and repeat the conversation.

Landlady: Hello?

Paula: Hi, I'm calling about the apartment for rent. Can you tell me about it?

Landlady: Sure. There are two bedrooms and a large living room.

Paula: Is there a laundry room?

Landlady: No, there isn't. But there's a laundromat down the street.

Paula: I see. Is there a park nearby?

Landlady: Yes, there is—just around the corner.

4 PRACTICE

A PAIRS. Practice the conversation. Then make new conversations. Use the information in the boxes.

A: Hello?

B: Hi, I'm calling about the apartment for rent. Can you tell me about it?

A: Sure. There are two bedrooms and a _____ .

B: Is there a _____ ?

A: No, there isn't. But there's _____ .

B: I see. Is there a _____ nearby?

A: Yes, there is—just around the corner.

sunny kitchen	dishwasher	**a microwave**	bus stop
new bathroom	parking lot	**free parking on the street**	shopping center
big closet	balcony	**a big window in the living room**	supermarket

B ROLE PLAY. PAIRS. Make your own conversations. Student A, imagine you are going to rent your house or apartment. Answer Student B's questions with true information. Student B, you want to rent a house or apartment. Ask questions.

Ask about an apartment

Grammar

There is / There are

Affirmative		Negative	
There is	a park nearby.	**There isn't a** / **There's no**	bus stop near here.
There are	two bedrooms.	**There aren't any** / **There are no**	restaurants in the neighborhood.

Questions			Short answers			
	Is there	a laundry room?	Yes,	**there is.** / **there are.**	No,	**there isn't.** / **there aren't.**
	Are there	a lot of windows?				
How many bedrooms	**are there?**		Two.	**(There are** two.)		

Grammar Watch

Use *there is* / *there are* to talk about a thing or things in a certain place.

1 PRACTICE

A Complete the sentences. Underline the correct words.

1. **There is** / **There are** a bus stop near the apartment.

2. **Is there** / **Are there** a bathtub?

3. **Are there** / **Is there** a lot of children in the neighborhood?

4. **There is** / **There are** two windows in the kitchen.

5. **There's** / **There isn't** no elevator in the building.

6. **There aren't** / **There isn't** a lot of traffic on this street.

B Complete the conversation. Use the correct form of *there is* / *there are*. Some sentences are negative.

A: So, tell me about your new apartment. How many bedrooms ___are there___?

B: ___There are___ two. And they're nice and big.

A: That's good. How are the neighbors?

B: Well, ___there's___ an older woman next door. She seems very friendly.

A: And how's the neighborhood?

B: I like it a lot. ___There are___ a lot of stores around the corner.

A: That's convenient. ___Are there___ any supermarkets?

B: No, ___there aren't___, but ___there's___ a convenience store down the street.

Getting Started
5 minutes

- Say: *We're going to study* there is *and* there are. *In the conversation on page 95, the landlady and Paula used this grammar.*
- Play CD 2, Track 10. Students listen. On the board, write: *There are two bedrooms* and *No, there isn't.* Underline *There are* and *there isn't.*

Presentation
15 minutes

There is / There are

- Copy the grammar charts onto the board or show Transparency 5.4 and cover the exercise.
- Read the Grammar Watch note.
- On the board, draw a word box with *is* and *are.* Side-by-side write: *1. There _____ a dishwasher. 2. There _____ shops nearby.* Say: *Look at item 1. What comes after the blank?* (*a dishwasher*) *Look at item 2. What comes after the blank?* (*shops*) *Which do you think is the answer for item 1,* is *or* are? (*is*) *Why?* (because *dishwasher* is singular) *Which do you think is the answer for item 2,* is *or* are? (*are*) *Why?* (because *shops* is plural)
- Point to item 1 on the board and ask: *How do I make this sentence negative?* Point to the grammar chart. Elicit and write under item 1: *There isn't a dishwasher. / There's no dishwasher.* Repeat with item 2 and write: *There aren't any shops. / There are no shops.*
- Point to item 1 on the board and ask: *How do I make this sentence into a question?* Point to the grammar chart. Elicit and write under item 1: *Is there a dishwasher?* Repeat with item 2 and write: *Are there any shops?*
- Elicit affirmative and negative short answers to each question and write them on the board.
- Tell students to point to the question with *How many* in the grammar chart. Read the question. Elicit other words to substitute for bedrooms when asking about an apartment (for example, *How many bathrooms / closets / windows are there?*).
- If you are using the transparency, do the exercise with the class.

Controlled Practice
25 minutes

1 PRACTICE

Ⓐ Complete the sentences. Underline the correct...

- Say: *Look at item 1. What comes after* There is / There are? (*a bus stop*) *Why is the answer* There is? (because *bus stop* is singular)
- Say: *Look at item 3. With* a lot of, *look at what comes after. Is* children *singular or plural?* (plural)
- To check answers, call on students to read the sentences out loud.

Ⓑ Complete the conversation. Use the correct form...

- Read the directions and the example.
- Point out that for *there is* students can also write *there's.*
- Students compare answers with a partner. Tell pairs to read the conversation out loud.
- *Optional:* Call on pairs to perform the completed conversation for the class.

EXPANSION: Grammar and writing practice for 1B

- Pair students and tell them to write sentences with *There is* and *There are* about their own house or apartment (for example, *There are two bedrooms. There's no dishwasher. There's a laundry room in the building. There are a lot of restaurants nearby.*).
- Say: *Student A, read your sentences to your partner. Student B, listen and take notes about your partner's home. Use abbreviations.*

Lesson 6 Ask about an apartment

2 PRACTICE

Read the answers. Write the questions. Use...

- Tell students to look at the *Questions* and *Short answers* boxes in the grammar charts on p. 96. Say one short answer from each line and elicit the corresponding question (for example, say: *Yes, there is.* Elicit: *Is there a laundry room?*).
- Read the directions and the example. Walk around and remind students to read Speaker B's answer before they write Speaker A's question.
- Say each item number and tell the class to call out their questions. Then tell students to check their questions and make sure they used question marks.
- *Optional:* Pair students and tell them to read the completed questions and answers out loud. Students switch roles after item 3.

Communicative Practice   15 minutes

Show what you know!

STEP 1. PAIRS. Student A, you are looking for...

- Divide the class in half and tell one group to play Student A and the other to play Student B. Read the directions.
- Form small groups within the Student A group. Tell them to look at the chart on page 97 and practice forming questions (for example, *How many bedrooms are there?*).
- Form small groups within the Student B group. Tell them to read the apartment ad on page 246 out loud, saying full words, not abbreviations. Tell them to say sentences about the apartment with *There is* and *There are* (for example, *There are three bedrooms.*).
- Direct students in the Student A group and then the Student B group to number off. Tell students with the same number to form a pair.

STEP 2. SAME PAIRS. Student A, ask about...

- Read the directions.
- Tell Student A to note Student B's responses in the chart on this page. Walk around and help as needed.

- To follow-up, tell Student A to check the information in the chart by reading it back to Student B (for example, Student A: *There are two bedrooms, right?* or *Are there two bedrooms?*).

STEP 3. SAME PAIRS. Change roles. Student A,...

- Read the directions.
- Tell Student B to note Student A's responses in the chart on page 246. Walk around and help as needed.
- To follow up, tell Student B to check the information in the chart by reading it back to Student A (for example, A: *There are three bedrooms, right?* or *Are there three bedrooms?*).

EXPANSION: Speaking and grammar practice for STEP 3

- Have students bring in apartment ads from the newspaper. Tell them to practice asking and answering questions about the ads.

EXPANSION: Grammar and writing practice for STEP 3

- Have students bring in apartment ads from the newspaper.
- Say: *Imagine your friend is looking for an apartment. Write your friend an e-mail message about the apartment in one of the ads. Make up a neighborhood name for the apartment. Use* There is / There are *and has / have (for example,* There's an apartment for rent in Mayfair. It has two bedrooms, and the rent is only $950! There's no fee.*).*

Progress Check

Can you . . . ask about an apartment?

Say: *We have practiced asking about apartments. Now, look at the question at the bottom of the page. Can you ask about an apartment?* Tell students to write a checkmark in the box.

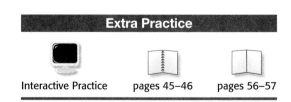

Extra Practice		
Interactive Practice	pages 45–46	pages 56–57

Read the answers. Write the questions. Use *Is there* and *Are there*.

1. **A:** _Is there a bus stop nearby?_

   B: Yes, there is. The #2 bus stop is across the street.

2. **A:** Are there families with children in the building?

   B: No. There are no families with children in the building.

3. **A:** Is there a supermarket nearby?

   B: Yes, there is. There's a supermarket 10 minutes from here.

4. **A:** Are there furnished apartments available?

   B: Sorry. There aren't any furnished apartments available.

5. **A:** Is there a laundry room in the building?

   B: Yes, there is. There's a laundry room in the basement.

6. **A:** How many closets are there?

   B: Four. There are four closets in the apartment.

Show what you know! Ask about an apartment

STEP 1. PAIRS. Student A, you are looking for an apartment. Look at the questions on this page. Student B, you have an apartment for rent. Look at your apartment information in the ad on page 246.

STEP 2. SAME PAIRS. Student A, ask about Student B's apartment. Take notes.

STEP 3. SAME PAIRS. Change roles. Student A, use the apartment ad on this page. Answer Student B's questions.

Ask about:	Notes
number of bedrooms	2
number of bathrooms	1
laundry room	no (near laundromat)
parking	yes
rent, fees, security deposit	$950/mo. + 1 mo. dep. no fee

APARTMENT FOR RENT. 3 BR, 2 BA, LR, DR. W/D in basement, nr. transportation, $1,200/mo. 1 mo. fee + 1 mo. sec. dep.

Can you...ask about an apartment? ☐

Reading

1 | BEFORE YOU READ

A Look at the map of the continental U.S. Write the region names on the map. Use the words in the box.

~~Midwest~~   Northeast   South   Southwest   West Coast   West

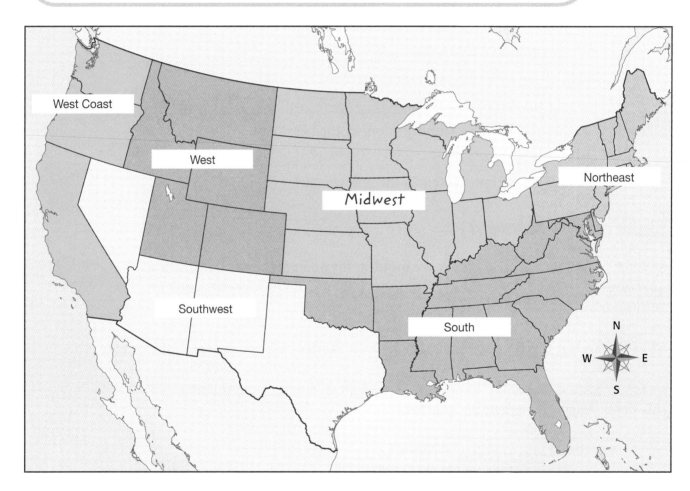

West Coast

West

Midwest

Northeast

Southwest

South

B PAIRS. Compare your answers.

C Skim the article on page 99. What is one of the important ideas discussed in the article?
Answers will vary but could include: The South and Southwest are the fastest growing regions in the U.S.

D PAIRS. Compare your answers.

Reading Skill:
Skimming

Skimming means you do not read every word. Instead, you read quickly to get the general idea of the article.

Getting Started   10 minutes

1 | BEFORE YOU READ

Ⓐ Look at the map of the continental U.S. Write...

- Tell students to find the compass on the map and to point to north, south, west, and east on the map.
- Read the directions. Say: *Write the names of the regions you know. Then use the compass to help you guess the other regions.*

Ⓑ PAIRS. Compare your answers.

- Say the directions on the compass and the region names in the box and ask the class to repeat.
- Students compare answers with a partner.
- Say the colors from the map and ask the class to call out the region names.
- Say each region name and elicit a few of the states that are in the region.
- Ask: *What region do we live in? What regions have you visited? Would you like to live in another region? Which one? Why?*

Ⓒ Skim the article on page 99. What is one of the...

- Read the Reading Skill note. Ask: *When you skim something, do you read it carefully or quickly?* (quickly) *Do you look for specific information or the general idea?* (the general idea)
- Read the directions. Give students a minute to skim the article.
- Ask: *What is one of the important ideas discussed in the article?* Tell students to write one idea.

Ⓓ PAIRS. Compare your answers.

- Pair students and tell them to ask each other the question from the directions.
- Ask: *What is one of the important ideas discussed in the article?* Call on each pair to say one idea (for example, *Springville is growing fast. People move to Springville for a lot of reasons. There are new problems in Springville.*).

Presentation
15 minutes

2 READ

Ⓐ **Listen. Read the article.**

- Tell the class to look at the newspaper article. Read the title and ask: *What's happening in Springville?* (It's growing fast. / A lot of people are moving there.) Explain that *record growth* means growing faster than it ever has before.
- Tell the class to look at the picture and ask: *What do you see?* (a lot of houses) Read the caption and ask: *Are the houses old or new?* (new) *Do we have new housing developments like this in our area? Do they cause any problems?*
- Play CD 2, Track 11. Students listen and read along silently.

Controlled Practice
20 minutes

3 CHECK YOUR UNDERSTANDING

Ⓐ Read the article again. Then answer the...

- Read the directions. Call on two students to read the questions.
- Tell students to read the article again and underline the reasons why people move to Springville and the problems caused by Springfield's growth. Ask: *How many reasons are there?* (four) *How many problems are there?* (two)
- Tell students to look at the information they underlined and write answers to the questions in their notebooks.
- Call on students to say answers and write them on the board.

Ⓑ PAIRS. Compare your community to Springville...

- Read the directions.
- On the board, draw a Venn diagram. Label the circles *Springville* and *[the name of your community]*. Point to the first reason on the board. Say: *There's warm weather in Springville. Is there warm weather in our community?* As a class, decide whether to write *warm weather* on the left side of the Venn diagram or in the middle.

- Tell pairs to decide where in the Venn diagram to write each reason and problem from Exercise 1B.
- Ask: *How is [our community] the same as Springville?* Call on pairs to say an item from the middle of their Venn diagram. Encourage them to use *There is / There are*. For example, *There are a lot of jobs here, too.* Repeat with: *How is [our community] different from Springville?*
- Ask: *Where would you like to live? Do you prefer Springville or [our community]? Why?* Discuss as a class.

Communicative Practice
15 minutes

Show what you know!

PRE-WRITING. NETWORK. PAIRS. Find a partner...

- Read the directions. On the board, draw a T-chart with the headings *I like* and *I don't like*. Tell students to copy the chart into their notebook.
- Tell pairs to look at their answers to the questions in Exercise 3B for ideas and to talk about things such as weather, jobs, cost of living, and traffic. Tell them to think of other things to add to their charts.
- Ask each pair to write something on the chart on the board. Tell them first to read what other pairs have written and not repeat.
- Read and discuss the chart on the board as a class.

WRITE. Write about your community...

Ask students to turn to page 270 and write about their community. See page T-xii for general notes about the Writing Activities.

Teaching Tip

You may want to collect student papers and provide feedback. Use the scoring rubric for writing on page T-xiv to evaluate vocabulary, grammar, mechanics, and how well he or she completes the task. You may want to review the completed rubric with the students.

Extra Practice

Interactive Practice	pages 46–47	pages 58–59

CD2 T11

Listen. Read the article.

Record Growth in Springville

Springville is growing fast. It is like many other cities in the South and Southwest. These are the fastest growing regions in the U.S. "Every day I meet another newcomer," says Amy Mark, a Springville real-estate agent.

New residents say they moved to Springville because of the warm weather, jobs, low cost of living, and natural beauty. The area is popular with people from the large, expensive cities of the Northeast and the West Coast. "We moved to Springville last year.

One of Springville's new housing developments

We exchanged a tiny apartment in Boston for this big, beautiful house," says Jim Walker. "We love it here."

But not everyone loves the growth. "We moved here from Philadelphia to get closer to nature, but instead we are stuck in traffic all the time," says Joanna Fields. Pam Foster, a longtime resident, agrees. "We're replacing the area's natural beauty with shopping malls and new houses. People come here to get away from the big city, but they're just bringing the big city with them."

A Read the article again. Then answer the questions on a separate piece of paper.

1. What are four reasons people move to Springville?
   warm weather, jobs, low cost of living, natural beauty
2. What are two problems caused by Springville growth?
   traffic, natural beauty replaced with malls and houses

B PAIRS. Compare your community to Springville. How is it the same? How is it different?

Show what you know!

PRE-WRITING. NETWORK. PAIRS. Find a partner who lives in your community. Talk about what you like and dislike about your community.

WRITE. Write about your community. See page 270.

Get directions

Listening and Speaking

1 BEFORE YOU LISTEN

A Look at the pictures. Write the directions on the lines.

> Turn right.   Turn left.   ~~Go straight.~~   Go through one traffic light.

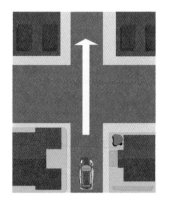
Go straight.

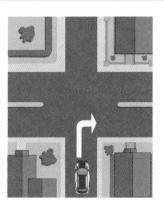
Turn right.

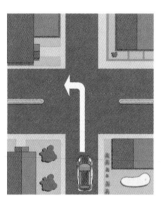
Turn left.

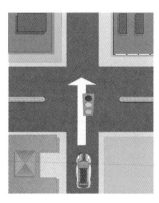
Go through one traffic light.

B CLASS. Imagine that you need directions to a place in your community. How do you usually get directions?

2 LISTEN

CD2 T12

A Listen to the phone message. Number the directions in the order you hear them.

___3___ turn right

___1___ turn left

___2___ go straight

___4___ go through one traffic light

CD2 T12

B Listen again. Find the "start here" box. Follow the directions on the map. Draw the route on the map. Then circle the library.

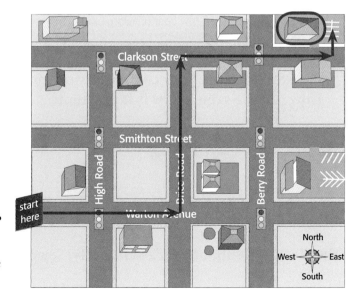

Getting Started   10 minutes

1 BEFORE YOU LISTEN

A Look at the pictures. Write the directions...

- Stand with your back to the class. Say and use your hand to indicate *straight*, *right*, and *left*. Do it again and ask the class to repeat.
- Read the directions. Students write the directions on the lines.
- Point to each picture and elicit the direction from the class.
- Point to each picture again, say the direction, and ask the class to repeat.

B CLASS. Imagine that you need directions to a...

- Read the directions.
- As a class, brainstorm and write on the board different ways to get directions (for example, *go online, use a GPS in your car, look at a map, call the place where you are going and ask*).
- *Optional:* Elicit some websites for getting directions and write the URLs on the board.

Presentation   5 minutes

2 LISTEN

A Listen to the phone message. Number...

- Read the directions. Tell students to read the directions silently.
- Play CD 2, Track 12. Students listen and number the directions.
- Play Track 12 again. Tell students to listen and check their answers.

Controlled Practice   10 minutes

B Listen again. Find the "start here"...

- Tell students to look at the map and find the red "start here" box. Ask: *What direction are we starting from?* (west)
- Read the directions. Tell students to take out a pencil and place it at the red "start here" box. Play Track 12 again. Students draw the route on the map and circle the library.
- Play Track 12 again. Tell students to listen and check the route they drew.
- Students compare routes with a partner.
- Ask the class: *Where is the library on the map?* (northeast) Ask a student to hold up the book and point to the library.

> **Teaching Tip**
>
> Remember that if students need additional support, they can read the Audio Script on page 301 as they listen.

EXPANSION: Speaking practice for 2B

- Pair students and tell them to practice giving directions from the "start here" box to the library.
- Tell students to choose another building on the map. Say: *Give your partner directions from the "start here" box to the building. Don't tell your partner which building it is. See if your partner can follow your directions and find the right building.*

Controlled Practice   20 minutes

3 CONVERSATION

A 🔊 **Listen. Then listen and repeat.**

- Read the Pronunciation Watch note.
- Tell students to practice the tongue position for the *th* sounds. Say: *Keep your tongue flat. Stick it out a little bit. Gently bite the tip of your tongue.*
- Tell students to keep their tongues in this position. Tell them to put their hands on their throats. Say: *To make the* th *sound in* then, *use your voice. You should feel vibration in your throat.* Say the voiced *th* sound several times and ask the class to repeat.
- Tell students to keep their tongues in position and their hands on their throats. Say: *To make the* th *sound in* thanks, *do not use your voice. You should not feel vibration in your throat.* Say the voiceless *th* sound several times and ask the class to repeat.
- Play CD 2, Track 13. Students listen.
- Resume playing Track 13. Students listen and repeat.

B 🔊 **Carrie has a new neighbor, Lan...**

- Tell students to look at the map. Tell them to circle the people and the Save-Rite Pharmacy.
- Ask: *What street are the people on?* (Third Street) *What street is the pharmacy on?* (Davis Road) *Are there any traffic lights or stop signs?* (Yes. There's a stop sign.) *Is the stop sign on Third Street or Davis Road?* (Third Street)
- Read the directions. Tell students to read the conversation silently and underline words that start with *th.* (*Third, the*) Ask: *Which word has a voiced* th? (*the*) *Which word has a voiceless* th? (*Third*) Say the words and ask the class to repeat.
- Play CD 2, Track 14. Tell students to follow the directions on the map with their finger as they listen and repeat.

4 PRACTICE

A PAIRS. **Practice the conversation. Then make new...**

- Pair students and tell them to practice the conversation in Exercise 3B. Tell them to take turns playing each role. Walk around and check students' pronunciation of *th* sounds.

- Then, in Exercise 4A, ask students to look at the maps. Say: *Speaker A asks for directions to a place in blue on the maps and Speaker B gives directions first with information that is green on the maps, then with information that is red, and finally with information that is yellow. Speaker A wants to make sure he remembers the directions and so repeats what Speaker B says.*
- Read the directions.
- Copy the conversation onto the board and use the color-coded map to fill in the blanks in the conversation.
- Ask two above-level students to model a new conversation.
- Tell pairs to take turns playing each role and to use the boxes to fill in the blanks. Tell Student A to follow the directions on the map and repeat them by completing his or her lines.
- Walk around and check that students are properly substituting information into the conversation. Tell partners to switch roles and choose different places.

▬▬▬ **MULTILEVEL INSTRUCTION for 4A**

Cross-ability The lower-level student plays Speaker A first. When it's the lower-level student's turn to play Speaker B, the higher-level student says Speaker A's first line, and then helps Speaker B to write the directions before they practice the rest of the conversation.

Communicative Practice   15 minutes

B ROLE PLAY. PAIRS. **Make your own...**

- Read the directions. If possible, post or distribute local maps for students to use.
- Model a conversation with an above-level student. Play Speaker B. Tell the student to look at the conversation in Exercise 4A and complete Speaker A's first line with a place in your community. Give directions to the place. Pause after each direction for Speaker A to repeat.
- Form pairs. Tell students to refer back to Exercise 1A on page 100 for help with giving directions.

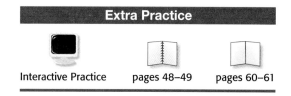

Extra Practice		
Interactive Practice	pages 48–49	pages 60–61

3 CONVERSATION

CD2 T13

A Listen. Then listen and repeat.

Then turn right.   It's on the left.
It's on Third Street.   Thanks.

> **Pronunciation Watch**
>
> There are two *th* sounds in English. To say the *th* sound in *then*, put your tongue between your teeth. Use your voice. To say the *th* sound in *thanks*, put your tongue between your teeth but do not use your voice.

CD2 T14

B Carrie has a new neighbor, Lan. Lan doesn't know her way around the neighborhood yet. Listen and repeat the conversation.

Lan: Can you give me directions to Save-Rite Pharmacy?
Carrie: Sure. Go straight on Third Street.
Lan: OK. Go straight on Third Street.
Carrie: All right. At the stop sign, turn right onto Davis Road.
Lan: At the stop sign, turn right onto Davis Road.
Carrie: Exactly. Save-Rite Pharmacy is on the left.

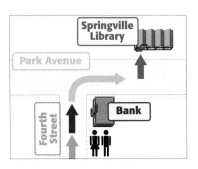

4 PRACTICE

A PAIRS. Practice the conversation. Then make new conversations. Use the directions on the maps.

A: Can you give me directions to   ?

B: Sure. Go straight on   .

A: OK. Go straight on   .

B: All right. At the   , turn   onto   .

A: At the   , turn   onto   .

B: Exactly.   is on the left .

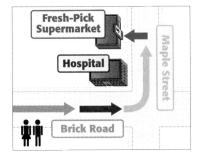

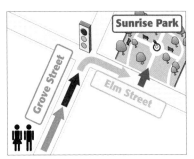

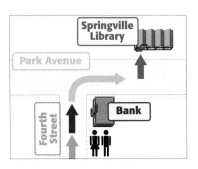

B ROLE PLAY. PAIRS. Make your own conversations. Ask for and give directions from school to places in your community.

1 GRAMMAR

A Imagine you are interested in renting an apartment. You want to know more about places in the neighborhood. Write questions with *Is there* and *Are there* and the words in parentheses.

1. (laundromat) _Is there a laundromat nearby?_

2. (bank) _Is there a bank nearby?_

3. (restaurants) _Are there restaurants nearby?_

4. (stores) _Are there stores nearby?_

5. (gas stations) _Are there gas stations nearby?_

6. (schools) _Are there schools nearby?_

7. (post office) _Is there a post office nearby?_

8. (park) _Is there a park nearby?_

B ROLE PLAY. PAIRS. Take turns. Ask the questions you wrote in Exercise A. Look at the neighborhood map. You are at the apartment for rent. Answer the questions. Tell where each place is located.

A: *Is there a laundromat nearby?*
B: *Yes, there is. There's a laundromat on First Avenue.*

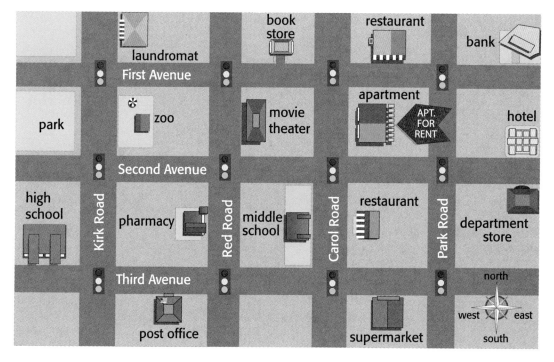

1 GRAMMAR

Ⓐ Imagine you are interested in renting an...

- Tell students to review the grammar chart on page 96 (*There is / There are*).
- Read the directions. Ask a student to read the example. Tell students to look at page 96 for other phrases to use in place of *nearby* (for example, *near here, in the neighborhood, near the apartment, on this street*).
- Students compare answers with a partner.
- Ask the class: *Which questions begin with* Is there? (items 1, 2, 7, and 8) *Which questions begin with* Are there? (items 3–6)

Ⓑ ROLE PLAY. PAIRS. Take turns. Ask the questions...

- Tell students to look at the map and find the apartment for rent. Tell students to point to the laundromat. Ask two students to read the example.
- Read the directions. Form new pairs.
- Students take turns asking and answering the questions from Exercise 1A.
- Call on pairs to ask and answer questions 2–8 for the class.

EXPANSION: Vocabulary and speaking practice for 1

- Ask students: *Which of these places is most important to have near your apartment? What other places do you want near your apartment?*
- Pair students and have them brainstorm additional places (for example, a bookstore, a coffee shop, a bus stop).
- Have students add the places they listed to the map on page 102. Then tell them to practice Exercise B again, using the new places.

2 GRAMMAR

Ⓐ WRITE. Look at the map on page 102. Write...

- Read the directions. Draw a people icon on the board. Point to it and say: *Choose a place to start. Draw a people icon on the map.* Then say: *Choose a place to finish. Circle the place on the map.*

- Ask students to review the directions on page 100 and the conversation on page 101. Tell students to then write directions from the people icon to the place they circled on the map.

Ⓑ PAIRS. Student A, read your directions from...

- Model the activity. Choose a starting and ending point. Tell the class the starting point and give directions. Tell the class to follow your directions on the map. Ask: *Where are you?*

- Pair students and tell them not to show each other their maps. Say: *Student A, tell your partner where to start. Read your directions from Exercise A. Then ask your partner:* Where are you? *If your partner answers incorrectly, check your directions and then repeat them. If your partner answers correctly, switch roles and repeat the activity.*

- For more practice getting directions, ask a couple of students to give the class a starting point, read their directions from Exercise 1A, and then ask the class: *Where are you?*

Ⓒ Complete the conversations with the present...

- Tell students to review the grammar chart on page 90 (Present continuous).

- Read the directions. Remind students to use the correct form of *be* and the verb + *-ing*. Read the example.

- Walk around and spot-check spelling of *-ing* verbs in item 2. Refer students to the spelling rules for *-ing* verbs on page 290 as needed.

- Students compare answers with a partner by reading the conversations out loud.

- Call on two pairs to read the conversations for the class. Discuss any errors.

- Ask: *What's the problem in Conversation 1?* (The light isn't working.) *Who's fixing the light?* (Dad and Uncle Jerry) *What's Mom doing?* (She's calling an electrician.) *Why?* (because Dad and Uncle Jerry aren't very good at fixing stuff)

- *Optional:* Call on pairs to perform the completed conversation for the class.

CD-ROM Practice

 Go to the CD-ROM for more practice.

If your students need more practice with the vocabulary, grammar, and competencies in Unit 5, encourage them to review the activities on the CD-ROM. This review can also help students prepare for the final role play on the following Expand page.

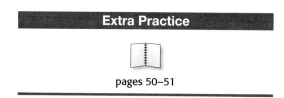

Extra Practice

pages 50–51

2 GRANMAR

A WRITE. Look at the map on page 102. Write directions from one place on the map to another place. Answers will vary.

> Start at the pharmacy. Go north on Red Road.

B PAIRS. Student A, read your directions from Exercise A. Student B, follow Student A's directions on the map on page 102. Where are you?

C Complete the conversations with the present continuous. Use contractions if possible.

1. **A:** I __'m looking for__ Dad. Is he home?
        (look for)

   B: Yes, he __'s looking at__ the light in my bedroom.
          (look at)

   It __isn't working__, and he __'s trying__ to fix it.
       (not work)   (try)

   A: But Dad isn't very good at fixing stuff.

   B: I know. Uncle Jerry is in my bedroom, too, and

   he __'s helping__ .
         (help)

   A: Does Uncle Jerry know how to fix a light?

   B: No. That's why Mom is on the phone right now.

   She's __calling__ an electrician!
          (call)

2. **A:** Hello?

   B: Hi, it's Alicia. Where are you?

   A: At home. Eddie and I __are sitting__ in the kitchen, and we __'re having__
                      (sit)   (have)
   some coffee. I __'m making__ a list of the things I need to do today.
                  (make)
   What about you?

   B: Well, I __'m having__ coffee too. I'm at the coffee shop, and
                  (have)

   I __'m waiting for__ you to meet me.
      (wait for)

   A: Oh, no! I'm so sorry. I forgot! That's not on my list!

 Go to the CD-ROM for more practice.

3 ACT IT OUT — What do you say?

STEP 1. CLASS. Review the Lesson 5 conversation between Paula and a landlady (CD 2 Track 10).

STEP 2. ROLE PLAY. PAIRS. Student A, you are talking to a landlord/landlady about an apartment. Ask questions about the apartment. Student B, you are the landlord/landlady. Answer Student A's questions. Make up the answers.

4 READ AND REACT — Problem-solving

STEP 1. Read about Anita's problem.

The lock on Anita's front door never worked well. Now the lock is broken. Anita calls the building manager. The building manager says it isn't his responsibility to fix the lock. He says "You break it. You fix it." She knows it is the building manager's responsibility.

STEP 2. PAIRS. What is Anita's problem? What can she do?
Here are some ideas.

- She can pay a locksmith to fix the lock.
- She can pay a locksmith to fix the lock and take the money out of her rent check.
- She can call the city housing office and ask for help.
- She can _____.

5 CONNECT

For your Study Skills Activity, go to page 251.
For your Team Project, go to page 278.

Which goals can you check off? Go back to page 85.

3   ACT IT OUT

STEP 1. CLASS. Review the Lesson 5 conversation...

- Tell students to review the conversation in Exercise 3B on page 95. Tell them to read the conversation silently and underline the questions. Tell students to review the questions at the top of page 94.
- Play CD 2, Track 10. Students listen.
- Tell students to write three questions to ask a landlord. Remind students that they can use *Is there, Are there,* and *How many . . . are there*?

STEP 2. ROLE PLAY. PAIRS. Student A, you are...

- Read the directions.
- Pair students. Tell A to ask his or her questions from Step 1. Tell B to make up answers to the questions.
- Walk around and check that students use *there is / there are* correctly.
- Call on pairs to perform for the class.
- While pairs are performing, use the scoring rubric on page T-xiii to evaluate each student's vocabulary, grammar, fluency, and how well he or she completes the task. You may want to review the completed rubric with the students.
- *Optional:* After each pair finishes, discuss the strengths and weakness of each performance either in front of the class or privately.

4   READ AND REACT

STEP 1. Read about Anita's problem.

- Say: *We are going to read about a student's problem, and then we need to think about a solution.*
- Read the directions.
- Read the story while students follow along silently. Pause after each sentence to allow time for students to comprehend. Periodically stop and ask simple *Wh-* questions to check comprehension (for example, *What is broken? Who does she call? What does he say? Why doesn't he want to fix the lock?*).

STEP 2. PAIRS. What is Anita's problem? What...

- Pair students. Read the ideas in the list. Give pairs a couple of minutes to discuss possible solutions for Anita.
- Ask: *Which ideas are good?* Call on students to say their opinion about the ideas in the list (for example, S: *I think she can call the city housing office and ask for help. This is a good idea.*).
- Now tell pairs to think of one new idea not in the box (for example, *She can write a letter to the landlord and explain the problem.*) and to write it in the blank. Encourage students to think of more than one idea and to write them in their notebooks.
- Call on pairs to say their additional solutions. Write any particularly good ones on the board and ask students if they think it is a good idea too (*Do you think this is a good idea? Why or why not?*).

MULTILEVEL INSTRUCTION for STEP 2

Cross-ability Tell students to read the ideas in the book and think about the pros and cons of each. Direct the higher-level student to say a pro and con for one idea and the lower-level student to identify the idea. For example, *She can pay a locksmith to fix the lock.* Pro: *It's easy. She doesn't have to discuss the problem.* Con: *It's expensive. She has to pay to fix the lock.*

5   CONNECT

Turn to page 251 for the Study Skills Activity and page 278 for the Team Project. See page T-xi for general notes about teaching these activities.

Progress Check

Which goals can you check off? Go back to page 85.
Ask students to turn to page 85 and check off any remaining goals they have reached. Call on students to say which goals they will practice outside of class.

6

In the Past

Classroom Materials/Extra Practice

CD 2
Tracks 15–30

Transparencies 6.1–6.6
Vocabulary Cards Unit 6

MCA
Unit 6

Workbook
Unit 6

Interactive Practice
Unit 6

Unit Overview

Goals
- See the list of goals on the facing page.

Grammar
- Simple past: Regular verbs
- Simple past: Irregular verbs
- Simple past: *Yes / No* questions and short answers
- Simple past: Information questions

Pronunciation
- Simple past *-ed* endings
- Question intonation with statements

Reading
- Read a biography of a famous person
- *Reading Skill:* Scanning for information

Writing
- Write about your past activities
- Write about milestones in your life
- Write a short autobiography

Life Skills Writing
- Write a note to a teacher to explain an absence

Preview
- Set the context of the unit by asking questions about the past (for example, *Where were you born? When did you come to the U.S.? Did you watch a movie last weekend?*).
- Hold up page 105 or show Transparency 6.1. Read the unit title and ask the class to repeat.
- Say: *Look at the picture. What do you think their relationship is?* (grandfather and grandson) *What are they looking at?* (photos / a photo album)
- Ask the Preview question: *What are the people talking about?* (the events in the photos / past events)

Goals
- Point to the Unit Goals. Explain that this list shows what the class will be studying in this unit.
- Tell students to read the goals silently.
- Say each goal and ask students to repeat. Explain unfamiliar vocabulary as needed:

    Recognize: to know what something is because you have learned about it in the past

    Milestones: very important events in a person's life
- Tell students to read the goals silently.
- Tell students to circle one goal that is very important to them. Call on several students to say the goal they circled.
- Write a checkmark (✓) on the board. Say: *We will come back to this page again. You will write a checkmark next to the goals you learned in this unit.*

In the Past

Preview

Look at the picture. What are the people talking about?

UNIT GOALS

- [ ] Identify events with family and friends
- [ ] Talk about past activities
- [ ] Recognize U.S. holidays
- [ ] Talk about milestones
- [ ] Talk about something that happened
- [ ] Write an absence note to a teacher

1 WHAT DO YOU KNOW?

A CLASS. Look at the pictures. Which events with family and friends do you know?

CD2 T15

B  Look at the pictures and listen. Listen again and repeat.

2 PRACTICE

A PAIRS. Student A, point to a picture and ask about the event. Student B, answer the question.

A: *Where are the people?*
B: *They're at an anniversary party.*

B WORD PLAY. GROUPS OF 3. Look at the pictures. For which events do you dress formally in your country? For which do you dress casually? For which do you give gifts? Complete the chart. Answers will vary.

Formal dress	Casual dress	Gift giving

C CLASS. Are the answers to Exercise B the same for events in the U.S.?

Lesson 1 Vocabulary

1 WHAT DO YOU KNOW?

A CLASS. Look at the pictures. Which events...

- Show Transparency 6.2 or hold up the book. Tell students to cover the list of words on page 107.
- Say: *Look at the pictures. Which events with family and friends do you know?* Elicit an event (for example, *Number 2 is a wedding.*).
- Students call out answers. Help students pronounce events if they have difficulty.
- If students call out an incorrect event, change the answer to a question for the class (for example, *Number 3 is a birthday party?*). If nobody can identify the correct event, tell students they will now listen to a CD and practice the vocabulary for events with family and friends.

Presentation   5 minutes

B 💿 Look at the pictures and listen. Listen...

- Read the directions. Play CD 2, Track 15. Pause after number 12 (*a surprise party*).
- Tell students to look at the pictures and vocabulary. Ask:

  Which event celebrates the date on which a husband and wife got married? (an anniversary party)

  Which event celebrates the end of a person's career? (a retirement party)

  Which event marks the end of a person's life? (a funeral)

  Which event is a meeting of related people who haven't seen each other for a long time? (a family reunion)

  Which event is a meal in which everyone invited brings a dish to share? (a potluck dinner)

- To check comprehension, say each event in random order and ask students to point to the appropriate picture.
- Resume playing Track 15. Tell students to listen and repeat.

2 PRACTICE

A PAIRS. Student A, point to a picture and ask...

- Read the directions. Read each line in the example and ask the class to repeat. Model correct intonation.
- Play Speaker A and model the example with an above-level student. Point to picture 3.
- Continue the conversation. Prompt Speaker B to point to a picture and ask: *Where are the people?*
- Pair students and tell them to ask about six pictures each.
- Walk around and help students correct each other's mistakes.

B WORD PLAY. GROUPS OF 3. Look at...

- Tell students to look at pictures 4 and 10. Say: *The people are dressed formally. What are they wearing?* (dark suits, ties, a dress)
- Tell students to look at pictures 5 and 9. Say: *The people are dressed casually. What are they wearing?* (shorts, jeans, T-shirts, sneakers)
- Read the directions.
- Tell students to complete the first column of the chart on their own and then compare events with their group members. Repeat with the second and third columns.

C CLASS. Are the answers to Exercise B the same...

- Draw the chart from Exercise 2B on the board. As a class, complete the chart for events in the U.S.
- Tell students to compare the chart on the board with their own chart. Ask: *Are there any differences?* Discuss as a class.
- Tell the class to look at the pictures again. Ask: *Are there any events that don't happen in your country? Do people have potluck dinners? Do they have family reunions?*

▬▬▬ EXPANSION: Speaking practice for 2C

- Tell students to circle an event on their chart for which the dress is different than in the U.S.
- Form pairs. Say: *What do you wear for this event in your country? What do you wear for this event in the U.S.? Tell your partner.*

Learning Strategy: Personalize

- Read the directions. Explain: Personalize *means to make something about you.*
- Provide each student with five index cards or tell students to cut up notebook paper.
- Model the strategy. Make a card for an event you have attended and show it to the class. Read the information on the card.
- Tell students to make cards for five events they have attended in the past.
- Walk around as students work. If misspellings occur, tell them to check the list on page 107.
- Say: *To practice the vocabulary, read the date and names on one side of the card and try to say the event.* Turn the card over to check your answer.
- Call on students to read their events.
- Say: *You can remember new vocabulary when you write about things that are important to you.* Remind students to use this strategy to remember other new vocabulary.

■■■ **EXPANSION: Graphic organizer practice**

- Draw a web diagram on the board. Tell students to choose a memorable event with family and friends. Tell them to write the event in the circle.
- At the ends of the lines radiating out from the circle, tell them to write as many details as they can about the event.
- To model the activity, complete the web diagram on the board with information about your own special event (for example, *My wedding: July 7, 2001; in Ventura, California; 120 guests; beautiful weather; steak and shrimp dinner; dancing.*).

Communicative Practice   20 minutes

Show what you know!

STEP 1. Look at the list of events with family and...

- Read the directions. Tell students to write their favorite event on the line.
- Ask them why they enjoy the event and tell them they will discuss their reasons in Step 2.

STEP 2. GROUPS OF 3. Talk about your favorite...

- Ask two students to read the example out loud.
- Tell students to note what they like about their favorite event.
- Model the activity. Prompt a student to ask you: *What's your favorite event?* Answer truthfully, in a manner similar to the example. Then ask an above-level student: *What's your favorite event? Why?*
- Form groups of 3.
- Walk around and listen to students' conversations. Help them explain their choices as needed.
- Call on groups to perform for the class.

■■■ **MULTILEVEL INSTRUCTION for STEP 2**

Cross-ability Before students practice the conversation, group them according to the same favorite event. Tell groups to brainstorm reasons why they enjoy the event. Ask an above-level student to record the reasons on a sheet of paper. Tell group members to choose a few reasons and note them in their books. For the activity, group students with different favorite events and, to the extent possible, of different levels.

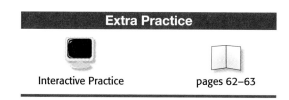

Extra Practice

Interactive Practice   pages 62–63

Events With Family and Friends

1. a birthday party
2. a wedding
3. an anniversary party
4. a funeral
5. a family reunion
6. a graduation party
7. a holiday meal
8. a baby shower
9. a barbecue
10. a retirement party
11. a potluck dinner
12. a surprise party

Learning Strategy

Personalize

Look at the list of events. Think of five events that you have attended. Make a card for each event. On one side of the card, write the vocabulary words. On the other side, write the date of the event and the names of some people who attended.

Show what you know!

STEP 1. Look at the list of events with family and friends. What is your favorite event?

_____

STEP 2. GROUPS OF 3. Talk about your favorite events. Explain your choices.

A: *What's your favorite event?*
B: *Weddings are my favorite event! Everyone is so happy. Everyone looks so beautiful.*

Listening and Speaking

1 BEFORE YOU LISTEN

CLASS. Look at the pictures. Which of these activities do you do with your family or friends?

| listen to family stories | look at old photos | stay up late | dance all night |

2 LISTEN

A CLASS. Look at the picture of Michelle and Sam. Guess: What are they talking about?

CD2 T16

B Listen to the conversation. Was your guess in Exercise A correct?

CD2 T16

C Listen again. Read the sentences. Circle *True* or *False*.

1. Michelle asks Sam about his weekend. (**True**) **False**

2. Sam was at a wedding last weekend. **True** (**False**)

3. Sam watched old movies last weekend. **True** (**False**)

4. Sam listened to family stories. (**True**) **False**

CD2 T17

D Listen to the whole conversation. What did Michelle do last weekend?

a.

b.

Getting Started

1 BEFORE YOU LISTEN

CLASS. Look at the pictures. Which of these...

- Tell the class to look at the pictures. Say each activity and ask the class to repeat.
- Ask: *Which of these activities do you do with your family or friends?* Tell students to put a checkmark next to the activities they do.
- Say: *Raise your hand if you do any of these: When you get together with family or friends, do you listen to family stories?* Repeat with the other three activities.

Presentation

2 LISTEN

Ⓐ CLASS. Look at the picture of Michelle and Sam....

- Tell the class to look at the picture. Ask: *Where are the people?* (at work / in an office break room) *What day is it?* (Monday) *What time is it?* (9:10)
- Say: *Point to Michelle. Point to Sam. What are they talking about? What do people talk about at work on Monday morning?*
- Elicit students' guesses and list them on the board (for example, *their weekends, their work, their lunch plans, the weather*).

> **Teaching Tip**
>
> *Optional:* Remember that if students need additional support, tell them to read the Audio Script on page 301 as they listen to the conversations.

Ⓑ 💿 Listen to the conversation. Was your...

- Read the directions.
- Play CD 2, Track 16.
- Ask: *What are they talking about?* Read the guesses on the board. Elicit and circle the best answer. (their weekends)

Ⓒ 💿 Listen again. Read the sentences....

- Read the directions.
- Play Track 16 again. Students listen and circle *True* or *False*.
- Students compare answers with a partner.
- Call on students to read the sentences. Tell the class to call out *True* or *False*.
- Write the false sentences on the board. As a class, change the false sentences to make them true. (2. Sam was at a <u>family reunion</u>. 3. Sam <u>looked at old pictures</u> last weekend.)
- Ask the class: *Does your family have family reunions?*

Ⓓ 💿 Listen to the whole conversation....

- Tell the class to look at the first picture. Ask: *What is the event?* (a birthday party) Tell the class to look at the second picture. Ask: *What are the people doing?* (talking, laughing, eating, drinking) *Is it a birthday party?* (No.) *Is it a party?* (Yes. / Maybe.)
- Read the directions and the question. Play CD 2, Track 17.
- Ask: *What did Michelle do last weekend? Did she have a birthday party?* (No.) *Did she have a party?* (Yes.) *Why was it a "surprise" party?* (because she didn't plan to have a party) *Who did she invite over?* (some friends) *Who else came?* (some other friends) *Which picture shows what Michelle did?* (b)

▬▬ **EXPANSION: Vocabulary practice for 2D**

- Tell students to refer back to page 27 and review the vocabulary for family members.
- Tell students to imagine they're planning a family reunion and that everyone can come. Say: *In your notebooks, list the names of family members you want to see at the family reunion and their relationship to you.* Then tell students to list the activities for the family reunion. Tell them to use the activities on page 108 and their own ideas. To prompt them, ask: *What does your family like to eat when they get together? What do they like to drink? What else does your family do? Sing? Listen to music? Play games?*
- Form pairs. Say: *Tell your partner who you really want to see at your family reunion. Tell your partner what your family is going to do at the reunion.*

Lesson 2 Talk about past activities

3 CONVERSATION

Ⓐ 💿 **Listen. Then listen and repeat.**

- Say: *Look at the words. What do they all end in?* (*-ed*)
- Write *invited* and *needed* on the board. Read the first sentence of the Pronunciation Watch note. Underline as follows: *invi<u>t</u>ed, nee<u>d</u>ed*. Pronounce *invited* and *needed*, emphasizing the /ɪd/ ending.
- Say: *The -ed ending does not add an extra syllable after other sounds.*
- Write *looked* and *dropped* on the board. Underline as follows: *loo<u>k</u>ed, dro<u>pp</u>ed*. Say: *After some sounds, the -ed ending sounds like* /t/. Pronounce *looked* and *dropped*, emphasizing the /t/ ending.
- Write *listened* and *showed* on the board. Underline as follows: *liste<u>n</u>ed, sho<u>w</u>ed*. Say: *After some sounds, the -ed ending sounds like* /d/. Pronounce *listened* and *showed*, emphasizing the /d/ ending.
- Play CD 2, Track 18. Students listen. Then resume playing Track 18. Students listen and repeat.

Ⓑ **Say the words to yourself. For which verbs does...**

- Tell students to look at the words and underline the letter or sound that comes before the *-ed* ending. Ask: *After which sounds does the -ed ending add a syllable?* (/t/ and /d/)

Ⓒ 💿 **Listen and check your answers.**

- Play CD 2, Track 19. Then ask: *For which verbs does -ed add a syllable?* Pronounce *visited* and *wanted* and ask the class to repeat.

Language Note

Ask: *For which verbs does -ed sound like* /t/? Play Track 19 again. Elicit and list on the board: *danced, watched, talked*. Add *looked* and *dropped* to the list. Tell students to copy the list into their notebooks and underline the letter or sound that comes before the *-ed* ending (*dan<u>c</u>ed, wat<u>ch</u>ed, tal<u>k</u>ed, loo<u>k</u>ed, dro<u>pp</u>ed*). Say the underlined sounds and ask the class to put their hands on their throats and repeat. Ask: *Did you feel any vibration when you said these sounds?* (No.) Explain: *These sounds are voiceless, so the ending* /t/ *is also voiceless.* Ask: *For which verbs does -ed sound like* /d/? Repeat the steps above. Ask: *Did you feel any vibration when you said these sounds?* (Yes.) Explain: *These sounds are voiced, so the ending* /d/ *is also voiced.*

Ⓓ 💿 **Listen and repeat the conversation.**

- Note: This conversation is the same one students heard in Exercise 2B on page 108.
- Tell students to read the conversation silently and underline any verbs that end in *-ed*.
- Ask: *What words did you underline?* (*showed, looked, listened*) Say: *Does the -ed ending add a syllable for any of these verbs?* (No.)
- Play CD 2, Track 20. Students listen and repeat.

Controlled Practice   25 minutes

4 PRACTICE

Ⓐ **PAIRS. Practice the conversation. Then make new...**

- Pair students and tell them to practice the conversation in Exercise 3D. Walk around and check pronunciation of the *-ed* endings.
- Then, in Exercise 4A, tell students to look at the information in the green and red boxes. Tell them to look at the verbs and underline the sound that comes before the *-ed* endings. Ask: *Does the -ed ending add a syllable for any of these verbs?* (No.)
- Ask two above-level students to practice a conversation for the class.

Communicative Practice   15 minutes

Ⓑ **MAKE IT PERSONAL. PAIRS. Talk about a...**

- Say: *Think of a past family event. What did you do?* Write your own family event and a couple of things your family did on the board.
- On the board, write: *How was your _____?* Prompt a student to ask you about your family event. Answer in a manner similar to Speaker B in the conversation in Exercise 4A. Use the information you wrote on the board.
- Pair students. Say: *Before you practice, tell your partner what your family event is.* Walk around and check that students form the past tense correctly.

Extra Practice

⬛

Interactive Practice

---

3 CONVERSATION

CD2 T18

(A) Listen. Then listen and repeat.

Extra syllable	No extra syllable	
invited	looked	listened
needed	dropped	showed

Pronunciation Watch

The *-ed* ending adds an extra syllable after the sound /t/ or /d/. It does not add an extra syllable after other sounds.

(B) Say the words to yourself. For which verbs does *-ed* add a syllable? Circle the numbers.

1. danced   (2.) visited   3. watched   (4.) wanted   5. talked   6. stayed

CD2 T19

(C) Listen and check your answers.

CD2 T20

(D) Listen and repeat the conversation.

Michelle: How was your weekend? How was the family reunion?

Sam: It was really nice, thanks. My whole family showed up.

Michelle: Sounds great.

Sam: Yeah, it was fun. We looked at old pictures and listened to family stories.

4 PRACTICE

(A) PAIRS. Practice the conversation. Then make new conversations. Use the information in the boxes.

A: How was your weekend? How was the _____ ?

B: It was really nice, thanks. My whole family showed up.

A: Sounds great.

B: Yeah, it was fun. We _____ and _____ .

(B) MAKE IT PERSONAL. PAIRS. Talk about a family event. What did you do?

anniversary party

barbecue

wedding

watched family movies

cooked a lot of food

stayed up late

talked about old times

played games

danced all night

Grammar

Simple past: Regular verbs

Affirmative		Negative	
I She **looked** at old pictures yesterday. They		I She **didn't cook** dinner last night. They	

1 PRACTICE

A Complete the letter. Use the simple past of the words in parentheses.

Grammar Watch

For most regular verbs, add -ed.
For example: want → wanted

For verbs that end in -e, add -d.
For example: invite → invited

Hi, Sis!

How are you? I know you really (want) ____wanted____ to go to Josh's

birthday party last Saturday. We (miss) ____missed____ you. Josh and Rebecca

(invite) ____invited____ a lot of people, and almost everyone (show up) ____showed up____.

There was a lot of food and I (help) ____helped____ in the kitchen. Then Josh

(play) ____played____ some music. We all (dance) ____danced____ and

(not want) ____didn't want____ to stop. We (not need) ____didn't need____ to get up early the

next day, so everyone (stay) ____stayed____ late. It was a fun party. Talk to you soon!

Gina

B Complete the conversation. Use the past tense forms of the words in the box.

> clean   ~~invite~~   not leave   stay up   visit   want   watch

A: You look a little tired this morning.

B: Yeah, I ____invited____ some friends over last night. They ____didn't leave____ until late

and then I ____cleaned____ the house. It was a mess! You look a little tired, too.

A: I am. I ____visited____ my cousin last night. We ____watched____ a soccer game on TV.

I ____wanted____ to see the end so I ____stayed up____ late.

Getting Started   6 minutes

- Say: *We're going to study simple past statements. In the conversation on page 109, Sam used this grammar.*
- Play CD 2, Track 20. Students listen. On the board, write: *We looked at old pictures and listened to family stories.* Underline *looked* and *listened.*

Presentation   10 minutes

Simple past: Regular verbs

- Copy the grammar charts onto the board or show Transparency 6.3 and cover the exercise.
- Tell students to look at the left grammar chart. Ask: *How do you form the simple past with regular verbs?* (add -ed to the base form of the verb) Say: *The form is the same with all subjects.* Read a sentence from the chart. Elicit a few other affirmative simple past statements and write them on the board.
- Tell students to look at the right grammar chart. Ask: *How do you form negative sentences in the simple past tense?* (*didn't* + base form of a verb) Say: *The form is the same with all subjects.* Read a sentence from the chart. Elicit a few other negative simple past statements and write them on the board.
- Say: *Look at the grammar charts again. Read the examples. What other words tell you these sentences describe past activities?* (*yesterday, last night*) Ask students to think of other past time expressions.
- If you are using the transparency, do the exercise with the class.

Controlled Practice   25 minutes

1 PRACTICE

A Complete the letter. Use the simple past of the...

- Read the first two sentences of the letter. Ask: *How do you form the simple past of* want? (add -ed) On the board, write: *want → wanted.* Ask: *How would you form the simple past of* not want? (*didn't + want*) On the board, write: *not want: didn't want.*
- Say: *If a verb ends in -e, just add -d to form the simple past.* Write *dance* on the board and ask the class how to form the past tense. Add *-d* to *dance.*

- Read the letter. Tell students to check their answers.
- Tell students to look at their answers. Ask: *For which verbs does -ed add a syllable?* (*wanted, invited*) Pronounce *invited* with the /ɪd/ ending and ask the class to repeat.
- *Optional:* Tell students to take turns reading the letter to a partner.

B Complete the conversation. Use the past tense...

- Read the directions. Tell students to use the words in the box only once.
- Students compare answers with a partner. Tell them to read the conversation. Walk around and check students' pronunciation of the /ɪd/ ending in *visited* and *wanted.*
- Call on two above-level students to read the conversation for the class.

Teaching Tip

Completion activities such as Exercises 1A and 1B are a great opportunity for students to demonstrate their reading comprehension. After Exercise 1A, ask: *What was the event?* (a birthday party) *What did people do?* (They listened to music. They danced. They stayed up late.) After Exercise 1B, ask: *What did A do last night?* (watched a soccer game on TV with his or her cousin) *What did Speaker B do last night?* (invited some friends over) *What did you do last night?* Write the questions on the board. Tell students to ask and answer the questions with a partner or copy the questions into their notebooks and write answers in class or for homework.

EXPANSION: Grammar and writing practice for 1B

- Ask: *What did you do last weekend?* Tell students to write at least five sentences using verbs on this page and pages 108 and 109 (for example, *I watched a movie on Friday night. I stayed up late. On Saturday, I cleaned the house. On Saturday night, I talked to my best friend on the phone. On Sunday, I cooked dinner for my family.*).

2 PRACTICE

A Read Kathy's to-do list. Then look at the pictures...

- Read the directions. Tell students to look at the pictures. Point to the first picture and ask: *What did Kathy do this morning?* (She visited Mrs. Parker.) Say: *Find* visit Mrs. Parker *on Kathy's list and check it.* Tell students to do the same for the other three pictures.
- Point to the second, third, and fourth pictures and ask: *What did Kathy do this morning?* (She watched a movie. She walked the dog. She baked cookies.) Then read each item on Kathy's list and ask the class to call out *yes* or *no.*

B PAIRS. Talk about what Kathy did and did not do...

- Read the directions.
- Tell students to look at the first two items on Kathy's list. Ask: *Did she visit Mrs. Parker?* (Yes.) *Did she call Joe?* (No.)
- Ask two students to read the example out loud.
- Tell students to look at the third item on Kathy's list. On the board, write: *She didn't finish homework.* Ask: *What's missing?* Add *her* before *homework.* Say: *You need to add words to some sentences.*
- Pair students and tell them to take turns talking about the items on Kathy's list. Remind students to add *-ed* to the verb for the things she did and to use *didn't* + the verb for the things she didn't do.

C WRITE. On a separate piece of paper, write five...

- Read the directions. Tell students to choose five items from Kathy's list but not to choose the first and second items.
- Tell students to use the sentences in Exercise 2B as a model. Remind students to start each sentence with a capital letter and end each sentence with a period.
- Ask students to write a sentence on the board for each item, beginning with *finish homework.* Read each sentence and correct as needed. Check that students added necessary words as follows: *She didn't finish her homework. She watched a movie. She didn't return the movie to the video store.*

▪▪▪ EXPANSION: Writing practice for 2C

- Tell students to write four additional sentences about what Kathy still needs to do (for example, *Kathy needs to call Joe.*).

Communicative Practice   20 minutes

Show what you know!

STEP 1. Complete the sentence with true...

- Model the activity. Think of one thing you did last week. On the board, write a sentence. Use a regular simple past verb (for example, *I baked banana bread last week.*).
- Tell students to think of one thing they did last week and to complete the sentence. Encourage them to use verbs from this unit.
- Walk around and check that students are using a regular simple past verb and the *-ed* ending.

STEP 2. GROUPS OF 5. Play the Memory Game....

- Read the directions. Ask three students seated in a row to read the example out loud. Then ask the same three students to model the activity by substituting their own names and activities into the example.
- Form groups of 5 and tell group members to count off. Say: *Student 1, read your sentence from Step 1. Student 2, say what Student 1 did and then read your own sentence. Student 3, say what Student 1 did, say what Student 2 did, and then read your own sentence, and so on.*
- Call on the fifth student in each group to report what all the people in his or her group did.

▪▪▪ MULTILEVEL INSTRUCTION for STEP 2

Cross-ability Instead of telling group members to count off, assign lower-level students number 1 or 2 and higher-level students number 4 or 5.

Progress Check

Can you . . . talk about past activities?

Say: *We have practiced talking about past activities. Now, look at the question at the bottom of the page. Can you talk about past activities?* Tell students to write a checkmark in the box.

Extra Practice		
Interactive Practice	pages 52–53	pages 64–65

A Read Kathy's to-do list. Then look at the pictures of the things she did after work today. Check the things Kathy did today on the list.

Kathy's to-do list

- ☑ visit Mrs. Parker
- ☐ call Joe
- ☐ finish homework
- ☑ watch movie
- ☐ return movie to video store
- ☑ walk the dog
- ☐ go to the supermarket
- ☑ bake cookies

B PAIRS. Talk about what Kathy did and did not do after work.

A: *Kathy visited Mrs. Parker.*
B: *She didn't call Joe.*

C WRITE. On a separate piece of paper, write five sentences about what Kathy did and did not do after work.

Show what you know!   Talk about past activities

STEP 1. Complete the sentence with true information. Use the simple past.

I _____ last week.

STEP 2. GROUPS OF 5. Play the Memory Game. Talk about what people did.

Talib: *I visited my sister.*
Minoru: *Talib visited his sister. I cooked dinner for my wife.*
Rita: *Talib visited his sister. Minoru cooked dinner for his wife.*
I watched three movies.

Can you...talk about past activities? ☐

Life Skills

1   RECOGNIZE U.S. HOLIDAYS

A **PAIRS.** Look at the calendars. Write the name of each holiday on the correct line.

> Christmas Day   Columbus Day   Independence Day   Labor Day
> Martin Luther King Jr. Day   Memorial Day   ~~New Year's Day~~   Presidents' Day
> Thanksgiving Day   Veterans' Day

1. New Year's Day
2. Martin Luther King Jr. Day
3. Presidents' Day
4. Memorial Day
5. Independence Day
6. Labor Day
7. Columbus Day
8. Veterans' Day
9. Thanksgiving Day
10. Christmas Day

B CD2 T21 Listen and check your answers. Then listen and repeat.

C CD2 T22 Look at the calendars. Listen to the conversations. Which U. S. holiday are they talking about? Write the name of each holiday on the line.

1. Independence Day
2. Thanksgiving Day
3. Christmas Day
4. Labor Day
5. New Year's Day

D **PAIRS.** Check your answers.

Lesson 4 Recognize U.S. holidays

Getting Started   10 minutes

Culture Connection

- Say: *On national holidays, people don't have to go to work or school. What are some national holidays in your country?*
- On the board, write the countries represented in your class. For each country, elicit a couple of important national holidays and list them on the board.
- Tell the class to look at the holidays on the board. Ask: *Which ones are also holidays in the U.S.? Circle the holidays that are also celebrated in the U.S.*
- Ask: *What's your favorite holiday in your country? When is it? Why do you like it?*

Presentation   20 minutes

1 RECOGNIZE U.S. HOLIDAYS

A PAIRS. **Look at the calendars. Write the name of...**

- Tell students to look at the names of national holidays in the box. Say each holiday for the class to repeat.
- Tell students to look at the pictures next to the calendars. Say: *Look at the picture next to January 21st. Who is this man?* (Martin Luther King Jr.) *Look at the picture next to February. Who are these men?* (George Washington, the 1st president of the U.S., Abraham Lincoln, the 16th president of the U.S.) *Look at the picture next to July. What do you see?* (fireworks) *Look at the picture next to September. What event is this?* (a barbecue) *Look at the picture next to November. What food is this?* (turkey) *Point to the pictures of soldiers. What months are they next to?* (May, November)
- Pair students and tell them to look at the calendars and pictures. Say: *Write the names of the holidays you know first. Cross them off in the box. Then try to guess the other holidays.*

B **Listen and check your answers. Then...**

- Play CD 2, Track 21. Tell students to circle any incorrect answers.
- Say: *Correct the answers you circled.*
- Play Track 21 again. Say: *Change any answers that are still not correct.*

- Review the difference between written and spoken numbers. On the board, write: *New Year's Day— January 1.* Say: *New Year's Day is on January 1st.* Ask: *When is Independence Day?* (on July 4th) Ask: *What do people usually call Independence Day?* (The Fourth of July) *When is your birthday?* Review ordinals as needed.
- Resume playing Track 21. Students listen and repeat.

EXPANSION: Vocabulary practice for 1B

- Tell students to look at the dates of the holidays in Exercise 1A. Ask: *Which holidays are celebrated on the same date every year? Which holidays change dates every year?*
- On the board, draw a T-chart with the headings *Same date every year* and *Change dates every year.* Number from 1 to 4 on the left side of the chart. Number from 1 to 6 on the right side of the chart.
- Call on students to complete the chart on the board.

Controlled Practice   30 minutes

C **Look at the calendars. Listen...**

- Play CD 2, Track 22. Pause after item 1. Ask: *What holiday has fireworks?* (Independence Day) On the board, write: *independence day.* Ask: *Is this correct?* (No.) *What do I need to do?* (begin each word with a capital letter) Cross out *independence day* and write *Independence Day.*
- Resume playing Track 22.

D PAIRS. **Check your answers.**

- Students compare answers with a partner and check that they capitalized each word.
- Ask a question for each item: *2. On which holiday do people usually eat turkey? 3. For which holiday do some people decorate a tree? 4. For which holidays do people often have a barbecue? 5. On which holiday do people stay up late the night before?*

EXPANSION Speaking practice for 1D

- Tell pairs to ask and answer questions about the dates of the holidays. On the board, write:

   A: When is New Year's Day?

   B: It's on January 1st. When is Thanksgiving Day?

   A: It's on the fourth Thursday in November. . . .

- Tell partners to ask about three holidays each.

2 PRACTICE

A Read the article about national holidays.

- Tell students to take out a piece of paper and number from 1 to 3. Tell students cover the article with the piece of paper.
- Say: *I'm going to ask you three questions about U.S. holidays. Write your guess.* Ask each question from the article.
- Number from 1 to 3 on the board. Repeat each question, elicit answers from the class, and write them on the board.
- Tell students to read the article silently and check the answers on the board.
- Read each question again. Point to each answer on the board and ask if it's correct. Correct as needed.
- *Optional:* Read the article out loud. Pause after each quiz question and answer and ask:

  1st question: *What are the "Big Six" holidays that many U.S. businesses observe?* (New Year's Day, Memorial Day, Independence Day, Labor Day, Thanksgiving Day, and Christmas Day) *Do you get these days off?*

  2nd question: *What did Martin Luther King Jr. do?* (He worked for the equality of all people.)

  3rd question: *Who do we remember on Memorial Day?* (U.S. military personnel who died in wars)

B Read the article again. Read the sentences....

- Read the example. Ask: *How do you know it's true? Where in the article does it say that there are ten national holidays?* Elicit and tell students to underline in the article: *There are ten national holidays.*
- Say: *For each item, underline the words in the article that give the answer.*
- Students compare answers with a partner.
- Tell pairs to look at their false answers. Say: *For each false answer, look at the words you underlined in the article.* Tell pairs to correct the false information in the sentences in Exercise 2B.
- Call on three students from different pairs to write corrected items 2 and 5 on the board (2. *Many businesses* in the U.S. *stay open* on national holidays. 4. President's Day celebrates *George Washington and Abraham Lincoln. / Martin Luther King Jr. Day* celebrates the life of Martin Luther King Jr.).

Culture Connection

- Explain: *In the U.S., the holiday season begins on Thanksgiving Day and ends on New Year's Day. During these five weeks, people say to each other, "Happy Holidays."*
- Ask: *Is there a special holiday season in your country? When is it? What do people say to each other?*
- Explain: *According to the calendar, summer begins on June 21st or 22nd and ends on September 21st or 22nd. Unofficially, summer begins on Memorial Day and ends on Labor Day in the U.S. For example, public swimming pools open on Memorial Day weekend and close on Labor Day weekend.*
- Ask: *Does any holiday or do special events mark the beginning and / or end of summer in your country? What are they?*

EXPANSION: Vocabulary and speaking practice for 2B

- For homework, tell students to bring a calendar for this year to class. Tell them to circle the national holidays.
- The following day, pair students. Tell Student A to write the dates for the six holidays with dates that change every year. Tell Student B to write the day of the week for the four holidays that are celebrated on the same date every year.
- Tell pairs to talk about the information they found. On the board, write:

  A: *What day is Christmas this year?*

  B: *What date is Martin Luther King Jr. Day this year?*
- Remind students to use ordinals to talk about dates.

Progress Check

Can you . . . recognize U.S. holidays?

Say: *We have talked about U.S. holidays. Now, look at the question at the bottom of the page. Can you recognize U.S. holidays?* Tell students to write a checkmark in the box.

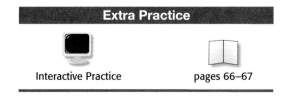

Extra Practice	
Interactive Practice	pages 66–67

A Read the article about national holidays.

What Do You Know About U.S. Holidays?

Take this quiz.

Q. How many national holidays are there in the United States?

A. There are ten national holidays, but most people don't know that because many businesses stay open on national holidays. Schools, banks, and government offices such as the post office are closed on all ten days. Many U.S. businesses observe only the "Big Six:" New Year's Day, Memorial Day, Independence Day, Labor Day, Thanksgiving Day, and Christmas Day.

Q. *Which holidays celebrate specific people?*

A. Presidents' Day, Martin Luther King Jr. Day, and Columbus Day celebrate specific people. Presidents' Day celebrates George Washington, the first president of the United States, and Abraham Lincoln, the sixteenth president. Martin Luther King Jr. Day celebrates Dr. King's work for the equality of all people. Columbus Day celebrates the day Columbus arrived in the Americas in 1492.

Q. *What's the difference between Veterans' Day and Memorial Day?*

A. Both holidays celebrate the U.S. military. On Veterans' Day, we celebrate all people in the U.S. military. On Memorial Day, we remember U.S. military personnel who died in wars.

B Read the article again. Read the sentences. Circle *True* or *False*. Correct the false information.

1. There are ten national holidays.	(True)	False
2. All businesses in the U.S. are closed on national holidays.	True	(False)
3. Government offices are closed on national holidays.	(True)	False
4. Presidents' Day celebrates the life of Martin Luther King Jr.	True	(False)
5. Columbus Day celebrates the day Columbus arrived in 1942.	(True)	False
6. Veterans' Day celebrates all people in the U.S. military.	(True)	False

Can you...recognize U.S. holidays? ☐

Talk about milestones

Listening and Speaking

1 BEFORE YOU LISTEN

CLASS. Look at the pictures of milestones.
What are some other important times in a person's life?

being born

growing up

graduating from school

getting a job

getting married

having children

2 LISTEN

CD2 T23

A Listen to the interview on a radio show. Which milestones do the people talk about?

☐ being born ☐ growing up ☐ going to school ☐ getting married

CD2 T23

B Listen again. Complete the sentences.

1. Daniel was born in _____.
   a. California   b. Colorado

2. Daniel wanted to be _____
   when he was a child.
   a. an actor   b. a plumber

3. Daniel _____ last night.
   a. went to a party   b. stayed home

Lesson 5 Talk about milestones

Getting Started   5 minutes

1   BEFORE YOU LISTEN

CLASS. Look at the pictures of milestones. What...

- Tell students to read the directions silently. Ask: *What are* milestones? (important times in a person's life)
- Say: *Look at the pictures of milestones in one person's life.* Say each milestone and ask the class to repeat. Say: *Imagine the pictures of your milestones. Check the milestones in your life.*
- Ask: *What are some other milestones?* Elicit students' ideas and list them on the board (for example, *moving, buying a house, retiring, becoming a grandparent*).

> **Language Note**
>
> On the board, write: *Being born is the first milestone.* Underline *being born* and ask if it's a noun or a verb. Point out that the *-ing* words at the beginning of the milestones act like nouns. Explain that *-ing* words that act like nouns are called *gerunds*.

EXPANSION: Graphic organizer and vocabulary practice for 1

- Draw a web diagram on the board. Write *Milestones* in the circle and ask students to copy the diagram into their notebooks.
- At the ends of the lines radiating from the circle, tell students to write the milestones they checked in Exercise 1. Tell them to draw circles around the milestones and then more lines radiating from each circle. On these lines, students note some details about each milestone, for example, a date, place, names.
- To model the activity, create your own web diagram on the board.

Presentation   20 minutes

2   LISTEN

A   Listen to the interview on a radio....

- Read the directions. Tell students to read the milestones silently.

- Play CD 2, Track 23. Tell students to listen and check the milestones the people talk about.
- Tell students to look at the picture again. Say: *Point to Amber Jenkins. Point to Daniel Lopez. Which one is the host / interviewer?* (Amber Jenkins)
- Say each milestone. Tell the class to call out *yes* or *no*.
- Ask: *Who is Daniel Lopez? / Why is Amber Jenkins interviewing him?* (He's a star / an actor / a celebrity.)

> **Teaching Tip**
>
> *Optional:* Remember that if students need additional support, tell them to read the Audio Script on page 302 as they listen to the conversations.

B   Listen again. Complete the sentences.

- Tell students to read the sentences and answer choices silently.
- Play Track 23 again. Students circle the letter of the correct answer.
- Students compare answers with a partner.
- Call on students to read the sentences.
- *Optional:* Tell students to cross out *Daniel* in the sentences and write *I*. Say: *Now complete the sentences with information about yourself.* For each item, call on several students to read their sentence.

EXPANSION: Graphic organizer and vocabulary practice for 2B

- Ask: *Are you interested in celebrities' lives? Who's your favorite actor / actress / singer / ... ?*
- Tell students to choose a celebrity and create a web diagram of his or her milestones.
- Pair or group students who like the same celebrity. If appropriate in your setting, allow students to research their celebrity online, or assign the activity for homework.
- Tell pairs / groups to copy their web diagram onto chart paper but leave off the celebrity's name. Number and post the web diagrams. Tell students to walk around, read the diagrams, and try to identify the celebrities. Tell them to write the numbers and names in their notebooks. Hold a competition to see who can identify the most celebrities.

3 CONVERSATION

Ⓐ Listen to the intonation of the...

- Say: *Sometimes you can make a statement into a question without changing word order.* On the board, write: *You were born in California.* Say the statement for the class to repeat. Then change the period into a question mark. Say the question for the class to repeat.
- Read the Pronunciation Watch note. Ask: *When can you say a statement as a question?* (to check understanding)
- On the board, write: *I was born in _____.* Call on several students to complete the statement. Model repeating the statement as a question to check understanding. For example, S: *I was born in Jakarta.* T: *You were born in Jakarta?* S: *Yes. / Right.*
- Play CD 2, Track 24. Say: *Listen to the intonation.*
- Say: *Now listen and repeat. Make your voice go up at the end.* Resume playing Track 24.

Ⓑ Listen to the sentences. Are they...

- Read the directions. Play CD 2, Track 25.
- Call on students to write the sentences with the correct punctuation on the board. Play Track 25 again. Ask the class to listen and check the sentences on the board. Correct as needed.
- Read the statements and then the questions for the class to repeat. Tell students to read the sentences with a partner.

Controlled Practice   20 minutes

Ⓒ Listen and repeat the conversation.

- Tell students to look at the picture. Ask: *Where are Fred and Chen?* (at work / in an office break room) Tell students to read the conversation silently and underline the milestones in Chen's life. Ask: *What did you underline?* Elicit: *born in a small village, grew up in Beijing, came to the U.S. five years ago, got an apartment in Long Beach, moved to San Francisco.*
- Tell students to read the conversation again and look for a clue to one more milestone in Chen's life. Tell students to circle the clue. Ask: *What did you circle?* (my wife) *What's the milestone?* (getting married)
- Play CD 2, Track 26. Students listen and repeat.

4 PRACTICE

Ⓐ PAIRS. Practice the conversation.

- Walk around and check that students are using question intonation in Fred's second line.

▉▉▉ EXPANSION: Speaking practice for 4A

- Tell one partner in each pair to close his or her book. This student tries to remember the events in Chen's life by making statements with question intonation (for example, *He's from China?*).
- The other partner looks at the conversation and answers *yes* or *no*. For *no* answers, he or she tells the first student to guess again.

Communicative Practice   15 minutes

Ⓑ MAKE IT PERSONAL. PAIRS. Ask your partner...

- Ask two above-level students to read the example.
- Write a few things you know about a student's life on the board (for example, *came to U.S. in 2007, studied English in El Salvador, two children*). Start a conversation with the student by asking: *Where are you from?* Then say statements as questions to check your understanding of the events in the student's life (for example, *You came to the U.S. in 2007? You studied English in El Salvador? You have two children?*). Correct the information on the board as needed.
- Tell pairs to ask each other: *Where are you from?* Say: *What do you already know about your partner? Use statements as questions to check information.*

Ⓒ Tell the class about your partner.

- Ask the student who played Angela in Exercise 4B to read the example.
- Use the information on the board to make statements (for example, *Hugo is from El Salvador. He came to the U.S. in 2007. He studied English in El Salvador. He has two children.*).
- Call on students to tell the class about their partner.

Extra Practice

Interactive Practice

3 CONVERSATION

CD2 T24

A 🖸 **Listen to the intonation of the sentences. Then listen and repeat.**

You were born in California?

Stella came to the U.S. last year?

Daniel always wanted to be an actor?

You got a job in a supermarket?

> **Pronunciation Watch**
>
> To check our understanding, sometimes we repeat a statement as a question. The voice goes up at the end.

CD2 T25

B 🖸 **Listen to the sentences. Are they statements or questions? Add a period (.) to statements. Add a question mark (?) to questions.**

1. Maria grew up in Houston.

2. You came to the U.S. in 1995?

3. Ali graduated from college two years ago.

4. She got married last year?

CD2 T26

C 🖸 **Listen and repeat the conversation.**

Fred: So, tell me . . . Where are you from?

Chen: China. I was born in a small village, but I grew up in Beijing.

Fred: And you came to the U.S. five years ago?

Chen: Right. First my wife and I got an apartment in Long Beach. Then we moved to San Francisco.

Fred: Your English is very good. Did you study English in China?

Chen: Yes, I did, but I didn't practice speaking a lot.

4 PRACTICE

A PAIRS. **Practice the conversation.**

B MAKE IT PERSONAL. PAIRS. **Ask your partner about events in his or her life.**

Angela: *Where are you from?*
Ivan: *Russia . . .*

C **Tell the class about your partner.**

Ivan is from Russia. He came to the U.S. in 2007. He studied English in Russia.

Grammar

Simple past: Irregular verbs

Affirmative		
I	**came**	to the U.S. ten years ago.

Negative		
I	**didn't come**	to the U.S. last year.

Grammar Watch

Here are some examples of past tense forms.
See page 286 for more past tense forms.

Base form	Past tense form	Base form	Past tense form
have	**had**	begin	**began**
go	**went**	come	**came**
get	**got**	leave	**left**
take	**took**	make	**made**
grow	**grew**	do	**did**

1 PRACTICE

A Complete the sentences. Underline the correct words.

1. I **don't grow** / **didn't grow** up in the U.S. I **grow** / **grew** up in Haiti.

2. Rosa **meets** / **met** Ricardo in 2006 and they **get** / **got** married in 2008.

3. Yao **took** / **takes** some college classes last year but he didn't **graduated** / **graduate**.

4. Last year they **leave** / **left** Colombia and they **came** / **come** to the U.S.

5. Ho-Jin **goes** / **went** to Los Angeles and he **finds** / **found** a good job there.

6. My grandmother **have** / **had** three brothers but she didn't **have** / **had** any sisters.

B Complete the sentences. Write the simple past of the words in parentheses.

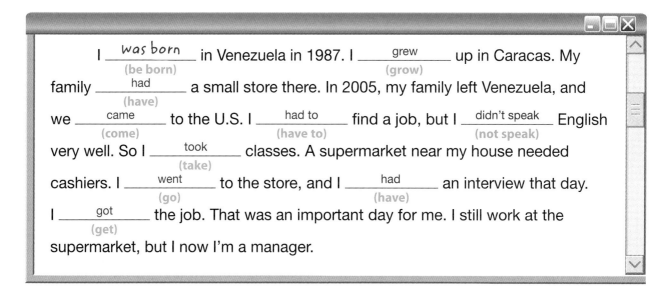

I ___was born___ in Venezuela in 1987. I ___grew___ up in Caracas. My
   (be born)   (grow)
family ___had___ a small store there. In 2005, my family left Venezuela, and
         (have)
we ___came___ to the U.S. I ___had to___ find a job, but I ___didn't speak___ English
      (come)   (have to)   (not speak)
very well. So I ___took___ classes. A supermarket near my house needed
                  (take)
cashiers. I ___went___ to the store, and I ___had___ an interview that day.
               (go)   (have)
I ___got___ the job. That was an important day for me. I still work at the
     (get)
supermarket, but I now I'm a manager.

Lesson 6 Talk about milestones

Getting Started 5 minutes

- Say: *We're going to study simple past statements using irregular verbs. In the conversation on page 115, Chen and Fred used this grammar.*
- Play CD 2, Track 26. Students listen. On the board, write *I grew up in Beijing.* and *And you came to the U.S. five years ago?* Underline *grew up* and *came.*

Presentation 10 minutes

Simple past: Irregular verbs

- Copy the grammar charts onto the board or show Transparency 6.4 and cover the exercise.
- Ask: *How do you form the simple past with regular verbs?* (add -ed) Write *graduate* on the board and elicit the past tense: *graduated.*
- Say: *Some verbs do not have -ed forms. They are irregular. Come is an irregular verb. Look at the top chart. What is the past form of* come? (*came*) Say the sentence in the top chart and ask the class to repeat.
- Ask a few students: *When did you come to the U.S.?* Note their names and responses on the board.
- Use the information on the board to form affirmative and negative simple past sentences with *come*. For example, *Ching Lie came to the U.S. three years ago. She didn't come to the U.S. six months ago.* Point out that the negative sentences are formed in the same way as regular verbs: *didn't* + base form of verb.
- Tell students to look at the Grammar Watch note. Say: *These are some of the verbs that have irregular simple past forms.* Say each past-tense form and ask the class to repeat.
- Say the base forms in random order and tell the class to call out the past-tense forms. Correct pronunciation as needed.
- Tell students to turn to page 286 and read the list of other verbs that are irregular in the simple past.
- If you are using the transparency, do the exercise with the class.

Community Building

Encourage students to quiz each other. Tell students to study the irregular past-tense forms. Then tell them to quiz a partner. Say: *Student A, close your book. Student B, say the past-tense form and tell Student A to say the base form. Then say the base form and tell Student A to say the past-tense form.*

Controlled Practice 15 minutes

1 PRACTICE

Ⓐ Complete the sentences. Underline the correct words.

- Tell students that all the sentences are in the past tense. Remind students to look at the Appendix on page 286 for past-tense forms of verbs that aren't in the Grammar Watch note.
- Students compare answers with a partner and take turns reading the sentences out loud.
- Call on students to read the sentences for the class.
- On the board, write *meet* and *find*. Elicit the past-tense forms and write them next to the base forms: *meet–met, find–found.* Say the past-tense forms and ask the class to repeat.

Ⓑ Complete the sentences. Write the simple past of...

- Ask: *What is the simple past of* be? (*was, were*) Tell students to look at the paragraph. Call on a student to read the first sentence.
- Remind students to use *didn't* + the base form of the verb with negative sentences.
- Walk around and spot-check students' spelling of irregular past forms.
- Students compare answers with a partner. Tell them to each read half of the paragraph out loud.
- Call on two above-level students to read the paragraph for the class. As they say the answers, write them on the board. Tell students to check their spelling.

EXPANSION: Grammar and vocabulary practice for 1B

- Tell students to read the paragraph in Exercise 1B again. Tell them to list five milestones in the person's life. Tell them to use the simple past tense.
- Pair students. On the board, write: *What was the first milestone?* Elicit the ordinal numbers *second* through *fifth* and list them under *first.* Say: *Take turns asking and answering the questions with a partner.*
- Review as a class: *1st—born in Venezuela, 2nd—grew up in Caracas, 3rd—came to the U.S., 4th—found a job, 5th—got a promotion.*

Presentation   15 minutes

Simple past

- Copy the grammar charts onto the board or show Transparency 6.4 and cover the exercise.
- Tell students to look at the left chart. Ask: *How do you form* Yes / No *questions in the simple past? What comes first? Next?* Elicit and write on the board: Did + *subject* + *base form of verb*.
- Tell students to look at the right chart. To elicit *Yes, I did.* and *No, I didn't.*, ask a few students: *Did you grow up in Ecuador?* Ask several more students: *Did you grow up in [Country]?*
- To elicit short answers with *he, she,* and *they,* ask students about their classmates: *Did [Student] grow up in [Country]? Did [Student] and [Student] grow up in [Country]?*
- Tell students to look at the Grammar Watch note. Ask a few students: *Were you born in Poland?* Elicit *Yes, I was.* or *No, I wasn't.* Ask several more students: *Were you born in [country]?* To elicit short answers with *he, she,* and *they,* ask students about their classmates: *Was [Student] born in [Country]? Were [Student] and [Student] born in [Country]?* On the board, write: *Yes, they were*.
- If you are using the transparency, do the exercise with the class.

2 PRACTICE

Write questions and answers. Use the correct...

- Write item 1 on the board. Elicit the question step-by-step, writing each part on the board: *What comes first? Next?* Then elicit the short answer and write it on the board. Call on two students to read the question and answer.
- Walk around and remind students to use the base form of the verb.
- Students compare answers with a partner and take turns asking and answering the questions.
- Call on pairs to read the questions and answers for the class.

Communicative Practice   15 minutes

Show what you know!

STEP 1. Write your name and four sentences...

- Tell students to look at the milestones on page 114. Point to each one and elicit the simple past form. Say: *To talk about your own milestones, say I . . .* Elicit: *was born, grew up, graduated from school, got a job, got married, had children.*
- Model the activity. Write your name and four sentences about events in your life (for example, *I grew up in California. I moved to the Northeast ten years ago. I got married in 2001. I had my daughter in 2003 and my son in 2004.*).

STEP 2. GROUPS OF 5. Mix up the papers from...

- Form groups of five. Read the directions.
- Ask one group to read the example. Assign the roles of A, B, C, D, and E.
- Ask another group to model the activity with a paper from their group. Tell one student to choose a paper and not show the rest of the group. Call on each of the other group members to ask a *Yes / No* question or make a guess. Help students form questions as needed.
- Walk around and check that students form *Yes / No* questions correctly and use short answers.

▬▬ MULTILEVEL INSTRUCTION for STEP 2

Cross-ability Allow a lower-level student in each group to play Speaker A first and answer *Yes, he / she did* or *No, he / she didn't.* This allows the student to hear appropriate *Yes / No* questions modeled before *he / she* has to ask them.

Progress Check

Can you . . . talk about milestones?

Say: *We have practiced talking about milestones. Now, look at the question at the bottom of the page. Can you talk about milestones?* Tell students to write a checkmark in the box.

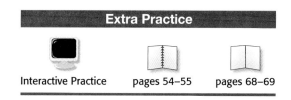

Extra Practice		
Interactive Practice	pages 54–55	pages 68–69

Simple past

Yes / No questions			
Did	you he she they	**grow up**	in Ecuador?

Short answers		
Yes,	I he she they	**did.**
No,		**didn't.**

··· Grammar Watch

Remember how to form past tense questions with *be*.

A: *Were you born in Poland?*
B: *Yes, I was.*

2 PRACTICE

Write questions and answers. Use the correct forms of the words in parentheses.

1. **A:** Did you grow up in a big city?
   (you / grow up / in a big city)
   B: No, I didn't.

2. **A:** Did Ana take English classes?
   (Ana / take / English classes)
   B: Yes, she did.

3. **A:** Did they move to San Diego?
   (they / move / to San Diego)
   B: No, they didn't.

4. **A:** Did Mr. Jung get a new job?
   (Mr. Jung / get / a new job)
   B: Yes, he did.

Show what you know!   Talk about milestones

STEP 1. Write your name and four sentences about milestones in your life. Use a separate piece of paper.

I grew up in Costa Rica.

STEP 2. GROUPS OF 5. Mix up the papers from Step 1. Student A, choose one paper. Other students, guess who wrote the paper. Take turns asking *Yes / No* questions.

B: *Did the person grow up in El Salvador?*
A: *No, she didn't.*
C: *Did she grow up in Costa Rica?*
A: *Yes, she did.*
D: *Did she come to the U.S. last year?*
A: *Yes, she did.*
E: *It's Patricia.*
A: *That's right!*

Can you…talk about milestones? ☐

Reading

1 **BEFORE YOU READ**

CLASS. **Scan the article. Who is Oprah Winfrey? When was she born?**
Oprah Winfrey is the host of a television show. She was born in 1954.

2 **READ**

CD2 T27

Listen. Read the article.

> **Reading Skill:**
> Scanning for Information
>
> Scanning an article means reading it quickly to find specific information. This is helpful when you need to find information such as names or dates quickly.

Oprah!

Oprah Winfrey is the host of *The Oprah Winfrey Show*. It is one of the most popular talk shows in the world. Oprah also has her own magazine, website, radio show, and book club.

Oprah was born in 1954. Her family was very poor, and her parents were not together. She had to move a lot. Her childhood was not easy. But Oprah was a fast learner and she did well in school. At the age of 17, Oprah got a job at a radio station as a newscaster. In 1973, she became the first African-American female television news anchor in Nashville, Tennesee. She was just 19.

In 1984, Oprah became the host of a talk show called *A.M. Chicago*. A year later, the TV network changed the name to *The Oprah Winfrey Show*. Today, millions of people in 132 countries watch the show every day.

But Oprah didn't stop there. In 1985, she acted in the movie *The Color Purple*. A year later she started a company, named Harpo Productions. It makes movies and TV specials. In 1996, she created Oprah's Book Club. It is now the largest book club in the world. In 2000, she started her first magazine, *O: The Oprah Magazine*.

These sucesses have made Oprah the richest African-American in the world. Oprah's charity, the Oprah Winfrey Foundation, gives millions of dollars to needy students and schools around the world. In 2007, Oprah spent $40 million to open the Oprah Winfrey Leadership Academy, a school for girls in South Africa.

Oprah on the set of *The Oprah Winfrey Show*

Oprah as Sofia in *The Color Purple*

Read a biography

Getting Started 10 minutes

1 BEFORE YOU READ

CLASS. Scan the article. Who is Oprah Winfrey?...

- Read the Reading Skill note.
- Ask: *What does* scanning *mean?* (reading quickly to find specific information) *What kinds of information can scanning help you find?* (names and dates)
- Ask a student to read the directions. Tell students to scan the article for answers to the questions. Tell them to underline this information in the article in pencil.
- Ask the class: *Who is Oprah Winfrey?* (host of *The Oprah Winfrey Show*) *When was she born?* (1954)
- Ask the class: *Have you watched* The Oprah Winfrey Show? Ask for a show of hands.

Presentation 15 minutes

2 READ

 Listen. Read the article.

- Play CD 2, Track 27. Students listen and read along silently.
- *Optional:* Play Track 27 again. Pause the CD after the following paragraphs and ask these questions:

  1st paragraph: *What does Oprah have in addition to her TV show?* (a magazine, a website, a radio show, and a book club)

  2nd paragraph: *Why was Oprah's childhood difficult?* (Her family was poor. Her parents were not together. She had to move a lot.)

3rd paragraph: *In how many countries do people watch* The Oprah Winfrey Show? (132)

4th paragraph: *What did she create in 1996?* (Oprah's Book Club)

5th paragraph: *What does the Oprah Winfrey Foundation do?* (It gives millions of dollars to needy students and schools around the world.)

Culture Connection

- Ask: *What is a book club?* Elicit or explain that it's a group of people who meet to discuss a book they have read.
- Say: *On her show, Oprah selects a book, discusses it on her show, and sometimes interviews the author. When Oprah announces a book club selection, sales of the book typically increase to more than a million copies.*
- Ask: *In your country, do people participate in book clubs? Are there any celebrities who promote reading?*
- Ask: *Would you like to join a book club?*

EXPANSION: Graphic organizer practice for 2

- Tell students to watch *The Oprah Winfrey Show* and create a web diagram with biographical information about the show's guest.

Controlled Practice   15 minutes

3 CHECK YOUR UNDERSTANDING

Ⓐ Read the article again. Complete the time line...

- Tell students to scan the article for dates. Tell them to circle all the dates in the article.
- Tell students to look at the time line. Ask: *What happened in 1954? When did Oprah become a TV news anchor?* Tell students to read the article again and write the missing milestones and dates on the time line.
- Students compare answers with a partner. On the board, write: *What happened in _____?* and *When did Oprah . . . ?* Tell students to take turns asking and answering the questions. Remind students to use the base form of the verb in the second question.
- Complete the questions on the board to elicit the missing information from the class. For example, *What happened in 1954?* (Oprah was born.) *What happened in 1971?* (She got a job at a radio station as a newscaster.) *When did she become a TV news anchor?* (in 1973)

Ⓑ PAIRS. What is Oprah's greatest success...

- Pair students and tell them to take turns reading the milestones on Oprah's time line.
- Ask: *What are Oprah's successes?* (She became a TV news anchor. She became the host of a television talk show. . . .) *Which one do you think is the most important?* Tell students to look at the time line and circle the success that they think is most important.
- Tell students to find the success they chose in the article. Tell them to underline the lines in the article about the success. Ask: *Why do you think it's Oprah's greatest success?* Tell students to note at least one reason.
- Tell partners to ask each other the questions in the directions.
- Read each success on the time line. Ask students who chose it as Oprah's greatest success to raise their hands. For each success, call on one student to say why he or she thinks it's the most important.

MULTILEVEL OPTION for 3B

Cross-ability Post six large sheets of paper in your classroom. Write one of Oprah's successes at the top of each. Group students who chose the same success as Oprah's greatest. Tell students to brainstorm and list reasons why it's the most important. Choose one above-level student to record the group's reasons. Choose another above-level student to report the group's reasons to the class. After the groups report, ask whether anyone changed their mind about which success is Oprah's greatest.

Communicative Practice   15 minutes

Show what you know!

PRE-WRITING. Write a time line of your life....

- Read the directions. Tell students to write the year they were born above *Birth* on the time line. Tell them to write the current year above *present* on the time line.
- Ask: *What are the other milestones in your life? When did they happen?* Tell students to write their important dates and events on the time line. Tell students to use the simple past tense.
- To model the activity, create your own time line on the board (for example, *1990—I graduated from college, 1998—I moved to the East Coast, 2001—I got married,* etc.).

WRITE. Write a short autobiography....

Ask students to turn to page 270 and write a short autobiography. See page T-xii for general notes about the Writing activities.

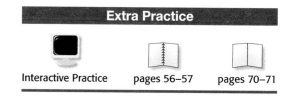

Extra Practice		
Interactive Practice	pages 56–57	pages 70–71

A Read the article again. Complete the time line with the correct year or milestone.

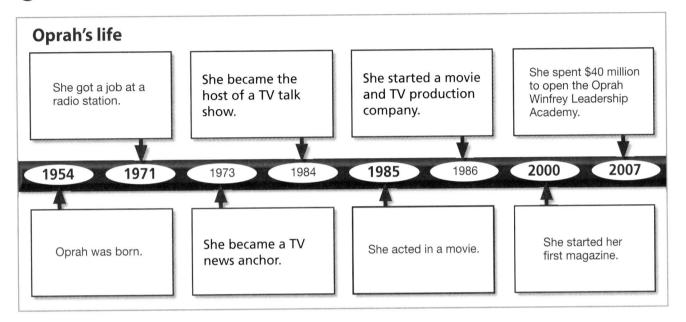

Oprah's life

| She got a job at a radio station. | She became the host of a TV talk show. | She started a movie and TV production company. | She spent $40 million to open the Oprah Winfrey Leadership Academy. |

| **1954** | **1971** | 1973 | 1984 | **1985** | 1986 | **2000** | **2007** |

| Oprah was born. | She became a TV news anchor. | She acted in a movie. | She started her first magazine. |

B PAIRS. What is Oprah's greatest success? Why do you think so?

Show what you know!

PRE-WRITING. Write a time line of your life. Start with the year you were born and end with this year. Use the time line in Exercise A as a model.

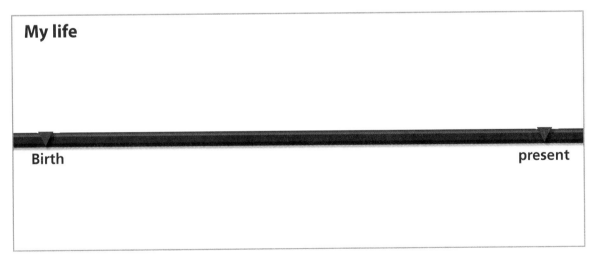

My life

Birth   present

WRITE. Write a short autobiography. See page 270.

Talk about something that happened

Listening and Speaking

1 BEFORE YOU LISTEN

CLASS. Look at the pictures. What are some other things that can happen on your way to school or work?

I had car trouble.

I overslept.

I got stuck in traffic.

I forgot my lunch.

I lost my keys.

This train is going to Fremont?

I took the wrong train.

2 LISTEN

CD2 T28

A Look at the picture of Maria and André having lunch. Listen to the conversation. Why does Maria ask, "Is everything OK?"

Because André looks _____.
a. sick   b. stressed out   c. nervous

CD2 T28

B Listen again. Put the events in the correct order.

___2___ André got stuck in traffic.

___3___ André got to work late.

___1___ André lost his car keys.

Talk about something that happened

Getting Started 10 minutes

1 BEFORE YOU LISTEN

CLASS. **Look at the pictures. What are some...**

- Say: *Think about bad things that happened on your way to school or work. What happened? Look at the pictures. Did any of these things happen to you?*
- Ask for a show of hands about each bad thing (for example, *Who had car trouble? Who overslept?*).
- Say each thing that can happen on the way to work or school and ask the class to repeat.
- Ask: *What are some other things that can happen?* Elicit student's ideas and write them on the board (for example, *I missed the bus. There wasn't any hot water. I forgot my school / work bag.*). Ask: *How do you feel when things like this happen to you?*

EXPANSION: Vocabulary practice for 1

- Act out one of the things that can happen on your way to school or work, for example, by pretending to grip a steering wheel and honk the horn. Ask the class to guess what happened. (You got stuck in traffic.)
- Form groups of three. Group members take turns acting out the things that can happen. Group members guess.

EXPANSION: Vocabulary and grammar practice for 1

- As a class, form a *Yes / No* question from each statement in Exercise 1 (for example, *Did you have car trouble? Did you oversleep?*). Also form *Yes / No* questions about the other events that the class thought of. Tell students to copy the questions into their notebooks. Tell students to think about the last bad morning they had. Then tell students to stand, mingle, and by asking the *Yes / No* questions try to find one classmate who had each problem. Tell them to write the classmate's name next to the question.
- As a follow-up, ask: *Who had car trouble? Who overslept?* Call on students to say classmates' names.

Presentation 5 minutes

2 LISTEN

A **Look at the picture of Maria and...**

- Tell students to look at the picture. Ask: *What are the people doing?* (eating)
- Read the directions. Ask: *What is the woman's name?* (Maria) *What does she ask André?* (Is everything OK?)
- Say: *How does André look? Does he seem sick, stressed out, or nervous? What does* nervous *mean?* (worried about something, like a test or a job interview)
- *Listen to find out why Maria asks, "Is everything OK?"* Play CD 2, Track 28. Students listen and circle the letter of the correct answer.
- Read the item with each answer choice. Tell the class to raise their hands for the sentence that is correct.

Teaching Tip

Optional: Remember that if students need additional support, tell them to read the Audio Script on page 302 as they listen to the conversations.

Controlled Practice 10 minutes

B **Listen again. Put the events in the...**

- Tell students to read the items silently. Tell them to look at the pictures in Exercise 1A. Say: *Which two bad things happened to André? Circle them.* (André got stuck in traffic. André lost his keys.)
- Read the directions. Tell students to write the numbers 1, 2, and 3 next to the items. Play Track 28 again. Students number the items.
- Students compare answers with a partner.
- Call on a student to read the events in the correct order for the class.

C **Listen to the whole conversation....**

- Tell students to read the questions and answer choices silently.
- Play CD 2, Track 29. Students listen and circle the answers.
- Students compare answers with a partner by taking turns reading the questions and answers.
- Call on two pairs to read the questions and answers.

Presentation   5 minutes

3   CONVERSATION

 Listen and repeat the conversation.

- Note: This conversation is the same one students heard in Exercise 2A on page 120.
- Play CD 2, Track 30. Students listen and repeat.

Controlled Practice   15 minutes

4   PRACTICE

A **PAIRS. Practice the conversation. Then...**

- Pair students and tell them to practice the conversation in Exercise 3. Tell them to take turns playing each role.
- Then, in Exercise 4A, ask students to look at the information in the boxes. Say each word or expression and ask the class to repeat. Review unfamiliar vocabulary as needed. Ask: *What does* upset *mean?* (unhappy and worried because something bad has happened) *What does* exhausted *mean?* (very tired)
- Read the directions.
- Copy the conversation onto the board and complete it with words from the boxes.
- Ask two above-level students to model a new conversation. Tell Student A to choose one blue item. Tell Student B to choose one green item and one red item.
- Tell pairs to take turns playing each role and to use the boxes to fill in the blanks.

- Walk around and, as needed, remind students to switch roles and practice both parts.
- Tell students to stand, mingle, and practice the conversation with several new partners.
- Call on pairs to perform for the class.

Communicative Practice   15 minutes

B MAKE IT PERSONAL. PAIRS. **Tell your partner...**

- Read the directions. Tell students to look at the conversation in Exercise 3. Tell them to underline André's lines and read them again silently.
- Read Speaker B's lines from Exercise 3. Add *I got to work* to the beginning of Speaker B's last line. Say: *Use B's lines as a model for talking about your own bad morning.*
- Tell the class about a bad morning you had (for example, *I had a rough morning last Monday. First, I overslept. Then I got stuck in traffic. I got to work / school at 9:30. I was really late.*).
- Call on pairs to perform for the class.

▬▬   MULTILEVEL INSTRUCTION for 4B

Pre-level Tell partners to underline Speaker B's lines in Exercise 4A. Tell them to add *I got to work* to the beginning of Speaker B's last line. Tell them to fill in the blanks in the conversation with information about their own bad morning. Tell them to change any other words in Speaker B's lines as needed. Tell them to read their version of Speaker B's lines to their partner.

Above-level After above-level pairs complete the activity, ask them to join another above-level pair and tell them about their partner's bad morning (for example, *[My partner] had a rough morning yesterday. First, she had car trouble . . .*).

Extra Practice

Interactive Practice

C Listen to the whole conversation. Then answer the questions. Circle the correct answers.

1. What day is it?
   (a.) Tuesday   b. Thursday

2. What mistake did André make?
   (a.) He went to work on his day off.   b. He didn't go to work.

3 CONVERSATION

Listen and repeat the conversation.

Maria: Is everything OK? You look stressed out.
André: Well, I had a rough morning.
Maria: Why? What happened?
André: First I lost my car keys.
Maria: Oh, no!
André: Then I got stuck in traffic.
Maria: When did you get to work?
André: At 10:00. I was really late.

4 PRACTICE

A PAIRS. Practice the conversation. Then make new conversations. Use the information in the boxes.

A: Is everything OK? You look   .

B: Well, I had a rough morning.

A: Why? What happened?

B: First I   .

A: Oh, no!

B: Then I   .

A: When did you get to work?

B: At 10:00. I was really late.

> upset
> unhappy
> exhausted

> lost my wallet
> overslept
> forgot my lunch

> had car trouble
> missed the bus
> took the wrong train

B MAKE IT PERSONAL. PAIRS. Tell your partner about a bad morning you had.

Talk about something that happened

Grammar

Simple past: Information questions

| What | | you | **do**? |
| Where | **did** | he | **go**? |

| Why | | she | **oversleep**? |
| When | **did** | Angel | **get to work**? |

1 PRACTICE

A Write questions about the past. Use the correct forms of the words in parentheses.

1. (What time / you / get up yesterday) _What time did you get up yesterday?_

2. (Where / you / go this morning) Where did you go this morning?

3. (What / you / have for lunch yesterday) What did you have for lunch yesterday?

4. (What time / you / get to school today) What time did you get to school today?

5. (What / you / do last night) What did you do last night?

B PAIRS. Ask and answer the questions in Exercise A.

A: *What time did you get up yesterday?*
B: *I got up at 7:00. I had to work at 8:00.*

C Complete the conversations. Read the replies. Write information questions about the underlined words.

1. **A:** _What did Saul forget?_

   B: Saul forgot <u>his wallet</u>.

2. **A:** When did Jane finish work?

   B: Jane finished work <u>at 10:45</u>.

3. **A:** Why did In-Ho miss the bus?

   B: In-Ho missed the bus <u>because he overslept</u>.

4. **A:** Where did Nadia find her car keys?

   B: Nadia found her car keys <u>in the kitchen</u>.

2 LIFE SKILLS WRITING

Write an absence note to a teacher. See page 261.

Getting Started   5 minutes

- Say: *We're going to study simple past information questions. In the conversation on page 121, Maria used this grammar.*
- Play CD 2, Track 30. Students listen. On the board, write: *When did you get to work?* Underline *did* and *get*.

Presentation   10 minutes

Simple past: Information questions

- Copy the grammar charts onto the board or show Transparency 6.5 and cover the exercise.
- On the board, write: *Did you grow up in Ecuador?* Say: *This is a* Yes / No *question in the simple past.*
- Cross out *in Ecuador*. Add *Where* to the beginning of the question. Rewrite the question: *Where did you grow up?* Say: *This is an information question in the simple past.*
- Call on four students to read the examples from the grammar charts.
- If you are using the transparency, do the exercise with the class.

Controlled Practice   15 minutes

1 PRACTICE

A Write questions about the past. Use the correct...

- Write item 1 on the board. Ask: *What do you need to add to form a question about the past?* (*did*) *Where do you need to add it?* (between *What time* and *you* / between the question word and the subject) Insert *did* into the words on the board. Read the example: *What time did you get up yesterday?*
- Walk around and remind students to begin their questions with a capital letter and end with a question mark.

B PAIRS. Ask and answer the questions in...

- Tell students to look at Exercise 1A and to circle the verb in each item. Then say each verb and ask the class to call out the past tense for statements (1. *get up–got up*, 2. *go–went*, 3. *have–had*, 4. *get–got*, 5. *get–got*, 6. *do–did*).

- Ask two above level students to read the example out loud. Prompt Student A to ask B the next question: *Where did you go this morning?*
- Pair students and tell them to take turns answering and asking the questions in Exercise A.
- Walk around and check that B is using the correct simple past forms of the irregular verbs.
- Call on a pair to ask and answer each question for the class.

EXPANSION: Speaking practice for 1B

- On a piece of paper, tell students to write answers to the questions in Exercise 1A in complete sentences.
- Then tell them to try to find classmates who did the same things. Tell students to look at their answers and try to remember the questions.
- When students find a classmate who did the same thing, tell them to sign their name next to each other's answers.
- Call on several students to report what both they and a classmate did (for example, *Daniel and I got up at 6:30 yesterday.*).

C Complete the conversations. Read the replies...

- Read the directions.
- Write item 1 on the board. Point to *his wallet* and ask: *What, Where, Why,* or *When*? Write *What* on the line. Elicit the rest of the question and write it on the line. Ask: *What form of the verb do we use with* did? (the base form)
- Walk around and spot-check for word order and the base form of the verbs.
- Students compare answers with a partner by reading the conversations.
- Call on pairs to read the conversations for the class.

2 LIFE SKILLS WRITING

Turn to page 261 and ask students to complete the absence note. See page T-xii for guidelines.

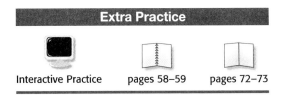

Extra Practice

Interactive Practice   pages 58–59   pages 72–73

Show what you know!

1 GRAMMAR

A Read the replies. Write questions about the...

- Tell students to review the grammar charts on pages 117 (Simple past *Yes / No* questions) and 122 (Simple past: Information questions). Then tell students to close their books.
- Write item 1 on the board (without the answer). Tell students to look at the underlined word in Speaker B's answer. Ask: *Is Speaker A's question a Yes / No question or an information question?* (*Yes / No* question) Write *Did* on the line. Ask: *What's the subject in Speaker B's reply?* (*I*) So, what's the subject of the question? Write *you* on the line. Ask: *What's the past-tense verb in Speaker B's reply?* (*went*) *What's the base form of* went? Write *go* on the line. Elicit the rest of the question and write it on the line.
- Write item 2 on the board. Tell students to look at the underlined words in Speaker B's reply. Ask: *Is Speaker A's question a Yes / No question or an information question?* (information question) To elicit the question, ask the following questions and write the answers on the line: *What's the question word?* (*When*) *What word comes after* When? (*did*) *What's the subject?* (*John and Ellen*) *What's the base form of* got married? (*get married*)
- Tell students to open their books and complete the exercise. Walk around and check the word order of students' questions and that they are using the base form of the verbs.
- Students compare answers with a partner. Tell them to take turns reading the questions and answers out loud.
- Call on pairs to read the questions and answers for the class.

EXPANSION: Grammar and speaking practice for 1A

- Tell students to look at the milestones on page 114 and to circle the milestones in their life.
- Pair students and tell them to show each other the milestones they circled. For each circled milestone, tell students to write one information question to ask their partner.

- To model the activity, write a milestone in your life on the board.
- As a class, brainstorm information questions (for example, for *being born*: *Where were you born? When were you born?*). Tell pairs to ask and answer the questions they wrote.

B Complete Nora's conversation with her...

- Tell students to also review the grammar charts on pages 110 (Simple past: Regular verbs) and 116 (Simple past: Irregular verbs).
- Read the directions. Tell students that most of the verbs are irregular. Tell them to use the Grammar Watch note on page 116 and Appendix page 286 to check past-tense forms as needed.
- Walk around and remind students to use *did* and the base form of the verb to form questions.
- Students compare answers with a partner by reading the conversation.
- Call on two students to read the conversation for the class.

EXPANSION: Grammar and speaking practice for 1B

- Form cross-ability pairs. Tell partners to write past-tense questions to ask someone about their wedding, baby shower, graduation party, retirement party, or a surprise party given for them. Tell them to use the questions in Exercise 1B as a model. Tell both partners to write the questions on a sheet of paper.
- Then tell students to stand, mingle, and find a classmate who's had the event they chose by asking: *Did you have a . . . ?* Tell them to ask the classmate their questions.

CD-ROM Practice

 Go to the CD-ROM for more practice.

If your students need more practice with the vocabulary, grammar, and competencies in Unit 6, encourage them to review the activities on the CD-ROM. This review can also help students prepare for the final role play on the following Expand page.

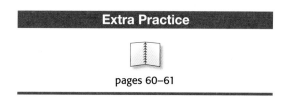

Extra Practice

pages 60–61

1 GRAMMAR

A **Read the replies. Write questions about the underlined words.**

1. **A:** _Did you go to Wilson Adult School?_

   B: <u>Yes</u>, I did. I went to Wilson Adult School.

2. **A:** _When did John and Ellen get married?_

   B: John and Ellen got married <u>last year</u>.

3. **A:** Where did Samuel grow up?

   B: Samuel grew up <u>in Namibia</u>.

4. **A:** Why did you move?

   B: We moved <u>because we didn't like cold weather</u>.

5. **A:** Did you visit your aunt and uncle?

   B: <u>No</u>, we didn't. We didn't visit our aunt and uncle.

6. **A:** When did Todd get that job?

   B: Todd got that job <u>in 2005</u>.

B **Complete Nora's conversation with her grandmother, Jane. Write the correct past forms of the verbs in parentheses.**

Nora: Grandma, you never _____told_____ me about your wedding day.
      (tell)

      _____Where did you get_____ married?
      (where / you / get)

Jane: We _____had_____ our wedding in a beautiful garden.
      (have)

Nora: _____Did you invite_____ a lot of people?
      (you / invite)

Jane: No, we didn't. It was a small wedding.

Nora: _____Did you feel_____ nervous?
      (you / feel)

Jane: Yes, I did. But I was really excited, too.

Nora: _____How did you know_____ that Grandpa was the right man for you?
      (how / you / know)

Jane: I just _____knew_____ it in my heart. And look at our life now—your
      (know)

      grandfather and I have two children and five beautiful grandchildren.

Expand   Show what you know!

2 ACT IT OUT   What do you say?

STEP 1. CLASS. Review the Lesson 5 conversation between Fred and Chen (CD 2 track 26).

STEP 2. PAIRS. Student A, tell your partner about the milestones of your life. Student B, ask questions about the milestones.

3 READ AND REACT   Problem-solving

STEP 1. Read about Yusef's problem.

Yusef started a new job at a hospital. Last night he had to clean the floors. His boss taught him how to use a floor cleaning machine. He used the machine, but then it stopped working. Yusef thinks he broke the machine.

STEP 2. PAIRS. What is Yusef's problem? What can he do? Here are some ideas.

- He can tell his boss, "I'm sorry, I broke the machine."
- He can tell his boss, "Someone broke the machine."
- He can say nothing about the broken machine.
- He can _____.

4 CONNECT

For your Study Skills Activity, go to page 251.
For your Team Project, go to page 279.

Which goals can you check off? Go back to page 105.

2 ACT IT OUT

STEP 1. CLASS. Review the Lesson 5...

- Tell students to read the conversation in Exercise 3C on page 115 silently and then practice it with a partner.
- Play CD 2, Track 26. Students listen and repeat the conversation.

STEP 2. PAIRS. Student A, tell your partner...

- Read the directions and the guidelines for Student A and Student B.
- Tell the class to look at the pictures and at the milestones on page 114. Ask: *What is the milestone for the baby?* (being born) *What is the milestone for the parents?* (having children)
- Tell the class to look at the new parents in the picture. Say: *Imagine that your partner is the mother or father in the picture. What questions could you ask about this milestone?* On the board, write:

  A: I had my son. / My son was born.

  B:

- As a class, brainstorm a few questions for Student B and write them on the board (for example, *Where did you have your son? When was he born?*).
- Tell students to note a few milestones in their lives.
- Pair students. Read the directions again. Tell Student A to use the simple past tense. Tell Student B to use *did* and the base form of a verb to ask *Yes / No* and information questions. Point out that Student B can also use simple past statements as questions to check Student A's information.
- Walk around and observe partners interacting. Check pairs' use of the simple past tense in statements, *Yes / No* questions, and information questions.
- Call on pairs to perform for the class.
- While pairs are performing, use the scoring rubric on page T-xiii to evaluate each student's vocabulary, grammar, fluency, and how well he or she completes the task.
- *Optional:* After each pair finishes, discuss the strengths and weaknesses of each performance either in front of the class or privately.

3 READ AND REACT

STEP 1. Read about Yusef's problem.

- Say: *We are going to read about a student's problem, and then we need to think about a solution.*
- Tell the class to look at the picture. Ask: *What is Yusef's job?* (custodian / janitor) *What is he doing?* (cleaning the floors)
- Read the story while students follow along silently. Pause after each sentence to allow time for students to comprehend. Periodically stop and ask simple *Wh-* questions to check comprehension. For example, *What happened?* (The floor cleaning machine broke.) *Why is Yusef upset?* (He thinks he broke the machine.)

STEP 2. PAIRS. What is Yusef's problem? What...

- Ask: *What is Yusef's problem?* (He thinks he broke the floor cleaning machine.) *What can Yusef do?*
- Pair students. Read the ideas in the list. Give pairs a couple of minutes to discuss possible solutions for Yusef.
- Ask: *Which ideas are good?* Call on students to say their opinion about the ideas in the list (for example, S: *I think he can tell his boss, "I'm sorry, I broke the machine." This is a good idea.*).
- Now tell pairs to think of one new idea not in the box (for example, *He can try to fix the floor cleaning machine.*) and to write it in the blank.
- Call on pairs to say their additional solutions. Write any particularly good ones on the board and ask students if they think it is a good idea too (*Do you think this is a good idea? Why or why not?*).

4 CONNECT

Turn to page T-251 for the Study Skills Activity and page T-279 for the Team Project. See page T-xi for general notes about teaching these activities.

Progress Check

Which goals can you check off? Go back to page 105.

Ask students to turn to page 105 and check off any remaining goals they have reached. Call on students to say which goals they will practice outside of class.

Health Watch

Classroom Materials/Extra Practice

CD 2
Tracks 31–46

T
Transparencies 7.1–7.6
Vocabulary Cards Unit 7

MCA
Unit 7

Workbook
Unit 7

Interactive Practice
Unit 7

Unit Overview

Goals
- See the list of goals on the facing page.

Grammar
- Prepositions of time: *at / by / in / on / from . . . to*
- Simple past: Irregular verbs
- Ways to express reasons (*because* + a subject and a verb; *for* + a noun)

Pronunciation
- Linking a consonant to a vowel sound
- Pronunciation of *t* between two vowel sounds
- Pauses to organize sentences into thought groups

Reading
- Read an article about ways to manage stress
- *Reading Skill:* Using formatting clues

Writing
- Write about the stress in your life
- Write about an injury

Life Skills Writing
- Complete a medical history form

Preview
- Set the context of the unit by asking questions about health (for example, *How do you feel today? What do you do when you're sick? Do you go to the doctor?*).
- Hold up page 125 or show Transparency 7.1. Read the unit title and ask the class to repeat.
- Explain: Health Watch *means paying attention to your physical condition and to medical information.*
- Say: *Look at the picture.* Ask the Preview questions: *Where is the person?* (She's at home. / She's on the sofa.) *What is she doing?* (She's eating soup / drinking orange juice / reading / watching TV.) *How does she feel?* (bad / sick)
- Write the word *health* on the board and check that students understand (for example, T [pointing to the picture]: *Is she in good health?* Ss: *No, she's sick.* T: *What do people do when they have health problems?* Ss: *Go to the doctor. / Take medicine. / Rest. / Miss work.*).

Goals
- Point to the Unit Goals. Explain that this list shows what the class will be studying in this unit.
- Tell students to read the goals silently.
- Say each goal and ask the class to repeat. As needed, explain: *An injury:* what happens when you get hurt; for example, you can have an injury to your arm or leg.
- Tell students to circle one goal that is very important to them. Call on several students to say the goal they circled.

Health Watch

Preview

**Look at the picture.
Where is the person?
What is she doing?
How does she feel?**

UNIT GOALS

☐ Identify health problems

☐ Make a doctor's appointment

☐ Read medicine labels

☐ Complete a medical history form

☐ Talk about an injury

☐ Call in when you have to miss work

1   WHAT DO YOU KNOW?

A   **CLASS.** Look at the pictures. Which health problems do you know?

CD2 T31

B   Look at the pictures and listen. Then listen and repeat.

2   PRACTICE

A   **WORD PLAY.** Some expressions for health problems have the word *a* or *an* before them. Some have the word *the* before them. And some have no word before them.

CD2 T32

Listen and complete the chart. Write the health problems in the correct columns.

I have a _____.	I have _____.
headache	chest pains
cough	heartburn
I have the _____.	**I have an _____.**
flu	earache
chills	upset stomach

B   **PAIRS.** Point to the pictures. Ask and answer questions about the people.

A: *What's the matter?*
B: *She has a headache. What's the matter?*
A: *He has chest pains.*

1

2

5

6

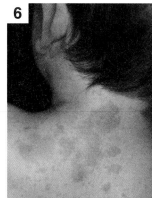
9

10

13

14

Lesson 1 Vocabulary

Getting Started   10 minutes

1 WHAT DO YOU KNOW?

A CLASS. **Look at the pictures. Which health...**

- Show Transparency 7.2 or hold up the book. Tell students to cover the list of words on page 127.
- Read the directions. Elicit a health problem and write in on the board (for example, *Number 2 is a sore throat.*).
- Students call out answers. Help students pronounce health problems if they have difficulty.
- If students call out an incorrect health problem, change the student's answer into a question for the class (for example, *Number 5 is a cold?*). If nobody can identify the correct health problem, tell students they will now listen to a CD and practice the health problems vocabulary.

Presentation   5 minutes

B 💿 **Look at the pictures and listen....**

- Read the directions. Play CD 2 Track 31. Pause after number 14 (*chest pains*).
- To check comprehension, say each health problem in random order and ask students to point to the appropriate picture.
- Resume playing Track 31. Students listen and repeat.

Controlled Practice   20 minutes

2 PRACTICE

A WORD PLAY. **Some expressions for health...**

- Read the directions.
- Tell students to look at the list of words on page 127. Elicit one health problem with *a* before it and one with *an*. Write them on the board. Ask: *Why does* earache *have* an *before it instead of* a*? (because* earache *begins with a vowel sound)*
- Elicit one health problem with *the* before it and one with no word before it. Write them on the board.
- Use the four health problems on the board in sentences with *I have _____.* As you say each sentence, act out the meaning (for example, hold your throat and say: *I have a sore throat.*).

💿 **Listen and complete the chart. Write...**

- Play CD 2, Track 32. Students listen and complete the chart.
- Copy the chart onto the board. Call on students to write in answers.
- Correct any mistakes on the board. To wrap up, act out the health problems in the chart (in random order) and call on students to say the sentences.

▦ **EXPANSION: Vocabulary practice for 2A**

- Pair students. One partner acts out the health problems in the chart. The other guesses by saying the sentences.

B PAIRS. **Point to the pictures. Ask and answer...**

- Read the directions. Play Speaker B and model the example with a student. Tell the student to point to picture 1 and ask: *What's the matter?* As you ask *What's the matter?*, point to picture 12.
- Say *What's the matter?* and ask the class to repeat.
- Pair students and tell them to take turns playing Speakers A and B. Walk around and check that students are using *a, an, the*, or no word appropriately before each health problem.
- To wrap up, point to pictures 1–14 and ask: *What's the matter?* The class calls out sentences with *He / She has . . .*

▦ **MULTILEVEL INSTRUCTION for 2B**

Cross-ability Ask higher-level students to cover the list of words on page 127 as they practice. Lower-level students can consult the list as needed and also use it to check their partner's use of vocabulary and *a, an, the*, or no word before each health problem.

Community Building

Model the activity and how students should correct each other's mistakes. Ask an above-level student to play Speaker B and make a mistake. Play Speaker A as follows:
A: [points to picture 1] *What's the matter?*
B: *She has an earache.*
A: *No, try again.*
B: *She has a headache.*
A: *Yes. Good!*

Lesson 1 Vocabulary

Learning strategy: Use your language

- Provide each student with five index cards or tell students to cut up notebook paper into five pieces.
- Read the directions. If you have students with low first-language skills, pair them with more capable peers if possible.
- Walk around as students work. If misspellings occur, tell them to check the list on page 127.
- Say: *You can use your language to help you remember new words.* Remind students to use this strategy to remember other new vocabulary.

Teaching Tip

As you visit with students, show them you are an active language learner yourself by trying to pronounce health problems in their native languages.

Community Building

Ask several students to present their cards to the class and teach the class to say health problems in their native languages. This is a fun way to build class community and value other students' languages.

Communicative Practice   15 minutes

Show what you know!

STEP 1. Do you go to the doctor? When?....

- Read the directions.
- Model the activity. Complete the sentence with a health problem from the list. Write your sentence on the board (for example, *I go to the doctor when I have a fever.*).
- Tell students to complete the sentence with a health problem from the list or their own health problem.

STEP 2. GROUPS OF 3. Talk to your classmates....

- Form groups of 3 and read the directions.
- Model the activity with an above-level student. Prompt the student to ask you: *When do you go to the doctor?* Point to and read your sentence on the board.
- Tell students to take turns asking and answering the question.

EXPANSION: Speaking practice for STEP 2

- On the board, write: *I don't go to the doctor when I _____.* Tell students to complete the sentence and then ask group members: *When do you not go to the doctor?*

EXPANSION: Writing and grammar practice for STEP 2

- Ask a student: *When do you go to the doctor?* On the board, write a sentence about the student (for example, *José goes to the doctor when he has a sore throat.*).
- Tell students to write a sentence about each of their partners.

EXPANSION: Speaking practice for STEP 2

- Tell students to stand, mingle, and ask as many classmates as they can: *When do you go to the doctor?* For each response, tell students to make a checkmark next to a health problem on the list.
- After a few minutes, tell students to stop, count their checkmarks, and identify the top three reasons to go to the doctor.
- On the board, write:

  Top 3 reasons to go to the doctor:

  1.

  2.

  3.
- Complete the list with the class's input.

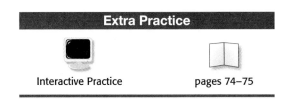

Extra Practice	
Interactive Practice	pages 74–75

3

4

7

8

11

12

Health Problems

1. **a** headache
2. **a** sore throat
3. **a** cough
4. **a** cold
5. **a** fever
6. **a** rash
7. **a** stiff neck
8. **an** earache
9. **an** upset stomach
10. **the** flu
11. **the** chills
12. heartburn
13. diarrhea
14. chest pains

Learning Strategy

Use your language

Look at the list of health problems. Make cards for five new words. Write the word in English on one side of the card. Write the word in your language on the other side.

Show what you know!

STEP 1. **Do you go to the doctor? When? Complete the sentence.**

I go to the doctor when I _____.

STEP 2. **GROUPS OF 3.** **Talk to your classmates. When do you go to the doctor?**

Listening and Speaking

1 BEFORE YOU LISTEN

CLASS. Look at the pictures and read the symptoms. When do people have these symptoms?

She's dizzy.

He's nauseous.

It's itchy.

It's swollen.

2 LISTEN

A **CLASS.** Look at the pictures. Guess: Where is the woman? Where is the man?

CD2 T33
B Listen to the conversation. Was your guess in Exercise A correct?

CD2 T33
C Listen again. What is the matter with Roberto? Check all of his symptoms.

☑ He has a fever.   ☑ He's nauseous.

☐ He has heartburn.   ☐ He's dizzy.

CD2 T33
D Listen again. Complete the information on the appointment card. Check the day and write the time of the appointment.

Roberto Cruz
has an appointment on

☐ Mon. ☑ Tue. ☐ Wed. ☐ Thu. ☐ Fri. ☐ Sat.

Date _____ *October 14* _____ At ____ 9 ____ (A.M.) P.M.

Daniel Silver, M.D.
194 Commerce Street, Suite 201
Dallas, Texas 75231

If you are unable to keep your appointment, kindly give us 24 hrs. notice.
Telephone (214) 555-8185

Make a doctor's appointment

Getting Started   10 minutes

1 BEFORE YOU LISTEN

CLASS. Look at the pictures and read the...

- Read the directions.
- Read each sentence and ask the class to repeat.
- Explain any unfamiliar vocabulary through modeling, if possible. For example, to demonstrate *dizzy*, spin around a couple of times, act unsteady, and say: *I'm dizzy.*
- Write the symptoms on the board. Ask: *When do people have these symptoms?* Tell students to review the vocabulary on page 127 for ideas. List students' responses under each symptom (for example, for dizzy: *when they have a headache, when they have an earache*).

Language Note

Point out that the symptoms in Exercise 1 are adjectives, while the health problems on page 127 are nouns.

Presentation   10 minutes

2 LISTEN

Ⓐ CLASS. Look at the pictures. Guess: Where...

- Read the directions. Ask: *Where is the woman? Where is the man?*
- Call on students to answer. Write guesses on the board (for example, *The woman in an office / in a doctor's office. The man is at home / in bed.*).

Ⓑ 💿 Listen to the conversation. Was...

- Read the directions.
- Play CD 2, Track 33. Students listen.
- Ask: *Where is the woman?* Read the guesses on the board. Elicit and circle the best answer. Repeat with *Where is the man?*

Controlled Practice   10 minutes

Teaching Tip

Optional: Remember that if students need additional support, tell them to read the Audio Script on page 129 as they listen to the conversations.

Ⓒ 💿 Listen again. What is the matter...

- Tell students to look at the pictures again and point to Mr. Cruz. Ask: *What do you think is the matter with him?* (He has a fever.)
- Read the directions and symptoms. Act out each symptom (for example, by placing your palm on your forehead for *He has a fever.*) or call on students to act them out.
- Play Track 33 again.
- To review, ask: *What is the matter with Roberto Cruz?*

Ⓓ 💿 Listen again. Complete the...

- Read the directions.
- Tell students to look at the appointment card and find the checkboxes for the days of the week and the space for the time. Tell students to circle A.M. or P.M. when they write the time.
- Play Track 33 again. Students listen and complete the appointment card.
- To review, ask: *When is Mr. Cruz's appointment?*

Culture Connection

- Tell students to look at the appointment card. Read the notice at the bottom of the card (*If you are unable . . .*). Ask: *If Mr. Cruz can't come to his appointment, when does he need to call?* (before Monday, October 13, at 9:00 A.M.)
- Say: *In the United States, some doctor's offices charge you for missed appointments. To avoid charges, call at least 24 hours ahead of time to cancel an appointment you can't keep.*
- Ask: *In your country, do doctor's offices charge for missed appointments?*

Lesson 2 Make a doctor's appointment

Presentation
10 minutes

3 CONVERSATION

Ⓐ 💿 Listen to the sentences. Notice...

- On the board, write: *I have a fever.* Point to and pronounce distinctly each word in the sentence.
- Read the Pronunciation Watch note. Mark the linking in the sentence on the board as you say: *I ha-va fever.* Ask students to repeat.
- Read the directions. Point to the linking symbol in the sentence on the board. Ask: *What's the consonant sound?* Write *v* under the linking symbol. Ask: *What's the vowel sound?* Write *a* under the linking symbol. Point to *va* and say: *We say the* v *from* have *together with the next word,* a.
- Play CD 2, Track 34. Students listen.
- Resume playing Track 34. Students listen and repeat.

Controlled Practice
5 minutes

Ⓑ 💿 Listen and repeat the conversation.

- Note: This conversation is the same one students heard in Exercise 2B on page 128.
- Tell students to read the conversation silently.
- Tell students to look for sentences and phrases that are the same or similar to the ones in Exercise 3A and mark the linking (*make an appointment, have a, come on*).
- Call on volunteers to write the sentences or phrases on the board and mark the linking.
- *Optional:* Tell students to look for other words in the conversation that start with vowels. Tell them to mark the linking (*fever and, and I'm, How about, about at*).
- Play CD 2, Track 35. Students listen and repeat.

4 PRACTICE

Ⓐ PAIRS. Practice the conversation. Then make new...

- Pair students and tell them to practice the conversation in Exercise 3B. Walk around and help with pronunciation as needed. Pay particular attention to students' pronunciation of the linked sounds they marked.

- Then, in Exercise 4A, tell students to look at the information in the boxes. Say each word or phrase and ask the class to repeat. Model each pair of symptoms (in random order) and ask the class to identify them. For example, scratch your leg and elicit: *rash / my leg is itchy.*
- Tell students to look at the words in blue and write *a, an, the,* or no word before them (*a cough, a headache, a rash*).
- Ask two above-level students to practice a conversation in front of the class. Tell B to choose a pair of symptoms. Tell A to choose a day and time from the same row in the boxes.
- Walk around and check that students are using *a* before the health problems in blue.
- Call on pairs to perform for the class.

▬▬ MULTILEVEL INSTRUCTION for 4A
Pre-level Before they practice each role, tell students to fill in the blanks in the conversation. Tell B to choose a pair of symptoms and write them in B's second line. Tell A to choose a day and time and write them in A's last line.
Above-level After they practice each role, tell students to cover the conversation and look only at the information in the boxes. Tell pairs to practice without looking at the conversation.

Communicative Practice
15 minutes

Ⓑ ROLE PLAY. PAIRS. Make your own...

- Tell students to note a pair of symptoms and a day and time. Tell them to use the vocabulary on page 127 and at the top of page 128.
- Pair students and tell them to practice the conversation.
- Walk around and check the symptoms and days that students have noted. Make corrections as necessary.
- Call on pairs to perform for the class.

▬▬▬ Extra Practice

Interactive Practice

3 CONVERSATION

A 🔘 **Listen to the sentences. Notice how we link a consonant sound to a vowel sound. Then listen and repeat.**

Pronunciation Watch

We often link words together without a break when we speak.

I have a fever.   Can you come at eight?

Can I make an appointment?   We close at noon on Friday.

CD2 T35

B 🔘 **Listen and repeat the conversation.**

Receptionist: Hello. Westview Clinic.
Roberto: Hi. This is Roberto Cruz. I need to make an appointment, please.
Receptionist: All right. What's the matter?
Roberto: I have a fever and I'm nauseous.
Receptionist: OK. Can you come on Tuesday morning? How about at 9:00?
Roberto: Yes, that's fine.

4 PRACTICE

A PAIRS. **Practice the conversation. Then make new conversations. Use your own names and the information in the boxes.**

A: Hello. Westview Clinic.

B: Hi. This is _____. I need to make an appointment, please.

A: All right. What's the matter?

B: I have a _____ and _____.

A: OK. Can you come _____? How about at _____?

B: Yes, that's fine.

cough	my throat is swollen	on Thursday	noon
headache	I'm dizzy	this afternoon	3:00
rash	my leg is itchy	first thing tomorrow	8:30

B ROLE PLAY. PAIRS. **Make your own conversations. Use your own names and different information.**

Grammar

Prepositions of time: *on / at / by / in / from ... to*

Can you come	**on**	Tuesday morning?
Roberto's appointment is	**at**	9:00 A.M.
Please get here	**by**	5:00 today.
I'm going to see the doctor	**in**	an hour.
The pharmacy is open	**from**	8:00 A.M. **to** 9:00 P.M.

········· **Grammar Watch**

- Use *on* with a day or date.
- Use *at* with a specific time on the clock.
- Use *by* with a specific time in the future.
- Use *in* with an amount of time in the future, with a month or year, or with *the morning/afternoon/evening*.
- Use *from . . . to* with a starting time and an ending time.

1 PRACTICE

A Underline the correct word.

1. Can you come **on** / **at** 9:15 A.M. on April first?

2. You need to get here **by** / **in** 5:00.

3. The clinic is open from 8:00 A.M. **at** / **to** 5:00 P.M.

4. The office is closed **on** / **in** Saturday and Sunday.

5. The doctor can see you **from** / **in** an hour.

6. Dr. Evans has openings **at** / **from** 3:40 to 5:00 P.M.

7. My appointment is **at** / **in** 2:30 this afternoon.

B Complete the sentences. Write *on, at, by, in,* or *from . . . to.*

1. The dentist has appointments available __on__ June 6 and 7.

2. The doctor can call you back __in__ a few minutes.

3. My son's appointment is __at__ 4:30 today.

4. The clinic has openings __from__ 3:30 __to__ 5:00 tomorrow afternoon.

5. The doctor's office closes __at__ noon for lunch.

6. Can I come __on__ Monday?

7. The doctor wants to see you again __in__ a week.

8. The drugstore is open __from__ 9:00 A.M. __to__ 7:00 P.M.

9. You need to call __by__ 5:00 P.M. because the office closes then.

10. Is the office open __on__ Saturdays?

Getting Started 5 minutes

- Say: *We're going to study prepositions of time. In the conversation on page 129, the receptionist used this grammar.*
- Play CD 2, Track 35. Students listen. Write on the board: *on Tuesday morning* and *at 9:00.* Underline *on* and *at.*

Presentation 10 minutes

Prepositions of time: *at / by / in / on / from . . . to*

- Copy the grammar chart onto the board or show Transparency 7.3 and cover the exercise.
- Read the sentences in the chart and tell the class to repeat.
- Explain expressions as needed: Please get here by 5:00 today *means arrive here before 5:00. 5:00 is the latest you can arrive. After 5:00 is too late.*
- Say: I'm going to see the doctor in an hour *means I'm going at [say the time one hour from now].*
- Say: The pharmacy is open from 8:00 A.M. to 9:00 P.M. *means the pharmacy opens at 8:00 A.M. and closes at 9:00 P.M.*
- Read the Grammar Watch note and ask the class to read along silently.
- Say: *Let's use prepositions of time to talk about when our English class is.* On the board, draw a web diagram and write *English class* in the circle. Write the prepositions of time at the ends of the lines out from the circle.
- Read the first bulleted item in the Grammar Watch note. Point to *on* in the web diagram and ask: *When is our English class?* Elicit and write the day(s) your class meets (for example, *on Tuesdays and Thursdays*). Repeat with the other bulleted items. For *by*, ask about the due date for a homework assignment. For *in*, ask when today's class is over.
- If you are using the transparency, do the exercise with the class.

Controlled Practice 25 minutes

1 **PRACTICE**

Ⓐ Underline the correct word.

- Read the directions and the example. Ask: *Why is the answer* at? (because 9:15 is a specific time on the clock)
- Students compare answers with a partner.
- Call on students to read the sentences. Correct as needed.

EXPANSION: Grammar practice for 1A

- Write item 1 on the board. Cross out *at* and the rest of the sentence. Circle *on.* Say: *Rewrite the sentence with* on. Elicit and write an alternative ending to the sentence with *on* (for example, *on Wednesday*). Read the new sentence: *Can you come on Wednesday?*
- Tell students to rewrite items 2–7 using the other preposition. For item 3, tell students to cross out from *from* to the end of the sentence.

Ⓑ Complete the sentences. Write...

- Read the directions and the example. Ask: *Why is the answer* on? (because June 6 and 7 are dates)
- Students compare answers with a partner.
- Call on students to read the sentences. Correct as needed.

2 PRACTICE

Ⓐ Look at the appointment card. Answer...

- Tell students to look at the appointment card. Ask: *Who is the patient?* (Elizabeth Ruiz) *What is her doctor's name?* (Dr. Medeiros)
- Say: *Point to the day of Elizabeth's appointment. Point to the time. Point to the hours the office is open.*
- Read the notice at the bottom of the appointment card. Ask: *Does Elizabeth need to arrive on time for her appointment, or does she need to arrive early?* (early) *How early?* (10 minutes) *What time is that?* (10:05)
- Read the directions and the example. Ask: *Why do we use* on? (because *Wednesday* is a day)

Ⓑ PAIRS. Compare your answers.

- Pair students and tell them to take turns reading the questions and answers. Tell them to talk about any answers that are different and make corrections as necessary.
- Read each question and call on students to read the answers.

▬▬ EXPANSION: Speaking practice for 2B

- On the board, write the day, date, and time of an appointment that you have. Use *on* and *at* to talk about when your appointment is. Use *in* to talk about how soon your appointment is.
- Tell students to note the day, date, and time of an appointment or plan they have. Tell students they can make up the information.
- Form small groups and tell students to talk about when and how soon their appointments are (for example, *My appointment is on . . . at. . . . It's in . . .*).

Communicative Practice 20 minutes

Show what you know!

PAIRS. Student A, look at the notes on this page....

- Pair students and assign roles of A and B. Read the first paragraph of the directions. Walk around and check that Student A is looking only at the notes on page 131 and Student B is looking only at the notes on page 247.

- Read the second paragraph of the directions. Write the example on the board. Ask an above-level pair to model the activity. Tell the pair to read and complete the example. Tell Student A to write the missing information. Tell Student B to ask Student A a question (for example, *When is Gloria's checkup?*).
- Say: *Use the questions in Exercise 2A as a model.*
- Walk around and help students form questions as needed. Check students' use of prepositions of time in their answers.
- To check their work, tell pairs to read the notes out loud. Say: *Student A, read the apple, flower, and banana notes. Student B, listen and check the information. Student B, read the grapes and moon notes. Student A, listen and check the information.*

▬▬ MULTILEVEL INSTRUCTION

Pre-level Before pairs do the activity, group As and Bs and tell them to form the questions they need to ask. Tell them to practice the questions and then return to their partners.

Above-level Tell students to review the questions in Exercise 2A. Tell them to also ask questions with *What day* and *How soon*.

Progress Check

Can you . . . make a doctor's appointment?

Say: *We have practiced making doctor's appointments. Now, look at the question at the bottom of the page. Can you make a doctor's appointment?* Tell students to write a checkmark in the box.

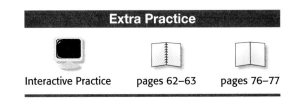

Extra Practice		
Interactive Practice	pages 62–63	pages 76–77

A Look at the appointment card. Answer the questions. Complete the sentences with *on*, *at*, *by*, *in*, or *from . . . to.*

John R. Medeiros, M.D.
114 Main St., Springfield, IL 62702
Office hours: M–F 8:00–5:00   (909) 555-1234

APPOINTMENT

FOR: ___Ms. Elizabeth Ruiz___

DATE: ___Wed., Oct. 6___   TIME: ___10:15 A.M.___

Please arrive at least 10 minutes before the time of your appointment.

1. What day is Elizabeth's appointment?

   It is ___on Wednesday___.

2. What time is her appointment?

   It is ___at 10:15 A.M.___.

3. When is the doctor's office open?

   It is open ___from 8:00 to 5:00___.

4. It is now 8:15 A.M. on October 6. How soon is Elizabeth going to see the doctor?

   She is going to see him ___in two hours___.

5. What time does Elizabeth need to arrive at the doctor's office?

   She should be there ___by 10:05 A.M.___.

B PAIRS. Compare your answers.

Show what you know! Make a doctor's appointment

PAIRS. Student A, look at the notes on this page. Student B, look at the notes on page 247.

Read the notes about the Lee family's appointments. Some information is missing. Take turns. Ask questions with *When* and *What time.* Write the missing information.

A: *When is Walter's dentist appointment?*
B: *On Friday at . . .*

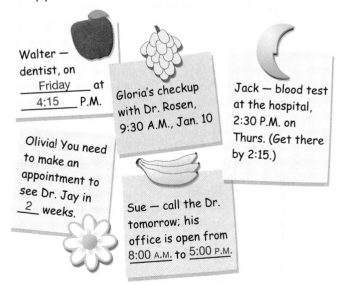

Walter —
dentist, on
___Friday___ at
___4:15___ P.M.

Gloria's checkup
with Dr. Rosen,
9:30 A.M., Jan. 10

Jack — blood test
at the hospital,
2:30 P.M. on
Thurs. (Get there
by 2:15.)

Olivia! You need
to make an
appointment to
see Dr. Jay in
___2___ weeks.

Sue — call the Dr.
tomorrow; his
office is open from
8:00 A.M. to 5:00 P.M.

Can you... make a doctor's appointment? ☐

Read medicine labels

Life Skills

1 READ OTC MEDICINE LABELS

A CLASS. What over-the-counter medicine do you buy?

B PAIRS. Read the definitions. Then read the medicine label. Find words that have the same meaning as the definitions. Write the words on the lines.

You can buy over-the-counter (OTC) medicine such as aspirin from any drugstore. For other medicine, you need to get a prescription from a doctor first.

1. for a short time: _temporarily_

2. make better: relieve

3. because of: due to

4. make less: reduce

5. do not use after this date: expiration date

Extra-Strength Pain Reliever

Active Ingredient: Acetaminophen 500 mg

Uses: Temporarily relieves the aches and pains due to
- headache
- the common cold
- backache
- toothache

Temporarily reduces fever

Directions
- Adults and children 12 years and over: Take 2 caplets every 6 hours.
- Do not take more than 8 caplets in 24 hours.
- Children under 12: Do not use this extra-strength product.

Expiration date: 11/10

C Read the medicine label again. Match the questions and answers.

1. __b__ What is this medicine for?   a. November 2010.

2. __e__ Who can take this medicine?   b. Aches and pains, and fever.

3. __c__ How much do I take?   c. Two caplets every six hours.

4. __d__ Who cannot use this product?   d. Children under 12.

5. __a__ What is the expiration date?   e. Adults and children over 12.

Lesson 4 Read medicine labels

Getting Started 5 minutes

- Ask: *Do you take medicine? When?* On the board, write: *I take medicine when I _____.* Model the activity by completing the sentence yourself (for example, say: *I take medicine when I have a headache.*). Tell students to copy and complete the sentence in their notebooks.
- Form small groups. Say: *Talk to your classmates. When do you take medicine?*

Presentation 10 minutes

1 READ OTC MEDICINE LABELS

A CLASS. What over-the-counter medicine do...

- Hold up your book and point to the note on the right side of the directions. Tell students to read the note silently.
- Ask: *What's a prescription?* (a piece of paper on which a doctor writes what medicine you need) *Do you need a prescription for over-the-counter medicine?* (No.) *Where can you buy OTC medicine?* (at any drugstore)
- *Optional:* Bring in a container from a prescription medicine and a container from an OTC medicine. Hold up the containers and ask: *Which one is an over-the-counter medicine? Which one can I buy at any drugstore?*
- Read the directions. Write *aspirin* (and the name of the OTC medicine from the container you brought in) on the board. Ask: *What other OTC medicine do you buy?* Write the names of medicines that students say on the board.

> **Culture Connection**
> - Ask: *Are there any medicines that you can buy over-the-counter in your country but need a prescription for here?*
> - List students' responses on the board.

B PAIRS. Read the definitions. Then read the...

- Read the directions and the definitions. Tell students to read the medicine label silently.
- Read the example. Tell students to find *temporarily* on the label and underline it. Say: Temporarily *means for a short time. Now find a word that means* make better.

- Pair students. Tell students to underline the words on the label and write them on the lines.
- Number from 1 to 5 on the board. Write the answer for item 1. Ask students to write answers 2–5.
- Say each answer and ask the class to repeat.
- Tell students to close their books. Say the definitions in random order and tell students to call out the words.

MULTILEVEL INSTRUCTION for 1B
Pre-level Tell students which words to find and underline on the label.
Above-level Give students the following additional definitions to match with terms on the label: *stronger than usual* (extra-strength), *the medicine that works* (active ingredient).

Controlled Practice 10 minutes

C Read the medicine label again. Match...

- Tell students to read the medicine label again silently.
- Read the directions. Ask two students to read the example.
- Students compare answers with a partner. Tell them to take turns reading the questions and answers.
- Read the questions and call on students to say answers. After each question and answer, check comprehension by asking an additional question: 1. *What kinds of aches does this medicine relieve?* (headaches, backaches, toothaches) 2. *Is this medicine safe for 13-year-olds?* (Yes.) 3. *What are caplets?* (Students can point to the picture.) 4. *Is this medicine safe for ten-year-olds?* (No.) 5. *What should you do with this medicine in December 2010?* (throw it in the trash)

EXPANSION: Speaking practice for 1C
- Ask students to bring in labels from OTC medicines.
- Tell students to read their labels and find answers to the questions in Exercise 1C.
- Pair students and direct them to ask each other the questions in Exercise 1C. Students answer using information from their label.
- *Optional:* Tell students to exchange labels with a classmate (not their partner). Repeat the activity.

Lesson 4   Read medicine labels

Presentation   20 minutes

2   READ PRESCRIPTION MEDICINE LABELS

Ⓐ CLASS. Look at the prescription...

- Read the directions. Say: *Point to the prescription. Point to the medicine label.* Ask: *Who gives you a prescription?* (a doctor) *Can you buy this medicine at any drugstore?* (No.)
- Tell students to read the questions silently and look for answers on the prescription and label.
- Read the questions and elicit answers from the class.
- Tell students to cover the medicine label. Say the specific pieces of information from the label in random order. Point to the board and tell students to call out the type of information (for example, T: *Do not take with aspirin.* Class: *Warning*).
- *Optional:* Pair students and tell them to take turns asking and answering the questions.

Ⓑ Read the medicine label in Exercise A again...

- Read the directions. Tell students to look at the example. Read the question and elicit the answer from the class.
- Students compare answers with a partner.
- Write *dosage* on the board. Read item 2 and elicit the answer. Ask the class what *dosage* means and write a definition (for example, *how much medicine you take*). Repeat with *refills*. Read item 5 and elicit a definition (for example, *times that you can get more medicine with the same prescription*).

Ⓒ 💿 Listen and check your answers...

- Play CD 2, Track 36. Students listen and check their answers.
- Say: *Now listen and repeat. Practice the questions because you're going to ask them in Exercise 3.* Resume playing Track 36.

Communicative Practice   15 minutes

3   PRACTICE

PAIRS. Take turns being the customer and the...

- Read the directions. Tell students to look at Exercise 2B. Point to the questions and ask: *Who asks the questions?* (the customer) *Who answers the questions?* (the pharmacist)
- Tell students to look at the medicine labels. On the board, write: *an eyedropper, a tube of ointment.* Ask: *What's the picture next to the first label?* (an eyedropper) Ask: *What's the picture next to the second label?* (a tube of ointment)
- Pair students. Say: *Talk to your partner. Decide who's going to be the pharmacist for the eyedrops and who's going to be the pharmacist for the ointment.*
- Tell students to look at the questions in Exercise 2B and find answers to the questions on their label.
- Say: *Take turns being the customer and the pharmacist. The customer asks the questions in Exercise 2B. The pharmacist answers the questions using the underlined information on his or her label.*
- Call on pairs to perform for the class.

▬▬ MULTILEVEL INSTRUCTION for 3
Cross-ability Tell the higher-level students to play the pharmacist first.

4   LIFE SKILLS WRITING

Turn to page 262 and ask students to complete the medical history form. See pages Txi–Txii for general notes about Life Skills Writing activities.

Progress Check

Can you . . . read medicine labels?

Say: *We have practiced reading medicine labels. Now, look at the question at the bottom of the page. Can you read medicine labels?* Tell students to write a checkmark in the box.

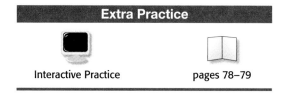

Extra Practice

Interactive Practice   pages 78–79

A CLASS. Look at the prescription and the medicine label. Answer the questions.

Leora Fishman, M.D.
Greenville Clinic
1123 W. Main St., Ft. Lauderdale, FL 33312
(954) 555-8732

Name _Kate Reed_ Age _36_

Address _25 Scenic Drive, Apt. 21B,_
Fort Lauderdale, FL 33312

Date _06/05/10_

R _Milacam 15 MG_

Signature _Leora Fishman_

Bio-Med Pharmacy
Doctor: Leora Fishman
Patient: Kate Reed
Dosage: Take 2 tablespoons by mouth
once a day. Take with food.
Warning: Do not take with aspirin.

Milacam 15 MG

2 Refills   Exp: 10/05/12

Who wrote the prescription? Dr. Leora Fishman
Who is it for? Kate Reed
Who do you give a prescription to? a patient
Where can you get this medicine? at a pharmacy / drugstore
What information is on the label?
doctor, patient, dosage, warning, medicine name, refills, expiration date

B Read the medicine label in Exercise A again. Match the questions and answers.

1. __e__ What is the name of the medicine?   a. Two.

2. __d__ How often do I take it?   b. Two tablespoons.

3. __b__ What is the dosage?   c. October 2012.

4. __c__ What is the expiration date?   d. Once a day.

5. __a__ How many refills can I get?   e. Milacam.

CD2 T36

C Listen and check your answers. Then listen and repeat.

3 PRACTICE

PAIRS. Take turns being the customer and the pharmacist. Ask and answer the questions in Exercise B about the prescription medicine.

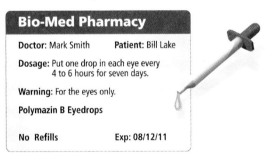

Bio-Med Pharmacy

Doctor: Mark Smith   Patient: Bill Lake

Dosage: Put one drop in each eye every
4 to 6 hours for seven days.

Warning: For the eyes only.

Polymazin B Eyedrops

No Refills   Exp: 08/12/11

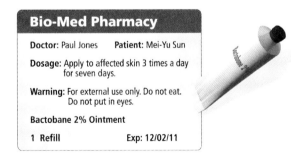

Bio-Med Pharmacy

Doctor: Paul Jones   Patient: Mei-Yu Sun

Dosage: Apply to affected skin 3 times a day
for seven days.

Warning: For external use only. Do not eat.
Do not put in eyes.

Bactobane 2% Ointment

1 Refill   Exp: 12/02/11

4 LIFE SKILLS WRITING   Complete a medical history form. See page 262.

Can you...read medicine labels?

Talk about an injury

Listening and Speaking

1 BEFORE YOU LISTEN

A Look at the pictures. Match each picture with a sentence from the box.
Write the sentences on the lines.

1. ___I fell.___

2. ___I broke my arm.___

3. ___I cut my finger.___

4. ___I sprained my ankle.___

5. ___I hurt my head.___

6. ___I burned my hand.___

I burned my hand.
I sprained my ankle.
I cut my finger.
I broke my arm.
~~I fell.~~
I hurt my head.

B PAIRS. Compare your answers.

2 LISTEN

A CLASS. Look at the picture. Where are Manolo and Ellie?

CD2 T37

B Listen to the conversation.
Read the sentences. Circle *True* or *False*.

1. Ellie broke her arm. (True) False

2. Ellie had an accident at a soccer game. True (False)

3. Manolo thinks he sprained his ankle. (True) False

CD2 T38

C Listen to the whole conversation. What happened
to Manolo? Circle the letter.

a.

(b.)

Talk about an injury

Getting Started   10 minutes

1   BEFORE YOU LISTEN

A **Look at the pictures. Match each picture...**

- Say: *Look at the pictures. What's an* injury? (when a person gets hurt / has an accident)
- As a warm up, ask the class if anyone has an injury. Help students describe their injuries.
- Read the directions and the example.
- Read the sentences in the box. Tell students to underline the parts of the body. Say: *If you know these parts of the body, you can match the pictures with the sentences.*

B **PAIRS. Compare your answers.**

- Say each sentence from the box in Exercise 1A and ask the class to repeat.
- Pair students and tell them to take turns reading the sentences.
- Walk around and spot-check students' written answers.
- Tell students to look at item 4 in Exercise 1A. Read the sentence. Explain that *sprains* are injuries to joints, or parts of your body that can bend. On the board, write: *I sprained my . . .* Demonstrate bending each joint. Elicit and list on the board the parts of the body that a person can sprain (*ankle, knee, elbow, wrist, fingers*).

Presentation   10 minutes

2   LISTEN

A **CLASS. Look at the picture. Where...**

- Direct students to look at the picture. Ask: *How many people are in the picture?* (three) *What do they all have?* (an injury)
- Read the directions. Say: *Point to Manolo. Point to Ellie.* Ask: *What are they doing?* (sitting, waiting, talking) *Where are they?* (in the waiting room at a doctor's office or hospital)

B 📀 **Listen to the conversation. Read...**

- Direct students to look at the picture again. Ask: *What part of his body did Manolo hurt?* (his ankle or foot) *What part of her body did Ellie hurt?* (her arm)
- Read the directions and the sentences. Play CD 2, Track 37.
- Read the sentences and call on students to say the answers.
- Tell students to rewrite item 2 to make it true (<u>Manolo</u> had an accident at a soccer game.).

Controlled Practice   10 minutes

> **Teaching Tip**
>
> *Optional:* Remember that if students need additional support, tell them to read the Audio Script on page 302 as they listen to the conversations.

C 📀 **Listen to the whole conversation....**

- Read the directions. Direct students to look at the pictures. Ask: *What do you think happened to Manolo?* Tell students to guess what happened and underline a or b.
- Play CD 2, Track 38.
- Students compare answers with a partner.
- Ask: *What happened to Manolo?* Ask students to look at the pictures and say what happened. (a. He sprained/hurt his ankle at a soccer game. b. He fell [down the bleachers]). Write their responses on the board. Ask: *Which is true?* Elicit and circle a. Ask: *Was your guess correct?*

▬▬▬ **EXPANSION: Graphic organizer practice for 2C**

- Say: *Think about an accident you had or an accident a friend or family member had when you were with them.*
- Draw a *Wh-* question chart on the board (with What, Where, When, and How as headings) and complete it with information about an accident you or your friend/family member had. In the *What?* box, write a sentence similar to the ones in the box in Exercise 1A. Write short answers in the other boxes.
- Tell students to draw a complete *Wh-* question chart about their accident.

Lesson 5 Talk about an injury

Presentation   5 minutes

3 CONVERSATION

Ⓐ 💿 Listen to the sentences. Notice...

- Write the first sentence on the board. Point to each word and pronounce it distinctly. Ask: *Is this how people speak?* (No.)
- Say the sentence again, running *What* and *are* together as you would in normal speech. Point to the underlined *t* in the sentence, say the sentence and ask: *What sound do you hear?* (/d/)
- Read the Pronunciation Watch note. Point to the underlined *t* and ask: *Is it between two vowel sounds?* (Yes.) *What does it sound like?* (/d/)
- Write the second sentence on the board. Ask: *Is the underlined* t *between two vowel sounds?* (Yes.) Say the sentence and ask: *Does the* t *sound like a quick* /d/? (Yes.) Repeat with the third sentence.
- Play CD 2, Track 39. Students listen.
- Resume playing Track 39. Students listen and repeat.

Controlled Practice   10 minutes

Ⓑ 💿 Listen to the sentences. Which underlined...

- Write item 1 on the board. Ask: *Is the underlined* t *between two vowel sounds?* (Yes.) Say the sentence and ask: *Does the* t *sound like a quick* /d/? (Yes.) Circle the item number.
- Play CD 2, Track 40.
- Play Track 40 again as needed.
- Write items 2–4 on the board. Say each sentence and ask: *Is the underlined* t *between two vowel sounds? Does the* t *sound like a quick* /d/?
- Have pairs practice saying items 1 and 4.

Ⓒ 💿 Listen and repeat the conversation.

- Note: This conversation is the same one students heard in Exercise 2B on page 134.
- Tell students to read the conversation silently. Tell them to find and underline the three *t*'s that are pronounced like quick /d/'s (*Wha*t *are you doing here? / Wha*t *about you? / a*t *a soccer game*)
- Play CD 2, Track 41.

4 PRACTICE

Ⓐ PAIRS. Practice the conversation. Then make...

- Pair students and tell them to practice the conversation in Exercise 3C.
- Then, in Exercise 4A, tell students to look at the information in the boxes. Point to the blue box. Call on volunteers to act out the meaning of the sentences. Say each sentence and ask the class to repeat. Point to the green box. Say the words and ask the class to point to the part of the body and repeat.
- Ask two above-level students to practice a conversation for the class. Tell them to use their own names.
- Tell pairs to use their names and the information in the boxes to fill in the blanks.

Communicative Practice   15 minutes

Ⓑ ROLE PLAY. PAIRS. Make your own...

- Brainstorm and write on the board a list of body parts people hurt. Say the words and ask the class to point to the part of the body and repeat. If possible, draw a green box around the list.
- Choose a body part from the list and elicit the class's help to make sentences about injuries. Tell students to look at the sentences in the box in Exercise 1A on page 134. Ask: *Can you burn your [leg]?* On the board, write: *I burned my leg.* Continue with the other sentences. Remind students that *sprains* only occur at joints. Draw a blue box around the sentences.
- Pair students and tell them to substitute information on the board or their own information into the conversation in Exercise 4A.
- Call on pairs to perform for the class.

Extra Practice

Interactive Practice

CONVERSATION

Pronunciation Watch

When the letter *t* is between two vowel sounds, it often sounds like a quick /d/ in North American English.

A CD2 T39

Listen to the sentences. Notice the pronunciation of the underlined *t*'s. Then listen and repeat.

Wha<u>t</u> are you doing here?
I was a<u>t</u> a soccer game.
What's the ma<u>tt</u>er?

B CD2 T40

Listen to the sentences. Which underlined *t*'s have the sound /d/? Circle the numbers.

(1.) Wha<u>t</u> about you?
2. I hur<u>t</u> my ankle.
3. Tha<u>t</u>'s too bad.
(4.) See you la<u>t</u>er.

C CD2 T41

Listen and repeat the conversation.

Manolo: Hi, Ellie. What are you doing here?
Ellie: Oh, hi, Manolo. I had an accident. I broke my arm.
Manolo: Oh, no! I'm sorry to hear that.
Ellie: Thanks. What about you?
Manolo: I hurt my ankle at a soccer game. I think I sprained it.
Ellie: That's too bad.

4 **PRACTICE**

A PAIRS. Practice the conversation. Then make new conversations. Use your own names and the information in the boxes.

A: Hi, _____. What are you doing here?
B: Oh, hi, _____. I had an accident.
A: Oh, no! I'm sorry to hear that.
B: Thanks. What about you?
A: I hurt my _____ at a soccer game. I think I sprained it.
B: That's too bad.

I cut my hand.
I burned my finger.
I fell.

foot
wrist
back

B ROLE PLAY. PAIRS. Make your own conversations. Use your own names and different information.

Talk about an injury

Grammar

Simple past: Irregular verbs
Affirmative
Ellie **had** an accident.
She **broke** her arm.
Manolo **got** hurt.
He **hurt** his ankle.

Grammar Watch

Common irregular verbs

Base form	Past-tense form	Base form	Past-tense form
break	**broke**	get	**got**
cut	**cut**	have	**had**
fall	**fell**	hurt	**hurt**

• See page 286 for more past-tense forms.

1 PRACTICE

A Complete the sentences. Underline the correct verbs.

1. I don't want my son to play soccer. Sometimes players **get** / got hurt.
2. Oh, no! I think I break / **broke** my leg.
3. Pilar cuts / **cut** her finger and went to the hospital.
4. He hurts / **hurt** his ankle on the stairs yesterday.
5. My grandfather sometimes **falls** / fell in the house. I'm worried.
6. They have / **had** an accident last Saturday.
7. My son breaks / **broke** his foot and went to the emergency room.
8. My daughter is sick today. She **has** / had a sore throat.

B Write sentences about the past. Use a verb from the box.

~~break~~   cut   fall   get   have   hurt

1. Oscar / his ankle _____Oscar broke his ankle._____

2. my son / his finger / with a knife ___My son cut his finger with a knife.___

3. you / a fever / last night ___You had a fever last night.___

4. we / sick ___We got sick.___

5. my grandmother / in the bathroom ___My grandmother fell in the bathroom.___

6. Sun-Ah / her arm ___Sun-Ah hurt her arm.___

Getting Started   5 minutes

- Say: *We're going to study the simple past tense of irregular verbs. You heard this grammar in Exercise 3C on page 135.*
- Play CD 2, Track 41. Students listen. Write on the board: *I had an accident, I broke my arm, I hurt my ankle.* Underline *had*, *broke*, and *hurt*.

Presentation   15 minutes

Simple past: Irregular verbs

- Write *burn* and *sprain* on the board. Ask: *How do we usually form the past tense?* Elicit the answer and add *-ed* to the words on the board. Say *burned* and *sprained* and ask the class to repeat.
- Say: *Some verbs do not have -ed forms. They have irregular past-tense forms.* Tell students to look at the sentences on the board. Ask: *What is the past-tense form of* have? (*had*) Repeat with *break* and *hurt*. Say: *Have, break, and* hurt *have irregular past-tense forms.*
- Copy the grammar charts onto the board or show Transparency 7.4 and cover the exercise. Point to the right chart and ask: *What other verbs have irregular past-tense forms?* (*cut, fall, get*) Say the irregular past-tense forms and ask the class to repeat.
- Tell students to look at the left chart. Point to the picture of Manolo and Ellie on page 134. Ask: *What happened to Ellie? What happened to Manolo?* Elicit the sentences in the chart. Then read the sentences and ask the class to repeat.
- If you are using the transparency, do the exercise with the class.

▰▰ EXPANSION: Grammar practice

- Tell students to look at the Grammar Reference on page 286. Say the past-tense forms and ask the class to repeat.
- Give students time to study the irregular past-tense forms on page 136 and in the Grammar Reference on page 286.

- Tell students to close their books. Say base forms in random order and ask the class to call out the past-tense forms.
- Pair students and tell them to quiz each other. Tell students to mark the verbs their partner doesn't know.
- Provide students with index cards or tell them to cut up notebook paper. Tell them to make flashcards for the verbs they need to practice more.

Controlled Practice   20 minutes

 PRACTICE

Ⓐ Complete the sentences. Underline the...

- Read the directions. Write the example on the board and point to the answer. Ask: *Is the verb present or past tense?* (present tense) *Why?* (You use *sometimes* with the present tense)
- Say: *Read the sentences carefully before you answer. Decide whether each sentence is present or past tense. Look for clues like* sometimes, today, *and* yesterday.
- Students compare answers with a partner.
- Call on students to read the completed sentences.

Ⓑ Write sentences about the past. Use a verb...

- Read the directions. Write item 1 on the board and point to the answer. Ask: *Which verb from the box is used?* (*break*) *What is the past-tense form of* break? (*broke*) Read the sentence.
- Say each verb in the box and ask the class to call out the past-tense form.
- Say: *First, choose the correct verb. Then write a past-tense sentence.*
- Students compare answers with a partner. Walk around and spot-check students' spelling of the past-tense forms.
- Call on students to read the completed sentences.

2 PRACTICE

Ⓐ PAIRS. Look at the pictures. What happened...

- Read the directions. Tell students to underline *last weekend.* Ask: *Are you going to use the present or the past tense?* (past tense)
- Say: *Look at item 1. What happened to Jessica last weekend?* Write the example on the board. Ask the class to complete the second sentence. On the board, write: *cut her hand.*
- Pair students. Say: *Look at the other pictures. What happened to David, Emery, and Denise last weekend? Talk to your partner. Try to think of two things to say about each picture. To get ideas, look at the exercises on page 136.*
- For items 2–4, ask: *What happened to [David]?* Call on pairs to give their answers. For each item, ask if there are any different answers.

Ⓑ WRITE. On a separate piece of paper, write...

- Read the directions and the sentences about Jessica on the board. Say: *Use the sentences as an example.*
- Remind students to start each sentence with a capital letter and end with a period. Tell students to check their spelling of irregular past-tense verbs by looking at the chart on page 136 and the Grammar Reference on page 286.
- For items 2–4 in Exercise 2A, ask students to write their sentences on the board. Correct as needed.
- Call on different students to read the sentences.

▨ EXPANSION: Speaking practice for 2B

- Tell students to read the conversation in Exercise 3C on page 135 again.
- Choose two pictures from Exercise 2A. With the class, create a phone conversation between the two people. Write it on the board. For example:

  Jessica: Hi, Denise. How was your weekend?

  Denise: Terrible. I got sick. I had a fever.

  Jessica: That's too bad.

  Denise: What about you? How was your weekend?

  Jessica: Not great. I had an accident in the kitchen. I cut my hand.

  Denise: Oh, no! I'm sorry to hear that.

- Form like-ability pairs. Instruct pre-level pairs to practice the conversation on the board. Instruct above-level pairs to create a conversation between the other two people in Exercise 2A.

Communicative Practice 20 minutes

Show what you know!

STEP 1. Complete the questions.

- Read the directions. To demonstrate the meaning of *Did you ever . . . ?,* ask: *Did you ever cut your finger? Did you ever sprain your ankle?* For each question, ask for a show of hands and ask a student whose hand is raised: *When?*
- Advise students to review the vocabulary on page 127 for help with completing the last question.
- Elicit a variety of endings for each question and write three complete questions on the board.

STEP 2. GROUPS OF 5. Ask your partners your...

- Form groups of 5. Read the directions and example.
- Model the activity. Next to your questions on the board, write the names of four above-level students as column headings of a chart. Point to the names and say: *This is my group.*
- Demonstrate asking each group member a question and taking notes on the chart.
- Tell students to create charts for their group and to continue asking questions until they complete their charts.

STEP 3. Tell the class about your partners.

- Tell students to look at their charts and circle the most interesting answer from each partner.
- Remind students to use the past tense. Point to the verbs in the questions on the board and elicit the past-tense forms (*hurt, broke, had*).

Progress Check

Can you . . . talk about an injury?

Say: *We have practiced talking about injuries. Now, look at the question at the bottom of the page. Can you talk about an injury?* Tell students to write a checkmark in the box.

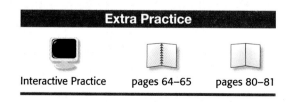

Extra Practice		
Interactive Practice	pages 64–65	pages 80–81

A PAIRS. Look at the pictures. What happened last weekend? Decide together.

Answers will vary.

Jessica had an accident in the kitchen. She . . .

1.

2.

3.

4.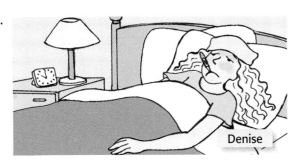

B WRITE. On a separate piece of paper, write two sentences about each picture in Exercise A. Write about what happened. Answers will vary.

Show what you know! Talk about an injury

STEP 1. **Complete the questions.** Answers will vary.

Did you ever hurt _____?

Did you ever break _____?

Did you ever have _____?

STEP 2. GROUPS OF 5. **Ask your partners your questions. Take notes.**

A: *Did you ever break your toe?*
B: *No, but I broke my finger at work last year.*

STEP 3. **Tell the class about your partners.**

Can you...talk about an injury? ☐

Reading

1 BEFORE YOU READ

A CLASS. **What is stress? When do you feel stressed?**

B PAIRS. **Scan the article. Look at the words and sentences in color. Answer the questions.**

1. What two questions does the article answer?
   What causes stress? How can you manage stress?
2. What are four causes of stress?
   change, loss of control, negative attitudes, unhealthy habits

> **Reading Skill:** Using Formatting Clues
>
> Authors sometimes use formatting such as boldface type, bullets, and color to help readers find the main points.

2 READ

CD2 T42

 Listen. Read the article.

STRESS

Everyone feels stress sometimes. But some people have so much stress that they become sick.

What causes stress?

Change   The biggest source of stress is change. It may be a bad change, like losing a job or getting divorced. But even a good change, like going on vacation, causes stress!

Loss of Control   You also feel stress in situations that are out of your control. Maybe you are stuck in traffic or your kids are sick. When you can't change the bad things in your life, you feel stress.

Negative Attitudes   The way you think can cause stress. For example, you worry a lot or you think too much about the bad things in your life. These kinds of negative attitudes cause stress.

Unhealthy Habits   Finally, the way you live can cause stress. Do you eat too much junk food? Do you work too many hours? These kinds of unhealthy habits add stress to your life.

How can you manage stress?

• Find out what causes stress in your life. Pay attention to the times you feel stressed out.

• Think about ways to change the things that cause you stress.

• Accept the things you can't change. Sometimes you can't avoid a stressful situation. You need to find a way to live with it.

• Talk about it. Sometimes you need help. Talk about your stress with a family member, friend, counselor, or doctor.

Getting Started
10 minutes

1 BEFORE YOU READ

A CLASS. What is stress? When do you feel...

- Write *STRESS* on the board. Ask: *What is stress?* Use the word *STRESS* as the center of a web diagram and note students' ideas on the board (for example, *worry, no time, too much work, can't relax, tired*). If students need help, tell them to look at the picture in the article.
- Ask: *When do you feel stressed?* Elicit a variety of responses and write them on the board.

B PAIRS. Scan the article. Look at the words and...

- Read the Reading Skills note about using formatting clues. Explain that *boldface type* is print that is thicker and darker than normal. Tell students to look at the article. Ask: *What words are in boldface type?* (*What causes stress?*, *Change*, etc., *How can you manage stress?*) Say: *These are the main points of the article.*
- Say: *Find the bullets in the article. How many are there?* (four) Hold up your book and point to the bullets.
- Pair students. Read the directions. Ask: *What colors are used in the article?* (blue and red) Tell pairs to look at the words and sentences in blue and red and answer the questions.
- Read item 1. Ask: *What color are the questions?* (blue) Elicit the two questions. Read item 2. Ask: *What color are the causes of stress?* (red) Elicit the four causes of stress and write them on the board as headings.

Presentation
15 minutes

2 READ

 Listen. Read the article.

- Instruct students to close their books. Point to each cause of stress on the board and ask the class for examples. For example, point to *Change* and ask: *What are some changes that can cause stress?* List students' ideas under each cause of stress on the board.
- Play CD 2, Track 42. Students listen and read along silently.
- *Optional:* Play Track 42 again. Pause the CD after each cause of stress and ask the class to add examples to the list on the board. For example, if they are not already on the board, add under *Change: losing a job, getting divorced*, and *going on vacation.*

Culture Connection

- Say: *Stress is a major health problem in the U.S. Money and work are the main causes of Americans' stress.*
- Ask: *Is stress a major problem in your country? What are the causes of people's stress? Do you feel more stress here or in your own country?*

Controlled Practice   20 minutes

3 CHECK YOUR UNDERSTANDING

A Read the article again. Circle *True* or *False*.

- Tell students to read again and highlight the answers in the article.
- Students compare answers with a partner.
- Call on students to say the answers.
- *Optional:* Tell students to rewrite items 3 and 4 to make them true (3. *Eating too much junk food is an example of* <u>an unhealthy habit</u>. 4. *You* <u>can't</u> *always avoid stressful situations.*).

B Take the stress quiz. Then count your...

- Tell students to look at the stress quiz. Read the quiz directions (*Circle the number . . .*) Ask what answers numbers 1, 3, and 5 represent (*Never, Sometimes,* and *Every day*). Ask: *What about numbers 2 and 4?* Elicit an adverb of frequency for each and write them on the board (*2—hardly ever, 4—often*). If students have difficulty, tell them to review the grammar charts on page 70.
- Tell students to read the quiz items silently and underline any words they don't understand. Explain unfamiliar vocabulary as needed.
- Read the directions. Walk around and, as needed, demonstrate adding the points in each column and writing the total on the line. Tell students to circle how much stress they have—*Not Much Stress, Some Stress,* or *A Lot of Stress.*
- Ask volunteers: *How much stress do you have?*

C PAIRS. Compare your scores. Talk about...

- Read the directions and the example. Tell students to look at the stress quiz. Tell them to circle their total score and the items on which they scored the highest.
- Pair students. To model the activity, talk about how stress affects your life. Say your score and the items you scored highest. Say how much stress you have.
- Call on a few volunteers to talk about how stress affects their lives.

Communicative Practice   15 minutes

Show what you know!

PRE-WRITING. Write a list of things in your life...

- Read the directions. Tell students to look at the examples on the board. Or tell students to read the *What causes stress?* section of the article again and underline things that cause stress. (*losing a job, getting divorced,* etc.)
- Tell students to write the things on the board or in the article that cause stress in their lives. Tell them to add other things that cause them stress.

NETWORK. Find classmates with the same...

- On the board, write: *What causes stress in your life?* Tell students to stand, mingle, and ask classmates the question. Say: *When you find a classmate with some of the same causes of stress, stay together. Look for other classmates with the same causes.*
- When all students have found at least one partner, tell students to stop and sit with the classmate(s) they found.
- Tell the class to look at the article again. Ask: *Where can you find information about how to manage stress?* (under *How can you manage stress?*)
- Tell partners to take turns reading the bullet points out loud. On the board, write: *Change, Accept, Talk.* Say: *Brainstorm ideas about how to manage your stress. What can you change? What can you not change? Who can you talk to?*

▬▬ MULTILEVEL INSTRUCTION

Cross-ability Ask the highest-level partner in each group to record the group's ideas and present them to the class.

WRITE. Write about the stress in your life...

Turn to page 271 and ask students to complete the activities. See page T-xii for general notes about Writing activities.

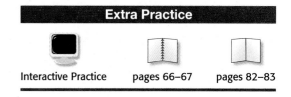

Extra Practice		
Interactive Practice	pages 66–67	pages 82–83

CHECK YOUR UNDERSTANDING

A **Read the article again. Circle *True* or *False*.**

1. Even good changes, like getting married, can cause stress.   (True)   False
2. Being in a situation you can't control causes stress.   (True)   False
3. Eating too much junk food is an example of a negative attitude.   True   (False)
4. You can always avoid stressful situations.   True   (False)
5. Talking with someone can help you manage stress.   (True)   False

B **Take the stress quiz. Then count your points. How much stress do you have?**

Answers will vary.

Stress Quiz

Circle the number that is true for you.

	Never		Sometimes		Every day
1. I get headaches.	1	2	3	4	5
2. I get stomachaches.	1	2	3	4	5
3. I have trouble sleeping.	1	2	3	4	5
4. I can't concentrate.	1	2	3	4	5
5. I worry about small things.	1	2	3	4	5
6. I get angry easily.	1	2	3	4	5
7. I want to be alone.	1	2	3	4	5
8. I argue with my friends and family.	1	2	3	4	5
Total Score	___ +	___ +	___ +	___ +	___ = ___

Not Much Stress 8–18   Some Stress 19–29   A lot of Stress 30–40

C **PAIRS.** **Compare your scores. Talk about how stress affects your life.**

My score is 30. I get headaches at work and have trouble sleeping . . .

Show what you know!

PRE-WRITING. **Write a list of things in your life that cause stress.**

NETWORK. **Find classmates with the same causes of stress. Form a group. Talk about ways you can manage stress.**

WRITE. **Write about the stress in your life. See page 271.**

Call in when you have to miss work

Listening and Speaking

1 BEFORE YOU LISTEN

A READ. CLASS. **Look at the picture and read about Hugo. Then answer the questions.**

> Hugo is at the dental clinic. He woke up with a bad toothache this morning. He was supposed to work from 10:00 A.M. to 6:00 P.M. today. At 9:30, he called his supervisor and explained his problem. He had to miss work today.

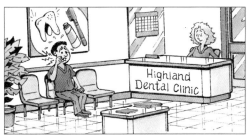

1. What is Hugo's problem?   He has a toothache.

2. Why did Hugo call his work supervisor?   He had to miss work.

B CLASS. **Have you ever had to miss work or school?**

2 LISTEN

CD2 T43

A 💿 **Look at the pictures of Soo-Jin calling her work supervisor. Listen to the conversation. Answer the questions.**

1. Why is Soo-Jin calling?
   a. She's going to be late.
   b. She's going to miss work.

2. Where is Soo-Jin going?
   a. to the hospital
   b. to the doctor's office
   c. to the dentist's office

CD2 T44

B 💿 **Listen to the whole conversation. What is Soo-Jin going to do later?**

a. call her supervisor
b. go to work
c. call the doctor

Lesson 8 Call in when you have to miss work

Getting Started
10 minutes

1 BEFORE YOU LISTEN

Ⓐ READ. CLASS. Look at the picture and read...

- Read the directions. Direct students to look at the picture. Ask: *Where is Hugo?* (at the dentist's office / at the Highland Dental Clinic) *What's the matter with Hugo?* (His tooth hurts.)
- Ask students to read the paragraph and the questions silently. Tell them to underline answers to the questions in the paragraph.
- Read the paragraph and each question and call on students to answer.

Ⓑ CLASS. Have you ever had to miss work...

- Read the question. Tell students to think about the last time they missed work or school.
- Talk about a time when you missed work. Mention the reason and who you called.
- Ask several students: *Have you ever had to miss work or school? What was the problem? Did you call someone? Who?* Call on above-level students first.

Culture Connection

- Say: *When you miss work because of sickness or injury, some employers require a doctor's note. If you're not sure, ask the doctor or dentist for a note just in case.*
- Ask: *Do employers in your country require a doctor's note when you miss work?*
- Say: *Some doctors ask, "Do you need a note for your employer?" If your doctor doesn't ask, what can you say?* Write students' ideas on the board (for example, *Can you please write a note for my boss?* or *I need a note for my employer.*).

Presentation
25 minutes

2 LISTEN

Ⓐ Look at the pictures of Soo-Jin...

- Read the directions. Say: *Point to Soo-Jin. Point to her work supervisor. How does Soo-Jin look?* (sick / like she has a headache / like she doesn't feel well)
- Tell students to read the questions and answer choices silently.
- Play CD 2, Track 43.
- Read the questions and call on students to say the answers.

Teaching Tip

Optional: Remember that if students need additional support, tell them to read the Audio Script on page 303 as they listen to the conversations.

Ⓑ Listen to the whole conversation....

- Read the directions. Tell students to read the answer choices silently.
- Play CD 2, Track 44.
- Read the question again. Call on a student to say the answer.

Call in when you have to miss work

3 CONVERSATION

A 🎧 **Listen to the sentences. Notice...**

- Read the Pronunciation Watch note.
- Write the first sentence on the board. Ask: *Where is the pause?* (between *sorry* and *to*) *What are the two thought groups?* (*I'm sorry* and *to hear that*) Read the sentence, pausing between the two thought groups, and ask the class to repeat.
- Play CD 2, Track 45. Students listen.
- Resume playing Track 45. Students listen and repeat.

Controlled Practice   20 minutes

B 🎧 **Listen and repeat the conversation.**

- This conversation is the same one students heard in Exercise 2A on page 140.
- Tell students to read the conversation silently. Tell them to look for sentences similar to the examples and mark the pauses (*I can't come in / today; I have to / go to the doctor; Sorry / to hear that*).
- While students are reading, write the conversation on the board. Ask students who have marked the pauses correctly to mark them on the board.
- Say: *I'm going to read the conversation. Listen for one more pause to mark.* Point out that periods and commas also represent pauses, but that it's not necessary to mark them. Read the conversation, pausing between *today* and *because*. Ask the class where the pause was and mark it on the board.
- Play CD 2, Track 46. Tell students to practice pausing between thought groups. As needed, say the lines and ask students to repeat.

   EXPANSION: Pronunciation practice for 3B

- Form groups of 4. Say: *Look at the Pronunciation Watch note. Each sentence in the Pronunciation Watch note has three thought groups. Read each sentence and talk about where to mark the pauses.*
- Instruct partners to count off from 1 to 4. Tell Student 1's to underline the first sentence in the Pronunciation Watch note, Student 2's the second sentence, etc.
- Designate areas of the classroom for Student 1's, 2's, 3's, and 4's to sit. Say: *Talk about the sentence you underlined with your new partners. Compare answers. Decide where to mark the two pauses.*

- Ask a student from each group to write the group's sentence on the board and mark the pauses. Read the sentences on the board with pauses as marked. Make corrections as needed.
- Call on students to read the sentences on the board with the correct pauses.

4 PRACTICE

A **PAIRS. Practice the conversation. Then...**

- Pair students and tell them to practice the conversation in Exercise 3B. Remind them to practice pausing between thought groups.
- Then, in Exercise 4A, tell students to look at the information in the boxes. Say each phrase or sentence and ask the class to repeat.
- Point to the first blue phrase and ask: *Take who to the clinic?* (my son) *What pronoun goes with* my son? (*he*) Tell students to underline *my son*, *he*, and *he* in the top row in the boxes.
- Ask two above-level students to practice a conversation in front of the class. Tell them to use their own names and information from the same row in the boxes to fill in the blanks.
- Call on pairs to perform for the class.

Communicative Practice   15 minutes

B **ROLE PLAY. PAIRS. Make your own...**

- Brainstorm other situations and explanations with the class and write them on the board.
- Read the directions.
- Play Speaker B and make up a conversation with an above-level student. Use the information you wrote on the board. Prompt Student A to choose a red phrase from Exercise 4A and change the pronoun as needed.
- Walk around and check that Student A uses a pronoun that matches Student B's information.
- Call on pairs to role play for the class.

Extra Practice
Interactive Practice

3 CONVERSATION

CD2 T45

A 💿 **Listen to the sentences. Notice the thought groups. Then listen and repeat.**

I'm sorry / to hear that.
Do you think / you'll be in / tomorrow?
I have to / take my son / to the clinic.

CD2 T46

B 💿 **Listen and repeat the conversation.**

Paula: Hello. Paula Charles speaking.

Soo-Jin: Hi, Paula. This is Soo-Jin. I can't come in today because I have to go to the doctor. I don't feel well.

Paula: Sorry to hear that. Thanks for calling, and take care of yourself.

Soo-Jin: Thanks.

4 PRACTICE

A **PAIRS. Practice the conversation. Then make new conversations. Use your own names and the information in the boxes.**

A: Hello. _____ speaking.

B: Hi, _____. This is _____. I can't come in today because

I have to _____.

A: Sorry to hear that. Thanks for calling, and _____.

B: Thanks.

take my son to the clinic	He has a fever.	I hope he feels better
take care of my mother	She's sick.	I hope she gets well soon
go to the dentist	I broke my tooth.	good luck

B **ROLE PLAY. PAIRS. Make your own conversations. Use your own names and different information.**

Call in when you have to miss work

Grammar

Ways to express reasons

Soo-Jin missed work yesterday	**because**	she didn't feel well.
She went to the doctor	**for**	a prescription.

••••••• **Grammar Watch**

- Use *because* + a subject and a verb.
- Use *for* + a noun.

PRACTICE

A Complete the sentences. Write *because* or *for*.

1. I can't go to school ___because___ I have a cold.

2. I have to go to the drugstore ___for___ some medicine.

3. My wife is going to the doctor ___for___ a blood test.

4. Carlo went to the clinic ___because___ he hurt his back.

5. I went to the store ___for___ some cold medicine.

6. I was absent yesterday ___because___ I had a fever.

B Look at the words. Where do the people have to go? Why? Write one sentence with *because* and one sentence with *for*.

1. Jack / the pharmacy / some medicine

   Jack has to go to the pharmacy because he needs some medicine.

   Jack has to go to the pharmacy for some medicine.

2. Janelle / the doctor / a flu shot

   Janelle has to go to the doctor because she needs a flu shot.

   Janelle has to go to the doctor for a flu shot.

3. Gladys / the dentist / a checkup

   Gladys has to go to the dentist because she needs a checkup.

   Gladys has to go to the dentist for a checkup.

Getting Started 5 minutes

- Say: *We're going to study ways to express reasons with* because *and* for. *In the conversation on page 141, Soo-Jin used this grammar.*
- Play CD 2, Track 46. Students listen. Write on the board: *I can't come in today because I have to go to the doctor.* Underline *because.*

Presentation 10 minutes

Ways to express reasons

- Copy the grammar chart onto the board or show Transparency 7.5 and cover the exercise.
- Read the sentences in the chart. Ask: *Why did Soo-Jin miss work yesterday?* (because she didn't feel well) *Why did she go to the doctor?* (for a prescription)
- Underline and read *she didn't feel well* and *a prescription.* Ask: *Which is a noun?* (*a prescription*) *Which is a subject and a verb?* (*she didn't feel well*)
- Read the Grammar Watch note.
- *Optional:* Review parts of speech. Read the first sentence in the grammar chart. Point to the underlined portion and ask: *What is the subject?* (*she*) *What is the verb?* (*didn't feel*) Read the second sentence. Point to the underlined portion. Circle *a* and say: *Nouns often have* a, an, *or* some *before them.*
- On the board, write: *He went to the doctor because* . . . and *He went to the doctor for* . . . Elicit several endings to each sentence and write them on the board (for example, . . . *because he had chest pains / he sprained his ankle / he needed a prescription; for a physical / eye drops / an X-ray*).
- If you are using the transparency, do the exercise with the class.

Controlled Practice 15 minutes

> **PRACTICE**

A **Complete the sentences. Write** *because* **or** *for.*

- Read the directions and the example. Tell students to underline *I have a cold.* Ask: *Why is the answer* because? (because there's a subject and a verb in *I have a cold*)
- Tell students to look at what comes after the blank in each sentence and decide whether it's a subject and a verb or a noun.
- Students compare answers with a partner.
- Call on students to say answers.
- *Optional:* Tell students to read the sentences again and find the two items that match the picture. (items 1 and 5)

B **Look at the words. Where do the people...**

- Read the directions.
- Tell students to look at the items. To review the modal *have to,* ask where each person has to go. Elicit complete sentences (for example, T: *Where does Jack have to go?* S: *He has to go to the pharmacy.*).
- Ask: *Are you going to write sentences in the simple past or the simple present?* (simple present)
- On the board, write: because + *a subject and a verb.* Tell students to look at item 1. Read the example. Say: *Look at the part of the sentence after* because. *What's the subject?* (*he*) *Why* he? (*he* is the pronoun for *Jack*) *What's the verb?* (*needs*) *Why* need_s_? (with *he,* the simple present verb ends in -*s*)
- On the board, write: for + *a noun.* Ask the class to help write the second sentence for item 1. Write the answer on the board.
- Walk around and check that students add a subject and verb after *because.* Check that students are using correct subject pronouns and subject-verb agreement.
- Call on students to write answers on the board.

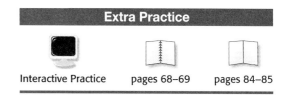

Extra Practice

Interactive Practice   pages 68–69   pages 84–85

1 GRAMMAR

A Complete the sentences. Use the simple past...

- Read the directions. Tell students to refer back to the grammar charts on page 136 (Simple past: Irregular verbs) as needed.
- Students compare answers with a partner. Walk around and check students' spelling of irregular verbs.
- Before reviewing answers, say each verb in the box and ask the class to call out the past tense.
- Call on students to read the sentences.

B Complete the conversations. Use the words...

- Read the directions. Tell students to refer back to the grammar charts on page 130 (Prepositions of time: *on / at / by / in / from . . . to*) and page 142 (Ways to express reasons) as needed.
- Students compare answers with a partner by reading the conversations.
- Call on two pairs to read the conversations for the class. Discuss any errors.
- *Optional:* Call on pairs to perform for the class.

CD-ROM Practice

 Go to the CD-ROM for more practice.

If your students need more practice with the vocabulary, grammar, and competencies in Unit 7, encourage them to review the activities on the CD-ROM. This review can also help students prepare for the final role play on the following Expand page.

Extra Practice
pages 70–71

1 GRAMMAR

A Complete the sentences. Use the simple past of a verb from the box.

> break   cut   fall   get   ~~have~~

1. I ___had___ a cold for three weeks, but now I feel fine.
2. Poor Rosa! She ___fell___ down the stairs and hurt her back.
3. Henry had an accident at work and ___broke___ a bone in his foot.
4. Be careful with that knife. Jim ___cut___ his hand with it yesterday.
5. I went to the doctor's office, and I ___got___ a prescription.

B Complete the conversations. Use the words in the boxes.

> at   by   for   ~~on~~

1. **A:** What are you doing ___on___ Wednesday afternoon?

   B: I'm going ___for___ a checkup.

   A: When is your appointment?

   B: It's ___at___ 4:30, but I need to go early. They want me to

   be there ___by___ 4:15.

> at   because   by   from   in   to

2. **A:** I need to see a doctor ___because___ I think I have an infection.

   B: Can you be here ___in___ an hour?

   A: I'm sorry, I can't. I work ___from___ 3:00 ___to___ 11:00.

   B: How about tomorrow? We have an opening ___at___ 9:00.

   A: That's fine. Thank you.

   B: OK. Please be here ___by___ 8:45.

Go to the CD-ROM for more practice.

2 ACT IT OUT   What do you say?

STEP 1. CLASS. Review the Lesson 2 conversation between the receptionist and Roberto (CD 2 track 33).

STEP 2. ROLE PLAY. PAIRS. Student A, you are the patient. Student B, you are the receptionist at the doctor's office.

Student A:
- Call the doctor's office and ask for an appointment.
- Explain your medical problem.
- Agree on a time you can come.

Student B:
- Ask about the patient's health problem.
- Suggest a time for the appointment.

3 READ AND REACT   Problem-solving

STEP 1. Read about Ramona's problem.

Ramona has a coworker named Mike. Mike often calls in late or sick to work. Tonight he calls in sick again. Ramona knows that he is not sick. She knows that Mike plans to attend a baseball game tonight. Ramona's boss asks her to cover Mike's hours. Ramona doesn't want to work late tonight.

STEP 2. PAIRS. What is Ramona's problem? What can she do? Here are some ideas.

- She can work late.
- She can tell her boss that Mike is not really sick.
- She can say, "I'm sorry, I can't work late tonight."
- She can _____.

4 CONNECT

For your Goal-setting Activity, go to page 252.
For your Team Project, go to page 280.

2 ACT IT OUT

STEP 1. CLASS. Review the Lesson 2 conversation...

- Tell students to review the conversation in Exercise 3B on page 129.
- Tell them to read the conversation silently and then practice it with a partner.
- Play CD 2, Track 33. Students listen.
- As needed, play Track 33 again to aid comprehension.

STEP 2. ROLE PLAY. PAIRS. Student A, you are the...

- Read the directions and the guidelines for A and B.
- Pair students. Tell A to make up a medical problem but to use real information about his or her schedule. Tell B to think of a name for the doctor's office. Remind pairs to pretend they are talking on the phone.
- Walk around and observe partners interacting. Check pairs' use of prepositions of time when they talk about the appointment time.
- Call on pairs to perform for the class.
- While pairs are performing, use the scoring rubric on page T-xiii to evaluate each student's vocabulary, grammar, fluency, and how well he or she completes the task.
- *Optional:* After each pair finishes, discuss the strengths and weakness of each performance either in front of the class or privately.

3 READ AND REACT

STEP 1. Read about Ramona's problem.

- Say: *We are going to read about a student's problem, and then we need to think about a solution.*
- Read the directions.
- Read the story while students follow along silently. Pause after each sentence to allow time for students to comprehend. Periodically stop and ask simple *Wh-* questions to check comprehension (for example, *Who is Mike? What does Mike often do? Where is Mike going tonight? Who has to cover Mike's hours?*).

STEP 2. PAIRS. What is Ramona's problem?...

- Ask: *What is Ramona's problem?* (Ramona's boss asked her to cover her co-worker Mike's hours. Ramona doesn't want to work late tonight.)
- Pair students. Read the ideas in the list. Give pairs a couple of minutes to discuss possible solutions for Ramona.
- Ask: *Which ideas are good?* Call on students to say their opinion about the ideas in the list (for example, S: *I think she can say, "I'm sorry I can't work late tonight." This is a good idea.*).
- Now tell pairs to think of one new idea not in the list (for example, *She can talk to Mike. She can say, "When you call in sick, I have to work late."*) and to write it in the blank. Encourage students to think of more than one idea and to write them in their notebooks.
- Call on pairs to say their additional solutions. Write any particularly good ones on the board and ask students if they think it is a good idea too (*Do you think this is a good idea? Why or why not?*).

▄▄ MULTILEVEL INSTRUCTION for STEP 2

Cross-ability If possible, pair students with the same first language. The higher-level partner helps the lower-level student to say his or her idea in English.

4 CONNECT

Turn to page 252 for the Goal-setting Activity and page 280 for the Team Project. See page T-xi for general notes about teaching these activities.

Progress Check

Which goals can you check off? Go back to page 125.
Ask students to turn to page 125 and check off any remaining goals they have reached. Call on students to say which goals they will practice outside of class.

Job Hunting

Classroom Materials/Extra Practice

CD 2
Tracks 47–58

Transparencies 8.1–8.6
Vocabulary Cards Unit 8

MCA
Unit 8

Workbook
Unit 8

Interactive Practice
Unit 8

Unit Overview

Goals
- See the list of goals on the facing page.

Grammar
- *Can* to express ability: affirmative and negative statements, *Yes / No* questions and short answers
- Time expressions with *ago*, *last*, *in*, and *later*
- Ways to express alternatives: *or*, *and*

Pronunciation
- *Can* and *can't*
- Intonation of questions with *or*

Reading
- Read an article about jobs in the U.S.
- *Reading Skill:* Predicting the topic

Writing
- Write about your dream job
- Write about your job skills and work history
- Write about the job you want in five years

Life Skills Writing
- Complete a job application

Preview

- Set the context of the unit by asking questions about jobs (for example, *Do you work? What's your job? What things do you have to do for your job? Do you like your job?*).
- Hold up page 145 or show Transparency 8.1. Read the unit title and ask the class to repeat.
- As needed, explain: Job hunting *means looking for a new job.*
- Say: *Look at the picture.* Ask the Preview question: *What are the people doing?* (shaking hands, talking)
- Say: *Look at the picture and the unit title. What is the reason for this meeting?* (It's a job interview.) Point to the man and ask: *What does he want?* (a new job) Point to the papers on the table and ask: *What do you think these are?* (a job application)

Goals

- Point to the Unit Goals. Explain that this list shows what the class will be studying in this unit.
- Tell students to read the goals silently.
- Say each goal and ask the class to repeat. Explain unfamiliar vocabulary as needed:

    Duties: things you have to do for a job

    Skills: things you can do, abilities you have

    Help-wanted ads: section of the newspaper that lists job openings

    Availability: when you can work

- Tell students to circle one goal that is very important to them. Call on several students to say the goal they circled.

Job Hunting

Preview

Look at the title of the unit and the picture. What are the people doing?

UNIT GOALS

- ☐ Identify job duties

- ☐ Talk about your skills at a job interview

- ☐ Read help-wanted ads

- ☐ Complete a job application

- ☐ Answer questions about work history

- ☐ Answer questions about availability

1 WHAT DO YOU KNOW?

A CLASS. Look at the pictures. Which jobs do you know? Use words from the box.

> computer system administrator
> food service worker
> manager
> nurse assistant
> receptionist
> sales associate
> stock clerk
> warehouse worker

B CLASS. Look at the pictures. What are some duties, or things you have to do, for each job?

CD2 T47
C Listen to the job duties. Then listen and repeat.

2 PRACTICE

A PAIRS. Student A, say a job from *What do you know?* Student B, say two job duties for that job.

A: *Manager.*
B: *Plan work schedules. Supervise employees.*

B WORD PLAY. GROUPS OF 3. Look at the list of job duties. On a separate piece of paper, write another job duty for each job.

1A

1B

3A

3B

5A

5B

7A

7B

Getting Started   15 minutes

1 WHAT DO YOU KNOW?

Ⓐ CLASS. Look at the pictures. Which jobs...

- Show Transparency 8.2 or hold up the book. Tell students to cover the list of words on page 147.
- Tell students to look at the jobs in the box. Say the jobs and ask the class to repeat.
- Number from 1 to 7 on the board. Read the directions. Tell students to match the jobs from the box with the pairs of pictures.
- As students call out answers (for example, *Number 2 is a nurse assistant.*), write them on the board: *1. computer system administrator, 3. warehouse worker, 4. sales associate/stock clerk, 5. receptionist, 6. food service worker, 7. manager.* Help students pronounce the jobs if they have difficulty.
- If students call out an incorrect job, change the student's answer into a question for the class (for example, *Number 5 is a manager?*).
- Tell students to label the pairs of pictures or write the picture numbers next to the jobs in the box.
- Point to each pair of pictures, say the job, and ask the class to repeat again.

Ⓑ CLASS. Look at the pictures. What are some...

- Show Transparency 8.2 or hold up the book. Tell students to cover the list of words on page 147.
- Read the directions. Say: *Look at the pictures. What are the people doing?*
- Brainstorm duties and write them next to the jobs on the board. (Phrase the duties in the same way as the job duties listed on page 147, beginning with the base form of a verb.) Try to brainstorm at least one duty for each job.

Presentation   5 minutes

Ⓒ 💿 Listen to the job duties. Then...

- Read the directions. Play CD 2 Track 47. Pause after number 7B (*plan work schedules*).
- Say each job duty in random order and ask students to point to the appropriate picture.
- Resume playing Track 47. Students listen and repeat.

Teaching Tip

To make sure students are connecting the new words with their meanings, tell them to point to the pictures as they listen / listen and repeat.

Controlled Practice   15 minutes

2 PRACTICE

Ⓐ PAIRS. Student A, say a job from *What do you...*

- Read the directions. Ask two on-level students to read the example.
- Ask an above-level student to stand up and play Speaker A. Tell the class that they are Speaker B. The above-level student says a few jobs and the class calls out the corresponding duties.
- Pair students. Tell them to take turns playing Speakers A and B.
- To wrap up, say each pair of job duties and ask the class to call out the job.

▰▰ MULTILEVEL INSTRUCTION for 2A

Cross-ability The higher-level student covers the list of job duties on page 147. The lower-level student consults the list to say job duties and to check the higher-level student's answers.

Ⓑ WORD PLAY. GROUPS OF 3. Look at the list...

- Read the directions.
- On the board, write: *1. computer system administrator: A. install computer hardware, B. help with computer problems, C. _____.* Point to *C* and ask: *What other things do computer system administrators do?* List students' ideas on the board.
- Form groups of 3. Assign a recorder in each group. Tell groups to brainstorm ideas and then choose one additional duty for each job.
- *Optional:* If students have Internet access in your classroom, allow them to search using the job title and duties.
- Write the jobs as headings on the board. Ask one student from each group (not the recorder) to write a duty for each job on the board. Read the additional duties for each job. Make corrections as necessary.

Learning Strategy: Make connections

- Provide each student with five index cards or tell students to cut up notebook paper into five pieces.
- Read the directions. Draw two rectangles on the board representing the two sides of a card. Write a job duty in one and the corresponding job in the other.
- Walk around as students work. If misspellings occur, tell them to check the list on page 147.
- Say: *You can learn new words by pairing them with related words.* Remind students to use this strategy to remember other new vocabulary.

Communicative Practice   15 minutes

Show what you know!

STEP 1. Think of your dream job. What is the title...

- Tell students to look at the list of job duties and underline the duties they would like to do for a job.
- Read the directions. Say: *A dream job is a job that you would love to have.*
- Write your dream job title and three duties on the board and read them.
- Tell students to choose a job from the list on page 146 or a different job. Say: *To get an idea of what job you would enjoy, look at the duties you underlined.*
- Walk around and help students who choose a different job.

STEP 2. GROUPS OF 3. Tell your classmates...

- Read the directions. Form groups of 3.
- Model the activity. Tell the class about your dream job. Point to the job title and duties on the board. Say: *My dream job is _____. The duties are . . .*
- *Optional:* Say: *Or you can add -s to the verbs and say what a person with your dream job does.* Point to the job title and duties on the board. Say: *My dream job is _____. A [your dream job] . . . (helps, prepares, plans,* etc.).

MULTILEVEL INSTRUCTION

Pre-level Provide a prompt. On the board, write: *My dream job is _____. The duties are . . .*

Above-level Walk around and encourage students to use the third-person singular -s to talk about the duties of their dream job.

Extra Practice	
Interactive Practice	pages 86–87

2A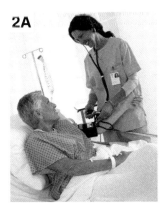

2B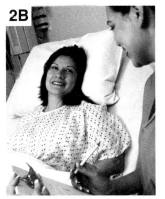

4A

4B

6A

6B

Job Duties

1A. install computer hardware
1B. help with computer problems

2A. take care of patients
2B. record patient information

3A. receive shipments
3B. unload materials

4A. assist customers
4B. stock shelves

5A. greet visitors
5B. handle phone calls

6A. prepare food
6B. clean kitchen equipment

7A. supervise employees
7B. plan work schedules

Learning Strategy

Make connections

Look at the list of job duties. Make cards for five new words. Write a job duty on one side of the card. Write a job that matches that duty on the other side.

Show what you know!

STEP 1. Think of your dream job. What is the title of your job? Answers will vary.
What are the duties?

Job title: _____

Job duties: _____ _____ _____

STEP 2. GROUPS OF 3. Tell your classmates about your dream job.

Talk about your skills at a job interview

Listening and Speaking

1 BEFORE YOU LISTEN

CLASS. Look at the job skills. Which skills do you have?

operate a forklift

use a word-processing program

use a cash register

order supplies

type

CUSTOMER SERVICE
Hablo español.
speak Spanish

2 LISTEN

A CLASS. Look at the picture of Albert and Manny. Guess: What is happening?

CD2 T48

B Listen to the conversation. Was your guess in Exercise A correct?

CD2 T48

C Listen again. Complete the sentences.

1. _____ is a store manager.
   a. Manny   (b.) Albert

2. _____ is looking for a job.
   (a.) Manny   b. Albert

3. Manny assists customers and _____ at his job.
   (a.) stocks shelves   b. orders supplies

4. Manny _____ use a cash register.
   a. can   (b.) can't

Talk about your skills at a job interview

Getting Started
10 minutes

1 BEFORE YOU LISTEN

CLASS. Look at the job skills. Which skills do you...

- Tell students to look at the job skills. Say each skill and ask the class to repeat.
- Act out each skill in random order. As you act, talk about what you're doing. For example, sit down at your computer and say: *I'm writing a letter.* Tell the class to call out the skill (*use a word-processing program*).
- Read the directions.
- Talk about your skills. Say: *I can . . . I can't . . .*
- Tell students to circle the skills they have.
- For each skill, ask the class: *Who can (operate a forklift)?* Ask for a show of hands.

EXPANSION: Vocabulary and writing for 1

- Ask students to look at the job duties on page 147 and circle the skills they have.
- Tell student to write a list of their skills, using the vocabulary from pages 147 and 148.
- Say: *Exchange lists with a partner. Read your partner's list and suggest a job for him or her. You can say: I think _____ is a good job for you.*

Presentation
15 minutes

2 LISTEN

A CLASS. Look at the picture of Albert and...

- Read the directions.
- Tell students to look at the picture and label Albert (on the left) and Manny.
- Ask: *What is happening?*
- Elicit students' guesses and list them on the board.
- Tell students they will listen for the answer in Exercise B.

B Listen to the conversation. Was your...

- Read the directions.
- Play CD 2, Track 48. Students listen.
- Ask: *What is happening?* Read the guesses on the board. Elicit and circle the best answer. (Albert is interviewing Manny.)

Teaching Tip

Optional: Remember that if students need additional support, tell them to read the Audio Script on page 303 as they listen to the conversations.

C Listen again. Complete...

- Read the directions. Tell students to read the sentences and answer choices silently.
- Play Track 48 again. Students listen and complete the sentences.
- Call on students to read the sentences.
- Tell students to look at the picture and ask: *What does Albert have in his hand?* (Manny's application)
- To review, ask: *What are Manny's duties in the job he has now?* (assist customers, stock shelves) Tell students to look at the list of job duties on page 147. Ask: *What is Manny's current job?* (sales associate / stock clerk)

Culture Connection

- Tell students to look at the picture of Albert and Manny. Ask: *How is Manny dressed for his interview?* (professionally—dress shirt and pants, tucked-in shirt, belt) Explain: *Even if regular employees dress casually, you should wear business clothes for your interview. It's important to be neat and clean. Don't wear too much jewelry, perfume, or aftershave.*
- Tell students to look at the picture again. Ask: *Where is Manny looking?* (at Albert's eyes) Explain: *It's important to look an interviewer in the eye. In the U.S., making eye contact shows confidence. If you avoid making eye contact, you'll make the interviewer uncomfortable—and he or she may even think that you're not telling the truth.*
- Tell students to look at the picture once more. Ask: *What are Albert and Manny doing?* (shaking hands) Explain: *It's a good idea to shake hands at the beginning and end of a job interview. Your handshake should be firm, and you should make eye contact and speak as you shake. At the beginning of an interview, you can say:* Nice to meet you. *At the end of an interview, you can say:* Thank you for your time.
- Tell students to practice a firm handshake with a partner. Remind them to make eye contact and speak as they shake.

Lesson 2 Talk about your skills at a job interview

Controlled Practice 10 minutes

3 CONVERSATION

A 🔊 **Listen. Then listen and repeat...**

- Read the first two sentences of the Pronunciation Watch note.
- Tell students to look at the sentences and underline *can*. Write the three sentences with *can* on the board. Point to *can* in each sentence and ask: *Does another word come after it?* In *I can learn* and *Can you speak Chinese?*, label *can: weak*.
- Read the third sentence of the Pronunciation Watch note. Point to *Yes, I can* on the board. Ask: *Does* can *have a weak or a strong pronunciation?* Label *can* in this sentence: *strong*.
- Read the last sentence of the Pronunciation Watch note. Write *I can't use a cash register* on the board. Underline *can't* and ask: *Does it have a weak or a strong pronunciation?* Label *can't: strong*.
- Play CD 2, Track 49. Students listen.
- Resume playing Track 49. Students listen and repeat.

B 🔊 **Listen and repeat the conversation.**

- Note: This conversation is the same one students heard in Exercise 2B on page 148.
- Tell students to read the conversation silently and underline *can* and *can't*.
- Tell students to read the Pronunciation Watch note again and label each *can* or *can't* they underlined *weak* or *strong*.
- Play CD 2, Track 50. Students listen and repeat. Tell them to pay particular attention to their pronunciation of *can / can't*.

Communicative Practice 25 minutes

4 PRACTICE

A **PAIRS. Practice the conversation. Then make new...**

- Pair students and tell them to practice the conversation in Exercise 3B. Walk around and help with pronunciation. Pay particular attention to students' pronunciation of *can* and *can't*.

- Then, in Exercise 4A, tell students to look at the information in the boxes. Say the duties / skills in each row and ask the class to repeat. At the end of each row, ask: *What job are these duties / skills for?* (row 1: warehouse worker; row 2: receptionist; row 3: food service worker)
- Ask two above-level students to practice a conversation for the class. Tell Student B to choose a blue and a green duty from the same row in the boxes. Tell Student A to use the red skill from the same row.
- Tell pairs to use information from the same row in the boxes to fill in the blanks.
- Walk around and check that students correctly substitute names and information into the conversation. Listen for correct pronunciation of *can* and *can't* in the last two lines of the conversation.
- Call on groups to perform for the class.

B **ROLE PLAY. PAIRS. Make your own...**

- Model the activity. On the board, write a job from the list on page 146. Ask: *What are three duties / skills for this job?* Write the duties / skills on the board. For example: *nurse assistant—take care of patients, record patient information, speak Spanish.*
- Label the first two duties / skills on the board: *B*. Label the last duty / skill: *A*.
- Play Speaker B and practice the conversation in Exercise 4A with an above-level student. Use the first two duties / skills on the board. Prompt Student A to use the third one.
- Tell students to choose a job they would like from the list on page 146 or a different job. Tell them to note three duties / skills for the job. Direct them to label the first two duties / skills: *B* and the last duty / skill: *A*.
- Pair students and tell them to practice the conversation.
- Walk around and check that students correctly substitute names and information into the conversation. Listen for correct pronunciation of *can* and *can't* in the last two lines of the conversation.
- Call on pairs to perform for the class. Ask the class to listen and guess the job that Student B is applying for.

Extra Practice

Interactive Practice

3 CONVERSATION

Pronunciation Watch

Can often has a weak pronunciation with a short, quiet vowel when another workd comes after it. It sounds like "c'n." *Can* has a strong pronunciation at the end of a sentence. *Can't* always has a strong pronunciation.

CD2 T49

A 🔘 **Listen. Then listen and repeat the sentences.**

I can't use a cash register.   I can learn.

Can you speak Chinese?   Yes, I can.

CD2 T50

B 🔘 **Listen and repeat the conversation.**

Albert: Manny? Hi, I'm Albert Taylor, the store manager. Please have a seat.

Manny: Thank you. It's nice to meet you.

Albert: I have your application here. I see that you are working now. What are your job duties?

Manny: Well, I assist customers and stock shelves.

Albert: OK. Tell me about your skills. Can you use a cash register?

Manny: No, I can't, but I can learn.

4 PRACTICE

A PAIRS. **Practice the conversation. Then make new conversations. Use your own names and the information in the boxes.**

A: _____? Hi, I'm _____, the store manager. Please have a seat.

B: Thank you. It's nice to meet you.

A: I have your application here. I see that you are working now. What are your job duties?

B: Well, I   and   .

A: OK. Tell me more about your skills. Can you   ?

B: No, I can't, but I can learn.

receive shipments	unload materials	**operate a forklift**
greet visitors	handle phone calls	**type**
prepare food	clean equipment	**order supplies**

B ROLE PLAY. PAIRS. **Make your own conversations. Use different information.**

Grammar

Can to express ability

Affirmative		
You Manny We	**can**	stock shelves.

Negative			
I They She	**cannot** **can't**	**speak**	Chinese.

Yes/No questions		
Can	you	**use** a cash register?

Short answers					
Yes,	I	**can.**	**No,**	I	**can't.**

Grammar Watch

- Use *can* + the base form of the verb.
- *Can't = cannot.* We use *can't* more often.

---

1 PRACTICE

A **Look at the pictures. Write one question with *can* for each picture.**

Answers will vary but could include:

1. <u>Can Nadia lift heavy boxes?</u>

   No, she can't.

2. Can Mike fix a leaky sink?

   No, he can't.

3. Can Jerome and Lisa use a cash register?

   No, they can't.

B **PAIRS. Ask and answer the questions in Exercise A.**

A: *Can Nadia lift heavy boxes?*
B: *No, she can't.*

Getting Started   6 minutes

- Say: *We're going to study* can *to express ability. In the conversation on page 149, Albert and Manny used this grammar.*
- Play CD 2, Track 50. Students listen. Write on the board: *Can you use a cash register? No, I can't, but I can learn.* Underline *Can, can't,* and *can.*

Presentation   15 minutes

Can to express ability

- Copy the grammar charts onto the board or show Transparency 8.3 and cover the exercise.
- Read the sentences in the charts and tell the class to repeat.
- Read the Grammar Watch note out loud and ask the class to read along silently.
- On the board, write: *I can speak English.* Underline *can* and *speak* and say: *Use* can + *the base form of a verb.*
- Point to the sentence on the board and elicit two ways to make it negative. On the board, write: *I can't speak English. / I cannot speak English.* Ask: *Which do we use more often?* (*I* can't *speak English.*)
- Point to the sentence *I can speak English* and ask the class to make a *Yes / No* question. Write: *Can you speak English?* Ask a few students the question and elicit the short answer: *Yes, I can.* Ask a few students: *Can your mother / father / grandparents speak English?* to elicit the short answer: *No, she / he / they can't.*
- If you are using the transparency, do the exercise with the class.

Language Note

Ask: *What is the negative of* can? Number from 1 to 3 on the board. Elicit and write *can't* and *cannot.* Say: *Use* can't *in informal conversation: I can't go to the party. In more formal speech and writing, don't use abbreviations.* On the board, write: *The president cannot / can not attend the event.* Point to *cannot* and say: *Both spellings are correct, but* cannot *as one word is more usual.* Write *cannot* next to number 3.

Controlled Practice   20 minutes

1   PRACTICE

Ⓐ Look at the pictures. Write one question with *can...*

- Read the directions and the example.
- Elicit another question for item 1: *Can Nadia type / use a computer?*
- Remind students to use the base form of the verb and to begin each question with a capital *C* and end with a question mark.
- Walk around and help with vocabulary and spelling as needed. Check that students form *Yes / No* questions correctly.

Ⓑ PAIRS. Ask and answer the questions in Exercise A.

- Read the directions.
- Play Speaker A and model the example with an above-level student. Model continuing the activity by asking another question: *Can Nadia type?* Elicit the short answer: *Yes, she can.*
- Pair students. Walk around and check Student B's use of pronouns.
- Call on three pairs to ask and answer the questions for the class. Make corrections as necessary.

■■■ **MULTILEVEL INSTRUCTION FOR 1B**
Cross-ability Direct the lower-level student to play the role of Speaker A first so that he or she has the short answers modeled before having to produce them.

■■■ **EXPANSION: Grammar and speaking practice for 1B**

- Tell students to change the subject of the questions in Exercise 1A to *you.*
- Direct pairs to ask each other the questions in Exercise 1A (for example, A: *Can you lift heavy boxes?* B: *Yes, I can.*).

2 PRACTICE

Ⓐ PAIRS. Look at Luisa's job application. Ask...

- Read the directions.
- Tell students to look at the application. Say the skills and ask the class to repeat. Explain: Sort materials *means organize them. For example, a warehouse worker puts boxes that are going to New York, Philadelphia, and Washington, D.C., in different areas of the warehouse.* To illustrate, draw boxes labeled *NYC, Phila.,* and *D.C.* in three separate areas on the board.
- Tell students to look at the example. Read A's question. Tell students to point to *use a computer* on the application. Ask: *Did Luisa check* use a computer? (No.) *Can she use a computer?* (No.)
- Pair students. Say: *One partner asks questions about Luisa's office skills. The other partner asks questions about Luisa's warehouse skills.*
- Call on one pair to ask and answer questions about Luisa's office skills. Call on another pair to ask and answer questions about Luisa's warehouse skills.

Ⓑ WRITE. Write sentences about Luisa's skills. Use...

- Read the directions. Tell students to write one sentence for each skill on the application.
- Remind students to use the base form of the verbs. Remind them to begin each sentence with a capital letter and end with a period.
- Walk around and spot-check students' grammar and punctuation.

EXPANSION: Pronunciation practice for 2B

- Pair students and direct them to take turns reading the sentences in Exercise 2B out loud. Tell them to practice the weak pronunciation of *can* and the strong pronunciation of *can't.*
- Walk around and monitor students' pronunciation. Model as needed.

Ⓒ WRITE. Look at the skills on the application...

- Read the directions.
- Tell students to look at the application and check the skills they have. Direct them to make their checkmarks to the right of each skill.
- Model the activity by writing one sentence about your skills on the board (for example, *I can use a computer.*).

Communicative Practice   20 minutes

Show what you know!

STEP 1. Write three questions to ask your group...

- Read the directions.
- Tell students to choose three skills and complete the questions in the chart. Tell them to look at the vocabulary on pages 147 and 148 and Luisa's application for ideas.
- Draw the chart on the board. Ask three students to come to the board and complete the questions.

STEP 2. GROUPS OF 4. Interview each member...

- Read the directions.
- Use the chart on the board to model the activity. Ask three students the questions on the chart. Record the students' names and answers.
- Form groups of 4. Direct students to ask each partner one question. Remind students to use short answers: *Yes, I can* or *No, I can't.*

STEP 3. Tell the class about your group's job skills.

- Read the directions.
- Use the chart on the board to model the activity. Point to each row of the chart and form a sentence with *can* or *can't* about the student's skills.
- Call on students to talk about their group's job skills.

MULTILEVEL INSTRUCTION for STEP 3

Pre-level Students write sentences about their group's skills before they report to the class.

Progress Check

Can you . . . talk about your skills at a job interview?

Say: *We have practiced talking about skills at a job interview. Look at the question at the bottom of the page. Can you talk about your skills at a job interview?* Tell students to write a checkmark in the box.

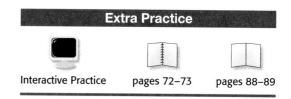

Extra Practice		
Interactive Practice	pages 72–73	pages 88–89

PRACTICE

A PAIRS. **Look at Luisa's job application. Ask and answer questions about Luisa's skills. Use** *can*.

A: *Can Luisa use a computer?*
B: *No, she can't.*

Luisa Ruiz

Please check the skills you have.

Office skills
❑ use a computer
☑ answer the phone
☑ record information

Warehouse skills
❑ operate a forklift
☑ sort materials
❑ lift up to 50 lbs.

B WRITE. **Write sentences about Luisa's skills. Use** *can* **and** *can't*.

1. Luisa can't use a computer.

2. Luisa can't operate a forklift.

3. Luisa can't lift up to 50 lbs.

4. Luisa can answer the phone.

5. Luisa can record information.

6. Luisa can sort materials.

C WRITE. **Look at the skills on the application in Exercise A. Write sentences about things you can and can't do.** Answers will vary.

1. _____

2. _____

3. _____

4. _____

Show what you know! Talk about your skills at a job interview

STEP 1. **Write three questions to ask your group about their job skills.**
Answers will vary.

Question	Name	Answer
Can you use a computer?	Paola	Yes
1. Can you		
2. Can you		
3. Can you		

STEP 2. GROUPS OF 4. **Interview each member of your group. Ask one of your questions. Complete the chart in Step 1.**

STEP 3. **Tell the class about your group's job skills.**

Paola can use a computer. Juan can . . .

Can you… talk about your skills at a job interview? ❑

Life Skills

1 READ HELP-WANTED ADS

A CLASS. Look at the help-wanted ads. Where can you find these ads? Where else can people find out about jobs?

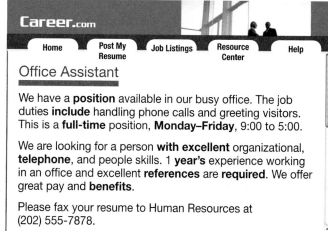

B Read the help-wanted ads. Look at the words in bold. Match the words and the abbreviations. Write the full words.

1. hr. ___*hour*___

2. M–F ___Monday–Friday___

3. PT ___part-time___

4. FT ___full-time___

5. excel. ___excellent___

6. yr. ___year___

7. tel. ___telephone___

8. pos. ___position___

9. bnfts. ___benefits___

10. req. ___required___

11. pref. ___preferred___

12. exp. ___experience___

13. ref. ___references___

14. incl. ___include___

15. w/ ___with___

16. eve. ___evening___

C PAIRS. Compare your answers.

D PAIRS. Read the help-wanted ads again. Student A, describe the car service driver job. Student B, describe the office assistant job.

Getting Started   5 minutes

Culture Connection

- Ask: *Did you have a job in your home country? How did you find it? How do people usually find out about jobs in your country?*
- List students' responses on the board. If *help-wanted ads* is on the board, circle it and say: *We're going to read help-wanted ads in English.* If *help-wanted ads* is not on the list, ask: *Do people use help-wanted ads to find jobs in your home country?*

Presentation   20 minutes

1   READ HELP-WANTED ADS

A CLASS. Look at the help-wanted ads. Where can...

- Direct students to look at the help-wanted ads and circle the names of the websites (*Job-ads.com* and *Career.com*). Ask: *Where can you find these ads?* (on the Internet)
- Ask the class if they know any job-search websites. List them on the board.
- Ask: *Where else can people find out about jobs?* (the newspaper, local newsletters, community bulletin boards, job fairs, friends and family) Ask: *Do you work? Where did you find out about your job?*

B Read the help-wanted ads. Look at the words...

- Read the help-wanted ads. After you read each ad, ask: *What is the job?* (driver; office assistant) *What skill(s) do you need for the job?* (drive; organizational, telephone, and people skills)
- Read the directions.
- Direct students to look at item 1. Tell them to find and point to the word *hour* in the ads.
- Direct students to look at item 2. Say: *Look at the words in bold in the ads. What do you think M–F is an abbreviation for?* (Monday–Friday)
- Tell students to match as many words and abbreviations as they can.

C PAIRS. Compare your answers.

- Pair students and tell them to fill in missing answers and make corrections as necessary.
- Say the correct answers and ask the class to repeat.

- Optional: Review unfamiliar vocabulary, as needed, by asking questions about the ads:

    part-time / full-time: *Which job is part-time?* (driver) *Which job is full-time?* (office assistant) *What are the hours of the full-time job?* (Monday–Friday, 9:00–5:00) *How many hours a week is that?* (40 hours) *How many hours a week is a part-time job?* (fewer than 40 hours)

    benefits: *Which job offers benefits?* (office assistant) *What types of benefits do some people get from their jobs?* (health insurance, dental insurance, retirement plans, paid vacation, etc.)

    required / preferred: *Which job do you need experience for?* (office assistant) *What word in the ad tells you that experience is necessary?* (required) *Do you need experience for the driver job?* (No.) *Would the car service company like to find a driver with experience?* (Yes.) *What word in the ad tells you that experience is important but not necessary?* (preferred)

    references: *Which job do you need references for?* (office assistant) *What is the sentence in the ad with the word* references? (1 year's experience . . . and excellent references . . .) *So, if* references *are related to your experience, what do you think* references *are?* (people you have worked for in the past who can talk about your skills and say that you would be good for the job)

EXPANSION: Writing practice for 1C

- Tell students to rewrite one of the ads using the abbreviations in place of the words in bold.

Communicative Practice   5 minutes

D PAIRS. Read the help-wanted ads again....

- Read the directions. Pair students.
- List talking points on the board: *hours, experience, pay, how to apply.* Tell students to highlight or underline this information in their ad.
- Call on students to describe the jobs for the class.

MULTILEVEL INSTRUCTION for 1D

Cross-ability Direct the higher-level student to play Speaker A and talk first. The lower-level student (playing Speaker B) can say the talking point (for example, *hours*) and then read the highlighted information in the office assistant ad.

Controlled Practice   15 minutes

2 PRACTICE

A **Read the help-wanted ads. Then read the sentences....**

- Tell students to read the help-wanted ads silently.
- Read the directions and the example. Ask: *What is the abbreviation for part-time?* (*PT*) Tell students to highlight or underline *PT* in ad c.
- Say: *When you find an answer, highlight or underline the information in the ad.*

B **PAIRS. Compare your answers.**

- Students compare answers with a partner and make corrections as necessary.
- Call on one student to read the sentences about job a, one student to read the sentences about job b, and one to read the sentences about job c.

▬ **EXPANSION: Vocabulary practice for 2B**

- Pair students. Tell partners to choose one ad each from Exercise 2A.
- Tell students to read the ad to their partner, substituting full words for the abbreviations.

Communicative Practice   15 minutes

C **GROUPS OF 3. Look at the ads on this page and...**

- Draw the following chart on the board:

	PT	FT	eve./ weekend hrs.	exp.	ref.	bnfts.
job a		✓				
job b						
job c						

- Complete the row for job a as a class. Ask: *Is job a part-time?* (No.) *Is it full-time?* (Yes.) *Do you have to work evenings and/or weekends?* (No.) *Do you need experience?* (Yes.) *Do you need references?* (No.) *Does it offer benefits?* (Yes.) Make checkmarks in the appropriate columns for *yes* answers.
- Tell students to complete the rows for jobs b and c.

- Ask two students to complete the chart on the board. Ask the class if the chart is correct. Make corrections as necessary.
- Read the directions.
- On the chart on the board, circle *job a* and the checkmark under *FT*. Read the example.
- Tell students to look at the chart and circle the job they're interested in and the reason(s).
- Form groups of 3. Walk around and help students phrase their reason as needed.
- To wrap up, ask: *Which job are you interested in?* Ask for a show of hands for the receptionist job, the store manager job, and the sales associate job. Write the most popular job on the board. Ask: *Why?* Elicit reasons from the class and list them on the board.

▬ **MULTILEVEL INSTRUCTION for 2C**

Pre-level Direct students to write a sentence similar to the example before they talk with their group.

Above-level Direct students to give several reasons why they are interested in the job.

3 LIFE SKILLS WRITING

Turn to page 263 and ask students to complete the job application. See pages T-xi–T-xii for general notes about Life Skills Writing activities.

Progress Check

Can you . . . read help-wanted ads?

Say: *We have practiced reading help-wanted ads. Now, look at the question at the bottom of the page. Can you read help-wanted ads?* Tell students to write a checkmark in the box.

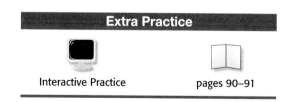

Extra Practice	
Interactive Practice	pages 90–91

A Read the help-wanted ads. Then read the sentences. Write the letter of the job.

HELP WANTED

RECEPTIONIST	STORE MANAGER	SALES ASSOCIATE AT JOE'S COOL CLOTHES
FT pos. M-F in busy medical office. 2 yr. exp. req. Need good computer and tel. skills. Great pay and bnfts. FAX resume to (802) 555-2149 or send to gmoss@HealthPractice.com.	FT pos. avail. Duties incl. supervise employees, plan work schedule, assist customers. Looking for a person w/ excel. people skills. 1 yr. manager exp. req. Exp. in office supply stores pref. Excel. ref. req. Some weekend hrs. Call Manuel for an interview at (802) 555-9814.	PT. eve. and weekend hrs. $10/hr. No exp. necessary. Apply in person at store. Liberty Mall. No calls, please.
a	**b**	**c**

1. __c__ This is a part-time job.

2. __a__ This job has good benefits.

3. __c__ This job pays $10 an hour.

4. __c__ Go to the store to apply for this job.

5. __b__ Call the store to apply for this job.

6. __a__ Send a résumé to apply for this job.

7. __b__ You need excellent people skills for this job.

8. __b__ You need excellent references to get this job.

9. __a__ You need two years' experience for this job.

10. __c__ You don't need experience for this job.

B PAIRS. Compare your answers.

C GROUPS OF 3. Look at the ads on this page and on page 152. Which job are you interested in? Why?

I'm interested in the receptionist job because I need a full-time job.

3 **LIFE SKILLS WRITING**   Complete a job application. See page 263.

Can you...read help-wanted ads?   ☐

Listening and Speaking

1 BEFORE YOU LISTEN

A CLASS. **Look at the people. Read the reasons they changed jobs. What are some other reasons people change jobs?**

B PAIRS. **Have you ever changed jobs? What was the reason?**

I'd like to make more money.

I'd like a different schedule.

I'd like a job closer to home.

I'd like to do something different.

2 LISTEN

CD2 T51

A 💿 **Listen to more of Manny's job interview. Put the events in the order they happened.**

1. __3__ Manny got a job as a stock clerk.

2. __1__ Manny came to the U.S.

3. __2__ Manny got a job as a gardener.

CD2 T51

B 💿 **Listen again. Why does Manny want to change jobs?**
His life changed, and he wants to do something different.

CD2 T52

C 💿 **Listen to the whole conversation. Manny says he was unemployed. What does *unemployed* mean?**
out of work

CD2 T52

D 💿 **Listen to the whole conversation again. Answer the questions.**

1. When was Manny unemployed?
   a. two months ago   (b.) two years ago

2. Why was Manny unemployed?
   (a.) His mother was sick.   b. He was sick.

3. How long was Manny unemployed?
   a. for two years   (b.) for two months

Lesson 5 Answer questions about work history

Getting Started
10 minutes

1 BEFORE YOU LISTEN

A CLASS. **Look at the people. Read the reasons...**

- Say: *Look at the people. Read the reasons they changed jobs.*
- Read the reasons and ask: *What are some other reasons people change jobs?* Brainstorm reasons and write them on the board. Begin each reason with *I'd like . . .* (for example, *I'd like to learn new skills / a job with benefits / a promotion / to move to a new city.*).

B PAIRS. **Have you ever changed jobs? What was...**

- Read the directions.
- Ask an above-level student to ask you each question (for example, S: *Have you ever changed jobs?* T: *Yes. First I was a business manager. Then I got a job as a teacher.* S: *What was the reason?* T: *I wanted to do something different.*).
- On the board, write: *old job:* _____ / *new job:* _____ / *reason for change:* _____. Tell students to write their answers in their notebooks.
- Pair students and tell them to ask each other the questions in the directions.
- Call on a few students to answer the questions for the class.

MULTILEVEL INSTRUCTION for 1B
Pre-level Students can answer the first question *yes* or *no*.
Above-level Students can explain their reason (for example, *I wanted a job closer to home because I wanted to spend more time with my family.*).

Presentation
25 minutes

2 LISTEN

A **Listen to more of Manny's job...**

- Say: *Point to Albert. Point to Manny.* Ask: *What do you remember about them? What is Albert's job?* (store manager) *What is Manny doing?* (interviewing for a new job) *Does Manny have a job now?* (Yes.)

- Read the directions. Tell students to read the events silently. Play CD 2, Track 51. Tell students to write *1* on the space next to the event that happened first, *2* for the next event, and *3* for the last.
- Call on a student to read the events in order.

B **Listen again. Why does Manny...**

- Ask: *What is Manny's job now?* (stock clerk)
- Review the reasons to change jobs. Say them and ask the class to repeat.
- Read the directions. Tell students to listen for one of the reasons.
- Play Track 51 again. Ask: *Why does Manny want to change jobs?* (He'd like to do something different.) If the class can't answer, play Track 51 again.
- Elicit the answer and write it on the board.

Teaching Tip

Optional: Remember that if students need additional support, tell them to read the Audio Script on page 303 as they listen to the conversations.

C **Listen to the whole conversation....**

- Read the directions. Write *unemployed* on the board. Tell students to listen for Albert to say *unemployed* and then listen to Manny's explanation.
- Play CD 2, Track 52. Students listen.
- Ask: *What do you think* unemployed *means?* (He didn't have a job.) If the class can't answer, do Exercise 2D and then ask again: *What does* unemployed *mean?*
- Say *unemployed* and ask the class to repeat.

Language Note

Point out that the prefix *un-* means *not*. Explain that someone who is *unemployed* is *not* employed, or doesn't have a job.

D **Listen to the whole conversation again....**

- Read the directions. Direct students to read the questions and answers silently.
- Play Track 52 again. Students listen and circle the letter of the correct answers.
- Read the questions. The class calls out the answers.

Presentation 5 minutes

 3 CONVERSATION

 Listen and repeat the conversation.

- Note: This conversation is the same one students heard in Exercise 2A on page 154.
- Tell students to read the conversation silently.
- Read the directions. Play CD 2, Track 53. Students listen.
- Resume playing Track 53. Students listen and repeat.

Controlled Practice 10 minutes

4 PRACTICE

Ⓐ PAIRS. **Practice the conversation. Then make new...**

- Pair students and tell them to practice the conversation in Exercise 3. Tell them to take turns playing each role.
- Then in Exercise 4A, tell students to look at the information in the boxes.
- Read the directions.
- Copy the conversation onto the board with blanks. Read through the conversation. When you come to a blank, ask what color it is. Point to the box that is the same color and fill in the blank with the first item in the box.
- Ask two on-level students to practice the conversation on the board for the class.
- Erase the words in the blanks and ask two above-level students to make up a new conversation for the class.
- Tell pairs to take turns playing Speakers A and B and use the information in the boxes to fill in the blanks.
- Tell students to stand, mingle, and practice the conversation with several new partners.
- Call on pairs to practice for the class.

Communicative Practice 10 minutes

Ⓑ ROLE PLAY. PAIRS. **Make your own...**

- Provide pens or highlighters in blue, green, red, and yellow, or tell students to write the color name next to each piece of information as follows.

  Ask: *When did you come to the U.S.?* On the board, write: _____ *ago.* Tell students to note their answer in blue.

  Ask: *What was your first job in the U.S.?* Tell students to note their answer in green. (Direct students who don't work or haven't changed jobs to make up the work history information.)

  Ask: *What job do you have now?* Tell students to note their answer in red.

  Ask: *What was the reason for your job change?* Tell students to note their answer in yellow.

- Pair students and tell them to substitute their own information into the conversation in Exercise 4A.
- Walk around and remind students to switch roles.
- Call on pairs to perform for the class.

Teaching Tip

While pairs are performing role plays, using the scoring rubric for speaking on page T-xiii to evaluate each student's vocabulary, grammar, fluency, and how well he or she completes the task. You may want to review the complete rubric with the students.

Extra Practice

Interactive Practice

3 CONVERSATION

CD2 T53

🔊 **Listen and repeat the conversation.**

Albert: So, tell me more about your work experience.

Manny: Well, I came to the U.S. three years ago. First, I got a job as a gardener. Then last year I got a job as a stock clerk.

Albert: OK. So now you're a stock clerk. Why are you looking for another job?

Manny: Things in my life have changed, and now I'd like to do something different.

4 PRACTICE

Ⓐ **PAIRS. Practice the conversation. Then make new conversations. Use the information in the boxes.**

A: So, tell me more about your work experience.

B: Well, I came to the U.S. _____ ago. First, I got a job as

a _____ . Then last year I got a job as a _____ .

A: OK. So now you're a _____ . Why are you looking for

another job?

B: Things in my life have changed, and now I'd like _____ .

a year	warehouse worker	**truck driver**	to make more money
a few years	nurse assistant	**receptionist**	a different schedule
ten months	food service worker	**cook**	a job closer to home

Ⓑ **ROLE PLAY. PAIRS. Make your own conversations. Use different information.**

Answer questions about work history

Grammar

Time expressions with *ago*, *last*, *in*, and *later*

I came to the U.S.	**three years 10 months**	**ago.**	**One month**	I started school.
I got a job	**last**	**year. week.**	**Two days**	**later,** I got a better job.
I changed jobs	**in**	**July. the fall.**	**A week**	I was unemployed.

1 PRACTICE

A Complete the sentences. Use the words in the boxes.

1. ~~ago~~
    in
    last

    Teresa came to the U.S. two years ___ago___. She studied

    English ___last___ year. She got a job ___in___ December.

2. ago
    last
    later

    Six months ___ago___, Mei-Li came to the U.S. She started work in a

    factory one month ___later___. She left that job ___last___ week

    because she got a better job.

3. in
    last
    later

    ___In___ 2004, Mohammed came to the U.S. One year ___later___,

    he got a job in a supermarket. He got a new job in a warehouse

    ___last___ month.

B Write each statement a different way. Use *ago* or *in*. Answers will vary but could include:

1. Tina got a new job last month. *Tina got a new job a month ago.*

2. Inez learned to use a computer in 2001. In 2001, Inez learned to use a computer.

3. Frank got his job a year ago. A year ago, Frank got his job.

4. Walter left his job in January. In January, Walter left his job.

5. Louise started school six months ago. Six months ago, Louise started school.

6. Beatriz changed jobs last week. A week ago, Beatriz changed jobs.

Getting Started   5 minutes

- Say: *We're going to study time expressions with ago, last, in, and* later. *In the conversation on page 155, Manny used this grammar.*
- Play CD 2, Track 53. Students listen. Write on the board: *I came to the U.S. three years ago. Then last year I got a job as a stock clerk.* Underline *three years ago* and *last year.*

Presentation   10 minutes

Time expressions with *ago, last, in,* and *later*

- Copy the grammar chart onto the board or show Transparency 8.4 and cover the exercise.
- Read the sentences in the grammar chart and ask the class to repeat.
- Ask: *When did this class meet for the first time?* Write a date on the board (for example, *September 2009*). Use the date to compose sentences with *ago, last,* and *in* about when the class started (for example, *The class started four months ago. The class started last fall. The class started in September.*). Write the sentences on the board.
- Think of an event that has happened since the start of school (for example, the arrival of a new student), and write the event and date on the board. Compose a sentence with *later* (for example, *Two months later, Juan joined the class.*).
- Read the sentences on the board and ask the class to repeat.
- If you are using the transparency, do the exercise with the class.

EXPANSION

- Direct students to substitute the times in the grammar chart with their own information. Tell them to write four sentences.
- On the board, write: *I came to the U.S. _____ ago. I got a job last _____. I changed jobs in _____. _____ later, I. . . .* (Tell students to choose one of the three sentence endings.)
- Pair students and tell them to read their sentences to their partner.

Controlled Practice   30 minutes

1 PRACTICE

A Complete the sentences. Use the words in the boxes.

- Read the directions. Write the example on the board and point to the answer. Ask: *Why is the answer* ago? (because *in* and *last* go before a time)
- Students compare answers with a partner.
- Call on students to read the completed items.

B Write each statement in a different way. Use...

- Read the directions. Write the example on the board. Underline *last month* and *a month ago.* Say: *The meaning is the same.* Ask: *What month was last month?* Elicit the answer and say: *Another possible answer is:* Tina got a new job in [last month]. Write this sentence on the board.
- Write the current date on the board. Tell students to use today's date to figure out how long ago or in what month or year the events happened.
- Students compare answers with a partner.
- Call on students to read the completed sentences.

2 PRACTICE

A WRITE. Look at the time line. Write a short...

- Say: *Here is a time line about Aram's life in the U.S. You're going to write a paragraph about it.*
- Tell students to read the directions and the events on the time line silently.
- Write the example on the board. Explain: *There's another way to write about this.* Write: *Aram came to the U.S. _____ years _____.* Write the current year on the board and *2005* and elicit the class's help to rewrite the sentence with *ago*.
- Tell students to look at the first and second events on the time line. Elicit a sentence about the second event with *later* (*One / A month later, he started English classes.*).
- Tell students to write one sentence about each event. Using *in*, *ago*, and *later* at least once each. For sentences with *ago*, tell students to compare the event date with today's date. For sentences with *later*, tell students to compare an event date with the event date right before it.

B PAIRS. Compare your paragraphs.

- Pair students and tell them to exchange books and read each other's paragraphs.
- Tell partners to point out differences in their paragraphs and help each other make corrections.
- Call on a few students to read different versions of the paragraph.

Communicative Practice   15 minutes

Show what you know!

STEP 1. Answer the questions about yourself. Use...

- Read the directions.
- Ask an above-level student the questions. Write the student's answers on the board. If the student doesn't use *in*, *ago*, or *later* (or uses them incorrectly), prompt the class to help rephrase the student's response using one of the time expressions.
- Point out that students can't use *later* to answer question 1. Elicit the class's help to rephrase the student's answer to question 2 using *later*.

STEP 2. GROUPS OF 5. Take turns asking *When...*

- Ask five students: *When did you come here?* Note their names and arrival month or year on the board. If a student uses *ago* to answer, ask the class to figure out the arrival month or year.
- Elicit the class's help to put the dates on the board in order. Ask: *Who came here first? . . . Second?* etc.
- On the board, draw a time line like the one in the example with the students' names and arrival dates.
- Form groups of 5. Tell group members to count off from 1 to 5. Say: *Number 1, you are the recorder. Take notes. Write down each group member's name and arrival date.*
- Read the directions and the example. Say: *Each group member asks the person to the right:* When did you get here? *Go around the circle until everyone has asked and answered the question.*
- Say: *Now use the recorder's notes to create a time line showing when each person in your group came here. Number 2, draw the time line.*

▬▬ MULTILEVEL INSTRUCTION for STEP 2

Cross-ability Instead of telling students to count off in their groups, assign lower-level students numbers 2 and 3, higher-level students numbers 4 and 5, and on-level students number 1.

STEP 3. Draw your time line on the board. Explain...

- Point to the time line on the board and say a sentence about each event in order from left to right. Use *in*, *ago*, and *later* at least once each.
- Say: *Practice talking about your time line. Then, Number 3, draw the group's time line on the board.*
- Call on students 4 and 5 from each group to come to the board and explain the time line to the class.

Progress Check

Can you . . . answer questions about work history?

Say: *We have practiced answering questions about work history. Look at the question at the bottom of the page. Can you answer questions about work history?* Tell students to write a checkmark in the box.

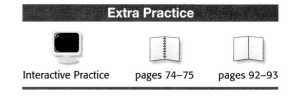

Extra Practice

Interactive Practice   pages 74–75   pages 92–93

A WRITE. Look at the time line. Write a short paragraph about Aram.
Use *in*, *ago*, and *later*. There is more than one correct answer. Answers will vary but could include:

| May, 2005 came to the U.S. | June, 2005 started English classes | January, 2006 got his first job | July, 2007 got a better job | December, 2009 became a supervisor |

Aram came to the U.S. in May, 2005. A month later, he started English classes. He

got his first job in January, 2006. Seven months later, Aram got a better job. In December 2009,

he became a supervisor.

B PAIRS. Compare your paragraphs.

Show what you know! Answer questions about work history

STEP 1. Answer the questions about yourself. Use *in*, *ago*, or *later*. Answers will vary.

1. When did you come to this country?_____
2. When did you start school here? _____

STEP 2. GROUPS OF 5. Take turns asking *When did you come here?*
Draw a time line to show when each person in the group came here.

Viktor: *I came here in July.*
Indira: *I came here four months ago.*

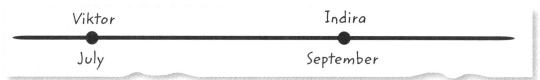

Viktor   Indira
July   September

STEP 3. Draw your time line on the board. Explain it to the class.

Can you... answer questions about work history? ☐

Reading

1 BEFORE YOU READ

A CLASS. Look at the pictures. Talk about the job market for these fields of employment in your area. Which fields have many jobs available?

agriculture

technology

health care

manufacturing

B CLASS. Look at the title of the article and the pictures. Predict: What do you think is the topic of the article?
What fields have the most jobs right now?

Reading Skill: Predicting the Topic

You can often guess what an article is about by looking at the title and any pictures. This will prepare you to understand what you read.

2 READ

CD2 T54

Listen. Read the article. Was your guess in Exercise B correct?

Today's Hot Jobs

The U.S. job market is changing fast. In 1900, 41 percent of workers had jobs on farms. Now only 2 percent of workers have agricultural jobs. In 1950, 25 percent of workers had jobs in manufacturing. Now only 12.5 percent have manufacturing jobs. So what fields of employment are growing today?

Health Care
Many of the fastest-growing jobs are in health care. The U.S. population is getting older. These older Americans need medical care and help with daily living. The greatest need is for home health aides

and physician assistants. Home health aides take care of patients in their homes. Physician assistants help doctors in a clinic or hospital.

Technology
As the field of technology changes, the jobs change, too. In the 1980s, most technology workers

were computer programmers. Now there is more need for network analysts, web designers, and software engineers. Network analysts make sure e-mail and Internet communications are working well. Web designers create Internet sites. Software engineers develop software like games and word-processing programs.

Today's jobs are in health care and technology. The job market continues to change quickly. Where will tomorrow's jobs be?

Source: U.S. Department of Labor

Getting Started   10 minutes

1   BEFORE YOU READ

Ⓐ CLASS. Look at the pictures. Talk about...

- On the board, write *job market* and explain: *When people talk about the* job market, *they're talking about whether it's easy or difficult to find jobs now and what fields the jobs are in.*
- Tell students to look at the pictures of job fields. Say each field and ask the class to repeat.
- Tell students to look at the list of jobs on page 146. Ask: *Which job is in technology?* (computer system administrator) *Which job is in health care?* (nurse assistant)
- Tell students to point to the *agriculture* picture. Ask: *Where do people with jobs in agriculture usually work?* (on a farm) Tell students to point to the *manufacturing* picture. Ask: *Where do people with jobs in manufacturing usually work?* (in a factory)
- Read the directions. Ask: *Where are the jobs in [your area]? What fields are they in?* Tell students to circle the field that it's easiest to find jobs in. Write the fields on the board. Ask: *What field did you circle?* Say each field and ask for a show of hands. Keep a tally on the board. Circle the top field(s) in your area.

  EXPANSION: Speaking practice for 1A

- Point to each of the top fields in your class and ask: *Who in the class works in (health care)? What are the job duties? What skills do you need? Do you have to interview for a job in this field? Do you need experience? Are the jobs usually full-time or part-time? Is the pay good? Do the jobs have good benefits?*
- Group students by field to the extent possible. Write the questions on the board. Tell groups to discuss and write answers.
- Ask groups to present the information to the class. Prompt students by pointing to the questions on the board.

Ⓑ CLASS. Look at the title of the article and...

- Read the Reading Skill note about predicting the topic.
- Read the directions. Ask: *What is the title of the article?* On the board, write: *Today's Hot Jobs.* Underline *hot* and say: *If something is* hot, *it's popular.* Point to the fields and tally on the board from Exercise 1A. Ask: *What jobs are hot in our area?*
- Tell students to look at the pictures in the article. Point to each picture and ask: *What field is this?* (health care; technology)
- Say: *So, the title of the article is* Today's Hot Jobs, *and the pictures show the health care and technology fields. What do you think the topic of the article is?* (The popular job fields right now are health care and technology.) Write the class's prediction on the board.

Presentation   15 minutes

2   READ

  Listen. Read the article. Was your guess...

- Play CD 2, Track 54. Students listen and read silently.
- Read the prediction from Exercise 1B on the board and ask: *Was your guess correct?*
- *Optional:* Play Track 54 again. Pause the CD after the following paragraphs and ask:

  First paragraph: *What field was hot in 1900?* (agriculture) *What field was hot in 1950?* (manufacturing) *Are these fields hot now?* (No.)

  Second paragraph: *What is one field that has many jobs available today?* (health care) *Why?* (because the U.S. population is getting older)

  Third paragraph: Ask: *What's another field that has many jobs available today?* (technology) *What was the hot technology job in the 1980s?* (computer programmer) *Is it a hot job today?* (No.)

- Ask: *Which field are you more interested in? Health care? Or technology?* Ask for a show of hands.

Controlled Practice   20 minutes

3   CHECK YOUR UNDERSTANDING

A Read the article again. What is the main idea?

- Read the directions and answer choices.
- Remind students that the *main idea* is the most important idea in the article. Ask: *Where can you usually find the main idea?* (in the first paragraph)
- Tell students to read the first paragraph again silently and then circle the letter of the main idea.
- Ask: *What is the main idea?* Write it on the board.

B Read the sentences. Circle *True* or *False*.

- Read the directions. Students compare answers with a partner. Call on students to read the sentences and say the answers.
- Tell pairs to rewrite the false sentences to make them true. Call on students to write true sentences on the board (1. In 1900, <u>41</u> percent of workers in the U.S. had agricultural jobs. 6. <u>Web designers</u> plan and make Internet sites. 7. <u>In the 1980s</u>, most technology workers <u>were</u> computer programmers. / Most technology workers are <u>network analysts, web designers, and software engineers</u>.)

C What are the fastest-growing jobs in the following...

- Point to the main idea on the board. Ask: *How is the U.S. job market changing? Where were the jobs in the past?* (agriculture and manufacturing) *Where are the jobs now?* (health care and technology)
- Read the directions. Tell students to read the article again and underline the fastest-growing jobs.
- Draw the chart on the board. Ask: *What are the fastest-growing jobs in health care? In technology?* Elicit the answers and complete the chart.

Communicative Practice   15 minutes

Show what you know!

PRE-WRITING. What job do you want to have....

- Read the directions.

- Tell students to look at the jobs they underlined in the article. Say: *Read about each job. On the chart in Exercise 3C, circle the job you're most interested in. Next to the chart, write what a person with this job does. For example,* Home health aides take care of patients in their homes.
- Ask: *What job do you want to have in five years? What do you need to do to get that job?* Tell students to note their ideas. Prompt students by asking: *What do you need to learn? Where can you learn these skills? Do you know someone who works in this field? Can you talk to this person?*

> **Teaching Tip**
>
> Increase the relevance of classroom activities with authentic materials. Bring in information from local community colleges and/or other programs that offer classes, training, and/or certification in the health care and technology fields. Tell students to look for classes they can take to help them get the job they want.

NETWORK. Find classmates who want to have...

- Tell students to stand, mingle, and ask classmates: *What job do you want to have in five years?* Say: *When you find a classmate who wants to have the same job, stay together. Look for other classmates who want to have the same job.*
- Tell students to stop and sit with their groups. Say: *Take turns talking about the things you need to do to get the job. Continue until everyone has said all their ideas. Listen and add to your notes.*

▨▨▨ MULTILEVEL INSTRUCTION
Cross-ability Direct lower-level students to say their ideas first. Higher-level students will have to produce more original ideas, such as *take a class in web design.*

WRITE. Write about the job you want in five years....

Turn to page 271 and ask students to complete the activities. See page T-xii for general notes about Writing activities.

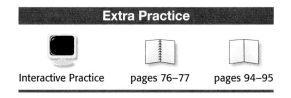

Extra Practice		
Interactive Practice	pages 76–77	pages 94–95

CHECK YOUR UNDERSTANDING

A Read the article again. What is the main idea?

    a. The number of jobs in the U.S. is growing.
    (b.) The U.S. job market is changing fast.
    c. Many of the fastest-growing jobs are in health care.

B Read the sentences. Circle *True* or *False*.

1. In 1900, 2 percent of workers in the U.S. had agricultural jobs.	True	**(False)**
2. Today, 12.5 percent of workers have jobs in manufacturing.	**(True)**	False
3. The field of health care is growing because people are getting older.	**(True)**	False
4. The number of home health aides is increasing.	**(True)**	False
5. Employers need workers with Internet skills.	**(True)**	False
6. Network analysts plan and make Internet sites.	True	**(False)**
7. Most technology workers are computer programmers now.	True	**(False)**

C What are the fastest-growing jobs in the following fields?
Complete the chart.

Health Care	home health aides	physician assistants	
Technology	network analysts	web designers	software engineers

Show what you know!

PRE-WRITING. What job do you want to have in five years? What do you need to do to get that job? Write notes.

> *nurse assistant —learn English, . . .*

NETWORK. Find classmates who want to have the same job in five years. Form a group. Talk about the things you need to do to get the job.

WRITE. Write about the job you want in five years. See page 271.

Answer questions about availability

Listening and Speaking

1 BEFORE YOU LISTEN

A **PAIRS.** Read the information about job interviews. Look at the words in boldface. What do the words mean?

> At a job interview, the interviewer asks you about your **availability**. For example,"Which **shift** can you work, day or night? and "Can you work on weekends?" The interviewer may ask if your hours are **flexible**. For example, "Can you work different hours if the schedule changes?" The interviewer also asks when you can start. If you are working, you should give your boss one or two weeks' **notice** that you are leaving your job. This will help your boss find a new employee to fill your position when you leave.

B **CLASS.** Do you work? What are your work hours? Do you like your work schedule?

2 LISTEN

CD2 T55

A 🔘 Listen to the end of Manny's interview. When does Manny prefer to work? Check all the correct answers.

☑ mornings ☐ afternoons

CD2 T55

B 🔘 Listen again. When can Manny start work?

a. tomorrow (b.)in two weeks c. in two days

CD2 T56

C 🔘 Listen to the whole conversation. Answer the questions.

1. Manny asks, "When can I expect to hear from you?" What does this mean? "When will I know if I got the job?"

2. At the end of the interview, does Manny know if he got the job? No

Getting Started 10 minutes

1 BEFORE YOU LISTEN

A PAIRS. **Read the information about job...**

- Read the directions.
- Tell students to look at the paragraph. Ask: *What are the words in boldface?* On the board, write: *availability*, *shift*, *flexible*, and *notice*.
- Tell students to read the paragraph silently.
- Read the first two sentences out loud, stressing *For example.* Ask the class: *What do you think* availability *means?* Elicit a definition and write it on the board (for example, *when you can work*).
- Pair students and tell them to read the first two sentences again and write a definition for *shift.* Call on pairs to read their definition. Write a definition on the board (for example, *the time of day when you work*).
- Tell pairs to read the next two sentences (starting with *The interviewer may ask . . .*) and write a definition for *flexible.* Call on pairs to read their definition. Write a definition on the board (for example, *you can change your hours if necessary*).
- Tell pairs to read the last three sentences (starting with *The interviewer also asks . . .*) and write a definition for *notice.* Call on pairs to read their definition. Write a definition on the board (for example, *telling your boss that you are leaving your job*).
- Say each word in boldface and ask the class to repeat.

B CLASS. **Do you work? What are your work...**

- Read the first two questions. Tell students who work to note their hours. Tell students who don't work to note their availability.
- Note your work hours on the board. Ask an above-level student to ask you each question in the directions. Talk about your work hours (PT or FT, M–F or evening / weekend hrs.) and whether or not you like your work schedule.
- Ask the class: *Who works?* Ask a few students who raise their hands: *What are your work hours? Do you like your work schedule?*

Presentation 20 minutes

2 LISTEN

A 🖸 **Listen to the end of Manny's interview....**

- Ask: *What do you think Albert and Manny are talking about now?* (Manny's availability)
- Read the directions and answer choices. Tell students to underline *prefer.*
- Play CD 2, Track 55.
- Ask: *When does Manny prefer to work?* (mornings)
- Ask: *Manny prefers the morning shift, but can he work the afternoon shift if Albert needs him to?* (Yes. He's flexible.)

B 🖸 **Listen again. When can Manny...**

- Read the directions and answer choices.
- Play Track 55 again. Read the question again. Call on a student to say the answer.
- Ask: *Why can't he start tomorrow?* (because he needs to give two weeks' notice at his job)

C 🖸 **Listen to the whole conversation....**

- Read the directions. Tell students to read the questions silently.
- Play CD 2, Track 56.
- Read the questions and elicit answers from the class. If the class can't answer, play Track 56 again.
- To wrap up, ask: *When can Manny find out if he got the job?* (next week)

Culture Connection

- Ask: *What does Manny ask in his interview?* (When can I expect to hear from you?)
- Say: *In the U.S. it's OK to ask questions in an interview. In fact, it's a good idea to prepare a few questions before an interview. Make sure your questions are about the company or the job. Remember not to ask about salary and benefits; wait until the interviewer brings them up.*
- Brainstorm a few questions to ask in an interview and write them on the board (for example, *Can you describe a typical day for someone in this job? What are the job duties? What skills are most important for this job? What new skills can I learn on the job?*).

Lesson 8 Answer questions about availability

3 CONVERSATION

Ⓐ 💿 Listen to the questions. Then listen...

- Read the Pronunciation Watch note.
- Tell students to look at the questions and circle *or*.
- Play CD 2, Track 57. Students listen.
- Resume playing Track 57. Students listen and repeat.

Controlled Practice   15 minutes

Ⓑ 💿 Listen and repeat the conversation.

- Note: This conversation is the same one students heard in Exercise 2A on page 160.
- Tell students to read the conversation silently.
- Direct students to find a question from Exercise 3A in the conversation. Tell them to circle *or* and mark the voice going up on the first choice and down on the last choice.
- Say: *Do you prefer mornings or afternoons?* Ask the class to repeat. Model again and ask individual students to repeat.
- Read the directions. Play CD 2, Track 58.

4 PRACTICE

Ⓐ PAIRS. Practice the conversation. Then make new...

- Pair students and tell them to practice the conversation in Exercise 3B. Tell them to take turns playing each role. Remind them to practice the correct pronunciation of the question with *or*.
- Then, in Exercise 4A, tell students to look at the information in the blue box. Tell them to circle *or* and mark the voice going up on the first choice and down on the last choice. Say: *Do you prefer first or second shift?* and *Do you prefer days or nights?* Ask the class to repeat.
- Explain that *first shift* is usually morning to afternoon and *second shift* is afternoon to evening.
- Copy the conversation onto the board with blanks. Read through the conversation. When you come to a blank, fill it in with information from the first row in the boxes. As you fill in each blank, say the color of the answer space and point to the same-color word or phrase you choose from the boxes.
- Ask two on-level students to read the conversation in front of the class.

- Tell pairs to take turns playing each role and to use information from the same row in the boxes to fill in the blanks. Walk around and check that students are using correction intonation.
- Tell students to stand, mingle, and practice the conversation with several new partners.
- Call on pairs to perform for the class.

Communicative Practice   15 minutes

Ⓑ ROLE PLAY. PAIRS. Make your own...

- Tell students to look at the conversation in 4A. Ask: *Who is Speaker A?* (the manager) Read Speaker A's first line. On the board, write: *Do you prefer _____?* Tell students to look at the information in the blue box. Ask: *What other choices related to availability can the manager ask about?* Brainstorm ideas and write them on the board (for example, *mornings or afternoons*, *part-time or full-time*). Draw a box around this information and label it *blue*. Ask students to come to the board and mark the pronunciation / intonation.
- Tell students to look at the conversation in 4A. Read Speaker A's second line. On the board, write: *Can you work on _____?* Tell students to look at the information in the red box. Brainstorm and write on the board other days the manager can ask about (for example, *weekends*, *Friday nights*, *holidays*). Draw a box around this information and label it *red*.
- Read the directions. Play Speaker A and make up a conversation with an above-level student. Use the information on the board.
- Pair students and tell them to take turns playing Speakers A and B.
- Call on pairs to role play for the class.

▬▬ MULTILEVEL INSTRUCTION for 4B
Pre-level Students fill in the blanks in the conversation in 4A before they practice.
Above-level On the board, write: *A: Do you have any questions for me? B: When can I expect to hear from you?* Tell pairs to extend the conversation.

Extra Practice

Interactive Practice

3 CONVERSATION

CD2 T57

A Listen to the questions. Then listen and repeat.

Do you prefer mornings or afternoons?

Can you work first shift or second shift?

Do you work days or nights?

CD2 T58

B Listen and repeat the conversation.

Albert: Let me ask you a few questions about your availability.
Do you prefer mornings or afternoons?

Manny: Well, I prefer mornings, but I'm flexible.

Albert: All right. Can you work on weekends?

Manny: Yes, I can.

Albert: Great. And when could you start?

Manny: In two weeks. I need to give two weeks' notice at my job.

Pronunciation Watch

Some questions with *or* ask the listener to make a choice. In these questions, the voice goes up on the first choice and down on the last choice.

4 PRACTICE

A PAIRS. Practice the conversation. Then make new conversations. Use the information in the boxes and your own information.

A: Let me ask you a few questions about your availability.

Do you prefer   ?

B: Well, I prefer   , but I'm flexible.

A: All right. Can you work on   ?

B: Yes, I can.

A: Great. And when could you start?

B: In two weeks. I need to give two weeks' notice at my job.

| first or second shift | first shift | Saturdays |
| days or nights | days | Sundays |

B ROLE PLAY. PAIRS. Make your own conversations. Use different information.

Grammar

Ways to express alternatives: *or, and*

He can work mornings	**or**	afternoons.
They can work Saturdays	**and**	Sundays.
I can't work Mondays	**or**	Tuesdays.

Grammar Watch

Use *or* (not *and*) in negative statements.

PRACTICE

A Complete the conversations. Write *and* or *or*.

1. **A:** Which shift do you prefer?

   B: I'm flexible. I can work first shift _____*or*_____ second shift.

2. **A:** Can you work weekends?

   B: Sure! I can work both Saturday _____*and*_____ Sunday. I want a lot of hours.

3. **A:** Can you work both Saturday and Sunday?

   B: I'll be happy to work Saturday _____*or*_____ Sunday, but I can't work both days.

4. **A:** Can you take classes in the morning _____*or*_____ in the evening?

   B: In the morning. I can't take classes in the evening because I work second shift.

B Look at Carlos's and Nadia's job applications. Write two sentences about each person's availability. Use *or* with *can* and *can't*.

1. Carlos can work second shift or third shift.

2. Carlos can't work first shift or weekends.

_____

Carlos Hernandez

When can you work? Check the boxes.

first shift ☐ second shift ☑ third shift ☑ weekends ☐

3. Nadia can work first shift or second shift.

4. Nadia can't work third shift or weekends.

_____

Nadia Perez

When can you work? Check the boxes.

first shift ☑ second shift ☑ third shift ☐ weekends ☐

C WRITE. Write two sentences about your own work availability. Use *or* with *can* and *can't*.

Getting Started

5 minutes

- Say: *We're going to study ways to express alternatives with* or *and* and*. In the conversation on page 161, Albert used this grammar.*
- Play CD 2, Track 58. Students listen. Write on the board: *Do you prefer mornings or afternoons?* Underline *or*.

Presentation

10 minutes

Ways to express alternatives: *or, and*

- Copy the grammar chart onto the board or show Transparency 8.5 and cover the exercise.
- Read the sentences in the chart.
- Read the first sentence in the chart again. Ask: *Can he work both mornings and afternoons?* (No.) Say: *He can work only at one time of day. He can work mornings, or he can work afternoons.*
- Read the second sentence in the chart again. Ask: *Can they work both Saturdays and Sundays?* (Yes.)
- Read the Grammar Watch note. Read the third sentence in the chart again. Ask: *Can this person work Mondays?* (No.) *Can this person work Tuesdays?* (No.) Say: *So, both days are not OK for this person. Why* or, *not* and*? (because the sentence is negative)
- If you are using the transparency, do the exercise with the class.

Controlled Practice

15 minutes

 PRACTICE

A Complete the conversations. Write *and* or *or*.

- Read the directions and the example. Ask: *Why is the answer* or*? (because this person can work first shift, or this person can work second shift—but not both)
- Students compare answers with a partner by reading the conversations.
- Call on pairs to read the conversations.

B Look at Carlos's and Nadia's job applications....

- Read the directions.
- Tell students to look at Carlos's job application. Read the example. Say: *Now write a sentence with can't.* Allow time for students to complete item 2.
- Elicit the sentence and write it on the board. Ask: *Can Carlos work first shift?* (No.) *Can he work weekends?* (No.) Say: *So, both times are not OK for Carlos. Why* or, *not* and*? (because the sentence is negative)
- Students check answers with a partner.
- Call on students to write answers on the board.

C WRITE. Write two sentences about your own...

- Remind students that *first shift* is from morning to afternoon and *second shift* from afternoon to evening. Ask: *When do you think third shift is?* (usually from evening to early morning) Explain: *In workplaces that are open 24 hours, usually:*

  First shift—8:00 A.M. to 4:00 P.M.
  Second shift—4:00 P.M. to 12:00 A.M.
  Third shift—12:00 A.M. to 8:00 A.M.

- Tell students to write a set of blank application checkboxes in their notebooks. Say: *When can you work? Check the boxes.* Tell students to check the two shifts they prefer.
- Read the directions. Tell students to write one sentence with *can* and one sentence with *can't* using the sentence in Exercise B as a model.
- Ask one student to write a sentence with *can* on the board and one student to write a sentence with *can't*.

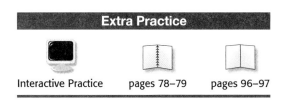

Extra Practice		
Interactive Practice	pages 78–79	pages 96–97

1 GRAMMAR

Ⓐ Complete the parts of a job interview. Use *can...*

- Read the directions. Tell students to refer back to the grammar charts on page 150 (*Can* to express ability) as needed.
- Remind students to use a capital letter at the beginning of the questions.
- Tell students to refer back to the Pronunciation Watch note on page 149. Tell them to circle the words in the conversation (*can* or *can't*) that have a strong pronunciation. Remind them to practice the weak pronunciation of *can* in the other sentences.
- Students role-play the completed conversation with a partner to check answers.
- Walk around and listen for the correct pronunciation of *can / can't*.
- *Optional:* Call on pairs to perform the completed conversation for the class.

Ⓑ Complete the sentences. Use *ago, and, in, last...*

- Read the directions. Tell students to refer back to the grammar charts on page 156 (Time expressions with *ago, last, in,* and *later*) and page 162 (Ways to express alternatives: *or, and*) as needed.
- Students compare answers with a partner by reading one paragraph each out loud.
- Call on two students to read the paragraphs for the class. Discuss any errors.

CD-ROM Practice

 Go to the CD-ROM for more practice.

If your students need more practice with the vocabulary, grammar, and competencies in Unit 8, encourage them to review the activities on the CD-ROM. This review can also help students prepare for the final role play on the following Expand page.

Extra Practice
📖
pages 80–81

1 GRAMMAR

A Complete the parts of a job interview. Use *can* and *can't*. Use the words in parentheses.

Manager: _____Can you use_____ a cash register?
                          (you / use)

Terry: No, I _____can't_____, but _____I can learn_____.
                                                        (I / learn)

Manager: OK, well, maybe _____you can stock_____ shelves at first.
                                           (you / stock)

Terry: Sure. _____I can do_____ that.
                          (I / do)

Manager: Do you prefer afternoons or evenings?

Terry: _____I can work_____ in the afternoon or in the evening. I'm flexible.
                  (I / work)

Manager: _____Can you work_____ on weekends?
                       (you / work)

Terry: Sure. On the weekend, _____I can work_____ mornings, afternoons,
                                             (I / work)
or evenings.

Manager: _____Can you start_____ tomorrow?
                       (you / start)

Terry: Yes, _____I can_____.

B Complete the sentences. Use *ago, and, in, last, later,* and *or.*

Ali Osman came to the U.S. _____in_____ 2005. One month _____later_____,
                                    1.   2.
he started school. He got his first job _____in_____ 2006. It was in a hospital, and
                                                 3.
he worked nights. Ali didn't like his work schedule. A few weeks _____later_____, his
                                                                              4.
boss asked, "Ali, do you prefer days _____or_____ nights?" Ali said, "I prefer days."
                                               5.
A week _____later_____, he changed his hours.
                6.

Ali continued to go to school. _____Last_____ year, he had classes three nights a
                                           7.
week: on Monday, Tuesday, _____and_____ Thursday. This year, he's going to school
                                      8.
_____in_____ the morning. He changed jobs a few weeks _____ago_____. He has a
      9.   10.
better job at a different hospital. But now he works from 12:00 P.M. to 8:00 P.M., so
he can't go to class in the afternoon _____or_____ the evening.
                                               11.

2 ACT IT OUT   What do you say?

STEP 1. CLASS. Review Albert and Manny's job interview in Lessons 2, 5, and 8 (CD 2 tracks 48, 51, and 55).

STEP 2. PAIRS. Student A, you are a job interviewer. Student B, you are applying for a job.

> **Student A**: ask about the applicant's:
> • job skills
> • work history
> • availability

> **Student B**: answer the interviewer's questions about your skills, work experience, and availability.

3 READ AND REACT   Problem-solving

STEP 1. Read about Marco's problem.

Marco is unemployed. He has a job interview tomorrow. At his last job, he had a problem. He made a mistake and his boss fired him. Marco does not think his boss was right. Marco is worried that the interviewer will ask, "Why did you leave your last job?" He doesn't know how to answer the question.

STEP 2. PAIRS. What is Marco's problem? What can he do? Here are some ideas.

• He can say, "I left my last job because I wanted a different schedule."
• He can say, "I was fired" and then explain what he learned.
• He can say, "I was fired" and explain why his boss was not fair.
• He can _____.

4 CONNECT   For your Community-building Activity, go to page 252.
For your Team Project, go to page 281.

2 ACT IT OUT

STEP 1. CLASS. Review Albert and Manny's...

- Tell students to review the conversations in Exercise 3B on page 149, Exercise 3 on page 155, and Exercise 3B on page 161.
- Tell students to read all three conversations silently.
- Tell students to practice the conversations with a partner. Students should keep the same roles for all three conversations.
- Play CD 2, Tracks 48, 51, and 55. Students listen.

STEP 2. PAIRS. Student A, you are a job interviewer....

- Read the directions and the guidelines for A and B.
- Pair students. Say: *Student A, you need to ask about Student B's job skills, work history, and availability. Look at the conversations again and underline the lines Albert uses to ask about each of these (Tell me about your skills. Can you . . . ? on page 149; So, tell me more about your work experience on page 155; and Let me ask you a few questions about your availability. Do you prefer . . . ? on page 161).*
- Tell Student B to note his or her skills, work experience, and availability.
- Walk around and observe partners interacting. Check pairs' use of *can* to talk about skills, time expressions to talk about work history, and *or / and* to talk about availability.
- Call on pairs to perform for the class.
- While pairs are performing, use the scoring rubric on page T-xiii to evaluate each student's vocabulary, grammar, fluency, and how well he or she completes the task.
- *Optional:* After each pair finishes, discuss the strengths and weakness of each performance either in front of the class or privately.

3 READ AND REACT

STEP 1. Read about Marco's problem.

- Say: *We are going to read about a student's problem, and then we need to think about a solution.*
- Read the story while students follow along silently. Pause after each sentence to allow time for students to comprehend. Periodically stop and ask simple *Wh-* questions to check comprehension (for example, *What does Marco have tomorrow? Why is Marco unemployed? What interview question is Marco worried about?*).

STEP 2. PAIRS. What is Marco's problem? What...

- Ask: *What is Marco's problem?* (He was fired from his last job. He has an interview tomorrow, and he doesn't know how to answer the question "Why did you leave your last job?") *What can Marco do?*
- Pair students. Read the ideas in the list. Give pairs a couple of minutes to discuss possible solutions for Marco.
- Ask: *Which ideas are good?* Call on students to say their opinion about the ideas in the list (for example, S: *I think he can say, "I was fired" and then explain what he learned. This is a good idea.*).
- Now tell students to think of one new idea not in the list (for example, *He can say, "I made a mistake, and I was fired. It won't happen again."*) and to write it in the blank. Encourage students to think of more than one idea and to write them in their notebooks.
- Call on pairs to say their additional solutions. Write any particularly good ones on the board and ask students if they think it is a good idea too (*Do you think this is a good idea? Why or why not?*).

▨▨▨ MULTILEVEL INSTRUCTION for STEP 2

Pre-level Students work in groups of 4 to come up with an idea.

Above-level Tell pairs to cover the list of ideas and to come up with three of four of their own ideas first. Then they can look at the list in the book to compare.

4 CONNECT

Turn to page 252 for the Community-building Activity and page 281 for the Team Project. See page T-xi for general notes about teaching these activities.

Progress Check

Which goals can you check off? Go back to page 145.

Ask students to turn to page 145 and check off any remaining goals they have reached. Call on students to say which goals they will practice outside of class.

Parents and Children

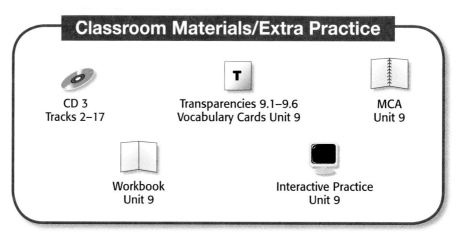

Classroom Materials/Extra Practice

CD 3
Tracks 2–17

Transparencies 9.1–9.6
Vocabulary Cards Unit 9

MCA
Unit 9

Workbook
Unit 9

Interactive Practice
Unit 9

Unit Overview

Goals
- See the list of goals on the facing page.

Grammar
- Future with *will*
- Adverbs of manner
- Object pronouns
- Possessive nouns

Pronunciation
- *Will* and the contraction *'ll*
- Possessive endings *'s* and *s'*

Reading
- Read an article about the cost of going to college
- *Reading Skill:* Use information in charts and tables

Writing
- Write about the progress of students you know
- Write about your educational goals

Life Skills Writing
- Write a telephone message
- Complete a school enrollment form

Preview
- Set the context of the unit by asking questions about parents and children (for example, *Do you have children? How many children do you have? Would you like to have children in the future?*).
- Hold up page 165 or show Transparency 9.1. Read the unit title and ask the class to repeat.
- Say: *Look at the picture.* Ask the Preview questions: *Who are the people?* (a mother and son) *What are they doing?* (studying / doing homework / The mother is helping her son with his homework.).
- On the board, write: *parents = mother and _____, children = son and _____.* Elicit *father* and *daughter* and write them on the board.

Goals
- Point to the Unit Goals. Explain that this list shows what the class will be studying in this unit.
- Tell students to read the goals silently.
- Say each goal and ask the class to repeat. Explain unfamiliar vocabulary as needed:

    Enrollment: signing up to attend a school

    Progress: how a person is learning, developing, improving over time

    Behavior: the way a person acts
- Tell students to circle one goal that is very important to them. Call on several students to say the goal they circled.

Parents and Children

Preview

Look at the picture.
Who are the people?
What are they doing?

UNIT GOALS

- [ ] Identify school subjects

- [ ] Make plans for school events

- [ ] Take a phone message

- [ ] Complete a school enrollment form

- [ ] Talk about progress in school

- [ ] Discuss your child's behavior in school

Vocabulary

1 WHAT DO YOU KNOW?

A CLASS. Look at the pictures. Which school subjects do you know?

CD3 T2

B  Look at the pictures and listen. Then listen and repeat.

2 PRACTICE

A WORD PLAY. PAIRS. Choose a school subject from the vocabulary list. Don't tell your partner. Write three clues for the word. Your partner will guess the word.

art: paint, draw, color

Student A, read your clues. Student B, guess after each clue. Take turns.

A: *Paint.*
B: *Art?*
A: *Right!*

B What schools are in your community? Find out and write the names of schools you know. Talk about your list with the class. Answers will vary.

School	Name of school
preschool	
elementary school	
middle school	
high school	

Lesson 1 Vocabulary

Getting Started   5 minutes

1 WHAT DO YOU KNOW?

A CLASS. Look at the pictures. Which school subjects...

- Show Transparency 9.2 or hold up the book. Tell students to cover the list of words on page 167.
- Read the directions . Elicit a school subject and write it on the board (for example, *Number 6 is music.*).
- Students call out answers. Help students pronounce school subjects if they have difficulty.
- If students call out an incorrect school subject, change the student's answer into a question for the class (for example, *Number 4 is English?*). If nobody can identify the correct school subject, tell students they will now listen to the CD and practice the school subjects vocabulary.

Presentation   5 minutes

B Look at the pictures and listen. Then...

- Read the directions. Play CD 3, Track 2. Pause after number 10 (*science*).
- To check comprehension, say each school subject in random order and ask students to point to the appropriate picture.
- Resume playing Track 2. Students listen and repeat.

Controlled Practice   15 minutes

2 PRACTICE

A WORD PLAY. PAIRS. Choose a school subject...

- Read the directions and write the example on the board. Ask: *What's the subject?* (art) *What are the clues?* (paint, draw, color)
- Tell the class to look at the list of words on page 167 and choose another school subject—not *art*. Elicit students' ideas for clues and write them on the board.
- Pair students. Tell them to choose another school subject—not the ones on the board. Walk around and offer ideas for clues as needed.

Student A, read your clues. Student B, guess after...

- Read the directions. Play Student A and model the example with a student. Ask a pair to model the other example on the board.
- Say: *If your partner guesses incorrectly, say no and read another clue.*
- To wrap up, ask students to read their clues and the class to guess.

MULTILEVEL INSTRUCTION for 2A

Cross-ability A lower-level student can work with a higher-level partner to write clues. Direct the students to find a new partner for the second part of the activity.

B What schools are in your community? Find out and...

- Note: If you are not familiar with the names of schools in your area, research this information before class.
- Tell students to complete as much of the chart as they can with names of local schools they know.
- Write *preschool, elementary school*, etc., as headings on the board. Ask volunteers to come to the board and list schools.

Culture Connection

- Explain: *In the U.S., children have to attend school until they are 16 years old. This is the law. Public schools provide a free education. Local property taxes pay for public schools.*
- Elicit or provide the grades / ages for each level of education in the U.S. Note the grades and ages next to each heading on the board (example, *preschool: usually 3–4 year olds; elementary school: K–5th grade; middle school: 6th–8th grade; high school: 9th–12th grade*). Ask: *About how old are pre-schoolers?* (4 years old) *Kindergartners?* (5 years old) *6th graders?* (11) *9th graders?* (14)
- Explain: *Public education usually begins in kindergarten, but some districts have preschool.*
- Ask: *Do children have to go to school in your country? What are the laws? Are there schools that children can attend for free?*

Lesson 1 Vocabulary

Learning Strategy: Use your language

- Provide each student with five index cards or tell students to cut up notebook paper into five pieces.
- Read the directions. If you have students with low first-language skills, pair them with more capable peers if possible.
- Walk around as students work. If misspellings occur, tell them to check the list on page 167.
- Say: *You can use your language to help you remember new words in English.* Remind students to use this strategy to remember other new vocabulary.

Teaching Tip

As you visit with students, show them you are an active language learner yourself by trying to say school subjects in their native languages.

Communicative Practice   15 minutes

Show what you know!

STEP 1. GROUPS OF 3. What are the three...

- Read the directions.
- On the board, write the subject you think is most important and explain why (for example, *I think math is the most important because you need to be able to manage your money.*).
- Tell students to write the subject they think is most important and note why they think it's important.
- Form groups of 3. Say: *Tell your group what subject you think is most important and why.*
- Say: *Do you agree with your partners? Write the other two subjects you think are most important. Use your partners' ideas or your own ideas.*

■■■ MULTILEVEL INSTRUCTION for STEP 1

Cross-ability Allow lower-level students to look at their partners' notes and write why each subject is important.

STEP 2. Tell the class your ideas.

- Read the directions.
- Ask: *What are the three most important subjects for students to learn? Why?* Call on volunteers to answer. Write answers on the board and tell students to copy them into their notebooks.

■■■ EXPANSION: Vocabulary practice for STEP 2

- Hang ten large sheets of paper around your classroom. Write one school subject at the top of each sheet.
- Tell students to walk around and write reasons why the subjects are important on the sheets.
- Ask ten students to stand and read the reasons on one sheet.

■■■ EXPANSION: Vocabulary and speaking practice for STEP 2

- Ask: *What was your favorite school subject when you were a child? Why?* Tell students to write their answer in their notebooks.
- Form groups of 3. Say: *Tell your group what your favorite school subject was when you were a child and why.*
- Call on a few students to say what a partner's favorite subject was as a child and why.

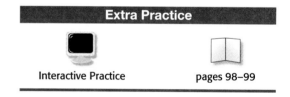

Extra Practice	
Interactive Practice	pages 98–99

3

4

7

9

School Subjects

1. math
2. language arts/English
3. P.E. (physical education)
4. social studies/history
5. art
6. music
7. technology
8. community service
9. world languages
10. science

Learning Strategy

Use your language

Look at the list of school subjects. Make cards for five new words. Write the word in English on one side of the card. Write the word in your language on the other side.

Show what you know!

STEP 1. GROUPS OF 3. What are the three most important subjects for students to learn? Why?

_____   _____   _____

STEP 2. Tell the class your ideas.

Make plans for school events

Listening and Speaking

1 BEFORE YOU LISTEN

READ. CLASS. Look at the pictures and read the
information. Then answer the questions.

A parent-teacher conference is a meeting between a
student's teacher and his or her parents. The teacher and
parents discuss the child's progress in school.

PTO stands for Parent-Teacher Organization. A PTO
is a group of teachers and parents of students in a school.
They work together to improve the school.

1. What is the purpose of a parent-teacher conference?

2. What is the purpose of a PTO?

parent-teacher conference

parent-teacher organization
(PTO)

2 LISTEN

A CLASS. Look at the picture. Mr. and Mrs. Duval
have a notice from their son's school.
Guess: What is the notice about?

CD3 T3

B Listen to the conversation. Was your
guess in Exercise A correct?

CD3 T3

C Listen again. Answer the questions.

1. When is the parent-teacher conference?
   a. Tuesday the 19th at 6:00
   b. Thursday the 19th at 6:00
   c. Thursday the 19th at 9:00

2. What does Mr. Duval have to do on the day of the conference?
   a. go to work   b. go to class   c. watch the kids

CD3 T4

D Listen to the whole conversation. What is Mr. Duval going
to do on Monday the 23rd?

a. go to work   b. go to the parent-teacher conference   c. go to a band concert

Make plans for school events

Getting Started   10 minutes

1   BEFORE YOU LISTEN

READ. CLASS. **Look at the pictures and read...**

- Read the directions.
- Tell students to look at the pictures. Read the captions under the pictures and ask the class to repeat.
- Tell students to read the two paragraphs silently.
- Read the first paragraph out loud. Tell students to look at the first picture. Ask: *What are the parents and teacher talking about?* (the child's progress in school) As needed, explain that *progress* is how well the child is doing in school, for example, the child's learning, grades, and behavior.
- Read the second paragraph out loud. Tell students to look at the second picture. Ask: *Who are the people?* (teachers and parents) *What are they talking about?* (how to improve the school) Ask: *What does* improve *mean?* (make better)
- Read each question. Elicit answers and write them on the board. 1. to discuss a child's progress in school, 2. to work together to improve the school.
- *Optional:* Write *parent-teacher conference* and *PTO meeting* on the board. Brainstorm things people talk about in each setting. List students' ideas on the board (for example, for *parent-teacher conference: grades, attendance, behavior, homework;* for *PTO meeting: school events, fundraisers*).

Presentation   10 minutes

2   LISTEN

A CLASS. **Look at the picture....**

- Read the directions. Ask: *What is the notice about?*
- Elicit students' guesses and list them on the board. Tell students they will listen for the answer in Exercise B.

Teaching Tip

Optional: Remember that if students need additional support, tell them to read the Audio Script on page 304 as they listen to the conversations.

B 💿 **Listen to the conversation. Was your...**

- Read the directions. Play CD 3, Track 3.
- Ask: *What is the notice about?* Read the guesses on the board. Elicit and circle the best answer. (a parent-teacher conference)

Controlled Practice   20 minutes

C 💿 **Listen again. Answer the questions.**

- Tell students to read the questions and answers.
- Play Track 3 again.
- Read the questions and ask the class to call out the answers. If students call out incorrect answers, play Track 3 again.

D 💿 **Listen to the whole conversation....**

- Read the directions and answer choices.
- Play CD 3, Track 4.
- To review, ask: *What is Mr. Duval going to do on Monday the 23rd?* Elicit the answer.
- *Optional:* On the board, write: *The parent-teacher conference is _____ Thursday the 19th at 6:00. Carlo's band concert is four days _____.* Ask the class to fill in the blanks. (*on, later*)
- *Optional:* Ask: *What school subject do you think Carlo likes?* (music)

3 CONVERSATION

A Listen to the sentences. Then...

- Read the Pronunciation Watch note. Tell students to underline *'ll / will* in the sentence.
- Read the directions. Play CD 3, Track 5.
- Say each of the pronouns contracted with *will* in the first four sentences. Ask the class to repeat. Ask: *What other pronouns are there?* Write the contractions of the board (*you'll, it'll, they'll*). Pronounce them and ask the class to repeat.

B Listen and repeat the conversation.

- Note: This conversation is the same one students heard in Exercise 2B on page 168.
- Tell students to read the conversation silently.
- Tell students to underline *will* and the contraction *I'll* in the conversation.
- Play CD 3, Track 6. Students listen and repeat.

Communicative Practice   20 minutes

4 PRACTICE

A PAIRS. Practice the conversation. Then...

- Pair students and tell them to practice the conversation in Exercise 3B. Tell them to take turns playing each role. Walk around and help with pronunciation as needed. Pay particular attention to students' pronunciation of *will* and *I'll*.
- Then for exercise 4A, tell students to look at the information in the boxes. Say each word or phrase and ask the class to repeat.
- Tell students to look at the school events in the blue box. To check comprehension, describe the events in random order and ask the class to call out the event: *parents and teachers talking about how to improve the school* (PTO meeting), *students acting on stage with parents and friends watching in the audience* (school play), *students showing their projects on things like health, technology, the environment, and space* (science fair).
- Copy the conversation onto the board with blanks. Read it and when you come to a blank, fill it in with information from the boxes.

- Ask two on-level students to practice the conversation on the board for the class.
- Erase the words in the blanks and ask two above-level students to make up a new conversation in front of the class.
- Tell pairs to take turns playing Speakers A and B and to use the information in the boxes.
- Walk around and check students' pronunciation of *will* and *I'll*. As needed, pronounce the words and ask students to repeat.
- Tell students to stand, mingle, and practice the conversation with several new partners.
- Call on pairs to practice for the class.

B ROLE PLAY. PAIRS. Make your own...

- Read the directions.
- Point to the blue box and ask: *What other school events can you think of?* (a parent-teacher conference, a band concert, an art show, a baseball game, a college fair)
- Point to the green box and ask: *What else can you do to leave work early?* (change my shift, take personal / vacation time, talk to my boss)
- Pair students and tell them to practice the conversation.
- Walk around and check students' pronunciation of *will* and *I'll*.
- Call on pairs to perform for the class.

▮▮▮ MULTILEVEL INSTRUCTION for 4B

Pre-level Before they role play, tell students to

write down a school event in blue and a way to leave work early in green.

Above-level Direct students to change other information in the conversation, such as dates, times, names, and who will watch the kids.

Extra Practice

Interactive Practice

3 CONVERSATION

CD3 T5

A 💿 **Listen to the sentences. Then listen and repeat.**

I'll try.
We'll both go.
He'll be at work.
She'll meet him there.
My mother will watch the kids.

CD3 T6

B 💿 **Listen and repeat the conversation.**

Mrs. Duval: Carlo brought a notice home from school today.
There's a parent-teacher conference in two weeks.

Mr. Duval: Oh, yeah? What day?

Mrs. Duval: Thursday the 19th at 6:00. My mother will watch the kids.
That way we can both go.

Mr. Duval: Oh, I have to work that day until 9:00, but I'll try to
change my shift.

> **Pronunciation Watch**
>
> The word *will* usually has a short, weak pronunciation. After a pronoun (such as *I* or *we*), we usually use the contraction *'ll*.

4 PRACTICE

A PAIRS. **Practice the conversation. Then make
new conversations. Use the information in the boxes.**

A: Carlo brought a notice home from school today.
There's a _____ in two weeks.

B: Oh, yeah? What day?

A: Thursday the 19th at 6:00. My mother will watch
the kids. That way we can both go.

B: Oh, I have to be at work that day until 9:00,
but I'll _____ .

school play
PTO meeting
science fair

switch hours with someone
ask if I can leave early
change my schedule

B ROLE PLAY. PAIRS. **Make your own conversations.
Use different information.**

Grammar

Future with *will*

Affirmative				Negative			
My mother	**will**	**watch**	the kids.	Frank	**will not**	**go**	to the PTO meeting.
She	**'ll**			They	**won't**		

1 PRACTICE

A **Complete the sentences. Use *will* for the future.**

Grammar Watch

- Use *will* + the base form of a verb.
- *won't = will not.*
- Use contractions with *will* for speaking and informal writing.

1. Anwar ___will work___ the evening shift this week.
   (work)
   He changed his schedule.

2. Laura ___will play___ on the soccer team next year.
   (play)

3. The PTO ___will have___ a bake sale in October.
   (have)

4. Raphael ___won't be___ home until 5:30. He gets help with his homework after school.
   (not / be)

5. The Technology Club ___won't meet___ this week because Monday is a holiday.
   (not / meet)

6. Andre ___will be___ late for dinner. He has football practice today.
   (be)

7. The kids ___won't have___ school on Friday because the teacher has a conference all day.
   (not / have)

B **Complete the conversation. Use *will* for the future and the words in the box. Use contractions if possible.**

> play   go   ~~be~~   check

A: Can you go to Jimmy's baseball game this Thursday night?

B: I'm sorry, I can't. I have to work.

A: That's too bad. Jimmy ___will be___ sad. He wanted you to come.

B: Well, they _'ll play___ again next week, right?

A: I think there's a game next Friday. I _'ll check____ the schedule.

B: OK. I _'ll go____ to the next game. I promise.

Lesson 3 Make plans for school events

Getting Started
5 minutes

- Say: *We're going to study the future with* will. *In the conversation on page 169, Mr. and Mrs. Duval used this grammar.*
- Play CD 3, Track 6. Students listen. Write on the board: *My mother will watch the kids* and *I'll try to change my shift*. Underline *will* and *I'll*.

Presentation
10 minutes

Future with *will*

- Copy the grammar charts onto the board or show Transparency 9.3 and cover the exercise.
- Read the sentences in the charts and tell the class to repeat.
- Read the first item in the Grammar Watch note and the first sentence in the left chart (*My mother will watch the kids.*).
- Read the second item in the Grammar Watch note. Tell students to look at the right chart. Read all four possible sentences (*Frank will not / won't go to the PTO meeting. They will not / won't go to the PTO meeting.*).
- Read the third item in the Grammar Watch note and the second sentence in the left chart (*She'll watch the kids.*).
- On the board, write: *He will change his schedule.* Ask the class to change the sentence to what people say (*He'll change his schedule.*). Then ask the class to change the sentence to make it negative (*He won't change his schedule.*).
- If you are using the transparency, do the exercise with the class.

Controlled Practice
25 minutes

1 PRACTICE

A Complete the sentences. Use *will*...

- Read the directions and the example.
- Students compare answers with a partner.
- Call on students to read the sentences. Correct as needed.

B Complete the conversation. Use *will*...

- Read the directions.
- Write the example on the board. Point to the answer and ask why it's not a contraction. (because *Jimmy* is a name) Then ask: *When do you usually use contractions?* (with pronouns)
- On the board, write: *My mother will watch the kids.* Ask the class to change the sentence to a question. Write the question on the board: *Will your mother watch the kids?*
- Students compare answers with a partner by reading the conversation.
- Call on pairs to perform the conversation for the class. Correct as needed.

2 PRACTICE

Complete the e-mail. Use the future with *will*...

- Read the directions. Ask: *Is an e-mail to a friend formal or informal writing?* (informal) *Is it OK to use contractions?* (Yes.)

- Students compare answers with a partner.

- Call on a higher-level student to read the e-mail out loud.

- To wrap up, ask a few comprehension questions: *What is the event?* (Sue's school play) *Will Anita's husband, Jack, go?* (No.) *Who will go?* (Anita and her kids) *What time does Anita have to work until?* (6:30) *What time is the play?* (at 8:00) *When will Anita call Jane?* (on Sunday)

Communicative Practice   20 minutes

Show what you know!

STEP 1. GROUPS OF 5. Look at the pictures....

- Tell students to look at the pictures. Say the events and ask the class to repeat.

- Tell students to look at the picture of a school bake sale and ask: *What is for sale?* (cookies, cupcakes, bread) Explain that at a school bake sale the members of a school group or club make desserts like cookies and cupcakes and sell them to make money for the school or group.

- Tell students to look at the picture of an international party and ask: *What are the people wearing?* (traditional dress from their countries) *What are the people doing?* (talking, eating) *Where is the food from?* (Italy, Mexico, South Korea)

- Read the directions and the example.

- Draw the chart on the board. Say each event task and ask the class to repeat. Ask: *What's a flyer?* (a piece of paper advertising something) If possible, show the class flyers for events at your school or in your community.

- Model the activity. Ask four higher-level students to stand up. Say: *We are a group.* Ask the group: *Which event should we choose, a school bake sale or an international party?* Write the event on the chart. For each event task on the chart, ask: *Who wants to . . . ?* and write the name of a group member on the chart.

- Form groups of 5. Tell group members to take turns asking *Who wants to . . .?* Direct each group member to volunteer to do one task.

▬▬ EXPANSION: Vocabulary Practice for STEP 1

- Explain that a *bake sale* is a type of *fundraiser*—an event to make money for a specific cause or group.

- Ask: *Can you think of any other types of school fundraisers?* (a car wash, a candy sale, a school fair / carnival)

STEP 2. Tell the class about your plans.

- Read the directions.

- Model the activity. Tell the class to look at the chart on the board. Point to each row and say who will do each task. Use *will* (for example, *Phuong will get permission from the school. Arturo will design a flyer.* etc.).

- One student from each group tells the class about the group's plans.

▬▬ EXPANSION: Writing and Speaking Practice for STEP 2

- Brainstorm what information to include on an event flyer. Make a list on the board (for example, *when the event is, where the event is, the cost of the event*).

- Direct each group to create a flyer for their event. If possible, provide students with poster paper and markers. Tell students to first plan on a sheet of notebook paper.

- Ask one student from each group to show the flyer to the class and talk about when and where the event will take place.

Progress Check

Can you . . . make plans for school events?
Say: *We have practiced making plans for school events. Now, look at the question at the bottom of the page. Can you make plans for school events?* Tell students to write a checkmark in the box.

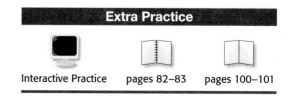

Extra Practice

Interactive Practice   pages 82–83   pages 100–101

Complete the e-mail. Use the future with *will* and the words in parentheses.

✉ invitation

To: jane@abc.com
Subject: Invitation

Hi Jane,

Thank you for inviting us to Sue's school play next Friday night. Unfortunately, Jack has a

class, so he ___won't be___ there. But the kids and I __'ll come__. I usually get out of
    (1. not / be)   (2. come)

work at around 6:30, but I __'ll leave__ early if I can. The kids and I __'ll eat__
                (3. leave)   (4. eat)

a quick dinner, and we __'ll get__ to the school around 8:00. Don't worry—we
                (5. get)

___won't be___ late! I'm going out now, so I ___won't call___ you tonight. I __'ll call__
    (6. not / be)   (7. not / call)   (8. call)

you on Sunday, and we __'ll talk__ some more then.
                (9. talk)

Anita

Show what you know!   Make plans for school events

**STEP 1. GROUPS OF 5. Look at the pictures.
Choose one event. Look at the event tasks in the chart.
Decide who will do each task. Complete the chart.**

A: *Who wants to get permission from the school?*
B: *I'll call the principal tomorrow.*

Event:	
Event task	**Group member**
get permission from the school	
design a flyer	
decide who will bring what	
set up before the event	
clean up after the event	

STEP 2. Tell the class about your plans.

a school bake sale

an international party

Can you…make plans for school events? ☐

Take a phone message

1 TAKE A PHONE MESSAGE

(A) **PAIRS.** Look at the picture. Guess: Why is the woman calling the school?

CD3 T7

(B) 🔘 Listen to the conversation. Was your guess in Exercise A correct?

CD3 T7

(C) 🔘 Read the phone messages. Listen to the conversation again. Circle the number of the correct message.

1.

Date __3/9__ Time __1:15__

To __Mr. Taylor__

While You Were Out

From __Elsa Vega (Maria's teacher)__

Phone __(718) 555-4343__

Message: __Will call back.__

_____

②

Date __3/9__ Time __1:15__

To __Mr. Taylor__

While You Were Out

From __Elsa Vega (Maria's mom)__

Phone __(718) 555-4343__

Message: __Please call back.__

_____

CD3 T8

(D) 🔘 Listen. Mr. Taylor is returning Ms. Vega's call. Ms. Vega's son Beto answers the phone and takes a message. Complete the message.

(E) **PAIRS.** Compare your answers.

Mom,

_____Mr. Taylor_____ called.

Please call him back. His

number is _____718-555-8185_____.

— Beto

Getting Started
5 minutes

- Ask: *Do you take phone messages at home? Where do you write them?*
- Ask the class: *Do you answer the phone at work? What do you do if someone's not available to take a call?*

Presentation
20 minutes

1 TAKE A PHONE MESSAGE

Ⓐ PAIRS. Look at the picture. Guess: Why is the...

- Read the directions. Pair students.
- Give pairs time to come up with an answer to the question. Then point to the woman in the right half of the picture and ask: *Why is the woman calling the school?* (to talk to her child's teacher)
- Elicit students' guesses and list them on the board.

> **Teaching Tip**
>
> *Optional:* Remember that if students need additional support, tell them to read the Audio Script on page 304 as they listen to the conversations.

Ⓑ 🔘 Listen to the conversation....

- Read the directions. Play CD 3, Track 7.
- Ask: *Why is the woman calling the school?* Read the guesses on the board. Elicit and circle the best answer.
- Ask: *What does the woman have a question about?* (her daughter's math homework)

Ⓒ 🔘 Read the phone messages. Listen...

- Read the directions. Tell students to read the messages silently. Tell them to circle what is different in each message (1. *Will call back.* 2. *Please call back.*).
- Say: *Now listen again.* Point to the woman in the right half of the picture and ask: *Is she Maria's teacher or Maria's mom? Who will call back, Ms. Vega or Mr. Taylor?*
- Play CD 3, Track 7.
- Repeat the questions above and elicit answers (*Maria's mom; Mr. Taylor will call back.*) Then ask the class to call out the number of the correct message.
- *Optional:* To review prepositions of time, ask: *When did Elsa Vega call?* (on March 9th at 1:15)

Ⓓ 🔘 Listen. Mr. Taylor is returning...

- Read the directions. Tell students to read the message silently.
- Play CD 3, Track 8. Tell students to write the phone number in the same way as in the messages in Exercise 1C.

Ⓔ PAIRS. Compare your answers.

- Students compare answers with a partner by reading the message out loud to each other.
- Say: *Raise your hand if you and your partner wrote the same number.* Play Track 8 again as needed.
- Call on a student to read the message. Write the phone number on the board.
- *Optional:* Point out that when taking a message, it's a good idea to repeat a phone number back to a caller, like Beto does.

Controlled Practice · 15 minutes

2 PRACTICE

A Complete the conversation with words from the box.

- Say: *This is the conversation from Exercise 1B on page 172.*
- Read the directions. Say the words in the box and ask the class to repeat.
- Tell students to cross out words in the box as they use them.

B PAIRS. Compare your answers. Then...

- Read the directions. Pair students.
- Partners compare answers and then practice the conversation. Tell partners to switch roles and practice both parts.
- *Optional:* Call on pairs to perform the conversation for the class.

Communicative Practice · 15 minutes

C PAIRS. Make your own conversations....

- Read the directions.
- Tell pairs to use the conversation in Exercise 2A as a model. Tell them to cross out the A's in Exercise 2A and replace them with *Secretary* and to cross out the B's and replace them with *Parent*.
- Say: *Student A, before you practice, write down your phone number with area code or a made-up phone number to use in the conversation. Also note the reason you are calling Mr. Taylor.*
- Say: *Student B, complete the message during the conversation. If you're not sure how to spell Student A's name, ask:* How do you spell that? *Repeat Student A's phone number to make sure you wrote it correctly.*
- Walk around and help as needed. Remind students to switch roles and practice both parts.
- Call on pairs to perform for the class.

▨ MULTILEVEL INSTRUCTION for 2C

Pre-level Highlight or underline the information in Exercise 2A that students need to change when they play Speaker A: *Elsa Vega, my daughter Maria's,* and *718-555-4343*. Tell them to write in the information they will use.

Above-level After they practice a few times while looking at the conversation in the book, ask pairs to cover the exercise and continue practicing.

3 LIFE SKILLS WRITING

Turn to page 264 and ask students to complete the school enrollment form. See page T-xii for general notes about Life Skills Writing activities.

Progress Check

Can you . . . take a phone message?

Say: *We have practiced taking phone messages. Now, look at the question at the bottom of the page. Can you take a phone message?* Tell students to write a checkmark in the box.

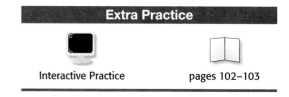

Extra Practice	
Interactive Practice	pages 102–103

A Complete the conversation with words from the box.

> available   call me back   give him
> take a message   ~~This is~~

A: Winter Hill Elementary School.

B: Hello. _____*This is*_____ Elsa Vega. May I speak to Mr. Taylor please?

A: I'm sorry. He's not ____available____ right now. May I ____take a message____?

B: Yes, please. I have a question about my daughter Maria's math homework.

Please ask him to ____call me back____.

A: Sure. What's your number?

B: It's (718) 555-4343.

A: OK. I'll ____give him____ the message.

B: Thank you.

B PAIRS. Compare your answers. Then practice the conversation.

C PAIRS. Make your own conversations.

Student A: You are the parent. Call Mr. Taylor at the Winter Hill Elementary School. Leave a message with the secretary.

Student B: You are the secretary. Take the message. Use today's date and time.

Date _____ Time _____

To _____

While You Were Out

From _____

Phone _____

Message: _____

_____

3 LIFE SKILLS WRITING

Complete a school enrollment form. See page 264.

Can you...take a phone message? ☐

Listening and Speaking

1 BEFORE YOU LISTEN

READ. CLASS. **Look at the picture. Read the information. What are some ways students can get extra help with school?**

Sometimes students have trouble in their classes. Students can get help from their parents and older brothers and sisters. Sometimes they can get extra help from teachers or older students before or after school. Most local libraries also have programs to help students with their schoolwork.

2 LISTEN

A CLASS. **Look at the picture. Guess: Where is Carlo's mother? Who is she talking to?**

CD3 T9

B Listen to the conversation. **Was your guess in Exercise A correct?**

CD3 T9

C Listen again. **Answer the questions.**

1. What subject is Carlo doing well in?

   <u>   Math   </u>

2. What subject *isn't* Carlo doing well in?

   <u>   Social Studies   </u>

CD3 T10

D Listen to the whole conversation. **What does Carlo's teacher suggest?**

  (a.) help from older students
  b. extra homework
  c. help from his parents

Getting Started   10 minutes

1 BEFORE YOU LISTEN

READ. CLASS. Look at the picture. Read...

- Tell the class to look at the picture. Ask: *Who are the people?* (a mother and son / a teacher and student) *What are they doing?* (schoolwork / homework) *What subject is it?* (math)
- Read the directions. Tell students to read the paragraph silently.
- Ask: *What are some ways students can get extra help with school?* Tell student to read again and underline the people and place students can go to for extra help.
- Ask again: *What are some ways students can get extra help with school?* Elicit and list on the board: *parents, older brothers and sisters, teachers (before or after school), older students (before or after school), local libraries.*

Presentation   10 minutes

2 LISTEN

Ⓐ CLASS. Look at the picture. Guess: Where is...

- Read the directions. Ask: *Where is Carlo's mother?* (at Carlo's school / in Carlo's classroom)
- Elicit students' guesses and list them on the board.
- Ask: *Who is Carlo's mother talking to?* (Carlo's teacher)
- Elicit students' guesses and list them on the board.

Ⓑ 💿 Listen to the conversation. Was...

- Read the directions.
- Play CD 3, Track 9.
- Ask: *Where is Carlo's mother?* Read the guesses on the board. Elicit and circle the best answer. Repeat with: *Who is she talking to?*

Controlled Practice   10 minutes

> **Teaching Tip**
> *Optional:* Remember that if students need additional support, tell them to read the Audio Script on page 304 as they listen to the conversations.

Ⓒ 💿 Listen again. Answer the questions.

- Tell students to look at the picture again. Point to the woman and ask: *What is Carlo's mother's name?* (Mrs. Duval) If students don't remember, tell them to look back at Exercise 2A on page 168. Point to the man and ask: *What is Carlo's teacher's name?* (Mr. Thomson) Write *Mrs. Duval* and *Mr. Thomson* on the board.
- Read the directions and the questions.
- Play Track 9 again.
- Students compare answers with a partner by asking and answering one question each.
- Ask the questions and call on students to say the answers.

Ⓓ 💿 Listen to the whole conversation....

- Read the directions and the answer choices.
- Play CD 3, Track 10.
- Ask students to raise their hands for each answer choice.
- To review, ask: *What does Carlo's teacher suggest?* (homework help after school / help from older students)
- *Optional:* Ask: *Is the homework help program before or after school?* (after school) *How much does it cost?* (It's free.)

Talk about progress in school

Presentation

5 minutes

3 CONVERSATION

C **Listen and repeat the conversation.**

- Note: This conversation is the same one students heard in Exercise 2B on page 174.
- Tell students to read the conversation silently.
- Read the directions. Play CD 3, Track 11.

Controlled Practice

10 minutes

4 PRACTICE

A PAIRS. **Practice the conversation. Then make new...**

- Pair students and tell them to practice the conversation in Exercise 3. Tell them to take turns playing each role.
- Then, in Exercise 4A, tell students to look at the information in the boxes. Say each word or phrase and ask the class to repeat.
- Read the directions.
- Copy the conversation onto the board with blanks. Read through the conversation. When you come to a blank, ask what color it is. Point to the box that is the same color and fill in the blank with the first item in the box. Fill in black blanks with first and last names from your class. In Speaker B's first blank, use *mother* for a female student and *father* for a male student.
- Ask the two students whose names you used to practice the conversation on the board for the class.
- Erase the words in the blanks and ask two above-level students to make up a new conversation in front of the class. Prompt Speaker B to fill in the blue blank with the same subject A chose.
- Tell pairs to take turns playing Speakers A and B. Tell them to use their names and the information in the boxes to fill in the blanks.
- Tell students to stand, mingle, and practice the conversation with several new partners.
- Call on pairs to practice for the class.

Communicative Practice

15 minutes

B MAKE IT PERSONAL. PAIRS. **Talk about your...**

- Read the directions and the example.
- On the board, write the heading *English ability*. Under *English ability*, list *pronunciation*, *writing*. Brainstorm other aspects of language ability and write them on the board (for example, *listening, speaking, reading, vocabulary, spelling, grammar*).
- Create a chart by writing the heading *Ways to improve* to the right of *English ability*. For each aspect of English ability, brainstorm at least one way to improve and write it on the board in the *-ing* form (for example, for *listening: listening to the news or talk radio in English*).
- Tell students to think about their English ability. Tell them to look at the list on the board and write down one thing they do well and one thing they have trouble with.
- Play Speaker A and model the activity. Talk about your ability in another language. Point to the thing you have trouble in. Prompt Student B to suggest the way to improve that is on the board.
- Pair students. Read the directions again. Tell them to follow the example and use information from the chart on the board.
- Walk around and remind students to switch roles.
- Call on pairs to perform for the class.

MULTILEVEL INSTRUCTION for 4B

Pre-level Highlight students' examples to show where they need to substitute their own information. In Student A's line, highlight *pronunciation* and *writing* in one color. In Student B's line, highlight *writing in a journal* in another color. Draw boxes in corresponding colors around the columns of the chart.

Above-level After pairs have practiced, call on students to say what their partner will do to improve his or her English (for example, *Raja will read children's books in English.*).

Extra Practice

Interactive Practice

CD3 T11

🎧 Listen and repeat the conversation.

Mr. Thomson: Hi, I'm Harold Thompson, Carlo's teacher. Nice to meet you.

Mrs. Duval: I'm Carlo's mother, Annette Duval. Nice to meet you, too. So, how's Carlo doing?

Mr. Thomson: Carlo's a good student. I enjoy having him in class.

Mrs. Duval: That's good to hear.

Mr. Thomson: He does very well in math. He works carefully.

Mrs. Duval: He likes math a lot. What about social studies?

Mr. Thomson: Well, he's having a little trouble in that class. He needs to do his homework.

Mrs. Duval: OK. I'll talk to him.

4 PRACTICE

Ⓐ **PAIRS.** Practice the conversation. Then make new conversations. Use the information in the boxes.

A: Hi, I'm _____, Carlo's teacher. Nice to meet you.

B: I'm Carlo's _____, _____. Nice to meet you, too. So, how's Carlo doing?

A: Carlo's a good student. I enjoy having him in class.

B: That's good to hear.

A: He does very well in _____. He _____.

B: He likes _____ a lot. What about _____?

A: Well, he's having a little trouble in that class.

He needs to _____.

B: OK. I'll talk to him.

Ⓑ **MAKE IT PERSONAL. PAIRS.** Talk about your English ability. What do you do well? What do you have trouble in? Suggest ways your partner can improve his or her English.

A: *My pronunciation is good. I have trouble with writing.*
B: *How about writing a journal in English?*

science

social studies

language arts

learns quickly

studies hard

writes well

language arts

science

math

ask more questions

spend extra time on it

study a little more

Grammar

Adverbs of manner

Adjective		
Carlo is a	**careful** **quick** **good**	worker.

Adverb	
Carlo works	**carefully**. **quickly**. **well**.

· · · · · · · · · **Grammar Watch**

Grammar Watch

- For most adverbs of manner, add -*ly* to the adjective. See page 287 for more spelling rules.

- A few adverbs of manner are irregular:
  good → well
  hard → hard
  fast → fast

1 PRACTICE

A Complete the sentences. Look at the underlined adjective. Write the adverb of manner.

1. Sonia is a <u>careless</u> writer. She writes ___carelessly___.

2. Vahan's pronunciation is <u>clear</u>. He speaks ___clearly___.

3. Amadi is a <u>fast</u> learner. He learns ___fast___.

4. Your children are <u>good</u> students. They do ___well___ in school.

5. My son is a <u>hard</u> worker. He works ___hard___ on his homework.

6. May-Ling is very <u>quiet</u> in class. She plays ___quietly___ with the other children.

7. Meng's handwriting is <u>neat</u>. He writes ___neatly___.

B Change the adjectives in the box to adverbs of manner. Use the adverbs to complete the sentences.

> careful   creative   good   hard   ~~poor~~   quick

1. Darren never practices the piano. He plays ___poorly___.

2. Nuncia gets good grades. She does ___well___ in school.

3. We don't have much time. Please work ___quickly___.

4. Amina works fast, but she makes mistakes. She needs to work ___carefully___.

5. Ernesto had a lot of great ideas for his science project. He always thinks ___creatively___.

6. John has a test tomorrow. He needs to study ___hard___.

Lesson 6 Talk about progress in school

Getting Started   5 minutes

- Say: *We're going to study adverbs of manner. In the conversation on page 175, Mr. Thomson used this grammar.*
- Play CD 3, Track 11. Students listen. Write on the board: *He does very well in math. He works carefully.* Underline *well* and *carefully.*

Presentation   10 minutes

Adverbs of manner

- Copy the grammar charts onto the board or show Transparency 9.4 and cover the exercise.
- Read the sentences in the left chart. Say: *Careful, quick, and* good *are adjectives. What word do they describe?* (worker) *What part of speech is* worker? (a noun) Write *(noun)* above *worker* on the chart and say: *An adjective describes a noun.*
- Read the sentences in the right chart. Say: *Carefully, quickly, and* well *are adverbs. What word do they describe?* (works) *What part of speech is* works? (a verb) Write *(verb)* above *works* on the chart and say: *An adverb describes the action of a verb. These adverbs tell you how Carlo works.*
- Read the first item in the Grammar Watch note. On the board, write: *careful + -ly = carefully, quick + -ly = quickly.* Say the first two sentences from the right side of the chart and ask the class to repeat.
- Read the second item in the Grammar Watch note. Say the last sentence from the right side of the chart and ask the class to repeat.
- If you are using the transparency, do the exercise with the class.

Controlled Practice   15 minutes

1 PRACTICE

A Complete the sentences. Look at...

- Read the directions and the example. Ask: *Why is the answer* carelessly? On the board, write: *careless + -ly = carelessly.*
- Remind students that a few adverbs of manner are irregular (for example, *good, hard,* and *fast*). Ask the class to call out the adverbs (*well, hard,* and *fast*).
- Students compare answers with a partner. Tell them to take turns reading the sentences.
- Call on students to read the completed sentences.

B Change the adjectives in the box to adverbs....

- Read the first sentence of the directions. Tell students to add *-ly* to the adjectives in the box or write the irregular form.
- Say the adjectives in the box and ask the class to call out the adverbs of manner.
- Read the second sentence of the directions and the example.
- Students compare answers with a partner. Tell them to take turns reading the sentences.
- Call on students to read the completed sentences.

Lesson 6 Talk about progress in school

Presentation 10 minutes

Object pronouns

- Copy the grammar charts onto the board or show Transparency 9.4 and cover the exercise. Say: *We're going to study object pronouns.*
- Read the sentences from the charts and ask the class to repeat.
- Read the Grammar Watch note while the class reads along silently.
- On the board, write: *Carlo needs to do his homework. His mother will talk to _____.* Ask: *What noun are we going to replace?* Underline *Carlo.* Ask: *What object pronoun takes the place of Carlo?* Write *him* in the blank.
- Circle *to* in the second sentence on the board. Ask: *In this sentence, does the object pronoun come after a verb or a preposition?* (a preposition)
- If you are using the transparency, do the exercise with the class.

Controlled Practice 5 minutes

2 PRACTICE

Complete the sentences. Write the correct object...

- Read the directions. Write the example on the board and ask: *Why is the answer* her? *What noun does* her *take the place of?* Underline *Ms. Carson.*
- Tell students to underline the noun in the first sentence before they write the object pronoun in the second sentence.
- Students compare answers with a partner. Tell them to take turns reading the sentences.
- Call on students to read the completed sentences.

Communicative Practice 15 minutes

Show what you know!

STEP 1. WRITE. Think of three students you know...

- Read the directions. Model the activity. On the board, list the names of three students you know (for example, your children, nieces, nephews, and neighbors—not students in your class).

- Next to the name of each student on the board, write: *is doing well in school* or *is doing poorly in school.* Underline *well* and *poorly* and say: Well *and* poorly *are adverbs of manner.*
- Continue each sentence by writing *because* and a reason. Use an adverb of manner in at least one of your reasons (for example, *she learns quickly, he studies hard, she writes carelessly, he doesn't work hard*). Write at least one reason without an adverb of manner (for example, *She has a good teacher. He doesn't do his homework.*).
- Tell students to look at the sentences in Exercises 1A and 1B on page 176 for ideas.

STEP 2. GROUPS OF 3. Read your sentences....

- Form groups of 3. Read the directions.
- Read the example. Explain: *You can talk more about the people.* Elaborate on the example by saying: *My daughter is doing well in school because she works hard. She does her homework carefully and studies hard for tests.*
- Model the activity by reading the sentences you wrote on the board for Step 1 and elaborating.

STEP 3. Tell the class about the students...

- Read the directions.
- Tell each student to choose one sentence from Step 1 to read to the class.

▮▮▮ MULTILEVEL INSTRUCTION

Pre-level Students can simply read the sentence(s) they wrote in Step 1.

Above-level Ask students to elaborate and also to ask lower-level students questions (for example, *Does your daughter do her homework? How many hours does she study at night?*).

Progress Check

Can you . . . talk about progress in school?

Say: *We have practiced talking about progress in school. Now, look at the question at the bottom of the page. Can you talk about progress in school?* Tell students to write a checkmark in the box.

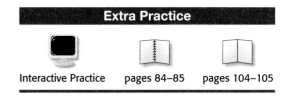

Extra Practice		
Interactive Practice	pages 84–85	pages 104–105

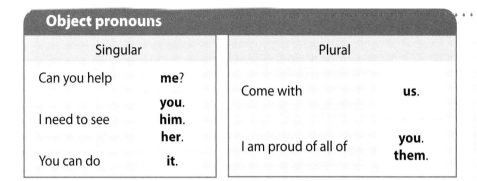

Object pronouns

Singular	
Can you help	**me**?
	you.
I need to see	**him**.
	her.
You can do	**it**.

Plural	
Come with	**us**.
I am proud of all of	**you**.
	them.

········ **Grammar Watch**

An object pronoun takes the place of a noun:

*I need to call <u>Bill</u>. I need to call **him**.*

Use an object pronoun:

• after a verb: *Call **me**. I know **her**.*

• after a preposition: *Talk to **me**. He's standing next to **her**.*

2 PRACTICE

Complete the sentences. Write the correct object pronoun.

1. Ms. Carson was at the parent-teacher conference. I met _____*her*_____.

2. There is a PTO meeting on Friday. We can't attend _____it_____.

3. Emily and Mary are doing very well in school. We're proud of _____them_____.

4. My daughter is not doing well in science. I am worried about _____her_____.

5. My son needs help in math class. Can you help _____him_____?

6. Are you busy? I need to talk to _____you_____.

7. When we don't understand something, our teacher helps _____us_____.

8. Art class is hard for me. I don't like _____it_____.

9. My son does his homework every day. I never have to remind _____him_____.

Show what you know!   Talk about progress in school

STEP 1. WRITE. Think of three students you know. How are they doing in school? Write a sentence about each person on a separate piece of paper. Use an adverb of manner.

> *My daughter is doing well in school because she works hard.*

STEP 2. GROUPS OF 3. Read your sentences. Talk about the people.

STEP 3. Tell the class about the students you talked about.

Can you... talk about progress in school?   ☐

Reading

1 BEFORE YOU READ

CLASS. **Read the chart. What types of colleges are there in your community?**

	Community college	College	University
Degrees offered	Associate's Degree (2 years)	Bachelor's Degree (4 years)	Bachelor's Degree (4 years)
			Master's Degree (2 more years)
			Doctor of Philosophy (4–7 more years)

2 READ

CD3 T12

Listen. Read the article.

Going to College

Thinking of going to college? Here are some things you should know.

Rising College Enrollment

According to the U.S. Census Bureau, 49 percent of high school graduates in 1980 went to college. Fifty-nine percent went to college in 1990. In 2007, over 66 percent of high school graduates went to college. Every year more and more Americans decide that going to college is a way to a better future.

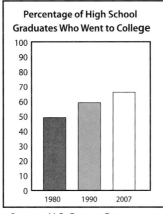

Percentage of High School Graduates Who Went to College

Source: U.S. Census Bureau

The Cost of College

But going to college costs a lot. Today, the average cost of tuition is between $2,000 and $22,000 a year. This does not include the cost of books, housing, and food. These can cost between $8,000 and $16,000 more a year.

Average Cost of Tuition	
Private College	$22,000
Public College	$ 6,000
Community College	$ 2,000

Paying for College

How do people pay for tuition? Many students get financial aid—scholarships, grants, and loans. Many students get loans. Some students get scholarships because their grades are good. Some students get grants because their income is low. Scholarships and grants are the best kind of financial aid because you don't have to pay them back. You do have to pay back student loans after you graduate. Most students use a combination of scholarships, grants, and loans to pay the high cost of college.

Getting Started

10 minutes

 BEFORE YOU READ

CLASS. Read the chart. What types of colleges...

- Ask questions about the chart, for example, *What type of degree can you get at a community college?* (an Associate's Degree); *How many years does it take?* (2 years); *How many years does it take to get a Master's Degree?* (4 years + 2 more years = 6 years); *Where can you get a Master's Degree?* (at a university).
- Read the question in the directions. Ask: *Are there community colleges in our community?* Write the names of local community colleges on the board. Repeat with colleges and universities.

Presentation

15 minutes

 READ

 Listen. Read the article.

- Ask: *What is the title?* (Going to College) Say: *Look at the charts. What is the article about? Guess.* Call on students to say what they think the article is about. (information about going to college)
- Play CD 3, Track 12. Students listen and read silently.

- If students have difficulty following along, play Track 12 again and pause at various points.
- Ask if there are words they do not understand and explain them, for example:

  tuition: what you pay to go to college

  housing: what you pay to live at college

- *Optional:* Play Track 12 again. Pause the CD after the following sections and ask these questions:

  Rising College Enrollment: *Did more Americans go to college in 1980 or in 1990?* (in 1990) *Did more Americans go to college in 1990 or in 2007?* (in 2007) *Is college enrollment going up or down?* (up)

  The Cost of College: *About how much does a year of college cost?* (between $2,000 and $22,000) *What other costs are there?* (books, housing, and food)

  Paying for College: Ask the class: *What types of financial aid can students get to help them pay for college?* On the board, write: *scholarships, grants,* and *loans.* Ask: *Which is money you borrow and pay back after you graduate?* (loans) *Which is money colleges give for good grades or some other specific reason?* (scholarships) *Which is money students get if their families don't earn a lot?* (grants)

Controlled Practice   20 minutes

3 CHECK YOUR UNDERSTANDING

Ⓐ PAIRS. Read the article again. What are the three...

- Read the directions.
- Pair students and tell them to read the article again.
- Tell students to underline one sentence in each section that tells the main idea, or most important idea (Section 1: *Every year more and more Americans decide that going to college is the way to a better future.* Section 2: *But going to college costs a lot.* Section 3: *Most students use a combination of scholarships, grants, and loans to pay for the high cost of college.*). Point out that the first or last sentence of a paragraph usually tells the main idea.
- Students compare underlined sentences with a partner.

▬ EXPANSION: Writing practice for 3A

- Tell pairs to look at the blue boldface type in the article and read the sentence they underlined for each section. Tell them to write a simple sentence that tells the main point in their notebooks.
- Write *1*, *2*, and *3* on the board. Ask students to come to the board and write a sentence giving the main point of each section. Read and compare the sentences for each section of the article (for example, 1. *More Americans are going to college / College enrollment is rising.* 2. *College is expensive.* 3. *Students can get scholarships, grants, and loans to help pay for college.*).

Ⓑ Look at the graph about high school...

- Read the Reading Skill note while the class reads along silently.
- Tell students to look at the article and point to the graph and then the table. Ask: *Which main point does the graph support?* (More Americans are going to college.) *Which main point does the table support?* (College is expensive.)
- Read the directions.
- Students compare answers with a partner. Tell them to take turns reading the questions and answers.
- Read the questions and call on students to answer.

- Ask more questions about the graph: *What percentage of high school graduates went to college in 1990?* (59 percent) *In 2007?* (over 66 percent) *To figure out how many high school graduates went to college in 2007, what do you need to know?* (the total number of high school graduates in 2007)

Ⓒ Read the statements. Circle *True* or *False*.

- Read the directions.
- Say: *You will use the table to answer one item.*

Ⓓ PAIRS. Compare your answers. Correct...

- Students compare answers with a partner. Tell pairs to correct the false statements to make them true (1. <u>more</u> high school graduates; 3. $2,000; 5. ~~grants and~~ loans).
- Call on students to say the answers and correct the false statements.
- Ask: *For which item did you use the table to answer?* (item 3)
- *Optional:* Ask more questions about the table.

Communicative Practice   15 minutes

Show what you know!

PRE-WRITING. PAIRS. Is going to college...

- Read the directions. Say: *Answer the question yes or no. Find a partner with the same answer.*
- Say to pairs: *If you think a college education is worth the cost, talk about what you can do with a college degree. Write your ideas in your notebooks. If you think a college education isn't worth the cost, talk about why not and what other things you can do with the money. Write your ideas.*

WRITE. Write about your educational goals....

- Turn to page 272 and ask students to complete the activities. See page T-xii for general notes about Writing activities.

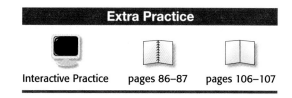

Extra Practice		
Interactive Practice	pages 86–87	pages 106–107

A PAIRS. Read the article again. What are the three main points of the article? 1) More students are going to college. 3) People pay for college with loans, 2) Going to college costs a lot. scholarships, and grants.

B Look at the graph about high school graduates in the article. Answer the questions.

> **Reading Skill:**
> Use Information in Charts and Tables
>
> Authors sometimes use graphs and tables to present information. This information supports the author's main ideas.

1. What do the numbers on the left side of the graph mean?

   a. the percentage of high school graduates who went to college
   b. the number of high school graduates who went to college

2. What percentage of high school graduates went to college in 1980?

   a. 50   b. 60

3. How many high school graduates went to college in 2007?

   a. 65,000   b. the graph doesn't say

C Read the statements. Circle *True* or *False*.

1. Today, fewer high school graduates go to college than in the past.   True   False

2. The cost of books, housing, and food for one year can be between $8,000 and $16,000.   True   False

3. One year of tuition at a community college is $6,000.   True   False

4. Three types of financial aid are scholarships, grants, and loans.   True   False

5. You have to pay back grants and loans.   True   False

D PAIRS. Compare your answers. Correct the false statements.

Show what you know!

PRE-WRITING. PAIRS. Is going to college one of your goals? Explain your answer.

WRITE. Write about your educational goals. See page 272.

Discuss your child's behavior in school

Listening and Speaking

1 BEFORE YOU LISTEN

CLASS. Look at the pictures. Do students in your country behave in this way?

☐ bully other kids

☑ not pay attention

☐ not get along with others

☐ fool around in class

☐ be disrespectful

Where is Steve?

☑ skip class

2 LISTEN

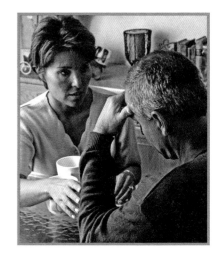

CD3 T13

A 🎵 **Listen to the conversation. Mr. and Mrs. Herrera got a call from their son Luis's teacher. What trouble is Luis having in school? Check the boxes in Before You Listen.**

CD3 T13

B 🎵 **Listen again. What are Luis's parents going to do?**

(a.) talk to Luis
b. call the principal
c. go to a parent-teacher conference

CD3 T14

C 🎵 **Listen to the whole conversation. Underline the correct words.**

Luis usually **does well** / **has problems** in school.

Getting Started   10 minutes

1 BEFORE YOU LISTEN

CLASS. Look at the pictures. Do students in your...

- Note: The checkboxes are for Exercise 2A.
- Tell students to look at the pictures. Say: *These students are behaving badly.* Say the behaviors and ask the class to repeat.
- To check understanding, describe the pictures in random order and ask the class to call out the behaviors. Say:

  Steve's not in class today, but he's not sick. (skip class)

  The girl is not listening to her math teacher. (not pay attention)

  The girl is arguing with another student. (not get along with others)

  The student is making fun of the teacher. (be disrespectful)

  The boy is frightening a smaller and weaker student. (bully other kids)

  The boy is playing in class. (fool around in class)

- Ask: *Do students in your country behave in this way?* Say each behavior and ask students to raise their hands if the behavior is common in schools in their country.

Culture Connection

- Tell students to look at the behaviors in Exercise 1 again. Ask: *In your country, what happens to students who behave in this way?* Write students' responses on the board.
- Ask: *In the U.S., what happens to students who behave in this way?* Elicit students' ideas. Talk about common forms of punishment in U.S. schools, for example, moving a student to another seat or to the front of the classroom, not allowing a student to participate in recess or some other fun activity, detention (making a student spend extra time at school, either before or after school), suspension (not allowing a student to attend school for a certain period of time), and expulsion (for serious offenses, making a student leave a school permanently).
- Explain: *In most states in the U.S., there are laws against using physical punishment to correct bad behavior in schools.*

Presentation   20 minutes

2 LISTEN

A Listen to the conversation. Mr. and...

- Read the directions. Tell students to look at the picture.
- Say: *Point to Mr. Herrera. Point to Mrs. Herrera.* Ask: *Who is Luis?* (their son) *Who called them?* (Luis's teacher) *Why are they upset?* (because Luis is having trouble in school)
- Tell students to underline the question in the directions: *What trouble is Luis having in school?* Tell students to listen and check the boxes in Exercise 1.
- Play CD 3, Track 13.
- Repeat the question and call on students to say which boxes they checked.

B Listen again. What are Luis's parents...

- Read the directions and the answer choices.
- Tell students to underline the question in the directions: *What are Luis's parents going to do?*
- Play Track 13 again. Students listen and circle the letter of the answer.
- Repeat the question. Say each answer choice and ask students to raise their hand for the answer they chose. If many students answered incorrectly, play Track 13 again.
- *Optional:* On the board, write: *Luis's parents _____ talk to Luis tonight after dinner.* Ask the class to complete the sentence. (*will*)

C Listen to the whole conversation....

- Read each answer choice: *Luis usually does well in school. Luis usually has problems in school.*
- Play CD 3, Track 14. Students listen and underline the correct words.
- Ask the class: *Which words did you underline?* On the board, write: *Luis usually does well in school.*
- *Optional:* Ask the class: *Why do you think Luis is having problems in school now? What are some reasons why students behave badly?*

Lesson 8 Discuss your child's behavior in school

3 CONVERSATION

A 🔘 **Listen to the possessive nouns. Then...**

- Write a few possessive nouns that don't add a syllable on the board (for example, *Justin's band, Brianna's job, the baby's seat*). Say them and ask the class to repeat.
- Write the names from the Pronunciation Watch note on the board. Point to and pronounce the underlined sound in each name. Say: *After these sounds, the 's ending adds an extra syllable.*
- Add an *'s* ending to each name and a noun (for example, *Luis's parents, Liz's homework, Josh's teacher, Mitch's class, George's grades*). Say each phrase and ask the class to repeat.
- Play CD 3, Track 15. Students listen.
- Resume playing Track 15. Students listen and repeat.

B 🔘 **Listen again. Underline the possessive...**

- Read the directions. Read the Pronunciation Watch note again. Tell students to look at Exercise 3A. Ask: *Which possessive nouns do you think add a syllable?* (boss's, Alex's, George's)
- Play CD 3, Track 16. Students listen and underline.
- Ask: *Were you correct?* Say *boss's, Alex's*, and *George's* and ask the class to repeat.

Controlled Practice   20 minutes

C 🔘 **Listen and repeat the conversation.**

- Note: This conversation is the same one students heard in Exercise 2A on page 180.
- Tell students to read the conversation silently and to underline the possessive nouns.
- Ask: *What did you underline?* (*friend's*) *Does the 's ending in* friend's *add an extra syllable?* (No.) Say *friend's* and ask the class to repeat.
- Read the directions. Play CD 3, Track 17.

4 PRACTICE

A **PAIRS. Practice the conversation. Then...**

- Pair students and tell them to practice the conversation in Exercise 3C. Tell them to take turns playing each role.

- Then, in Exercise 4A, tell students to look at the information in the boxes. Say each phrase and ask the class to repeat.
- Copy the conversation onto the board with blanks. Read through it and fill it in with information from the top row in the boxes.
- Ask two on-level students to read the conversation in front of the class.
- Tell pairs to take turns playing each role and to use information from the same row in the boxes to fill in the blanks.
- Tell students to stand, mingle, and practice the conversation with several new partners.
- Call on pairs to perform for the class.

Communicative Practice   10 minutes

B **MAKE IT PERSONAL. GROUPS OF 3. What...**

- Read the directions.
- Review by asking: *What trouble is Luis having in school?* (not paying attention and skipping class) *What are Luis's parents going to do?* (talk to Luis)
- Say: *When Luis's parents talk to him, what should they say? What can they do to change his behavior?* Tell students to write a couple of ideas in their notebooks (for example, *They need to find out what's going on. They need to ask why he's not paying attention and skipping class. They can ask for a parent-teacher conference. They can get him help with his schoolwork. They can punish him.*).
- Form groups of 3. Tell group members to take turns saying their ideas and talking about them.
- Ask: *What's your group's best idea?* Ask each group to write one idea on the board. Read and talk about the ideas on the board.

▬▬ **EXPANSION: Speaking Practice for 4B**

- Assign each group of 3 one bad behavior from Exercise 1 on page 180. Ask: *What should the parents of the student in the picture do?*
- Tell groups to brainstorm and record ideas. Tell them to choose one creative solution to present to the class.

Extra Practice
⬛
Interactive Practice

3 CONVERSATION

Pronunciation Watch

The **'s** or **s'** possessive ending adds an extra syllable after the sounds at the end of *Luis, Liz, Josh, Mitch* and *George*. It does not add an extra syllable after other sounds.

CD3 T15

A Listen to the possessive nouns. Then listen and repeat.

my boss's name

his friend's house

Alex's friend

Sue's homework

George's class

her parent's car

CD3 T16

B Listen again. Underline the possessive nouns that add a syllable.

CD3 T17

C Listen and repeat the conversation.

Mrs. Herrera: Where's Luis?

Mr. Herrera: He's at a friend's house. Why? What's up?

Mrs. Herrera: Well, his teacher called. He's having some trouble at school.

Mr. Herrera: Uh-oh. What kind of trouble?

Mrs. Herrera: She said he's not paying attention and skipping class.

Mr. Herrera: What? Well, we need to talk to him right away.

Mrs. Herrera: Definitely. Let's all talk tonight after dinner.

4 PRACTICE

A PAIRS. Practice the conversation. Then make new conversations. Use the information in the boxes.

A: Where's Luis?

B: He's at a friend's house. Why? What's up?

A: Well, his teacher called. He's having some trouble at school.

B: Uh-oh. What kind of trouble?

A: She said he's _____ and _____ .

B: What? Well, we _____ right away.

A: Definitely. Let's all talk tonight after dinner.

not getting along with others
getting to school late
being disrespectful to his teachers

bullying some other kids
not doing his homework
fooling around in class

need to find out what's going on
have to have a talk with him
need to have a family meeting

B MAKE IT PERSONAL. GROUPS OF 3. What should Luis's parents do?

Grammar

Possessive nouns

Singular	Plural
Their son**'s** name is Luis.	Their son**s'** names are Minh and Sang.
	The children**'s** classroom is down the hall.

······· **Grammar Watch**

To form a possessive noun:

• Add '*s* to most singular nouns: *a boy's name.*

• Add only an apostrophe to plural nouns that end in -*s*: *my parents' car.*

• Add '*s* to plural nouns that do not end in -*s*: *the men's hats*

• See page 287 for more spelling rules.

PRACTICE

A **Underline the correct word.**

1. Who is your **daughters / <u>daughter's</u>** teacher?

2. My **<u>sons</u> / son's** are in the first and second grades.

3. The **teachers / <u>teacher's</u>** first name is Alex.

4. Sometimes a teacher calls a **students / <u>student's</u>** parents.

5. I know the names of all my **<u>classmates</u> / classmates'**.

6. My **daughter's / <u>daughters'</u>** names are Alicia and Rita.

7. The guidance **<u>counselor's</u> / counselors'** name is Ms. White.

B **Find and correct the error in each sentence.**

1. My ~~sons~~ ^{son's} grades are poor, so I need to talk to his teacher.

2. The new ~~teacher's~~ ^{teachers'} names are Ms. Trudeau and Ms. Appleton.

3. Where is the school ~~nurse'~~ ^{nurse's} office?

4. My ~~daughters~~ ^{daughter's} report card was good, but my son is having a hard time.

5. The principal will try to answer all the ~~parents's~~ ^{parents' or parent's} questions.

6. Teachers like to meet their ~~students~~ ^{students'} parents.

C **PAIRS. Check your answers.**

Getting Started   5 minutes

- Say: *We're going to study possessive nouns. In the conversation on page 181, Mr. Herrera used this grammar.*
- Play CD 3, Track 17. Students listen. Write on the board: *He's at a friend's house.* Underline *friend's.*

Presentation   10 minutes

Possessive nouns

- Copy the grammar charts onto the board or show Transparency 9.5 and cover the exercise.
- Above the singular sentence in the left chart, write: *They have a son.* Read the two sentences. Underline *son* and *son's.* Ask: *Which noun is possessive?* (*son's*) Say: *Possessive nouns are followed by another noun. They show that one thing or person belongs to or is related to another thing or person.* Point to the singular sentence in the left chart and ask: *What belongs to their son?* (his name)
- Read the singular sentence in the left chart. On the board, write *son name* with space between the two words. Ask: *What do you add to a singular noun to make it possessive?* Add *'s* to *son.*
- Read the first plural sentence in the right chart. On the board, write *sons names* with space between the two words. Ask: *What do you add to a plural noun that ends in -s to make it possessive?* Add an apostrophe to *sons.*
- Read the second plural sentence in the right chart. On the board, write *children classroom* with space between the two words. Ask: *What do you add to a plural noun that doesn't end in -s to make it possessive?* Use a different color to add *'s* to *children.*
- Tell students to read the Grammar Watch note silently. Then tell them to turn to page 287 and read the spelling rules for possessive nouns.
- If you are using the transparency, do the exercise with the class.

Controlled Practice   15 minutes

PRACTICE

Ⓐ Underline the correct word.

- Read the directions.

- Write the example on the board. Point to the answer and ask: *Why is the answer* daughter's? (because it's followed by another noun / because it's possessive)
- Note: In items 1–5, students determine whether the nouns are possessive or not. In items 6–7, students choose the correct possessive form.
- Students compare answers with a partner.
- Call on students to write the answers on the board.

Ⓑ Find and correct the error in each sentence.

- Read the directions.
- Write the example on the board. Point to the answer and ask: *Why is* sons *incorrect?* (because it's followed by another noun and should be possessive) Read the sentence. Underline *his* and ask: *Is it one son or more than one son?* (one son) Write *son* on the board and ask: *What do you add to a singular noun to make it possessive?* Use a different color to add *'s* to *son.*
- Tell students that every sentence has one error. Direct them to cross out the noun that has an error and write the correct form above. Tell them to look at the rest of the sentence for clues to whether the noun is singular or plural.

Ⓒ PAIRS. Check your answers.

- Call on students to write answers on the board.
- Tell students to check their own answers and then ask a partner to double-check them.

■■■ EXPANSION: Grammar Practice for C

- Tell students to write sentences telling the names of people in their family.
- Model the activity by writing your own sentences on the board (for example, *My parents' names are Robert and Karen. My husband's name is William. My sons' names are Lucas and Shawn. My daughter's name is Samantha.*).
- Tell students to ask a partner to check their possessive forms and correct any errors.

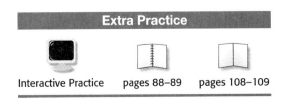

Extra Practice		
Interactive Practice	pages 88–89	pages 108–109

1 GRAMMAR

Ⓐ Complete the school newsletter. Use the future...

- Read the directions. Tell students to refer back to the grammar charts on page 170 (Future with *will*) as needed.
- Students compare answers with a partner. Tell them to read about one event each.
- Call on two students to read about the events.

> **Community Building**
>
> - Provide information (event, date, place, activities) about upcoming school or community events.
> - Form groups of 4. Tell each group to choose a different event (or their own event) and write a paragraph like the ones in Exercise 1A.
> - Tell groups to exchange papers and check spelling, grammar, and punctuation.
> - Compile the paragraphs to create a newsletter. Post the newsletter in your classroom. Offer extra credit to students who post information about events classmates might be interested in throughout the term.

Ⓑ Complete the conversations. Write the possessive...

- Read the directions. Tell students to refer back to the grammar charts on page 182 (Possessive nouns) and page 176 (Adverbs of manner) as needed.
- For the spelling of the adverb in item 4B, tell students to look at page 287 of the Grammar Reference.
- Students compare answers with a partner by reading the conversations.
- Call on pairs to read the conversations for the class. As students read, write the answers on the board.

Ⓒ Cross out the underlined nouns and write...

- Read the directions. Tell students to refer back to the grammar charts on page 177 (Object pronouns) as needed.
- Students compare answers with a partner.
- Call on students to read the sentences.

CD-ROM Practice

 Go to the CD-ROM for more practice.

If your students need more practice with the vocabulary, grammar, and competencies in Unit 9, encourage them to review the activities on the CD-ROM. This review can also help students prepare for the final role play on the following Expand page.

Extra Practice
pages 90–91

1 GRAMMAR

A Complete the school newsletter. Use the future with *will*.

March Events Oak Grove Middle School

Bake Sale

The fourth grade (1. have) __will have__
a bake sale on March 6 at 12:30 P.M. in the
cafeteria. Students (2. sell) __will sell__
cookies, cupcakes, and other baked goods.

PTO Meeting

The Oak Grove PTO (3. meet) __will meet__
on March 9. Members (4. discuss) __will discuss__
new school programs for this year. Please
join us!

B Complete the conversations. Write the possessive forms of the nouns in parentheses. Change the adjectives in parentheses to adverbs of manner.

1. **A:** How are my (son) ____son's____ grades in math?

   B: Fine. He's doing very (good) ____well____.

2. **A:** How were the (children) ____children's____ grades?

   B: Great! They're working (hard) ____hard____ in school.

3. **A:** I didn't hear the (little girl) ____little girl's____ name.

   B: I think she said, "Mimi." She speaks (quiet) ____quietly____.

4. **A:** I can't read the (student) ____student's____ handwriting.

   B: I know. He writes (sloppy) ____sloppily____.

C Cross out the underlined nouns and write object pronouns.

1. Do you know Mr. Jones? I like ~~Mr. Jones~~ a lot. *him*

2. My daughter Eliza is having a hard time. Can you help ~~Eliza~~? *her*

3. Brad's homework is hard. He doesn't understand ~~his homework~~. *it*

4. Asha's schoolbooks are heavy. It's hard for her to carry ~~her schoolbooks~~. *them*

5. I want to meet my children's teachers. I want to talk to ~~the teachers~~. *them*

2 ACT IT OUT — What do you say?

STEP 1. CLASS. Review the Lesson 2 conversation between Mr. and Mrs. Duval (CD 3 track 3).

STEP 2. ROLE PLAY. PAIRS. You are the parents of two children. Your daughter Sandra is in the seventh grade. Your son Kyle is in the ninth grade. Read the school events notices. Make plans to attend your children's events.

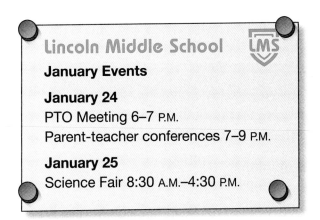

Lincoln Middle School — LMS

January Events

January 24
PTO Meeting 6–7 P.M.
Parent-teacher conferences 7–9 P.M.

January 25
Science Fair 8:30 A.M.–4:30 P.M.

Melrose High School — MELROSE
This week's school events

January 24
Band Concert 7–8 P.M.

January 25
PTO Meeting 5–6 P.M.
Parent-teacher conferences 6–9 P.M.

3 READ AND REACT — Problem-solving

STEP 1. Read about Mai's problem.

Mai's daughter Kalaya is twelve years old. Mai received a note from Kalaya's teacher. The teacher wrote that Kalaya is misbehaving in class. She is not getting along with another student. Kalaya says that the other student is bullying her. Mai believes Kalaya. She doesn't think that the teacher is being fair.

STEP 2. PAIRS. What is Mai's problem? What can she do?
Here are some ideas.

- She can talk to the teacher.
- She can talk to the school principal.
- She can talk to the other student's parents.
- She can _____.

4 CONNECT

For your Study Skills Activity, go to page 253.
For your Team Project, go to page 282.

Which goals can you check off? Go back to page 165.

EXPAND   Show what you know!

2   ACT IT OUT

STEP 1. CLASS. Review the Lesson 2 conversation...

- Tell students to review the conversation in Exercise 3B on page 169.
- Ask them to read the conversation silently and then practice it with a partner.
- Play CD 3, Track 3. Students listen.
- As needed, play Track 3 again to aid comprehension.

STEP 2. ROLE PLAY. PAIRS. You are the parents...

- Read the directions.
- Pair students. Ask: *What's the name of your daughter's school?* (Lincoln Middle School) *What's the name of your son's school?* (Melrose High School)
- Say: *Parent A, start a conversation by saying:* Sandra brought a notice home from school today. There's a .... *Parent B, ask when the event is. Tell Parent A about Kyle's events. Talk about which events you'll go to, who will go, and when you'll go.*
- As needed, suggest that students review prepositions of time on page 130.
- Walk around and observe partners interacting. Check pairs' use of *will*, especially contractions with *will*, and possessive nouns (*Sandra's parent-teacher conference, Kyle's band concert*).
- Call on pairs to perform for the class.
- While pairs are performing, use the scoring rubric on page T-xiii to evaluate each student's vocabulary, grammar, fluency, and how well he or she completes the task.
- *Optional:* After each pair finishes, discuss the strengths and weakness of each performance either in front of the class or privately.

3   READ AND REACT

STEP 1. Read about Mai's problem.

- Say: *We are going to read about a student's problem, and then we need to think about a solution.*
- Read the directions.
- Read the story while students follow along silently. Pause after each sentence to allow time for students to comprehend. Periodically stop and ask simple *Wh-* questions to check comprehension (for

example, *Who is Kalaya? What trouble is Kalaya having in school? According to Kalaya, what is really happening? Who does Mai believe?*).

STEP 2. PAIRS. What is Mai's problem? What can...

- Ask: *What is Mai's problem?* (Her daughter Kalaya's teacher says Kalaya is misbehaving in class. Kalaya says another student is bullying her.) *What can Mai do?*
- Pair students. Read the ideas in the list. Give pairs a couple of minutes to discuss possible solutions for Mai.
- Ask: *Which ideas are good?* Call on students to say their opinion about the ideas in the list (for example, S: *I think she can talk to the teacher. This is a good idea.*).
- Now tell pairs to think of one new idea not in the list (for example, *She can ask the teacher to move Kalaya to a different seat, away from the other student.*) and to write it in the blank. Tell students to think of more than one idea and to write the ideas in their notebooks.
- Call on pairs to say their additional solutions. Write any particularly good ones on the board and ask students if they think it is a good idea, too (*Do you think this is a good idea? Why or why not?*).

▬▬ MULTILEVEL INSTRUCTION for STEP 2
Pre-level Ask pairs to agree on one good idea.
Above-level Ask pairs to rank the ideas in the list (including their new idea) on a scale of 1–4 (1 = the best).

4   CONNECT

Turn to page 253 for the Study Skills Activity and page 282 for the Team Project. See page T-xi for general notes about teaching these activities.

Progress Check

Which goals can you check off? Go back to page 165.
Ask students to turn to page 165 and check off any remaining goals they have reached. Call on students to say which goals they will practice outside of class.

10

Let's Eat!

Classroom Materials/Extra Practice

CD 3
Tracks 18–32

T
Transparencies 10.1–10.6
Vocabulary Cards Unit 10

MCA
Unit 10

Workbook
Unit 10

Interactive Practice
Unit 10

Unit Overview

Goals
- See the list of goals on the facing page.

Grammar
- Count nouns / Non-count nouns
- *How much / How many*
- Comparative adjectives with *than*
- Quantifiers with plural and non-count nouns

Pronunciation
- Weak pronunciation of *to*, *the*, *a*, and *of*

Reading
- Read an article about the nutrients in food
- *Reading Skill:* Read about the effects of caffeine

Writing
- Write a food shopping list
- Write a radio commercial for a food product
- Keep a caffeine journal

Life Skills Writing
- Complete a healthy eating log

Preview
- Set the context of the unit by asking questions about eating habits (for example, *Where do you shop for food? Do you try to eat a healthy diet? How often do you eat out?*).
- Hold up page 185 or show Transparency 10.1. Read the unit title and ask the class to repeat.
- Say: *Look at the picture.* Ask the Preview questions: *Where are the people?* (at the supermarket) *What are they doing?* (shopping for food / reading a label)

Goals
- Point to the Unit Goals. Explain that this list shows what the class will be studying in this unit.
- Tell students to read the goals silently.
- Say each goal and ask the class to repeat. Explain unfamiliar vocabulary as needed:

  Quantity: an amount of something that can be counted or measured (Use items in your classroom to demonstrate; for example, *10 paperclips is a quantity. Half a glass of water is a quantity.*)

  Nutrition information: the amount of calories, fat, cholesterol, etc., in a food product (Bring in a food product or container and point to the nutrition information on the label.)

  Log: a record; a list of dates, times, and facts
- Tell students to circle one goal that is very important to them. Call on several students to say the goal they circled.

Let's Eat!

Preview

Look at the picture.
Where are the people?
What are they doing?

UNIT GOALS

- [ ] Identify food containers and quantities

- [ ] Ask for quantities of food

- [ ] Read nutrition information

- [ ] Complete a healthy eating log

- [ ] Compare information in food ads

- [ ] Read a menu

- [ ] Order food in a restaurant

1   WHAT DO YOU KNOW?

A   **CLASS.** Look at the pictures. Which foods do you know? Which containers and quantities do you know?

CD3 T18

B   Look at the pictures and listen. Then listen and repeat.

2   PRACTICE

CD3 T19

A   Look at the pictures and listen. Check the pictures of the words you hear.

B   **PAIRS.** Check your answers.

C   **WORD PLAY. GROUPS OF 3.** Which foods come in these containers? Use the foods in the pictures and your own ideas.   Answers will vary but could include:

a bag of
- *oranges*
- rice
- potato chips
- _____

a box of
- cereal
- cookies
- crackers
- _____

a can of
- tomatoes
- soup
- tuna
- _____

a jar of
- mayonnaise
- jelly
- pickles
- _____

1

6

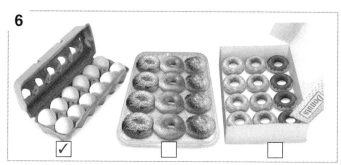

8   **9**

12   **13**

14

Lesson 1 Vocabulary

Getting Started 10 minutes

1 WHAT DO YOU KNOW?

Ⓐ CLASS. Look at the pictures. Which foods...

- Show Transparency 10.2 or hold up the book. Tell students to cover the list of words on page 187.
- Say: *Look at the pictures. Which foods do you know?* Elicit a food (for example, *Number 6 has donuts.*).
- Students call out answers. Help students pronounce foods if they have difficulty.
- Say: *Look at the pictures. Which containers and quantities do you know?* Elicit a container or quantity and write it on the board (for example, *Number 4 is "box."*).
- If students call out an incorrect container or quantity, change the student's answer into a question for the class (for example, *Number 8 is "jar?"*). If nobody can identify the correct container or quantity, tell students they will now listen to a CD and practice the food containers and quantities vocabulary.

Presentation 10 minutes

Ⓑ Look at the pictures and listen. Then...

- Play CD 3, Track 18. Students listen. Pause after number 14 (*pound*).
- To check comprehension, say each container or quantity in random order and ask students to point to the appropriate picture.
- Resume playing Track 18. Students listen and repeat.

Teaching Tip

To make sure students are connecting the new words with their meanings, tell them to point to the pictures as they listen / listen and repeat.

Controlled Practice 25 minutes

2 PRACTICE

Ⓐ Look at the pictures and listen. Check...

- Read the directions. Say: *For example, when you hear "a bag of potato chips," write a checkmark in the box under the potato chips.*
- Tell students to look at the pictures and read the labels on the food containers.
- Play CD 3, Track 19. Students listen and write a checkmark under the correct items.

Ⓑ PAIRS. Check your answers.

- Pair students and tell them to compare checkmarks.
- *Optional:* Tell pairs to look at the pictures they didn't check and identify the container or quantity and the food.
- *Optional:* If you are using the transparency, as the class listens, check the pictures on Transparency 10.2.

Ⓒ WORD PLAY. GROUPS OF 3. Which foods...

- Read the directions.
- On the board, write: *a bag of . . .* Ask: *Which picture shows bag?* (picture 1) *What foods are in picture 1?* On the board, list: *potato chips, rice, oranges.* Ask: *What other foods come in a bag?* Use students' responses to add to the list on the board (for example, *pasta, flour, pretzels, frozen vegetables*).
- Form groups of 3. Walk around and check spelling. If you see a misspelled food, write the word correctly on the board.

Learning Strategy: Draw pictures

- Provide each student with four index cards or tell students to cut up notebook paper into four pieces.
- Read the directions. If you have students with low first-language skills, pair them with more capable peers if possible.
- Walk around as students work. If misspellings occur, tell them to check the list on page 187.
- Say: *You can make cards with pictures to remember new words.* Remind students to use this strategy to remember other new vocabulary.

Community Building

When students make cards for vocabulary words, they can use them to quiz each other.

Communicative Practice   15 minutes

Show what you know!

STEP 1. Think about the food you have at home....

- Read the directions.
- Write the examples on the board. Underline *of* in each item. Add *a dozen eggs* to the list. Point out that we use *of* after all the containers and quantities except *dozen*.
- Model the activity. Write your own list of several food items on the board (for example, *a box of cereal, a bag of pretzels, a bottle of apple juice, a half-gallon of milk, a dozen bagels*). Underline *a* and *of* in each item.
- Walk around and spot-check students' spelling. Remind students to use *a* and *of* (except with *dozen*).

STEP 2. GROUPS OF 4. Compare your lists. Circle...

- Read the directions.
- Model the activity. Ask three students to read you their lists. As each student reads, check the items that are also on your list. Circle the items on your list that have three checkmarks.
- Form groups of 4. Students take turns reading their lists. Group members listen and check the items that are also on their list.

STEP 3. Tell the class about the food your group has...

- Read the directions and the example.
- Point to the circled items on your list on the board and say: *We all have . . .*
- Tell groups to check that all members circled the same items.
- Tell groups to write a sentence similar to the example and practice telling the class about the food the group has at home.
- Call on one student from each group to report to the class.

EXPANSION: Listening Practice for STEP 3

- As each group reports to the class in Step 3, tell students to listen and check the circled items that are also on their list.
- Ask the class: *Are there any foods that everyone in the class has at home?* Write these on the board.

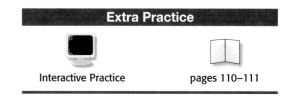

Extra Practice	
Interactive Practice	pages 110–111

2  ✓ ☐ ☐

3 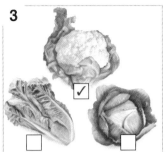 ✓ ☐ ☐

4  ✓ ☐ ☐

5  ☐ ✓ ☐

7  ☐ ☐ ✓

Food Containers and Quantities

1. bag
2. bunch
3. head
4. box
5. can
6. dozen
7. jar

8. bottle
9. container
10. pint
11. quart
12. half-gallon
13. gallon
14. pound

Learning Strategy

Draw pictures

Look at the list of food containers. Make cards for three or four food containers. On one side, write the word. On the other side, draw a picture of the container.

10  ✓ ☐ ☐

11  ✓ ☐ ☐

Show what you know!

STEP 1. Think about the food you have at home. Write a list of ten food items. Use container and quantity words.

> a gallon of milk
> a head of lettuce

STEP 2. GROUPS OF 4. Compare your lists. Circle the foods that everyone in your group has at home.

STEP 3. Tell the class about the food your group has at home.

We all have a gallon of milk and . . .

Ask for quantities of food

Listening and Speaking

1 BEFORE YOU LISTEN

CLASS. Where do you go food shopping? What kind of store is it? Find classmates who shop at the same kind of stores. Talk about why you shop there.

a supermarket

a convenience store

an outdoor market

2 LISTEN

A CLASS. Look at the picture of two roommates, Agnes and Yuka. Guess: What are they talking about?

CD3 T20

B Listen to the conversation. Was your guess in Exercise A correct?

CD3 T20

C Listen again. What does Agnes need from the grocery store? What does Yuka need? Write *A* for Agnes and *Y* for Yuka.

Y

Y

A

CD3 T21

D Listen to the whole conversation. Complete the sentence.

Agnes needs to _____.

a. find her purse   b. get something from the refrigerator   c. write the things down

Getting Started   10 minutes

1   BEFORE YOU LISTEN

CLASS. Where do you go food shopping? What...

- Tell the class to look at the pictures. Say each type of store and ask the class to repeat.
- To check understanding, ask questions: *Which is bigger, a supermarket or a convenience store?* (a supermarket) *Which one usually has better prices?* (a supermarket) *Where can you find the freshest fruits and vegetables?* (at an outdoor market)
- Ask: *Where do you go food shopping?* Tell students to write down the name of the store where they usually shop for food. Ask: *What kind of store is it?* Tell students to circle the kind of store.
- Tell students to stand, mingle, and ask each other: *Where do you go food shopping? What kind of store is it?* Say: *When you find a classmate who shops at the same kind of food store, stay together. Look for other classmates who shop at the same kind of food store. When you've formed a small group, sit down and talk about why you shop there.*
- Write the three types of store on the board as headings. Ask a member from each group to come to the board and write a couple of the group's reasons under the appropriate heading.
- Read the reasons why students shop at each kind of store. Ask the class: *Which type of store is most popular? Why?*

Presentation   5 minutes

2   LISTEN

Ⓐ CLASS. Look at the picture of two roommates....

- Read the directions. Ask: *What are they talking about?*
- Elicit students' guesses and list them on the board. Students will listen for the answer in Exercise B.

> **Teaching Tip**
>
> *Optional:* Remember that if students need additional support, tell them to read the Audio Script on page 305 as they listen to the conversations.

Ⓑ Listen to the conversation. Was your...

- Read the directions. Play CD 3, Track 20. Students listen.
- Ask: *What are they talking about?* Read the guesses on the board. Elicit and circle the best answer. (Answer: what they need from the grocery store)

Controlled Practice   10 minutes

Ⓒ Listen again. What does Agnes need...

- Tell students to look at the picture again. Say: *Point to Agnes. Point to Yuka.* Ask: *Which roommate is going to the grocery store?* (Agnes)
- Read the directions.
- Point to each picture and ask the class to call out the food item (*a can of tomatoes, onions, milk*)
- Play Track 20 again. Students listen and write *A* or *Y* next to the pictures.
- To review, ask: *What does Agnes need from the grocery store?* (milk) *What does Yuka need?* (a can of tomatoes and two onions)

Ⓓ Listen to the whole conversation....

- Read the directions.
- Tell students to read the item and answer choices silently.
- Play CD 3, Track 21. Students listen and circle the letter of the correct answer.
- Call on a student to read the sentence.

▬▬ EXPANSION: Vocabulary and listening practice for 2D

- Tell students they will write Agnes's complete grocery list. Tell them to first write the items pictured in Exercise 2C.
- Play CD 3, Track 21.
- Students listen to the whole conversation and write three more items. Tell them to use the food containers and quantities vocabulary from page 187.
- Play Track 21 as many times as needed to aid comprehension.
- Call on students to list the items on the board (*a can of tomatoes, two onions, a jar of mayonnaise, a loaf of bread, a box of cereal*).

Lesson 2   Ask for quantities of food

Presentation   5 minutes

 3   CONVERSATION

Listen and repeat the conversation.

- Note: This conversation is the same one students heard in Exercise 2B on page 188.
- Tell students to read the conversation silently.
- Play CD 3, Track 22. Students listen and repeat.

Controlled Practice   15 minutes

4   PRACTICE

Ⓐ PAIRS. Practice the conversation. Then....

- Pair students and tell them to practice the conversation in Exercise 3. Walk around and help with pronunciation as needed.
- Read the directions.
- Tell students to look at the pictures of food items. Ask the class to call out the foods. Say each food and ask the class to repeat. Use the plurals *cucumbers*, *apples*, and *oranges*.
- Copy the conversation onto the board with blanks. Read through the conversation. When you come to a blank, fill it in with a student's name or information from the same row in the boxes. As you fill in each blank, say the color of the answer space and point to the picture in the same-color box.
- Ask two students to read the conversation on the board. Ask the student whose name you used to play B.
- Ask two on-level students to practice a new conversation in front of the class.

- Tell pairs to take turns playing each role and to use information from the same row in the boxes to fill in the blanks.
- Walk around and check that students use the plurals *cucumbers*, *apples*, and *oranges* when appropriate.
- Tell students to stand, mingle, and practice the conversation with several new partners.
- Call on pairs to perform for the class.

Communicative Practice   15 minutes

Ⓑ ROLE PLAY. PAIRS. Make your own....

- Read the directions.
- On the board, write as headings: *some* _____, *a can of* _____, and *two* _____. Brainstorm and list one food item under each heading.
- Tell students to look at the headings and example and think of their own three food items. Tell them to write their food items under the pictures in Exercise 4A. Walk around and check that the food items students choose work with *some*, *a can of*, and *two* respectively.
- Pair students and tell them to use B's food items in the conversation from Exercise 4A. Walk around and make sure partners take turns playing each role.
- Call on pairs to perform for the class.

▅▅▅ **MULTILEVEL INSTRUCTION for 4B**

Cross-ability Direct the higher-level student to play A first and model by repeating B's food items in A's second and third lines.

Extra Practice

Interactive Practice

3 CONVERSATION

CD1 T26

Listen and repeat the conversation.

Agnes: Hi, Yuka. I'm going to the grocery store for some milk. Do you need anything?

Yuka: Uh, let me see. Could you get a can of tomatoes?

Agnes: A can of tomatoes? Sure, no problem.

Yuka: Oh, and I need some onions.

Agnes: How many onions?

Yuka: Two.

Agnes: All right. A can of tomatoes and two onions. I'll be back in a little while.

4 PRACTICE

A PAIRS. Practice the conversation. Then make new conversations. Use your own names and the information in the boxes.

A: Hi, _____. I'm going to the grocery store for some _____. Do you need anything?

B: Uh, let me see. Could you get a can of _____?

A: A can of _____? Sure, no problem.

B: Oh, and I need some _____.

A: How many _____?

B: Two.

A: All right. A _____ and two _____. I'll be back in a little while.

B ROLE PLAY. PAIRS. Make your own conversations. Talk about the food you need.

Ask for quantities of food

Grammar

Count nouns/Non-count nouns

Singular count nouns	Plural count nouns	Non-count nouns	
an onion a sandwich	two onions some sandwiches	bread fish	milk rice

Yes/No questions		Affirmative/Negative answers			
Are	onions?	**Yes,** **No,**	**are** **aren't**	**some** **any**.	on the counter. Sorry.
there **any**		there			
Is	milk?	**Yes,** **No,**	**is** **isn't**	**some** **any**.	in the fridge. Sorry.

Grammar Watch

- There is = there's
- See page 288 for spelling rules for plurals.
- See page 289 for more examples of non-count nouns.

1 PRACTICE

A Complete the questions with *Is/Are there any*. Complete the answers with *There's/There are* or *There isn't/aren't*.

1. **A:** _____Is there any_____ bread?

   B: Yes, _____there's_____ some on the counter.

2. **A:** _____Are there any_____ tomatoes?

   B: No, _____there aren't_____ any.

3. **A:** _____Is there any_____ coffee?

   B: Yes, _____there's_____ some in the pot.

4. **A:** _____Are there any_____ carrots?

   B: Yes, _____there are_____ some in the refrigerator.

5. **A:** _____Is there any_____ butter?

   B: No, _____there isn't_____ any, but we have margarine.

6. **A:** _____Are there any_____ bananas?

   B: No, _____there aren't any_____. I ate the last one.

B PAIRS. Practice the conversations in Exercise A.

Getting Started 5 minutes

- Say: *We're going to study count nouns and non-count nouns. In the conversation on page 189, Agnes and Yuka used this grammar.*
- Play CD 3, Track 22. Students listen. Write on the board: *I'm going to the store for some milk*; *Oh, and I need some onions*; and *two onions*. Underline *some milk*, *some onions*, and *two onions*.

Presentation 15 minutes

Count nouns / Non-count nouns

- Copy the grammar charts onto the board or show Transparency 10.3 and cover the exercise.
- Point to the top charts. Ask: *What are the singular count nouns?* Underline *an* and *a* in *an onion* and *a sandwich*. Ask: *What are the plural forms of the count nouns?* Underline the plural endings in *onions* and *sandwiches*.
- Ask: *What are the non-count nouns?* (*bread, fish, milk*, and *rice*) Next to the heading *Non-count nouns*, write and then cross out *a, an* and *-s*:

Say: *Do not use* a *or* an *with non-count nouns. Non-count nouns do not have plural forms.*
- Point to the bottom charts. To the left, label the top row *plural count nouns* and the bottom row *non-count nouns*.
- Read the sentences for the plural count nouns across the charts (*Are there any onions? Yes, there are some on the counter. / No there aren't any. Sorry.*) and ask the class to repeat. Say: *Use* there are *with plural count nouns.*
- Read the statements for the non-count nouns across the charts (*Is there any milk? Yes, there is some in the fridge. / No there isn't any. Sorry.*) and ask the class to repeat. Say: *Use* there is *with non-count count nouns.*
- Read the *Yes / No* questions and the negative answers again and ask the class to repeat. Say: *Use* any *in questions and negative sentences.*
- Read the affirmative answers and ask the class to repeat. Say: *Use* some *in affirmative sentences.*
- Tell students to read the Grammar Watch note silently. Tell them to turn to pages 288–289 and read more about nouns.
- If you are using the transparency, do the exercise with the class.

Controlled Practice 10 minutes

1 PRACTICE

A Complete the questions with *Is / Are there any...*

- Read the first sentence of the directions. Write the first line of the example on the board. Ask: *Why is the answer* Is there any? (because *bread* is non-count)
- Read the second sentence of the directions. Write the second line of the example on the board. Ask: *Why is the answer* there's? (because *bread* is non-count and the answer is affirmative)
- Tell students to look at the noun in each item. Remind students that nouns with plural endings are count nouns.
- Walk around as students complete the exercise and spot-check students' answers. If you see an incorrect answer, ask the student to circle the noun in the item and then ask: *Is the answer* Is there any *or* Are there any? *or* Is the answer *There's* or *There are?* If the error is with affirmative / negative, tell the student to circle *Yes* or *No* in the second line.

B PAIRS. Practice the conversations in Exercise A.

- Pair students and tell them to compare answers by asking and answering the questions.
- Call on pairs to ask and answer the questions for the class. Correct as needed.

EXPANSION: Speaking Practice for 1B

- Tell students to look at the foods on pages 186–187 and make a list of five count and five non-count nouns. Model by writing the headings *count* and *non-count* on the board and numbering from 1 to 5. Elicit and list on the board a couple of count nouns (for example, *oranges, eggs*) and a couple of non-count nouns (for example, *rice, olive oil*).
- Pair students. Say: *Ask your partner about the food in his or her fridge or cupboard at home. Use* Are there any *or* Is there any *and the foods on your lists.* Model by pointing to a count noun on the board and asking an above-level student: *Are there any [eggs] in your fridge?* Then point to a non-count noun and ask the same student: *Is there any [rice] in your cupboard?*

Lesson 3 Ask for quantities of food

Presentation 5 minutes

How much / How many

- Copy the grammar chart onto the board or show the chart on Transparency 10.3 and cover the exercise.
- Read the sentences and ask the class to repeat.
- Ask: *Do we use* How many *or* How much *with plural count nouns like* eggs *or* oranges? (*How many*) *What do we use with non-count nouns like* chicken *or* sugar? (*How much*)
- Point out that containers and quantities can be used to make non-count nouns countable. *Optional:* For practice with this, write on the board: *rice—2, soda—5, yogurt—8, milk—3, meat—1.* Tell students to use containers or quantities to write the amounts (*2 bags of rice, 5 bottles of soda, 8 containers of yogurt, 3 gallons of milk, a pound of meat*)
- On the board, write: *How _____ rice? How _____ bags of rice?* Ask the class to complete the questions. (*much, many*)

Controlled Practice 10 minutes

2 PRACTICE

Ⓐ Complete the conversation. Underline the correct...

- Read the directions and the example. Ask: *Why is the answer* many? (because *potatoes* is a plural count noun)
- Remind students to refer to page 289 for more examples of non-count nouns.
- Students compare answers by reading the conversation with a partner.
- Call on two higher-level students to read the conversation for the class.

Ⓑ WRITE. Write Beatriz's shopping list.

- Read the directions. Read the first two lines of the conversation in Exercise 2A. Then point to the shopping list and read: *5 lbs. of potatoes.*
- On the board, write: *lbs. = pounds, lb. = pound.*
- Call on students to write the items on Beatriz's shopping list on the board.

Communicative Practice 15 minutes

Show what you know!

STEP 1. What food do you like to take on a picnic....

- Read the directions. To model, elicit a couple of ideas and write them on the board.
- Walk around and check that students use plural count nouns or non-count nouns (no -*s*).
- Ask several students to write three items each on the board. Ask the class to check that the count nouns end in -*s* and the non-count nouns don't.

STEP 2. GROUPS OF 5. Plan a picnic. Decide...

- Form groups of 5. Read the directions.
- Ask a group to model the example. Assign roles of A, B, C, D, and E. A, B, and C read the example. Prompt D to suggest a food item from his or her list (*Let's take some . . .*). Prompt E to ask: *How much / How many do we need?* Say: *OK. We have [five chicken sandwiches] and [two bags of potato chips]. What else will we take?*
- Say: *Every group member should take a turn suggesting a food item to take. You can say: Let's take some . . . . Every group member should ask* How much / How many do we need? *about another member's suggestion.*
- Walk around and make sure all group members take a turn suggesting a food item and asking *How much / How many do we need?* about another member's suggestion.

▬▬▬ MULTILEVEL INSTRUCTION for STEP 2
Cross-ability Assign roles of D and E to higher-level students in the group.

Progress Check

Can you . . . ask for quantities of food?
Say: *We have practiced asking for quantities of food. Now, look at the question at the bottom of the page. Can you ask for quantities of food?* Tell students to write a checkmark in the box.

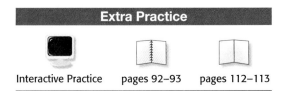

Extra Practice		
Interactive Practice	pages 92–93	pages 112–113

How much / How many			
How	**much**	chicken oil	do we need?
	many	eggs cans of soup	

2 PRACTICE

A **Complete the conversation. Underline the correct words.**

Ana: How **much** / <u>**many**</u> potatoes do we have? Do we need more?

Beatriz: Yes. I'll get a five-pound bag at the store.

Ana: OK. Are you going to get <u>**cheese**</u> / **cheeses**?

Beatriz: Yeah. But how <u>**much**</u> / **many** cheese do we need?

Ana: Oh, a pound is fine. We need some <u>**fruit**</u> / **fruits**, too.

Beatriz: OK. I'll get three **orange** / <u>**oranges**</u>.

Ana: How <u>**much**</u> / **many** milk do we have?

Beatriz: None. I'll get a half-gallon.

Ana: Could you get some <u>**sugar**</u> / **sugars**, too?

Beatriz: Sure. How <u>**much**</u> / **many** sugar do you want?

Ana: One pound is enough.

Shopping List

5 lbs. of potatoes

1 lb. of cheese

3 oranges

1½-gallon of milk

1 lb. of sugar

_____

B **WRITE.** **Write Beatriz's shopping list.**

Show what you know! Ask for quantities of food

STEP 1. **What food do you like to take on a picnic? Write a list.**

STEP 2. GROUPS OF 5. **Plan a picnic. Decide where to go and what food you will take.**

A: *Let's go to Central Park.*
B: *OK. Let's take some chicken sandwiches.*
C: *Good idea. How many do we need? I think . . .*

Can you . . . ask for quantities of food? ☐

Life Skills

1 READ FOOD LABELS

A **CLASS.** Do you eat a healthy diet? How do you know the foods you eat are healthy?

B Scan the article. What is a nutrient?

What's in My Food?

Carbohydrates, cholesterol, fiber, protein, sodium, and sugar are some of the nutrients in food. All of these nutrients are good for you, but only in the right amounts.

Carbohydrates give you energy for several hours. Foods such as pasta, bread, and potatoes have a lot of carbohydrates.

Cholesterol is only in animal fat. Foods such as butter, mayonnaise, red meat, and eggs have a lot of cholesterol. Too much cholesterol is not good for you.

Fiber is from plants. Foods such as vegetables, fruits, and grains all have lots of fiber. Fiber is good for you. It helps your stomach digest food.

Protein makes your body strong. Foods such as chicken, fish, and beans have a lot of protein.

Sodium is another word for salt. Foods such as potato chips, canned soups, and olives have a lot of sodium. Too much sodium is not good for you.

Sugar gives you quick energy. Candy, cookies, and soda have a lot of sugar. Too much sugar is not good for you. Watch out! Sometimes sugar has a different name, such as high-maltose corn syrup or high-fructose corn syrup.

How do you find out what's in your food?

Read the ingredient and nutrition labels on your food packages. An ingredient label lists all the ingredients in the food. The ingredients are listed in the order of amount. The first ingredient on the list is the main (or largest) ingredient. The last ingredient is the smallest one. A nutrient label lists the amount of each nutrient in one serving of the food. To eat a healthy diet, you need to ask, "What's in my food?" and make sure you eat the right amounts of each nutrient.

C Read the article. Write the missing food item for each nutrient category.

1. **carbohydrates:** bread, potatoes, _____*pasta*_____

2. **cholesterol:** butter, mayonnaise, red meat, _____eggs_____

3. **fiber:** vegetables, grains, _____fruits_____

4. **protein:** chicken, beans, _____fish_____

5. **sodium:** potato chips, olives, _____canned soups_____

6. **sugar:** candy, soda, _____cookies_____

Lesson 4 Read nutrition information

Getting Started 5 minutes

- Ask: *When you go food shopping, do you read food labels? What nutrition information do you look for?*
- Write students' responses on the board (for example, *calories, sugar, fat, fiber, sodium*).

Presentation 35 minutes

 READ FOOD LABELS

A CLASS. **Do you eat a healthy diet? How do you...**

- Ask: *Do you eat a healthy diet?* Ask for a show of hands.
- Ask students who raised their hands: *How do you know the foods you eat are healthy? What fresh foods are healthy?* (fruit, vegetables, fish, nuts) *What packaged foods are healthy?* Elicit a couple of ideas and then ask: *How do you know?*
- Say: *To find out what packaged foods are healthy, you can read the nutrition information on the food label.* Point to students' responses from Getting Started on the board. Point to each one and ask: *What's healthy? High [fiber] or low [fiber]?* Write *high* or *low* in front of each response.

B Scan the article. **What is a nutrient?**

- Read the directions.
- Remind students: Scanning an article *means reading it quickly to find specific information. Look quickly at the article to find the word* nutrient.
- Allow about a minute for students to scan the article. Ask where they found *nutrient* (in the first paragraph).
- Ask: *What is a nutrient?* (*Possible answers:* what's in food; the things in food that are good for you; things like carbohydrates, cholesterol, fiber.) Write students' responses on the board.

C Read the article. **Write the missing food item...**

- Direct students to read the article silently.
- Read the directions and the example. Tell students to find the part of the article that talks about carbohydrates and underline the foods that have a lot of carbohydrates.

- Students compare answers with a partner.
- Say each nutrient category and ask the class to repeat.
- Tell students to close their books. Say the groups of food items in random order and ask the class to call out the nutrient categories.

EXPANSION: Speaking and Vocabulary Practice for 1C

- Tell students to look at the food items in Exercise 1C and underline the ones they eat often. Ask: *What nutrients do you eat a lot of?*
- On the board, write: *For a healthy diet, eat foods that are high in _____. Eat foods that are low in _____, _____, and _____.* Tell students to read the article again and complete the sentences (*high in fiber; low in cholesterol, sodium, and sugar*).
- Pair students. Say: *Tell your partner what foods you will eat less of and why. Tell your partner what foods you will eat more of and why.* Write on the board: *I will drink / eat less _____. I will drink / eat more _____.* Model by talking about your own diet. Say: *I will drink less soda because it has a lot of sugar. I will eat more fruits and vegetables because they have a lot of fiber.*

EXPANSION: Graphic Organizer for 1C

- Draw a chart on the board with the column headings: *Nutrient, Foods with a lot, What it does,* and *Eat a lot or a little?* Use the nutrient categories as row headings.
- Tell students to read the article again and complete the chart. Tell them that some information will be missing from the chart.
- To model, read the *Carbohydrates* section of the article and fill in the first row of the chart: *pasta, bread, potatoes; gives you energy.* Explain to students that for *carbohydrates*, they can leave the last column blank, since the article does not provide information about how many carbohydrates to eat.

Lesson 4 Read nutrition information

D **Read the nutrition labels for a gallon of whole milk...**

- Say: *Read the nutrition labels for a gallon of whole milk and a gallon of non-fat milk.*
- Ask: *What nutrient does milk have that makes your body strong?* (protein) *How many grams of fat does whole milk have?* (8 grams) *How many grams of fat does non-fat milk have?* (0 grams)
- Say: *Greasy, oily foods like French fries, donuts, and butter have a lot of fat. Too much fat is not good for you.* On the board, write: *For a healthy diet, eat foods that are high / low in fat.* Tell the class to call out the answer. Circle *low.*
- Tell students to find *calories* on the labels. Explain: *Calories are a measure of how much energy a food can produce. People need a certain amount of calories every day to stay healthy. We burn calories through exercise and everyday activities. People gain weight when they eat a lot of calories and don't burn them.* On the board, write: *If you aren't trying to gain weight, eat foods that are high / low in calories.* Tell the class to call out the answer. Circle *low.*
- Read the example. Tell students to find *servings per container* on each label. Ask: *How much milk is in one serving?* (one cup) Say: *The nutrition information on each label is for one cup of milk.*

E **PAIRS. Check your answers.**

- Students compare answers with a partner. Tell them to take turns reading the sentences out loud.
- Tell pairs to correct the false sentences (3. <u>8 grams</u>, 6. <u>0 grams</u>, 8. <u>8 grams</u>).

Communicative Practice   15 minutes

2 PRACTICE

A **GROUPS OF 3. Look at the two nutrition labels...**

- Form groups of 3.
- Say: *Look at the two nutrition labels in Exercise D again. Circle the numbers that are different for each.*
- Ask groups: *Which milk do you think is better for your health? Why?* Say: *Take turns completing the example with one reason. Each group member should try to give a different reason.*
- Ask the class: *Which milk do you think is better for your health? Why?* Elicit and write on the board: *It's lower in calories. It's lower in fat. It's lower in cholesterol.*

MULTILEVEL INSTRUCTION for 3A

Cross-ability Direct higher-level students to say a reason why non-fat milk is better for your health first, modeling the language to use. Direct lower-level students to say a reason second.

B **PAIRS. Look at the labels. Circle...**

- Read the directions.
- Tell students to silently re-read the last section (*How do you find out what's in your food?*) of the article on page 192.
- Pair students and tell them to find the sentence in the article that tells which ingredient is the main ingredient. (*The first ingredient on the list . . .*) Students circle the main ingredient on each label.
- Tell students to silently re-read the *Sugar* section of the article. Then tell pairs to find the other names for sugar (*high-maltose corn syrup, high-fructose corn syrup*). Students underline the sugar ingredients on each label.
- To review, ask: *What's the main / largest ingredient in the peanut energy bar?* (peanuts) *What's the main / largest ingredient in the orange drink?* (water) *What are the sugar ingredients in the peanut energy bar?* (high-maltose corn syrup, sugar, high-fructose corn syrup) *What are the sugar ingredients in the orange drink?* (high-fructose corn syrup, sugar)

3 LIFE SKILLS WRITING

Turn to page 265 and ask students to complete the healthy eating log. See page T-xii for general notes about the Life Skills Writing activities.

Progress Check

Can you . . . read nutrition information?

Say: *We have practiced reading nutrition information. Now, look at the question at the bottom of the page. Can you read nutrition information?* Tell students to write a checkmark in the box.

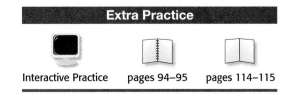

Extra Practice		
Interactive Practice	pages 94–95	pages 114–115

Nutrition Facts
Serving Size 1 Cup
Servings Per Container 16

Amount Per Serving	
Calories 160 Calories from Fat 71	
Total Fat 8 g	
Cholesterol 35 mg	
Sodium 125 mg	
Total Carbohydrate 13 g	
Dietary Fiber 0 g	
Sugar 12 g	
Protein 8 g	

whole milk

Nutrition Facts
Serving Size 1 Cup
Servings Per Container 16

Amount Per Serving	
Calories 90 Calories from Fat 0	
Total Fat 0 g	
Cholesterol 5 mg	
Sodium 130 mg	
Total Carbohydrate 13 g	
Dietary Fiber 0 g	
Sugar 12 g	
Protein 8 g	

non-fat milk

D Read the nutrition labels for a gallon of whole milk and a gallon of non-fat milk. Read the sentences. Circle *True* or *False*.

> g = grams
> mg = milligrams

1. There are 16 servings in a gallon of milk. **(True)** False
2. The whole milk has 160 calories per serving. **(True)** False
3. The whole milk has zero grams of total fat per serving. True **(False)**
4. The non-fat milk has 5 milligrams of cholesterol per serving. **(True)** False
5. The whole milk has 125 milligrams of sodium per serving. **(True)** False
6. Non-fat milk has 12 grams of dietary fiber per serving. True **(False)**
7. Both kinds of milk have 12 grams of sugar per serving. **(True)** False
8. The non-fat milk has zero grams of protein per serving. True **(False)**

E PAIRS. Check your answers.

2 PRACTICE

A GROUPS OF 3. Look at the two nutrition labels in Exercise D again. Which milk do you think is better for your health? Why?

I think non-fat milk is better because . . .

B PAIRS. Look at the labels. Circle the main ingredient. Underline the sugar ingredients.

Ingredients: peanuts, high-maltose corn syrup, sugar, rolled oats, high-fructuse corn syrup.

SUNSHINE ORANGE DRINK

Ingredients: water, high-fructose corn syrup, sugar, 2% or less of each of the following juices — orange, apple, lime, grapefruit.

3 LIFE SKILLS WRITING

Complete a healthy eating log. See page 265.

Can you... read nutrition information? ☐

Listening and Speaking

1 BEFORE YOU LISTEN

CLASS. **Look at the people. Read the reasons that they buy food. What's important to *you* when you buy food?**

Convenience is important to me. I buy food that's easy to prepare.

I buy food that **tastes good**. That's all I care about.

I think about **price**. I get store brands and things on sale.

I buy **healthy** food like low-fat milk and whole wheat bread.

I like **fresh** fruits and vegetables. I don't buy frozen or canned food.

2 LISTEN

CD3 T23

A **Listen to the food commercial. What is the commercial for?**

a.

b.

c.

CD3 T23

B **Listen again. Check the words you hear.**

☑ better taste   ☑ better for you

☑ healthier meals   ☑ fresher

☐ lower price   ☐ easier to prepare

Getting Started
10 minutes

1 BEFORE YOU LISTEN

CLASS. Look at the people. Read the reasons...

- Read the directions. Tell students to read the reasons silently.
- Read the reasons. Say the boldfaced words and ask the class to repeat.
- Write the boldfaced words on the board, and tell students to close their books. Say the following and ask the class to call out a word or phrase from the board:

  It doesn't cost a lot. (price)

  It's not frozen or canned. (fresh)

  It's easy to prepare. (convenience)

  It's good for you. (healthy)

  I like to eat it. (tastes good)

- Tell students to open their books. Ask: *What's important to you when you buy food? Draw a star next to the reason that's most important to you.* Say each reason and ask for a show of hands. Tally the responses on the board and circle the most popular answer.

Presentation
10 minutes

2 LISTEN

Ⓐ Listen to the food commercial...

- Point to each picture and ask the class to call out the food item (fish, meat, chicken).
- Read the directions. Play CD 3, Track 23.
- Ask: *What is the commercial for?* Ask the class to call out the answer.

> **Teaching Tip**
>
> *Optional:* Remember that if students need additional support, tell them to read the Audio Script on page 305 as they listen to the conversations.

Controlled Practice
10 minutes

Ⓑ Listen again. Check the words...

- Read the directions.
- Play Track 23 again.
- Ask the class: *How many boxes did you check?* Ask for a show of hands: *One box? Two boxes?* etc. Play Track 23 again as needed.
- Call on students to say the answers.

▬▬ EXPANSION: Vocabulary Practice for 1B

- Tell students to number the people in Exercise 1 from 1 to 5.
- Tell pairs to look at the answers for Exercise 2B. Ask: *According to the ad, who should buy French's Chicken?* (person 2, person 4, and person 5).

Compare information in food ads

Controlled Practice   20 minutes

3   CONVERSATION

A CLASS. **Look at the picture of Lucy and her...**

- Tell students to cover Exercise 3C. Read the directions. Ask: *What is Estela holding?* (a can of coffee) Ask: *What are they talking about?*
- Elicit students' guesses and list them on the board.

B 📀 **Listen to the conversation....**

- Read the directions. Play CD 3, Track 24. Students listen.
- Ask: *What are Lucy and her mother talking about?* Read the guesses on the board. Elicit and circle the best answer. (reasons to buy the brand of coffee— better taste, lower price)

C 📀 **Listen and repeat the conversation.**

- Tell students to uncover Exercise 3C and read the conversation silently. Ask: *What brand of coffee does Estela buy?* (Franklin) *Why?* (It tastes great and it's not expensive.)
- Play CD 3, Track 25. Students listen and repeat.

4   PRACTICE

A PAIRS. **Practice the conversation. Then make new...**

- Pair students and tell them to practice the conversation in Exercise 3C.
- Then, in Exercise 4A, tell students to look at the information in the boxes. Say each word or phrase and ask the class to repeat.
- Read the directions.
- Copy the conversation onto the board with blanks. Read through the conversation. When you come to a blank, ask what color it is. Point to the box that's the same color and fill in the blank with the first item in the box.
- Ask two on-level students to practice the conversation on the board for the class.
- Erase the words in the blanks and ask two above-level students to make up a new conversation in front of the class.

- Tell pairs to take turns playing A and B. Tell them to use information from the same row in the boxes to fill in the blanks.
- Tell students to stand, mingle, and practice the conversation with several new partners.
- Call on pairs to practice for the class.

Communicative Practice   10 minutes

B MAKE IT PERSONAL. GROUPS OF 3. **Talk...**

- Read the directions. Tell students to think about a product they like. Tell them to draw a simple picture of the product that shows the brand name. Do the same on the board.
- Model a conversation with an above-level student. Ask an above-level student to read A's lines from Exercise 4A, substituting your brand and product in the first line. Respond with B's lines from Exercise 4A. For B's last line, give your own two reasons.
- Pair students and tell them to practice the conversation. Tell A to ask about the product in B's drawing. Tell B to give two reasons for liking the product.
- Walk around and remind students to switch roles and practice both parts.
- Call on pairs to perform for the class.

■■■■ **MULTILEVEL INSTRUCTION for 4B**
Pre-level Direct students to write down two reasons why they like their product.
Above-level Tell pairs to talk about a few products.

■■■■ **EXPANSION: Listening and Graphic Organizer Practice for 4B**

- Draw a six-column chart on the board with the headings: *Brand and product, Convenient, Tastes good, Low price, Healthy,* and *Fresh.*
- As students listen to classmates' conversations, tell them to write the brand and product in the first column of the chart, then check the reasons they hear.

Extra Practice

Interactive Practice

3 CONVERSATION

A CLASS. Look at the picture of Lucy and her mother, Estela, in the supermarket. Guess: What are they talking about?

CD3 T24
B 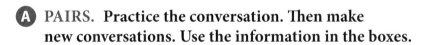 Listen to the conversation. Was your guess in Exercise A correct?

CD3 T25
C Listen and repeat the conversation.

Lucy: Oh, you buy Franklin brand coffee. Is it good?

Estela: Yes, it's excellent. I think it's better than all the other brands.

Lucy: Really? Why?

Estela: It tastes great and it's not expensive.

4 PRACTICE

A PAIRS. Practice the conversation. Then make new conversations. Use the information in the boxes.

A: Oh, you buy   brand   . Is it good?

B: Yes, it's excellent. I think it's better than all the other brands.

A: Really? Why?

B: and it's not expensive.

Sunshine	orange juice	It tastes good
Captain Cook	fish	It's always fresh
Dairy Glenn	ice cream	It's low-fat

B MAKE IT PERSONAL. GROUPS OF 3. Talk about a product you like. Explain why you like it.

Compare information in food ads

Grammar

Comparative adjectives with *than*

| This coffee is | fresh. tasty. expensive. | It's | **fresher** **tastier** **more expensive** | **than** | the other brands. |

---

1 PRACTICE

A Write the comparative forms with *-er* or *more*.

1. fresh — *fresher*
2. fast — faster
3. good — better
4. delicious — more delicious
5. sweet — sweeter
6. expensive — more expensive
7. healthy — healthier
8. fattening — more fattening
9. salty — saltier

Grammar Watch

To form comparative adjectives:

- from one-syllable adjectives, add *-er*.
- from two-syllable adjectives ending in *y*, change *y* to *i* and add *-er*.
- from adjectives of two or more syllables, use *more* + an adjective.
- Some comparative adjectives are irregular. For example: *good* → *better*.
- See page 289 for more spelling rules.

B Complete the sentences. Write the comparative form of the adjective in parentheses. Add *than*.

1. Bananas are (sweet) __*sweeter than*__ apples.
2. Margarine is (cheap) __cheaper than__ butter.
3. Fresh orange juice tastes (good) __better than__ frozen orange juice.
4. I think homemade meals are (tasty) __tastier than__ fast food.
5. Fresh fruit is (nutritious) __more nutritious than__ canned fruit.
6. Canned soup is (convenient) __more convenient than__ homemade soup.
7. Vegetables are (good for you) __better for you than__ cookies.
8. Sandwiches are (easy to make) __easier to make than__ hamburgers.

Lesson 6 Compare information in food ads

Getting Started
5 minutes

- Say: *We're going to study comparative adjectives with* than. *In the conversation on page 195, Estela used this grammar.*
- Play CD 3, Track 25. Students listen. Write on the board: *I think it's better than all the other brands.* Underline *better than.*

Presentation
10 minutes

Comparative adjectives with *than*

- On the board, write: *fresh, tasty,* and *expensive.*
- Read the first item from the Grammar Watch note. Point to and say: *fresh.* Ask: *How many syllables does* fresh *have?* (one) *How do we form the comparative?* Add *-er* to *fresh* on the board. Say *fresher* and ask the class to repeat.
- Read the second item from the Grammar Watch note. Point to and say: *tasty.* Ask: *How many syllables does* tasty *have?* (two) Draw a line between *ta* and *sty. Does it end in* -y? (Yes.) *How do we form the comparative?* On the board, change the *y* in *tasty* to *i* and add *-er.* Say *tastier* and ask the class to repeat.
- Read the third item from the Grammar Watch note. Point to and say: *expensive.* Ask: *How many syllables does* expensive *have?* (three) Draw lines between *ex* and *pen* and *pen* and *sive. How do we form the comparative?* Write *more* in front of *expensive* on the board. Say *more expensive* and ask the class to repeat.
- Tell student to read the fourth item from the Grammar Watch note silently. Say: *There are no rules for forming irregular comparatives. You have to study and practice them.*
- Tell students to turn to page 289 for more examples of spelling rules.
- Copy the grammar chart onto the board or show Transparency 10.4 and cover the exercise.
- Read the sentences in the grammar chart and ask the class to repeat. Point out that the first sentence in each pair describes one thing—*this coffee*—and the second compares two things—*this coffee* and *the other brands.*
- If you are using the transparency, do the exercise with the class.

Controlled Practice
20 minutes

1 PRACTICE

A Write the comparative forms with *-er* or *more.*

- Read the directions and the example.
- Tell students to say the adjectives and count the syllables. Walk around and pronounce adjectives for students as needed.
- Students compare answers with a partner.
- Call on students to write answers on the board and correct as needed. Say the comparative adjectives and ask the class to repeat.
- *Optional:* Draw a four-column chart on the board with the headings: *one syllable: add* -er; *two syllables ending in* -y: y → i, *add* -er; *2+ syllables:* more _____; *irregular.* Ask students who come to the board to write answers in the appropriate column. Say the comparative adjectives in each column and ask the class to repeat.

B Complete the sentences. Write the comparative...

- Read the directions and the example.
- Tell students to look at their answers and check that they all include *than.*
- Students compare answers with a partner. Tell them to take turns reading the sentences.
- Call on students to read the completed sentences. Ask students who read items 4 and 8 to spell *tastier* and *easier.*

▬▬ EXPANSION: Grammar Practice for 1B

- Tell students to use the answers from Exercise 1B in new sentences.
- Model by writing your own sentence with *sweeter than* on the board (for example, *Ice cream is sweeter than yogurt.*).
- Pair students. Say: *Student A, read your sentences to your partner. Student B, say whether you agree or disagree with each statement.* On the board, write: *I agree, I disagree.*

2 PRACTICE

A PAIRS. Compare the food in the supermarket ad....

- Read the directions. Say the adjectives in the box and ask the class to call out the comparatives.
- *Optional:* Direct students to write the comparative forms next to the adjectives in the box.
- Read the example. Tell students to look at the supermarket ad. Ask: *How much is a small salad?* ($2.99) *How much is a large salad?* ($4.99) Elicit another comparison from the class (for example, *The potato chips are saltier than the pretzels.*).
- Pair students. Walk around and check that students are using the correct comparative forms and *than.*

B On a separate piece of paper, write six sentences...

- Read the directions. Tell students to use the example in Exercise 2A as a model.
- To provide an additional model, call on a pair to say a comparison. Write the sentence on the board. Correct as needed.
- Tell partners to exchange papers and check each other's sentences. Tell students to check that the sentences are true, that the comparative forms are correct and correctly spelled, and that the sentences contain *than.*
- Call on students to write sentences on the board with each of the adjectives from the box. Read them and correct as needed.

Communicative Practice   25 minutes

Show what you know!

STEP 1. GROUPS OF 3. You are the owners of...

- Read the directions.
- Form groups of 3. Tell groups to decide on a product and invent a brand name. Say: *Each group member, think of one reason why your product is better than other brands. Groups, write three sentences.* Point out that students can use adjectives from the box in Exercise 2A.
- Walk around and check that groups write three complete sentences with correct comparatives and *than.*

STEP 2. WRITE. SAME GROUPS OF 3. Write...

- Read the directions and the example.
- Play CD 3, Track 23, the commercial for French's Chicken, again.
- Tell groups to use their sentences from Step 1 in a radio commercial.

STEP 3. Read your commercial to the class....

- Read the directions.
- Tell students to take turns reading their commercial in their groups. Tell them to choose one group member to read the commercial to the class.
- As students read their commercials, write the brand name and product on the board. When all groups have read, say each brand and product and ask students to raise their hands for the best one.
- Circle the best product. Ask the class: *Why did you like this product?*

▪▪▪ MULTILEVEL INSTRUCTION for STEP 3

Cross-ability Make sure there is at least one higher-level student in each group to help write the commercial. In Step 3, direct the higher-level student to read the commercial first, modeling for other group members.

▪▪▪ EXPANSION: Listening and Writing Practice for STEP 3

- For homework, tell students to listen to radio or TV commercials in English.
- For five commercials, tell them to write down the brand name, product, and one reason why the product is better than other brands.

Progress Check

Can you . . . compare information in food ads?

Say: *We have practiced comparing information in food ads. Now, look at the question at the bottom of the page. Can you compare information in food ads?* Tell students to write a checkmark in the box.

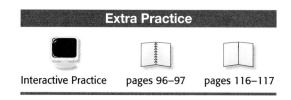

Extra Practice		
Interactive Practice	pages 96–97	pages 116–117

A **PAIRS.** Compare the food in the supermarket ad.
Use adjectives from the box or other adjectives.

Answers will vary but could include:

A small salad is cheaper than a large salad.

Potato chips are more fattening than pretzels.
Pizza is more fattening than a salad.
A salad is more nutritious than pretzels.

cheap
delicious
expensive
fattening
fresh
good
nutritious
salty

B On a separate piece of paper, write six sentences comparing the food in the supermarket ad.

Show what you know!   Compare information in food ads

STEP 1. GROUPS OF 3. You are the owners of a food company. Think of a food or drink you will sell. Write three reasons why your product is better than other brands.

> *Old South fried chicken is more delicious than other brands. It is ...*

STEP 2. WRITE. SAME GROUPS OF 3. Write a radio commercial for your product.

> *Are you hungry? Then try Old South fried chicken. Old South fried chicken is more delicious than other brands ...*

STEP 3. Read your commercial to the class. As a class, vote on the best product.

Can you... compare information in food ads?   ☐

Reading

1 **BEFORE YOU READ**

A **CLASS.** What do you know about the drug caffeine?
How does it make people feel? Is it good for you or bad for you?

B Look at the products. Check the products that have caffeine.
Circle the product that has the most caffeine.

☑ Cola ☐ Chewing gum ☑ Coffee ☑ Tea ☑ Chocolate ☑ Headache medicine ☐ Lemon/lime soda

CD3 T26
C Listen and check your answers. Are you surprised by this information?

2 **READ**

CD3 T27
Listen. Read the article.

Caffeinated Nation

You have a cup of coffee for breakfast. Later in the day, you have a cola with your lunch.
After work, you take some pain reliever for a headache. You may not know it, but each
of these products **contains** caffeine. Almost everyone **consumes**
caffeine. Ninety percent of people living in the U.S. **consume**
caffeine every day. Most people get caffeine from coffee, but others
get it from tea, cola, chocolate, or even some medicines.

What is caffeine?
Caffeine is a chemical found in coffee beans, tea leaves, cocoa
beans, and other plants.

What are the effects of caffeine?
Fifteen minutes after caffeine enters your body, you start to feel
changes. Your heart beats faster. You may have more energy and
feel more awake. You feel happier. These **effects** can last for several
hours. When they go away, you may feel a little tired and sad.

Lesson 7 Read about the effects of caffeine

1 BEFORE YOU READ

A CLASS. **What do you know about the drug...**

- Ask: *What do you know about the drug caffeine?* Elicit students' responses and write them on the board (for example, *It's in coffee. It helps you wake up / stay awake. Pregnant women shouldn't have too much.*).
- Ask: *How does it make people feel?* Elicit students' responses and write them on the board (for example, *awake, energetic, focused, nervous, shaky*).
- Ask for a show of hands: *Is it good for you? Or bad for you?* Ask students who raised their hands for *good for you*: *Why?* Ask students who raised their hands for *bad for you*: *Why?*

B **Look at the products. Check the products...**

- Tell students to look at the products but cover the words. Ask: *Can you name the products?* Point to each picture and ask the class to call out the product.
- Ask: *Which products do you think have caffeine? Write a checkmark next to them. Which product do you think has the most caffeine? Circle it.*
- Ask the class: *Which product do you think has the most caffeine?* Ask for a show of hands for each product. Write the most popular guess on the board.

C **Listen and check your answers. Are you...**

- Read the directions.
- Play CD 3, Track 26. Tell students to listen and use a different color to check and circle the products in Exercise 1B.
- Ask the class: *Which products have caffeine?* (cola, coffee, tea, chocolate, headache medicine) *Were your guesses correct? Which product has the most caffeine?* (coffee) Point to the guess on the board and ask: *Was our guess correct?*
- Ask: *Are you surprised by this information? Is there a product that you didn't know had caffeine?*

2 READ

Listen. Read the article.

- Play CD 3, Track 27. Students listen and read silently.
- Play Track 27 again. Pause the CD after the first paragraph and ask: *What percentage of Americans has caffeine every day?* (90 percent)
- Resume playing Track 27.
- Pause the CD after the *What are the effects of caffeine?* section and ask:

    What is caffeine? (a chemical found in coffee beans, tea leaves, cocoa beans, and other plants)

    How does caffeine make people feel? (Your heart beats faster. You have more energy. You feel more awake. You feel happier.)

    How do they feel several hours later? (tired and sad)

- Finish playing Track 27. Ask: *Is some caffeine bad for you?* (No.) *Is too much caffeine bad for you?* (Yes.) *Why? What can it do?* (can make you feel nervous and irritable, can give you a headache or an upset stomach, can make it difficult to sleep) *How can you find out whether products have caffeine?* (read the labels) Explain to students that some product labels do not include information about caffeine. Brainstorm with the class a list of additional caffeine-containing products (for example, *energy drinks, some bottled water, green tea*).

Controlled Practice   20 minutes

3 **CHECK YOUR UNDERSTANDING**

Ⓐ Look at the words in bold in the article. Guess...

- Read the Reading Skill note as students read along silently.
- Read the directions. Say the words and ask the class to repeat.
- Tell students to find the word *contain* in the article. Tell them to read the sentence before the sentence with *contain*, the sentence with *contain*, and the sentence after the sentence with *contain*.
- Tell students to read the definitions and find the one for *contain*.
- Read the sentences around *contain*, from *After work . . .* to *consumes caffeine.* Ask: *What does contain mean?* (have something inside it)
- Tell students to find each word in the article, read the sentences around the word, and choose the definition.
- Students compare answers with a partner.
- Call on students to read the definitions for the words.
- *Optional:* Write the words on the board. Tell students to close their books. Read the definitions in random order and ask the class to call out the words.

▬▬ **EXPANSION: Vocabulary Practice for 3A**

- Tell students to use the words from Exercise 3A in their own sentences.
- Model the activity by asking the class to compose a sentence with *contain* (for example, *Milk contains protein.*).
- Students compare sentences in small groups.

Ⓑ Read the article again. Complete the statements.

- Read the directions.
- Write item 1 on the board. Ask: *What does consume mean?* (eat or drink something) Elicit the answer to item 1 and complete the sentence on the board.

Ⓒ PAIRS. Check your answers.

- Students compare answers with a partner. Tell partners to take turns reading the sentences in Exercise 3B. Say: *If you and your partner have a different answer, refer back to the article.*
- Call on students to read the sentences in Exercise 3B.

Communicative Practice   15 minutes

Show what you know!

PRE-WRITING. PAIRS. Is caffeine bad for you....

- Read the directions. Tell students to read the *Is caffeine bad for you?* section of the article again.
- Pair students and tell them to read items 4–6 in Exercise 3B.
- On the board, write the questions: *How much coffee is it OK to drink?* (2–3 cups a day) *When is caffeine harmful?* (when you have too much) *What are the bad effects of caffeine?* (It can make you feel nervous or irritable, or it can give you a headache or an upset stomach.) Tell pairs to talk about each question.
- Ask pairs: *Is caffeine bad for you?* Tell pairs to write a few sentences explaining their answer (for example, *It's OK to drink two to three cups of coffee a day. Too much caffeine is bad for you. It can make you feel irritable, can give you an upset stomach, or can make it difficult to sleep.*).
- Call on pairs to read their answers.

WRITE. Keep a caffeine journal. See page 272.

Turn to page 272 and ask students to complete the activities. See page T-xii for general notes about Writing activities.

Extra Practice	
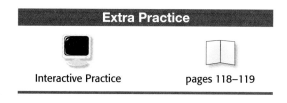	
Interactive Practice	pages 118–119

Is caffeine bad for you?

For most people, caffeine in average amounts does not cause health problems. Research shows that drinking two to three cups of coffee a day is not **harmful**. However, too much caffeine can be bad for your health. It can make you feel nervous and **irritable**. It may give you a headache or an upset stomach. If you **consume** caffeine too late in the day, you may find it difficult to sleep at night. It's a good idea to read the labels on medicines, foods, and **beverages** to find out if they **contain** caffeine.

3 CHECK YOUR UNDERSTANDING

A Look at the words in bold in the article. Guess the meaning of the words from context. Match the words and the definitions.

1. __e__ contain   a. a drink
2. __b__ consume   b. eat or drink something
3. __d__ effect   c. causing a health problem or injury
4. __c__ harmful   d. the way that something changes a person
5. __f__ irritable   e. have something inside it
6. __a__ beverage   f. getting a little angry quickly and easily

> **Reading Skill:**
> Getting Meaning from Context
>
> You can sometimes guess the meaning of a word from the words or sentences around it.

B Read the article again. Complete the statements. Answers will vary but could include:

1. Almost all Americans consume _____ caffeine _____ every day.

2. Some medicine such as _____ a pain reliever _____ has caffeine.

3. There is caffeine in beverages such as _____ coffee _____ and _____ tea _____.

4. Drinking more than _____ three _____ cups of coffee a day can affect your health.

5. Too much caffeine can give you a _____ headache _____ or an _____ upset stomach _____.

6. If you consume caffeine late in the day, you may find it difficult to _____ sleep _____.

C PAIRS. Check your answers.

Show what you know!

PRE-WRITING. PAIRS. Is caffeine bad for you? Explain your answer.

WRITE. Keep a caffeine journal. See page 272.

Listening and Speaking

1 BEFORE YOU LISTEN

CLASS. Look at the menu. Which foods do you know? Which foods look good?

Mom's Café

Main Dishes

Main dishes are served with a house salad and your choice of one side.

All Main Dishes $9.95

meatloaf

roast chicken

pork chops

Asian noodles   hamburger   fish sandwich   macaroni and cheese

Sides

coleslaw   French fries

mixed vegetables   onion rings

mashed potatoes

Drinks

soda   bottled water
apple juice   iced tea

2 LISTEN

CD3 T28

A 🔘 Ernesto and Angela are ordering lunch in a restaurant. Listen to the conversation. Look at the guest check. Complete their order.

CD3 T29

B 🔘 Listen to the whole conversation. Why is the waitress surprised?

a. The woman wants to change her order.
b. The man ordered a lot of food.
c. The people decide to leave the restaurant.

Guest Check

TABLE **3**   SERVER **Sally**   CHECK # **088207**

2 iced teas

1 meatloaf   with

mixed vegetables

1 hamburger   with

onion rings

TAX

TOTAL

Lesson 8 Order food in a restaurant

Getting Started 10 minutes

1 BEFORE YOU LISTEN

CLASS. Look at the menu. Which foods...

- Tell students to look at the menu. Ask: *What's the name of the restaurant?* (Mom's Café) *How much are the main dishes?* ($9.95) *What do the main dishes come with?* (a house salad and one side) Say: *Point to the sides. Do you have to pay extra for the salad or the sides?* (No.)
- Say each main dish, side, and drink and ask the class to repeat.
- Ask: *Which foods do you know?* Tell students to write a checkmark next to the foods they know.
- Ask: *Which foods do you not know?* Call on students to name foods they don't know. Describe these foods or elicit descriptions from other students (for example, S: *I don't know macaroni and cheese.* T / classmate: *It's pasta with cheese sauce. My kids love it!*).
- Ask: *Which foods look good?* Call on a few students to answer. Then ask questions with comparatives: *Which looks better, the hamburger or the fish sandwich? Which looks tastier, the French fries or the mashed potatoes?*

EXPANSION: Speaking Practice for 1

- Form groups of 3. Ask groups: *If you're trying to eat a healthy diet, what can you order at Mom's Café?* Tell groups to talk about the main dishes, sides, and drinks and choose the healthiest one in each group. Ask: *Which foods and drinks are not healthy? Why? Why is the food or drink you chose healthier than the others?*
- Say: Talk about one choice and explain your choice to your group. Provide an example: *Mixed vegetables are healthy. Vegetables have fiber. French fries and onion rings have more sodium (also more calories, fat, and cholesterol) than mixed vegetables.*

Presentation 20 minutes

2 LISTEN

A **Ernesto and Angela are ordering...**

- Read the directions.

- Tell students to look at the guest check. Ask: *What drinks did Ernesto and Angela order?* (iced teas) *What sides did they order?* (mixed vegetables and onion rings) *What's missing from the guest check?* (the main dishes)
- Play CD 3, Track 28. Students listen for the main dishes and write them on the guest check.
- Call on students to say the answers.
- Tell students to point to the pictures of *meatloaf, mixed vegetables, hamburger,* and *onion rings* in Exercise 1.

B **Listen to the whole conversation....**

- Ask a student to read the directions and answer choices.
- Play CD 3, Track 29. Read the question again. Call on a student to say the answer.

EXPANSION: Speaking Practice for 2B

- On the board, write:

  Angela: I'd like the _____.

  Waitress: And what would you like with that?

  Angela: _____.

- Pair students and tell partners to take turns ordering for Angela.

Culture Connection

- Tell students to fill in the prices on the guest check. Assign a price for the drinks, such as $1.50 each. Write the sales tax for your state on the board. Tell pairs to calculate the tax and total.
- Elicit the total and write it on the board. Ask: *How much should Ernesto and Angela leave for a tip?* Explain that in the U.S. a tip is not included in the bill (except for large groups). Point out that servers in the U.S. are usually paid a low wage because it's expected that they will receive a tip from every table.
- Next to the total on the board, write: *15–20% tip.* Say: *Tip 15% for normal service. Tip 20% for really good service.* Ask pairs to calculate a 15% tip and a 20% tip for Ernesto and Angela's waitress.
- Ask: *Do servers usually receive tips in your country? Is the tip / service included in the bill? How much do customers generally tip?*

Lesson 8 Order food in a restaurant

3 CONVERSATION

A Listen to the sentences. Notice...

- Read the Pronunciation Watch note.
- Read the directions. Play CD 3, Track 30. Students listen.
- Resume playing Track 30. Students listen and repeat.

B Listen to the sentences. Complete...

- Read the directions. Play CD 3, Track 31.
- Write the items on the board. Call on students to write the answers.
- Read the sentences with the weak pronunciation of *a*, *to*, *the*, and *of*. Ask the class to repeat.
- Tell students to take turns reading the sentences to a partner. Tell them to practice the weak pronunciation of *a*, *to*, *the*, and *of*. Walk around and listen. Model as needed.

Controlled Practice   10 minutes

C Listen and repeat the conversation.

- Note: This conversation is the same one students heard in Exercise 2A on page 200.
- Tell students to look at the picture. Say: *Point to the waitress. Point to Ernesto. What is Ernesto's wife's name?* (Angela)
- Tell students to read the conversation silently. Tell them to underline *to*, *the*, *a*, and *of*.
- Read the directions. Play CD 3, Track 32.
- As students repeat, listen carefully for the weak pronunciation of *to*, *the*, *a*, and *of*.

4 PRACTICE

A PAIRS. Practice the conversation.

- Pair students and tell them to practice the conversation in Exercise 3C. Remind them to practice the weak pronunciation of *to*, *the*, *a*, and *of*.

Communicative Practice   20 minutes

B ROLE PLAY. GROUPS OF 3. **Make your own...**

- Read the directions.
- Model a conversation with two above-level students. Play C (the waiter or waitress). To prompt A and B, write *I'd like the _____* on the board. Ask: *Are you ready to order? And what would you like with that? And for you?* Repeat A's and B's orders back to them. End the conversation by saying: *I'll be right back with your salads.*
- Tell students to look at the conversation in Exercise 3C and underline language they can use when they're the waiter or waitress (*Are you ready to order? And what would you like with that?*). Brainstorm and write on the board how to ask for the second customer's order (for example, *And for you? What would you like? What can I get for you?*).
- Tell students to look at the menu on page 200 and circle the two main dishes and two sides they will order. Say: *You'll play a customer twice. What will you order each time?*
- Form groups of 3. Tell groups that each member should take a turn playing the waiter or waitress.
- Walk around and check that C takes A's and B's orders. Listen for the weak pronunciation of *to*, *the*, *a*, and *of*.
- Call on pairs to role play for the class.
- *Optional:* As pairs role play, tell students to listen and write down their orders.

MULTILEVEL INSTRUCTION for 4B

Pre-level Direct students to cross out the food in Ernesto's lines in Exercise 3C and write in new foods.

Above-level Direct students to also take their customers' drink orders. Provide language as necessary: *What would you like to drink? Can I get you (started with) some drinks?*

Extra Practice

Interactive Practice

3 CONVERSATION

CD3 T30

A 🔘 **Listen to the sentences. Notice the pronunciation of *to, the, a,* and *of.* Then listen and repeat.**

Are you ready to order?
I'd like the meatloaf.
A side of mixed vegetables.

> **Pronunciation Watch**
>
> The words *to, the, a,* and *of* usually have a weak pronunciation. The vowel sound is short and quiet.

CD3 T31

B 🔘 **Listen to the sentences. Complete each sentence with *to, the, a* or *of.***

1. I'd like ____a____ soda.

2. I'm ready ____to____ order now.

3. I'll have ____the____ roast chicken.

4. Could I have a side ____of____ coleslaw?

CD3 T32

C 🔘 **Listen and repeat the conversation.**

Waitress: Here are your iced teas. Are you ready to order?
Ernesto: Yes. I'd like the meatloaf.
Waitress: And what would you like with that?
Ernesto: A side of mixed vegetables.
Waitress: OK. Meatloaf with mixed vegetables.
Ernesto: And a hamburger with a side of onion rings.
Waitress: A hamburger with onion rings.
Ernesto: Oh, and could we have some sugar?
Waitress: Sure. Here you go. I'll be right back with your salads.

4 PRACTICE

A PAIRS. Practice the conversation.

B ROLE PLAY. GROUPS OF 3. Make your own conversations. Students A and B, you are the customers. Order food from the menu on page 200. Student C, you are the waiter or waitress. Take the customers' orders.

Grammar

Quantifiers with plural nouns

Affirmative			Negative		
We have	**many** **a lot of** **some** **a few**	apples.	We don't have	**many** **a lot of** **any**	apples.

Quantifiers with non-count nouns

Affirmative			Negative		
We have	**a lot of** **some** **a little**	sugar.	We don't have	**a lot of** **any** **much**	sugar.

PRACTICE

A Underline the correct words.

1. Apple juice has **many** / **a lot of** sugar.

2. You should eat **some** / **a few** fruit every day.

3. Vegetables have **a lot of** / **many** fiber.

4. Athletes eat **much** / **a lot of** carbohydrates to get energy.

5. There aren't **a few** / **many** nutrients in a bag of candy.

6. There is usually **a lot of** / **much** salt and fat in cheese.

Grammar Watch

Don't use *much* + a non-count noun in affirmative statements.
Example: *We eat a lot of rice.*
(**Not:** *We eat ~~much rice~~.*)

B Complete the conversations. More than one answer may be possible. Answers will vary but could include:

1. **A:** Do you eat ___a lot of___ eggs? You know, they have a lot of cholesterol.

   B: No, not really. I eat only ___two___ eggs a week.

2. **A:** I really like fish. Do you eat ___any___ fish?

   B: Yes, I love it! It's good for you.

3. **A:** What would you like to drink?

   B: I'd like ___some___ water, please.

Lesson 9 Order food in a restaurant

Getting Started
5 minutes

- Say: *We're going to study quantifiers with plural nouns and non-count nouns. In the conversation on page 201, Ernesto used this grammar.*
- Play CD 3, Track 32. Students listen. Write on the board: *Oh, and could we have some sugar?* Underline *some*.

Presentation
15 minutes

Quantifiers with plural nouns

- Copy the top grammar charts onto the board or show the top charts on Transparency 10.5 and cover the exercise.
- Read each affirmative sentence, and then its corresponding negative sentence (*We have many apples, We don't have many apples,* etc.).
- Ask: *Which quantifiers for plural nouns can you use in the affirmative and the negative?* (*many, a lot of*) *Which ones can only be used in the affirmative?* (*some, a few*) *What do* some *and* a few *change to in the negative?* (*any*)

Quantifiers with non-count nouns

- Copy the bottom grammar charts onto the board or show all the charts on Transparency 10.5 and cover the exercise.
- Read the affirmative sentences with plural nouns and with non-count nouns. Ask: *Which quantifiers can you use with plural nouns and non-count nouns?* (*a lot of, some*) Say: *a lot of apples, a lot of sugar, some apples, some sugar.*
- Ask: *Which quantifiers can only be used with plural nouns?* (*many, a few*) Say: *many apples, a few apples.*
- Ask: *Which quantifier can only be used with non-count nouns?* (*a little*) Say: *a little sugar.*
- Read the sentences under *Quantifiers with non-count nouns*. Read each affirmative sentence and then its corresponding negative sentence (*We have a lot of sugar, We don't have a lot of sugar,* etc.).
- Ask: *Which quantifier for non-count nouns can be used in the affirmative and the negative?* (*a lot of*) *Which ones can only be used in the affirmative?* (*some, a little*) *What does* some *change to in the negative?* (*any*) *What does* a little *change to in the negative?* (*much*)

- Tell students to read the Grammar Watch note silently.
- If you are using the transparency, do the exercise with the class.

Controlled Practice
15 minutes

> **PRACTICE**

A Underline the correct words.

- Read the directions and the example. Ask: *Why is the answer* a lot of? (because the sentence is affirmative and *sugar* is non-count)
- Students compare answers with a partner. Tell them to take turns reading the sentences out loud.
- Call on students to read the sentences.

B Complete the conversations. More than one...

- Read the directions.
- Write item 1 on the board. Read the conversation. Point to: *I eat only _____ eggs a week.* Ask: *Is the sentence affirmative or negative?* (affirmative) *Is* eggs *a plural noun or a non-count noun?* (a plural noun) Point to the top left chart. Ask: *What are the possible answers?* (*many, a lot of, some, a few*) Read the conversation again and ask: *What is the best answer?* (*a few*)
- Walk around and spot-check students' answers. If you see an incorrect answer, ask questions (*Affirmative or negative? Plural or non-count?*) to help the student determine the correct chart to choose an answer from.
- Students compare answers with a partner by reading the conversations.
- Call on pairs to read the conversations.

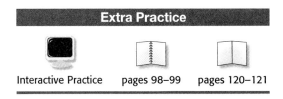

Extra Practice

Interactive Practice   pages 98–99   pages 120–121

1 GRAMMAR

A **Complete the conversation. Underline the correct...**

- Read the directions. Tell students to refer back to the grammar charts on page 190 (Count nouns / Non-count nouns), page 191 (*How much / How many*), and page 202 (Quantifiers with plural nouns and non-count nouns) as needed.

- Students compare answers with a partner by reading the conversation.

- Call on an above-level pair to read the conversation for the class. Discuss any errors.

- *Optional:* Tell students to read the conversation again and write the shopping list.

B **Compare two foods. Write four sentences. Use...**

- Read the directions. Tell students to refer back to the grammar chart on page 196 (Comparative adjectives with *than*) as needed.

- Tell students that they can use different foods in each sentence if they wish.

- Walk around and spot-check students' sentences for correct comparative forms and *than*. Remind students to start sentences with a capital letter and end with a period.

- Tell students to read their sentences to a partner. Students say whether or not they agree with each of their partner's sentences. On the board, write: *I agree, I disagree.*

- For each adjective in the box, call on a few students to read a sentence. Discuss any errors.

CD-ROM Practice

 Go to the CD-ROM for more practice.

If your students need more practice with the vocabulary, grammar, and competencies in Unit 10, encourage them to review the activities on the CD-ROM. This review can also help students prepare for the final role play on the following Expand page.

Extra Practice
pages 100–101

1 GRAMMAR

A Complete the conversation. Underline the correct words.

Cook: Do we have enough **meat** / **meats** for tomorrow?

Assistant: I think so. There's **much** / **a lot** of meat in the refrigerator. But there isn't **much** / **many** fish.

Cook: OK. Put it on the list. What about vegetables? Are there **much** / **many** potatoes?

Assistant: About 100 pounds. But there are only **a little** / **a few** carrots.

Cook: How **much** / **many** onions?

Assistant: Onions? There aren't **any** / **some**.

Cook: OK. Then we need **any** / **some** carrots and onions. Put **rice** / **rices** on the list, too.

Assistant: OK. How **much** / **many** pounds of rice?

Cook: Fifty. And how about **fruit** / **fruits**? I need **much** / **a lot of** apples for tomorrow's apple pies.

Assistant: I'll put them on the list. We have **some** / **any**, but only **a little** / **a few**. I think we need some **sugar** / **sugars** for the pies, too.

B Compare two foods. Write four sentences. Use the comparative forms of adjectives from the box or other adjectives. Answers will vary but could include:

> delicious   easy to cook   fattening   good for you   sweet   tasty

Apples are better for you than candy bars.

1. Tuna is more delicious than chicken.

2. Salad is better for you than candy.

3. Oranges are sweeter than apples.

4. Potato chips are more fattening than pretzels.

2 ACT IT OUT   What do you say?

PAIRS. Read the nutrition labels. Compare the brands.
Use the words in the box. Tell the class which brand you would buy.
Explain your answer.

fattening   good for you   nutritious   salty   tasty

3 READ AND REACT   Problem-solving

STEP 1. Read about Amalya's problem.

Amalya has a full-time job. After work, she also has to cook for
her family and do the housework. Often she does not have enough
time to prepare a healthy meal for her family. Also, fresh fruit and
vegetables are expensive in her neighborhood.

**STEP 2. PAIRS. What is Amalya's problem? What can she do?
Here are some ideas.**

- She can buy inexpensive frozen vegetables.
- She can ask her family to help with shopping, cooking, and washing dishes.
- She can shop at a farmer's market for fresh fruits and vegetables.
- She can _____.

4 CONNECT   For your Community-building Activity, go to page 253.
For your Team Project, go to page 283.

Which goals can you check off? Go back to page 185.

2 ACT IT OUT

PAIRS. Read the nutrition labels. Compare...

- Read the directions. Ask: *Which chicken do you think tastes better? Which chicken do you think is better for your health?*
- Pair students. Tell them to say which brand they would buy and to say at least two reasons why each. Remind pairs to use the comparative forms of the verbs in the box and *than.*
- Walk around and observe partners interacting. Check pairs' use of comparatives and *than.*
- Call on pairs to perform for the class.
- While pairs are performing, use the scoring rubric on page T-xiii to evaluate each student's vocabulary, grammar, fluency, and how well they complete the task.
- *Optional:* After each pair finishes, discuss the strengths and weakness of each performance either in front of the class or privately.

3 READ AND REACT

STEP 1. Read about Amalya's problem.

- Say: *We are going to read about a student's problem, and then we need to think about a solution.*
- Read the directions.
- Read the story while students follow along silently. Pause after each sentence to allow time for students to comprehend. Periodically stop and ask simple *Wh-* questions to check comprehension (for example, *How many hours a week does Amalya work? What does she have to do after work? What does she not have time to do? Why doesn't she buy fresh fruit and vegetables?*).

STEP 2. PAIRS. What is Amalya's problem? What...

- Ask: *What is Amalya's problem?* (She doesn't have time to prepare a healthy dinner for her family, and fruits and vegetables are expensive in her neighborhood.) *What can Amalya do?*
- Pair students. Read the ideas in the list. Give pairs a couple of minutes to discuss possible solutions for Amalya.

- Ask: *Which ideas are good?* Call on students to say their opinion about the ideas in the list (for example, S: *I think she can ask her family to help with shopping, cooking, and washing dishes. This is a good idea.*).
- Now tell students to think of one new idea not in the list (for example, *She can prepare healthy meals on the weekend and freeze them.*) and to write it in the blank. Encourage students to think of more than one idea and to write them in their notebooks.
- Call on pairs to say their additional solutions. Write any particularly good ones on the board and ask students if they think it is a good idea too (*Do you think this is a good idea? Why or why not?*).

■■■ MULTILEVEL INSTRUCTION for STEP 2
Pre-level Ask: *Which ideas save time? Which ideas save money?* Pair lower-level students and tell them to draw a two-column chart with the headings *save time* and *save money.* Tell pairs to write the ideas from the book and the board in the chart.

Above-level Tell pairs to compare two ideas for saving time and two ideas for saving money. Tell them to write two sentences (for example, *Asking her family to help is easier than preparing meals on the weekend. Buying frozen vegetables is cheaper than shopping at a farmer's market.*).

4 CONNECT

Turn to page 253 for the Community-building Activity and page 283 for the Team Project. See page T-xi for general notes about teaching these activities.

Progress Check

Which goals can you check off? Go back to page 185.
Ask students to turn to page 185 and check off any remaining goals they have reached. Call on students to say which goals they will practice outside of class.

Call 911!

Classroom Materials/Extra Practice

CD 3
Tracks 33–48

T
Transparencies 11.1–11.6
Vocabulary Cards Unit 11

MCA
Unit 11

Workbook
Unit 11

Interactive Practice
Unit 11

Unit Overview

Goals
- See the list of goals on the facing page.

Grammar
- Present continuous: Statements and questions
- *There was / There were*
- Compound imperatives

Pronunciation
- Stressed syllables
- The sound /h/ at the beginning of words

Reading
- Read an article about causes of home injuries
- *Reading Skill:* Identifying supporting details

Writing
- Write about what people are doing
- Describe emergency situations
- Write about the safety of your home

Life Skills Writing
- Complete an employee accident report

Preview
- Set the context of the unit by asking questions about emergencies (for example, *How do you react in an emergency? Are you calm or nervous and scared? Can you think clearly, or do you panic?*).
- Hold up page 205 or show Transparency 11.1. Read the unit title and ask the class to repeat.
- Ask: *What's the first thing you should do in an emergency?* (Call 911!) *What's 911?* Explain: *In the United States and Canada, it's the telephone number for emergency police, fire, or ambulance services.*
- Say: *Look at the picture.* Ask the Preview questions: *Who are the people?* (emergency medical technicians, or EMTs / paramedics) *What is happening?* (There's a medical emergency. / Someone is very sick or hurt, and an ambulance is taking the person to the hospital.)
- Say: *Look at the picture and the unit title. How did the EMTs know to come and help the woman?* (Someone called 911.)

Goals
- Point to the Unit Goals. Explain that this list shows what the class will be studying in this unit.
- Tell students to read the goals silently.
- Say each goal and ask the class to repeat. Explain unfamiliar vocabulary as needed:

    Procedures: the correct way of doing something
- Tell students to circle one goal that is very important to them. Call on several students to say the goal they circled.

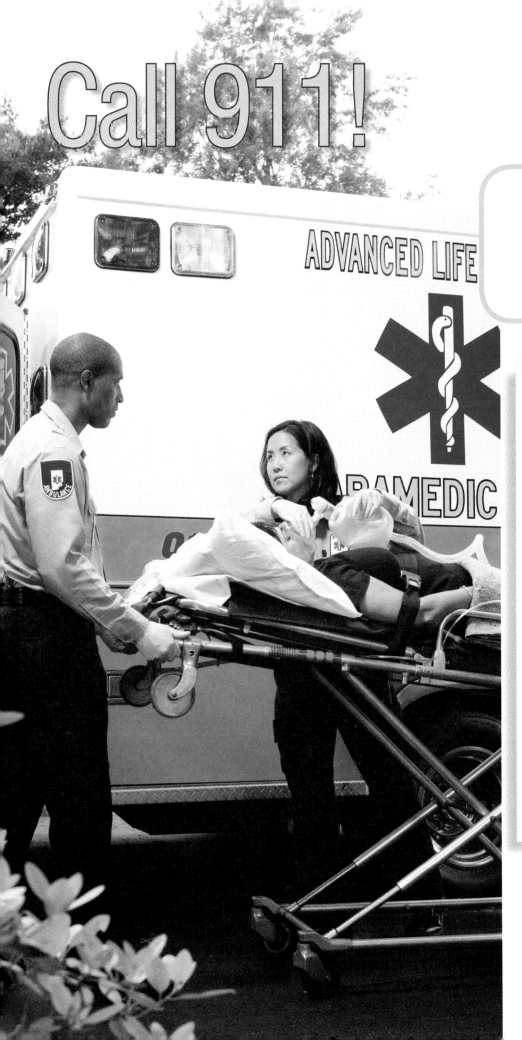

Call 911!

Preview

Look at the picture.
Who are the people?
What is happening?

UNIT GOALS

☐ Identify medical emergencies

☐ Call 911 to report a medical emergency

☐ Talk about medical emergencies

☐ Understand fire safety procedures

☐ Describe an emergency

☐ Respond to a police officer's instructions

☐ Complete an employee accident report

Lesson 1   Vocabulary

1 WHAT DO YOU KNOW?

A CLASS. Look at the pictures. Which medical emergencies do you know?

CD3 T33

B Look at the pictures and listen. Listen again and repeat.

2 PRACTICE

A PAIRS. Student A, point to the pictures. Ask about the emergencies. Student B, identify the emergencies.

A: *What's the emergency?*
B: *She's unconscious.*

B WORD PLAY. PAIRS. Look at the list of medical emergencies on page 207. Write the words in the correct column.

Happening right now	Happened in the past
She's bleeding. He's choking. She's having trouble breathing. He's having a heart attack. She's unconscious. He's having an allergic reaction.	He swallowed poison. She burned herself. He fell.

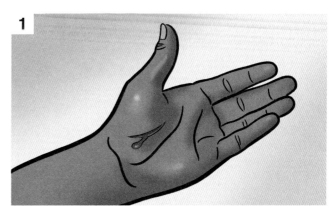

1

4

6

8

9

Lesson 1 Vocabulary

1 WHAT DO YOU KNOW?

Ⓐ CLASS. Look at the pictures. Which...

- Show Transparency 11.2 or hold up the book. Tell students to cover the list of words on page 207.
- Say: *Look at the pictures. Which medical emergencies do you know?* Elicit a medical emergency (for example, *In number 9, he fell.*).
- Students call out answers. Help students pronounce medical emergencies if they have difficulty. As needed, restate students' responses to match the vocabulary on page 207.
- If students call out an incorrect medical emergency, change the student's answer into a question for the class (for example, *In number 4, he's choking?*). If nobody can identify the correct medical emergency, tell students they will now listen to a CD and practice the vocabulary for medical emergencies.

Presentation   5 minutes

Ⓑ 💿 Look at the pictures and listen. Listen...

- Read the directions. Play CD 3, Track 33. Pause after number 9 (*He fell.*).
- To check comprehension, act out several medical emergencies in random order and ask students to call out the medical emergency (for example, for *choking*, pretend to take a bite of food, then grab your neck and try to speak without any sound coming out).
- Resume playing Track 33. Students listen and repeat.

Teaching Tip

Acting out new vocabulary is especially helpful for kinesthetic learners. Call on volunteers to act out a medical emergency for the class to guess.

2 PRACTICE

Ⓐ PAIRS. Student A, point to the pictures. Ask...

- Read the directions. Read each line in the example and ask the class to repeat.
- Play A and model the example with an above-level student. Point to picture 5 and ask: *What's the emergency?* Point to another picture and ask: *What's the emergency?*
- Model changing roles. Tell the student to point to a picture and ask you: *What's the emergency?*
- Pair students and tell them to take turns playing A and B.

Ⓑ WORD PLAY. PAIRS. Look at the list of medical...

- Read the directions. Say: *You're going to look at the list of medical emergencies and decide which ones are happening now and which ones happened in the past. How can you tell?* Elicit students' ideas.
- Copy the chart onto the board and read the example. Underline *right now*, *'s*, and *-ing* in the left side of the chart.
- Point to *Happened in the past* and ask: *What is the ending for regular past-tense verbs?* (*-ed*) Remind students that some verbs are irregular in the past tense.
- Pair students and tell them to look at each medical emergency and decide where to write it in the chart.
- Call on students to write the medical emergencies in the chart on the board. Correct as needed.

Language Note

Point to the left side of the chart and ask: *Which emergency isn't present continuous?* Write *She's unconscious* on the board. Underline *unconscious* and ask: *What part of speech is* unconscious? (adjective) Point to the right side of the chart and ask: *Which emergency had an irregular past-tense verb?* (*He fell.*) *What's the base form of* fell? (*fall*)

Learning Strategy: Use your language

- Provide each student with five index cards or tell students to cut up notebook paper into five pieces.
- Read the directions. If you have students with low first-language skills, pair them with more capable peers if possible.
- Walk around as students work. If misspellings occur, tell them to check the list on page 207.
- Say: *You can use your language to help you remember new words in English.* Remind students to use this strategy to remember other new vocabulary.

Communicative Practice 20 minutes

Show what you know!

GROUPS OF 3. Have you or someone you know...

- Read each question and note your own answers on the board (for example, *my aunt—fell off her bike, broke her wrist; my uncle—drove her to the ER*).
- Ask a student to ask you each question from the directions. Answer with real information. Use your notes on the board (for example, *My aunt fell off her bike. She broke her wrist. My uncle drove her to the emergency room.*).

- Tell students to think of a medical emergency that they, a family member, or friend had. If students have trouble thinking of something, tell them to think of a medical emergency from a TV show or movie. Tell them to note answers to the three questions in their notebooks. Students should use the vocabulary on this page and can also refer back to Unit 7 (pages 127, 128, and 134) for more ideas.
- Show students how to make the present continuous medical emergencies past tense. On the board, write: *She's bleeding.* Cross out *'s* and write *was*.
- Form groups of 3 and tell each student to take a turn asking and answering the questions.
- Walk around and check students' use of the past tense.

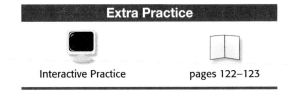

Extra Practice	
Interactive Practice	pages 122–123

2

3

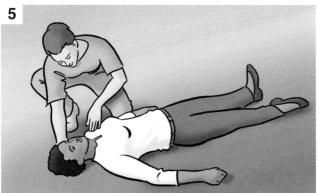

5

7

Medical Emergencies

1. **She's** bleeding.
2. **He's** choking.
3. **She's** having trouble breathing.
4. **He's** having a heart attack.
5. **She's** unconscious.
6. **He's** having an allergic reaction.
7. **He** swallowed poison.
8. **She** burned herself.
9. **He** fell.

Learning Strategy

Use your language

Look at the list of medical emergencies. Make cards for four or five new medical emergencies. Write the sentence in English on one side of the card. Write the sentence in your language on the other side.

Show what you know!

GROUPS OF 3. Have you or someone you know ever had a medical emergency? What happened? What did you do?

Listening and Speaking

1 BEFORE YOU LISTEN

Call 911 when there is an emergency situation. Calling 911 is free from any telephone in the U.S.

READ. CLASS. Read about 911 emergency calls. Then look at each picture. What is the situation? Should you call 911?

2 LISTEN

A **CLASS. Look at the picture. Guess: What is happening?**

CD3 T34

B Listen to the conversation. Was your guess in Exercise A correct?

CD3 T34

C Listen again. What does the 911 operator ask? Check the questions.

- ☑ What's your emergency?
- ☐ Where are you?
- ☑ What's the location of the emergency?
- ☑ What are the cross streets?
- ☐ What are you doing?
- ☑ What's your name?

CD3 T34

D Listen again. Where is the emergency?

Write the names of the cross streets. _____17th and 18th Avenues_____

CD3 T35

E Listen to the whole conversation. How is the man going to get to the hospital? Circle the letter.

(a.) an ambulance   b. a taxi

Call 911 to report a medical emergency

Getting Started   10 minutes

1 BEFORE YOU LISTEN

READ. CLASS. **Read about 911 emergency calls....**

- Write *911* on the board. Say *nine-one-one* and ask the class to repeat.
- Tell students to read the note about 911 emergency calls silently.
- To check comprehension, ask: *When should you call 911?* (when there is an emergency situation) *How much does it cost to call 911?* (It's free.)
- Direct students to look at the first picture. Ask the class: *What is the situation?* (She fell. She hurt her knee.) *Is it an emergency?* (No.) *Should you call 911?* (No.)
- Repeat with pictures 2–4 (2. He's having a heart attack. Yes. Yes; 3. She swallowed poison. Yes. Yes; 4. He has a cold. No. No.)

Culture Connection

- Say: *911 is the emergency telephone number for the U.S. and Canada. It is only for emergencies. For non-emergencies, call the local police or fire station or your doctor's office.* List local police and fire station numbers on the board for students to copy.
- Ask: *Is there an emergency telephone number in your home country? What is it?* List countries and their emergency telephone numbers on the board.
- *Optional:* Provide additional examples: Australia—000; European Union—112; United Kingdom—999.

Presentation   25 minutes

2 LISTEN

A CLASS. **Look at the picture. Guess: What is...**

- Read the directions. Ask: *What is happening?*
- Elicit students' guesses and list them in two columns on the board under the headings *Man* and *Woman.* Students will listen for the answer in Exercise B.

B **Listen to the conversation. Was your...**

- Read the directions. Play CD 3, Track 34. Students listen.
- Ask: *What is happening?* Read the guesses on the board. Elicit and circle the best answer. (The man is having a heart attack. The woman is calling 911.)

Teaching Tip

Optional: Remember that if students need additional support, tell them to read the Audio Script on page 306 as they listen to the conversations.

C **Listen again. What does the 911...**

- Read the directions. Play Track 34 again. Students listen and check the questions they hear.
- Ask the class: *How many questions did you check?* (Students should have checked four questions.) Play Track 34 again as needed.
- Call on students to read the questions they checked.

D **Listen again. Where is...**

- Read the directions.
- Explain: *A cross street is a street that crosses another street.* On the board, draw and label the street your school is on. Mark the location of the school. Then draw and label the two nearest cross streets on either side of your school. Say: *[Peach Avenue] and [Cherry Street] are the nearest cross streets to our school.*
- Play Track 34 again.
- On the board, draw and label Elm Street and mark the location of Dave's Sports Shop. Then draw two streets crossing Elm on either side of Dave's. Ask: *What are the cross streets?* Label the cross streets: *17th Avenue* and *18th Avenue*
- Tell students to write the nearest cross streets for their home and work in their notebooks.

E **Listen to the whole conversation....**

- Read the directions and the answer choices. Play CD 3, Track 35.
- Ask the class: *How is the man going to get to the hospital?*

Lesson 2 Call 911 to report a medical emergency

Presentation   10 minutes

3 CONVERSATION

Ⓐ **Listen to the words. Notice the stressed...**

- Read the Pronunciation Watch note.
- Write *allergic* on the board and pronounce it slowly. Ask: *How many syllables does* allergic *have?* (three) Pronounce *allergic* again, exaggerating the stress on the second syllable. Ask: *Which syllable is longer and louder?* Mark the stress on the second syllable. Pronounce *allergic* again and ask the class to repeat.
- Play CD 3, Track 36. Students listen.
- Resume playing Track 36. Students listen and repeat.

Ⓑ **Listen to the words. Mark (•) the...**

- Tell students to listen and mark the stress over the vowel in the syllable that is longer and louder than the other syllables.
- Play CD 3, Track 37. Repeat as needed.
- Write the words on the board. Call on students to mark the stress. Make corrections as needed.
- Pronounce the words and ask the class to repeat.

Controlled Practice   5 minutes

Ⓒ **Listen and repeat the conversation.**

- Note: This conversation is the same one students heard in Exercise 2B on page 208.
- Tell students to read the conversation silently and to look for words from Exercises 3A and 3B in the conversation and mark the stressed syllables.
- Call on volunteers to write the words on the board and mark the stressed syllables (*emergency*, *location*)
- Play CD 3, Track 38. Students listen and repeat.
- Walk around and check that students are stressing the correct syllables in *emergency* and *location*.

Communicative Practice   10 minutes

4 PRACTICE

Ⓐ PAIRS. **Practice the conversation.**

- Pair students and tell them to practice the conversation in Exercise 3C. Walk around and help with pronunciation as needed. Pay particular attention to students' pronunciation of *emergency* and *location*.

Ⓑ ROLE PLAY. PAIRS. **Make new conversations....**

- Read the directions.
- Model the activity. On the board, write:
  Emergency:
  Location:
  Cross streets:
- Fill in the information you will use in your conversation.
- Ask an on-level student to play A and read the questions. Play B and answer the questions using the information on the board.
- Tell students to fill in the blanks (in pencil) with an emergency, a location, and cross streets to use when they play B. Remind students to refer back to the list of medical emergencies on page 207.
- Pair students and tell them to practice the conversation.
- Walk around and check A's pronunciation of *emergency* and *location*. Check that B correctly provides information about an emergency.
- Call on pairs to perform for the class.

▬▬▬ MULTILEVEL INSTRUCTION for 4B
Cross-ability Direct lower-level students to play A first.

Extra Practice
Interactive Practice

3 CONVERSATION

CD3 T36

A 🔘 **Listen to the words. Notice the stressed syllable. Then listen and repeat.**

Many words in English have more than one syllable. One syllable in these words is stressed. It is longer and louder than the other syllables.

•   •   •   •   •

allergic   location   situation   ambulance   emergency

CD3 T37

B 🔘 **Listen to the words. Mark (•) the stressed syllable.**

1. electric   2. reaction   3. conversation   4. unconscious

CD3 T38

C 🔘 **Listen and repeat the conversation.**

Operator: 9-1-1. What's your emergency?

Olivia: I think a man is having a heart attack.

Operator: OK. What's the location of the emergency?

Olivia: Dave's Sports Shop at 103 Elm Street.

Operator: What are the cross streets?

Olivia: 17th and 18th Avenues.

Operator: All right. What's your name?

Olivia: Olivia Ramos.

4 PRACTICE

A PAIRS. Practice the conversation.

B ROLE PLAY. PAIRS. Make new conversations.
Use different emergencies and locations. Answers will vary.

A: 9-1-1. What's your emergency?

B: _____.

A: OK. What is the location of the emergency?

B: _____.

A: What are the cross streets?

B: _____ and _____.

A: All right. What's your name?

B: _____.

Talk about medical emergencies

Grammar

Present continuous: Statements and questions

Affirmative		
A man	**is having**	a heart attack.

Negative		
He	**is** not	**breathing**.

Yes / No questions		
Is	he	**bleeding**?

Short answers					
Yes,	he	**is**.	**No**,	he	**'s not**.

Information questions			
What		they	**doing**?
	are		
Where		you	**going**?
What		**happening**	now?
	is		
Who		**calling**	911?

Answers		
They	**'re waiting**.	
I	**'m going**	to the clinic.
He	**'s talking**	to the police.
The driver	**is calling**.	

1 PRACTICE

Complete the sentences. Use the correct present continuous form of the verb in parentheses.

1. Help! Call 911! My mother __is choking__ !
   (choke)

2. A man just fell down in the parking lot. He __isn't breathing__.
   (not breathe)

3. __Are__ you __talking__ to the 911 operator now?
   (talk)

   Tell him we need an ambulance right away.

4. A woman __is lying__ on the ground. I think she's unconscious.
   (lie)

5. They are taking Frank to the hospital. Who __'s going__ with him?
   (go)

6. The police __are leaving__. Where __are__ they __going__?
   (leave)   (go)

7. What __'s happening__? There are a lot of fire trucks in the street.
   (happen)

8. I fell off my bicycle and hurt my knee. It's sore, but it __isn't bleeding__.
   (not bleed)

9. I'm taking Mike to the emergency room. I think he __'s having__
   (have)

   an allergic reaction to some food he ate.

Grammar Watch

- You can use contractions in the present continuous.

  She's bleeding.
  They aren't breathing.
  What's happening?

- See page 290 for spelling rules for *-ing* verbs.

Lesson 3 Talk about medical emergencies

Getting Started   5 minutes

- Say: *We're going to study the present continuous. In the conversation on page 209, Olivia used this grammar.*
- Play CD 3, Track 38. Students listen. Write on the board: *I think a man is having a heart attack.* Underline *is having.*

Presentation   20 minutes

Present continuous: Statements and questions

- Copy the grammar charts onto the board or show Transparency 11.3 and cover the exercise.
- Remind students: *Use the present continuous for events happening at the present time.* Ask: *What's happening in our classroom right now?* Elicit a few present continuous sentences and write them on the board (for example, *You are talking. We are listening. Wen is looking at the clock.*). Underline *am, is,* or *are* in the sentences and *-ing.*
- Read the sentences in the top four charts and ask the class to repeat.
- Tell students to turn to Exercise 2B on page 206 and choose one medical emergency from the *Happening right now* side of their charts. On the board, write:

  Affirmative:

  Negative:

  Yes / No question:

  Short answer:

- Tell students to write the affirmative statement, make it negative, use it to form a *Yes / No* question, and write short answers. Do one example on the board with students: *He is choking. He is not choking. Is he choking? Yes, he is. No, he's not.* Direct students to choose another emergency and write the four types of sentences in their notebooks.
- Tell students to read their sentences to a partner. Walk around and check that students are forming the present continuous correctly.

- Read the Grammar Watch note and ask the class to read along silently. Tell students to rewrite their affirmative and negative statements using contractions (for example, *He's choking. He's not choking. He isn't choking.*). Ask: *When do we use contractions?* (in conversation and informal writing)
- From the two bottom charts, read each information question and its answers and ask the class to repeat.
- Tell students to look at the picture in Exercise 2A on page 208 and write a couple of information questions. Call on students to write questions on the board (for example, *What is happening? What is the woman / Olivia doing? Who is calling 911?*). Make corrections as needed. Read the questions and call on students to answer using the present continuous.
- If you are using the transparency, do the exercise with the class.

Controlled Practice   15 minutes

 1   PRACTICE

Complete the sentences. Use the correct...

- Read the directions and the example. On the board, write: *choke.* Cross out the *e* and write *-ing.* Review the spelling rules for *-ing* verbs on page 290 as needed.
- Walk around and encourage students to use contractions.
- Students compare answers with a partner, taking turns reading the sentences.
- Call on students to read the sentences. Write the answers on the board. Write all possible answers (for example, for item 2: *is not breathing, isn't breathing, 's not breathing*). Tell students to check their spelling.

2 PRACTICE

Complete the phone conversation between...

- Read the directions.
- Ask two students to read the first two lines of the conversation. Write the example on the board. Circle *'s* and say: *Remember, we use contractions in the present continuous in conversation.*
- Walk around and check that students use *is* or *'s* and the verb + *-ing.*
- Students compare answers by reading the conversation with a partner.
- Ask a pair to read the conversation for the class. Write the answers on the board. Tell students to check their spelling.
- *Optional:* Call on pairs to perform for the class.

Communicative Practice   20 minutes

Show what you know!

STEP 1. PAIRS. Student A, look at the picture on...

- Ask the class: *Where are the people?* (in the emergency room of a hospital / in an ER)
- Pair students and assign partners roles of A and B. Tell Student A to look only at the picture on this page and Student B to look only at the picture on page 247.
- Say: *Study your picture. What are the people doing?* Tell students to read the example and write six sentences in their notebooks.

   ▬▬▬ **MULTILEVEL INSTRUCTION for STEP 1**

   Cross-ability In Step 1, pair or group lower-level and higher-level students with the same role. Direct them to work together to write six sentences about the people in their picture.

STEP 2. SAME PAIRS. Talk about your pictures....

- Ask two students to read the example.
- Say: *Take turns. Student A, talk about a person in your picture. Student B, say what the same person is doing in your picture. Then, Student B, talk about a person in your picture. Student A, say what the same person is doing in your picture.*
- Say: *If you're not sure which person your partner is talking about, ask what clothes the person is wearing.*
- Tell pairs to number the differences in the picture as they find them.
- Walk around and help as needed. Check that students use the present continuous correctly.
- To check answers, draw a T-chart on the board with the headings *A's picture* and *B's picture.* Number from 1 to 6. Call on pairs to say differences. Write the differences in the chart on the board.
- Tell partners to look at each other's pictures.

Progress Check

Can you . . . talk about medical emergencies?

Say: *We have practiced talking about medical emergencies. Now, look at the question at the bottom of the page. Can talk about medical emergencies?* Tell students to write a checkmark in the box.

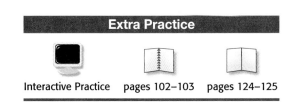

Extra Practice		
Interactive Practice	pages 102–103	pages 124–125

Complete the phone conversation between two friends. Use the correct present continuous form of the verb in parentheses.

A: You won't believe this. There was an accident in front of my house!

B: Oh, no! What <u>'s happening</u>?

(happen)

A: Well, one man is <u>calling</u> 911. Wait … Now I see an ambulance.

(call)

It <u>'s coming</u> down the street. And a fire truck.

(come)

B: Is anyone hurt?

A: I'm not sure. A man <u>'s helping</u> a woman. He <u>'s talking</u> to her

(help) (talk)

and she <u>'s holding</u> her head. I think she <u>'s bleeding</u>.

(hold) (bleed)

Show what you know! Talk about medical emergencies

STEP 1. PAIRS. Student A, look at the picture on this page. Student B, look at the picture on page 247.

Student A, study the picture. What are the people doing? Write six sentences.

> A baby is crying.

STEP 2. SAME PAIRS. Talk about your pictures. What is different? Find at least six differences.

A: *In my picture, a baby is crying.*
B: *In my picture, a baby is sleeping.*

Can you...talk about medical emergencies? ☐

Life Skills

1 IDENTIFY FIRE HAZARDS

PAIRS. Look at the picture. Match the fire hazards to their descriptions.

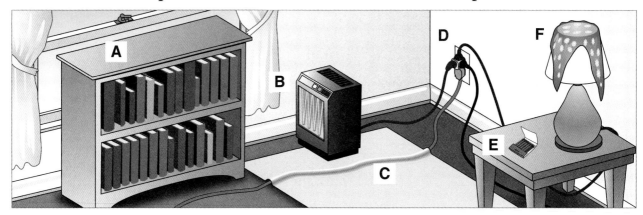

1. __F__ cloth on a lamp

2. __D__ too many plugs in an electrical outlet

3. __C__ an electrical cord under a rug

4. __A__ no window exit

5. __E__ matches available to children

6. __B__ a heater close to a curtain

2 IDENTIFY FIRE SAFETY WORDS

(A) What fire safety words do you know? Write the words from the box.

an escape plan   exits   a fire escape   ~~a fire extinguisher~~   a smoke alarm

1.

a fire extinguisher

2.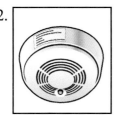

a smoke alarm

3.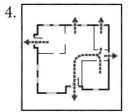

a fire escape

4.

an escape plan

5.

exits

CD3 T39

(B) Listen and check your answers. Then listen and repeat.

(C) GROUPS OF 3. What are other home fire hazards? What can people do to make their home safer?

Lesson 4 Understand fire safety procedures

Getting Started 5 minutes

- List the following words from Exercise 1 on the board: *lamp, cord, rug, window, heater, curtain.*
- Say the words and ask the class to repeat.
- Ask: *Do we have any of these objects in our classroom?* Call on students to point out the objects.
- *Optional:* Ask volunteers to write the words on cards and label the objects in your classroom.

Presentation 15 minutes

1 IDENTIFY FIRE HAZARDS

PAIRS. Look at the picture. Match the fire hazards...

- Explain: Hazards *are things that may be dangerous or cause accidents.* Fire hazards *are things that may cause a fire.*
- Read the directions. Pair students and tell them to look for words from the board in the descriptions.
- Read each description and ask the class to call out the letter of the fire hazard.
- Say: *Read the descriptions again. Do you have any of these fire hazards in your home?*
- *Optional:* Tell students to copy the fire hazards into their notebooks and check their own homes for fire hazards.

2 IDENTIFY FIRE SAFETY WORDS

A What fire safety words do you know? Write...

- Read the directions and the words from the box.
- Tell students to match as many fire safety words and pictures as they can.

B Listen and check your answers....

- Read the directions.
- Play CD 3, Track 39. As needed, pause to allow students to fill in missing answers and / or make corrections.
- Resume playing Track 39. Tell students to point to the pictures in Exercise 2A as they listen and repeat.
- Say: *Look at the fire safety pictures and words again. Which things does your home have?*

Communicative Practice 10 minutes

C GROUPS OF 3. What are other home fire hazards....

- Form groups of 3.
- Say: *Look at the fire hazards in Exercise 1. What are other home fire hazards?* Elicit a couple of ideas (for example, *a kitchen towel close to the stove, a lighter available to children*).
- Say: *Look at the fire safety words in Exercise 2A. What can people do to make their homes safer?* Elicit a couple of ideas (for example, *have a fire extinguisher on each floor of the house, install smoke alarms*).
- Tell groups to take out two sheets of paper and write the titles *Home fire hazards* and *Ways to make your home safer.* Ask two students in each group to be recorders. Tell groups to brainstorm and list their ideas.
- Direct the third student in each group to write one idea from each list on the board. Tell students to try to choose ideas that are not already on the board.
- Read the ideas in each list on the board. Correct as needed.
- Tell students to write down one thing they will do to make their home safer.
- *Optional:* Tell students to rank the ideas for making a home safer in order of importance.

MULTILEVEL INSTRUCTION
Cross-ability Direct the two higher-level students in each group to be the recorders.

Lesson 4 Understand fire safety procedures

Presentation   20 minutes

3 LEARN FIRE SAFETY TIPS

Ⓐ 💿 Listen to the fire safety tips. Then...

- Ask: *Do you know what to do in case of a fire?* List students' ideas on the board.
- Tell students to read the fire safety tips silently.
- Play CD 3, Track 40. Students listen.
- Play Track 40 again. Students listen and complete the tips.
- Students compare answers with a partner by reading the sentences.
- Call on students to read the sentences. Write the answers on the board. Tell students to check their spelling.
- Ask a few comprehension questions: *When should you call 911?* (after you leave your home) *What should you take with you?* (nothing) *What should you do before you open a door?* (feel it) *Should you open a hot door?* (No.) *What should you do if you smell smoke?* (stay close to the floor, cover your mouth and nose with a wet cloth)

Ⓑ READ. PAIRS. Read about Carmen. Which of the...

- Tell students to read the paragraph silently.
- Read the directions.
- Pair students. Tell pairs to read the paragraph again and highlight the fire safety tips Carmen followed in one color and the mistakes she made in another color.
- Ask the class: *Which of the fire safety tips from Exercise 3A did Carmen follow?* Call on students to read the sentences they highlighted (*She touched the front door to her apartment, but it was not hot. She opened the door. She didn't take the elevator. She waited across the street from the building until the firefighters said it was OK to go back inside.*).
- Ask the class: *What mistakes did Carmen make?* Call on students to read the sentences they highlighted. For each mistake, ask the class to identify the tip she didn't follow and then read the tip (for example, S: *First, she called 911.* T: *Which tip did she not follow?* Class: *Number 2.* T: *Don't stop to call 911 . . .*). (Other mistakes: *Then she got her wallet and keys . . .—Tip number 1. She smelled smoke so she ran . . .—Tip number 5.*)

Communicative Practice   10 minutes

4 TALK ABOUT FIRE ESCAPE PLANS

PAIRS. Look at the Pierre family escape plan....

- Say: *Look at the Pierre family escape plan. It shows how family members will exit the house quickly and safely if there is a fire.*
- Pair students and tell them to answer the questions about the Pierre family escape plan. Tell students to write their answers.
- Call on pairs to ask and answer each question. Explain each answer. For example, for item 1, count on your fingers as you say: (1) *Mom and Dad's bedroom,* (2) *Aunt Fran's bedroom,* (3) *Jack and John's bedroom.* For item 3, point to the windows on the diagram and count.
- Say: *Fire escape plans should have two ways out of each room. They should have a family meeting place away from the home. Do you have a fire escape plan?*

▬▬ EXPANSION: Life Skills Practice for 4

- For homework, tell students to create a family escape plan like the one shown in Exercise 4.
- Direct students to exchange papers and answer the questions from Exercise 4 about their partner's escape plan.

Progress Check

Can you . . . understand fire safety procedures?

Say: *We have practiced understanding fire safety procedures. Now, look at the question at the bottom of the page. Can you understand fire safety procedures?* Tell students to write a checkmark in the box.

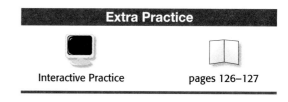

Extra Practice	
Interactive Practice	pages 126–127

3 **LEARN FIRE SAFETY TIPS**

CD3 T40

A 💿 **Listen to the fire safety tips. Then listen again. Complete the tips.**

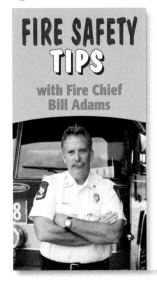

FIRE SAFETY TIPS

with Fire Chief
Bill Adams

1. Leave your ____home____ immediately. Do not take anything with you.

2. Don't stop to call ____911____. Call from a neighbor's house outside of your building.

3. Don't use an ____elevator____ to exit your building. Use the stairs.

4. Feel every closed ____door____ before opening it. Do not open a door that is hot. Try to find another exit.

5. If you smell ____smoke____, stay close to the floor. Cover your mouth and nose with a wet cloth.

6. When you get outside, do not go back into your home for any reason. Tell ____firefighters____ about anyone still inside the building.

B **READ. PAIRS. Read about Carmen. Which of the fire safety tips from Exercise A did she follow? Did she make any mistakes?**

Last night there was a fire in Carmen's apartment building. First, she called 911. Then she got her wallet and keys from her bedroom. she touched the front door to her apartment, but it was not hot. She opened the door. She smelled smoke so she ran to the stairs. She didn't take the elevator. She waited across the street from the building until the firefighters said it was OK to go back inside.

4 **TALK ABOUT FIRE ESCAPE PLANS**

PAIRS. Look at the Pierre family escape plan. Answer the questions.

1. How many bedrooms are there? 3

2. How many people live there? 5

3. How many windows are there? 11

4. How many exits are there in each bedroom? 4, 2, 4
   Where are they? entrance and windows

5. Where is the family meeting place?
   the mailbox across the street

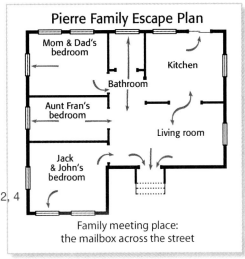

Pierre Family Escape Plan

Mom & Dad's bedroom

Kitchen

Bathroom

Aunt Fran's bedroom

Living room

Jack & John's bedroom

Family meeting place:
the mailbox across the street

Can you . . . understand fire safety procedures? ☐

Listening and Speaking

1   BEFORE YOU LISTEN

CLASS. Look at the dangerous situations. What are some other dangerous situations?

a construction accident   a car accident   a robbery   an explosion

2   LISTEN

A   **CLASS. Look at the picture. Guess: What are Mr. and Mrs. Novak talking about?**

a. traffic   (b.) the news   c. the weather

CD3 T41

B   Listen to the conversation. Was your guess in Exercise A correct?

CD3 T41

C   Listen again. Which story are they talking about?

a.

MORNING HERALD
Fire Destroys Hotel, No Injuries Reported

b.
Greenville Times
Route 52 Car Accident Leaves Two Hospitalized

(c.)
Village News
Gas Explosion Injures Two

d.
Journal News
First Federal Bank Robbed, No One Hurt

CD3 T42

D   Listen to the whole conversation.

What problem did the emergency situation cause?   1. traffic / 2. closed streets

Getting Started

1 BEFORE YOU LISTEN

CLASS Look at the dangerous situations. What are...

- Say: *Look at the dangerous situations.* Say each dangerous situation and ask the class to repeat.
- Ask: *What are some other dangerous situations?* Write students' ideas on the board (for example, *a fire, a natural disaster [a hurricane, an earthquake, a tornado], a fall, a wild animal*).

Presentation

2 LISTEN

Ⓐ CLASS. Look at the picture. Guess: What are...

- Read the directions. Ask: *What are Mr. and Mrs. Novak talking about?*
- Write the answer choices on the board and read them. Call on students to guess.

Ⓑ 💿 Listen to the conversation. Was your...

- Play CD 3, Track 41. Students listen.
- Circle the correct answer on the board. Ask: *Was your guess correct?*

> **Teaching Tip**
>
> *Optional:* Remember that if students need additional support, tell them to read the Audio Script on page 306 as they listen to the conversations.

Controlled Practice

Ⓒ 💿 Listen again. Which story...

- Tell students to read the newspaper headlines silently and underline the dangerous situations.
- Say each newspaper name and ask the class to call out the dangerous situation (a. *fire*, b. *car accident*, c. *gas explosion*, d. *bank robbery*).
- Play Track 41 again. Students listen and circle the letter of the story they hear.
- Ask: *Which story are they talking about?* Call on a student to answer.
- Ask the class: *How many people were hurt?* (two)

Ⓓ 💿 Listen to the whole conversation.

- Tell students that the gas explosion caused another problem.
- Play CD 3, Track 42. Students listen and write the answer to the question.
- Students compare answers with a partner.
- Ask: *What problem did the emergency situation cause?* Ask the class to call out the answer. (Traffic is bad. A lot of streets are closed downtown.) Write the answer on the board.

▬ EXPANSION: Graphic Organizer Practice for 2D

- Draw a *Wh-* question chart on the board. In the *What?* box, write *gas explosion.* Play Track 42 again. Tell students to listen for the *Who? Where? When?* and *Why?* of the story.
- Elicit the class's help to complete the chart on the board (*Who? two people hurt; Where? downtown; When? yesterday; Why? They don't know yet.*)
- Ask: *What is the name of our local newspaper? What were the headlines today?*
- Bring in newspapers or tell students to look at the local paper for homework. Tell students to choose a story about a dangerous situation and complete a *Wh-* question chart with information from the story.

Lesson 5 Describe an emergency

3 CONVERSATION

Ⓐ 💿 **Listen to the pairs of words. Notice...**

- Model pronouncing the /h/ sound. Say: *First, open your mouth. Then use your throat to breathe out.* Say the /h/ sound and ask the class to repeat.
- Read the directions. Play CD 3, Track 43. Students listen.
- Resume playing Track 43. Students listen and repeat.

Controlled Practice   20 minutes

Ⓑ 💿 **Listen to each pair of words. Are the....**

- Read the directions. Play CD 3, Track 44. Students listen and write *S* or *D*.
- Play Track 44 again if students have difficulty.
- Say each pair of words and ask the class to call out *same* or *different*.

Ⓒ 💿 **Listen and repeat the conversation.**

- Note: This conversation is the same one students heard in Exercise 2B on page 214.
- Tell students to read the conversation silently. Tell them to find words that begin with *h* and underline the *h* (*h*ear, *h*appened, *h*appened, *h*urt, *h*ospital). Say the words and ask the class to repeat.
- Play CD 3, Track 45. Students listen and repeat.

4 PRACTICE

Ⓐ **PAIRS. Practice the conversation. Then make new...**

- Pair students and tell them to practice the conversation in Exercise 3C.
- Then, in Exercise 4A, tell students to look at the information in the boxes.
- Say the dangerous situations in the blue box and ask the class to repeat.
- Say the sentences in the red box and ask the class to repeat. Ask: *Which two sentences have the same meaning?* (*No one was hurt. There were no injuries.*)
- Copy the conversation onto the board with blanks. Read it and when you come to a blank, ask what color it is. Point to the box that's the same color and fill in the blank with the first item in the box.

- Ask two on-level students to practice the conversation on the board for the class.
- Tell pairs to take turns playing A and B. Tell them to use the information in the boxes to fill in the blanks.
- Walk around and check students' pronunciation of the /h/ sound at the beginning of *hear, happened,* and *hurt*. As needed, pronounce the words and ask students to repeat.
- Tell students to stand, mingle, and practice the conversation with several new partners.
- Call on pairs to practice for the class.

Communicative Practice   15 minutes

Ⓑ **MAKE IT PERSONAL. PAIRS. Make your own...**

- Ask the class: *Do you read the newspaper? Where do you get your news?*
- Pair students. Say: *Think about an emergency situation you have heard about. In your notebooks, write down the type of situation and the number of injuries and / or deaths.*
- *Optional:* Bring in newspapers and tell students to look for stories about dangerous emergency situations. Tell them to write down the type of situation and the number of injuries. Tell partners to choose different stories.
- Say: *Student A, talk about the information you wrote down. Begin the conversation by saying:* Did you hear what happened yesterday?
- Call on pairs to perform for the class.

▬▬▬ MULTILEVEL INSTRUCTION for 4B

Pre-level Tell students to write down the type of dangerous emergency situation. Tell them to write a sentence, similar to the sentences in the red box in Exercise 4A, about injuries. Direct pairs to use their information in the conversation in Exercise 4A.

Above-level Tell higher-level pairs to talk about the information they wrote in their notebooks without looking at the conversation in Exercise 4A.

Extra Practice

Interactive Practice

---

3 CONVERSATION

CD3 T43

A 🔊 **Listen to the pairs of words. Notice the sound /h/ at the beginning of the second word in each pair. Then listen and repeat.**

1. ear hear
2. I high
3. art heart
4. ow how

CD3 T44

B 🔊 **Listen to each pair of words. Are the two words the same (S) or different (D)? Write S or D.**

1. _S_   2. _D_   3. _D_   4. _S_   5. _D_   6. _S_

CD3 T45

C 🔊 **Listen and repeat the conversation.**

Mr. Novak: Did you hear what happened yesterday?
Mrs. Novak: No. What happened?
Mr. Novak: There was a gas explosion downtown.
Mrs. Novak: Oh my gosh. That's terrible. Was anybody hurt?
Mr. Novak: Yes. Two people went to the hospital.

4 PRACTICE

A PAIRS. Practice the conversation. Then make new conversations. Use the information in the boxes.

A: Did you hear what happened yesterday?

B: No. What happened?

A: There was a _____ downtown.

B: Oh my gosh. That's terrible. Was anybody hurt?

A:

robbery
car accident
construction accident

No one was hurt.
There were no injuries.
Four people were hurt.

B MAKE IT PERSONAL. PAIRS. Make your own conversations. Talk about an emergency situation you have heard about.

Grammar

There was / There were

Affirmative				Negative		
There	**was**	a gas explosion	yesterday.	**There**	**wasn't**	a fire.
	were	two car accidents	last week.		**was no**	fire.
					weren't	any injuries.
					were no	injuries.

Yes / No questions			Short answers						
Was	**there**	a fire?	Yes,	**there**	**was.**	No,	**there**	**wasn't.**
Were		any injuries?			**were.**			**weren't.**

1 PRACTICE

Complete the conversations. Use *there* and *was* or *were*.

1. **A:** What happened downtown last night?

   B: _____There was_____ a robbery at the jewelry store.

   A: _____Were there_____ any customers there?

   B: Yes, _____there were_____. But no one was hurt.

2. **A:** _____There was_____ a problem at the high school last night.

   B: I know. _____There was_____ a fight after the basketball game.

   A: Wow! Did the police come?

   B: Yes, _____there were_____ five police cars in the parking lot.

3. **A:** _____There was_____ an explosion at the factory yesterday.

   B: Was anybody hurt?

   A: No, luckily _____there were_____ no injuries.

4. **A:** _____Was there_____ an accident on Main Street this morning?

   B: Yes, _____there was_____. I heard about it on the radio.

   A: I thought so. _____There was_____ a lot of traffic and I was late to work.

Getting Started 5 minutes

- Say: *We're going to study* There was *and* There were. *In the conversation on page 215, Mr. Novak used this grammar.*
- Play CD 3, Track 45. Students listen. Write on the board: *There was a gas explosion downtown.* Underline *There was.*

Presentation 15 minutes

There was / There were

- On the board, draw a word box with *was* and *were*. Side-by-side, write: *1. There ___ a gas explosion yesterday. 2. There ___ two car accidents last week.* Say: *Look at sentence 1. What comes after the blank?* (*a gas explosion*) *Look at sentence 2. What comes after the blank?* (*two car accidents*) *Which do you think is the answer for number 1,* was *or* were? (*was*) *Why?* (because *explosion* is singular) *Which do you think is the answer for number 2,* was *or* were? (*were*) *Why?* (because the word *accidents* is plural)
- Underline *last week* and *yesterday* in the sentences on the board. Say: *Use* there was / there were *to talk about the past.*
- Copy the grammar charts onto the board or show Transparency 11.4 and cover the exercise.
- Read the sentences in the top two charts and ask the class to repeat.
- Point to sentence 1 on the board and ask: *How do I make this sentence negative?* Tell students to look at the top left grammar chart. Elicit and write under sentence 1: *There wasn't a gas explosion yesterday. There was no gas explosion yesterday.* Repeat with sentence 2 and write: *There weren't any car accidents last week. There were no car accidents last week.*

- Read the sentences in the bottom two grammar charts and ask the class to repeat.
- Point to sentence 1 on the board and ask: *How do I make this sentence into a question?* Tell students to look at the grammar chart. Elicit and write under sentence 1: *Was there a gas explosion yesterday?* Repeat with sentence 2 and write: *Were there any car accidents last week?*
- Elicit affirmative and negative short answers to each question and write them on the board.
- If you are using the transparency, do the exercise with the class.

Controlled Practice 20 minutes

1 PRACTICE

Complete the conversations. Use *there* and *was* or *were*.

- Read the directions. Write the example on the board and point to the answer. Ask: *Why is the answer* There was? (because *robbery* is singular)
- Students compare answers with a partner by reading the conversations.
- *Optional:* Pair students and ask them to practice the completed conversations. Call on pairs to perform the completed conversations for the class.

Lesson 6 Describe an emergency

2 PRACTICE

Ⓐ WRITE. Look at the pictures of emergency...

- Read the directions.
- Say the words from the box and ask the class to repeat.
- Say the words from the box again and ask the class to call out *singular* or *plural*. Tell students to look at the first noun. Explain: A lot of smoke *is singular* because smoke *is non-count. You use* There was *with a lot of and* There were *with lots of.*
- Tell students to look at picture 1. Read the example.
- Say: *For each picture, use your own idea to write the first sentence and words from the box to write the second sentence. There is more than one correct answer.*

Ⓑ PAIRS. Compare your answers.

- Tell pairs to take turns reading their sentences for each picture.
- Ask the class: *Were there many differences between your sentences and your partner's sentences? What situation did you say there was in picture 4? What situation did your partner say there was?*
- Call on a couple of students to read their sentences for each picture.

Communicative Practice   20 minutes

Show what you know!

STEP 1. GROUPS OF 3. Student A, tell about...

- Read the directions.
- Ask two on-level students to read the example.
- Ask for a show of hands: *Did you watch the news on TV last night? Did you read the newspaper this morning? Did you listen to the news on the radio today or yesterday? Did you read the news online today or yesterday?*
- Tell students to think of an emergency situation they have heard about. Tell them to write down where they heard about it and the information they remember—the situation, where it happened, when it happened, the number of injuries.

- As a class, brainstorm questions that B and C can ask to get more information. Write them on the board (for example, *Was anybody hurt? Were there any injuries? Where / When / How did it happen? Did the police / firefighters / an ambulance come? Was there a lot of smoke / traffic?*).
- Model the activity. Play A and tell about an emergency situation you have heard about. Say where you heard about the situation, what the situation was, and where it happened (for example, *I read the newspaper this morning. There was a robbery at Community Bank on Lincoln Highway.*). Call on volunteers to ask you questions from the board or their own questions. Answer the questions.

STEP 2. Tell the class about an emergency situation.

- Read the directions.
- Model the activity. Tell the class about the emergency situation you described in Step 1. Begin in the same way (for example, *I read the newspaper this morning. There was a robbery . . .*). Include the information elicited by students' questions.
- Tell students to practice telling a partner about the emergency situation from Step 1.
- Call on students to tell the class about their emergency situation. Check that students use *There was / There were* correctly.

░░░ EXPANSION: Listening and Writing Practice for STEP 2

- For homework, tell students to watch the local news on TV in English.
- Tell students to write two sentences with *There was / There were* about three different emergency situations.
- Call on students to tell the class about one emergency situation.

Progress Check

Can you . . . describe an emergency?

Say: *We have practiced describing emergencies. Now, look at the question at the bottom of the page. Can you describe an emergency?* Tell students to write a checkmark in the box.

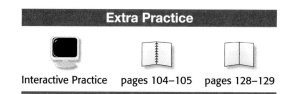

Extra Practice		
Interactive Practice	pages 104–105	pages 128–129

A **WRITE.** Look at the pictures of emergency situations from the news last night. Write two sentences to describe each picture. Use *there was* or *there were* and words from the box or your own ideas. Answers will vary.

> a lot of smoke   a traffic jam   a crowd of people   lots of police

> *There was a fire last night. There was a lot of smoke.*

1.

2.

3.

4.

B **PAIRS.** Compare your answers.

Show what you know!   Describe an emergency

STEP 1. GROUPS OF 3. Student A, tell about an emergency situation you have heard about. Students B and C, ask questions to get more information.

A: *I watched the news on TV last night. There was a fire on Center Street.*
B: *Was anybody hurt?*
A: *Some people went to the hospital.*

STEP 2. Tell the class about an emergency situation.

Can you...describe an emergency? ☐

Reading

1 BEFORE YOU READ

CLASS. Look at the pictures of everyday objects in the home.
Which of these objects can be dangerous?

candy

cleaning supplies

a bathtub

a stove

a balloon

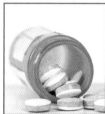
medicine

2 READ

CD3 T46

Listen. Read the article. Were your guesses in Before You Read correct?

Accidents Will Happen

What do you think of when you think of home?
Do you think of comfort and safety? Well, think
again! Every four seconds a person in the U.S.
gets injured in the home. In fact, one-third of
all injuries happen at home. Every year about
10 million people visit hospital emergency
rooms because of household accidents.

What are the most common causes of home injuries?

1 **Falls** are the most common cause of home
injuries. More than 5 million people are
injured by falls each year. Falls are especially
dangerous for people age 65 and older.

Safety tips: Make sure halls and stairs have
enough light. Keep your floors clear of
clothes, toys, and other things. Put nonslip
rubber mats in bathtubs and showers.

2 **Poisonings** are the second most
common cause of home injuries. There are
2.3 million poisonings every year. Poisonings
can happen to people of all ages.

Safety tips: Keep all medicine and cleaning
supplies away from children. Keep all your
medicines in their original containers so you
don't take the wrong medicine.

Read about causes of home injuries

Getting Started — 10 minutes

1 BEFORE YOU READ

CLASS. Look at the pictures of everyday objects...

- Say: *Look at these pictures of everyday objects.* Say each object and ask the class to repeat.
- Ask: *Which of these objects can be dangerous?* Tell students to circle the words for the objects they think can be dangerous.
- Ask: *Which objects did you circle?* Call on a few students to answer.

Presentation — 20 minutes

2 READ

  Listen. Read the article. Were your guesses...

- Play CD 3, Track 46. Students listen and read silently.

- *Optional:* Play Track 46 again. Pause the CD after each cause of home injuries and ask the class:

    How many people are injured each year?
    (1. 5 million; 2. 2.3 million; 3. 261, 000; 4. no information)

    Who is most affected? (1. people age 65 and older; 2. people of all ages; 3. people in the kitchen; 4. children younger than five)

- Tell students to read the article again and underline the everyday objects from Exercise 1 that are in the article. (They are all mentioned in the article.) Ask: *Which everyday objects from* Before You Read *can be dangerous?* (all of them) *Were your guesses correct?*

- Say the most common causes of home injuries (*falls, poisonings, burns,* and *choking*) and ask the class to repeat. Say the everyday objects from Exercise 1 and ask the class to call out the type of home injury it can cause (for example, T: *candy,* Ss: *choking*).

Controlled Practice 15 minutes

3 CHECK YOUR UNDERSTANDING

Ⓐ GROUPS OF 3. Look at paragraphs 2, 3, and 4...

- Read the Reading Skill note. Ask: *What are supporting details?* (reasons, examples, steps, or other kinds of information) *What do they help explain?* (the main ideas)

- Tell students to read paragraph 1 (*Falls*) in the article again. Read the example. Tell students to underline the main idea sentence in the paragraph. Ask: *Which sentences help explain the main idea?* (*More than 5 million people are injured by falls each year.* and *Falls are especially dangerous for people age 65 and older.*) Say: *These are the supporting details.*

- Write the example on the board and complete it with the two sentences above.

- Read the directions.

- Form groups of 3. Tell each member to choose a different paragraph. Tell students to first underline the main idea sentence in their paragraph.

- Tell group members to take turns talking about their paragraphs. Remind them to use the example as a model.

- Call on students to say the main idea and supporting details for paragraphs 2, 3, and 4.

▰▰▰ **EXPANSION: Graphic Organizer Practice for 3A**

- Ask: *Can you guess what the fifth most common cause of home injuries is?* (drowning)

- Draw three boxes on the board. In the top box, write: *Main idea.* In the middle and bottom boxes, write: *Supporting detail.*

- Say: *Pretend we're going to write a paragraph about drowning. What can the main idea sentence be? To write sentences with supporting details, what do we need to find out?* Elicit answers and write them in the boxes on the board:

    Main idea: Drowning is the fifth most common cause of home injuries.

    Supporting detail: how many people are injured by drowning each year

    Supporting detail: who is most affected by drowning

Ⓑ GROUPS OF 3. Read the safety tips for each...

- Read the directions and the example.

- Tell students to read the safety tips for each kind of home injury again and to underline the things that they do.

- Say: *Each group member should take a turn asking and answering:* Which of the tips do you do?

- Ask: *Which of the tips do you do?* Call on a few students.

Communicative Practice 15 minutes

Show what you know!

PRE-WRITING. PAIRS. How safe is your home...

- Read the directions.

- Tell students to look at the safety tips they didn't underline in Exercise 3B. Ask: *Which of these tips can you follow to make your home safer?*

- To model the activity, talk about something you can do to make your home safer (for example, *I can keep my floors clear of toys. I can ask my kids to clean up their toys when they are finished playing.*).

- Pair students. Tell partners to take turns asking each other: *What can you do to make your home safer?*

WRITE. Write about the safety of your home....

- Turn to page 273 and ask students to complete the activities. See page T-xii for general notes about Writing activities.

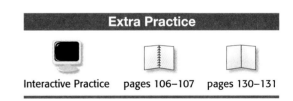

Extra Practice		
Interactive Practice	pages 106–107	pages 130–131

3 **Burns** are the third leading cause of home injuries. There are 261,000 fire and burn injuries every year. Most burns happen in the kitchen while cooking or eating food.

Safety tips: Stay in the kitchen while food is cooking. Turn pot handles inward, so they don't stick out from the stove. Don't wear loose clothes while cooking.

4 **Choking** accidents are the fourth leading cause of home injuries. Children—especially those younger than five—can easily choke on food and small objects. Candy causes 20 percent of all childhood choking accidents. Any object that can fit inside a paper towel roll can cause choking.

Safety tips: Don't give young children small pieces of candy. Keep small objects like coins, jewelry, balloons, and toys with small parts out of their reach. Be sure to read toy labels for warnings.

Source: www.homesafetycouncil.org

3 CHECK YOUR UNDERSTANDING

A GROUPS OF 3. **Look at paragraphs 2, 3, and 4. Each person choose a paragraph. Say which sentence in each paragraph gives the main idea. Say which sentences contain supporting details.**

In paragraph one, the main idea sentence is Falls are the most common cause of home injuries. *The supportive details are . . .*

B GROUPS OF 3. **Read the safety tips for each kind of home injury. Which of the tips do you do?**

I have rubber mats in my bathtub.

> **Reading Skill:**
> Identifying Supporting Details
>
> Supporting details are reasons, examples, steps, or other kinds of information. Authors use supporting details to help explain the main ideas.

Show what you know!

PRE-WRITING. PAIRS. **How safe is your home? What can you do to make it safer?**

WRITE. **Write about the safety of your home. See page 273.**

Listening and Speaking

1 BEFORE YOU LISTEN

A CLASS. Do you know what to do if you are pulled over by the police?

B Take the quiz. Check *True* or *False*.

Do you know...
what to do if you get pulled over?

		True		False
1.	You should always pull over to the left.	☐ True		☑ False
2.	After you pull over, you should get out of your car.	☐ True		☑ False
3.	Keep your hands on the steering wheel when the police officer talks to you.	☑ True		☐ False
4.	Give the police officer your driver's license, registration, and proof of insurance.	☑ True		☐ False
5.	Don't argue with the police officer.	☑ True		☐ False
6.	If a police officer gives you a ticket, you need to pay the police officer immediately.	☐ True		☑ False

2 LISTEN

CD3 T47

A 🔊 Listen to the police officer talking about what to do if you're pulled over. Then check your answers on the quiz.

B PAIRS. Discuss the quiz. Did any of the answers surprise you? What did you learn from the police officer's talk?

Lesson 8 Respond to a police officer's instructions

Getting Started   10 minutes

1 BEFORE YOU LISTEN

A CLASS. **Do you know what to do if you are pulled...**

- Read the question.
- Tell students to look at the picture. Ask: *What does it mean to be* pulled over by the police? (A police car signals—usually with its lights and its siren—that you should drive to the side of the road and stop.)
- Repeat the question. Elicit students' ideas and write them on the board.

B **Take the quiz. Check** *True* **or** *False*.

- Tell students to look at the quiz. Explain unfamiliar vocabulary. Say: *Look at numbers 1 and 2. What phrase means* drive to the side of the road and stop? (*pull over*) Tell students to look at number 4. If possible, bring in your car registration and proof-of-insurance card to show the class.
- Read the quiz title. Read each quiz item and ask students to raise their hands for *True* or *False*.
- Tell students they will now listen to the CD to check their answers.

Culture Connection

- Explain that laws about car registration and car insurance vary from state to state in the U.S.
- Say: *In most states, you go to the Department of Motor Vehicles (DMV) to register a car. You show your owner's certificate, pay a fee, and receive a registration card, license plate(s), and a sticker for your car window that shows your registration is valid for one year.*
- Say: *Most states require car insurance—to cover the cost of damage, medical expenses, etc. if you are in an accident. Many states require drivers to carry proof of insurance, a card from the insurance company that has your policy number and the dates your insurance is valid.*
- Ask: *What are the laws about car registration and car insurance in your home country? Are they similar to the laws in the U.S.?*

Presentation   20 minutes

2 LISTEN

A Listen to the police officer talking...

- Play CD 3, Track 47. Students listen and check their answers.
- To aid comprehension, pause the CD after each sections and / or play Track 47 as many times as needed.
- Ask the class: *Did you change any of your answers? Which ones?* Tell students to circle the item number of any answers they changed.
- Play Track 47 again. Pause after each answer in the recording, read the quiz item, and elicit the correct answer.

EXPANSION: Listening Practice for 2A

- Play Track 47 again. Tell students to listen and correct the false items in the quiz (1, 2, and 6).
- Students compare answers with a partner.
- Call on students to read the corrected items: 1. . . . pull over to the <u>right</u>. 2. . . . you should <u>stay in</u> your car. 6. If a police officer gives you a ticket, <u>don't</u> pay the police officer . . .

B PAIRS. **Discuss the quiz. Did any of the answers...**

- Say: *Look at the item numbers you circled on the quiz. What did you think the answer was? What did you learn?*
- Pair students. Say: *Ask each other the questions from the directions. Tell your partner which answers surprised you and what you learned.*
- To wrap up, ask a few students the questions from the directions.

Culture Connection

- Tell students to close their books and listen again to the police officer talking about what to do if you're pulled over. Play Track 47 again.
- Say: *Now do you know what to do if you are pulled over by the police? Tell a partner what you can remember about what to do.*
- Ask: *What do you do if you are pulled over by the police in your country? Which things are the same? Which things are different?*

3 CONVERSATION

Ⓐ CLASS. Look at the traffic violations. What are...

- Tell students to look at the traffic violations. Say each violation and ask the class to repeat.
- To check comprehension, say: *Look at the violations. Which one means driving too fast?* (speeding) *Which one means driving too close to the car in front of you?* (tailgating) *Which one means not stopping?* (running a red light)
- Ask the class: *What are some other violations you know of?* List students' ideas on the board (for example, *running a stop sign, making an illegal turn, not using car seats for young children, passing a school bus, driving too slowly, talking on a cell phone* [in some states]).

Controlled Practice   15 minutes

Ⓑ 💿 Listen and repeat the conversation.

- Read the directions. Play CD 3, Track 48. Students listen and repeat.
- Ask: *What did the police officer ask for?* (license, registration, and proof of insurance) *Did the driver wait for the police officer to ask for his documents before he got them out?* (Yes.) *Why did the officer pull him over?* (for speeding) *Did he argue with the officer?* (No.)
- As needed, explain *glove compartment.* Ask: *Where is the* glove compartment *in a car?* (in front of the passenger's seat) *What did the driver from the conversation have in his glove compartment?* (registration and proof of insurance) *What do you have in your glove compartment?*
- *Optional:* Play Track 48 again to aid comprehension and give students more practice saying the new vocabulary.

4 PRACTICE

Ⓐ PAIRS. Practice the conversation. Then make new...

- Pair students and tell them to practice the conversation in Exercise 3B.
- Say: *Now make new conversations. Use different traffic violations.* Tell pairs to underline the information in the conversation in Exercise 3B that they will need to change. Ask the class: *What*

did you underline? (speeding) Point out that students may also want to change *pocket* to *purse, pocketbook, backpack,* etc.

- Tell pairs to substitute traffic violations from the top of the page or the board for *speeding* in the conversation in Exercise 3B.
- Tell students to stand, mingle, and practice the conversation with several new partners.

Communicative Practice   15 minutes

Ⓑ MAKE IT PERSONAL. GROUPS OF 3. Talk...

- Model the activity. Talk about a time when you or someone you know was pulled over (for example, *My husband was pulled over for making an illegal turn in San Francisco. There was a sign, but we didn't see it. We apologized and explained that we weren't from the city. The police officer didn't give us a ticket!*).
- On the board, write: *. . . was pulled over for . . .* Ask: *What did you / someone you know do? What did the police officer do?*
- Walk around and listen to students' conversations. Ask questions to elicit more information.

▮▮▮ MULTILEVEL INSTRUCTION for 4B

Above-level Encourage students to elaborate on their stories and ask each other questions to get more information.

Pre-level Ask students to note who was pulled over and what the violation was. Tell them to use this information to complete the prompt on the board.

Extra Practice
Interactive Practice

---

3 CONVERSATION

A **CLASS.** Look at the traffic violations. What are some other violations you know of?

running a red light

tailgating

not wearing a seat belt

speeding

CD3 T48

B 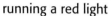 **Listen and repeat the conversation.**

A: I need to see your license, registration, and proof of insurance.

B: OK. My license is in my pocket. The other things are in the glove compartment.

A: That's fine. You can get them.

B: Here you go.

A: I'll be back in a moment. Please turn off your engine and stay in your car.

[a few minutes later]

A: Do you know why I pulled you over?

B: I'm not sure.

A: I pulled you over for speeding.

B: I see.

4 PRACTICE

A **PAIRS.** Practice the conversation. Then make new conversations. Use different traffic violations.

B **MAKE IT PERSONAL.** **GROUPS OF 3.** Talk about a time you or someone you know was pulled over.

Respond to a police officer's instructions

Grammar

Compound imperatives				
Affirmative				
Turn off	your engine	**and**	**stay**	in your car.
Negative				
Don't get out	of your car	**or**	**take off**	your seat belt.

····· **Grammar Watch**

• Connect two affirmative imperatives with *and*.

• Connect two negative imperatives with *or*.

PRACTICE

A Read the driving rules. Complete each sentence with *and* or *or*.

1. Drive carefully ___and___ obey all traffic laws.

2. Be sure to wear your seat belt ___and___ use car seats for young children.

3. Don't use your cell phone ___or___ read a map while driving.

4. Drive more slowly ___and___ put on your headlights in bad weather.

5. Don't tailgate ___or___ change lanes without signaling.

B Read the advice about what to do during a traffic stop. Rewrite each pair of sentences as two imperatives with *and* or *or*.

1. You should use your turn signal. You should pull over to a safe spot.

   Use your turn signal and pull over to a safe spot.

2. You should wait for the police officer. You should roll down your window.

   Wait for the police officer and roll down your window.

3. You should be polite. You should follow the officer's instructions.

   Be polite and follow the officer's instructions.

4. You should not argue with the officer. You should not offer money to the officer.

   Don't argue with the officer or offer him / her money.

5. You should not start your car. You should not leave until the officer gives you permission to go.

   Don't start your car or leave until the officer gives you permission to go.

Lesson 9 Respond to a police officer's instructions

Getting Started   5 minutes

- Say: *We're going to study compound imperatives, or how to connect two commands. In the conversation on page 221, the police officer used this grammar.*
- Play CD 3, Track 48. Students listen. Write on the board: *Please turn off your engine and stay in your car.* Underline *turn off* and *and stay.*

Presentation   10 minutes

Compound imperatives

- To review, say: *Imperatives are the form of the verb you use when you give someone a command, directions, or advice. To form imperatives, use the base form of a verb or* don't + *the base form of a verb.* On the board, write: *Call 911. Don't call 911.*
- Say: *Compound imperatives are two imperatives joined together in the same sentence.*
- Copy the grammar chart onto the board or show Transparency 11.5 and cover the exercise.
- On the board, write: *Turn off your engine. Stay in your car.*
- Read the first item from the Grammar Watch note. Write *and* between the two affirmative imperatives on the board. Read the first sentence in the chart and ask the class to repeat.
- On the board, write: *Don't get out of your car. Don't take off your seat belt.*
- Read the second item from the Grammar Watch note. Write *or* between the two negative imperatives on the board and cross out *Don't* in the second one. Read the second sentence in the chart and ask the class to repeat.
- If you are using the transparency, do the exercise with the class.

Controlled Practice   15 minutes

 PRACTICE

Ⓐ Read the driving rules. Complete each sentence...

- Read the directions and the example. Ask: *Why is the answer* and? (because *drive carefully* and *obey all laws* are affirmative)

- *Optional:* Tell students to circle *Don't* in the sentences. Say: *If* Don't *is at the beginning of a sentence, use* or.
- Students compare answers with a partner. Tell pairs to take turns reading the sentences.
- Call on students to read the completed sentences.

Ⓑ Read the advice about what to do during a traffic...

- Read the directions.
- Write item 1 on the board. Cross out *You should* in both sentences. Write *and* between the two sentences. Read the example.
- Walk around and check students' work. If you see mistakes in items 4 and 5, write item 4 on the board; cross out *You should not* in both sentences and write *or* between the sentences.
- Students compare answers with a partner. Tell pairs to take turns reading the sentences.
- Call on students to read the sentences.

■■■ EXPANSION: Grammar practice for B

- Tell students to read the fire safety tips on page 213 again.
- On the board, write: *If there's a fire . . .*
- Pair students. Tell them to choose two affirmative imperatives and combine them with *and.* Tell them to choose two negative imperatives and combine them with *or.*
- Call on pairs to read their sentences (for example, *Leave your house immediately and call 911 from a neighbor's house. Don't take anything with you or stop to call 911.*).

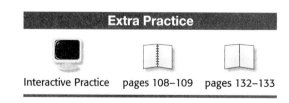

Extra Practice		
Interactive Practice	pages 108–109	pages 132–133

1 GRAMMAR

Complete the phone conversations. Use the correct...

- Read the directions. Tell students to refer back to the grammar charts on page 210 (Present continuous: Statements and questions) and page 216 (*There was / There were*) as needed.
- Remind students to use a capital letter when an answer begins a sentence.
- Students compare answers with a partner by reading the conversations.
- Call on two pairs to read the conversations for the class. As pairs read, write the correct answers on the board. Discuss any errors. Tell students to check their spelling.
- *Optional:* Call on pairs to perform for the class.

2 LIFE SKILLS WRITING

Turn to page 266 and ask students to complete the employee accident report. See page T-xii for general notes about Life Skills Writing activities.

CD-ROM Practice

Go to the CD-ROM for more practice.

If your students need more practice with the vocabulary, grammar, and competencies in Unit 11, encourage them to review the activities on the CD-ROM. This review can also help students prepare for the final role play on the following Expand page.

Extra Practice
pages 110–111

1 GRAMMAR

Complete the phone conversations. Use the correct present continuous form of the verb in parentheses, or use the correct form of *there be* in the past.

1. **Bill:** Hi, Ann. Listen, I'm going to be late. I ___*am sitting*___ in my car.
   (sit)

   I'm stuck in a traffic jam. ___There was___ an accident near Lakeland.
   (there be)

   Ann: Oh, no! Was anyone hurt?

   Bill: I'm not sure. ___There was___ an ambulance
   (there be)
   here a few minutes ago.

   Ann: ___Are___ you ___moving___?
   (move)

   Bill: Actually, a police officer ___is directing___
   (direct)
   traffic now. Got to go. I'll see you soon.

2. **Sue:** Hi, Rita. I hope I ___'m not calling___ at a bad time?
   (not call)

   Rita: No, I ___'m not working___ today. The factory is closed.
   (not work)

   ___There was___ an explosion yesterday.
   (there be)

   Sue: You're kidding!

   Rita: No, it's true. Luckily, ___there were___ no injuries.
   (there be)

   Sue: That's amazing. ___was there___ a fire?
   (there be)

   Rita: Yeah, a big one. ___There were___ ten or twelve fire trucks there.
   (there be)

   Sue: Wow.

2 LIFE SKILLS WRITING   Complete an employee accident report. See page 266.

3 ACT IT OUT What do you say?

STEP 1. CLASS. Review the Lesson 2 conversation between the 911 operator and Olivia (CD 3 track 34).

STEP 2. ROLE PLAY. PAIRS. Student A, you see an emergency situation. Student B, you are the 911 operator.

Student A:
- Think of an emergency situation.
- Role-play calling 911. Describe the emergency.
- Answer the 911 operator's questions.

Student B:
- Ask about the emergency.
- Ask about the location of the emergency.
- Ask for the caller's name.

4 READ AND REACT Problem-solving

STEP 1. Read about Fahad's problem.

Fahad had an accident at work. He burned himself and he is in a lot of pain. Fahad went to a clinic and the doctor said he should not work for one week. Fahad is afraid to tell his boss about the accident. He doesn't want to lose his job.

STEP 2. PAIRS. What is Fahad's problem? What can he do? Here are some ideas.

- He can report his accident to his boss.
- He can say nothing and continue working.
- He can ask a co-worker to cover his hours for the week.
- He can _____.

5 CONNECT

For your Study Skills Activity, go to page 254.
For your Team Project, go to page 284.

3 ACT IT OUT

STEP 1. CLASS. Review the Lesson 2 conversation...

- Tell students to review the conversation in Exercise 3C on page 209.
- Tell them to read the conversation silently and then practice it with a partner.
- Play CD 3, Track 34. Students listen.
- As needed, play Track 34 again to aid comprehension.

STEP 2. ROLE PLAY. PAIRS. Student A, you see...

- Read the directions and the guidelines for A and B.
- Tell A to think of an emergency situation and location. Suggest that A review the medical emergencies on page 207 and the dangerous situations on page 214. Tell A to start the conversation by pretending to dial 911.
- Tell B to highlight or underline questions from the Lesson 2 conversation that he she can ask.
- Remind A to use the present continuous or simple past with a medical emergency (for example, *She's bleeding* or *He swallowed poison.*) or *There was / There were* with a dangerous situation. Suggest that B can also ask *Was anybody hurt?* about a dangerous situation.
- Walk around and observe partners interacting. Check A's use of the present continuous, simple past, or *there was / there were*.
- Call on pairs to perform for the class.
- While pairs are performing, use the scoring rubric on page T-xiii to evaluate each student's vocabulary, grammar, fluency, and how well they complete the task.
- *Optional:* After each pair finishes, discuss the strengths and weakness of each performance either in front of the class or privately.

4 READ AND REACT

STEP 1. Read about Fahad's problem.

- Say: *We are going to read about a student's problem, and then we need to think about a solution.*
- Read the directions.
- Read the story while students follow along silently. Pause after each sentence to allow time for students to comprehend. Periodically stop and ask simple

Wh- questions to check comprehension (for example, *What happened to Fahad? What did the doctor say? What is Fahad afraid to do? Why?*).

STEP 2. PAIRS. What is Fahad's problem? What...

- Ask: *What is Fahad's problem?* (Fahad can't work for one week because he had an accident. He's afraid to tell his boss.). *What can Fahad do?*
- Pair students. Read the ideas in the list. Give them a couple of minutes to discuss possible solutions for Fahad.
- Ask: *Which ideas are good?* Call on students to say their opinion about the ideas in the list (for example, S: *I think he can report his accident to his boss. This is a good idea.*).
- Now tell students to think of one new idea not in the list (for example, *He can call in sick.*) and to write it in the blank. Encourage students to think of more than one idea and to write them in their notebooks.
- Call on pairs to say their additional solutions. Write any particularly good ones on the board and ask students if they think it is a good idea too (*Do you think this is a good idea? Why or why not?*).

▬▬▬ MULTILEVEL INSTRUCTION for STEP 2
Cross-ability Tell students to read the ideas in the book and think about the pros and cons of each. Direct the higher-level student to say a pro and con of one idea and the lower-level student to identify the idea (for example, *He can report his accident to his boss.* Pro: *It's honest. He can stay home and get well.* Con: *He might lose his job.*).

5 CONNECT

Turn to page 254 for the Study Skills Activity and page 284 for the Team Project. See page T-xi for general notes about teaching these activities.

Progress Check

Which goals can you check off? Go back to page 205.
Ask students to turn to page 205 and check off the goals they have reached. Call on students to say which goals they will practice outside of class.

12 The World of Work

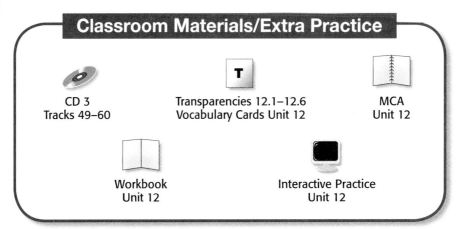

Classroom Materials/Extra Practice

CD 3
Tracks 49–60

T
Transparencies 12.1–12.6
Vocabulary Cards Unit 12

MCA
Unit 12

Workbook
Unit 12

Interactive Practice
Unit 12

Unit Overview

Goals
- See the list of goals on the facing page.

Grammar
- Expressions of necessity: *must / have to*
- Expressions of prohibition: *must not / can't*
- Information questions with *Who*
- Information questions with *What / Which / When / Where*
- *Can / Could* to ask permission

Pronunciation
- Rising intonation in *Yes / No* questions
- Falling intonation in statements and *Wh-* questions

Reading
- Read a FAQ about the Social Security program
- *Reading Skill:* Think about what you know

Writing
- Write about your responsibilities
- Write about your life after you retire

Life Skills Writing
- Complete a vacation request form

Preview
- Set the context of the unit by asking questions about work (for example, *Do you work? Where do you work? What are your job duties? What are your hours?*).
- Hold up page 225 or show Transparency 12.1. Read the unit title and ask the class to repeat.
- As needed, explain: The world of work *means all about work.*
- Say: *Look at the picture.* Ask the Preview questions: *Where is the woman?* (at work) *What is she doing?* (clocking in / out) As needed, explain: *When you clock in, you record the time you arrived at work. When you clock out, you record the time you left work.*

Goals
- Point to the Unit Goals. Explain that this list shows what the class will be studying in this unit.
- Tell students to read the goals silently.
- Say each goal and ask the class to repeat. Explain unfamiliar vocabulary as needed:

    Policies: similar to procedures or rules; the way things are done at a particular place

    Pay stub: a piece of paper that's attached to your paycheck; it shows how much money you earned and how much money was taken out for taxes, insurance, etc. (Show the art on page 232.)

    Cover your hours: to work for you when you can't come to work
- Tell students to circle one goal that is very important to them. Call on several students to say the goal they circled.

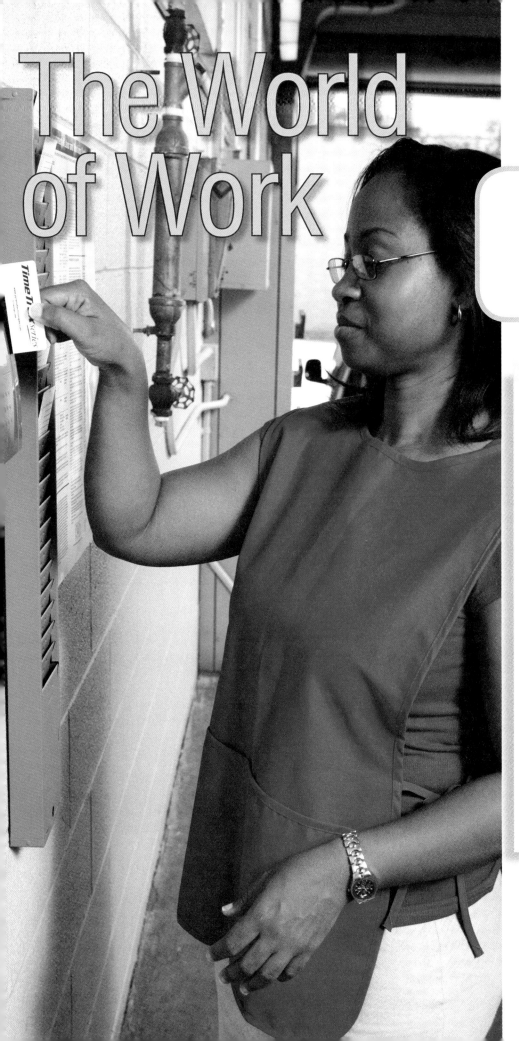

The World of Work

Preview

Look at the picture.
Where is the woman?
What is she doing?

UNIT GOALS

☐ Identify job
responsibilities

☐ Ask about
policies at work

☐ Talk about
responsibilities

☐ Read a pay stub

☐ Ask a co-worker
to cover your
hours

☐ Ask about work
schedules

☐ Request a
schedule change

☐ Complete a
vacation request
form

1 WHAT DO YOU KNOW?

A CLASS. Look at the pictures. What are the people doing? Which job responsibilities do you know?

CD3 T49

B Look at the pictures and listen. Listen again and repeat.

2 PRACTICE

A PAIRS. What are the job responsibilities for each of the following jobs?

| computer system administrator | nurse assistant |
| sales assistant | warehouse worker |

A: *What are the responsibilities of a nurse assistant?*
B: *Wash hands, wear latex gloves . . .*

B WORD PLAY. GROUPS OF 3. Look at the categories of job responsibilities. Complete the chart with job responsibilities from the list on page 227. There may be more than one correct answer.

Answers will vary but could include:

Category	Job responsibility
Wear the right clothing	*wear a uniform*
Follow health and safety rules	wear latex gloves
Be on time	clock in / out
Communicate with others	work as a team
Use equipment correctly	ask questions

Lesson 1 Vocabulary

Getting Started   10 minutes

1 WHAT DO YOU KNOW?

A CLASS. **Look at the pictures. What are the people...**

- Show Transparency 12.2 or hold up the book. Tell students to cover the list of words on page 227.
- Say: *Look at the pictures. What are the people doing? Which job responsibilities do you know?* Elicit a job responsibility (for example, *Number 7 is wash hands.*).
- Students call out answers. Help students pronounce job responsibilities if they have difficulty.
- If students call out an incorrect job responsibility, change the student's answer into a question for the class (for example, *Number 9 is wear a uniform?*). If nobody can identify the correct job responsibility, tell students they will now listen to a CD and practice the job responsibilities vocabulary.

Presentation   5 minutes

B **Look at the pictures and listen. Listen...**

- Read the directions. Play CD 3, Track 49. Pause after number 12 (*store the equipment*).
- Tell students to look at picture 5. Explain: Work as a team *means work together to do a job*.
- Tell students to look at pictures 11 and 12. Explain: Maintain the equipment *means take care of the equipment*. Store the equipment *means put the equipment away properly*.
- To check comprehension, say each job responsibility in random order and ask students to point to the appropriate picture.
- Resume playing Track 49. Students listen and repeat.

Controlled Practice   20 minutes

2 PRACTICE

A PAIRS. **What are the job responsibilities for...**

- Read the directions.
- Say the jobs from the box and ask the class to repeat.

- Ask: *Do you remember these jobs from Unit 8? Ask: Who receives shipments and unloads materials?* (a warehouse worker) *Who installs computer hardware and helps with computer problems?* (a computer system administrator) *Who takes care of patients and records patient information?* (a nurse assistant) *Who assists customers and sometimes stocks shelves?* (a sales assistant) Point out that *sales assistant* is the same as *sales associate*.
- Ask: *What are other responsibilities of these jobs?* Ask two students to read the example.
- Pair students. On the board, write: *What are the responsibilities of a _____?* Say: *Student A, ask about the responsibilities of a job from the box. Student B, say at least two job responsibilities from the list on page 227. Then switch roles.*
- Walk around and help as needed. Tell students that there is more than one correct answer. Encourage students to guess if they're not sure about the responsibilities of a job. Remind students to switch roles.
- Write each job from the box as a heading on the board. Ask the class: *What are the responsibilities of a computer system administrator?* List students' ideas on the board (for example: *maintain the equipment, ask questions, work as a team*). Repeat with the other jobs from the box.

B WORD PLAY. GROUPS OF 3. **Look at...**

- Read the directions.
- Say: *Look at the example.* Wear a uniform *is a job responsibility in the category* Wear the right clothing. *What's another job responsibility in this category?* (wear latex gloves / wear safety gear)
- Form groups of 3. Ask: *What's a job responsibility in the category* Follow health and safety rules? Tell groups to talk about job responsibilities for each category and to choose one to write in the chart.
- List the categories on the board. Ask one student from each group to write the group's answers to the right of each category on the board. Tell the students to write only answers that are not already on the board.
- Read the categories and job responsibilities on the board. Talk about how the job responsibilities fit into the categories (for example, say: *A uniform is clothing, so* wear a uniform *can go in the* Wear the right clothing *category.*).

Learning Strategy: Learn words that go together

- Provide each student with six index cards or tell students to cut up notebook paper into six pieces.
- Read the directions.
- Walk around as students work. If misspellings occur, tell them to check the list on page 227.
- Say: *You can remember new vocabulary when you write words that go together.* Remind students to use this strategy to remember other new vocabulary.

Communicative Practice   15 minutes

Show what you know!

STEP 1. Look at the list of job responsibilities. Think...

- Read the directions.
- Model the activity. List the responsibilities for your job on the board (for example, *Teacher: follow directions, ask questions, work as a team*).
- Tell students to think about the job they have now or a job they want. Tell them to look at the list of job responsibilities and circle the responsibilities for their job.
- Tell students to write the job title and list the responsibilities.

STEP 2. PAIRS. Tell your partner about the job and...

- Read the directions.
- Model the activity. Tell the class about your job. Point to the job title and responsibilities on the board. Say: *I am a teacher. Teachers have to follow directions, ask questions, and work as a team.*
- Write on the board: *I want to be a* _____. Ask an above-level student to tell the class about a job he or she wants and the responsibilities.
- Pair students. Tell them to take turns describing their job's responsibilities.
- To wrap up, ask a few students to tell the class about the job his or her partner has or wants.

■■■ MULTILEVEL INSTRUCTION for STEP 2
Cross-ability The higher-level student describes the job he or she wants first. Then, as needed, the higher-level student can prompt the lower-level student by asking questions, for example, *Do cooks have to wear a uniform?*

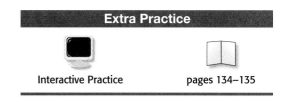

Extra Practice	
Interactive Practice	pages 134–135

2

3

Job Responsibilities

1. clock in/out
2. call in late
3. follow directions
4. report problems with the equipment
5. work as a team
6. wear a uniform
7. wash hands
8. wear latex gloves
9. wear safety gear
10. ask questions
11. maintain the equipment
12. store the equipment

5

Learning Strategy

Learn words that go together

Choose six job responsibilities from the vocabulary list. Make vocabulary cards. Write the verb on the front of the card and the other words on the back. For example, *wear / a uniform.*

7

EMPLOYEES MUST WASH HANDS

8

10

11

Show what you know!

STEP 1. Look at the list of job responsibilities. Think of a job you have or want. List the responsibilities for that job.

STEP 2. PAIRS. Tell your partner about the job and the responsibilities.

Ask about policies at work

Listening and Speaking

1 BEFORE YOU LISTEN

A **CLASS.** Look at the picture of a customer and an employee at the Greenville Hotel. Imagine you are the manager of the hotel. What is the employee doing wrong?

B **CLASS.** What other things are employees usually not allowed to do at work?

2 LISTEN

CD3 T50

A Listen to Michelle Rivera talking to new employees at their orientation meeting. What does Michelle talk about?

☑ wearing the right clothing

☐ wearing safety gear

☑ being on time

☐ working as a team

CD3 T50

B Listen again. Complete the sentences. Write the words you hear.

1. You must wear your ___employee ID___ badge during your work shift.

2. Employees in housekeeping and food service must ___wear a uniform___.

3. During your 6-hour shift you must take a 30-minute ___break___.

4. You must not ___clock in___ or ___clock out___ for another employee.

New employee orientation

Getting Started   10 minutes

 BEFORE YOU LISTEN

A CLASS. Look at the picture of a customer and...

- Read the directions. Say: *Point to the customer. Point to the employee.* Ask: *Where are they?* (at the Greenville Hotel)
- Ask: *What is the employee doing wrong?* Elicit students' ideas and write them on the board. (*Possible answers:* He's eating. He's drinking. He's talking on the phone and not helping the customer. He isn't wearing the right clothing. He isn't helping the customer.)

Teaching Tip

If you notice that students are not using the present continuous, do a mini-review by prompting students to rephrase responses in the present continuous. For example, if a student says *He has food*, write *He's* on the board and elicit *eating*.

B CLASS. What other things are employees...

- Say: *Employees are usually not allowed to eat, drink, talk on the phone, wear shorts or wild clothing, or not pay attention to customers.*
- Ask: *What other things are employees usually not allowed to do at work?* Elicit students' ideas and list them on the board (for example, *chew gum, smoke, text, wear too much jewelry, arrive late, use alcohol or drugs*).

Presentation   20 minutes

2 LISTEN

Teaching Tip

Optional: Remember that if students need additional support, tell them to read the Audio Script on page 307 as they listen to the conversations.

A **Listen to the Michelle Rivera...**

- Read the directions.
- Tell students to look at the picture and point to Michelle. Ask: *Who is Michelle talking to?* (new employees) *What kind of meeting is this?* (an orientation) *What is an orientation?* (a meeting for new employees) Say: *At an orientation, new employees learn about company policies, or what they are expected to do and what they are not allowed to do.*
- Tell students to read the directions and answer choices silently.
- Play CD 3, Track 50. Students listen and check the boxes of topics they hear.
- Students compare answers with a partner.
- Ask: *What does Michelle talk about?* Call on students to say the answers.
- Write *dress code* on the board. Ask: *Which of the four answers has the same meaning as* dress code? (wearing the right clothing) Tell students to write *dress code* next to *wearing the right clothing*.

B 🔘 **Listen again. Complete the sentences....**

- Read the directions.
- Tell students to read the sentences silently.
- Play Track 50 again. Students listen and write the answers.
- Play Track 50 again to aid comprehension. Students compare answers with a partner. Tell them to take turns reading the sentences.
- Call on students to read the sentences. Write the answers on the board. Tell students to check their spelling.
- Ask: *What's an ID badge?* Tell students to point to Michelle Rivera's ID badge in the picture. Tell students to look at the picture in Before You Listen. Ask: *Is the employee wearing his ID badge?* (No.) *Do you wear an ID badge at your job?*
- *Optional:* Say: *Housekeeping and food service are two departments at the Greenville Hotel. What department does Michelle Rivera work in?* Play the beginning of Track 50 again. Tell students to listen for her department. Repeat the question. Elicit and write on the board: *human resources.* Explain: Human resources *is the department in a company that deals with employing, training, and helping people. Most people call it* H.R.

Lesson 2   Ask about policies at work

3   CONVERSATION

A 💿 **Listen to the questions. Then listen...**

- Read the Pronunciation Watch note and the directions.
- Tell students to look at the questions. Ask (with rising intonation): *Are they all* Yes / No *questions?* (Yes.) Say: *Listen for the voice to go up at the end of each question. Then practice making your voice go up at the end of each question.*
- Play CD 3, Track 51. Students listen.
- Resume playing Track 51. Students listen and repeat.

Controlled Practice   15 minutes

B 💿 **Monica is a new employee at...**

- Read the directions. Ask: *Who's Monica?* (a new employee at the Greenville Hotel)
- Tell students to read the conversation silently and underline the *Yes / No* questions.
- Ask: *Which questions did you underline?* Write *Can I ask you a question?* and *Am I allowed to wear sneakers?* on the board and mark the intonation with an arrow as in Exercise 3A. Tell students to mark the sentences in their books. Say the questions and ask the class to repeat.
- *Optional:* Point out that *What do you want to know?* is an information question and has different intonation / pronunciation.
- Play CD 3, Track 52. Students listen and repeat.
- Ask: *Are employees at the Greenville Hotel allowed to wear sneakers?* (No.) *What do they have to wear?* (black shoes) Say: *Look at the picture in Exercise 1A on page 228 again. Is the employee wearing black shoes?* (No.) *What is he wearing?* (sneakers)

4   PRACTICE

A **PAIRS. Practice the conversation. Then make...**

- Pair students and tell them to practice the conversation in Exercise 3B. Walk around and pay particular attention to students' intonation in the *Yes / No* questions.
- Read the directions.
- Tell students to look at the information in the boxes. Say each phrase and ask the class to repeat.

- Copy the conversation onto the board with blanks. Read it and when you come to a blank, fill in a student's name or information from the same row in the boxes. As you fill in each blank, say the color of the answer space and point to the same-color phrase you choose from the boxes.
- Ask the student whose name you used and another on-level student to practice the conversation.
- Tell pairs to take turns playing each role and to use information from the same row in the boxes to fill in the blanks.
- Walk around and check that A uses rising intonation in the *Yes / No* questions.
- Tell students to stand, mingle, and practice the conversation with several new partners.
- Call on pairs to perform for the class.

Communicative Practice   15 minutes

B **ROLE PLAY. PAIRS. Make your own...**

- Read the directions. Write: *Am I allowed to _____?* and *No, you aren't. You have to _____.* as headings on the board. As a class, brainstorm pairs of phrases to complete the sentences and write them on the board (for example, *wear shorts / wear pants, drink in the warehouse / drink in the break room, leave early / talk to a manager*).
- Pair students and tell them to practice the conversation in Exercise 4A with the information on the board or their own information.
- Walk around and check that pairs substitute information correctly and that A uses rising intonation in the *Yes / No* questions.
- Call on pairs to perform for the class.

▬▬ **EXPANSION: Speaking Practice for 4B**

- Pair students.
- Say: *What are you not allowed to do at your job? Tell your partner. If you don't work, talk about what a family member's not allowed to do at work.*
- Call on several students to say something their partner (or their partner's family member) is not allowed to do at their job.

Extra Practice
⬛
Interactive Practice

3 CONVERSATION

A CD3 T51 Listen to the questions. Then listen and repeat.

Pronunciation Watch

In *Yes / No* questions, the voice usually goes up at the end.

Can I ask you a few questions?

Do we have to clock out?

Are we allowed to wear sneakers?

B CD3 T52 Monica is a new employee at the Greenville Hotel. She's asking Michelle Rivera a question. Listen and repeat the conversation.

Monica: Hi, Michelle. Can I ask you a question?

Michelle: Sure. What do you want to know?

Monica: Am I allowed to wear sneakers?

Michelle: No, you aren't. You have to wear black shoes.

Monica: OK. Thanks. I'm glad I asked.

4 PRACTICE

A PAIRS. Practice the conversation. Then make new conversations. Use your partner's name and the information in the boxes.

A: Hi, _____. Can I ask you a question?

B: Sure. What do you want to know?

A: Am I allowed to _____?

B: No, you aren't. You have to _____.

A: OK. Thanks. I'm glad I asked.

eat at my desk	eat in the break room
park anywhere	park in the back
trade shifts	talk to a manager

B ROLE PLAY. PAIRS. Make your own conversations. Use different information.

Grammar

Expressions of necessity: *must / have to*

You	have to / must	wear	black shoes.
He	has to / must		

·············· Grammar Watch

We almost never use *must* for questions. Use *have to* for questions.

Do we have to wear a uniform?

Expressions of prohibition: *must not / can't*

You	must not / can't	wear	sneakers.

1 PRACTICE

Complete the conversations. Use *must, must not, have to*, or *can't* and a verb. There may be more than one correct answer. Answers will vary but could include:

1. **A:** Are you going to the orientation meeting today?

   B: Yes. All new employees ___*have to go*___ to the meeting.

2. **A:** Can we smoke in the break room?

   B: No, we ___can't smoke___ anywhere in the building.

   There's a smoking area outside.

3. **A:** What's the uniform for front desk employees?

   B: Front desk employees ___must wear___ dark suits and black shoes.

4. **A:** How do I take a sick day?

   B: You just call your manager. But you ___have to call___ your

   manager at least 30 minutes before the start of your shift.

5. **A:** I'm going to eat lunch at my desk.

   B: Sorry, it's not allowed. You ___can't eat___ at your desk.

   You ___must eat___ in the break room.

Getting Started   5 minutes

- Say: We're going to study *must, have to, must not,* and *can't.* In the conversation on page 229, Michelle used this grammar.
- Play CD 3, Track 52. Students listen. Write on the board: *You have to wear black shoes.* Underline *have to wear.*

Presentation   10 minutes

Expressions of necessity: *must / have to*

- Copy the top grammar chart onto the board or show Transparency 12.3 and cover the exercise.
- Read the first two sentences in the top chart. On the board, write: *have to wear = must wear.* Say: *These two sentences have the same meaning:* You need to wear black shoes.
- Read the first and third sentences in the top chart. On the board, write: *have / has to + base form of a verb.*
- Read the second and fourth sentences in the top chart. On the board, write: *must + base form of a verb.* Explain: *Must* does not change, and we don't use to *after* must.
- Read all of the sentences in the top chart and tell the class to repeat.
- Read the Grammar Watch note and ask the class to read along silently. Underline *He has to wear black shoes* in the top chart. Ask the class to make it into a question. Elicit and write on the board: *Does he have to wear black shoes?*

Expressions of prohibition: *must not / can't*

- Copy the bottom grammar chart onto the board or show Transparency 12.3 and cover the exercise.
- Read the two sentences in the bottom chart and tell the class to repeat. Say: *These two sentences have the same meaning: Don't wear sneakers.*
- On the board, write: must not / can't + *base form of a verb.*
- If you are using the transparency, do the exercise with the class.

Controlled Practice   20 minutes

1 **PRACTICE**

Complete the conversations. Use *must, must not...*

- Read the directions and the example. Ask: *What is another possible answer? (must go) How do we know to use the verb* go? Underline *Are you going* in A's line.
- Students compare answers with a partner by reading the conversations. Remind students that there is more than one correct answer.
- There are two possible answers for each item. Elicit both answers by calling on two pairs to read each conversation. For each item, write both possible answers on the board.
- *Optional:* Call on pairs to perform the completed conversations for the class.

2 PRACTICE

A READ. Read the information. Answer the questions.

- Ask students to read the information silently and write answers to the questions.
- Read the information out loud. Ask the class the questions and elicit answers.

B Complete the statements about Jack's...

- Tell students to look at the information again. Say: *Jack is an employee. What are his responsibilities?* Read the directions.
- Write the example on the board. Point out that *have to* changes to *has to* because *Jack* is the subject. Ask: *How do we know to use the verb* be? Tell students to circle *Be* in the first reminder in the list *Your Duties as an Employee*. Ask: *What is another possible answer?* (*must be*)
- Remind students to use verbs from *Your Duties as an Employee*. Say: *There is more than one correct answer.*

C PAIRS. Compare your answers.

- Pair students. Students compare answers by taking turns reading the sentences.
- Say: *If you both have the same answer, talk about the other possible answer. Write the other possible answer to the right of each sentence.*
- Call on students to read the sentences. Elicit both possible answers for each item.

Communicative Practice   20 minutes

Show what you know!

STEP 1. NETWORK. Are you an employee...

- Read the directions.
- Ask for a show of hands as you ask the questions from the directions: *Are you an employee? A student? A parent?*

- Designate an area of the classroom for employees, students, and parents to meet. If groups are very disproportionate, switch students who are members of more than one group to the smaller groups.

STEP 2. SAME GROUPS. What responsibilities...

- Read the directions.
- Tell all students to take out one sheet of paper. Provide groups with tape.
- Tell groups to think of responsibilities and form sentences with *have to* or *can't*. Say: *Ask one group member to write each sentence in large print on their sheet of paper. Ask two other group members to check the sentence. Then tape the sheet of paper on the wall for the whole group to see.*
- Remind groups to write and post at least five sentences.

STEP 3. CLASS. Write three lists of responsibilities...

- On the board, write the headings: *Your Duties as an Employee, Your Duties as a Student,* and *Your Duties as a Parent.*
- Read the directions.
- Ask two students from each group to collect the sheets of paper and copy the responsibilities onto the board.
- Call on two different students from each group to take turns reading their group's sentences.
- Ask the class: *Which group has the most responsibilities: employees, students, or parents?* Count the sentences and circle the answer.

Progress Check

Can you . . . talk about responsibilities?

Say: *We have practiced talking about responsibilities. Now, look at the question at the bottom of the page. Can you talk about responsibilities?* Tell students to write a checkmark in the box.

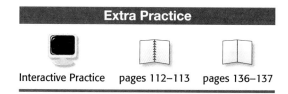

Extra Practice		
Interactive Practice	pages 112–113	pages 136–137

2 PRACTICE

A READ. Read the information. Answer the questions.

1. Who is the information for?
   employees
2. What is the information about?
   employee responsibilities

B Complete the statements about Jack's responsibilities. Use the correct form of *have to, must, must not,* or *can't.* Answers will vary but could include:

Your Duties as an Employee

To make your work more successful, here is a list of reminders:
- Be on time. This is very important.
- Call your supervisor if you are going to be late.
- Begin and end your breaks at the scheduled times.
- Don't forget to clock in and out.
- Don't clock in or out for other employees.
- Don't make personal calls at work.

1. Jack _has to be_ on time for work.

2. He _must call_ if he's going to be late.

3. He _must end_ his breaks on time.

4. He _has to clock_ in and out.

5. He _can't clock in_ for other employees.

6. He _must not make_ personal calls at work.

C PAIRS. Compare your answers.

Show what you know! Talk about responsibilities

STEP 1. NETWORK. Are you an employee? A student? A parent? Form three groups. If you are a member of more than one of these three groups, choose one.

STEP 2. SAME GROUPS. What responsibilities do members of your group have? Write at least five responsibilities using *have to* and *can't.*

> Students have to be on time for class.

STEP 3. CLASS. Write three lists of responsibilities on the board. Which group has the most responsibilities: employees, students, or parents?

Can you...talk about responsibilities? ☐

Read a pay stub

Life Skills

1 READ A PAY STUB

A **PAIRS.** Look at Frank's pay stub. How much money did he earn? How much money did he get?

1 — days you worked for this paycheck

Frank Martin	Pay Date 10/29		Pay Period 10/17–10/23		Rate of Pay $10.00

2 — amount of money you get per hour

Description	Hours	Earnings	Deductions	Amount
Regular	40	$400.00	Federal tax	$40.00
			State tax	$20.00
			Social Security	$30.00
			Medicare	$7.20
			State Disability Insurance (SDI)	$6.00

					Net Pay $296.80
Total Gross Pay		$400.00	**Total Deductions**	$103.20	

3 — amount of money you get *before* deductions

4 — money taken out to pay for taxes and insurance

5 — amount of money you get *after* deductions

B Look at Frank's pay stub again. Match the deductions with the definitions.

1. ___e___ Federal tax
2. ___a___ State tax
3. ___b___ Social Security
4. ___d___ Medicare
5. ___c___ SDI

a. tax you pay the state government

b. money for older people not working now

c. money for workers who are disabled and can't work

d. money for health care for older people

e. tax you pay the U.S. government

C Look at Frank's pay stub again. Correct the incorrect statements.

1. Frank's pay stub is for ~~two weeks~~ of work. *one week*

2. Frank's company paid him on ~~10/23~~ for this pay period. *10/29*

3. Frank gets paid ~~$40~~ per hour. *$10*

4. ~~Four~~ deductions were taken out of Frank's paycheck. *Five*

5. Frank paid the U.S. government ~~$20~~ in taxes. *$40*

6. Frank got ~~$400~~ after all deductions were taken out. *$296.80*

Lesson 4 Read a pay stub

Getting Started

5 minutes

- Ask: *Do you work? When you get your paycheck, do you look at the pay stub?* (Explain as needed: *The* pay stub *is the piece of paper that's attached to your paycheck.*) *What information is on your pay stub?* (how much money you earned and how much money was taken out for taxes, insurance, etc.)

Presentation

15 minutes

 READ A PAY STUB

Ⓐ PAIRS. Look at Frank's pay stub. How much...

- Write *deductions* on the board. Tell students to look at the pay stub and find the definition for deductions. Ask: *What are deductions?* (money taken out [of your paycheck] to pay for taxes and insurance)
- Read the directions.
- Pair students. Tell them to read the pay stub and circle the answers to the two questions.
- Ask: *How much money did Frank earn?* ($400) Say: *$400 is his* gross pay, *the amount of money he earns* before *deductions.*
- Ask: *How much money did Frank get?* ($296.80) Say: *$296.80 is his* net pay, *the amount of money he gets* after *deductions.* Net pay *is also called* take-home pay.
- Ask: *How much money was taken out of Frank's paycheck?* ($103.20) *What did this money pay for?* (federal tax, state tax, Social Security, Medicare, and State Disability Insurance)

Ⓑ Look at Frank's pay stub again. Match...

- Read the directions.
- Say the deductions and ask the class to repeat. Do the same for the definitions. Explain that someone who is *disabled* has a physical or mental condition that can make it difficult for him or her to work.
- Students compare answers with a partner.
- Say the deductions and call on students to read the definitions.
- Tell students to close their books. Say the definitions in random order and tell students to call out the deductions.

Controlled Practice

25 minutes

Ⓒ Look at Frank's pay stub again. Correct...

- Tell students to look at Frank's pay stub again. Say: *Point to the* pay date. Ask the class: *What is the meaning of* pay period? (days you worked for this paycheck) *What is the meaning of* rate of pay? (amount of money you get per hour)
- Read the directions. Write the example on the board. Ask: *Why is the answer* one week? (because the pay period is 10/17–10/23: seven days)
- Students compare answers with a partner.
- Call on students to read the corrected sentences.

Teaching Tip

Encourage students to keep a personal dictionary with English words and definitions in their notebooks. When definitions are provided (as pay stub terms and kinds of deductions are here), they can copy the words and definitions into their notebooks.

Culture Connection

- Ask: *What is Social Security?* (money for older people not working now) *What is Medicare?* (money for health care for older people)
- Say: *Social Security and Medicare are employment taxes collected by the U.S. government.* Ask: *Are they state or federal programs?* (federal)
- Explain: *Social Security and Medicare are social insurance programs. Social Security provides money for retired people, disabled people, and the children of workers who die. Medicare provides health insurance coverage to people who are 65 years old and over.*
- Ask: *Do older people receive money and health care from the government in your home country? Is money deducted from people's paychecks to pay for these programs?*

2 PRACTICE

A Read Alex's pay stub. Answer the questions.

- Read the directions and note. Ask: *When do you get overtime pay?* (when you work more than 40 hours a week) *Do you get paid more or less for overtime?* (more)
- Read the example. Tell students to highlight or underline the pay period on Alex's pay stub. Ask: *How many weeks of work is this?* (two weeks)
- Tell students to refer back to the explanations of Frank's pay stub on page 232 as needed.

B PAIRS. Check your answers.

- Students compare answers with a partner. Tell them to take turns asking and answering the questions.
- Read the questions and call on students to say the answers.
- Ask additional questions: *How many deductions were taken out of Alex's paycheck?* (four) *How much did Alex pay the U.S. government in taxes?* ($114) *What are the other deductions on Alex's pay stub?* (state tax, Social Security, and Medicare)
- Explain: *Social Security and Medicare taxes are employment taxes collected by the U.S. government. FICA, or Federal Insurance Contributions Act, is the law that requires employees and employers to pay Social Security and Medicare taxes.*

Communicative Practice 15 minutes

C PAIRS. Look at the pay stub in Exercise A. Look...

- Read the note about overtime pay again. On the board, write: *overtime = 1.5 x regular rate of pay.*
- Tell students to look back at Frank's pay stub on page 232. Ask the class to calculate Frank's overtime pay rate. Elicit and write on the board: *1.5 x $10.00 = $15.00.*
- Read the directions.
- Tell students to circle Alex's overtime earnings ($180.00). Ask: *How many overtime hours did Alex work?* (10 hours)
- Pair students and tell them to calculate Alex's overtime pay rate. Tell them to show two different ways to calculate it.
- Ask two students to show how to calculate Alex's overtime pay rate on the board: *$180/10 = $18.00 per hour; 1.5 x $12.00 = $18.00 per hour.*
- *Optional:* Tell students to calculate their own overtime rate of pay.

Progress Check

Can you . . . read a pay stub?

Say: *We have practiced reading pay stubs. Now, look at the question at the bottom of the page. Can you read pay stubs?* Tell students to write a checkmark in the box.

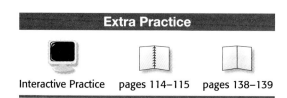

Extra Practice		
Interactive Practice	pages 114–115	pages 138–139

PRACTICE

Note: When you work more than 40 hours a week, you get a special overtime rate of pay. It is one and a half times your regular rate.

A Read Alex's pay stub. Answer the questions.

Alex Simon	**Pay Date** 12/22		**Pay Period** 12/02–12/16	**Rate of Pay** $12.00	
Description	**Hours**	**Earnings**	**Deductions**	**Amount**	
Regular	80	$960.00	Federal tax	$114.00	
Overtime	10	$180.00	State tax	$57.00	
			FICA ⎡Social Security	$85.50	
			⎣Medicare	$20.50	
Total Gross Pay		$1,140.00	**Total Deductions**	$277.00	**Net Pay** $863.00

1. How long is the pay period? _From December 2 to December 16_

2. On what day did the company pay Alex for this pay period? _December 22_

3. How many overtime hours did Alex work? _10_

4. How many total hours did Alex work? _90_

5. What is Alex's regular rate of pay? _$12.00_

6. What is Alex's gross pay? _$1,140.00_

7. How much money was taken out in deductions? _$277.00_

8. What is Alex's net pay? _$863.00_

B PAIRS. Check your answers.

C PAIRS. Look at the pay stub in Exercise A. Look at Alex's overtime earnings. How much did Alex get paid per hour for overtime? _$18.00 per hour_

Can you...read a pay stub? ☐

Listening and Speaking

1 BEFORE YOU LISTEN

A READ. **Look at the picture. Read the information about Ron and Jim. Answer the questions.**

Ron is a manager at Discount Music. One of his employees, Jim, calls the store. He can't work his shift because he has to baby-sit his niece. It is only an hour before his shift starts. Ron can't find anyone to cover Jim's shift. There are a lot of customers and Ron has to work very hard.

Answers may vary.
1. Why can't Jim work his shift?
   He has to baby-sit his niece.
2. What problems does this cause?
   Ron has to cover Jim's shift.

B GROUPS OF 3. **What should employees do if they are going to miss work?**

2 LISTEN

A CLASS. **Luis and Rachel are co-workers. Look at the picture. Guess: What are they talking about?**

CD3 T53
B Listen to the conversation. Was your guess in Exercise A correct?

CD3 T53
C Listen again. Answer the questions.

1. Luis asks Rachel for a favor. What's the favor?
   He asks her to work his shift.
2. Does Rachel agree to do the favor? Yes.

CD3 T54
D Listen to the whole conversation. Answer the question.

Luis and Rachel check the schedule. What do they want to know?

a. who is working that day   b. what time the shift starts   c. what time the shift ends

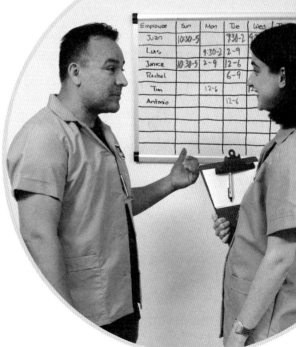

Getting Started 10 minutes

 BEFORE YOU LISTEN

A READ. Look at the picture. Read the information...

- Tell students to look at the picture. Ask: *Where are the people?* (at a music store) Say: *Point to the employee. Point to the customers. How does the employee look?* (stressed, tired, upset) *How do the customers look?* (angry, impatient, annoyed)
- Read the directions. Tell students to read the information silently.
- Ask: *Who is the employee in the picture?* (Ron) *What is his position?* (manager) *Who is Jim?* (one of Ron's employees)
- Tell students to read the questions and underline the answers in the paragraph.
- Ask the questions and elicit answers.

B GROUPS OF 3. What should employees do if...

- Ask the class: *When does Jim call to say he can't work his shift?* (an hour before his shift starts)
- Read the directions. Form groups of 3. Tell groups to assign a recorder, listener, and reporter.
- Tell groups to brainstorm and reporters to list their group's ideas (for example, *call as soon as they know they will miss work, ask another employee to work their shift, trade shifts with another employee, find another solution for a personal situation to avoid missing work*).
- Ask: *What should employees do if they are going to miss work?* Call on the reporter from each group to say one idea. To avoid repetition, tell the listeners to look at the group's list and make checkmarks next to ideas other groups say.

Presentation 20 minutes

2 LISTEN

A CLASS. Luis and Rachel are co-workers. Look...

- Read the directions. Direct students to look at the picture. Say: *Point to Luis. Point to Rachel.* Ask: *Are they wearing uniforms?* (Yes.) *What do you think their job is?* (nurse assistants)

- Ask: *What are they talking about?*
- Elicit students' guesses and list them on the board.
- Tell students to look at the schedule behind Luis and Rachel. Ask the class: *When is Luis working?* (on Monday from 9:30 to 2:00 and on Tuesday from 2:00 to 9:00) *When is Rachel working?* (on Tuesday from 6:00 to 9:00)

B Listen to the conversation. Was your...

- Read the directions.
- Play CD 3, Track 53.
- Ask: *What are they talking about?* Read the guesses on the board. Elicit and circle the best answer. (trading shifts)

> **Teaching Tip**
>
> *Optional:* Remember that if students need additional support, tell them to read the Audio Script on page 307 as they listen to the conversation.

C Listen again. Answer the questions.

- Read the directions.
- Tell students to read the questions silently. Ask: *What's a favor?* (something that you do for someone in order to help them)
- Play Track 53 again. Students listen and answer the questions.
- Students compare answers with a partner. Tell them to take turns reading the questions and answers.
- Read the questions and call on students to answer.
- Say: *Rachel will cover Luis's hours on Monday.* Tell students to write this change on the schedule in the picture.

D Listen to the whole conversation....

- Read the directions. Tell students to read the question and answer choices silently.
- Play CD 3, Track 54. Students listen and answer the questions.
- Read the question and answer choices. Ask students to raise their hands for their answer.
- *Optional:* Ask: *Do you ever ask co-workers to cover your hours? Do you ever cover hours for your co-workers? Who do you like to work with?*

Lesson 5 Ask a co-worker to cover your hours

A 🔘 **Listen to the sentences. Then listen...**

- Read the Pronunciation Watch note.
- *Optional:* Ask: *What kind of intonation do* Yes / No *questions have?* (rising intonation) *What kind of intonation do information questions and statements have?* (falling intonation)
- Tell students to look at the sentences. Say: *Point to the information questions. Point to the statements.*
- Write the sentences on the board and mark the intonation. For each sentence, ask: *What's the most important word in the sentence?* (up, start, study, 9:30)
- Read the directions. Say: *Listen for the voice to jump up on the most important word in each sentence and then go down at the end of each sentence.*
- Play CD 3, Track 55. Students listen.
- Resume playing Track 55. Students listen and repeat.

Controlled Practice   15 minutes

B 🔘 **Listen and repeat the conversation.**

- Note: This conversation is the same one students heard in Exercise 2B on page 234.
- Tell students to read the conversation silently, find the *Yes / No* questions, and mark the rising intonation. (*Can I ask you a favor? Can you take my shift for me?*) Tell them to find the information questions and mark the falling intonation (*What is it? What's up? What time do you start?*)
- On the board, write these statements: *I'm on the schedule for Monday, but I can't come in. I have to study for a test.* Mark the falling intonation and ask the class to repeat. Tell students to mark the intonation in the conversation.
- Read the directions. Play CD 3, Track 56. As students repeat, listen carefully for the correct intonation.

A PAIRS. **Practice the conversation. Then make new...**

- Pair students and tell them to practice the conversation in Exercise 3B.

- Then, in Exercise 4A, tell students to look at the information in the boxes. Write the red questions on the board. Ask: *Rising or falling intonation?* Mark the falling intonation. Say the questions and ask the class to repeat.
- Say the blue phrases and ask the class to repeat.
- Read the directions.
- Copy the conversation onto the board with blanks. Read it and use the name of an on-level student in the first blank. When you come to the second blank, ask what color it is. Point to the box that's the same color and fill in the blank with the first item in the box.
- Ask the student whose name you used and another on-level student to practice the conversation on the board for the class.
- Erase the words in the blanks and ask two above-level students to make up a new conversation in front of the class.
- Tell pairs to take turns playing A and B. Tell them to use their names and the information in the boxes to fill in the blanks.
- Walk around and check students' intonation.
- Tell students to stand, mingle, and practice the conversation with several new partners.
- Call on pairs to practice for the class.

Communicative Practice   15 minutes

B ROLE PLAY. PAIRS. **Make your own...**

- Read the directions.
- Brainstorm and write on the board different reasons for missing work. Begin each reason with the base form of a verb (for example, *go to my daughter's parent-teacher conference, go to the doctor, study for a test, stay home and wait for the plumber*). If possible, draw a blue box around the list.
- Pair students and tell them to practice the conversation, using information on the board or their own information.
- Walk around and remind students to switch roles. Check that students are using correct intonation.
- Call on pairs to perform for the class.

Extra Practice
🔲
Interactive Practice

3 CONVERSATION

CD3 T55

A 🅰 Listen to the sentences. Then listen and repeat.

What's up?   I have to study.

What time do you start?   I start at 9:30.

CD3 T56

B 🅱 Listen and repeat the conversation.

Luis: Hi, Rachel. Can I ask you a favor?

Rachel: Sure. What is it?

Luis: I'm on the schedule for Monday, but I can't come in.

Rachel: Oh. What's up?

Luis: I have to study for a test. Can you take my shift for me?

Rachel: What time do you start?

Luis: 9:30.

Rachel: No problem.

Pronunciation Watch

Information questions and statements usually end with falling intonation. The voice jumps up on the most important word in the sentence and then goes down at the end.

4 PRACTICE

A PAIRS. Practice the conversation. Then make new conversations. Use your partner's name and the information in the boxes.

A: Hi, _____. Can I ask you a favor?

B: Sure. What is it?

A: I'm on the schedule for Monday, but I can't come in.

B: Oh.

A: I have to _____. Can you take my shift for me?

B: What time do you start?

A: 9:30.

B: No problem.

What's going on?
What's happening?
Why not?

baby-sit my niece
go to the dentist
pick up my in-laws at the airport

B ROLE PLAY. PAIRS. Make your own conversations. Use different reasons for missing work.

Grammar

Information questions with *Who*

	Who = subject		Answers
Who	**works** **wrote**	on Mondays? the schedule?	Luis and I work on Mondays. Mary wrote the schedule.

	Who = object				Answers
Who	**do** **did**	I she	**give** **see**	my timesheet to? yesterday?	Give your timesheet to your supervisor. She saw Jeff.

Grammar Watch

- To ask about the subject, use *Who* + a verb.
- To ask about the object, use *Who* + a helping verb + a subject + a verb.

1 PRACTICE

A Put the words in order. Write questions. Capitalize the first word.

1. who / extra hours / needs ___Who needs extra hours?___

2. I / ask / who / do / about sick time ___Who do I ask about sick time?___

3. the schedule / makes up / who ___Who makes up the schedule?___

4. I / call / do / who / about trading shifts ___Who do I call about trading shifts?___

5. goes / on break / who / at 10:45 A.M. ___Who goes on break at 10:45 A.M.?___

B Write questions with *Who* to ask for the underlined information.

1. **A:** ___Who needs a favor?___

   B: <u>Bill</u> needs a favor.

2. **A:** ___Who do you usually work with?___

   B: I usually work with <u>Jung-Su</u>.

3. **A:** ___Who does Jim need to call?___

   B: Jim needs to call <u>his supervisor</u>.

4. **A:** ___Who do they need to see?___

   B: They need to see <u>Fran</u>.

5. **A:** ___Who helped you out?___

   B: <u>Jose and Carlos</u> helped me out.

Lesson 6   Ask about work schedules

Getting Started
5 minutes

- Say: *We're going to study information questions with* Who. *In the conversation you listened to in Exercise 2D on page 234, Rachel used this grammar.*
- Play CD 3, Track 54. Students listen. Write on the board: *By the way, who's working that day?* Underline *who's working.*

Presentation
10 minutes

Information questions with *Who*

- Copy the grammar charts onto the board or show Transparency 12.4 and cover the exercise.
- Tell students to look at the answers in the right charts. Point to each answer and ask: *Who?* Underline: *Luis and I, Mary, your supervisor,* and *Jeff.* Point to the underlined people in the first two answers and say: *They are subjects.* Point to the underlined people in the last two answers and say: *They are objects.* Label subjects and objects on the board.
- Tell students to look at the questions. Read the questions in the bottom left chart. Say: *When* who *is the object of the question, use normal question word order.* Write on the board: Who + *does, do, or* did + *subject + base form of verb.*
- Read the first two questions. Say: *When* who *is the subject of the question, don't use* does, do, *or* did. *Don't change the verb, except to make third-person plural verbs singular.* Write on the board: Who + *verb.* Then write: *Luis* works *on Mondays.* → *Who* works *on Mondays? / Luis and I* work *on Mondays* → *Who* works *on Mondays.*
- Read the first item in the Grammar Watch note. Then read the questions and answers in the top grammar charts and ask the class to repeat.
- Read the second item in the Grammar Watch note. Then read the questions and answers in the bottom grammar charts and ask the class to repeat.
- If you are using the transparency, do the exercise with the class.

Controlled Practice
15 minutes

1   PRACTICE

A Put the words in order. Write questions. Capitalize...

- Read the directions.
- Tell students to read the Grammar Watch note again and underline Who + *a verb* and Who + *a helping verb + a subject + a verb.*
- Write the example on the board. Point to *Who* and *needs* in the answer and say: Who + *a verb.*
- Tell students to find items in the exercise that have *do* and to mark those sentences *Object.* Tell them to review the grammar charts as they do the exercise.
- Walk around and spot-check for capitalization. Remind students to use questions marks. If students have difficulty, suggest that they cross out the words as they use them.
- Students compare answers with a partner. Tell them to take turns reading the questions.
- Call on students to read the questions.

EXPANSION: Grammar Practice for 1A

- Tell pairs to write answers to the questions in Exercise 1A. Tell them to use classmates' names (for example, *Sergio needs extra hours. Ask Minh about sick time.*).
- Call on pairs to read questions and answers.

B Write questions with *Who* to ask for...

- Read the directions. Write item 1 on the board and point to the answer. Ask: *Why is the answer* Who *needs a favor?* (because Bill is the subject) Ask two students to read the example.
- Say: *Before you write a question, look at the underlined information in B's response. Decide if it's the subject or the object.* Read the Grammar Watch note again.
- Students compare answers with a partner by reading the conversations. Walk around and spot-check for capitalization and question marks.
- Call on pairs to read the conversations. Write the questions on the board. Discuss any errors.

Lesson 6 Ask about work schedules

Presentation 5 minutes

Information questions with *What / Which / When / Where*

- Copy the grammar charts onto the board or show Transparency 12.4 and cover the exercise.
- Read the questions and answers in the charts and ask the class to repeat.
- Tell students to look back at the Grammar Watch note on page 236. Ask the class: *Which pattern do these questions follow?* On the board, write: *question word + a helping verb + a subject + a verb.* Ask: *What are the helping verbs?* List *does, do,* and *did* under *a helping verb.* Ask: *What form of the verb do you use?* Write *base form* under *a verb.*
- Tell students to close their books. On the board, write: *Which days, Where,* and *What time.* Say: *at 3:00 P.M., the break room, Thursday and Friday* and ask the class to call out the question word(s).
- If you are using the transparency, do the exercise with the class.

Controlled Practice 10 minutes

2 PRACTICE

Complete the conversations. Write information...

- Read the directions. Tell students to underline the question words in the directions.
- Ask two students to read the example. Repeat the question. Point to *question word + a helping verb + a subject + a verb* on the board. Ask the class: *What are the question words? What's the helping verb? What's the subject? What's the verb?* As students answer, write each word or phrase from the question under its corresponding label.
- Tell students to first look at the responses and decide *what time, which,* or *where.*
- Walk around and spot-check for capitalization and question marks.
- Students compare answers with a partner by reading the conversations.
- Call on pairs to read the conversations for the class. Write the questions on the board. Discuss any errors.

Communicative Practice 15 minutes

Show what you know!

GROUPS OF 3. Look at the work schedule. Student...

- Form groups of 3.
- Read the directions. Ask: *What does Student A do?* (chooses one employee) *Does Student A tell the group which employee?* (No.) *What do Students B and C do?* (guess the employee) *How?* (They ask questions with *What, Which,* and *When.*)
- Ask a group to read the example. Ask: *Who can it be?* (Ivan, Marco, or Will)
- Tell students to look at the work schedule. Brainstorm other questions students can ask and write them on the board (for example, *Which days does he have off? What time does he get breaks? What time does he finish work?*).
- Tell Students B and C to take turns asking Student A questions.

▮▮▮ MULTILEVEL INSTRUCTION

Pre-level Direct students to use the questions on the board when they play B and C. Point out that all the employees are men, so they don't need to make any changes to the questions.

Above-level Direct students not to look at the questions on the board when they play B or C.

▮▮▮ EXPANSION: Speaking Practice

- Tell pairs to choose two employees with different hours from the work schedule and to role-play asking their partner to cover their hours.

Progress Check

Can you . . . ask about work schedules?

Say: *We have practiced asking about work schedules. Now, look at the question at the bottom of the page. Can you ask about work schedules?* Tell students to write a checkmark in the box.

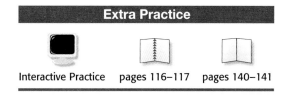

Extra Practice		
Interactive Practice	pages 116–117	pages 140–141

Information questions with *What / Which / When / Where*					Answers
What time	**does**	my shift	**begin**?		At 3:00 P.M.
Which days	**do**	I	**have off**	this week?	Thursday and Friday.
When	**did**	you	**start**	your break?	Five minutes ago.
Where	**do**	we	**go**	to clock in?	The break room.

2 PRACTICE

Complete the conversations. Write information questions. Use *What time*, *Which*, *When*, *Where* and the words in parentheses. Answers will vary but could include:

1. **A:** (day / you / have off) _Which day do you have off?_

   B: Tuesday.

2. **A:** (my shift / start) _When does my shift start?_

   B: At 3:00 P.M.

3. **A:** (I / get / a vacation) _When do I get a vacation?_

   B: After six months on the job.

4. **A:** (I / clock in) _Where do I clock in?_

   B: Outside the employee break room. The time clock is on the wall.

5. **A:** (we / get / breaks) _What time do we get breaks?_

   B: At 10:15 A.M. and 2:30 P.M. Check with your supervisor.

Show what you know! Ask about work schedules

GROUPS OF 3. Look at the work schedule. Student A, choose one employee. Students B and C, guess the employee. Ask questions with *What*, *Which*, and *When*.

A: *OK, I'm ready.*
B: *What does the employee do?*
A: *He's a cashier.*
C: *What time does he start work?*

	Mon.	Tues.	Wed.	Thu.	Fri.	Sat.	Sun.
Eduardo, stock clerk	OFF	OFF	6–2 Break: 11–11:30	6–2 Break: 11–11:30	6–2 Break: 11–11:30	6–2 Break: 11–11:30	6–2 Break: 11–11:30
Stan, stock clerk	OFF	OFF	6–1 Break: 11–11:30	6–1 Break: 11–11:30	6–1 Break: 11–11:30	6–2 Break: 11–11:30	6–2 Break: 11–11:30
Deng, stock clerk	6–2 Break: 12–12:30	6–2 Break: 12–12:30	6–1 Break: 12–12:30	6–1 Break: 12–12:30	OFF	OFF	6–2 Break: 12–12:30
Ivan, cashier	OFF	OFF	8–2 Break: 11–11:30	8-2 Break: 11–11:30	8-2 Break: 11–11:30	8-2 Break: 11–11:30	8-2 Break: 11–11:30
Marco, cashier	8–2 Break: 12–12:30	8–2 Break: 12–12:30	8–2 Break: 12–12:30	8-2 Break: 12–12:30	OFF	OFF	8–2 Break: 12–12:30
Will, cashier	OFF	9–2 Break: 12–12:30	9–2 Break: 12–12:30	9–2 Break: 12–12:30	9–2 Break: 12–12:30	OFF	9–2 Break: 12–12:30

Can you...ask about work schedules? ☐

Reading

1 BEFORE YOU READ

A READ. PAIRS. Look at the pictures. Read about Fran and Al. Why did they stop working?

Fran   Al

> Fran is 70 years old. She is retired. She stopped working in 2007.
>
> Al can't work. He was in an accident and now he is disabled.

B CLASS. Social Security is a government program. What do you know about it?

2 READ

CD3 T57

Listen. Read the FAQ (Frequently Asked Questions).

> **Reading Skill:**
> Think About What You Know
>
> Before you read, think about what you already know about the topic. This information will help you understand the article.

Social Security FAQ

Home   Contact Us   Help   Search

What is Social Security?
Social Security is a U.S. government program. It pays money (benefits) to people age 62 or older who have retired. It also provides money for people who can't work because of a disability.

How did Social Security start?
The U.S. government created Social Security in 1935 to help needy Americans. At that time, many Americans were poor. People had to work their whole lives. People who were too old or too sick to work had to get help from family members. People without families had a difficult time.

How does Social Security work?
Workers pay a Social Security tax. The money is automatically taken out of each paycheck. This money is used to pay the benefits of people who are retired or disabled today.

Lesson 7 Read about the Social Security program

Getting Started — 10 minutes

1 BEFORE YOU READ

A READ. PAIRS. Look at the pictures. Read about...

- Read the directions.
- Pair students and tell them to read about Fran and Al silently. Tell them to underline the reasons why they stopped working.
- Read the sentences about Fran and Al. Ask: *How old is Fran?* (70 years old) *Why did Fran stop working?* (She retired.) *What happened to Al?* (He was in an accident.) *Why did he stop working?* (He is disabled.)
- Say: *When you stop working because of your age, you . . .* Elicit *retire* from the class. Say: *Someone who can't work because of an injury is . . .* Elicit *disabled* from the class. Say *retired* and *disabled* and ask the class to repeat.

B CLASS. Social Security is a government program...

- Read the Reading Skill note and the directions.
- Tell students to look back at Exercise 1B on page 232. Ask: *What is Social Security?* (money for older people not working now)
- Draw a K-W-L chart (a three-column chart with the headings *Know*, *Want to know*, and *Learned*). Under *Know*, list: *government program* and *money for older people not working now*. Ask: *What else do you know about Social Security?* Add students' ideas to the list under *Know* (for example, *a federal / U.S. government program, a deduction from your paycheck, for retired people*).
- Point to the second column in the chart and ask: *What do you want to know about Social Security?* Elicit a couple of questions and write them in the chart (for example, *How old do you have to be to get Social Security? Do you have to pay Social Security? Do you have to be a U.S. citizen to get Social Security?*).

Presentation — 20 minutes

2 READ

Read and listen to the FAQ...

- Tell the class to look at the reading. Ask: *Where can you find this information?* (online) *What is the title?* (Social Security FAQ)
- Tell students to look at the directions. Ask: *What is FAQ?* (Frequently Asked Questions) Explain: Frequently Asked Questions *is a list of questions that many people ask about a particular topic and their answers.*
- Tell students to look at the reading. Ask: *What are the Frequently Asked Questions about Social Security?* (*What is Social Security? How did Social Security start? How does Social Security work? How much do people pay?* etc.) Tell students to look at the K-W-L chart on the board. Ask: *Are any of these questions the same as the questions on our chart?*
- Play CD 3, Track 57. Students listen and read along silently.
- Read your class's questions in the *Want to know* column of the chart on the board. Play Track 57 again. Pause the CD after each question and answer and ask if any answers were given to the questions in the chart. Write answers under *Learned* on the chart. Ask: *What else did you learn?* For each question and answer in the reading, write one thing students learned on the chart.
- Tell students to take turns reading the information under *Learned* in the chart to a partner.

Controlled Practice   20 minutes

3 CHECK YOUR UNDERSTANDING

Ⓐ Read the FAQ again. Read the statements. Circle...

- Read the directions.
- Students compare answers with a partner.
- Read the statements and call on students to say the answers. For false items, call on another student to read the question and answer from the FAQ that gives the correct information (2. Every retired person in the U.S. <u>does not get</u> Social Security benefits. 3. You have to work a total of <u>ten</u> years to get Social Security benefits. 4. <u>U.S. citizens and noncitizens</u> can get Society Security benefits. 5. Everyone does <u>not</u> get the same Social Security payment.)

Ⓑ PAIRS. Look at the boldfaced questions in...

- Tell students to read the Social Security FAQ again silently.
- Pair students. Read the directions. Say: *Student A, ask your partner the boldfaced questions from the Social Security FAQ. Student B, close your book and answer the questions in your own words. Look at the chart on the board if you need help.*
- Model the activity. Ask a higher-level student: *What is Social Security?* If the student gives incorrect information, change the student's answer into a question (for example, *Social Security is for people 65 and older?*).
- Walk around and help as needed. Continue to model how to change incorrect information into a question.

▰▰▰ MULTILEVEL INSTRUCTION FOR 3B

Cross-ability Direct the lower-level student to ask the questions first. When it's the lower-level student's turn to answer the questions, direct the higher-level student to ask more specific questions as needed to prompt his or her partner (for example, *Is it a U.S. government program or a state program? What age do you have to be?*).

Communicative Practice   10 minutes

Show what you know!

Culture Connection

- Ask: *How old do you have to be to get Social Security?* (62 years old) Explain: *You can get some Social Security benefits at 62, but to get full benefits you have to be 67.*
- Ask: *What is the retirement age in your home country? What age do you have to be to receive retirement benefits?*
- Say: *In the U.S., older people live on Social Security and also other money they have saved for retirement. There are many types of retirement plans. They allow workers to save money for retirement and pay less in taxes now. The two most popular types of retirement plans are 401Ks and IRAs. You contribute money to a 401K plan through your employer. IRA stands for Individual Retirement Account. You can go in to any bank to open an IRA.*
- Ask: *How do people save for retirement in your home country?*

PRE-WRITING. PAIRS. Someday you will retire...

- Read the directions. Ask: *What age do you want to retire at? What year will that be?*
- Ask: *Are you saving for your retirement? Do you have any retirement accounts? Are there any deductions from your paycheck for retirement? What money will you live on when you retire?*
- Model the activity. Say, for example, *I will retire in 2030. I have a 401K. When I'm 62, I'll get Social Security.*
- Pair students. Tell partners to ask each other the questions.

WRITE. Write about your life when you are retired....

Turn to page 273 and ask students to complete the activities. See page T-xii for general notes about Writing activities.

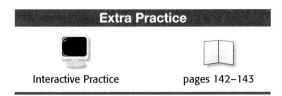

Extra Practice	
Interactive Practice	pages 142–143

How much do people pay?
Workers pay 6.2 percent of their earnings. Their employers pay another 6.2 percent. Self-employed workers pay 12.4 percent of their earnings.

Can everyone get Social Security benefits?
No. To get Social Security payments, you have to work and pay Social Security taxes for a total of ten years.

Can a noncitizen of the United States get Social Security benefits?
Yes. Any person who works legally in the U.S. and pays Social Security taxes for ten years can get benefits.

Does everyone get the same amount?
No. People who work longer and pay more Social Security taxes get a bigger retirement benefit. The average Social Security payment is now over $1,000 a month.

Top of page

3 CHECK YOUR UNDERSTANDING

A Read the FAQ again. Read the statements. Circle *True* or *False*.

1. The U.S. government created the Social Security program in 1935. (True) False

2. Every retired person in the U.S. gets Social Security benefits. True (False)

3. You have to work a total of twenty years to get Social Security benefits. True (False)

4. Only U.S. citizens can get Social Security benefits. True (False)

5. Everyone gets the same Social Security payment. True (False)

B PAIRS. Look at the boldfaced questions in the FAQ. Ask and answer the questions in your own words.

Show what you know!

PRE-WRITING. PAIRS. Someday you will retire. What year will that be? What money will you live on when you retire?

WRITE. Write about your life when you are retired. See page 273.

Request a schedule change

Listening and Speaking

1 BEFORE YOU LISTEN

CLASS. Look at some reasons that people change their work schedules. What are some other reasons?

My son is starting school.

I'm taking classes now.

My wife needs the car during the day.

My husband's work schedule changed.

2 LISTEN

A **CLASS. Look at the picture of Linda and Ron. Guess: What is their relationship?**

a. a customer and a manager
b. an employee and a manager

CD3 T58
B Listen to Linda and Ron's conversation. Was your guess in Exercise A correct?

CD3 T58
C Listen again. Answer the questions.
Answers will vary but could include:
1. Why does Linda need to talk to Ron? _She needs to change her schedule._

2. When does Linda work now? _mornings_

3. When does she want to work? _evenings_

4. Why does she ask for a schedule change? _She plans to take classes._

CD3 T59
D Listen to the whole conversation. What kind of class is Linda planning to take? Business classes.

Request a schedule change

Getting Started

1 BEFORE YOU LISTEN

CLASS. Look at some reasons that people change...

- Say: *Look at some reasons that people change their work schedules.* Say the reasons and ask the class to repeat.
- Ask: *What are some other reasons that people change their work schedules?* Write students' ideas on the board (for example, *I want to work part-time / full-time. My child-care situation changed. I want to be home with my children after school. I need to get a ride with another employee.*).
- Optional: Ask: *Have you ever asked to change your work schedule? What was the reason?*

Presentation

2 LISTEN

Ⓐ CLASS. Look at the picture of Linda and Ron....

- Read the directions. Ask: *What's their relationship?*
- Write the answer choices on the board and read them.
- Call on students to guess. They will listen for the answer in Exercise B.

Ⓑ 🎧 Listen to Linda and Ron's...

- Read the directions. Play CD 3, Track 58.
- Circle the correct answer on the board. Ask: *Was your guess correct?*
- Ask: *Who is the employee?* (Linda) *Who is the manager?* (Ron)

Controlled Practice

Ⓒ 🎧 Listen again. Answer the questions.

- Read the directions.
- Tell students to read the questions silently.
- Play Track 58 again. Students listen and write answers to the questions.
- Walk around as students listen. If students have incomplete or incorrect answers, play Track 58 again.
- Read the questions and call on students to say the answers. Write the answers on the board.

Teaching Tip

Remember that if students need additional support, they can read the Audio Script on page 307 as they listen.

Ⓓ 🎧 Listen to the whole conversation....

- Read the directions.
- Play CD 3, Track 59. Students listen.
- Read the question again. Call on a student to say the answer.
- Optional: Ask: *Why is Linda taking business classes?* (because she wants to be a manager) *What kinds of classes would help you get a better job?*

Lesson 8 Request a schedule change

Presentation   5 minutes

3 **CONVERSATION**

 Listen and repeat the conversation.

- Note: This conversation is the same one students heard in Exercise 2A on page 240.
- Read the directions. Play CD 3, Track 60. Students listen and repeat.

Controlled Practice   15 minutes

4 **PRACTICE**

Ⓐ PAIRS. Practice the conversation. Then make new...

- Pair students and tell them to practice the conversation in Exercise 3.
- Then, in Exercise 4A, tell students to look at the information in the boxes. Say each word or phrase and ask the class to repeat.
- Copy the conversation onto the board with blanks. Read through the conversation. When you come to a blank, fill it in with an on-level student's name or information from the top row in the boxes. As you fill in each blank, say the color of the answer space and point to the same-color word or phrase you choose from the boxes.
- Ask the two students whose names you used to read the conversation in front of the class.
- Tell pairs to take turns playing each role and to use information from the same row in the boxes to fill in the blanks.
- Tell students to stand, mingle, and practice the conversation with several new partners.
- Call on pairs to perform for the class.

Communicative Practice   15 minutes

Ⓑ ROLE PLAY. PAIRS. Make your own...

- Read the directions.
- Review the reasons for asking for a schedule change in Exercise 1 on page 240. Say the reasons and ask the class to repeat. Review the additional reasons the class brainstormed on the board. Say the reasons and ask the class to repeat.
- Say: *Pretend you need to ask for a schedule change at work.* On the board, write: *When do you work now? Why do you need to change your schedule? What schedule do you want to change to?* (If possible, write the first question in blue, the second in green, and the third in red.) Tell students to write down their answers.
- Model the activity. Write your own answers to the questions on the board. Play Student A and role-play a conversation with an above-level student. Substitute your answers into the conversation in Exercise 4A. At B's blue blank, prompt the student to use your first answer.
- Pair students and tell them to practice the conversation, substituting the information they wrote into the conversation.
- Walk around and remind students to switch roles.
- Call on pairs to perform for the class.

5 **LIFE SKILLS WRITING**

Turn to page 267 and ask students to complete the vacation request form. See page T-xii for general notes about Life Skills Writing activities.

Extra Practice

Interactive Practice

---

3 CONVERSATION

CD3 T60

Listen and repeat the conversation.

Linda: Excuse me, Ron. Can I speak to you for a minute?

Ron: Sure, Linda. What's up?

Linda: I need to talk to you about my schedule.

Ron: OK. Right now you work in the mornings, right?

Linda: Yes. But I'm planning to take classes now. Could I change to evenings?

Ron: Well, let me look at the schedule. I'll get back to you.

Linda: OK. Thanks.

4 PRACTICE

A PAIRS. Practice the conversation. Then make new conversations. Use your partner's name and the information in the boxes.

A: Excuse me, _____. Can I speak to you for a minute?

B: Sure, _____. What's up?

A: I need to talk to you about my schedule.

B: OK. Right now you work _____, right?

A: Yes. But _____. Could I change to _____ ?

B: Well, let me look at the schedule. I'll get back to you.

A: OK. Thanks.

the second shift	Tuesdays and Thursdays	full-time
my daughter is starting school	my hours changed at my other job	my mom can't take care of my son anymore
the first shift	Mondays and Wednesdays	part-time

B ROLE PLAY. PAIRS. Make your own conversations. Use different reasons for asking for a change in schedule.

5 LIFE SKILLS WRITING

Complete a vacation request form. See page 267.

Request a schedule change

Grammar

Can / Could to ask permission

Can Could	I	speak change have	to you? to evenings? Friday off?	Sure. Of course. Yes, you **can**.

Grammar Watch

- *Could* is more formal than *can* to ask permission.
- Answer a *could* permission question with *can*.

PRACTICE

A Complete the conversations. Write questions with *can* or *could*. Answers will vary but could include:

1. **A:** Can I take a break now?

   B: Sure, you can take a break. But please wait till Marlena comes back.

2. **A:** Can we trade shifts on Friday?

   B: Sure. No problem. We can trade shifts on Friday.

3. **A:** Could I have Friday off?

   B: I'm sorry, but you can't have Friday off. We need you on Friday.

4. **A:** Could we talk about the schedule?

   B: Yes, we can talk about the schedule. Come into my office.

5. **A:** Can you cover my hours tomorrow?

   B: Sorry, I can't cover your hours tomorrow. I have plans.

6. **A:** Could I leave early tonight?

   B: Go ahead. You can leave a little early tonight. We're not that busy.

7. **A:** Could I have more hours next week?

   B: OK. I think I can give you more hours next week. I'll see what I can do.

B PAIRS. Student A, ask for permission to do something. Use the ideas in the box or your own ideas. Student B, answer Student A's questions.

> use your dictionary   borrow your pen   copy your notes

Request a schedule change

Getting Started   5 minutes

- Say: *We're going to study ways to use* Can / Could *to ask permission. In the conversation on page 241, Linda used this grammar.*
- Play CD 3, Track 60. Students listen. Write on the board: *Can I speak to you for a minute?* and *Could I change to evenings?* Underline *Can . . . speak* and *Could . . . change.*

Presentation   5 minutes

Can / Could to ask permission

- Copy the grammar charts onto the board or show Transparency 12.5 and cover the exercise.
- Read the Grammar Watch note.
- On the board, write: *Can I speak to you?* and *Could I speak to you?* Ask: *Which one is more formal?* (*Could I speak to you?*) *Which one would you use probably use with your manager?* (*Could I speak to you?*) *Which one would you probably use with a co-worker?* (*Can I speak to you?*) Point to the answer *Yes, you can* and ask: *Which one is this an answer for?* (both)
- Read the questions and answers in the charts and ask the class to repeat.
- If you are using the transparency, do the exercise with the class.

Controlled Practice   10 minutes

PRACTICE

Ⓐ Complete the conversations. Write questions with...

- Read the directions and the example. Ask: *What is the other possible question?* (*Could I take a break now?*) Point out that both *Can I take a break now?* and *Could I take a break now?* are correct.
- *Optional:* Tell students to look at the responses. Say: *If it sounds like a manager, use* Could. *If it sounds like a co-worker, use* Can.
- Students compare answers with a partner by reading the conversations.
- Call on two pairs to read each conversation, one with *Can* and one with *Could.*

Communicative Practice   10 minutes

Ⓑ PAIRS. Student A, ask for permission to do...

- Read the directions.
- Say: *Look at the first idea in the box. What question can Student A ask?* On the board, write:

    A: *Can / Could I use your dictionary?*
    B:

- Tell students to study the grammar charts and Exercise A. Ask: *How can Student B answer?* List ideas on the board (for example, *Sure. Of course. Yes, you can. No problem. I'm sorry, but you can't. Go ahead.*). Say the responses and ask the class to repeat.
- Pair students. Tell students to take out their supplies so their partner can see what they have.
- Walk around and check that students form questions with *Can / Could* correctly.
- Call on pairs to perform for the class.

▬▬ EXPANSION: Grammar Practice for B

- Write the following list of people on the board: *a manager, a co-worker, a police officer, a waiter or waitress, your child's teacher, a doctor, a sales associate, a family member, your teacher, a celebrity.*
- Pair students. Say: *Copy the list of people. Ask each person for permission to do something. Write a question with* Can *or* Could.
- Tell students to change partners and compare their questions.

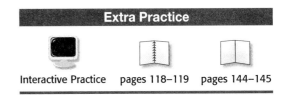

Extra Practice		
Interactive Practice	pages 118–119	pages 144–145

REVIEW   Show what you know!

1 GRAMMAR

Ⓐ Complete the conversation. Use *can, can't, could*...

- Read the directions. Tell students to refer back to the grammar charts on page 230 (Expressions of necessity: *must / have to*) and page 242 (*Can / Could* to ask permission) as needed.
- Tell student to read the Safety Reminder.
- Students compare answers with a partner by reading the conversation.
- Call on a pair to read the conversation. Where *can* and *could* are both correct, elicit the alternate answer from the class.

Ⓑ Complete the conversations. Write information...

- Read the directions.
- Tell students to refer back to the grammar charts on page 236 (Information questions with *Who*) and page 237 (Information questions with *What / Which / When / Where*) as needed as they fill in the blanks.
- Students compare answers with a partner by reading the conversations.
- Call on pairs to read the conversations for the class. Discuss any errors.

CD-ROM Practice

 Go to the CD-ROM for more practice.

If your students need more practice with the vocabulary, grammar, and competencies in Unit 12, encourage them to review the activities on the CD-ROM. This review can also help students prepare for the final role play on the following Expand page.

Extra Practice
pages 120–121

1 GRAMMAR

A Complete the conversation. Use *can*, *can't*, *could*, and *have to*. Answers will vary but could include:

Nora: Excuse me. This is my first day. _____Can_____ I ask you something?

Olga: Sure. What do you want to know?

Nora: Well, do we have to wear these uniforms?

Olga: No, we don't. We _____can_____ wear our own shirts and pants if we want. But we _____have to_____ wear work boots. No sneakers or sandals. It's for safety.

> **Safety Reminder**
> All employees must wear work boots. No sneakers or sandals allowed!

Nora: I see. One more thing. _____Can_____ I ask you a favor?

Olga: What is it?

Nora: I'm supposed to work Monday, but I _____can't_____. You're not on the schedule for Monday. _____Could_____ you take my shift?

Olga: Sure. But ask Mr. Wang first. We _____have to_____ get his permission.

B Complete the conversations. Write information questions with the words in parentheses.

1. **A:** (who) _Who do I give my vacation request form to?_

   B: Give your vacation request form to your supervisor.

2. **A:** (what time) _What time can Kevin take his break?_

   B: Kevin can take his break at 12:30.

3. **A:** (where) _Where do I store the floor cleaning equipment?_

   B: You store the floor cleaning equipment in the hall closet.

4. **A:** (which days) _Which days does Tanya work?_

   B: Tanya works on Thursday, Friday, and Saturday this week.

5. **A:** (when) _When did you work overtime?_

   B: I worked overtime on Thursday and Saturday.

2 ACT IT OUT   What do you say?

STEP 1. CLASS. Review the Lesson 2 conversation between Monica and Michelle (CD 3 track 52).

STEP 2. ROLE PLAY. PAIRS. Student A, you are a new employee. Student B, you are an experienced employee.

> **Student A:** Ask about what employees have to do and what they are not allowed to do.

> **Student B:** Explain company policy.

3 READ AND REACT   Problem-solving

STEP 1. Read about Ivan's problem.

Ivan started working in a warehouse eight years ago. He likes the job but he needs to work more hours. A few months ago Ivan's boss hired some new employees. His boss gave them a lot of overtime hours. Ivan almost never gets overtime. He doesn't think this is fair.

STEP 2. PAIRS. What is Ivan's problem? What can he do? Here are some ideas.

- He can talk to his boss.
- He can say nothing and get a second job.
- He can offer to cover other employees' hours.
- He can _____.

4 CONNECT

For your Goal-setting Activity, go to page 255.
For your Team Project, go to page 285.

2 ACT IT OUT

STEP 1. CLASS. Review the Lesson 2 conversation...

- Tell students to review the conversation in Exercise 3B on page 229.
- Tell them to read the conversation silently and then practice it with a partner.
- Play CD 3, Track 52. Students listen.
- As needed, play Track 52 again to aid comprehension.

STEP 2. ROLE PLAY. PAIRS. Student A, you are...

- Read the directions and the guidelines for A and B.
- Pair students. Tell A: *Ask if you are allowed to do something and if you have to do something.* Tell B to answer with what employees *must do, have to do, must not do,* or *can't do.*
- Walk around and observe partners interacting. Check pairs' use of expressions of necessity and prohibition.
- Call on pairs to perform for the class.
- While pairs are performing, use the scoring rubric on page T-xiii to evaluate each student's vocabulary, grammar, fluency, and how well they complete the task.
- *Optional:* After each pair finishes, discuss the strengths and weakness of each performance either in front of the class or privately.

3 READ AND REACT

STEP 1. Read about Ivan's problem.

- Say: *We are going to read about a student's problem, and then we need to think about a solution.*
- Read the directions.
- Read the story while students follow along silently. Pause after each sentence to allow time for students to comprehend. Periodically stop and ask simple *Wh-* questions to check comprehension (for example, *What is Ivan's job? When did Ivan start? What does Ivan need? What did the new employees get? Why is Ivan upset?*).

STEP 2. PAIRS. What is Ivan's problem? What can...

- Ask: *What is Ivan's problem?* (The new employees get a lot of overtime hours, but Ivan almost never gets overtime.). *What can he do?*
- Pair students. Read the ideas in the list. Give pairs a couple of minutes to discuss possible solutions for Ivan.
- Ask: *Which ideas are good?* Call on students to say their opinion about the ideas in the list (for example, S: *I think he can offer to cover other employees' hours. This is a good idea.*).
- Now tell students to think of one new idea not in the list (for example, *He can apply for a job in another department.*) and to write it in the blank. Encourage students to think of more than one idea and to write them in their notebooks.
- Call on pairs to say their additional solutions. Write any particularly good ones on the board and ask students if they think it is a good idea, too (*Do you think this is a good idea? Why or why not?*).

▬▬ MULTILEVEL INSTRUCTION for STEP 2

Pre-level Sit with students, say each idea in the list, and ask students to explain why they like or don't like each solution, for example, for idea 1, A: *I like this idea. Maybe the boss doesn't know that Ivan wants more hours.*

Above-level Pairs discuss the problems with each idea (for example, A: *He can't get a second job because commuting to two jobs is hard.*)

4 CONNECT

Turn to page 255 for the Goal-setting Activity and page 285 for the Team Project. See page T-xi for general notes about teaching these activities.

Progress Check

Which goals can you check off? Go back to page 225.

Ask students to turn to page 225 and check off any remaining goals they have reached. Call on students to say which goals they will practice outside of class.

Information Gap Activities

UNIT 1, PAGE 13

A Student B, look at Joseph Smith's identification card. Answer Student A's questions about Joseph Smith. Use the information on the identification card.

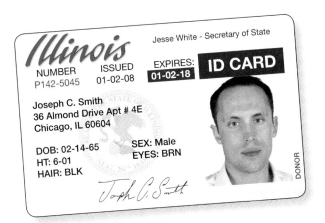

B Student B, ask questions. Complete the missing information on the application.

Name of Applicant			
First	Last	Middle	Suffix (Jr., Sr., III)
Ana	Martinez	Maria	–
Social Security Number (SSN)	Place of Birth	Date of Birth (mm–dd–yyyy)	
451-100-282	New York, NY	05-07-1987	

Sex		Height				Weight	
Male ☐	Female ☑	5 Feet	4 Inches			110 Pounds	

Eye Color	Hair Color	
Brown	Brown	

Residence Address	
Street	Apt. #
101 Chestnut St	–
City	State	Zip Code
Yonkers	NY	10701

UNIT 5, PAGE 91

STEP 1. PAIRS. Student B, Look at the picture. Don't show your picture to your partner.

STEP 2. SAME PAIRS. Talk about the pictures. What are the people doing? What problems do you see? Take notes. What are the differences in your pictures?

A: *In my picture, a man is fixing a sink in a kitchen.*

B: *In my picture, a man is cooking . . .*

UNIT 5, PAGE 97

STEP 1. PAIRS. Student B, you have an apartment for rent. Look at your apartment information in the ad.

STEP 2. SAME PAIRS. Student B, answer Student A's questions about your apartment.

STEP 3. SAME PAIRS. Change roles. Student B, ask about student A's apartment. Take notes.

> **APARTMENT FOR RENT**. 2 BR, 1 BA, LR, EIK, nr. laundromat and bus stop, parking avail. $950/mo. + 1 mo. sec. dep. No fee.

Ask about:	Notes
number of bedrooms	3
number of bathrooms	2
laundry room	in basement
parking	no – near transportation
rent, fees, security deposit	$1200/mo + 1 mo. fee + 1 mo. security deposit

UNIT 7, PAGE 131

Read the notes about the Lee family's appointments. Some information is missing. Take turns. Ask questions with *When* and *What time*. Write the missing information.

A: *When is Walter's dentist appointment?*
B: *On Friday at . . .*

UNIT 11, PAGE 211

STEP 1. PAIRS. Student B, study the picture. What are the people doing? Write six sentences.

A baby is sleeping.

STEP 2. SAME PAIRS. Talk about your pictures. What is different? Find at least six differences.

A: *In my picture, a baby is crying.*
B: *In my picture, a baby is sleeping.*

Persistence Activities

Unit 1   Name Game

A **GROUPS OF 5. Play the Name Game.**

Nellie: My name is Nellie.

Pablo: Her name is Nellie. My name is Pablo.

Jun: Her name is Nellie. His name is Pablo. My name is Jun.

Jai Yong: Her name is Nellie. Excuse me. What's your name again, please?

Pablo: Pablo.

Jai Yong: OK, thanks. Her name is Nellie. His name is Pablo. Her name is Jun. My name is Jai Yong.

Simone: Her name is Nellie. His name is Pablo. Her name is Jun. His name is Jai Yong. My name is Simone.

B How many classmates' names do you remember?

Unit 2   Things We Have in Common

A Read the sentences. Check (✓) all the statements that are true for you.

☐ I have a small family.
☐ I have a large family.

☐ Most of my family lives in this country.
☐ Most of my family lives in my country.

☐ I live with my family.
☐ I live with friends.

☐ I'm married.
☐ I'm single.

☐ I have children.
☐ I don't have children.

☐ I have a job.
☐ I don't have a job.

B Walk around the room. Ask your classmates questions. For example, *Do you have a large family?* Find classmates who have things in common with you. Take notes.

C CLASS. Report to the class.

Monica and I are both married. We both live with our families. Blanca and I both have two children.

Unit 3　Goal Visualization: *Where, Who, What*

Ⓐ CLASS. Look at the picture of Brigitte. She's an ESL student at The Greenville Adult School. Today, she's doing some food shopping. Answer the questions.

1. Where is Brigitte?

2. What is she doing?

3. What is she saying?

Ⓑ GROUPS OF 3. Think about your goals for learning English: Where do you want to speak English? Who do you want to speak to? What do you want to talk about or say? Tell your group.

Ⓒ Draw a picture of yourself speaking English. Show where you want to speak English and who you want to speak with. Write what you want to say or talk about.

Ⓓ CLASS. Show your picture to the class. Explain your goal.

Unit 4 Outside of Class

A Think about ways you can practice English outside of class. Complete the questionnaire. Which things do you do now? Which things do you want to do in the future? Check (✓) the boxes.

Activity	I do this now.	I want to do this.
I listen to the radio in English.	☐	☐
I listen to music in English.	☐	☐
I watch TV in English.	☐	☐
I read the newspaper in English.	☐	☐
I read magazines in English.	☐	☐
I read the mail in English.	☐	☐
I read books in English.	☐	☐
I read websites in English.	☐	☐
I read with my children in English.	☐	☐
I write letters in English.	☐	☐
I write e-mails in English.	☐	☐
Other: _____	☐	☐

B GROUPS OF 3. Talk about your answers to the questionnaire.

C What do you want to do next week? Choose one activity.
Write one goal for next week.

Next week, I will _____ in English.

D SAME GROUPS. Talk about your goals. Check with each other next week.
Did you complete your goal?

Unit 5 Daily Planner

A When do you study or practice English? Write a daily planner.
Use the planner below as a model. Make one planner for every day of the week.

Day: Monday

Activity	Time
English class	8:30 A.M.–11:30 A.M.
Use English at work	1:00 P.M.–5:00 P.M.
Listen to music in English	5:00 P.M.–5:30 P.M.
Do my homework	8:30 P.M.–9:00 P.M.

B GROUPS OF 3. Show your planners to your group.

Unit 6 My Vocabulary Learning Strategies

A CLASS. Look at the Learning Strategies on pages 7, 47, 67, and 87.

B Which strategies do you use to learn vocabulary? Check (✓) the strategies.

☐ Personalize   ☐ Use pictures

☐ Make connections   ☐ Make labels

☐ Other: _____

C GROUPS OF 5. Talk about the strategies you use.

A: *I personalize and I use pictures. What about you?*
B: *I . . .*

D Write your vocabulary goals for this week.

I want to learn _____ new words this week.
         (number)

I will use _____ to help me remember the new words.
         (title of Learning Strategy)

E SAME GROUPS. Talk about your goals. Check with each other next week.
Did you complete your goals?

Unit 7   Things That Make It Hard to Attend School

A CLASS. Think about things that make it hard for people to attend school. Make a chart on the board.

Things That Make It Hard to Attend School
The kids get sick.

B Copy the chart from Exercise A. Which things make it hard for you to attend school? Circle them.

C NETWORK. Find classmates who circled some of the same things as you. Form a group.

D GROUPS. What can you do to change the things you circled? Make a list of ideas.

Maybe my sister can watch my kids. I can watch her kids other times.

E SAME GROUPS. Make a plan. Tell your group.

I will talk to my sister about watching my kids.

Unit 8   Class Jobs

A CLASS. Look at the list of class jobs. These assistants help the teacher. Are there other jobs in your class? Write them in the list.

Assistant 1: Write today's date on the board.

Assistant 2: Erase the board.

Assistant 3: Give out supplies.

Assistant 4: Take attendance.

Assistant 5: Collect supplies.

Assistant 6: _____

Assistant 7: _____

B CLASS. Choose assistants to help your teacher. Write the students' names in the list. Change assistants every week.

(Note: For the Unit 9 Activity, each student should have a folder or binder, if possible.)

Unit 9   My Portfolio

A portfolio is a folder or binder of papers or drawings. For example, artists have portfolios of their work. You use your portfolio to keep things that show what you can do.

Ⓐ Create a portfolio of your written work in English. You can include your Life Skills writing, your paragraph writing, unit tests, workbook exercises, etc. Choose papers that you feel proud of. Make a list of the papers you include.

Ⓑ PAIRS. Show your portfolio to your partner. For each paper in your portfolio, tell your partner why you feel proud.

(*Note: For the Unit 10 Activity, you will need tea and cookies or other refreshments.*)

Unit 10   Getting to Know You Tea

Ⓐ CLASS. Bring tea and cookies to class. Take some of the tea and cookies. Sit with a classmate you don't know.

Ⓑ PAIRS. Take turns. Ask and answer the questions below.

Elena: *Hi. My name is Elena. What's your name?*
Dmitri: *My name is Dmitri. Hi. Where are you from? . . .*

- What's your name?
- Where are you from?
- Tell me about your family.
- What do you do? Tell me about your job.
- What is your favorite free-time activity?
- What do you like to do on the weekend?
- What kind of food do you like?
- What's your favorite holiday?
- What are your interests and special skills?

Ⓒ Report to the class. Say one new thing you learned about your partner.

Dmitri likes Mexican food.

Unit 11 Study Skills and Habits

A Do you have good study skills and habits? Take this questionnaire.

		Yes	No
In class	I come to class every day.		
	When I can't come to class, I make up the work.		
	I ask questions when I don't understand.		
	I participate in every exercise.		
Your study space	I have a specific place where I study outside of class.		
	I have good lighting where I study.		
	I sit on a comfortable chair at a table or a desk.		
	I don't watch TV or listen to music when I study.		
Your time	I study at the same time every day.		
	I plan my study schedule every week.		
	I set small study goals.		
Your studies	I review what we did in class every day.		
	I use the workbook for extra practice.		
	I look for ways to practice my English outside of class.		

B PAIRS. Compare answers.

C SAME PAIRS. Make a plan. Choose one thing you want to change about your study skills and habits. Tell your partner.

Unit 12   Now I Can . . .

A Look at the first page of each unit. Read the unit goals. Which goals did you check off? Choose one goal that you are proud of from each page. Write the goals in the chart.

Unit Number	Now I can . . .
1	
2	
3	
4	
5	
6	
7	
8	
9	
10	
11	
12	

B Report to the class. Tell the class one goal that you can do now.

Now I can write a personal check!

C CLASS. Stand up and clap for everyone. CONGRATULATIONS ON YOUR SUCCESS!

Life Skills Writing

Unit 1

A A driver's license is a common form of identification used in the U.S. Do you have a driver's license? If not, what type of identification card do you have?

B Read the form. Find *Learner permit*, *ID card*, and *Signature*. What do these words mean?

2 WRITE

Complete the form. Use true or made-up information.

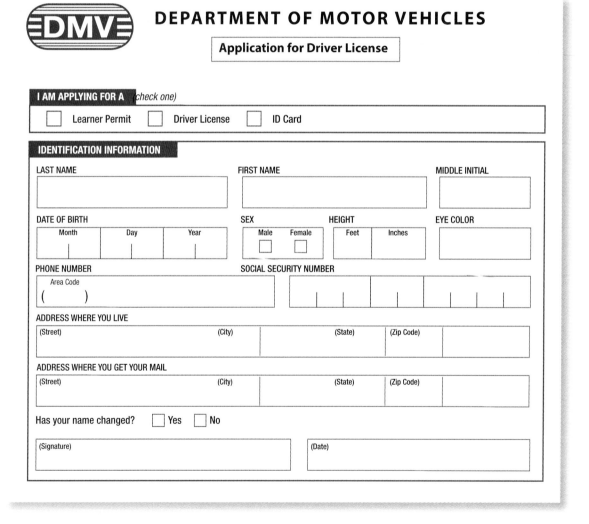

Can you...complete a driver's license application? ☐

Unit 2

BEFORE YOU WRITE

A A customs declaration form is used to mail packages from the U.S. to other countries. What information do you think you need to write on a customs declaration form?

B Read the form. Find *Gift, Documents, Commercial sample, Other,* and *Country of origin of goods*. What do these words mean?

2 **WRITE**

Imagine that you are sending a gift to a friend in another country. Complete the form. Use true or made-up information.

Postal Service **Customs Declaration**			Sender's Name and Address
☐ Gift ☐ Commercial sample			
☐ Documents ☐ Other			
Quantity and description of contents	Weight	Value (US $)	
			Addressee's Name and Address
For Commercial items only Country of origin of goods	Total Weight	Total Value (US $)	
I, the undersigned, whose name and address are given, certify that the particulars given in this declaration are correct and that this item does not contain any dangerous article or articles.			
Date and sender's signature			Date and Sender's Signature

`LC524307871US`

Can you...complete a post office customs form? ☐

Unit 3

A Read the check. Find: *Pay to the order of*, *In the amount of*, and *Memo*. What do these words mean?

Monica Butler   1379
14 Apple Lane
San Francisco,
CA 94105   DATE ____9/18/08____

PAY TO THE   *Pacific Gas and Electric Company* $ | *87.65*
ORDER OF

IN THE   *Eighty-seven and 65/100* _____ DOLLARS
AMOUNT OF

FIRST SAVINGS BANK
CA
MEMO *Utility bill*   *Monica Butler*

122213311:   5556665656   1379

B Read the check again. Complete the sentences.

1. The check is from _Monica Butler_____.

2. The check is to _Pacific Gas and Electric Company_____.

3. The date on the check is _9/18/08_____.

4. The amount of the check is _$87.65_____.

5. The check is payment for _a utility bill_____.

Imagine you are buying a jacket from the Oakville Department Store. The total is $59.95. Write the check. Use today's date.

                                                                    101

DATE _Answers will vary_____

PAY TO THE   Oakville Department Store $ | 59.95
ORDER OF

IN THE   Fifty-nine and 95/100 _____ DOLLARS
AMOUNT OF

National Bank
CA
MEMO jacket   (student's signature)

356621035:   8214600186   101

Can you...write a personal check? ☐

Unit 4

1 BEFORE YOU WRITE

A Have you ever visited your local library? Look at the list of things you can do at a library. Which would you like to do?

- ☐ check out books and movies
- ☐ bring your children to a story hour
- ☐ get help finding a job
- ☐ take an English class
- ☐ use a computer
- ☐ other: _____

B Look at the instructions on the library card application. What do you need to do to get a library card?

2 WRITE

Complete the library card application. Use true or made-up information.

III GREENVILLE PUBLIC LIBRARY III

Adult Library Card Application

Date: _____

You may apply for a Greenville Public Library card if you live or work in the city of Greenville. The library card is free to all Greenville residents. You are responsible for all materials checked out on your card.

Instructions:
Complete this application. Bring the application and one piece of identification to the circulation desk. Identification must include your name and address. Acceptable identification includes: a driver's license or state identification card, a utility bill, or a bank statement.

Please print. Enter only one letter or number in each box.

Name and Mailing Address

Last Name | First Name | Middle Initial

Mailing Address | Apt. #

City | State | Zip Code

(Area Code) | Telephone Number | Date of Birth (month/day/year) | Male | Female | Adult | Senior Citizen (Age 62 or over)

E-mail Address

Can you…complete a library card application? ☐

Unit 5

A Do you live in an apartment or a house? How long have you lived there?

B Read the form. Find *Landlord*, *Evicted*, *Salary*, and *References*.
What do these words mean?

Imagine you want to rent an apartment. Complete the form.
Use true or made-up information.

Apartment Rental Application

Full Name _____ Phone Number _____

Date of Birth _____ E-mail Address _____

List any pets you have _____

Rental History

Current Address _____

Month and year you moved in _____ Rent $ _____

Reasons for leaving _____

Landlord's Name _____ Landlord's Phone Number _____

Previous addresses for the last two years _____

_____

_____

Credit History

Have you ever not paid your rent on time? _____

Have you ever been evicted from an apartment? _____

Employment Information

Your employment status is: Full-time ☐ Part-time ☐ Student ☐ Unemployed ☐

Employer's Name _____ Employer's Phone Number _____

Salary $ _____ Dates of Employment _____

References

Please list three references and their contact information.

Name: _____ Phone: _____

Name: _____ Phone: _____

Name: _____ Phone: _____

Can you...complete an application for an apartment? ☐

Unit 6

A Read the note that Sofia's mother wrote to her teacher. Then answer the questions.

> March 25, 2010
>
> Dear Mrs. Roe,
>
> My daughter Sofia Ramos was absent on March 23 and March 24. She had a fever and a sore throat.
>
> Sincerely,
>
> *Carmen Ramos*

1. Who wrote the note? _____

2. When did she write the note? _____

3. What is Sofia's teacher's name? _____

4. When was Sofia absent from school? _____

5. Why was Sofia absent from school? _____

2 WRITE

Write a note to your teacher or your child's teacher to explain an absence.

Can you…write an absence note to a teacher? ☐

Unit 7

A Medical history forms provide information about your medical history to doctors and other health workers. Why is this information important?

B Read the form. Find *Allergies, Medications, Medical conditions, Health status, Deceased,* and *Concerns.* What do these words mean?

2 WRITE

Complete the form. Use true or made-up information.

MEDICAL HISTORY

Today's Date: _____

Patient's Name: _____

Date of Birth: _____

_____

Medical Allergies: _____

Food Allergies: _____

Other Allergies: _____

_____

Current medications you are taking: _____

_____

Current medical conditions: _____

Family Medical History			
Relation	**Age**	**Health Status**	**If Deceased: Cause/ Age at death**
Father			
Mother			
Siblings			

Please check all conditions which apply to yourself or any members of your family:

☐ asthma/allergies   ☐ headaches

☐ arthritis   ☐ seizures/epilepsy

☐ high blood pressure   ☐ stroke

☐ high cholesterol   ☐ lung disease

☐ diabetes   ☐ liver disease

☐ heart disease   ☐ ulcers

Other concerns: _____

_____

_____

Can you…complete a medical history form? ☐

Unit 8

BEFORE YOU WRITE

Job applications provide employers with important information. Read the form. Find *Under age 18*, *Position*, and *References*. What do these words mean?

2 **WRITE**

Imagine you are applying for a job as a stock clerk at Super Foods Supermarket. Complete the form. Use true or made-up information.

Super Foods Supermarket

Job Application
Personal Information

Full Name _____

Address _____

Phone Number _____ Are you under age 18? ☐ yes ☐ no

Position you are applying for _____ What day can you start work? _____

Days and hours you can work

☐ Monday from _____ to _____   ☐ Tuesday from _____ to _____

☐ Wednesday from _____ to _____   ☐ Thursday from _____ to _____

☐ Friday from _____ to _____   ☐ Saturday from _____ to _____

☐ Sunday from _____ to _____

Education

Name and Address of School   Degree or Diploma   Graduation Date

_____

_____

Employment History

Present or Most Recent Position

Employer _____

Address _____

Supervisor _____ Phone Number _____

Previous Position

Employer _____

Address _____

Supervisor _____ Phone Number _____

References

1. _____

2. _____

Can you...complete a job application? ☐

Unit 9

BEFORE YOU WRITE

A school enrollment form provides important personal information to a school. Read the form. Find *Gender, Last school attended,* and *Local emergency contact.* What do these words mean?

2 **WRITE**

Imagine you are enrolling your child in Franklin High School. Complete the form. Use true or made-up information.

Franklin High School
Enrollment Form

Student's Full Name: _____

Gender: M___ F___   Date of Birth: _____   Phone: _____

Street Address: _____ City: _____ State: _____ Zip: _____

Last School Attended: _____

Last School's Street Address: _____

City: _____ State: _____ Zip: _____

Dates Enrolled: _____

Parents' Full Names: _____

Father's Employer: _____ Phone: _____

Mother's Employer: _____ Phone: _____

Local Emergency Contact: _____

Country of Birth: _____ Student's First Language: _____

Main Language Spoken at Home: _____

Other Languages Spoken at Home: _____

Did student study English as a second language? _____

Parent or Guardian Signature: _____

Date: _____

Can you...complete a school enrollment form? ☐

Unit 10

A What kinds of foods do you think are healthy? Do you eat healthy foods?

B Read the form. Find *Calories, Fiber, Protein, Carbohydrates, Sugar, Fat,* and *Grams.* What do these words mean?

2 WRITE

Keep a record of the food you eat today. Complete the log. Use information from the nutrition labels on the food you eat.

Healthy Eating Log

Date: _____

Food or Beverage: _orange juice_____

Calories	Carbohydrates	Fat	Protein	Sugar	Fiber
110	26g	0g	2g	22g	0g

Food or Beverage: _____

Calories	Carbohydrates	Fat	Protein	Sugar	Fiber

Food or Beverage: _____

Calories	Carbohydrates	Fat	Protein	Sugar	Fiber

Daily Totals

Calories	Carbohydrates	Fat	Protein	Sugar	Fiber

Can you...complete a healthy eating log? ☐

Unit 11

A Have you ever been in an accident at work? What information do you think you should give to your employer if you are in an accident?

B Read the form. Find *Accident, Work location,* and *Required medical attention.* What do these words mean?

Imagine you had an accident at work. Complete the form with information about the accident.

Employee Accident Report
office of Human Resources

Employee name: _____

Employee Social Security number: _____

Address: _____

_____

Home phone number: _____

Job Title: _____

Date of birth: ___ _____

Date of accident: _____ Time of accident: _____

Place of accident: _____

Employee work location: _____

Employee required medical attention   ☐ Yes   ☐ No

Other information you would like to include: _____

_____

_____

Employee signature: _____ Today's date: _____

Can you...complete an employee accident report?   ☐

Unit 12

Before you can go on vacation, your employer might ask you to complete a vacation request form. Read the form. Find *Department*, *Requested*, and *Supervisor*. What do these words mean?

2 WRITE

Imagine you want to go on vacation. Complete the form. Use true or made-up information.

VACATION REQUEST FORM

Employee _____ Date of Hire _____

Department _____

Number of Vacation Days Requested _____

Dates Requested _____

Employee Signature _____ Date _____

Supervisor Signature _____ Date _____

Can you...complete a vacation request form? ☐

Writing

Unit 1

1 BEFORE YOU WRITE

A Read Cheong-Ah's tips for learning English.

> My Learning Tips   Cheong-Ah Lee
> • Make vocabulary cards with a word on one side and a picture
>   of the word on the other side.
> • Organize my notes into charts.
> • Watch movies with subtitles so I can read and listen at the same time.

B What is Cheong-Ah's learning style? Circle the letter.

a. auditory   (b.) visual   c. kinesthetic

2 WRITE

Think about your learning style. Write two tips for learning English. Use Cheong-Ah's tips as a model.

Writing Watch

Capitalize the first word of a sentence.

Unit 2

1 BEFORE YOU WRITE

A Read Yahia's list of responsibilities.

B Look at Yahia's list again. Do you have some of the same responsibilities? Check (✓) the ones you have, too.

> My responsibilities   Yahia El-kadi
> — work
> — pay the bills
> — watch my children when my wife is at work
> — go to English class
> — go food shopping for the family
> — go to the doctor with my mother

2 WRITE

Write a list of your responsibilities. Use Yahia's list as a model. Write a star (*) next to the most important ones.

Writing Watch

Use a dictionary to check the spelling of words you don't know.

Unit 3

1 **BEFORE YOU WRITE**

A Read about Zofia's next big purchase.

B Why is Zofia going to buy the computer with cash? Circle the letter.

a. She likes to make small payments every month.

(b.)She likes to know the total cost.

> *My Next Big Purchase   Zofia Nowak*
>
> *I want to buy a computer. I'm going to pay for it with cash. I don't like credit cards. With cash I know how much everything costs. There are no surprises!*

2 **WRITE**

Think about an expensive purchase you want to buy. How are you going to you pay for it? Why? Write about your next big purchase. Use Zofia's paragraph as a model.

Writing Watch

End each sentence with a period.

Unit 4

1 **BEFORE YOU WRITE**

A Read about what is rude and polite in Rafael's country.

> *Rafael Rodriguez*
>
> *In Venezuela it is polite to say hello when you walk into a room—even to people you don't know. It's polite to say goodbye when you leave a room, too. It's polite to stand when you meet someone new. You should stand up and shake hands.*

B What is rude in Spain? What is polite? Write *R* for rude and *P* for polite.

__P__ Say hello to strangers.

__P__ Say goodbye when you leave a room.

__R__ Sit when you are introduced to someone.

2 **WRITE**

Write about what is rude and polite in your home country. Use Rafael's paragraph as a model.

Writing Watch

Capitalize the names of countries.

Unit 5

1 BEFORE YOU WRITE

A Read about Manuel's community in the United States.

B What does Manuel like about his community? What does he dislike? Write *L* for *Like* and D for *Dislike*.

_L_	the schools	_D_	the cost of living
_L_	the jobs	_D_	the housing
_L_	the pay	_D_	the weather

> Living in Winston   by Manuel Vega
>
>   I live in Winston. It's a nice place to live. The schools are good. There is plenty of work and the pay is good. But there are some things I don't like about Winston. It's expensive to live here and the apartments are too small. Worst of all, the weather is very cold in winter.

2 WRITE

Write about what you like and dislike about your community. Use Manuel's paragraph as a model.

Writing Watch

Indent the first line of each paragraph.

Unit 6

1 BEFORE YOU WRITE

A Read Joseph's autobiography.

> My Life   Joseph Bernard
>   I was born in Gonaives, Haiti in 1984. In 1998, my family and I moved to the United States. In 2000, I got my first job. In 2003, I finished high school. In 2007, I got married to Josette Pierre.

B Read Joseph's autobiography again. Complete his time line.

born	moved to the U.S.	got first job	finished high school	got married
19 _84_	19 _98_	20 _00_	20 _03_	20 _07_

2 WRITE

Look at your time line on page 119. Write a short autobiography. Use Joseph's autobiography as a model.

Writing Watch

Use a comma between the name of a city and a country or a city and a state.

Unit 7

1 BEFORE YOU WRITE

A Read about something that causes stress in Yao's life.

Stress at work   Yao Wang
    My job can be stressful. I work in a restaurant. Sometimes it gets very busy.
Everyone is running around. We cannot work fast enough, and our boss gets angry.
I don't like it when it gets so busy. Everyone is upset.

B Is Yao Wang's job stressful all the time?   ☐ Yes   ☑ No

2 WRITE

Write about something that causes stress in your life.
Use Yao's paragraph as a model.

Writing Watch

Check that your subjects and verbs agree. For example, *he writes*, NOT *he write*.

Unit 8

1 BEFORE YOU WRITE

A Read about Marie's future job.

My Future Job   Marie Toussaint
    I want to get a job as a nurse assistant because I like to take care of people.
Nurse assistants work in hospitals, nursing homes, and people's homes. They help
patients with things like eating and taking a bath. I think this is a good job for me.

B Why does Marie want to be a nurse assistant? Circle the letter.

a. to earn good money   (b.) to take care of people   c. to work at home

2 WRITE

Write about the job you want in five years.
Write about why you want that job and what the
duties are. Use Marie's paragraph as a model.

Writing Watch

Use *because* to answer *Why* and to give a reason.

Unit 9

BEFORE YOU WRITE

A Read Khalid's paragraph.

B What is Khalid's educational goal?

a. a certificate

b. a bachelor degree

c. an associate degree

> My Educational Goal   Khalid Ali
> First, I need to improve my English. After that, I want to get an associate degree at a community college. I plan to study for two years. I want to study hotel and restaurant management. Then I can get a better job and I can earn more money.

2 **WRITE**

Write about your educational goals. Use Khalid's paragraph as a model.

Writing Watch

Use *First, After that*, and *Then* to show the order that things happen.

Unit 10

1 **BEFORE YOU WRITE**

A Read Fabio's caffeine journal.

B Do you think Fabio consumes a lot of caffeine?

> Caffeine Journal   Fabio Barreto
> Thursday, December 2
>
> | Time | Caffeine |
> |------|----------|
> | 6:30 A.M. | cup of coffee with milk |
> | 9:30 A.M. | chocolate muffin |
> | 11:30 A.M. | iced tea |
> | 2:30 P.M. | cola |

2 **WRITE**

A Keep a caffeine journal for one day. Write down every time you consume something with caffeine.

Time	Caffeine

Writing Watch

Write A.M. for times before noon and P.M. for times after noon.

B Look at your caffeine journal. Did you consume a lot of caffeine?

Unit 11

1 | BEFORE YOU WRITE

A Read about Aisha's ideas for making her home safer.

> How to Make My Home Safer   Aisha Said
>   There are some things I can do to make my home safer. My shower is slippery. I can put a mat in the shower. There are toys all over the living room. I can put the toys in the closet. Sometimes I leave food cooking on the stove and do other things. I can stay in the kitchen when I am cooking.

B Which areas of her home does Aisha plan to make safer? Check (✓) all that are true.

☑ bathroom   ☐ bedroom   ☑ living room   ☑ kitchen   ☐ stairs   ☐ yard

2 | WRITE

Write about what you can do to make your home safer.
Use Aisha's paragraph as a model.

Writing Watch

Include a subject and a verb in each sentence.

Unit 12

1 | BEFORE YOU WRITE

A Read about Blanca's retirement plans.

> My Retirement   Blanca Deras
>   I will retire in 2030. I will move back to my hometown in El Salvador. My family has a house there. I will take care of the garden and I will visit my family and friends.

B Read Blanca's paragraph again. Answer the questions.

1. What year will Blanca retire? _2030_____

2. Where will she live? _El Salvador_____

3. What will she do? _take care of the garden and visit family and friends_____

2 | WRITE

Write about your retirement plans. What year will you retire? Where will you live? What will you do?
Use Blanca's paragraph as a model.

Writing Watch

Proofread your writing for grammar, punctuation, capitalization, and spelling.

Team Projects

Unit 1 Meet Your Classmates MAKE A BOOKLET

Materials
- paper
- pens or markers
- stapler and staples
- camera (optional)

TEAMS OF 4 Captain, Co-captain, Assistant, Spokesperson

GET READY **Captain:** Ask your teammates, "Where are you from? Where do you live now? What do you do?" Give your teammates your information, too.
Assistant: Take notes.
Co-captain: Keep time. You have five minutes.

Name: _____

Home country: _____

Where he/she lives now: _____

Occupation: _____

Name: _____

Home country: _____

Where he/she lives now: _____

Occupation: _____

Name: _____

Home country: _____

Where he/she lives now: _____

Occupation: _____

Name: _____

Home country: _____

Where he/she lives now: _____

Occupation: _____

CREATE **Co-captain:** Get the materials. Then keep time. You have ten minutes.
Team: Create your booklet. Use one page for each person. Write the information on the page. Take a photo of each person if you want and put it on the page.

REPORT **Spokesperson:** Show your booklet to the class. Tell the class about your teammates.

COLLECT **Captains:** Collect the booklet pages from each group. Staple them together to make a booklet about your classmates.

UNIT 2 What We Have in Common <u>MAKE A POSTER</u>

TEAMS OF 4 Captain, Co-captain, Assistant, Spokesperson

GET READY **Captain:** Ask your teammates questions. Find out what you and your teammates have in common. Are your personalities the same or different?
Assistant: Complete the chart.
Co-captain: Keep time. You have five minutes.

Materials
- large paper
- markers
- camera (optional)

A: *I'm quiet. Are you?*
B: *Yes, I'm quiet, too. What about you, Than?*
C: *I'm usually quiet.*

How we are the same	How we are different

CREATE **Co-captain:** Get the materials. Then keep time. You have ten minutes.
Team: Create your poster. Write about what you have in common and how you are different. Take a photo of your team if you want.

REPORT **Spokesperson:** Show your poster to the class. Tell the class about your teammates.

Unit 3 Neighborhood Shopping MAKE A GUIDE

Materials
- 4 pieces of white paper
- pens or markers
- stapler and staples

TEAMS OF 4 Captain, Co-captain, Assistant, Spokesperson

GET READY **Captain:** Ask your teammates about their favorite stores in your area.
Assistant: Write the answers in the chart.
Co-captain: Keep time. You have five minutes.

Store name	Location	What you like to buy	Why you shop there
Shop Mart	Main Street	clothes for my kids	low prices

CREATE **Co-captain:** Get the materials. Then keep time. You have ten minutes.
Team: Create your shopping guide. Choose one store that you talked about. Write a page for that store. Include the information in your chart.

REPORT **Spokesperson:** Tell the class about the store.

COLLECT **Captains:** Collect the shopping guides from each group. Staple them together to make a neighborhood shopping guide.

Unit 4   Neighborhood Activities <u>MAKE A GUIDE</u>

Materials
- 4 pieces of white paper
- pens or markers
- stapler and staples

TEAMS OF 3 Captain, Co-captain, Assistant, Spokesperson

GET READY **Captain:** Ask your teammates, "What do you like to do on a special day? Where can you do that?" Ask for other information such as hours and cost.
Team: Plan three activities for a special day.
Assistant: Write the information in the chart.
Co-captain: Keep time. You have five minutes.

Activity	Location	Other information (hours, cost)
picnic	Greenville Park	open 7:30 A.M. - 9:00 P.M. free

CREATE **Co-captain:** Get the materials. Then keep time. You have ten minutes.
Team: Create your activity guide. Write a page about your three activities for a special day. Include the information in your chart. Add art if you want.

REPORT **Spokesperson:** Show your activity guide to the class. Tell the class about the activities.

COLLECT **Captains:** Collect the activity guides from each group. Staple them together to make a neighborhood activity guide.

Unit 5   The Perfect Home   MAKE A HOUSING CLASSIFIED AD

TEAMS OF 3   Captain, Co-captain, Assistant, Spokesperson

GET READY   You are a family of three.

Captain: Ask your teammates about the home you want or need.
Assistant: Complete the chart.
Co-captain: Keep time. You have five minutes.

Materials
- large paper
- markers

Number of bedrooms	
Number of bathrooms	
Size of rooms	
Cost	
Neighborhood	
Special features	☐ yard ☐ laundry ☐ fireplace ☐ garage ☐ other: _____

CREATE   **Co-captain:** Get the materials. Then keep time. You have ten minutes. **Team:** Create your ad. Write a heading with the number of bedrooms and bathrooms. Write the other information in your notes. Check the abbreviations. Add art if you want. Use the housing ads on page 93 as a model.

REPORT   **Spokesperson:** Show your ad to the class. Tell the class about your home.

COLLECT   **Class:** Walk around the room. Look at the ads. Which home is best for you?

Unit 6   Time to Celebrate   MAKE A HOLIDAY CALENDAR

Materials
- large paper
- markers
- rulers

TEAMS OF 4   Captain, Co-captain, Assistant, Spokesperson

GET READY   Your instructor/teacher will give you three months.
Captain: Ask your teammates about the holidays you celebrate during these three months. Ask, "What holidays do you celebrate? When are the holidays? How do you celebrate the holidays? What do you do?"
Assistant: Complete the chart.
Co-captain: Keep time. You have ten minutes.

Holiday	Date	How you celebrate
Halloween	October 31	wear costumes, give candy to children

CREATE   **Co-captain:** Get the materials. Then keep time. You have ten minutes.
Team: Create your calendar. Make a calendar page for each month. Write the holidays on the correct dates. Write a short paragraph/description about how people celebrate one of the holidays on your calendar pages. Add art if you want.

REPORT   **Spokesperson:** Show your calendar to the class. Tell the class about your holidays.

Unit 7 Home Remedies MAKE A BOOKLET

Materials
- 4 pieces of white paper
- pens or markers
- stapler and staples

TEAMS OF 4 Captain, Co-captain, Assistant, Spokesperson

GET READY **Team:** Home remedies are ways of treating an illness that is not serious at home. Choose illnesses from the box or use your own ideas.

Captain: Ask your teammates what home remedies they use.

A: *What do you do for a burn?*
B: *I put toothpaste on the burn.*

Assistant: Complete the chart.
Co-captain: Keep time. You have five minutes.

| a burn | a cold | a headache |
| a sore throat | a stomachache | a stuffy nose |

Illness	Home remedies
a burn	*put toothpaste on the burn* *put milk on the burn*

CREATE **Co-captain:** Get the materials. Then keep time. You have ten minutes.
Team: Create your booklet. Write a page for each home remedy. (Each student writes one.)

REPORT **Spokesperson:** Tell the class about your home remedies.

COLLECT **Captains:** Collect the booklet pages from each group. Staple them together to make a booklet about home remedies.

Unit 8   Job Skills and Requirements <u>MAKE A BOOKLET</u>

TEAMS OF 4 Captain, Co-captain, Assistant, Spokesperson

Materials
- 3 pieces of white paper
- pens or markers
- stapler and staples

hospital	hotel	school
restaurant	factory	other: _____

GET READY   **Team:** Choose a workplace. Each student chooses one job in this workplace.

Captain: Ask your teammates, "What skills do you need for this job? What education or experience do you need?"

Assistant: Write the answers in the chart.

Co-captain: Keep time. You have five minutes.

Workplace	Job	Skills	Education and/or experience

CREATE   **Co-captain:** Get the materials. Then keep time. You have ten minutes.

Team: Create your booklet. Make a page for each job. Write about the skills, education, and/or experience you need for this job.

REPORT   **Spokesperson:** Tell the class about one of the jobs.

COLLECT   **Captains:** Collect the booklet pages from each group. Staple them together to make a booklet about the skills you need for different jobs.

Unit 9 Ways to Improve Your English <u>MAKE A POSTER</u>

TEAMS OF 3 Captain, Co-captain, Assistant, Supervisor

Materials
- large paper
- markers

GET READY **Captain:** Ask your teammates, "What are ten ways to improve your English?"
Assistant: Take notes.
Co-captain: Keep time. You have five minutes.

Practice speaking outside of class. Read English books.

_____

_____

_____

_____

_____

CREATE **Co-captain:** Get the materials. Then keep time. You have ten minutes.
Team: Create your poster. Write the suggestions from your list.
Add pictures to the poster if you want.

REPORT **Spokesperson:** Show your poster to the class. Tell the class your suggestions.

Unit 10 Places to Shop for Food MAKE A FOOD SHOPPING GUIDE

TEAMS OF 4 Captain, Co-captain, Assistant, Spokesperson

GET READY **Captain:** Ask your teammates, "Where do you shop for food? Where is it located? Why do you shop there?"
Assistant: Complete the chart.
Co-captain: Keep time. You have five minutes.

Materials
- 3 pieces of white paper
- pens or markers
- stapler and staples

Name of store	Location	Reason for shopping there
Greenville Farmer's Market	Greenville Park	fresh fruits and vegetables, low prices

CREATE **Co-captain:** Get the materials. Then keep time. You have ten minutes.
Team: Create your shopping guide. Write where your team shops for food. Write about why your team shops at these places.

REPORT **Spokesperson:** Show your shopping guide to the class.
Tell the class about where your team shops.

COLLECT **Captains:** Collect the shopping guide from each group. Staple them together to make a class shopping guide.

Unit 11 Plan for a Fire Emergency <u>MAKE A POSTER</u>

TEAMS OF 3 Captain, Co-captain, Assistant, Spokesperson

Materials
- large paper
- markers

GET READY Imagine there is a fire in your school.
Captain: Ask, "What will you do if there is a fire at our school? Where will you go?"
Team: Draw a map of your school building. Mark all of the exits in your classroom. Talk about what to do and where to go in case of a fire.
Assistant: Write the instructions.
Co-captain: Keep time. You have five minutes.

Stay calm. Leave your books. Go to the hall. Turn . . .

_____

_____

_____

_____

CREATE **Co-captain:** Get the materials. Then keep time. You have ten minutes.
Team: Create your poster. Draw the escape plan. Write the instructions.

REPORT **Spokesperson:** Show your escape plan to the class. Read your instructions.

Unit 12   Your Dream Company   MAKE AN EMPLOYEE MANUAL

TEAMS OF 4   Captain, Co-captain, Assistant, Spokesperson

GET READY   You are opening your dream company.
Captain: Ask your teammates, "What kind of company is it?
What's the name of the company? What are the rules for your
employees? What are the rules for taking time off?"
Assistant: Write the answers in the chart.
Co-captain: Keep time. You have five minutes.

Materials
- 1 piece of white paper
- pens or markers
- stapler and staples

Type of business	
Company name	
Employee duties	
Time-off rules	

CREATE   **Co-captain:** Get the materials. Then keep time. You have ten minutes.
Team: Create your employee manual. Write the information from your charts.
Include the name of your company, the type of business, the employee duties, and
time-off rules. Each team member writes one part.

REPORT   **Spokesperson:** Tell the class about your company.

COLLECT   **Class:** Walk around the room. Look at the employee manuals.
Which company would you like to work for the most?

Grammar Reference

UNIT 1, Lesson 3, page 10

Contractions are short forms. Contractions join two words together. In a contraction, an apostrophe (') replaces a letter. Use contractions in speaking and informal writing.

Contractions with *be*

Affirmative			Negative		
I am	=	I'm	I am not	=	I'm not
you are	=	you're	you are not	=	you're not / you aren't
he is	=	he's	he is not	=	he's not / he isn't
she is	=	she's	she is not	=	she's not / she isn't
it is	=	it's	it is not	=	it's not / it isn't
we are	=	we're	we are not	=	we're not / we aren't
they are	=	they're	they are not	=	they're not / they aren't

Negative contractions with *do*

I do not	=	I don't
you do not	=	you don't
he does not	=	he doesn't
she does not	=	she doesn't
it does not	=	it doesn't
we do not	=	we don't
they do not	=	they don't

UNIT 6, Lesson 6, page 116 and UNIT 7, Lesson 6, page 136

Simple past: irregular verbs

Base form	Past tense form	Base form	Past tense form	Base form	Past tense form
be	was/were	get	got	run	ran
begin	began	give	gave	say	said
bleed	bled	go	went	see	saw
break	broke	grow	grew	send	sent
bring	brought	have	had	sing	sang
buy	bought	hurt	hurt	sit	sat
come	came	keep	keep	sleep	slept
cost	cost	know	knew	speak	spoke
cut	cut	leave	left	spend	spent
do	did	lose	lost	swim	swam
drink	drank	make	made	take	took
drive	drove	meet	met	teach	taught
eat	ate	oversleep	overslept	tell	told
fall	fell	pay	paid	think	thought
feel	felt	put	put	understand	understood
find	found	quit	quit	wake up	woke up
forget	forgot	read	read	write	wrote

UNIT 9, Lesson 6, page 176

Spelling rules for adverbs of manner

We can make many adverbs of manner from adjectives.

For most adverbs of manner, add -ly to an adjective. For example:

nice	$\longrightarrow$	nicely
quiet	$\longrightarrow$	quietly
normal	$\longrightarrow$	normally

If an adjective ends in y, change y to i and add -ly. For example:

happy	$\longrightarrow$	happily
noisy	$\longrightarrow$	noisily
angry	$\longrightarrow$	angrily

UNIT 9, Lesson 9, page 182

Spelling rules for possessive nouns

A possessive noun shows that a person or thing owns something.

Add 's to most singular nouns and names. For example:

student	$\longrightarrow$	student's
girl	$\longrightarrow$	girl's
Ming	$\longrightarrow$	Ming's

Add 's to singular nouns and names that end in -s. For example:

boss	$\longrightarrow$	boss's
Mr. Jones	$\longrightarrow$	Mr. Jones's
James	$\longrightarrow$	James's

Add ' to plural nouns that end in -s. For example:

parents	$\longrightarrow$	parents'
classmates	$\longrightarrow$	classmates'
boys	$\longrightarrow$	boys'

Add 's to plural nouns that do not end in -s. For example:

children	$\longrightarrow$	children's
people	$\longrightarrow$	people's
women	$\longrightarrow$	women's

Spelling rules for plurals and irregular nouns

Add -s to make most nouns plural. For example:

1 student	→	2 students
1 pencil	→	5 pencils
1 house	→	10 houses

Add -es to nouns that end with s, z, x, sh, or ch. For example:

1 sandwich	→	3 sandwiches
1 bus	→	4 buses
1 dish	→	5 dishes

For most nouns that end in o, just add -s. For example:

| 1 avocado | → | 2 avocados |
| 1 radio | → | 2 radios |

For some nouns that end in a consonant and o, add -es. For example:

1 potato	→	2 potatoes
1 tomato	→	8 tomatoes
1 hero	→	4 heroes

When a noun ends in a consonant + y, change y to i and add -es. For example:

1 baby	→	3 babies
1 country	→	15 countries
1 berry	→	20 berries

When a noun ends in f, change f to v and add -es. When a noun ends in fe, change fe to v and add -es. For example:

1 wife	→	2 wives
1 knife	→	9 knives
1 loaf	→	7 loaves

Some nouns have irregular plural forms. For example:

1 foot	→	2 feet
1 tooth	→	10 teeth
1 man	→	5 men
1 woman	→	8 women
1 child	→	7 children
1 person	→	12 people

UNIT 10, Lesson 3, page 190

Non-count nouns

Drinks	Some food		Materials	Subjects	Activities	Other
coffee	beef	meat	corduroy	art	baseball	advice
juice	bread	pasta	cotton	language arts	basketball	equipment
milk	butter	rice	denim	math	exercise	furniture
soda	cheese	salad	fleece	music	hiking	homework
tea	chicken	salt	glass	physical	jogging	information
water	chocolate	soup	leather	education	running	mail
	fish	spinach	metal	science	soccer	money
	fruit	sugar	nylon	social studies	swimming	news
	ice cream	yogurt	silk	technology	tennis	paper
	lettuce		vinyl	world languages		traffic
			wood			weather
			wool			work

UNIT 10, Lesson 6, page 196

Spelling rules for comparatives and irregular comparatives

To make comparative adjectives from one-syllable adjectives, add -*er*. For example:

cheap	$\longrightarrow$	cheaper
tall	$\longrightarrow$	taller
cold	$\longrightarrow$	colder

If a one-syllable adjective ends in *e*, add -*r*. For example:

nice	$\longrightarrow$	nicer
late	$\longrightarrow$	later
large	$\longrightarrow$	larger

If an adjective ends in one vowel and one consonant, double the consonant and add -*er*. For example:

hot	$\longrightarrow$	hotter
big	$\longrightarrow$	bigger
sad	$\longrightarrow$	sadder
thin	$\longrightarrow$	thinner

For two-syllable adjectives that end with -*y*, change *y* to *i* and add -*er*. For example:

busy	$\longrightarrow$	busier
pretty	$\longrightarrow$	prettier
easy	$\longrightarrow$	easier

UNIT 11, Lesson 3, page 210

Spelling rules for -ing verbs

For most verbs, add -ing to the base form of the verb. For example:

| work | $\longrightarrow$ | working |
| do | $\longrightarrow$ | doing |

For verbs that end in e, drop the e and add -ing. For example:

change	$\longrightarrow$	changing
leave	$\longrightarrow$	leaving
make	$\longrightarrow$	making

If the base form of a one-syllable verb ends with consonant, vowel, consonant, double the final consonant and add -ing. For example:

shop	$\longrightarrow$	shopping
run	$\longrightarrow$	running
cut	$\longrightarrow$	cutting
begin	$\longrightarrow$	beginning

Word List

UNIT 1

applicant, 12
application, 12
attractive, 8
auditory learner, 18
average height, 7
average weight, 7
bald, 7
beard, 7
beautiful, 8
bossy, 14
cheerful, 14
curly, 7

date of birth, 13
DOB (date of birth), 13
friendly, 15
funny, 15
goatee, 7
good-looking, 8
handsome, 8
heavy, 7
height, 7
identification card, 12
interesting, 15
kinesthetic learner, 18

laid-back, 14
learning style, 18
long hair, 7
mailing address, 12
moody, 14
mustache, 7
outgoing, 14
personality, 15
physical description, 7
pretty, 8
quiet, 15
short hair, 7

shoulder-length, 7
shy, 14
slim, 7
straight hair, 7
street address, 12
sweet, 14
talkative, 14
tall, 7
thin, 7
visual learner, 18
wavy, 7
weight, 7

UNIT 2

advice, 32
aunt, 27
brother, 27
Certificate of Mailing, 39
Certified Mail, 39
children, 27
Collect on Delivery
    (COD), 39
cousin, 27
daughter, 27
Delivery Confirmation, 39
envelope, 38
Express Mail, 38

family, 26
father, 27
father-in-law, 27
female, 26
fiancé, 27
fiancée, 27
First-Class Mail, 38
game show, 40
grandchildren, 27
granddaughter, 27
grandfather, 27
grandmother, 27
grandson, 27

have in common, 34
husband, 27
Insurance, 39
letter, 38
mailing service, 38
mailing tube, 38
male, 26
mother, 27
mother-in-law, 27
nephew, 27
niece, 27
package, 38
Parcel Post, 38

parents, 27
post office, 38
postcard, 38
pound, 38
Priority Mail, 38
Registered Mail, 39
relationship, 26
responsibility, 32
sister, 27
sister-in-law, 27
son, 27
uncle, 27
wife, 27

UNIT 3

ad, 52
ATM, 54
bakery, 55
bank, 55
big, 61
blouse, 61
boots, 47
broken, 60
button, 60
calculate change, 52
charades, 57
clearance sale, 48
clothes, 47
coat, 47
cold, 49
cool, 49
corduroy, 47

cotton, 47
credit card, 58
deli, 54
denim, 47
discount, 52
drugstore, 55
errand, 54
exchange, 50
fleece, 47
flip-flops, 52
gas station, 55
gloves, 47
grocery store, 55
hardware store, 54
hole, 60
hot, 49
jacket, 47

jeans, 47
laundromat, 54
leather, 47
library, 55
long, 61
loose, 60
material, 47
missing, 60
nylon, 47
raincoat, 47
receipt, 53
rent-to-own, 59
return (a purchase), 50
ripped, 60
sale, 52
scarf, 47
seam, 60

shorts, 49
silk, 47
sunglasses, 52
sweater, 61
sweatshirt, 47
swimsuit, 53
swimwear, 52
T-shirts, 61
tax, 52
tight, 60
too, 62
very, 62
vinyl, 47
windbreaker, 47
wool, 47
zipper, 60

UNIT 4

accept, 80
calendar, 72
clean the house, 75
club, 72
computer, 68
computer class, 68
cook, 74
decline, 80
do the dishes, 75
don't feel well, 80
errands, 81
exercise, 71
free-time, 67
get some coffee, 81
get up early, 75

go dancing, 67
go fishing, 67
go for a bike ride, 67
go for a walk, 67
go hiking, 67
go jogging, 67
go out to eat, 67
go shopping, 67
go swimming, 67
got to a meeting, 81
go to the beach, 67
go to the movies, 77
go to the park, 67
go to the zoo, 67
guitar class, 68

hate, 76
have other plans, 80
indoor, 66
invitation, 80
invite, 81
iron, 74
karate, 69
like, 76
love, 76
make some calls, 81
message board, 78
not like, 76
once, 71
outdoor, 66
painting, 69

polite, 78
read, 77
rude, 78
run some errands, 81
schedule, 73
spend time with family, 77
take a walk, 81
too busy, 80
twice, 71
use a computer, 77
vacuum, 74
watch TV, 74

UNIT 5

air-conditioning, 92
balcony, 95
basement, 92
bathroom, 92
broken, 87
building manager, 88
bulletin board, 93
bus stop, 95
ceiling, 86
clogged, 87
closet, 95
cost of living, 99
dining room, 92
dishwasher, 90
door, 86
dryer, 92
eat-in kitchen, 92

electrician, 88
elevator, 92
faucet, 86
fee, 92
fix, 88
furnished, 92
get directions, 100
go straight, 100
go through (a light), 100
heat, 87
hot water, 87
Internet posting, 93
kitchen, 95
landlady, 94
laundry room, 94
leaking, 87
living room, 92

lock, 86
locksmith, 88
mailbox, 87
microwave, 95
Midwest, 98
natural beauty, 99
newspaper ad, 93
Northeast, 98
(not) working, 87
paint, 91
pet, 92
plumber, 88
problem, 86
public transportation, 92
real estate agent, 93
region, 98
rent, 92

rental apartment, 92
security deposit, 92
sink, 86
South, 98
Southwest, 98
stove, 87
stuck, 87
toilet, 86
traffic, 99
turn left, 100
turn right, 100
utilities, 92
washer, 92
washing machine, 86
West, 98
West Coast, 98
window, 86

UNIT 6

anniversary party, 107
baby shower, 107
barbecue, 107
be born, 114
biography, 118
birthday party, 107
Christmas Day, 112
Columbus Day, 112
dance all night, 108
dress casually, 106
dress formally, 106
exhausted, 121
family reunion, 107

forget (your lunch), 120
funeral, 107
get a job, 114
get married, 114
get stuck in traffic, 120
give gifts, 106
graduate from
   school, 114
graduation party, 107
grow up, 114
have car trouble, 120
have children, 114
holiday, 107

holiday meal, 107
Independence Day, 112
Labor Day, 112
listen to family
   stories, 108
look at old photos, 108
lose (your keys), 120
Martin Luther King Jr.
   Day, 112
Memorial Day, 112
milestone, 105
New Year's Day, 112
oversleep, 120

potluck dinner, 107
Presidents' Day, 112
retirement party, 107
stay up late, 108
surprise party, 107
take the wrong train, 120
Thanksgiving Day, 112
time line, 119
to-do list, 111
unhappy, 121
upset, 121
Veterans' Day, 112
wedding, 107

UNIT 7

absence, 140
appointment, 128
appointment card, 128
break your arm, 134
break your tooth, 141
burn your hand, 134
call in sick/late, 144
chest pains, 127
cough, 127
create stress, 139
cut your finger, 134
diarrhea, 127
dizzy, 128
dosage, 133
due to, 132
earache, 127

expiration date, 132
eye drops, 133
fall, 134
feel better, 141
fever, 127
get well soon, 141
good luck, 141
have a cold, 127
have the chills, 127
have the flu, 127
headache, 127
health problem, 127
heartburn, 127
hurt your head, 134
injury, 134
itchy, 128

loss of control, 138
manage stress, 138
medical history, 133
medicine label, 132
miss work, 140
nauseous, 128
negative attitude, 138
ointment, 133
over-the-counter (OTC)
   medicine, 132
pharmacist, 133
pharmacy, 133
prescription, 132
rash, 127
reduce, 132
refill, 133

relieve, 132
sick, 141
sore throat, 127
sprain your ankle, 134
stiff neck, 127
stress, 138
supervisor, 140
swollen, 128
symptom, 128
tablespoon, 133
temporarily, 132
unhealthy habit, 138
upset stomach, 127

UNIT 8

agriculture, 158
assist customers, 147
availability, 160
benefits, 152
change jobs, 154
clean kitchen
   equipment, 147
computer system
   administrator, 146
experience, 152
field of employment, 158
flexible, 160
food service worker, 146
full-time, 152
give notice at work, 160

greet visitors, 147
handle phone calls, 147
health care, 158
help with computer
   problems, 147
help-wanted ad, 152
install computer
   hardware, 147
job application, 151
job duty, 146
job interview, 148
manager, 146
manufacturing, 158
nurse assistant, 146
operate a forklift, 148

order supplies, 148
part-time, 152
plan work schedules, 147
prefer, 152
prepare food, 147
receive shipments, 147
receptionist, 146
record patient
   information, 147
references, 152
résumé, 152
sales associate, 146
shift, 160
skill, 148
speak Spanish, 148

stock clerk, 146
stock shelves, 147
supervise employees, 147
take care of patients, 147
technology, 158
truck driver, 155
type, 148
unemployed, 154
unload materials, 147
use a cash register, 148
use a word-processing
   program, 148
warehouse worker, 146
work history, 154
work schedule, 160

UNIT 9

art, 166
Associate Degree, 178
Bachelor Degree, 178
be disrespectful, 180
behave, 180
behavior, 180
bully, 180
call someone back, 173
college, 178
college degree, 178
color, 166
community college, 178
community service, 167
Doctor of Philosophy, 178
draw, 166

elementary school, 166
financial aid, 179
fool around, 180
get along with others, 180
get extra help, 174
give someone a
   message, 173
grant, 179
high school, 166
language arts/English, 167
leave a message, 173
leave early, 169
loan, 179
Master Degree, 178
math, 167

meeting, 169
middle school, 166
misbehave, 180
music, 167
notice from school, 168
parent-teacher
   conference, 168
pay attention, 180
P.E. (physical
   education), 167
phone message, 172
preschool, 166
PTO (parent-teacher
   organization), 168
return a call, 172

science, 167
science fair, 169
scholarship, 179
school play, 169
school subject, 166
skip class, 180
social studies/history, 167
take a message, 172
technology, 167
try, 169
tuition, 179
university, 178
world languages, 167

UNIT 10

apple juice, 200
bag, 187
beans, 189
beverage, 199
bottle, 187
bottled water, 200
box, 187
bunch, 187
caffeine, 198
calories, 193
can, 187
carbohydrates, 192
cereal, 189
cheap, 196
chewing gum, 198
chocolate, 198
cholesterol, 192
coffee, 195
cola, 198
coleslaw, 200
commercial, 194
consume, 198
contain, 198

container, 187
convenience, 194
convenience store, 188
cucumber, 189
delicious, 196
dozen, 187
effect, 198
fat, 193
fattening, 196
fiber, 192
fish, 190
fish sandwich, 200
French fries, 200
fresh, 194
gallon, 187
good, 196
gram (g), 193
guest check, 200
half-gallon, 187
hamburger, 200
harmful, 199
head, 187
headache medicine, 198

healthy, 194
ice cream, 195
iced tea, 200
ingredient, 192
irritable, 199
jar, 187
lettuce, 187
lemon/lime soda, 198
low-fat, 195
macaroni and cheese, 200
mashed potatoes, 200
meatloaf, 200
menu, 200
milligram (mg), 193
mixed vegetables, 200
non-fat milk, 193
noodles, 200
nutrients, 192
nutrition label, 192
nutritious, 196
onion rings, 200
orange, 189
orange juice, 195

outdoor market, 188
picnic, 191
pint, 187
pork chop, 200
pound, 187
price, 194
protein, 192
quantity, 187
quart, 187
roast chicken, 200
salty, 196
serving, 193
shopping list, 191
soda, 200
sodium, 192
soup, 189
sugar, 192
supermarket, 188
taste, 194
tea, 198
tuna, 189
yogurt, 189

UNIT 11

911, 208
allergic reaction, 207
ambulance, 208
be hurt, 215
bleed, 207
burn yourself, 207
car accident, 214
choke, 207
cleaning supplies, 218
cloth, 212
construction
  accident, 214
cross street, 208
crowd of people, 217
curtain, 212

dangerous, 214
driver's license, 220
electric, 209
electrical cord, 212
electrical outlet, 212
electrical plug, 212
emergency, 206
escape plan, 212
exit, 212
explosion, 214
fall, 207
fire escape, 212
fire extinguisher, 212
fire hazard, 212

have trouble
  breathing, 207
heart attack, 207
heater, 212
injury, 215
location, 208
matches, 212
medical emergency, 207
police, 217
proof of insurance, 220
pull over, 220
reaction, 209
registration, 220
robbery, 214
rug, 212

run a red light, 221
safety procedure, 212
safety tip, 213
seat belt, 221
situation, 209
smoke alarm, 212
special, 221
steering wheel, 220
swallow poison, 207
tailgate, 221
taxi, 208
traffic jam, 217
traffic ticket, 220
unconscious, 207

UNIT 12

ask for a favor, 234
ask questions, 227
be on time, 226
call in late, 227
clock in/out, 227
cover someone's
  hours, 234
deduction, 232
disabled, 238
eat at my desk, 229
eat in the break
  room, 229

employee badge, 228
federal tax, 232
first shift, 241
follow directions, 227
full-time, 241
gross pay, 232
latex gloves, 227
maintain equipment, 227
manager, 228
Medicare, 232
miss work, 234
net pay, 232

orientation meeting, 228
overtime hour, 233
park, 229
part-time, 241
pay period, 232
pay stub, 232
rate of pay, 232
regular hour, 232
report a problem, 227
retired, 238
safety gear, 227
second shift, 241

Social Security, 232
Social Security benefits, 238
State Disability Insurance
  (SDI), 232
state tax, 232
store equipment, 227
talk to a manager, 229
trade shifts, 229
uniform, 227
wash hands, 227
work as a team, 227

Audio Script

UNIT 1

Page 8, Listen, Exercises A and B

Tania: Hi, Eva.

Eva: Hi, Tania. Are you coming to my party tonight?

Tania: Of course. Are you inviting your friend?

Eva: Which friend?

Tania: You know—he's handsome and he has short, black hair.

Page 8, Listen, Exercise C

Tania: Hi, Eva.

Eva: Hi, Tania. Are you coming to my party tonight?

Tania: Of course. Are you inviting your friend?

Eva: Which friend?

Tania: You know—he's handsome and he has short, black hair.

Eva: Does he have blue eyes?

Tania: No, he has brown eyes.

Eva: Oh. You mean Victor. He's not my friend, he's my brother! But of course I'll introduce him to you.

Page 14, Listen, Exercises A and B

Tania: So tell me more about Victor. What's he like?

Eva: Well, he's outgoing and he has a lot of friends.

Tania: Yeah? What else?

Eva: He's sweet but he's a little quiet.

Page 14, Listen. Exercise C

Tania: So tell me more about Victor. What's he like?

Eva: Well, he's outgoing and he has a lot of friends.

Tania: Yeah? What else?

Eva: He's sweet but he's a little quiet.

Tania: Quiet? That's not a problem.

Eva: But you're so talkative. Don't you like talkative guys?

Tania: No, I don't. I like guys who *listen* a lot!

Page 20, Listen, Exercises B and C

Eva: I want to introduce you to my friend. Victor, this is Tania. Tania, this is Victor.

Victor: Nice to meet you.

Tania: Nice to meet you, too.

Victor: So, are you a student?

Tania: Yes, I am. Eva and I are in the same English class.

Victor: Oh, that's nice. Where are you from?

Tania: Ecuador.

Victor: Really? What's it like?

Tania: It's a very beautiful country.

Page 20, Listen, Exercise D

Eva: I want to introduce you to my friend. Victor, this is Tania. Tania, this is Victor.

Victor: Nice to meet you.

Tania: Nice to meet you, too.

Victor: So, are you a student?

Tania: Yes, I am. Eva and I are in the same English class.

Victor: Oh, that's nice. Where are you from?

Tania: Ecuador.

Victor: Really? What's it like?

Tania: It's a very beautiful country. . . . So, how about you? Are you a student, too?

Victor: No, I'm not. I work at a restaurant. I'm a cook.

UNIT 2

Page 28, Listen, Exercise B

Amy: Tell me about your family.

Babacar: Well, I don't have a very big family. I have a brother and two sisters.

Amy: Do they live here?

Babacar: My sisters live in Senegal, but my brother lives here.

Page 28, Listen, Exercise C

Amy: Tell me about your family.

Babacar: Well, I don't have a very big family. I have a brother and two sisters.

Amy: Do they live here?

Babacar: My sisters live in Senegal, but my brother lives here.

Amy: Really? What does your brother do?

Babacar: He works in a hospital. He's a medical assistant.

Amy: And does he live near you?

Babacar: Yes. In fact, we live in the same apartment.

Amy: Wow, then he *really* lives near you!

Page 34, Listen, Exercises B and C

Ming: Tina, is this your sister? You two look alike.

Tina: Yeah, that's my sister, Lili.

Ming: Do you have a lot in common?

Tina: Actually, we do. She works in a bank, and I do, too. And we both have new babies.

Page 34, Listen, Exercise D

Ming: Tina, is this your sister? You two look alike.
Tina: Yeah, that's my sister, Lili.
Ming: Do you have a lot in common?
Tina: Actually, we do. She works in a bank, and I do, too. And we both have new babies.
Ming: That's nice.
Tina: What about you, Ming? Do you have any brothers or sisters?
Ming: I have two sisters, and we have a lot in common.
Tina: Really?
Ming: Yeah. I have two sisters, and they do, too. I don't have any brothers, and they don't, either!

Page 39, Practice

Customer: Hello. I'd like to mail this package.
Clerk: How do you want to send it?
Customer: How long does Parcel Post take?
Clerk: Two to nine days.
Customer: OK. I'll send it Parcel Post.
Clerk: Do you want Delivery Confirmation or Insurance?
Customer: Yes. Delivery Confirmation, please.

Page 40 Listen, Exercises A, B, and C

Oliver: Hello, I'm Oliver Marley, and welcome to *They're Your Family Now!*, the game show where we ask people questions about their in-laws. Please welcome our first contestant, Mr. Trevor Scanlon.
Trevor: Hello.
Oliver: Now, Trevor. Here are the rules of the game. Before the show, we asked your wife Ann ten questions about her family. Now I'm going to ask you the same questions. You get $100 for every question you answer correctly.
Trevor: OK! I'm ready.
Oliver: Great. Trevor, here's your first question. Where do your wife's grandparents live?
Trevor: Oh! That's easy. They live in San Antonio with the rest of her family.
Oliver: Right! Good start. OK. Here's your next question. How many brothers and sisters does your mother-in-law have?
Trevor: My mother-in-law?! . . . Well, there's Martha, Paula, Henry, Charles, . . . and what's his name? . . . Paul! OK. My mother-in-law has two sisters and three brothers. So that's five in total.

Oliver: That's right! Good job. Next question. What does your brother-in-law Alex do?
Trevor: Oh, wow . . . I know he works in an office . . . Um, he's an engineer?
Oliver: No, he's an accountant!
Trevor: Oh!
Oliver: Better luck on the next one. Here it is . . . When does your sister-in-law Danielle work?
Trevor: Oh, I know this one! Danielle works at night because her husband works during the day. She watches the baby all day, and he watches him at night!
Oliver: Correct! Well, so far you have three points. We have to take a break, but we'll be right back with *They're Your Family Now!*

UNIT 3

Page 48, Listen, Exercises A and B

Lindsey: Hi, this is Lindsey Campbell with WEYE's *Eye Around Town*, the program that tells you what's happening in town. So what's happening today? I'm here at the summer clearance at Big Deals, and the store is full of shoppers. Let's talk to a few of them . . . Excuse me. What's your name?
Alicia: Alicia Duran.
Lindsey: Hi, Alicia. Tell us, why are you here at Big Deals today?
Alicia: Well, I shop here a lot. They have great prices on everything you need.
Lindsey: And what do you need to buy today?
Alicia: Well, I don't *need* to buy anything, but I *want* to buy a new pair of jeans.
Lindsey: Well, I hope you find some, Alicia. Next . . . tell us your name, please.
Gladys: Gladys Flores.
Lindsey: Gladys, why are you here today?
Gladys: I'm here with my daughter. We don't need to buy anything today. We just need to return this dress. It's really easy to return things here if you have your receipt . . . Where *is* that receipt? I know it's here somewhere . . .
Lindsey: Uh . . . OK. And you, sir. Who are you, and why are you here at Big Deals today?
John: My name's John Nichols. I need to buy some shorts for my son.
Lindsey: Do you always shop here at Big Deals?

John:	Yeah. It's so convenient. They have everything here, so I don't need to go to a lot of different stores. I really don't like to shop.
Lindsey:	OK, well, we need to go back to the studio now, and I want to look for a jacket while I'm here! I'm Lindsey Campbell with your *Eye Around Town*. Now back to the studio.

Page 54, Listen, Exercises A and B

Debbie:	So, what are your plans for tomorrow?
Antonio:	Nothing. I'm going to relax. Why?
Debbie:	Well, I have a lot to do. First, I need to go to the ATM. Then I need to go to the hardware store. Then I'm going to stop at the supermarket.
Antonio:	Wow. You're going to be busy.

Page 54, Listen, Exercise C

Debbie:	So, what are your plans for tomorrow?
Antonio:	Nothing. I'm going to relax. Why?
Debbie:	Well, I have a lot to do. First, I need to go to the ATM. Then I need to go to the hardware store. Then I'm going to stop at the supermarket.
Antonio:	Wow. You're going to be busy.
Debbie:	I know. And you are, too.
Antonio:	What?
Debbie:	Yeah. You're going to help me. You're going to the laundromat, the deli, and the drug store.
Antonio:	OK. See you later.
Debbie:	Hey—where are you going?
Antonio:	To take a nap. I got tired just thinking about tomorrow.

Page 60, Listen, Exercises B and C

Shu-Chi:	Hi, Kelly. Where are you going?
Kelly:	I'm going to Kohn's. I need to return this jacket.
Shu-Chi:	How come?
Kelly:	The zipper is broken.
Shu-Chi:	That's annoying . . . Um, could you do me a favor?
Kelly:	What is it?
Shu-Chi:	Could you return a dress for me?
Kelly:	Sure. What's wrong with it?
Shu-Chi:	It's too short.

Page 60, Listen, Exercise D

Shu-Chi:	Hi, Kelly. Where are you going?
Kelly:	I'm going to Kohn's. I need to return this jacket.
Shu-Chi:	How come?
Kelly:	The zipper is broken.
Shu-Chi:	That's annoying . . . Um, could you do me a favor?
Kelly:	What is it?
Shu-Chi:	Could you return a dress for me?
Kelly:	Sure. What's wrong with it?
Shu-Chi:	It's too short.
Kelly:	Too short? Let me see it.
Shu-Chi:	Sure. It's in that bag.
Kelly:	Oh, no! Of course this is too short. It's a shirt, not a dress!

UNIT 4

Page 68, Listen, Exercises A and B

Mario:	What are you doing this weekend?
Bi-Yun:	I'm going to go to the beach with my family.
Mario:	Really? Sounds like fun.
Bi-Yun:	Yeah. We usually go to the beach on Sunday. What about you?
Mario:	Well, I have a guitar class. I have a guitar class every Saturday morning.

Page 68, Listen, Exercise C

Mario:	What are you doing this weekend?
Bi-Yun:	I'm going to go to the beach with my family.
Mario:	Really? Sounds like fun.
Bi-Yun:	Yeah. We usually go to the beach on Sunday. What about you?
Mario:	Well, I have a guitar class. I have a guitar class every Saturday morning.
Bi-Yun:	You play the guitar? Wow. That's really neat.
Mario:	Well, I don't really play . . .
Bi-Yun:	But you're taking classes, right?
Mario:	Yeah. But I don't know how to play. That's why I'm taking classes!

Page 73, Practice, Exercise A

This is the Greenville Community Center Information Line. The following information is for the month of September.

The Lunch Club meets at Hilda's Café on the second Friday of the month at 12:00 P.M.

We now have a dance class. The dance class meets on Thursdays from 3:00 to 4:00 P.M.

The Movie Club now meets on the second and fourth Saturday of the month. Movies begin at 7:00 P.M.

The ESL class meets every Monday and Wednesday from 7:00 to 9:00 P.M.

The Jogging Club meets every Saturday at 8:00 A.M.

We now have a Concert Club. The Concert Club meets on the first and third Friday of the month. Concerts start at 7:00 P.M.

Page 74, Listen, Exercises A and B

Katie: Welcome to our show. I'm your host, Katie Martin. We all have things that we need to do. And here's the problem: A lot of times we don't like the things we need to do. So, what's the solution? Well, today we're talking to Dr. Collin Goldberg, and he has some ideas. Welcome to the show, Dr. Goldberg.

Dr. Goldberg: Thanks, Katie. It's great to be here.

Katie: So, Dr. Goldberg, tell us about some of your ideas.

Dr. Goldberg: Sure. Here's the first one: When you need to do something you hate, do something you like *at the same time*. For example, if you hate to wash dishes, then do something you love *while* you wash the dishes. Wash the dishes and watch TV. Or wash the dishes and talk to a friend on the phone.

Katie: That way you're not thinking about the activity that you don't like.

Dr. Goldberg: Exactly.

Katie: That seems pretty easy. Do you have any other tips?

Dr. Goldberg: Sure. Here's another idea: Put a time limit on the activities you hate to do.

Katie: A time limit?

Dr. Goldberg: Exactly. For example, say it's 1:00 and you need to clean the house. Decide what time you're going to finish cleaning, say 3:00. When it's 3:00, you stop.

Katie: That's it?

Dr. Goldberg: Yes. It's an extremely simple idea, but it works. When you have a time limit, you know when the activity is going to end. And that can help a lot.

Katie: That makes sense.

Dr. Goldberg: Right. And here's one more: After you do something you hate, do something you like. For example, if you hate to do laundry, but you love to read, then say to yourself, "I'm going to do the laundry. Then I'm going to read for half an hour."

Katie: Dr. Goldberg, these sound like really good ideas. We have to take a break now, but we'll be back in a moment with more . . .

Page 80, Listen, Exercises B and C

Gloria: Do you want to get some lunch?

Yi-Wen: Sorry, I can't. I have to finish some work.

Gloria: Oh. Are you sure?

Yi-Wen: Yes, I'm sorry. I really can't.

Gloria: Well, how about a little later?

Yi-Wen: Thanks, but I don't think so. Not today.

Page 80, Listen, Exercise D

Gloria: Do you want to get some lunch?

Yi-Wen: Sorry, I can't. I have to finish some work.

Gloria: Oh. Are you sure?

Yi-Wen: Yes, I'm sorry. I really can't.

Gloria: Well, how about a little later?

Yi-Wen: Thanks, but I don't think so. Not today. I have a big meeting this afternoon. Hold on a second. Hello? Oh, hi, Bob. OK. Great. Thanks for calling. Guess what? My meeting was canceled.

Gloria: That's great! So now you can go to lunch?

Yi-Wen: Yes, I guess I can. Let me get my coat.

Page 81, Conversation, Exercise B

1. I have a test tomorrow.
2. I have to study.
3. He has to stay late.
4. He has a meeting.

UNIT 5

Page 88, Listen, Exercises B and C

Harry: Hello?

Joe: Hi, Harry. It's Joe.

Harry: Oh, hi, Joe. Can I call you back?

Joe: Sure. No problem.

Harry: Thanks. My radiator is broken and I'm trying to fix it.

Joe: You should call the building manager.

Page 88, Listen, Exercise D

Harry: Hello?

Joe: Hi, Harry. It's Joe.

Harry: Oh, hi, Joe. Can I call you back?

Joe: Sure. No problem.

Harry: Thanks. My radiator is broken and I'm trying to fix it.

Joe: You should call the building manager.

Harry: That's a good idea. There's just one problem.

Joe: What's that?

Harry: Well, I just got a new job. Now *I'm* the building manager!

Page 94, Listen, Exercises A and B

Landlady: Hello?
Paula: Hi, I'm calling about the apartment for rent. Can you tell me about it?
Landlady: Sure. There are two bedrooms and a large living room.
Paula: Is there a laundry room?
Landlady: No, there isn't. But there's a laundromat down the street.
Paula: I see. Is there a park nearby?
Landlady: Yes, there is—just around the corner.

Page 94, Listen, Exercise C

Landlady: Hello?
Paula: Hi, I'm calling about the apartment for rent. Can you tell me about it?
Landlady: Sure. There are two bedrooms and a large living room.
Paula: Is there a laundry room?
Landlady: No, there isn't. But there's a laundromat down the street.
Paula: I see. Is there a park nearby?
Landlady: Yes, there is—just around the corner.
Paula: Wow! And the ad says it's only $200 a month!
Landlady: Yes, sorry. That was a mistake. The rent is $2,000 a month, not $200.
Paula: Oh, well, thanks. I guess I don't need any more information. I'm looking for something under five hundred a month.

Page 100, Listen, Exercises A and B

Thank you for calling the Greenville Public Library. For directions, press 1.
Directions to the library: From the west, take Warton Avenue east. Turn left onto Brice Road. Go straight. Turn right onto Clarkson Street. Go through one traffic light. The library is on the left.
To repeat this message, press 2. To disconnect, press 0. Thank you. Good-bye.

UNIT 6

Page 108, Listen, Exercises B and C

Michelle: How was your weekend? How was the family reunion?
Sam: It was really nice, thanks. My whole family showed up.
Michelle: Sounds great.
Sam: Yeah, it was fun. We looked at old pictures and listened to family stories.

Page 108, Listen, Exercise D

Michelle: How was your weekend? How was the family reunion?
Sam: It was really nice, thanks. My whole family showed up.
Michelle: Sounds great.
Sam: Yeah, it was fun. We looked at old pictures and listened to family stories. How about you?
Michelle: My weekend was pretty good. I had a surprise party on Saturday night.
Sam: Really? Was it someone's birthday?
Michelle: No, it wasn't a birthday. I just invited some friends over. Then some other friends came over, and—surprise! It was a party!

Page 112, Recognize U.S. Holidays, Exercise C

Conversation 1
A: What time do the fireworks begin?
B: At 9:00. But let's go a little early so we can get a good spot.

Conversation 2
A: Oh, my! What a big turkey!
B: I'm so glad everyone in the family is coming to help eat it!

Conversation 3
A: Mmm. I love the smell of the tree in the house. Don't you?
B: Yes, and I love decorating the tree, too. Here are the lights!

Conversation 4
A: Well, this is it! Our last barbecue of the summer!
B: Yeah. I can't believe summer is over.
A: That's right! Tomorrow, it's back to work, and back to school!
B: Oohhh!

Conversation 5
A: How was the party last night?
B: We had a terrific time, but we didn't get home until really late. I'm glad it's a holiday today.
A: Yeah, it's a great way to start the new year!

Page 114, Listen, Exercises A and B

Amber: Welcome to *Star Talk*, the program where we talk to today's biggest stars. I'm your host Amber Jenkins, and today I'm very excited to welcome actor Daniel Lopez!

Daniel: Thanks. It's great to be here.

Amber: So, Daniel, tell us about yourself and your celebrity life.

Daniel: Uh—sure. But my life really isn't that interesting.

Amber: Your life? Not interesting? I don't believe it. I mean, you're a huge star. Now, let's start with your childhood. You were born in California?

Daniel: Yes, I was born in California, and that's where I grew up. I had a pretty normal childhood.

Amber: What about school?

Daniel: Uh, yeah. I went to school. I graduated from high school and went to college.

Amber: And you always wanted to be an actor?

Daniel: No, I didn't. Actually, I wanted to be a plumber when I was a kid. My dad was a plumber, and I wanted to be just like him. I started acting in college.

Amber: OK, so you had a normal childhood. You went to school. But now your life is very different, right? You probably do lots of interesting things.

Daniel: Uh, not really.

Amber: Oh, come on, tell us. What did you do last night? I'll bet you went to a big, fancy party.

Daniel: No, actually I stayed home. I watched some TV and went to bed early.

Amber: Went to bed early? That's not glamorous at all!

Daniel: I know, I'm telling you, I don't have a very glamorous life. I'm really just a regular guy.

Amber: Well, there you go, listeners—Daniel Lopez is just a regular guy. We need to take a break, but we'll be back . . .

Page 115, Conversation, Exercise B

1. Maria grew up in Houston.
2. You came to the U.S. in 1995?
3. Ali graduated from college two years ago.
4. She got married last year?

Page 120, Listen, Exercises A and B

Maria: Is everything OK? You look stressed out.

André: Well, I had a rough morning.

Maria: Why? What happened?

André: First I lost my car keys.

Maria. Oh, no!

André: Then I got stuck in traffic.

Maria: When did you get to work?

André: At 10:00. I was really late.

Page 121, Listen, Exercise C

Maria: Is everything OK? You look stressed out.

André: Well, I had a rough morning.

Maria: Why? What happened?

André: First I lost my car keys.

Maria: Oh, no!

André: Then I got stuck in traffic.

Maria: When did you get to work?

André: At 10:00. I was really late.

Maria: That's too bad.

André: Wait—It gets worse.

Maria: Really? What happened?

André: When I finally got to work, I realized it was Tuesday.

Maria: So?

André: So, I don't work on Tuesdays! Tuesday is my day off!

UNIT 7

Page 128, Listen, Exercises B, C, and D

Receptionist: Hello. Westview Clinic.

Roberto: Hi. This is Roberto Cruz. I need to make an appointment, please.

Receptionist: All right. What's the matter?

Roberto: I have a fever and I'm nauseous.

Receptionist: OK. Can you come on Tuesday morning? How about at 9:00?

Roberto: Yes, that's fine.

Receptionist: All right. What's your name again?

Roberto: Roberto Cruz.

Receptionist: Roberto Cruz. OK, Mr. Cruz, we'll see you on Tuesday at 9:00.

Roberto: OK. Thank you.

Page 134, Listen, Exercise B

Manolo: Hi, Ellie. What are you doing here?

Ellie: Oh, hi, Manolo. I had an accident. I broke my arm.

Manolo: Oh, no! I'm sorry to hear that.

Ellie: Thanks. What about you?

Manolo: I hurt my ankle at a soccer game. I think I sprained it.

Ellie: That's too bad.

Page 134, Listen, Exercise C

Manolo: Hi, Ellie. What are you doing here?

Ellie: Oh, hi, Manolo. I had an accident. I broke my arm.

Manolo: Oh, no! I'm sorry to hear that.

Ellie: Thanks. What about you?

Manolo: I hurt my ankle at a soccer game. I think I sprained it.

Ellie: That's too bad. I guess you can't play soccer for a while.

Manolo: Oh, I don't play soccer. I just watch.

Ellie: What? So how did you hurt your ankle?

Manolo: Well, I was at a soccer game. I was hungry, so I got some food. I had a drink and a sandwich in my hands, and I fell down the stairs on the way to my seat.

Page 140, Listen, Exercise A

Paula: Hello. Paula Charles speaking.

Soo-Jin: Hi, Paula. This is Soo-Jin. I can't come in today because I have to go to the doctor. I don't feel well.

Paula: Sorry to hear that. Thanks for calling, and take care of yourself.

Soo-Jin: Thanks.

Page 140, Listen, Exercise B

Paula: Hello. Paula Charles speaking.

Soo-Jin: Hi, Paula. This is Soo-Jin. I can't come in today because I have to go to the doctor. I don't feel well.

Paula: Sorry to hear that. Thanks for calling, and take care of yourself.

Soo-Jin: Thanks.

Paula: Do you think you'll be in tomorrow?

Soo-Jin: I'm not sure. I can call you later after I go to the doctor.

Paula: All right. That sounds good.

UNIT 8

Page 148, Listen, Exercises B and C

Albert: Manny? Hi, I'm Albert Taylor, the store manager. Please have a seat.

Manny: Thank you. It's nice to meet you.

Albert: I have your application here. I see that you are working now. What are your job duties?

Manny: Well, I assist customers and stock shelves.

Albert: OK. Tell me about your skills. Can you use a cash register?

Manny: No, I can't, but I can learn.

Page 154, Listen, Exercises A and B

Albert: So, tell me more about your work experience.

Manny: Well, I came to the U.S. three years ago. First, I got a job as a gardener. Then last year I got a job as a stock clerk.

Albert: OK. So now you're a stock clerk. Why are you looking for another job?

Manny: Things in my life have changed, and now I'd like to do something different.

Page 154, Listen, Exercises C and D

Albert: So, tell me more about your work experience.

Manny: Well, I came to the U.S. three years ago. First, I got a job as a gardener. Then last year I got a job as a stock clerk.

Albert: OK. So now you're a stock clerk. Why are you looking for another job?

Manny: Things in my life have changed, and now I'd like to do something different.

Albert: I see. By the way, you wrote on your application that you were unemployed two years ago. Can you explain that?

Manny: Sure. I left my job because my mother was sick, and I had to take care of her for two months. When she got better, I got a new job.

Page 160, Listen, Exercises A and B

Albert: Let me ask you a few questions about your availability. Do you prefer mornings or afternoons?

Manny: Well, I prefer mornings, but I'm flexible.

Albert: All right. Can you work on weekends?

Manny: Yes, I can.

Albert: Great. And when could you start?

Manny: In two weeks. I need to give two weeks' notice at my job.

Page 160, Listen, Exercise C

Albert: Let me ask you a few questions about your availability. Do you prefer mornings or afternoons?

Manny: Well, I prefer mornings, but I'm flexible.

Albert: All right. Can you work on weekends?

Manny: Yes, I can.

Albert: Great. And when could you start?

Manny: In two weeks. I need to give two weeks' notice at my job.

Albert:	OK. Well, everything looks good. Do you have any questions for me?
Manny:	Yes. When can I expect to hear from you?
Albert:	Well, I have some other interviews this week. I can let you know next week.
Manny:	OK. Thank you for the opportunity to talk with you. It was nice to meet you.
Albert:	You, too.

UNIT 9

Page 168, Listen, Exercises B and C

Mrs. Duval:	Carlo brought a notice home from school today. There's a parent-teacher conference in two weeks.
Mr. Duval:	Oh yeah? What day?
Mrs. Duval:	Thursday the 19th at 6:00. My mother will watch the kids. That way we can both go.
Mr. Duval:	Oh, I have to work that day until 9:00, but I'll try to change my shift.

Page 168, Listen, Exercise D

Mrs. Duval:	Carlo brought a notice home from school today. There's a parent-teacher conference in two weeks.
Mr. Duval:	Oh yeah? What day?
Mrs. Duval:	Thursday the 19th at 6:00. My mother will watch the kids. That way we can both go.
Mr. Duval:	Oh, I have to work that day until 9:00, but I'll try to change my shift.
Mrs. Duval:	I hope you can.
Mr. Duval:	Me, too. When is Carlo's band concert? I know it's coming up.
Mrs. Duval:	That's Monday the 23rd.
Mr. Duval:	OK. I'll definitely go to that.

Page 172, Take a phone message, Exercises B and C

Receptionist:	Winter Hill Elementary School.
Elsa:	Hello. This is Elsa Vega. May I speak to Mr. Taylor please?
Receptionist:	I'm sorry. He's not available right now. May I take a message?
Elsa:	Yes, please. I have a question about my daughter Maria's math homework. Please ask him to call me back.
Receptionist:	Sure. What's your number?
Elsa:	It's 718-555-4343.
Receptionist:	OK. I'll give him the message.
Elsa:	Thank you.

Page 172, Take a phone message, Exercise D

Beto:	Hello.
Mr. Taylor:	Hi. May I please speak with Ms. Vega?
Beto:	I'm sorry. She isn't here right now. May I take a message?
Mr. Taylor:	Yes, please. This is Mr. Taylor from Winter Hill Elementary School. Please ask her to call me back.
Beto:	OK. What's your number?
Mr. Taylor:	My number is 718-555-8185.
Beto:	718-555-8185. All right. I'll give her the message.
Mr. Taylor:	Thank you.

Page 174, Listen, Exercises B and C

Mr. Thompson:	Hi, I'm Harold Thompson, Carlo's teacher. Nice to meet you.
Mrs. Duval:	I'm Carlo's mother, Annette Duval. Nice to meet you, too. So, how's Carlo doing?
Mr. Thompson:	Carlo's a good student. I enjoy having him in class.
Mrs. Duval:	That's good to hear.
Mr. Thompson:	He does very well in math. He works carefully.
Mrs. Duval:	He likes math a lot. What about social studies?
Mr. Thompson:	Well, he's having a little trouble in that class. He needs to do his homework.
Mrs. Duval:	OK. I'll talk to him.

Page 174, Listen, Exercise D

Mr. Thompson:	Hi, I'm Harold Thompson, Carlo's teacher. Nice to meet you.
Mrs. Duval:	I'm Carlo's mother, Annette Duval. Nice to meet you, too. So, how's Carlo doing?
Mr. Thompson:	Carlo's a good student. I enjoy having him in class.
Mrs. Duval:	That's good to hear.
Mr. Thompson:	He does very well in math. He works carefully.
Mrs. Duval:	He likes math a lot. What about social studies?
Mr. Thompson:	Well, he's having a little trouble in that class. He needs to do his homework.
Mrs. Duval:	OK. I'll talk to him.
Mr. Thompson:	Have you thought about signing up Carlo for homework help after school?
Mrs. Duval:	Homework help? What's that?
Mr. Thompson:	It's an after-school program. Older kids from the high school come and help students with their homework. The program is free, and students can get the extra help they need.

Page 180, Listen, Exercises A and B

Mrs. Herrera: Where's Luis?

Mr. Herrera: He's at a friend's house. Why? What's up?

Mrs. Herrera: Well, his teacher called. He's having some trouble at school.

Mr. Herrera: Uh-oh. What kind of trouble?

Mrs. Herrera: She said he's not paying attention and skipping class.

Mr. Herrera: What? Well, we need to talk to him right away.

Mrs. Herrera: Definitely. Let's all talk tonight after dinner.

Page 180, Listen, Exercise C

Mrs. Herrera: Where's Luis?

Mr. Herrera: He's at a friend's house. Why? What's up?

Mrs. Herrera: Well, his teacher called. He's having some trouble at school.

Mr. Herrera: Uh-oh. What kind of trouble?

Mrs. Herrera: She said he's not paying attention and skipping class.

Mr. Herrera: What? Well, we need to talk to him right away.

Mrs. Herrera: Definitely. Let's all talk tonight after dinner.

Mr. Herrera: This is so strange. Luis never has problems at school.

Mrs. Herrera: I know. He's usually a great student.

UNIT 10

Page 186, Practice, Exercise A

1. a bag of potato chips
2. a bunch of grapes
3. a head of cauliflower
4. a box of cereal
5. a can of tuna fish
6. a dozen eggs
7. a jar of pickles
8. a bottle of soda
9. a container of yogurt
10. a pint of milk
11. a quart of orange juice
12. a half-gallon of ice cream
13. a gallon of water
14. a pound of cheese

Page 188, Listen, Exercises B and C

Agnes: Hi, Yuka. I'm going to the grocery store for some milk. Do you need anything?

Yuka: Uh, let me see. Could you get a can of tomatoes?

Agnes: A can of tomatoes? Sure, no problem.

Yuka: Oh, and I need some onions.

Agnes: How many onions?

Yuka: Two.

Agnes: All right. A can of tomatoes and two onions. I'll be back in a little while.

Page 188, Listen, Exercise D

Agnes: Hi, Yuka. I'm going to the grocery store for some milk. Do you need anything?

Yuka: Uh, let me see. Could you get a can of tomatoes?

Agnes: A can of tomatoes? Sure, no problem.

Yuka: Oh, and I need some onions.

Agnes: How many onions?

Yuka: Two.

Agnes: All right. A can of tomatoes and two onions. I'll be back in a little while.

Yuka: Wait a second, since you're going, we could use a jar of mayonnaise, a loaf of bread, and a box of cereal. Hey, what are you doing?

Agnes: I'm looking for a pen and paper. I need to write all this down!

Page 194, Listen, Exercises A and B

Your family is important to you. You want to take care of them. You want to give them food that tastes good and that's good for them. Better taste, healthier meals. That's what you get from French's Chicken. With no added chemicals, French's Chicken is better for you than any other brand of chicken. Never frozen, French's Chicken is fresher than other chicken. Try it. You'll taste the difference.

Page 198, Before you Read, Exercise C

The following products have caffeine: cola, coffee, tea, chocolate, and some headache medicines. Coffee has the most caffeine but some headache medicines have almost as much caffeine as coffee.

Page 200, Listen, Exercise A

Waitress: Here are your iced teas. Are you ready to order?
Ernesto: Yes. I'd like the meatloaf.
Waitress: And what would you like with that?
Ernesto: A side of mixed vegetables.
Waitress: OK. Meatloaf with mixed vegetables.
Ernesto: And a hamburger with a side of onion rings.
Waitress: A hamburger with onion rings.
Ernesto: Oh, and could we have some sugar?
Waitress: Sure. Here you go. I'll be right back with your salads.

Page 200, Listen, Exercise B

Waitress: Here are your iced teas. Are you ready to order?
Ernesto: Yes. I'd like the meatloaf.
Waitress: And what would you like with that?
Ernesto: A side of mixed vegetables.
Waitress: OK. Meatloaf with mixed vegetables.
Ernesto: And a hamburger with a side of onion rings.
Waitress: A hamburger with onion rings.
Ernesto: Oh, and could we have some sugar?
Waitress: Sure. Here you go. I'll be right back with your salads.
Angela: Excuse me. I want to order something, too.
Waitress: Oh! Aren't you having the hamburger?
Angela: Actually, no. The meatloaf and the hamburger are both for him.
Ernesto: Yeah. I'm pretty hungry!

UNIT 11

Page 208, Listen, Exercises B, C, and D

Operator: 9-1-1. What's your emergency?
Olivia: I think a man is having a heart attack.
Operator: OK. What's the location of the emergency?
Olivia: Dave's Sports Shop at 103 Elm Street.
Operator: What are the cross streets?
Olivia: 17th and 18th Avenues.
Operator: All right. What's your name?
Olivia: Olivia Ramos.

Page 208, Listen, Exercise E

Operator: 9-1-1. What's your emergency?
Olivia: I think a man is having a heart attack.
Operator: OK. What's the location of the emergency?
Olivia: Dave's Sports Shop at 103 Elm Street.
Operator: What are the cross streets?
Olivia: 17th and 18th Avenues.
Operator: All right. What's your name?

Olivia: Olivia Ramos.
Operator: All right, Ms. Ramos. An ambulance is on its way. But don't hang up. Stay on the line with me until the ambulance gets there.
Olivia: OK. I'll just tell the man that the ambulance is coming.

Page 214, Listen, Exercises B and C

Mr. Novak: Did you hear what happened yesterday?
Mrs. Novak: No. What happened?
Mr. Novak: There was a gas explosion downtown.
Mrs. Novak: Oh my gosh. That's terrible. Was anybody hurt?
Mr. Novak: Yes. Two people went to the hospital.

Page 215, Conversation, Exercise B

1. here, here 2. art, heart 3. high, I 4. Ow!, Ow!
5. ear, hear 6. high, high

Page 214, Listen, Exercise D

Mr. Novak: Did you hear what happened yesterday?
Mrs. Novak: No. What happened?
Mr. Novak: There was a gas explosion downtown.
Mrs. Novak: Oh my gosh. That's terrible. Was anybody hurt?
Mr. Novak: Yes. Two people went to the hospital.
Mrs. Novak: How did it happen? Do they know?
Mr. Novak: No, not yet. They're looking into the cause.
Mrs. Novak: I'll bet traffic is terrible around there.
Mr. Novak: Oh, yeah. It says here a lot of the streets are closed downtown.

Page 220, Listen, Exercise A

Hi, I'm Officer Ramirez, and I'm here today to talk to you about what to do if you're pulled over by a police officer.

So imagine: You're driving along, and everything's great. But suddenly you hear a siren, and behind you there's a police car with flashing lights. That can be really scary. But stay calm and follow this simple advice.

Anytime you see a police car with flashing lights or hear a siren, look for a place to pull over quickly. Always pull over to the right, even if you're in the left lane. Use your turn signal, and pull over to a safe spot.

After you stop your car, roll down your window. Wait for the police officer and stay in your car. Don't get out. If it's dark, turn on the light inside your car. Put your hands on the steering wheel where the officer can see them.

The officer will probably ask for your license, registration, and proof of insurance. Wait for the officer to ask for your documents. Then tell him what you're going to do. For example, say, "I'm going to get my wallet. It's in my purse."

Cooperate and be polite. Follow the officer's instructions. Do not argue with the officer. The officer will give you a warning or a ticket. If you get a ticket, there are instructions on the ticket about how to pay it. You don't pay the officer at that time. Never offer any money or other gifts to an officer.

Finally, don't start your car or leave until the officer gives you permission to go.

Remember, stay calm and listen to the police officer. Police officers want to help and protect you.

UNIT 12

Page 228, Listen, Exercises A and B

Hello, everybody. I'm Michelle Rivera from human resources. Welcome to the Greenville Hotel. I think that you will find this a great place to work. We're going to start our orientation meeting by talking about company policies, and then we'll take a tour of the building.

Let's start with employee responsibilities. We'll give you an employee ID badge at the end of this meeting. You must wear your employee ID badge during your work shift. This is very important.

Also, all employees must follow the dress code. Your manager will explain the dress code for your department. Employees in housekeeping and food service must wear a uniform. Please get your uniforms at the end of this orientation.

Here's another very important responsibility: You must clock in at the start of your shift and clock out at the end of the shift. Please be on time! And you must also clock in and out when you take your break. During your six-hour shift you must take a thirty-minute break. You must not clock in or clock out for another employee.

Are there any questions? No? OK. Now, some information about our sick day policy. Please open your company policy booklet to page 5 . . .

Page 234, Listen, Exercises B and C

Luis: Hi, Rachel. Can I ask you a favor?
Rachel: Sure. What is it?
Luis: I'm on the schedule for Monday, but I can't come in.
Rachel: Oh, what's up?
Luis: I have to study for a test. Can you take my shift for me?
Rachel: What time do you start?
Luis: 9:30.
Rachel: No problem.

Page 234, Listen, Exercise D

Luis: Hi, Rachel. Can I ask you a favor?
Rachel: Sure. What is it?
Luis: I'm on the schedule for Monday, but I can't come in.
Rachel: Oh, what's up?
Luis: I have to study for a test. Can you take my shift for me?
Rachel: What time do you start?
Luis: 9:30.
Rachel: No problem. I can use the extra hours. By the way, who's working that day?
Luis: I don't know. Let's check the schedule . . . . Oh, Tim's working that day.
Rachel: Tim? Oh, definitely! I like working with him!

Page 240, Listen, Exercises B and C

Linda: Excuse me, Ron. Can I speak to you for a minute?
Ron: Sure, Linda. What's up?
Linda: I need to talk to you about my schedule.
Ron: OK. Right now you work in the mornings, right?
Linda: Yes. But I'm planning to take classes now. Could I change to evenings?
Ron: Well, let me look at the schedule. I'll get back to you.
Linda: OK. Thanks.

Page 240, Listen, Exercise D

Linda: Excuse me, Ron. Can I speak to you for a minute?
Ron: Sure, Linda. What's up?
Linda: I need to talk to you about my schedule.
Ron: OK. Right now you work in the mornings, right?
Linda: Yes. But I'm planning to take classes now. Could I change to evenings?
Ron: Well, let me look at the schedule. I'll get back to you.
Linda: OK. Thanks.
Ron: By the way, what classes are you planning to take?
Linda: Business classes. Someday I want to be a manager.
Ron: Oh, that's great. Let me know if I can help.

Index